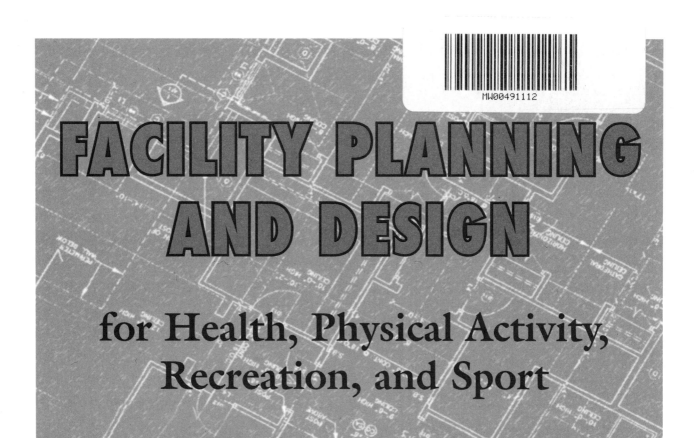

FACILITY PLANNING AND DESIGN

for Health, Physical Activity, Recreation, and Sport

12th Edition

Thomas H. Sawyer

Contributor and Editor-in-Chief

SAGAMORE PUBLISHING, Champaign, Illinois

©2009 Sagamore Publishing, L.L.C.

Published by Sagamore Publishing in cooperation with the
   American Association for Physical Activity and Recreation (AAPAR).

All rights reserved.

Publishers: Joseph J. Bannon and Peter L. Bannon

General Manager: M. Douglas Sanders

Director of Production: Susan M. Davis

Production Coordinator: Jason Pethtel

Cover design/interior layout: Jason Pethtel

ISBN: 978-1-57167-543-9

Library of Congress Catalog Card Number: 2009930746

Printed in the United States.

Sagamore Publishing L.L.C.
804 N. Neil Street
Champaign, IL 61820

www.sagamorepub.com

10 9 8 7 6 5 4 3 2 1

This book is dedicated to all the professionals who work daily with students and clients to develop new or renewed health, fitness, physical activity, recreation, and sports facilities worldwide.

———————————————————

Contents

Foreword ix

Acknowledgments xi

Prologue xiii
> Todd L. Seidler, University of New Mexico
> Bernie Goldfine, Kennesaw State University

Section I
Common Facility Components

Chapter 1... 3

Planning Facilities: Master Plan, Site Selection, and Development Phases
> Thomas H. Sawyer, Indiana State University
> Michael G. Hypes, Morehead State University

Chapter 2... 19

Planning Facilities for Safety and Risk Management
> Todd L. Seidler, University of New Mexico

Chapter 3... 27

Sustainable Design, Construction, and Building Operations
> Rick Gonzales, University of Wisconsin–Eau Claire

Chapter 4... 39

Universal and Accessible Design: Creating Facilities That Work for All People
> Richard J. LaRue, University of New England
> Donald Rogers, Indiana State University

Chapter 5... 49

Electrical, Mechanical, and Energy Management
> Richard J. LaRue, University of New England
> Thomas H. Sawyer, Indiana State University

Chapter 6... 73

Ancillary Areas
> Jeffrey C. Petersen, Baylor University
> Rick Gonzales, University of Wisconsin–Eau Claire

Chapter 7... 97

Graphics and Signage
> Michael G. Hypes, Morehead State University

Chapter 8... 105

Indoor Surfaces
> Hal Walker, Elon University
> Tony Weaver, Elon University

Chapter 9.. 121
Landscape Design, Sports Turf, and Parking Lots
    Richard J. LaRue, University of New England
    David A. LaRue, Landscape Architect
    Thomas H. Sawyer, Indiana State University

Section II
Field and Court Specifications

Chapter 10...139
Indoor and Outdoor Courts
    Bernie Goldfine, Kennesaw State University

Chapter 11... 161
Field Spaces
    Thomas H. Sawyer, Indiana State University

Chapter 12...175
Bleachers
    Michael G. Hypes, Morehead State University

Section III
Recreational Spaces

Chapter 13...185
Aquatic Facilities
    Leland Yarger, Ball State University
    Steven Dalcher, Ball State University

Chapter 14... 201
Playgrounds
    Donna Thompson, University of Northern Iowa
    Susan Hudson, University of Northern Iowa

Chapter 15... 217
Designing Facilities for Parks and Recreation
    Kimberly J. Bodey, Indiana State University
    Thomas H. Sawyer, Indiana State University

Chapter 16... 241
Campus Recreational Sports Centers
    Thomas H. Sawyer, Indiana State University

Chapter 17...247
Strength and Cardiovascular Training Facilities
    Lawrence W. Judge, Ball State University

Chapter 18..265
Adventure Programming Facilities
     Donald Rogers, Indiana State University

Chapter 19..281
Skateparks and Winter Sports Areas
     Thomas H. Sawyer, Indiana State University

Chapter 20..295
Camps and Camping
     Thomas H. Sawyer, Indiana State University

Section IV
Specialty Areas

Chapter 21..305
Track and Field and Cross-Country Facilities
     Lawrence W. Judge, Ball State University
     Thomas H. Saywer, Indiana State University

Chapter 22..323
Designing Facilities for K-12 Health, Physical Education, and Driver Education
     Thomas H. Sawyer, Indiana State University

Chapter 23..345
Designing Combative Areas for Boxing and Martial Arts
     Jason Winkle, Indiana State University
     Thomas H. Sawyer, Indiana State University

Chapter 24..355
Equestrian Spaces
     Michael G. Hypes, Morehead State University
     Julia Ann Hypes, Morehead State University

Chapter 25..363
Athletic Training Facilities
     Joe Brown, Emeriti Faculty, Austin Peay State University
     Michael G. Hypes, Morehead State University

Chapter 26..377
Shooting Facilities: Archery, Rifle, and Pistol
     Jason Winkle, Indiana State University

Section V
Trends and History

Chapter 27...389
Design Trends in Stadiums and Arenas
  Todd L. Seidler, University of New Mexico
  John J. Miller, Texas Tech University

Chapter 28...407
Trends in Equipment and Supplies
  Jeffrey C. Petersen, Baylor University

Chapter 29...419
History of the Council on Facilities
  Thomas H. Sawyer, Indiana State University
  Michael G. Hypes, Morehead State University

Chapter 30...427
Equipment and Facility Design Standards
  Thomas H. Sawyer, Indiana State University

Appendices
A Facility Specification Guide...437
B Listing of Skatepark Builders, Consultants, and Designers 454
C Planning Checklists for Outdoor Spaces 455
D Existing Facility Assessment and Future Planning Checklist..........461
E Indoor Activity Area Planning Checklist 462
F Cleaning and Maintenance Equipment Record Sheet 466
G Surface Selection Process 467
H DIN Standards 468
I Indoor Activity Dimensions..469
J Park and Recreation Open Space Standards 470
K Metric Conversion Formulas...489
L General Resources for Planning Facilities................................490
M Associations pertinent to Planning..491
N Association Pertinent to Planning for Accessibility 493
O Track and Field Layouts 494
P Retrofitting or Replacing Facilities 495
Q Sample ASHRAE Standards 497
R Facility Maintenance 499
S Academic Classrooms and Laboratories..................................508
T Dance Spaces 513

References...522
Glossary of Terms...533
Index...547

ACKNOWLEDGMENTS

Appreciation is expressed to the Editorial Committee members of the Council on Facilities and Equipment (CFE) for assuming initial responsibility for outlining the content and chapters for the text and selection of the chapter authors. While some served as authors/editors for specific chapters in the text, all served as reviewers for assigned chapter drafts. The Editorial Committee members for the 12th edition consisted of:

Dr. Thomas H. Sawyer, NAS Fellow, Chair and Editor-in-Chief, Contributor, 1999-2014 (9th, 10th, 11th, and 12th editions), Indiana State University, Chair CFE, 1995-97
Dr. Julia Ann Hypes, Morehead State University, Chair CFE, 2007-08
Dr. Michael G Hypes, Morehead State University, Chair CFE, 2008-2009
Dr. Jeffrey C. Peterson, Baylor University, Chair CFE, 2005-07
Ms. Mariah Burton Nelson, American Association for Physical Activity and Recreation, Executive Director, 2006-present

We are indebted to a number of authoritative sources for permission to reproduce material used in this text:

—The National Collegiate Athletic Association (NCAA) for permission to reproduce drawings from selected 1997 NCAA rulebooks. It should be noted that these specifications, like others, are subject to annual review and change.
—*Athletic Business* for permission to reprint selected drawings.
—Selected architectural firms for supplying photographs, line drawings, artists renderings, and other materials.

Special recognition is due to those professionals who served as chapter authors or assistant editors, including Kimberly Bodey, Joe Brown, Steven Dalcher, Bernie Goldfine, Rick Gonzales, Susan Hudson, Julia Ann Hypes, Michael G. Hypes (Contributor and Assistant Editor), Lawrence W. Judge, Richard LaRue, David LaRue, John Miller, Jeffrey Peterson, Donald Rogers, Gary Rushing, Todd Seidler, Donna Thompson, LeLand Yarger, Hal Walker, Todd Weaver, and Jason Winkle. These individuals worked diligently to present chapter material in an informative and useful manner.

Without great assistance from a number of very special and important folks, this book would not have been possible: Julia Ann Hypes, who was responsible for the glossary and author information; Meghan "Muffin" Sawyer Rosselli for her graphic and photography expertise; and Sagamore Publishing for invaluable advice, counsel, patience, and encouragement during the final edit of the manuscript.

PROLOGUE

Todd L. Seidler, University of New Mexico
Bernie Goldfine, Kennesaw State University

Have you ever seen a facility with so many design problems that it left you shaking your head in disbelief? Each facility presents its own unique design challenges; if these challenges are not addressed and overcome, the result is a facility with design problems. Typically, the larger a building project, the greater the likelihood that mistakes will be made in the planning and design process. Often, details are overlooked, and sometimes even major mistakes are made in the planning process and not discovered until after the facility is built and opened for use. For example, most of us have seen buildings with poor lighting, ventilation, or access control that could have been prevented with appropriate planning. In particular, one of the most common design flaws in recreational, physical education, and sports facilities is a lack of proper storage space. Surely, we have all visited buildings where hallways, classrooms, and even activity spaces were used for temporary or permanent storage of equipment.

Inadequate planning has resulted in countless design flaws in sports and recreation facilities. Can you imagine a high school football team playing on an 80-yard football field? What about a recreation center with access to the locker rooms available only by crossing the gym floor? Do you believe a facility designer would locate a locker room toilet one foot lower than the septic field it was supposed to drain into? How about a gymnasium with large picture windows directly behind the basketball backboards? And how safe is an indoor track constructed as part of a pool deck that has water puddles present in every running lane? Impossible? Unfortunately it is not.

These "building bloopers" are real and not as uncommon as we would like to believe. Such mistakes can be embarrassing, expensive, amazing, and sometimes humorous (if it is not your facility). These and many other design errors can usually be traced to insufficient planning. An example of an outrageous building blooper is Olympic Stadium in Montreal. Constructed as the track and field site for the 1976 Montreal Olympics, it has yet to be completed satisfactorily. Originally estimated to cost about $60 million, the price thus far is in excess of $1 billion.

Building bloopers are often caused by devoting insufficient time, effort, and/or expertise to the planning process. The earlier in the process that mistakes are discovered and corrected, the less they will cost to rectify. It is inexpensive to change some words on a paper, somewhat more expensive to change lines on a blueprint, and outrageously expensive or even impossible to make changes once the concrete has been poured. Furthermore, the impact of a poorly designed building is staggering when compared with other management problems. Problematic staff can be relieved of their responsibilities. Funds can be raised for underfinanced programs. However, the consequences of a poorly designed building will have to be endured for decades. Therefore, it is essential to devote all available resources early in the planning process.

All too often, facilities are planned without in-depth consideration of the programs that they will support. Basically, a facility is a tool. The better it is planned, designed, and constructed, the better it will support the objectives of the programs it will house. Strange as it may seem, sport facilities often are designed without a great deal of consideration given to programming and user desires. Aesthetics, the interests of one popular sport or program at the time, or the personal desires of decision-makers may, in fact, dictate the design of the facility. Implementing a new program in an existing or poorly planned facility often requires designing the programs based on the limitations of the facility. Poorly designed venues may limit or even prevent some activities from taking place. Conversely, a well-designed facility will support and enhance the desired programs. Planning and building a new facility is a great opportunity to ensure that it will optimally support these programs. Furthermore, well-planned venues allow for flexibility when the popularity of activities and user demand fluctuate. Planned with an eye toward future trends, these facilities are designed to be easily altered so that new activities can be added as needs change.

This book is intended to provide a basic understanding of the planning and design process as well as the unique features of many different areas and types of facilities. Although there is no such thing as a perfect building, with significant time, effort, and expertise devoted to the planning and design process, future building bloopers can be kept to a minimum. It is hoped that those of you involved with the planning of sports facilities will find this book to be a significant resource.

The National Council on Facilities and Equipment

Founded in 1946

Since 1946 the Council on Facilities and Equipment published and endorsed *Facility Planning and Design for Health, Physical Activity, Recreation, and Sport*. This book has been used worldwide by design specialists and facility and event management professionals. The expanded and updated 12th edition will continue the tradition established in 1946. It is the leader in the field. Its authors are well known for their expertise in the design fields.

Michael G. Hypes, D.A.
Morehead State University
Chairperson 2009-2011

Lawrence W. Judge, Ph.D.
Ball State University
Chair-Elect 2009-2011

SECTION I

COMMON
FACILITY
COMPONENTS

PLANNING FACILITIES: MASTER PLAN, SITE SELECTION, AND DEVELOPMENT PHASES

1

Thomas H. Sawyer, Indiana State University
Michael G. Hypes, Morehead State University

Anyone who has been involved in facility planning and development understands that errors are common during the planning and development process. The challenge is to complete a facility project with the fewest number of errors. Before becoming too deeply involved in the planning and development process, it is important to review some of the common errors that have been made in the past (Conklin, 1999). Conklin (1999), Farmer, Mulrooney, & Ammon (1996), Frost, Lockhart, & Marshall (1988), and Horine & Stotlar (2002) suggest these errors include, but are not limited to (see photos on next page): (1) failure to provide adequate and appropriate accommodations for persons with disabilities throughout the facility; (2) failure to provide adequate storage spaces; (3) failure to provide adequate janitorial spaces; (4) failure to observe desirable current professional standards; (5) failure to build the facility large enough to accommodate future uses; (6) failure to provide adequate locker and dressing areas for both male and female users; (7) failure to construct shower, toilet, and dressing rooms with sufficient floor slope and properly located drains; (8) failure to provide doorways, hallways, or ramps so that equipment may be moved easily; (9) failure to provide for multiple uses of facilities; (10) failure to plan for adequate parking for the facility; (11) failure to plan for adequate space for concessions and merchandising; (12) failure to provide for adequate lobby space for spectators; (13) failure to provide for an adequate space for the media to observe activities as well as to interview performers; (14) failure to provide for adequate ticket sales areas; (15) failure to provide adequate space for a loading dock and parking for tractor trailers and buses; (16) failure to provide adequate numbers of restroom facilities for female spectators; (17) failure to provide adequate security and access control into the facility and within the facility; (18) failure to provide adequate separation between activities (buffer or safety zones) in a multipurpose space; (19) failure to provide padding on walls close to activity area, padding and/or covers for short

fences, on goal posts, and around trees; (20) failure to plan for the next 50 years; (21) failure to plan for maintenance of the facility; (22) failure to plan for adequate supervision of the various activity spaces within the facility; and (23) failure to plan to plan.

Planning Facilities/Venues for Health, Fitness, Physical Activity, Recreation, and Sports

The planning process defined in this chapter should be used for planning any of the following facilities/venues:

- stadiums for baseball, football, soccer, softball, or track and field;
- arenas for basketball, football, or ice hockey;
- gymnasiums for public schools, colleges and universities, YM/WCAs, or Boys' and Girls' clubs;
- natatoriums;
- outdoor aquatic centers;
- municipal parks and recreation areas;
- skateboard parks;
- adventure areas, including rope courses, challenge courses and climbing walls, and combative areas.

Further, the process should include a planning committee, a master plan, pre-development review, a facility checklist, site selection, and development phases.

Development of a Master Plan

Master planning is a decision-making process that promotes changes that will accommodate new needs and search for ways to improve existing conditions. The master plan is very critical during periods of limited resources. The process of planning can and does change attitudes about the needs and utilization of current assets, as well

Dos

This is an example of proper use of safety fencing for a baseball or softball shelter. Notice the four-foot fence has a protective cover.

This is an example of proper use of a protective covering for a short fence that provides a greater measure of safety for the players.

This is a good example of proper design with a warning track, eight-foot fence with protective covering and a wind screen.

Don'ts

This is an example of an unsafe fence without a protective covering for a short fence.

This is an example of a proper 10-foot safety buffer zone, but with an unprotected wall. This wall should be covered with mats under the basket.

This is an example of poor planning with the exit doors located directly behind the basketball backboard.

Figure 1.1
Facilities Master Plan

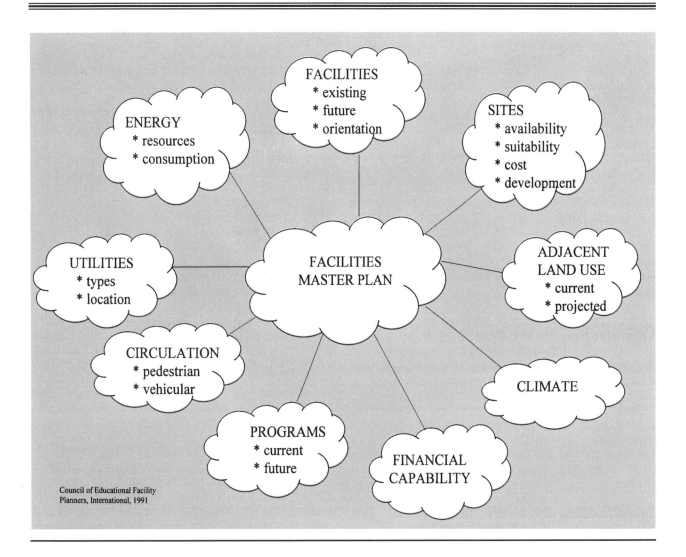

Council of Educational Facility
Planners, International, 1991

as provides a way for communicating with the stakeholders (Hewitt, 1997).

The master-planning process requires coordination and integration of program, financial, and physical planning. Such planning is cyclical in nature and requires the development of procedures and schedules implemented by the expertise of strategic and master planning staff to ensure that the various activities occur in the proper sequence (Hewitt, 1997) (see Figure 1.1).

Another important characteristic of the master-planning process is its ability to respond to changing needs. It must be a flexible and dynamic plan so that it is easy to amend, taking into consideration future projections as reflected by the realities of the present. This means the process is more important than the product (Hewitt, 1997).

Master planning is a process structured to promote cost-effective development decisions that best serve the goals and objectives of the organization. The process operates on the premise that the development of facilities and their ongoing management can best serve specific program needs if the organization's standards of space planning, facilities programming, design, and construction management are closely linked (Hewitt, 1997).

Typical Phases of a Master Plan

The master plan can be used to answer three common questions often raised: Where are we? Where do we want to go? How do we get there? This approach is flexible to allow the individual organization to reflect local conditions, priorities, and emphases.

Establishment of an Ad Hoc Program Committee and a Plan for Planning

The organization's ad hoc planning advisory committee (sometimes called the program committee) should be composed of the following members:

- program specialists

- end users
- financial consultants
- maintenance personnel
- community representatives
- management representatives
- facility consultants

The role of the planning advisory committee includes representing all of the organization's constituencies; overseeing and reviewing the ongoing work; communicating with the various stakeholders about the work in progress, findings, and results; validating the process; resolving unsettled issues; and endorsing the results and forwarding the master plan for approval.

The committee should be assisted by the office staff within the organization, who should keep the senior administration advised of the ongoing work, coordinate and schedule the planning efforts, serve as committee recorder, assist in communicating the ongoing work to the stakeholders, and represent the committee at planning work sessions and related meetings.

Organization Briefings and Initiation of Organization Master Plan Studies

The committee should organize and schedule information meetings to (a) notify the organization and the community of the organization's planning activity, purpose, method, and schedule; (b) solicit immediate concerns, comments, and suggestions; (c) encourage participation in the planning process and identify organization or community issues; and (d) identify the planning staff who will be available for further discussions of these and related matters.

Identification and Confirmation of the Organization's Goals and Objectives

Now detailed planning can begin with three concurrent studies: development of an organization profile, identification of capital improvements, and analysis of existing conditions. The development of the organization's program statement is intended to generally describe the organization's niche (see Figure 1.2). The statement should include, but not be limited to: a brief history of the organization; the organization's mission; the organization's programs, products, and services; the administrative structure; critical issues and strategic responses; goals and objectives for the organization; details about clientele; an outline of short-range planning, mid-range planning, and long-range planning; and other programmatic features that help describe the organization as a distinctive operational entity (see Figure 1.3). Finally, the statement should conclude with a descriptive overview of how the existing situation is expected to change strategically during the period covered by the proposed organization master plan and the implications and consequences such changes may have on the physical development of the organization.

It is important to compile a ten-year listing of projected capital improvements for the organization. Capital improvement items should include buildings, landscape, circulation (i.e., pedestrian and vehicular traffic), infrastructure (i.e., chilled air, electricity, roadways, sewage, sidewalks, steam, telecommunications, water, etc.), land acquisition, and actions that will change and modify the existing physical plant (e.g., new state highway right-of-way).

The objective of the survey of existing conditions is to discover and describe elements that, in combination, typically help create, inform, and/or express the organization as a physical place designed and operated as an organization for a specific purpose and located in a setting that has tangible physical characteristics. Certain items should be identified and defined in graphic and narrative formats so as to describe location, function, and physical character of elements. Such items include land ownership, land forms and topography; microclimate, soils and related subsurface conditions; recreational, social, and cultural patterns; land use; building use; buildings rated by physical condition; building entrances, exits, and service points; pedestrian and vehicular circulation systems; public transportation; parking; landscapes; ecological and natural settings, views, vistas, and related design features; major utilities by location, type, and condition; site history and heritage; site and building accessibility; and site and building problems.

Synthesis and Evaluation of Findings

After establishing an ad hoc planning advisory committee, completing briefings and initiating plan studies, and identifying and confirming master plan goals and objectives, it is time to synthesize and evaluate those findings. This effort should begin to clarify issues and opportunities that should be addressed by the organization and should establish and confirm the direction of the master plan. The issues and opportunities that should surface during the synthesis and evaluation effort relate to the following:

- The organization's image.
- A sense of place for the improvements.
- Existing and new initiatives that may require new building(s) and infrastructure, improvements and revitalization of existing physical resources, and potential demolition.
- Expansion of present facilities should occur only after careful and thorough evaluation of projected needs and capabilities of existing facilities.
- Once needs are established, the following approaches, listed in priority order, are generally considered the most appropriate way to proceed with the program requirements: (1) higher usage of existing

Figure 1.2
Program Statement

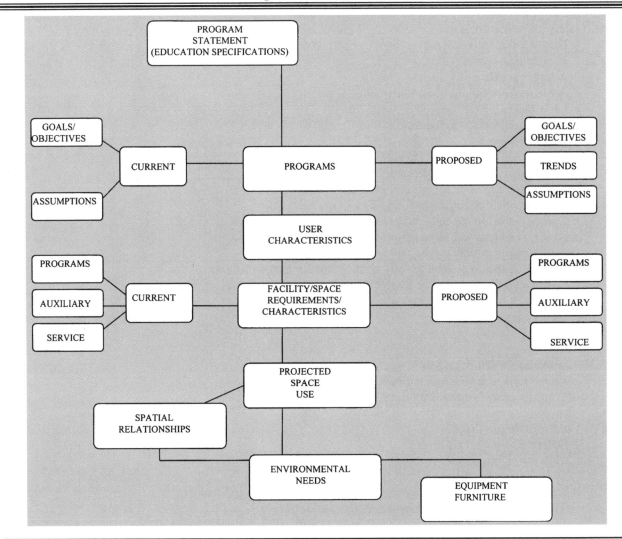

space, (2) renovation of existing structures, (3) infill (i.e., adding vertically or horizontally to existing structures), and (4) expansion of facilities into new areas on the organization's site.

The master plan, during this phase, needs to take into consideration generally accepted land use guidelines such as (1) the highest and best use should be made of all land, (2) avoid land-use conflicts (i.e., neighboring residential and commercial areas), (3) areas should complement each other and promote a visual interest and functionally fit the remainder of the organization's site, (4) facilities should be constructed only on sites that best meet programmatic and environmental objectives of the organization, and (5) the organization should develop a no-build policy relating to the preservation of historic sites or open spaces.

Further, the master plan should contain goals and objectives for circulation and transportation on the organization's site. These goals and objectives should include, but not be limited to: (1) general access to the organization, (2) vehicular circulation, (3) parking, (4) pedestrian and bicycle circulation, and (5) transit.

Another extremely important aspect of the master plan will be the utilities and service elements. A consolidated utility system consistent with the projected needs of the organization should be developed. This system should be designed for simplicity of maintenance and future needs for extension or expansion of the utility network.

The master plan should consider the landscape design. The primary landscape goal for the campus should be to present an image with a high degree of continuity and quality. The landscape design should take into consideration the organization's buildings and grounds, accessibility issues, fire, security, energy conservation, and desired development beyond the organization's property line.

Figure 1.3
Sample Building Program Statement Outline

Part I. Objectives of the Programs
       a. Instructional (professional service)
       b. Recreational sports
       c. Adapted activities
       d. Athletics (interscholastic and intercollegiate)
       e. Club sports
       f. Community/school programs
       g. Others

Part II. Basic Assumptions to be Addressed
       a. Facilities will provide for a broad program of instruction,
          adapted activities, intramural and other sports
       b. Demographics of the population who will use the facility
       c. Existing facilities will be programmed for use
       d. Basic design considerations. "What's most important?"
       e. Facility expansion possibilities will be provided for in the planning
       f. Outdoor facilities should be located adjacent to indoor facilities
       g. Consideration will be given to administration and staff needs
       h. Existing problems
       i. Others

Part III. Comparable Facility Analysis
       a. Visit comparable facilities that have been recently constructed
       b. Compare cost, design features, etc.

Part IV. Factors Affecting Planning
       a. Federal and state legislation
       b. Club sports movement
       c. The community education or "Lighted School" program
       d. Surge of new non-competitive activities being added to the curriculum
       e. Expansion of intramural sports and athletic programs
       f. Sharing certain facilities by boys and men and girls and women (athletic training
          rooms and equipment rooms)
       g. Coeducational programming
       h. Emphasis on individual exercise programs
       i. Physical fitness movement
       j. Systems approach in design and construction
       k. New products
       l. Others

Part V. Explanation of Current and Proposed Programming
       a. Instructional
       b. Intramural sports
       c. Club sports
       d. Adaptive programs
       e. Community/school
       f. Recreational programs
       g. Priority listing of programs
       h. Others

Part VI. Preliminary Data Relative to the Proposed New Facilities

The following steps assume an organization planning a new facility from the ground up.

Regional Analysis

Sufficient data must be gathered about the off-site surroundings to ensure that the project will be compatible with surrounding environments, both manmade and natural. This part of the design process is referred to as the regional analysis. It should include:

- Service area of the facility under construction (i.e., major facilities such as parks, large commercial areas facilities, and minor facilities, such as children's playgrounds, senior citizen centers, local library, etc.).
- User demand (i.e., determining the kind of use desired by clients, activity interests, demographic makeup of residents, local leadership, and calculating the number of users).
- Access routes (i.e., major and secondary routes).
- Governmental functions and boundaries (i.e., contact the local planning agency and local government offices).
- Existing and proposed land uses (i.e., gathering information about abutting land ownership, adjacent land uses, land use along probable access routes, off-site flooding and erosion problems, offsite pollution sources, views [especially of aesthetic and historic interest], and significant local architectural or land use characteristics).
- Regional influences (i.e., check for anything unusual or unique that could either enhance or cause problems to the project).

Site Analysis

The planning committee will need to consider various pieces of information prior to selecting the building site. The considerations for site selection (Fogg, 1986; Miller, 1997) include:

- Access to the site (i.e., ingress and egress, surrounding traffic generators, accessibility via public transportation).
- Circulation within the site (e.g., roads—paved and unpaved, bicycle trails, walks and hiking trails).
- Parking.
- Water supply.
- Sewage disposal.
- Electrical service.
- Telephone service.
- Other utilities, including oil/natural gas transmission lines, or cable TV.
- Structures to be constructed.
- Environmental concerns and conditions on and off property (e.g., noise, air, water, and visual pollution).
- Easements and other legal issues (e.g., deed restrictions, rights of way, and less-than-fee-simple ownership).
- Zoning requirements (i.e., changing the zoning is usually time consuming and expensive and frequently not possible).
- Historical significance.
- Any existing uses (activities) on the site.
- Climactic conditions prevalent in the area by season (e.g., temperature; humidity; air movement velocity, duration, and direction; amount of sunshine; precipitation—rain, sleet, snow; sun angles and subsequent shadows; special conditions—ice storms, hurricanes, tornadoes, heavy fog, heavy rainstorm, floods, and persistent cloud cover).
- Nuisance potentials (e.g., children nearby, noise, etc.).
- Natural features (e.g., topography, slope analysis, soil conditions, geology, hydrology, flora and fauna).
- Economic impact of a site (e.g., labor costs, growth trends, population shifts, buying power index, available work force, property taxes, surrounding competition, utility costs, incentives, area of dominant influence [ADI], designated market area [DMA], and established enterprise zones).
- Natural barriers and visibility.
- Supporting demographics (e.g., age, gender, occupation, marital status, number of children, expenditures, education, income, number of earners in the family, ethnic background, etc.) and psychographics (e.g., lifestyle data or lifestyle marketing).
- Security concerns (e.g., proximity of police, fire, emergency medical personnel, hospitals).

The most important aspects of site selection are location, location, and location. If the site is not in the most accessible location with a high profile for people to recognize, it will have a negative effect on the success of the venture.

The following seven steps apply to both new ventures and established organizations planning major overhauls:

1. Master Plan Agenda

The master plan agenda is a specific list of issues, opportunities, and projected physical improvements. The plan will include the number and type of structures to be constructed or renovated, the estimated capital costs over a set period of time, approximate locations of new structures, and probable priority to be considered in the preparation of the master plan (see Figure 1.4).

2. Review and Discussion

This step offers the organization and its stakeholders the opportunity to review and comment on the work completed on the master plan to date. The planning committee should be present at these open forums to answer questions and understand the issues and concerns raised. The presentations for these open forum meetings should include:

Figure 1.4
Developing a Master Plan

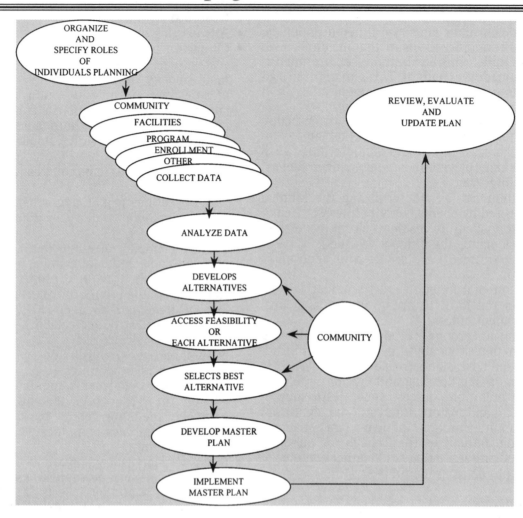

- a description of the process,
- a summary of the organization's profile,
- a review of the projected capital improvements,
- a summary of the surveys and analysis of existing conditions,
- an accounting of issues and opportunities,
- a list of items on the master plan agenda, and
- a description of the next steps in the planning process.

The committee should review and evaluate all reactions and concerns raised at the meeting(s).

Then the committee should determine appropriate modifications to the master plan.

3. Preparation of the Draft Master Plan

The preliminary master plan should be expressed in both general and specific terms. The former is intended to communicate the major features of the campus plan. The latter view enriches the vision by showing in greater detail the character, justification, feasibility, and phasing of selected significant improvements. The following components typically appear in a master plan: (1) new construction; (2) building and site reconstruction, renewal, and demolition; (3) revisions to and extension of the circulation systems; (4) new and improved landscape projects; (5) parking patterns; (6) transportation proposals; (7) infrastructure projects; (8) joint organization and community development; (9) drawings and illustrations; (10) block models; (11) organization design guidelines for buildings and building materials; and (12) landscape guidelines including views, boundary identification, major entrances and exits, service entrances and exits, building sites, vehicular and pedestrian circulation systems, parking, water features, rock formations, gardens, open spaces, and passive or recreational spaces.

4. Review of Preliminary Plan

The planning committee will present the preliminary plan to the organization's constituencies, administration, board, and community at large. These groups will review the preliminary plan. After careful review, a combined report will be generated with any suggested modifications and justifications for the modifications.

5. Revision of the Master Plan to Obtain Consensus and Approval

After the preliminary plan review has been completed, the master plan should be revised to include any recommended changes from the stakeholders. The revised plan should be published and distributed as a draft master plan for use in the plan-approval process. The master plan remains a dynamic and flexible document even after approval.

6. Documentation and Dissemination of the Master Plan

The ad hoc planning advisory committee is transformed into a standing planning advisory committee with the following responsibilities: (1) serve as a conduit for the organization's community to present issues and suggestions regarding the master plan; (2) review all capital expenditure projects; (3) confirm conformance to the campus plan; (4) expedite the resolution of nonconformance; (5) review, resolve, and recommend plan amendments; and (6) participate in an annual review of the master plan and cyclical master plan revisions.

7. Master Plan Amendment Process

The master plan will need to be amended periodically to stay current with new trends and developments. The standing planning advisory committee should plan to revise the master plan every five years. The process would be the same as the original process that established the master plan. The standing planning advisory committee will annually review the master plan. If a major new initiative has been approved by the administration and requires modification of the master plan or a major failure of a structure or utility occurs, the committee can request that a modification be made in the master plan. This recommendation would be forwarded to the administration and board for approval.

Implementation of Plan

After the master plan has been approved as a guideline for the organization's future planning, it is important to remember that the master plan is a guide for the entire organization. It is not a specific plan for a particular structure. Once approval and funding have been gained for a specific structure, then the developmental process begins for that structure. The common components that compose a development process for a single structure or complex include research; regional analysis; site

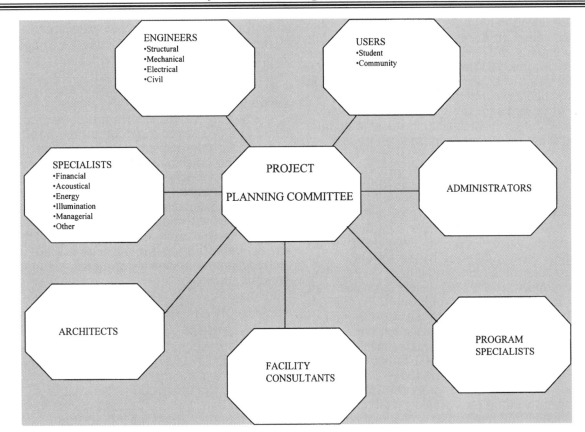

**Figure 1.5
Project Planning Committee**

analysis; program; functional analysis; combined site, function, land use; refinement and site plan/ overall design; construction documents; bidding; construction; and review.

Design Team

The design team (see Figure 1.5) is composed of the project planning committee, architect(s), engineers, facility consultant(s), interior designer(s), construction manager, acoustical consultant(s), and turf management specialist(s). Generally, the architectural firm selected by the organization employs engineers (e.g., civil, electrical, mechanical, and structural), interior designers, acoustical consultants, and turf management specialists. The organization often hires a facility consultant to work with the program committee and architect. However, in some cases, the architectural firm as part of the design team may employ the facility consultant.

A facility consultant can provide numerous services. If the consultant is part of the owner's team rather than the architectural team, this individual should serve as a liaison between the project planning committee and the architect. It is important to understand that the majority of architects employed by an organization have little or no experience in designing these types of facilities. It would be preferable to select an architectural firm familiar with these types of facilities. If this is not possible, then the facility consultant becomes very important to the process.

Selecting an Architectural Firm

The selection of an architectural team should be based solely on the reputation and experience of the company and a formal review process. Once a project is approved then an advertisement (a request for qualifications [RFQ]) should be placed in the news media seeking qualifications of interested architectural firms for the specific project. Later, a letter would be sent to specific firms who qualify, inviting them to submit proposals.

Tips for Drafting the Request for Proposal

The request for proposal, (or RFP), is composed of the following components: (1) Prepare an RFP and send to a broad list of applicants to ascertain their qualifications for this particular type of project (Noyes & Skolnicki, 2001). (2) Draft an evaluation sheet to be used by the selection committee to determine who is qualified. (3) Based on your responses to the RFQ, select no more than twenty firms to which to send the RFP. (4) Draft a second evaluation sheet to narrow the pool to three to five finalists for the selection committee. (5) Provide the applicants adequate time to prepare a proposal—between three and four weeks, and longer if holidays are involved. (6) Request the firms include in their proposals the following: a list of recently completed projects (last ten years), the estimated budgeted costs and actual costs for

each project, and in-house professionals available to work on the project. (7) The owner needs to provide the applicants with adequate background for the project. (8) The finalists will participate in an interview process.

Prior to the Interview

Prior to interviewing the finalists, the program committee, facility consultant, and administration representatives should travel to at least two facilities built by each firm and review the final result of their efforts. The travelers need to speak with the facility manager and users and ask about the best features of the facility and the worst features. What would they do differently? After completing the tours, draft a number of questions to ask the architect during the interview.

The Interview

After the field of applicants is narrowed to three to five, the firms should be interviewed. Each firm should demonstrate its competence and philosophy in the following areas (modified from the American Institute of Architects suggestions):

- client's role in the design process
- number and type of consultants required
- design or build versus conventional design versus fast-track process
- extent of engineering services
- construction supervision
- number of sets of plans or specifications to be provided
- construction cost
- factors that may influence construction
- time schedule and target dates for completion
- architectural fee and payment schedule
- development of a budget

Criteria for Selection

The successful firm should be open and flexible with the program committee and facility consultant, be experienced with this type of project, and be able to demonstrate that they have completed facilities within the budget developed (Noyes & Skolnicki, 2001). The firm should be able to demonstrate awareness, a user-friendly process, past success with other similar projects, and past fees as related to similar projects. Finally, the firm should be willing to provide accessibility to the architects and engineers during the planning and building phases.

Research for Facility Development

In its research, the planning committee should be concerned with (1) knowing and understanding the current and future needs and desires of the people who are involved in and/or affected by the proposed project and (2) knowing everything reasonably possible about the project function and/or activity and the space requirements.

Designers Design for People

At least four groups of people may need to be involved in the research and eventually be satisfied, including clients (board of directors, etc.), users, affected neighbors and/or public, managers and operators, and possibly others. Each of the relevant groups must be identified and its needs, concerns, and desires understood. There will almost certainly be some conflicts between the various groups. Understanding these problems in advance may make it possible to resolve them during the design phase.

Maintenance and Operations

Maintenance and operational needs, small but significant, must be clearly understood. They can make a project successful or doom it to future failure. The following are some specific items to consider:

1) *Maintenance*
- Will maintenance be conducted by in-house labor or by contract?
- Is special equipment used or needed (e.g., riding lawn mowers, etc.)?
- Does maintenance staff have any requirements for any standard equipment (e.g., motors, lights, shower heads, pumps, etc.) used or preferred by the maintenance staff?
- How capable is staff to maintain sophisticated equipment?
- What are maintenance space requirements, such as equipment clearance around motors and pumps, so routine maintenance can be performed, etc.?
- Are there any special fire protection requirements?
- What special storage requirements are needed for flammables and chemicals?

2) *Operations*
- Security—Is it needed? If so, what type (patrol, electronic, entrance only, dogs, by whom)? If patrolled, how—by foot, car, motorcycle, horse, bike, or boat?
- Hours of operation—Is night lighting required?
- Trash pickup—In-house? Contract? Kind of equipment used?
- Deliveries—Food, supplies, etc. When are separate entrances and exits needed?
- Communications system—Speakers, phone, radio, bell system, public address system?
- Safety/first aid—Are special facilities needed? Where? Extent? Emergency vehicle access?
- Peak use—How is it handled? Restrict use or provide overflow capacity?

3) *Special Programs*
- Will there be any? If so, what kind (e.g., concerts at noon, employee training, visitor information and/or education, arts and craft shows, special exhibits)?
- Any special space requirements for programs? Lighting? Service areas? Other utilities?

Facilities and Their Requirements

Most facilities have specific site requirements. Technical data must be gathered on all the proposed facilities. At a minimum, the following must be known:

- Size (actual dimensions plus any buffer spaces or required accessory space)
- Grade requirements (i.e., maximum and minimum)
- Any special construction requirements (e.g., tennis courts, ice hockey rinks)
- Utility needs (i.e., type and amount)

Predevelopment Review

Along with the master planning process, a thorough review of facility needs should be completed for a proposed new or renovated facility. This review should be completed before an architect or consultant is brought on board. This can save time and money as well as assuring that the structure will fit the proposed program. It is important to develop a checklist at the beginning, not the end, of the planning process. This will help focus and guide the dream and planning process. See the appendices for examples of specific checklists as a guide in developing your own checklist for the proposed project.

Program

Program, as used here, is the organization of the information needed for planning a project to provide an appropriate facility to meet the needs of the affected people (client, users, neighbors, and staff). Program needs should include a list of activities, facility needs for each activity listed, number of participants in each activity during peak periods, size of each facility ranging from minimum to ideal, and a description of the relationship between activities and facilities (i.e., can certain activities coexist with other activities at the same time in one facility?).

Functional Analysis

Functional analysis is the process of analyzing and organizing the information provided in programming and relationships by translating that analysis into graphic symbols. It establishes the preferred or ideal physical relationships of all the component parts of a project. The process commonly consists of four parts: space diagrams, relationship charts and/or diagrams, bubble diagrams, and land-use concepts. All of the elements contained in the activity/program must be considered and their desired functional and physical relationships accommodated.

Combined Site, Function, and Land Use

Two issues are key to land use: people needs and site constraints. At this point, the various constraints and opportunities presented by the site must become integrated with people needs. It is also the time when the reality of the site constraints may require changes in the program. This step combines the site analysis with the functional analysis. If changes are made in the program, the changes must be incorporated throughout the functional analysis phase. This step in the site design process is where analysis of the site data is most completely utilized.

If the site selected is too small, the following options should be considered:

- Physical modification of the site. This may be the least desirable option, because it is almost always undesirable from an environmental standpoint. It frequently is not aesthetically pleasing, and it is usually expensive.
- Expand the site if adjacent land is available. This is frequently not possible and can be expensive.
- Change to another site. This can be expensive, and alternate sites may not be available.
- Cancel the project. This is not usually desirable or possible.
- Creatively look at new ways of solving the problem.

The location is the most difficult choice. It is always difficult to abandon the proven acceptable way of designing and operating facilities. When successful, however, it can often lead to outstanding, innovative solutions.

Refinement and Site Plan/ Overall Design

After the land-use step has been completed, the planning committee needs to refine the focus of the building project before it moves to the site plan/overall design step. After the refinement is complete, then, and only then, should the planners consider site planning and overall design. A site plan shows the entire existing and proposed site features superimposed on a topographic base map at an appropriate scale. It functions as the coordinating plan that ensures that all the project parts fit together. This is the point in the site design process where imagination and creativity are really important. In addition, this plan is almost always the feature part of any presentation to the client and other interested parties. Finally, accompanying the site plan will be a number of drawings, including utilities (e.g., water sources, sewer lines, and electricity/communication lines), grading and drainage, circulation, scale drawings, relationships, and three-dimensional aspects.

Construction Documents

Construction documents control the actual constructed results and consist of two separate parts: working drawings and specifications, the written companion to the working drawings. Upon completion of the working drawings and specifications, the project is bid and, if the bids are satisfactory, the contract is awarded.

Working Drawings

All working drawings must be clear, concise, and understandable to the people who are going to construct the building. Only as much detail as is necessary to build the project should be included. More detail might give the client more control but will definitely cost more money for design and will result in higher bids. All pieces must be clearly presented in such a manner that will allow accurate building.

All construction drawings must be accurate, clearly labeled, and dimensioned. If in doubt as to the need for a label or a dimension, include it! Normally, written numbers on the plan take precedence over field-scaled distances.

A useful tool in outlining the numbers and kinds of construction drawings is a plan control list. Each drawing expected to be needed is listed by description. This enables the designer(s) to coordinate work and helps to ensure that all aspects of the project are included.

With the completed list of plans, an estimate of time required to complete the working drawing and the necessary scheduling of work assignments can be carried out. This plan control document will probably be revised during the preparation of drawings. In its final form, it will become the drawing index listing for Sheet 2 of the working drawings package.

The more detailed and elaborate the working drawings, the higher the cost of preparing them, and very frequently, the higher the cost of building the project. A rule of thumb: The smaller the job, the fewer the construction documents. Small contractors do not like excessive control and paperwork. They frequently will not bid on projects with elaborate specifications, and if they do, they bid high. Frequently, too much control will cause bids to be higher, but does not result in an increase in quality.

The construction drawings must be reviewed by the maintenance staff to 1) ensure compatibility of parts with existing facilities, 2) see if the project can be effectively maintained at reasonable cost, and 3) determine if alternative materials or design modifications would reduce the costs and/or simplify maintenance. A detailed cost estimate is almost always necessary at this point in the design process. If costs estimated for the time of construction are too high, then the project may have to be reduced in scope and/or redesigned. Be certain that lifetime operations and maintenance costs are also considered in the estimate.

The construction drawings should include the following: demolition and site preparation, utilities, landscape and site improvements, structural, architectural, mechanical/HVAC, mechanical/plumbing, mechanical/fire protection, and electrical/telecommunications.

Specifications

The written portion of the construction documents comes in three parts: bidding and contract requirements (including the bid documents)—Division 0; general requirements—Division 1; and construction specifications Divisions 2-16.

This part of the design process is often most disliked by designers because of the massive detail required. It is, however, of the utmost importance in ensuring that the design is actually built according to the way it was envisioned.

Specifications should be organized in the 16-division format developed by the Construction Specifications Institute (CSI) as follows:

Division 0:	Bidding requirements, contract forms, and conditions of the contract
Division 1:	General requirements/special conditions
Division 2:	Site work
Division 3:	Concrete
Division 4:	Masonry
Division 5:	Metals
Division 6:	Wood and plastic
Division 7:	Thermal and moisture protection
Division 8:	Doors and windows
Division 9:	Finishes
Division 10:	Specialties
Division 11:	Equipment
Division 12:	Furnishings
Division 13:	Special construction
Division 14:	Conveying systems
Division 15A:	Mechanical (HVAC)
Division 15B:	Mechanical (plumbing)
Division 16:	Electrical

General Notes

- Include everything in the specifications that you want to see in the final constructed product.
- Make sure that Division 1 includes the contractor providing "as-built" drawings, catalogue cuts, and, where appropriate, an operation manual and training of operating and maintenance staff.
- Include only information necessary to the specific project—especially if it is a small one. As with plans, small contractors don't like and frequently don't understand long, involved specifications; therefore, they will not bid or may increase their bids accordingly. The heavier, thicker, and more complicated the specifications are, the higher the bid.

- Conversely, the less detail you have in the specifications, the greater the opportunity for misunderstandings between the owner and contractor.
- All phases of specifications are readily adaptable to computerization and/or word processing. Much time can be saved if "canned" specifications are used, thus speeding up this tedious but crucial task. Computerization will probably lead to standardization of details and format.

Schematic Design Phase

In the schematic design phase, the architect prepares schematic design documents that consist of drawings and other documents illustrating the scale and relationship of project components. These are based on the mutually agreed-upon program with the owner, the schedule, and the construction budget requirements, and they are submitted to the owner for approval.

The products from this first phase of the project consist of the following: renderings (architect's conception of the building) and models, floor plans and elevations, narrative (a description of the project with sufficient detail to allow an initial review by the organization), outline specifications (e.g., exterior materials, interior finishes, mechanical and electrical systems, identification of significant discrepancies between the project requirements and the budget), and cost estimates.

The project management issues for this phase consist of cost and budget, program expansion, schedule slippage, design review, quality assurance, use of design and estimating contingencies, code compliance, and building committee(s).

Design Development Phase

Based on schematic design documents and any adjustments authorized by the owner in the program, schedule, or construction budget, the architect prepares further design development documents for approval by the owner. These consist of drawings and other documents to fix and describe the size and character of the project as to architectural, structural, mechanical, and electrical systems, materials, and other appropriate elements.

The products for this phase include: drawings (site and landscape, utilities, structural, architectural, mechanical, electrical, and special equipment), narrative, specifications, and cost estimates.

The project management issues for this phase consist of cost and budget, scope creep (common elements previously eliminated from the project that reappear in design development), design review, technical review (specific reviews initiated by the owner to ensure the organization's guidelines for design and construction are being complied with), and use of design contingencies.

Construction Approaches

The traditional approach is commonly known as the lump-sum contract. In this method, a general contractor is selected based on the lowest bid. The general contractor is responsible for selecting all subcontractors and selection of all construction materials. It is not advisable to enter into this type of contractual relationship, because the general contractor has too much control of the profit and loss for a job.

Many public projects employ a construction manager to oversee the progress of the construction through all phases. This method allows for multiple bids, such as one for mechanical, another for electrical, and another for general construction of the structure.

Another approach is called design and build. This method places the responsibility for completion of the project on the architect and builder who work for the same company. This option sets a fixed price, encourages interaction, and eliminates additional costs arising from design changes. A variation of design and build is called fast tracking. It is used in large projects in which contracts are let incrementally or sequentially so that the construction time may be reduced. This variation may be not be allowed in public projects due to federal or state mandates.

Construction Document Phase

Based on the approved design development documents and any further adjustments in the scope or quality of the project or in the construction budget authorized by the owner, the architect prepares construction documents for the approval of the owner. These consist of drawings and specifications setting forth in detail the requirements for the construction of the project.

Construction documents (developed by the American Institute of Architects [AIA] and the Associated General Contractors of America [AGCA] consist of the following: invitation to bid, instructions to bidders, information available to bidders, bid forms and attachments, bid security forms, construction agreement, performance bond, payment bond, certificates, contract conditions (i.e., general conditions, and supplementary conditions), specifications (Divisions 1-16), drawings, addendum(s), and contract modifications.

The program management issues for the phase consist of: code compliance, scope creep, schedule slippage, design review, technical review, quality assurance, use of design and estimating contingencies, design contract interpretation and enforcement, bidding and construction strategy (i.e., a lump-sum bid for all components or multiple bids for general contractor, mechanical, electrical, and add-ons or reductions), cost overruns or under runs, design-bid-build (i.e., project designed by an architectural firm and bid out to construction firms to build), design and build and a variation of design and build called fast tracking.

All designers must keep current on the latest product information available in their field of expertise. When the plans and specifications are completed, the project is ready for bid.

Bidding

Bids are opened in front of witnesses, usually the contractors or their representative(s), and an attorney (normally required by a government agency). The bidding process includes (a) bidding and advertising, (b) opening and review of bids, and (c) award of contract. The bid documents include invitation to bid, instructions to bidders, the bid form, other sample bidding and contract forms, and the proposed documents (e.g., drawings and specifications).

Bidding and Advertising

Bidding is the process of receiving competitive prices for the construction of the project. A bid form should be provided to ensure that all bids are prepared in the same manner for easy comparison. The bids can be received in many ways. The most common are:

- lump sum (one overall price),
- lump sum with alternatives (either add-ons or deletions), and
- unit prices.

All bids on large projects should be accompanied by some type of performance bond, ensuring that the contractor will perform the work as designed at the price bid in the time specified. This ensures that bidders are sincere in their prices.

The time and place of the receipt of the sealed bids must be clearly shown on all bid packages. No late bids can be received without compromising the entire bidding process.

Small Projects (Up to $25,000)

A bid of this size can normally be handled informally. The process of calling a selected list of local contractors will usually be sufficient and will probably result in obtaining the best price.

Larger Projects (Over $25,000)

A formal bid process is usually necessary to ensure fairness, accuracy, and a competitive result. The process starts with advertising for bids. Advertising frequently is initiated prior to the completion of the plans with an effective date for picking up the completed plans and specifications. The larger, more complex the project is, the wider the range of advertising necessary. Governmental agencies usually have minimum advertising standards. They advertise in the legal advertisement section of the local paper and papers in larger nearby cities and in professional construction journal(s). In addition, designers or clients frequently have a list of contractors who have successfully built past projects and/or who have indicated an interest in bidding on future projects.

As a minimum, the advertisement should consist of

- a description of the project and kind of work required,
- the date and place plans can be picked up,
- the cost of plans and specifications (usually only sufficient to cover printing costs),
- the bid date and time, and
- client identification.

The approximate value of the project is sometimes included although some designers and clients do not wish to give out this information. With complex projects, it is desirable to schedule a pre-bid conference to explain the design and bidding process to prospective bidders. During the bidding period, one or more prospective bidders frequently raise questions. If the questions require design modifications or clarifications, the questions must be answered in writing in the form of an addendum to all holders of plans.

Opening and Reviewing of Bids

The designers or their representatives are usually present at the bid opening. After the bids are opened and read, it is necessary to analyze them and decide to whom the contract is to be awarded. The technical analysis is usually by the designers who consider whether the bid is complete, the prices are reasonable, and the contractor is able to do the work. A recommendation is then made. The legal analysis by the attorney is conducted concurrently with examining whether bonds are attached, all necessary signatures are included, and all required in formation is provided.

Award of Contract

Assuming favorable analysis by all involved and that the bids are acceptable to the client, the contract will be awarded. Most contracts are awarded to the lowest qualified bidder. Sometimes, however, the low bidder is not large enough or does not have the expertise to do the work required. Occasionally some bids are improperly prepared. In these situations, they may be rejected and the next lowest qualified bidder will be awarded the contract, or the project is re-bid. This can lead to problems with the disqualified bids or bidders and is why an attorney should be present.

Construction Phases

The architect should visit the site at least twice monthly at appropriate intervals during the construction stage and make the owner generally familiar with the progress and quality of the work in writing. The architect has other responsibilities, including certifying the payments represented to the owner for payment.

The construction step of a project goes through several phases. The number of phases depends upon the scope of the project and the contracting agency. Two general guidelines govern the construction step: (1) the larger the project, the more steps required and (2) governmental projects usually have more contractual controls. At least some, and perhaps all, of the following steps will be required during construction.

Pre-Construction Conference

A meeting between the contracting agency and the contractor(s) prior to the commencement of construction to review the contract items and make sure there is an understanding of how the job is to be undertaken.

Construction

The actual construction begins this phase, which could take as much as five years, depending on the scope of the project. However, construction can generally be completed in 18 to 24 months on an average project.

Change Orders

Change orders are defined as official documents requested by either the contractor or the contracting agency that change the approved contract documents. These changes usually include an adjustment of the bid price and a benefit to the contractor. It is better to avoid all change orders. Where this is not possible, be prepared to pay a premium price and to accept delays in contract completion.

Pre-Final Inspection and Preparation of Punch List

The initial review of a completed construction project is called a pre-final inspection. This inspection should have all the affected parties' decision makers present including the owner or his or her representative, the architect, the contractor(s), and any subcontractors. At this time, it is also desirable to have the facility operation supervisor present. During this review, a "punch list" is prepared of any work that needs to be completed by the contractor prior to a final inspection. All items that are not completed or are not completed according to specifications should be included on the list. The punch list is then agreed upon and signed by all affected parties. The contractor must then correct and/or finish all the items on the list. When the punch list is completed, it is time to call for a final inspection.

As-Built Drawings and Catalogue Cuts

Defined as the drawings prepared by the contractor showing how the project was actually built. These drawings will be of great value to the operations and maintenance staffs. They must know exactly what facilities were actually built and their locations to be able to maintain the project effectively.

Catalogue cuts are printed information supplied by the manufacturers on materials and equipment used in the project construction. This material is necessary so that the operating staff will be able to learn about the material and equipment. In addition, it is needed for locating necessary replacement parts. It must also be included in working drawings and specifications of future renovations and/or expansion of the project.

Preparation of an Operations Manual

An operations manual contains written instructions on how to operate and maintain special equipment. The minimum data included should be how to start up, how to shut down, inspection(s) time intervals and what should be inspected, schedule of required maintenance, safety precautions, and who to contact for specialized repair assistance.

Training on How to Operate the Project

This contract item is usually included only for larger projects that are unfamiliar to the people who will operate them.

Final Inspection

The final inspection should concentrate on items not found acceptable during any previous inspections. The same review team that made the pre-final inspection should be assembled for the final inspection.

Acceptance of Completed Project

Assuming all the work has been completed as shown on the plans and described in the specifications, the project should be accepted and turned over to the owner or operator. Further, if the contractor has posted a performance bond guaranteeing the work, it should be released by the contracting agency.

If at all possible, avoid partial acceptances. Sometimes it is necessary to take over a part or parts of a project prior to completion of the entire project. If this becomes necessary, the contractor will have the opportunity to blame future problems and/or delays on having to work around the people using the project.

Maintenance Period

When living plants are involved, many contractors have a maintenance period included after the acceptance of the project. This can last anywhere from 30 days or more (for lawns) to 90 days for flowers and, frequently, one full growing season for ground cover, vines, shrubs, and trees.

Bond Period

Most government projects and some larger projects require the contractor to post not only a performance bond, but also a one-year (or some other specified period) warranty on the quality of the work. Usually the bond requires the contractor to replace or repair any defective or damaged items during the time covered by the bond. Typical items would be leaking roofs, infiltration of ground water into sewer lines, puddling of water in parking lots or tennis courts, etc.

Bond Inspection and Final Acceptance

At the end of the bond period, the original final inspection team holds another inspection. Prior to release of the bond, any problems that have been uncovered during this inspection must be rectified at no cost to the contracting agency. It is important to note that when the bond is released, the contractor no longer has any responsibility to the project.

Review

The project has been completed and turned over to the client. Does the project do what it was designed to from the standpoint of the (a) client, (b) user, (c) affected neighbors and/or public, (d) manager and operator, and (e) design team? There are two basic kinds of information to be gathered: information on people and on physical conditions.

PLANNING FACILITIES FOR SAFETY AND RISK MANAGEMENT

2

Todd L. Seidler, University of New Mexico

Sports and recreation facilities that are poorly planned, designed, or constructed often increase participants' exposure to hazardous conditions and not only render the facility harder to maintain, operate, and staff, but can also significantly increase the organization's exposure to liability. A poorly designed facility can usually be traced to a lack of effort or expertise of the planning and design team. It is not uncommon for a sport, physical education, or recreation facility to be designed by an architect who has little or no experience designing that type of building. For those without the proper background and understanding of the unique properties of sport and recreation facilities, many opportunities for mistakes exist that may lead to increased problems related to safety, operations, and staffing.

Design problems commonly seen in activity facilities include inadequate safety zones around courts and fields, poorly planned pedestrian traffic flow through activity areas, poor security and access control, lack of proper storage space, and the use of improper building materials. Often, safety problems related to design are difficult, expensive, or impossible to fix once the facility has been built. It is essential that these facilities be planned and designed by professionals with activity-related knowledge and experience.

In order to protect themselves from claims of negligence, managers of sport and recreation programs and facilities have a number of legal responsibilities they are expected to perform. In this case, negligence is the failure to act as a reasonably prudent and careful sport or facility manager would act in the same or similar circumstances. In general, facility managers are required to run their programs so as not to create an unreasonable risk of harm to participants, staff, and spectators. One of their specific legal duties is to ensure that the environment provided is free from foreseeable risks or hazards. Unsafe facilities are one of the leading claims made in negligence lawsuits related to sports and physical activity. When discussing facility liability, Page (1988, p. 138) called it "one of

the largest subcategories within the broad spectrum of tort law." More specifically, managers of sports facilities are expected to provide a reasonably safe environment and at least to carry out the following five duties:

- Keep the premises in safe repair.
- Inspect the premises to discover obvious and hidden hazards.
- Remove the hazards or warn of their presence.
- Anticipate foreseeable uses and activities by invitees and take reasonable precautions to protect the invitee from foreseeable dangers.
- Conduct operations on the premises with reasonable care for the safety of the invitee.

According to van der Smissen (1990, p. 235), "The design, layout, and construction of areas and facilities can provide either safe or hazardous conditions, enhancing or detracting from the activity in which one is engaged." A facility that has been properly planned, designed, and constructed will greatly enhance the ability of the facility manager to effectively carry out these legal duties. A look at common safety problems in sports facilities has determined that they can usually be traced to two primary causes: 1) poor facility planning and design and 2) poor management.

When discussing safe facilities, Maloy (2001, p. 105) states, "Most liability problems dealing with safe environment, however, stem from maintenance and operation of the premises, not their design and construction." Even though this may be true, it is important to understand that there are many things that can be done during the planning process that will enhance the sport manager's ability to safely and properly maintain and operate the premises. A well-designed facility makes the management process more effective and efficient. It follows that the easier it is to maintain a facility, the more likely it is that it will be done well. According to Jewell (1992, p. 111) in his book, *Public Assembly Facilities*, "Public safety begins with good architectural design . . . ." Therefore, the majority of this chapter will focus on the planning and design of safe facilities.

Planning Safe Facilities

In order to plan and build a facility that is safe, efficient, and that optimally supports the activities likely to occur in each area, a thorough understanding of those activities is required. During the planning process, each individual space within the facility must be studied in an attempt to identify every activity that will, or might take place in that space. After this has been done, the requirements of the space necessary for each of the activities must be determined. For example, if it is determined that a multipurpose room will house classes in aerobic dance, martial arts, yoga, and gymnastics, and will also act occasionally as a small lecture set-up with portable chairs, the needs of each of these activities must be met, even though some may be in conflict with others. After the design requirements have been identified for each activity, a master list for each area should be developed. This master list is then used to plan that area in order to reduce the number of design errors as much as possible. The following are areas where errors in planning often create hazardous situations within facilities.

Security and Access Control

When designing a facility, the following two kinds of access will be addressed: controlling access (1) to the facility and (2) within the facility. Controlling access to sport, recreation, and fitness facilities is an important function of facility managers. Legal liability, deterrence of vandalism and theft, member safety and satisfaction, and maintaining exclusivity and value for those who pay for the privilege of using the facility are a few of the reasons it is necessary to deny access to those who don't belong. A properly designed and equipped facility, along with the use of computerized controls and a well-trained staff, can make access control relatively easy to deal with.

Many facilities, especially older spectator facilities, can be a nightmare to control. Fire regulations require many outside doors for quick evacuation. When limited access is desired, how can these doors be secured, monitored, and controlled without violating fire codes?

When designing a facility, it is often advantageous to plan for one control point through which everyone entering or leaving the building must pass. This control point is usually staffed during open hours, so the appropriate fee is paid, ID card checked, or permission given to those who are eligible to enter. If a higher degree of control is desired, a door, gate, or turnstile can also be used.

Many computer software programs are now available to help with access control. If patrons and staff are issued ID cards, such as in a club, school, or corporate setting, systems with magnetic strip or bar code readers can be used to quickly check a person's status. Swiping the ID card through an electronic card reader can determine if the user is eligible to enter. In systems designed for high traffic flow, the computer can be connected directly to a turnstile. If, after scanning the ID, the computer determines that the person should be permitted to enter, it can send a signal to release the turnstile and allow the individual to come in. This, however, does not prevent an unauthorized person from using someone else's ID. For increased security, picture IDs are desirable to ensure that the person using the card is the legal owner. Other new systems of access control include software programs that, upon scanning an ID card, display a picture of the patron on a computer monitor. If a higher level of security is desired, some systems actually use biometric identification. These systems may scan a patron's fingerprint, palm print, or even retina and compare it to records in the computer's memory. Facial recognition systems are now being used in high-security situations to identify individuals that may pose a threat to a facility or event. These security/access control systems are not only used to admit members, but can also track attendance and adherence to fitness programs, determine patrons' attendance habits, help set staffing levels to provide services at the proper times of the day and to provide information for marketing efforts.

Another aspect of access control that is improving with advances in technology is the replacement of standard door locks and keys. Systems now exist that place an electronic card reader at each door. Instead of a key, each authorized person is issued a card that can be passed through, or near, any of the card readers. A central computer receives the information from the card and compares it with the information stored in memory. The computer determines if the person who was issued that card is authorized to open that particular door, and either unlocks it or refuses access.

This type of system has many advantages. The computer can be programmed to allow access only to certain areas for each individual cardholder. A part-time employee may have a card

Example of an illegal control mechanism.

that works only on certain doors, while the facility manager's card can be programmed to open them all, like a master key. Also, the computer may be programmed so that certain cards only work during specified hours.

In the case of regular locks, if someone loses a key, it is often necessary to re-key many of the locks in the building. New keys must then be issued to everyone, often at great expense. With the card system, if someone loses an access card, that card can simply be turned off on the computer and a new card issued to the owner. The old card then becomes useless.

Another feature of the card access system is that each time someone uses a card to open a door it can be recorded on the computer. For example, computer records may show not only that a certain door was opened on Tuesday night at 11:05, but also whose card was used and if the person went in or out through the door. This information can be extremely valuable for facility security. The system can also be connected to the fire alarm and programmed to automatically unlock any or all of the doors when the alarm is triggered. Though it may initially be more expensive to install the card reader system than to install standard locks, it will usually pay for itself in increased efficiency, convenience, and long-term cost.

It is often desirable to control access to certain areas within a facility. Most buildings limit access to areas such as equipment rooms, office areas, mechanical rooms, or storage, but when a multiuse facility has more than one event or activity taking place at the same time, it may also be desirable to separate different parts of the building. For example, in a college activity center, it is not uncommon to have a varsity basketball game in the main arena, while the rest of the facility is kept open for recreation. With good planning, this can be accomplished by physically separating the spaces through the use of different entrances and exits, different floors, and locking doors, gates, and fences that can quickly restrict passage from one area to another.

There are two basic concepts to be familiar with for controlling access within a facility: (1) horizontal and (2) vertical circulation control.

Horizontal circulation control is a common method of managing access to different parts of a facility when there is a need to separate areas on the same floor. In the above example, when the entire facility is open for recreation, an open access plan is utilized. However, when a varsity basketball game is scheduled, certain doors, gates, and fences can be opened or closed in order to restrict spectator access to the arena without having to close down the rest of the building.

Sometimes it may be most efficient to plan for managing access through vertical circulation control. For example, it may be desirable in a large arena to have limited access to the lower level. This level may include the playing floor, locker rooms, business offices, coaches' offices, training rooms, and storage areas. By limiting public access to the entire floor, it becomes much easier to secure each individual area. In some arenas and stadiums, the luxury suites are located on one floor, and access to that floor can be gained only by certain elevators, stairways, or gates. Patrons in general seating areas cannot gain access to the suite level, thereby enhancing security and also providing a feel of exclusivity for suite holders. If vertical circulation is needed for a large number of people, providing non-skid ramps with good handrails or escalators may provide a safer method than stairs.

Buffer Zones

Some activities require a certain amount of space surrounding the court, field, or equipment to enhance the safety of the participants. An inadequate amount of space for a buffer zone or safety zone can present foreseeable risks of injury. A number of lawsuits have been based on claims that an injury occurred as a result of an inadequate buffer or safety zone. Whether it is to separate two adjacent courts or to provide room between the court and a wall or another object, buffer zones must be considered.

Indoor

It is recommended that basketball courts be designed to have at least ten feet of clear space beyond the end lines that is free from walls, obstructions, or other courts (Dougherty & Seidler, 2007). This should be possible when designing a new facility but, if it's not, a very minimum of six feet is needed, and anything less than ten feet should be fully padded to soften the impact where players are likely to hit if they lose control while going out of bounds. As for the sidelines of the court, it is recommended that at least a six feet buffer space is provided between adjacent courts or to any obstruction including bleachers, walls, tables, benches, or stored equipment. It is important to remember that if cross-courts are used, then ad-

Failure to provide activity space free of obstruction.

equate buffer zones and padding must be provided beyond the end lines of those courts. However, the collegiate (NCAA) and high school (NFHS) rule books specify that a minimum of three feet of space is required around the perimeter of the court, but it is preferable to have a ten-foot clearance. All too often, facility planners see the three-foot minimum specified in the rulebook and design to that. It is the author's belief that a three-foot buffer zone is inadequate for safety, and anything less than six feet presents a foreseeable risk of collision. There is no reason for continuing to build brand new gymnasiums that contain dangerous conditions from the day they open. The smaller the buffer zone, the greater the risk of injuries occurring from collisions with walls, benches, bleachers, or tables. A full ten-foot buffer zone is recommended beyond the end line of basketball courts.

Because gyms are often used for many activities other than basketball, it is recommended that all walls and obstructions be fully padded. It is suggested that wall padding cover from no more than four inches off the floor to a height of at least 6'4" and extend at least the entire width of the court. On many existing courts, it is not uncommon to have padding begin six to 12 inches above the floor, rise only to five or six feet and extend only the width of the lane. In these facilities, players diving for a ball and sliding into the wall, those over six feet tall, or others outside the lane receive no protection.

Another problem that is common in basketball is with the scorer's table and team benches. These are commonly placed within three feet of the sideline and are often unpadded. Padded scorer's tables are available, but there are too few in use, especially at the high school level.

The American Society for Testing and Materials (ASTM) (2004) recently established standard specification F2440-04 in order to identify a minimum level of protection for impact and shock absorption properties for wall padding. The ASTM standard is an important step in the safety of sport and recreation facilities, and it is recommended that any padding that is purchased meet or exceed the ASTM standard.

Activity spaces and surrounding areas should also be designed to be free of obstructions such as doors, poles, columns, and supports. If any such obstruction cannot be moved or eliminated from the activity area or safety zone, it must be padded. All other protrusions that may cause a safety hazard in the gymnasium should be avoided if possible. Common examples of such protrusions include drinking fountains and fire extinguishers, which, during the planning process, can easily be moved or recessed into a wall. Standard doorknobs located in an activity area can also present a hazard, and alternative types of knobs that are recessed in the door are available. Such handles are commonly used on racquetball courts.

It should be recognized that an activity area such as a gymnasium might be used occasionally for activities other than those it was designed for. It is not uncommon for outdoor activities such as softball, ultimate frisbee, or track practice to be moved indoors during inclement weather. These activities must be considered when planning a safe gym. The main point is that not all activities will use the traditional court markings for their activity area. This means that the distance from out-of-bounds to the wall is not always a safety factor for those activities that ignore the floor markings. If these activities can be identified and planned for before construction, there is an opportunity to provide a safe environment for them also. Otherwise, it becomes a management concern and a potentially hazardous aspect of the facility that must be compensated for.

Allowing more than one activity to take place in one area can be dangerous. Playing more than one basketball game on two or more courts that overlap, such as using a side basket for one game and an end basket for another, produces a situation in which an injury is foreseeable.

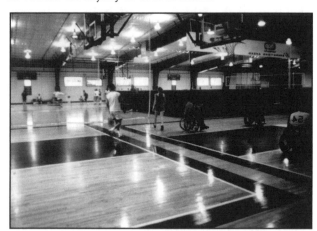

Dangerous overlap of adjacent activity areas.

Another area where buffer or safety zones are important and often overlooked is in the weight room. Placing weight equipment too close together can present a serious safety hazard. Most weight equipment should be spaced a minimum of three feet apart. This measurement should be made with the movement of the machine or exercise in mind. Some exercises require a horizontal movement, and the buffer zone should be measured from the extremes of this movement. An example occurs with many leg-extension machines. As the movement is executed, the legs straighten and extend another two feet or so out from the machine. The buffer zone should be measured from the point of full extension. Some exercises require more than a three-foot buffer zone. Certain free-weight exercises such as squats and power cleans require more room because of the amount of weight and relative lack of control typically encountered during such exercises.

Outdoor

Outdoor fields and courts have many of the same problems. Overlapping fields are a common occurrence and can cause a significant safety hazard if activities are allowed to take place simultaneously. A common example is two softball fields that share a part of the outfields. If games are being played at the same time on each field, the outfielders are at risk of collision. Overlapping courts and fields should be avoided if at all possible. An alternative might be to turn the fields around.

Two activity areas adjacent to each other can be just as dangerous as those that overlap. It is not uncommon to see a baseball field located next to a track. Sometimes this can lead to joggers on the track having to dodge errant baseballs. All adjacent activity areas must be planned with the idea that activities may occur simultaneously, so that foreseeably dangerous situations can be avoided.

Another common design that can produce several hazardous conditions is the typical football field that is surrounded by a track. Very often, facilities for field events are constructed inside the track and include asphalt runways and pit areas in addition to the track and pit areas constructed with concrete curbs. In this situation, there is often little distance between the football sidelines and the inner perimeter of the track, much less the runways, pits, and the commonly used concrete pole vault box.

Ideally, two activity areas, such as a football field and a track, should not be combined in one space. Realistically, though, there often is not sufficient space to construct the two separately, and they must be combined. If this type of mixed-use field is necessary, it is recommended that there be no obstructions within a minimum of 15 feet of the sidelines or end zone of the football field. At the very least, the jumping and vaulting runways can be placed outside the track. If bleachers on the opposite side of the field are not adequate to accommodate crowds, removable bleachers can be temporarily installed over those runways and pit areas. The high-jump approach as well as the shot put and discus pads can be located more than 15 feet from the end zone without encroaching on the track.

Other common obstructions that can create hazardous conditions are telephone, water, and/or electrical boxes used during football games that are often placed adjacent to the inner perimeter of the track. These are typically metal boxes mounted on poles several inches above the ground. A runner (either track or football) who is bumped, stumbles, or is tackled, can fall and strike the sharp metal receptacle and be severely injured. If such boxes are essential, they should be placed underground with the top flush with the field surface. Any obstructions that are within 15 feet of the field should be padded for safety. The primary problem with padding obstructions is that, even when padded, they are still a hazard. Also, the padding deteriorates over time, or disappears, or people get lax about installing it prior to usage of the field. It is better to plan and construct the area without such hazards in the first place.

Many fields have been built with steel manhole covers or storm drain grates in, or next to, the playing area. Also, fences are constructed or trees planted just outside the boundary lines, typically with no thought for the safety of the people using the field. It is important to understand that not all activities take place within the playing field. Whether chasing a fly ball into foul territory or getting tackled on the sideline, obstructions that are just out-of-bounds can be significant hazards. With proper planning, these can often be easily avoided.

Another common safety hazard often seen in high school baseball and softball facilities is open dugouts. All dugouts should be screened in front to protect those within from line-drive foul balls and errant throws. Providing protected access to and from the dugout is also important. Water fountains and bat racks should be placed inside or behind the dugout, with players being able to gain access to them from the dugout without being directly exposed to the field.

Portable soccer goals that are left out on fields also can create a very hazardous situation. Several children are killed or severely injured each year by climbing on goals that are not anchored to the ground. These goals are often heavy, poorly balanced and tend to tip over when someone hangs on them. Injuries typically occur when a child hangs from the crossbar and is then crushed as it tips over. These incidents can be prevented by either permanently anchoring soccer goals or using a chain or cable to lock them in place.

Pedestrian Traffic Flow

A common flaw in planning a facility that can cause safety problems is failure to properly plan

**Example of lack of adequate
storage space.**

for pedestrian traffic flow from one area to another. Requiring people to walk through an activity area in order to get to their desired destination can result in a needlessly high-risk situation. A very common example is when the main entrance to the locker room can only be reached by walking across the gym floor. The result is people entering and leaving the locker room while an activity is taking place in the same space.

Another example of poor traffic flow planning often occurs when pedestrians are forced to walk across a court or between two adjacent courts to get to another part of the facility. This also puts pedestrians in a situation where a collision with a participant is likely.

Planning pedestrian traffic flow within some activity areas is an important consideration. A weight room can be more hazardous if people do not have good, clear, open pathways to move around to different parts of the room. The design and layout of the weight room should take into account the movement of the users, especially during times of peak occupancy. Laying out the optimal pathways within the weight room that provide users with easy access to the more popular areas or machines will help prevent excess traffic between machines.

Storage

One of the most common complaints that facility managers report when asked about their facility is a lack of adequate storage space. The following is a typical example of how this often occurs. A new facility is planned with plenty of storage space in the early stages of planning. As the design is developed and the estimated cost of construction becomes clearer, it is determined that the project is over budget and something must be cut. Storage areas are often the first spaces to go.

Without proper storage space, equipment will usually be stored in a corner of the gym, in one of the hallways or on the side of the pool deck. Beside the fact that improperly stored equipment is much more likely to be vandalized or stolen, it may also attract children (see attractive nuisance below) or others to use or play with it, usually unsupervised and not in the manner for which it was designed. Equipment such as mats and port-a-pits, gymnastic apparatus, standards, nets, goals, chairs, hurdles, tables, ladders, maintenance equipment, etc., are often seen stacked in the corners of gyms. No longer a common sight, trampolines were often pushed into a corner and left unattended. This improper storage and poor supervision led to many catastrophic injuries and deaths and has resulted in the elimination of trampolines from most programs today. It is essential that adequate storage space be planned and constructed and that it be readily accessible and easily secured to prevent unauthorized use of the contents.

Lack of sufficient storage space for outdoor equipment is also often a problem. Providing a fenced, lockable storage area for items that are too large to be moved indoors for things such as blocking sleds is recommended. A fully enclosed storage area for pole vault and high-jump pits, hurdles, judges stands, and other moveable equipment will provide protection from the weather and vandals and will prevent creating an attractive nuisance.

Proper Materials

Many factors must be considered during the selection of materials to be used in the construction of a sport or recreation facility. Among these are initial cost, functionality, durability and expected life span, ease, and cost of maintenance and aesthetics. Another factor that is often overlooked is safety. Without proper consideration, building and finishing materials can play a large role in the inherent safety of the facility. The potential activities that may take place in every space must be studied thoroughly to ensure that the facility will optimally support each.

Flooring materials must be chosen with great care. Poor selection of the floor surface can contribute to significant safety hazards. One of the most dangerous examples commonly occurs in wet areas, such as locker rooms, shower areas, training rooms, and pool decks. The material selected for the floors in these areas should be a long-lasting, easily maintained, non-slip surface. All too often, these wet areas are constructed with a smooth finish, such as smooth or polished concrete, linoleum, or terrazzo. These are excellent surfaces in the proper situation and are usually selected for cost, durability, and ease of maintenance. But they all can become extremely slippery when wet. Many excellent non-slip surfaces are available for areas where they may get wet. One of the best surfaces for wet areas is rough-finish ceramic or quarry tile.

Inappropriate use of acoustical panels.

All wet areas should be designed to slope toward a floor drain to avoid standing water.

Wall surfaces also offer opportunities for hazards to be designed into a facility. A major hazard often introduced into a facility is the use of glass in or near activity areas. Glass in doors or windows or covering fire extinguishers is a common cause of injury. Even the use of glass embedded with wire mesh should be questioned in activity areas. This type of glass is often mistakenly considered safety glass, which it is not (Cohen, 2004). It is designed for fire protection and can be easily broken. If someone were to put their hand or head through such a window, the wire mesh would likely make the injury much worse than the same incident with regular glass.

Another relatively common problem has occurred with the use of glass in what most people think of as a non-activity area. The trophy case in the lobbies of most high school gyms is a good example. Planners often overlook the fact that lobby space is frequently used for activities, whether it's the wrestling team running in the halls during inclement weather, cheerleaders practicing, or just the everyday horseplay that occurs with teenagers. Safety glass of some sort should be used in this area. Mirrors used in weight rooms and dance studios must be selected and located with care. They should be high-strength, shatterproof glass designed for activity areas. Weight-room mirrors should be mounted about 18 inches above the floor to avoid contact with a barbell that may roll against the wall.

It is also important to select proper ceiling materials. Acoustic ceiling panels can be excellent for classrooms and offices but can become a maintenance headache and safety hazard when used in activity areas such as gyms. Acoustic panels are not meant to withstand abuse from balls and often break or shatter when hit.

The materials selected must be chosen with care in order to withstand the abuse likely to occur in each particular area. Lighting fixtures in activity areas must be appropriate to withstand the activities that will take place. In gyms where balls or other objects may hit the lights, each fixture must be designed to withstand potential punishment. The proper light typically has a plastic cover and a wire screen for protection. If the fixture is struck hard enough to shatter the bulb, the broken glass will be contained by the plastic cover and prevented from falling to the floor. Fixtures without this feature may shower broken glass on the participants below when struck.

Supervision

Designing a facility so that it can be supervised efficiently is a great advantage for two major reasons. First, a lack of proper supervision is one of the most common allegations made in lawsuits regarding negligence in sport and physical activity programs. The design and layout of the facility are often overlooked as a primary reason for poor supervision. Some facilities are inherently easy to supervise and some are not.

Second, a poorly designed facility may require five staff members to properly supervise activities, whereas a well-designed building of similar size

and offerings may require only three. Figuring the cost of paying even one extra supervisor, using the number of hours the facility is open each year

Emergency safety device.

over the life of the facility, can result in a dramatic increase in operating cost.

A well-designed facility can be adequately supervised by a minimum number of staff members. Design features that enhance efficiency of supervision include activity areas that are close together and easily monitored. Instead of spreading activity areas around the perimeter of the facility, one efficient method being used is to design a long central hallway or mall off of which are placed the activity areas. With proper windows or other means of observing, a supervisor can view many different areas in a short period of time.

Locker rooms are another area that are often poorly designed for adequate supervision. Concrete floors and walls, steel lockers with sharp corners, and standing water, all make locker rooms perhaps the single most dangerous facility in sport and recreation. In school settings, there is also a lot of unstructured time with classes coming and going, showering and changing clothes. It all adds up to a need for close, active supervision. Most locker rooms are laid out in rows of high lockers, which makes it difficult to supervise the activities and easy for someone to hide. All too often, the teacher/coaches' office is located in a position that does not allow an adequate view of the entire room. Providing the ability to easily and adequately supervise must be considered while planning and designing a locker room.

Another innovation that is seeing increased usage is Closed Circuit Television (CCTV) systems. A well-designed system can allow a supervisor in one location to visually monitor many diverse locations, both within and outside of the facility. Often the supervisor is equipped with a two-way radio in order to stay in constant communication with attendants on duty inside and outside the building. If a problem is observed on the CCTV monitor, the supervisor can direct an attendant to respond immediately. A properly planned system may allow for a smaller staff than might otherwise be required, while actually increasing supervisory coverage of the facility.

Miscellaneous Considerations

All facilities must be planned in compliance with all applicable codes. This includes all Occupational Safety and Health Administration (OSHA), Americans with Disabilities Act (ADA), fire, safety, and health codes that are appropriate for a given situation.

Humidity must be controlled throughout the facility. Excessive humidity not only reduces the comfort level but can cause corrosion and deterioration of building materials. Under the right conditions, high humidity can also condense onto activity floors, steps, walkways, etc., and create a dangerous condition. Lighting levels must be sufficient for the activity. Improper lighting can cause a hazardous situation, especially in areas where participants must visually track fast-moving objects such as in racquetball.

Signage can be an important part of a facility risk- management program. Rules, procedures, instructional and warning signs must be developed and posted in proper locations.

SUSTAINABLE DESIGN, CONSTRUCTION, AND BUILDING OPERATIONS

3

Rick Gonzales, University of Wisconsin - Eau Claire

The need to become more sensitive to global warming, rising energy prices, increased contamination, the increase in environmental related diseases and ailments, material shortages, overflowing landfills, and other related issues has caused significant concern, not just in the scientific community, but with the general public as well. Increased news coverage, Academy Award-winning documentaries, and Nobel Peace prizes, along with increased awareness has brought this issue to the forefront of human concern.

Figure 3.1

Background

People and organizations can have many different reasons why they adopt or promote sustainable design methods. Some reasons why such practices should be considered include, but are not limited to the following:

Altruistic objectives—such as demonstrating commitment to environmental stewardship and social responsibility by showing leadership in transforming the built environment.

Carbon reduction—is an essential ingredient of all fossil fuels (coal, oil, gasoline). When these fuels are burned to provide energy, carbon dioxide (CO_2), a greenhouse gas, is released into the Earth's atmosphere.

Greenhouse gases (GHG)—any gas that absorbs infrared radiation in the atmosphere. Greenhouse gases include, but are not limited to, water vapor, carbon dioxide (CO_2), methane (CH_4), nitrous oxide (N_2O), chlorofluorocarbons (CFCs), hydrochlorofluorocarbons (HCFCs), ozone (O_3), hydro fluorocarbons (HFCs), perfluorocarbons (PFCs), and sulfur hexafluoride (SF_6), (United States EPA, 2008).

Reduce energy consumption—any program that promotes the implementation of energy efficiency improvements in buildings to reduce energy consumption and create energy savings.

Reduce non-biodegradable waste generation—encouraging consumers to avoid using disposable products and designing products that use less material to achieve the same purpose. In construction, the challenge is to produce high-quality projects with minimal generation.

Conserve water—to reduce the withdrawal of fresh water from an ecosystem to stay within its natural replacement rate.

Reduce harmful greenhouse gas emissions (GHG)—primary sources of GHG include home heating and cooling, electricity consumption, agriculture, and transportation.

Protecting the rights of future generations—development that meets our own needs without compromising the ability of future generations to meet their needs. Implicit in this definition is the recognition of rights of future generations—the right to achieve a sustainable level of development and the right to be able to utilize natural resources, (*Encyclopedia of Sustainable Development*, 2000).

Improve air quality—eliminating sick building syndrome, improving occupant health and psyche, reducing lost work time, and improving productivity.

Reducing the production of toxic chemicals—moving away from chemicals that can harm human health or unnaturally enhance food production.

Moving America away from oil dependency—developing better fuel sources that are good for our national security, economy, and the environment.

Global warming—rising earth temperature's effects on species survival, food production, and weather.

Saving the wildlands—defending the wild places of our world, including our forests, parks, wetlands, and wilderness areas.

Reviving our oceans—over fishing, pollution, and habitat destruction.

Financial incentives—local communities, state agencies, and some federal agencies may give developers some type of financial incentive for building sustainable buildings. If the protection of an historic structure is involved, then there may also be financial incentives available for the restoration of such a structure.

Whatever the reasoning for deciding to proceed with sustainable objectives does not matter; it is the right thing to do. No reason is better than another.

There is no common definition of what sustainability means. Green design, socially responsible design, high performance buildings, ecologically efficient, environmentally friendly, healthy buildings, ecodesign, natural resource efficient, whole building design, and other terms are widely used synonymously.

From the Whole Building Design Guide

Figure 3.2. Whole Building Approach to High-Performance Buildings

To practice sustainable methods requires a complete "cradle-to-grave" approach. The cradle-to-grave approach is an analysis of the impact of a product from the beginning of its source-gathering processes, through the end of its useful life, to disposal of all waste products. Cradle–to–cradle is a related term signifying the recycling or reuse of materials at the end of their first useful life (*Green Building Encyclopedia*, 2007).

According to the *Green Building Encyclopedia* (2007), sustainability is the condition of being able to meet the needs of present generations without compromising those needs for future generations. It is achieving a balance among extraction and renewal and environmental inputs and outputs as to cause no overall net environmental burden or deficit. To be truly sustainable, a human community must not decrease biodiversity, must not consume resources faster than they are renewed, must recycle and reuse virtually all materials, and must rely primarily on resources of its own region.

There are many organizations that promote sustainable design practices. These organizations may stress a particular aspect of sustainability, such as site design, products and materials, recycling, or other key aspect in the cradle-to-grave approach.

Sustainable Design for Facilities/Venues for Health, Fitness, Physical Activity, Recreation, and Sports

Health, fitness, physical activity, recreational, and sports facilities fall behind other types of facilities with sustainable features in mind. There is no apparent reason why this industry has lagged behind others. U.S. Green Building Council (US-GBC) data for certified buildings in Figure 3.3 highlights this current disparity. This graphic is from 2006, and other facilities have come on line since that time, but the total number of sport and recreational facilities is still a small percentage of the total. Locating green facilities is not as easy as one might think. Facilities can be green but not be certified. There are also multiple certification programs available, each with certification criteria.

It is important to note that of the many LEED-[Leadership in Energy and Environmental Design] certified buildings, that only a small percentage qualify as facilities or venues for health, fitness, physical activity, recreation, and sports. According

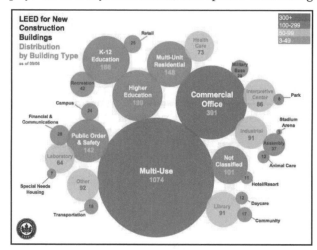

Figure 3.3. USGBC Certified Buildings by Building Type as of September 2006

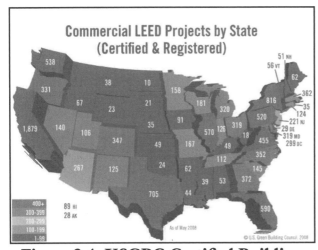

Figure 3.4. USGBC Certified Building by State as of July 2008

to Figure 3.4, the number of LEED-certified sport and recreational facilities are as follows:
- Recreation—forty-two
- Park—eight
- Stadium/arena—three

Known sustainable sport facilities that have been completed to date include the following:

- Los Angeles Community College Fieldhouse
- Harbor College PE/Wellness Center
- Montclair State
- Haverford College
- Grinnell College
- Dow Diamond
- Coors Field
- Great American Ball Park
- Detroit Lions HQ and Training Center
- University of South Carolina Baseball Stadium
- University of Connecticut Football Training Facility
- Murray State University

HOK Sport Photo

Figure 3.5. University of Connecticut Football Training Facility

The University of Connecticut facility was the first collegiate athletic facility to achieve LEED silver certification. This facility was just completed in 2006. This supports the concern that green industry is still in its infancy, especially when it comes to sport and recreation facilities.

Other sport facilities are planned but yet to be completed. The details of what will make them sustainable are unknown. In 2008, or shortly thereafter, other green sport facilities expected to be fully operational include, but are not limited to, the following:
- University of Connecticut Football Complex
- Minnesota Twins Ballpark
- Washington Nationals Ballpark
- University of Michigan Gymnastics facility
- Orlando Magic Arena
- Citi Field
- Thunder Bay Community Center
- Aquinas College Rec Center

HOK Sport Photo

Figure 3.6. Washington Nationals Ball Park

Vancouver, Canada plans to build numerous sustainable facilities for the 2010 Olympic Games and Paralympic Games.

The City of Chicago, in its bid for the 2016 Summer Olympic Games, has committed to constructing numerous green facilities. It is important to note that sustainability is a key concern of the International Olympic Committee (IOC). According to the IOC website, "environmental organizations and sports organizations have increasingly matching agendas when it comes to sustainability. It is about making sport more sustainable and sustainability more relevant. And it is about joining forces through partnerships. This was confirmed by today's presentations by environmental groups such as Greenpeace and the World Wildlife Fund, which showcased their initiatives in the context of the Olympic Games."

There has been significant movement to build sustainable schools and universities. These facilities may include gymnasiums that utilize sustainable design as well. These types of facilities are not broken down to a point that will allow for an easy analysis of the various green components that each educational facility may have.

The movement toward sustainable buildings is not just an American effort. Many countries have embraced the need for more environment-friendly structures in sport. The UK, Australia, Canada, and others are aggressively pursuing the benefits of sustainable buildings.

HOK Sport Photo

Figure 3.7. ANZ Stadium Sydney, Australia

Key Concepts of Sustainability Need for Integrated Design

To ensure design success on any project, not just sustainable building projects, requires an integrated approach to the process. This approach requires that all members of the design team, including the designers, stakeholders, and construction workers work together to set project objectives, select appropriate building materials, systems, and project delivery methods. In the U.S., most construction projects are structured on an adversarial level, where designers, owners, and constructors have different agendas and

there is little mutual trust. This is the "low-bid" mentality. Everyone is looking for a bargain, but sometimes, those bargains hurt everyone. No one wants the contractor who had a large mistake in tabulating his bid constructing his project. No one should want an unqualified design team to design a project just because they were willing to do the project for the lowest price or because they knew the right person.

Burgeoning Young Industry

Since this industry is still in its infancy, it could also be said that the number of professionals adequately trained to design and construct these specialized facilities is a small percentage of the total professional population. No one wants to be the one who pays for the on-the-job training of inexperienced professionals, and no one wants to be the proving ground for untried technology (DOE, 2003). For these two reasons, the number of sustainable projects underway as a percentage of all construction projects remains relatively small.

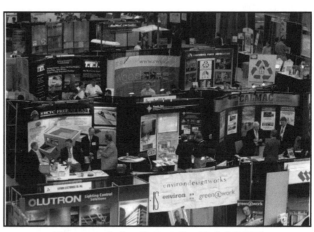

Figure 3.9. Greenbuild 2007 Conference Photo

The 2007 Conference held in Denver had over 700 exhibitors of green products, materials, and services on hand. More than 10,000 industry professionals attended the conference.

From the Whole Building Design Guide

Figure 3.8. Integrated Design Approach

Green Globes Green Building Initiative Logo

Figure 3.10. U. S. Green Building Council Logo

Building Certification Programs

There are multiple certification programs of various types in the marketplace, but there are two primary programs that focus on the advancement of responsible building practices and one that focuses on responsible product design and fabrication.

The USGBC has also compiled an extensive library of available resources that many industry professionals utilize, even if it is not their goal to achieve LEED certification. For this reason, many USGBC publications, periodicals, and data will be cited extensively in this chapter.

To date, LEED has the strong brand name recognition and appears to be the front runner among multiple certification methods. The LEED process has been adopted for use by the federal government and many state and local governments.

Another excellent certification program is the Green Globes program developed by the Green Building Initiative. This program has some similarities to the LEED format. The Green Globes process assesses potential points in seven areas that include the following:

- Project management
- Site
- Energy
- Water
- Resources
- Emissions, effluents, and other impacts
- Indoor environment

The primary reason for these similarities is that both share a common beginning. Both systems were based on the Building Research Establishment's Environmental Assessment Method (BREEAM) from the United Kingdom.

Figure 3.12. Energy Star Logo

The Green Globes method is less rigid, easier to use, and costs much less to certify a building. It is important to remember that a building does not have to be certified to be sustainable. The decision to certify is the choice of the building owner.

The Energy Star certification program developed by the EPA and the Department of Energy is a program that promotes energy-efficient products and practices for the benefit of American consumers.

By the end of 2007, more than 4,100 buildings and plants had earned Energy Star status. The total includes 1,500 office buildings, 1,300 supermarkets, 820 K-12 schools, and 250 hotels. According to the EPA, these facilities have saved nearly $1.5 billion annually in lower energy bills and also prevented carbon dioxide emissions.

It is not the intent of this chapter to promote any one sustainable design organization, but it is important to note that the USGBC LEED system is rapidly becoming the national norm. Many organizations in many fields promote sustainability methods, but few give guidelines as to how that goal can be achieved. The USGBC does provide more of a "how to" to sustainability, and that has significantly helped in the adoption of the program. This organization has experienced incredible growth in the last 11 years. In 1996, the USGBC membership was 61 members. By July of 2008, the membership had risen to 16,727.

LEED Rating System Product Portfolio

According to the USGBC, green design is the design and construction practices that significantly reduce or eliminate the negative impact of buildings on the environment and occupants. The LEED process varies by project type. To date, USGBC has developed multiple processes with sub-categories that include the following:

- New construction and major renovations (LEED-NC, Version 2.2)
- Existing buildings (LEED-EB, Version 2.0)
- Commercial interiors (Version 2.0)
- Core and shell (Version 2.0)
- Homes (Pilot Version 1.11a)
- Neighborhood development (Pilot Version)

Most projects that professionals in the sport and recreations industry may face should fall along the LEED-NC or LEED-EB process; for that reason, greater emphasis will be given to detailing those processes. LEED building certification is a voluntary consensus based national standard for developing high-performance, sustainable buildings.

LEED-NC and LEED-EB

These two processes for distinctively different types of projects have great similarities in what is measured. In both processes, the same six broad areas of concern are measured. These six broad areas are as follows:

- Sustainable site planning
- Safeguarding water and water efficiency
- Energy efficiency and renewable energy
- Conservation of materials and resources

- Indoor environmental quality
- Innovation in upgrades, operations, and maintenance

The six broad areas of concern may not vary by either measuring process, but how and what is measured does vary by process. The specific differences are as follows:

- *LEED-NC Process*
  Total points possible are 69.
  For certification, a project must earn the following point levels:
    -Platinum—52 to 69 points
    -Gold—39 to 51 points
    -Silver—33 to 38 points
    -Certified—26 to 32 points

- *LEED-EB Process*
  Total points possible are 85.
  For certification, a project must earn the following point levels:
    -Platinum—64 to 85 points
    -Gold—48 to 63 points
    -Silver—40 to 47 points
    -Certified—32 to 39 points

The higher number of available points for existing buildings diminishes the value of each point. There may be very little that an existing structure can do about its site configuration, thus making it hard to achieve points in that area. Existing buildings are prime candidates for improvement in the areas of energy and atmosphere, materials and resources, and environmental air quality.

Of all of the LEED-certified buildings, there are a very small number of platinum-certified buildings in any of the LEED processes. As of October 2007, the number of buildings per certification level for all of the LEED Rating Systems, regardless of project type, i.e., NC, EB, or any other LEED category were as follows:

- Platinum—61 or about 5% of the total
- Gold—317 or about 28% of the total
- Silver—372 or about 33% of the total
- Bronze—3 (no longer offered) or less than 1% of the total
- Certified—387 or about 34% of the total
- Total number of LEED certified buildings—1,540 as of May 2008

Benefits of Green Buildings
Sustainable practices can substantially reduce the impact on natural resource consumption. Green buildings can also reduce energy consumption. According to the USGBC (2006), sustainable buildings as an average consume:

    30% less energy
    30% less carbon

    30 to 50% less water usage
    50 to 90% less cost due to waste generation

In addition to the potential financial benefits, green buildings can also:

- Promote building occupant health and decreased risk management
- Reduce the impact on local infrastructures
- Increase building valuation
- Decrease vacancy in commercial buildings
- Be excellent for public relations
- Increase morale
- Reduce the growth of mold

The general public has a positive perception of brands and products that are aligned with social causes. According to the USGBC (2008):

89% choose brands aligned with social causes
74% listen to brands aligned with social causes
69% shop for brands aligned with social causes
66% recommend brands aligned with social causes

It is still unknown whether or not green buildings live up to expectations. Only time will tell whether or not these buildings actually deliver the intended benefits. Despite this fact, there are still perceived benefits to green buildings (USGBC, 2008). The perceived benefits of green buildings are as follows:

8 to 9% decrease in operating expenses
7.5% increase in building values
6.6% improvement in ROI
3.5% increase in occupancy
3% rent increase

If the Benefits Are So Great, Why Isn't Everyone Building Sustainable Buildings?
The sustainable products, materials, and equipment industry is still in its infancy. New items are becoming available every week. Only time will tell which of these will catch on and survive in the long term. At this point in time, the cost to construct sustainable structures does cost more than conventional construction, but the cost is decreasing at a reasonable rate (Kibert, 2005).

Kibert also found that compared to standard construction methods, the cost to construct sustainable facilities at LEED standards can cost above and beyond that of conventional construction as follows:

    Platinum—6.5% higher
    Gold—1.8% higher
    Silver—2.1% higher
    Certified—0.7% higher

Since the LEED certification process is relatively new, there is little hard data to examine so that it can be confirmed or refuted that sustainable facilities reduce operating costs over time. If costs are found to be reduced, then it is possible to recoup the high first-costs investment that these types of facilities require.

The California Sustainable Building Task Force (CSBTF) study (2003) that examined 33 LEED-certified projects concluded that there was a 2% cost increase to become LEED certified. As a follow-up to this study, a Greenspirit Strategies (GSL) study examined the results of the CSBTF study and concluded that data analysis was flawed and that the actual costs to become certified were probably more like a 4% increase to the total project cost.

In 2007, Compass Resource Management issued the report Towards a Green Building and Infrastructure Investment Fund in conjunction with the Vancouver 2010 Olympic and Paralympics Winter Games effort. In this report, the researchers conducted multiple surveys and studied multiple models to determine the increased cost of LEED-certified construction as well as the potential benefits. This report confirmed that LEED certification does increase cost above and beyond that of conventional construction as follows:

Platinum—4.7% to as high as 10.3% more
Gold—0.4% to as high as 8.1% more
Silver—0% to as high as 4.3% more
Certified—0% to as high as 2.4% more

It is important to note that this same study also found that LEED-certified buildings had significant impact on reducing the overall building consumption. The observed reductions were as follows:

Platinum—60%
Gold—47%
Silver—33%
Certified—24%

Rapidly rising energy costs will continue to rise, and reducing long-term operating costs could be a very attractive alternative to relatively low first costs required for construction. Not all of a project's incurred costs will provide a return on investment. The soft costs of a project, such as specialized design work, LEED certification process, etc., are actual costs but will not provide any financial return directly. Reducing water runoff or recycling resources do equate to benefits to society but do not equate to actual measurable savings (The American Chemistry Council, 2003).

Avoided costs are also hard to measure. For example, it may be harder than one would think to quantify productivity improvement or reduced maintenance costs. Sustainable buildings can contribute to savings in both of these; but will people actually work harder if they are more comfortable and less likely to become ill? In factory settings, this case can easily be made, but in office environments or classrooms, or even sport and recreation facilities, the effects will be undetectable. People will

do what they have to do and very seldom will they exceed that accepted limit. Reducing costs can also imply to some that there may be staff reductions, as less people will be required to do the same amount of work. The concept that people could lose their jobs because productivity is up and costs are down could make sustainable facilities a very hard sell (The American Chemistry Council, 2003).

Building owners and developers must also be sold on making investments in sustainable buildings. Higher first costs could mean higher rents or higher costs to be passed onto the consumer. Could doing the right thing price someone out of the marketplace? Renters of commercial or residential properties generally do not care about increased investment costs, as they know that those costs will be passed onto them (Brown, Southworth, & Stovall, 2005).

According to the *Whole Building Design Guide* (2007), the first cost of construction will only amount to about 2% of the total cost of building ownership in the first 30 years. If building owners and developers fully understood the negligible impact of the first cost of construction, would they be more likely to embrace sustainable design at a higher initial cost? The CSBTF study also found that going green would result in a 20% savings in the total life cycle cost of the structure.

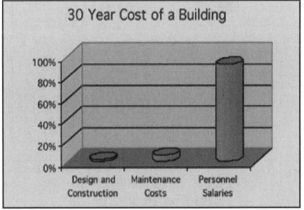

From the Whole Building Design Guide

Figure 3.13. Cost of an Average Building Over a 30-Year Lifetime

Other costs that cannot be easily quantified are the human and community benefits. How does one measure moral, decreased turnover, absenteeism, and other human factors? How does one begin to measure community factors such as reduced land erosion, controlled storm water runoff, and watershed pollution? For that matter, what is the moral responsibility of building owners?

It is important to note that as the sustainable products, materials, and services industry matures, the costs will continue to go down, thus reducing the first-cost premium. Government regulation of some type may also mandate the movement toward more sustainable buildings, thus making it more mainstream.

As many contractors are not savvy on the intricacies of sustainable development, there may be some wariness in bidding or pricing such structures. There can be an impact on cost when a contractor perceives the sustainable requirements as onerous or risky. When faced with uncertainty, the contractor will add a contingency to his pricing or refuse to participate if he believes that the contingencies will price them out of the project. If the bidding pool diminishes, then there is less competition, and the bid prices will most likely rise (Matthiessen, 2004). Proceeding with projects using the integrated design approach will help to prevent these types of problems.

Quantifying the Benefits

Understanding the life costs of a facility is an essential part of the design, construction, and operational stages, essential for making good decisions. In order to fully understand the concepts of life-cycle costing, it is necessary to understand

From the Whole Building Design Guide

Figure 3.14. Life Cycle of Building Products

the concepts of compounding, discounting, present value, and equivalent annual value.

Figure 3.14 graphically represents the cradle-to-grave concept of life-cycle costing. It is not the purpose of this chapter to delve into all of these concepts in detail, but there are a number of readily available sources to assist one's understanding of life-cycle costing concepts. Life-cycle costing could easily be a chapter in itself. Available resources include, but are not limited to, the following:

Building for Environmental Economic Sustainability (BEES)—this free software was developed by the National Institute of Standards and Technology (NIST) to assist users in measuring the environmental and economic performance of various building products.

Cost Effectiveness for Capital Asset Protection Version 3.0—this is another NIST-developed

product that allows the user to create models to compare risk mitigation strategies based on established economic evaluation practices.

The National Renewable Energy Laboratory (NREL) has published the Life-Cycle Inventory (LCI) database, which is a publicly available database for commonly used materials and products in the construction industry.

Green Building Initiative has a product called the Life Cycle Assessment (LCA) tool that allows designers to compare alternative design scenarios to assist in the decision-making process.

The American Society for Testing and Materials (ASTM) publishes many life-cycle costing standards; in fact, the organization has published 143 different standards that relate to building sustainability. These standards include, but are not limited to the following:

–ASTM E833-06 Standard Terminology of Building Economics
–ASTM E964-06e1 Standard Practice for Measuring Benefit-to-Cost and Savings-to-Investment Ratios for Buildings and Building Systems
–ASTM E917-05 Standard Practice for Measuring Life Cycle Costs of Buildings and Building Systems

A core group of facility management members have published a free product called the Asset Lifecycle Model for Total Cost of Ownership Management. This product can be useful for existing facilities that need to make good decisions on day-to-day operations. Core participants included the Association of Higher Education Facilities Officers, Federal Council, International Management Association, and the National Association of State Facilities Administrators.

The Athena Institute has developed the Eco-Calculator for Assemblies, which is a good tool for comparing different assemblies (exterior and interior walls, roofs, floors, windows, etc.) for comparative environmental impact.

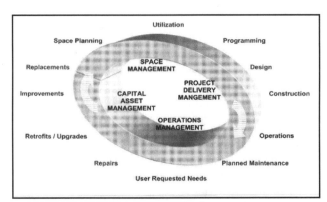

Figure 3.15. Building Life-Cycle Process from the Asset Lifecycle Model for Total Cost of Ownership Management

The Federal Energy Management Program (FEMP) also has a free product called the Building Life Cost Cycle (BLCC) program. There are multiple life-cycle costing models and software packages available for sale, but the free packages would serve most needs just fine.

Figure 3.15 graphically depicts that all projects are cyclical in nature and function in a never-ending loop. The only factor that is not shown in this graphic is the eventual demise of a structure. No structure will last forever, and all buildings will eventually need to be demolished.

One of the biggest obstacles to analyzing the potential benefits of LEED certification effectiveness is the inability to establish a baseline for measurement. Government regulation, building code requirements, or even the availability of resources may cause a move toward sustainability that would have happened anyway (The American Chemistry Council, 2003).

Financial Incentives

HUD, through its Brownfields Economic Development Initiative (BEDI), does offer loan guarantees to finance projects that redevelop abandoned, idle, or underutilized industrial or commercial facilities that may be burdened by real or potential environmental contamination. Detailed and up-to-date listings of financial incentives are available at the USGBC website_https://www.usgbc.org, or at the Database of State Incentives for Renewables and Efficiency (DSIRE) website http://www.dsireusa.org/. Financial incentives may include any of the following:

- Tax incentives
- Grants
- Bonds
- Lease purchase programs
- Loan programs
- Personal income tax incentives
- Property tax incentives
- Rebate programs
- Sales tax incentives

There are other types of incentives that are not financial in nature but are beneficial to a developer nonetheless. This other type of potential incentive is favorable zoning permissions. Some municipalities may grant preferable zoning or rezoning approvals to projects that meet municipal sustainability objectives. These incentives can also be found on the previous two websites.

According to the IPE Real Estate monthly newsletter (2007), there are a number of large, well-funded real estate portfolios that heavily invest in green projects worldwide. The interest in these properties is because of the higher rents that can be commanded, lower tenant turnover, quicker space absorption, and substantially reduced annual operating costs. Sustainable buildings may also receive high valuations from real estate appraisers, thus improving the value of the investment.

Sustainability and Government Regulation

There is little federal government support or requirement for sustainable facilities funded by the state, municipal, or the private sector. It is a mandate for most federal agencies, but that is the limit of federal involvement. A complete listing of requirements by state and municipalities can be found in the Database of State Incentives for Renewables and Efficiency (DSIRE) website http://www.dsireusa.org/.

Large societal paradigm shifts as to what we value will be required before substantial changes will occur. In the near term, simply bringing current building practices up to the level of best practices would yield tremendous energy and cost savings. Past studies have shown that many climate-friendly and cost-effective measures in the building sector are not fully utilized in the absence of policy intervention (Brown, Southworth, & Stovall, 2005). Studies suggest that significant improvements in the energy efficiency of buildings appear to be cost effective; but they are not likely to occur without extensive policy changes (ORNL, 2003).

Myths and Facts of Sustainability

According to the USGBC (2008), the environmental impact of buildings in the U.S. is as follows:

71% of total electricity consumption
39% of total primary energy use
36% of total greenhouse emissions
65% (136 million tons) of construction and demolition waste (about 2.8 lbs per person per day)
12% of potable water use

Globally, 40% of raw materials or three billion tons are consumed for use in buildings (USGBC, 2008).

Buildings cannot be sustainable unless a process such as LEED or Green Globes has officially certified it. False—the certification process can take time and money to achieve this status. Sustainable design can be built into any project and does not require certification. There are benefits to achieve certification, as it will draw positive attention to a building.

Existing buildings cannot be easily modified to make them more sustainable. False—an existing building does not have the flexibility in design and material selection as a new building, but energy and water savings features can be integrated after the fact. Other potential features can include use of recycled materials and mechanical systems upgrades to improve air quality. Existing buildings have an advantage over new construction in that reuse of an existing building reduces the amount of demolition waste or construction waste that a new or replacement structure would generate.

Only aluminum, paper, glass, and plastics can be recycled. False—fryer grease, motor oil, paint, tires, concrete, most organic materials, wood products, metals, toner cartridges, and many other items can be easily recycled. Look for resources in your area to determine what recycling opportunities exist.

Any low-flow fixtures are an excellent means to reduce water usage.—Can be true or false; low-water fixtures, such as showers, sometimes require showering for longer periods of time. Low-flow toilets can sometimes be problematic. Water flow is what initiates the removal of waste and promotes flow through waste piping. Sometimes these can lead to back-ups and overflows, thus requiring building repair and increased sanitation concerns. It is important to look for fixtures that will reduce water usage but also prevent adverse side effects as well.

Sustainable products and materials are regulated. False—there is no national standard for what constitutes a sustainable material or product. There are professional and not-for-profit organizations that do compile lists of acceptable products and materials.

Sustainable products and materials will last as long as non-sustainable materials and products. Can be true; but most likely is false. Recent studies have indicated that some green building products including some low VOC paints will not last as long as conventional paints. Bamboo, cork, and other green flooring materials will not wear as well as conventional flooring materials.

Any competent professional can design or build a sustainable building. False—in 2003, the Department of Energy (DOE) study found that less than 2% of all architects, engineers, or contractors had ever been involved in a sustainable building. As of July 2008, the USGBC had certified 57,417 professionals, but there is a big distinction between achieving certification and actually having meaningful professional experience. Much has changed in the last five years, but the ratio of sustainable buildings being constructed today to total number of buildings built today is such a small percentage that is unlikely that the experience factor has not increased significantly.

Sustainable Operations

In the day-to-day operations, there are a number of things that operations can do to promote sustainable operations. These operations can help to reduce operating costs, promote air quality, reduce pollutants, and conserve resources. Areas where sustainable practices can make a difference include, but are not limited to the following:

Green cleaning—use of biodegradable and environment friendly chemicals.

HVAC maintenance—use of HEPA filters, keeping ductwork free of dust and water collection.

Energy conservation—turn off lighting and equipment when not in use.

Water conservation—understand your current water usage and how that impacts your operating costs.

Develop a plan that works to reduce water usage. Identify in your plan areas where water consumption can be reduced, for example, the use of low-flow fixtures and low water use landscaping. Examine your operations for leaks and drips to reduce waste. Use automatic timers where possible on faucets, sprinklers, etc. Work with building occupants to change behavior through education.

Green vehicles—hybrid vehicles or all electric when possible.

Recycling programs—make recycling a routine process.

Food service operations—limit food waste, buy local products, use environment friendly chemicals, reduce water usage, recycle frying grease.

Green grounds keeping—use environment friendly or natural pesticides, use local plants, recycle clippings, reduce water usage, and xeriscape when possible.

The above is not a complete listing of all of what could be accomplished to make day-to-day operation sustainable. It is just a short list to give the reader an understanding that much is possible with a little of forethought.

Tips for a Successful Sustainability Program

Predesign:

- Select your design and construction team members carefully. Use the integrated design approach on the project.
- Develop a sustainability checklist of features that are desired for the project. Prioritize these features accordingly, as not all may be necessary to make the project a success.
- Determine if any financial incentives are available for the project before moving the plan forward.
- Facilities can be designed and constructed that meet all sustainable criteria. Is it necessary to certify the building?
- Stop the practice of building disposable buildings. This concept runs contrary to the practice of building new stadiums and arenas with the latest and greatest technology and amenities as part of the facilities "arms race" mentality. There is great truth to the old adage, "We don't build them like we used to." Save and reuse old structures rather than demolish them.
- Consider alternative energy options such as wind, photovoltaic, geothermal, anaerobic digestion, fuel cells, or solar power.

- Use native vegetation:
Drought-resistant or low-maintenance vegetation is also preferable.
- Orient facilities properly.
Always take advantage of south facing windows, use of trees to cool outside walls, use of wind to provide ventilation, or water to reduce the heat island effect.
- Do not overbuild. Design facilities that can be easily added onto when needed rather than building for a future that may never be required.
- Set your preliminary budgets accordingly. If you launch into a green project with a budget for a conventional project, there will be problems. Understand what your green project will entail, so that it can be accurately reflected in your first budget. Project funding will probably be based on this first budget, so work hard to get it right.

Design:

Keep it simple; you can go green with a tight budget. Don't limit yourself, explore all possibilities, and don't sacrifice performance for the sake of first-cost savings.

Set your project objectives early and stick to the plan. Don't allow "scope creep," unless it is absolutely necessary.

- Design in flexibility. Try to predict potential future uses as best as possible.
- Do not rely on technology. There are many things that you can do that are reasonable in cost, have good paybacks, and rely on simple and strait forward concepts.
There are tried and true products and materials available for use without taking undue risks. Again, do your research!
- Use low-flow water fixtures. Not all low-flow fixtures are made equal. Some low-water-use toilets can end up being more trouble than they are worth if these units fail to properly remove solid waste material. Low-flow toilets that require multiple flushes or fail to remove all waste are not solutions, but additional problems. Do your research before buying or specifying products.
- Use natural lighting whenever possible, but use it wisely. Too much lighting or glare of any kind can prove detrimental to any kind of sport, fitness, and recreation or for spectators.
- Properly select the products, finishes, and materials to be used.

Use of recycled or reclamated water may be possible. Check with local health and building code officials before proceeding.

Properly size the HVAC equipment for the intended use. Remember that building codes are minimums and not ideals. It is just as important to not undersize airflow and changes as it is to oversize a system. Make sure that all systems, new or existing, are properly balanced and operational.

Water harvesting:

- Capture rainwater to help offset the need for additional potable water for landscaping needs.
- Remember that life safety codes are minimums and not ideals. So don't under insulate buildings or under size ventilation systems, etc.
- Specify low-VOC products and materials. Low-VOC items will not contribute to poor indoor air quality.

Construction:

- Minimize construction waste. Make recycling easy by identifying where materials of different types can be stored and work to educate the construction staff.
- Reduce the tendency to clear the site. Save as many trees as possible and protect the site's topsoil.
- Use quality local products whenever possible.

Startup and Occupancy:

Consider the use of a qualified building commissioning firm. According to the Building Commissioning Association (BCA), commissioning provides documented confirmation that building systems function according to criteria set forth in the project documents to satisfy the owner's operational needs. Commissioning existing systems may require developing new functional criteria to address the owner's current requirements for system performance. According to the BCA, building commissioning can also be of use in existing buildings as well. The benefits of retrocommissioning is the systematic process for investigating, analyzing, and optimizing the performance of building systems by improving their operation and maintenance to ensure their continued performance over time. Retrocommissioning helps make the building systems perform interactively to meet the owner's current facility requirements.

Operations:

- Institute a comprehensive recycling program.
- Maintain all mechanical and electrical systems to ensure optimum performance and to prolong its useful life.

Use HEPA filters:

- Regularly change out filters to ensure optimum performance.
- Use green cleaning products and equipment.
- Use environmentally friendly pesticides and herbicides.
- Use recycled water.

Renovation:

No design project can accurately predict the future. All facilities will need some type of strategic renovation for any of a multitude of reasons. Keeping up with technological changes such as computerization, lighting, etc. might require some renovation in order to keep facilities fit for duty.

Demolition:

- Adapt and reuse existing facilities whenever possible. When you knock something down, the debris has to go somewhere.
- Remember that nothing will last forever and plan replacement facilities before it's too late.
- Do not let all of the possibilities overwhelm you and prevent you from doing the right thing. Utilize well-trained and experienced professionals to help you through the maze of this dynamic and ever-changing industry.

Potential Downsides to Green Buildings

The industry is still in its infancy, and only time will tell whether or not facilities live up to the green hype. Already there is a growing industry in lawsuits related to facilities that failed to live up to expectations. Potential legal questions and issues that could someday impact green buildings being designed and constructed today include the following:

- Does a green building add an additional layer of risk?

- Fraud, negligence, or breech of contract might happen if facilities fail to perform as expected.
- What are the legal implications if someone intends to build to a green certification level such as LEED, but not seek certification?
- Will there be insurance implications?
- Can there be trademark implications if the name of certifying organizations is used but no payments are made to that organization?
- Are there issues on the design professional's standard of care?
- How will standard contracts need to be modified?

Pitfalls to Avoid

Reliance on technology—going green does not require high technology. The federal government launched full speed into the construction of sustainable buildings and relied heavily on technology. The high cost of technology when the green marketplace was so young resulted in many high-profile design failures.

Use of untrained and experienced support professionals—select professionals for their unique and related experience. This should not be an on-the-job training opportunity. Not all professionals have the same credentials.

Avoid the low-bid mentality—even with public money, there are ways to select the most qualified design and construction firms without having to settle for the lowest offer.

UNIVERSAL AND ACCESSIBLE DESIGN: CREATING FACILITIES THAT WORK FOR ALL PEOPLE

4

Richard J. LaRue, University of New England
Donald Rogers, Indiana State University

This chapter presents historical, conceptual, and regulatory information as well as planning resources related to universal and accessible design. Primary to the regulatory development of accessibility planning today are the key statutes from the 1990 Americans With Disabilities Act (ADA) and information regarding the most recent accessibility guidelines as published by the Architectural and Transportation Barriers Compliance Board (Access Board). Given the nonspecific nature of the regulations, the interpretations of many ADA statutes have been tested in court. The results of this litigation have created a body of case law under each ADA title. When planning facilities where issues of accessibility are not clearly defined, it may be helpful to research the available case law. Generally, the government was unresponsive to early accessibility legislation such as the 1968 Architectural Barriers Act (ABA). Today, accessibility is not the overlooked factor that it once was in the design of public and private facilities. However, there are still many questions about compliance and how to best meet the access needs of people with disabilities.

Even with published standards and guidelines, plus regular updates, it is possible for planners and designers to make misinterpretations and oversights. This chapter attempts to provide facilities planners and designers with accessibility standards and guidelines associated with typical design features such as parking, restrooms, entryways, ramps, and information areas. Additional resources will be provided in the form of Web sites and other references to assist in locating information. It is important to realize that beyond all the supporting features associated with facilities addressed in this book, there are often specific activity space, program, and equipment accessibility features to consider.

In this chapter and in resources located on the Web and other places, differences between the terms "final rule," "guidelines," and "standards" may be difficult to understand. For example, in many of the documents found on the Access Board's Web site, the term final rule is used. This would seem to indicate that this is now an enforce-able mandate but, in fact, it may not be. There is a sequence that begins with the law, and then guidelines are developed, and finally they become standards or regulations after being reviewed and approved by the necessary agency or agencies. This means that when the Access Board publishes final rules, these are only guidelines until the Office of Management and Budget (OMB) reviews them, and then the entities responsible for enforcement must approve them and only then do they become enforceable standards or regulations. Enforcement responsibilities are also explained in this chapter. A unique situation exists with the ABA that allows final rules by the Access Board to become standards as soon as the OMB approves them. This happens because the Access Board is responsible for enforcing the ABA, while other entities are responsible for the ADA and its subsequent titles.

The goal of this detail is to reinforce the hope that planners will go beyond the minimum guidelines or standards, thereby creating spaces that meet the broadest needs of participants while making everyone feel welcome. In situations where guidelines have not been established, or standards and regulations are not in effect, the ADA is clear that all covered entities must still comply with the law, which prohibits discrimination against people with disabilities. In these situations, enforcement entities expect planners to use current best practices when designing and building for accessibility. Where guidelines have been published, but have not become standards, these guidelines then would probably constitute best practices or minimum requirements. When no guidelines exist, then it is the responsibility of the planners and designers to research what is being done with regard to accessibility in the types of facilities they are creating. It is very useful to involve people with disabilities in this type of information-gathering process to get a sense of what the real needs are and whether new design ideas or adaptations will be functional.

Terminology is an important consideration when discussing, writing about, and reporting on matters that involve people with disabilities. There are a number of trendy terms used in these situations; however, most violate basic principles of acceptable terminology. A deliberate effort was made in this chapter to follow what is known as "person-first" terminology. The federal government uses this approach and scholars writing in the field prefer it, and perhaps most importantly, it is widely endorsed by the professional community of people with disabilities. Its usage is prominently seen in the ADA and the Individuals With Disabilities Education Act. This approach acknowledges the person ahead of the disability, emphasizing that the disability is a fraction of the whole person. While a person can undeniably have a disability, he or she should not be considered disabled. The term *handicapped* is often used with regard to accessibility as with handicapped parking or a handicapped restroom stall. In fact, when these facilities meet code, they are actually accessible features. When they do not meet code, they present a barrier to a person with a disability, which creates a handicapping situation. Helping designers create accessible and universal facilities instead of "handicapped" facilities is the primary purpose of this chapter.

Two final topics of foundation knowledge and awareness are the concepts of accessible and universal design. Frequently, these two terms are used interchangeably when considering the access needs of people with disabilities. While they are related in some ways, each has a unique meaning. *Accessible* has a popular or nontechnical meaning, that suggests something is made usable or available through some type of adaptation for individuals who have disabilities. It also has well-developed legal meaning in the context of the ADA and ABA. Consider the situation where a ramp does not comply with *The Americans With Disabilities Act Accessibility Guidelines* (ADAAG). Some would say that the ramp provides access, even in cases where it is quite steep. Others who have knowledge of the ADA might reference the ADAAG indicating the requirement for an "accessible" ramp to be no steeper than 1:12. In either case, the term accessible is referring specifically to meeting the needs of people with disabilities.

The second term, *universal design*, moves beyond the narrow concept of accessible. Accessible design juxtaposes accessible components with typical construction in order to eliminate or minimize environmental barriers for people with disabilities. Universal design creates a broadly inclusive environment that effectively blends a variety of design concepts, including accessible, into a range of meaningful options for all users. In a universally designed facility, it is not evident that modifications have been made for a specific person or group. This approach facilitates inclusion by focusing on people's abilities and emphasizing socially meaningful roles.

Exploring the complexities of universal and accessible design can be an overwhelming prospect. There are so many codes and regulations that designers and planners are expected to follow in addition to accessibility that the process may seem restrictive to the point of stifling creativity.

While codes and regulations do present boundaries of a sort, they also provide concrete beginning points that can actually stimulate creative design ideas. A helpful suggestion is to envision a comprehensive plan of accessibility that goes beyond minimum standards while taking into consideration the many potential uses of the space by people with a wide range of needs and abilities.

Civil Rights Legislation for Persons With Disabilities

The ABA of 1968, PL 90-480, authorized four primary agencies to issue accessibility standards in accordance with its respective statutory authority. Those agencies are the General Services Administration (GSA), the Department of Defense (DOD), the Department of Housing and Urban Development (HUD), and the U.S. Postal Service (USPS). The problem that surfaced with this approach is that guidelines were inconsistent between the agencies, resulting in much confusion. To address the issue of compliance with the ABA, Congress established the Architectural and Transportation Barriers Compliance Board (ATBCB) [Access Board] in Section 502 of the Rehabilitation Act of 1973.

The Access Board is composed of representatives from the four initial agencies, seven other governmental agencies (Health and Human Services, Interior, Justice, Labor, and Transportation, and the Veterans Administration), and 12 members appointed from the general public by the president of the United States. A 1978 amendment to Section 502 of the Rehabilitation Act of 1973 added to the Access Board's functions. This amendment required the Access Board to issue minimum guidelines and requirements for the standards then established by the four standard-setting agencies (GSA, DOD, HUD, and USPS).

The final rule establishing the guidelines now in effect was published in the *Federal Register* on August 4, 1982 (Access Board, Retrieved February 6, 2001). These guidelines are referred to as the *Minimum Guidelines and Requirements for Accessible Design* (MGRAD).

The four standard-setting agencies determined that the adopted uniform standards would, as much as possible, conform to the 1982 Guidelines of the Access Board and be consistent with standards published by the American National Standards Institute (ANSI). "ANSI is a non-governmental national organization that publishes a wide variety of recommended standards. ANSI's standards for barrier-free design are developed by a committee made up of 52 organizations representing associations of handicapped people, rehabilitation professionals, design professionals, builders, and manufacturers" (Access Board, Retrieved February 6, 2001, p. 5).

It is important to note that ANSI's 1961 standards, "Specifications for Making Buildings and Facilities Accessible to, and Usable by, Physically Handicapped People," formed the technical basis for the first accessibility standards adopted by the federal government and most state governments. The development of ANSI's revised standards in 1980 was based upon research funded by HUD. The 1980 ANSI standards were generally accepted by the private sector including the Council of American Building Officials (Access Board, Retrieved February 6, 2001). A fully updated ICC/ANSI A117.1, *Architectural Features and Site Design of Public Buildings and Residential Structures for Persons with Disabilities* is now available.

In 1984, the Access Board updated the MGRAD and published the UFAS, which became the standard used by the four agencies responsible for accessibility to enforce the ABA. The UFAS followed the ANSI 1980 standards in format and, with regard to scope provisions and technical requirements, met or exceeded the comparable provisions of MGRAD (Access Board, Retrieved February 6, 2001).

The ADA of 1990 significantly expanded the role of the Access Board. Under the ADA, the Access Board became responsible for developing accessibility guidelines for entities covered by the Act and for providing technical assistance to individuals and organizations on the removal of architectural, transportation, and communication barriers.

In 1991, the Access Board published ADAAG, considered more stringent than the UFAS guidelines. The Access Board maintains responsibility for revisions of the ADAAG as well as the UFAS. In November 2000, the Access Board published a comprehensive proposal to update and merge both its ADA and ABA/UFAS accessibility guidelines into the *ADA-ABA Accessibility Guidelines*. This was intended to provide more consistency between the ADA and ABA, simplify and clarify the language, and broaden the scope of what is covered. After extensive review and public comment, the Access Board approved the guidelines in final form on January 14, 2004, and published them as revised guidelines on July 23, 2004 (available online: http://www.access-board.gov/ada-aba/final.cfm. On June 17, 2008, these proposed regulations were published in the *Federal Register*. These proposed guidelines are now enforceable laws.

The Access Board's recent efforts to update the ADA and ABA/UFAS guidelines and provide ANSI with guidance with A117.1 will produce standards that are highly consistent with each other. The new ADA/ABA version will read very much like model building codes and industry standards. This should be more helpful for designers, planners and architects as they integrate accessibility requirements into the vast array of building codes they must consider. The goals of the new standards include greater consistency across standards, added scoping to meet the needs of people with disabilities, and changing the formatting for improved usability and a "building code-like" presentation. It is projected that these changes will result in improved compliance with accessibility requirements.

On September 25, 2008, the president signed the Americans with Disabilities Act Amendments Act of 2008 ("ADA Amendments Act" or "Act"). The Act makes important changes to the definition of the term "disability" by rejecting the holdings in several Supreme Court decisions and portions of EEOC's ADA regulations. The Act retains the ADA's basic definition of 'disability' as an impairment that substantially limits one or more major life activities, a record of such an impairment, or being regarded as having such an impairment. However, it changes the way that these statutory terms should be interpreted in several ways. Most significantly, the Act:

- directs EEOC to revise that portion of its regulations defining the term "substantially limits";
- expands the definition of "major life activities" by including two non-exhaustive lists:
  —the first list includes many activities that the EEOC has recognized (e.g., walking) as well as activities that EEOC has not specifically recognized (e.g., reading, bending, and communicating);
  —the second list includes major bodily functions (e.g., "functions of the immune system, normal cell growth, digestive, bowel, bladder, neurological, brain, respiratory, circulatory, endocrine, and reproductive functions");
- states that mitigating measures other than "ordinary eyeglasses or contact lenses" shall not be considered in assessing whether an individual has a disability;
- clarifies that an impairment that is episodic or in remission is a disability if it would substantially limit a major life activity when active;
- provides that an individual subjected to an action prohibited by the ADA (e.g., failure to hire) because of an actual or perceived impairment will meet the "regarded as" definition of disability, unless the impairment is transitory and minor;
- provides that individuals covered only under the "regarded as" prong are not entitled to reasonable accommodation; and
- emphasizes that the definition of "disability" should be interpreted broadly.

EEOC will be evaluating the impact of these changes on its enforcement guidances and other publications addressing the ADA. Effective Date: The ADA Amendments Act is effective as of January 1, 2009. (U.S. Equal Employment Opportunity Commission, p. 1., available online: http://www.eeoc.gov/ada/amendments_notice.html.

Where these changes related to the enforcement of the ADA are most important to the design and operation of sport and recreation facilities, has yet to be thoroughly tested in court. However, this Act should be considered, especially with regard to ADA protections for employees, by employers. Therefore, when planning for and managing such facilities, the designer and employer have a responsibility to recognize the clarity this Act brings to these responsibilities.

A final rule (guidelines) covering recreation facilities was published in September 2002 as a supplement to ADAAG. These guidelines cover newly constructed and altered recreation facilities in the areas of amusement rides, boating facilities, fishing piers and platforms, miniature golf courses, golf courses, exercise equipment, bowling lanes, shooting facilities, swimming pools, wading pools, and spas (available online: http://www.access-board.gov/recreation/final.htm). These guidelines are following the same timetable as the above-mentioned changes to ADA/ABA and are part of the proposed rulemaking process. In addition, new guidelines for play areas were issued as a supplement to ADAAG on November 17, 2000. "The guidelines cover the number of play components required to be accessible, accessible surfacing in play areas, ramp access and transfer system access to elevated structures, and access to soft contained play structures. They address play areas provided at schools, parks, child care facilities (except those based in the operator's home, which are exempt), and other facilities subject to the ADA" (available online: http://www.access-board.gov/play/finalrule.pdf). These play area guidelines were issued as part of the 2004 final rule ADA/ABA guidelines and await adoption as law by the DOJ and other agencies.

As of the writing of this chapter, the Access Board has generated a report that contains the guidelines for outdoor developed areas, which includes trails, beaches, picnic areas, and campgrounds and is continuing to accept public comments and hold information meetings. For information about the progress of rule making on outdoor areas or to locate guidelines contact the Access Board (http://www.access-board.gov/outdoor/). Another source for information regarding outdoor recreation areas is available from the National Center on Accessibility (http://www.ncaonline.org/).

Proactively and concurrent with the Access Board, the U.S. Forest Service has developed accessibility guidelines to provide guidance for their own agency "to maximize accessibility while at the same time recognizing and protecting the unique characteristics of the natural setting of outdoor recreation areas and hiker/pedestrian trails. These guidelines apply to new or reconstructed areas within the National Forest System" (U.S. Forest Service, 2008; available online: http://www.fs.fed.us/recreation/programs/accessibility).

Presently, the only areas not covered by accessibility legislation in the United States are churches and private clubs. Exceptions include those churches that rent or lease facilities to the public; these facilities are covered. Private clubs must also demonstrate sufficient cause for existing as such. They cannot just charge a fee, generate a list of "members," and then expect to be exempt from accessibility law. An area that was considered exempt by some is historically significant facilities protected by the 1966 Historic Preservation Act. However, historic preservation law does not supersede accessibility law, and the reverse is also true. In such situations, it is expected that accessibility law be applied sensitively to these types of facilities with thoughtful designs that do not compromise important historical features while creating the greatest degree of access possible. A more detailed discussion with illustrations to assist in making historically significant facilities accessible can be found in Preservation Briefs 32: Making Historic Properties Accessible (available online: http://www.nps.gov/history/hps/tps/briefs/brief32.htm) from the National Park Service, Heritage Preservation Services Office in Washington, D.C. U.S. Department of Justice Guide to Disability in September 2005 the U.S. Department of Justice published a Guide to Disability Laws that includes a summary of all disability legislation (available online: http://www.ada.gov/cguide.htm#anchor63814).

The Telecommunications Act of 1996 requires the Access Board to develop and maintain accessibility guidelines for telecommunications and customer premises equipment (e.g., mandated

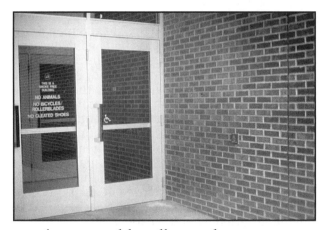

Automated handicapped entrance.

closed-captioning options on the newest models of televisions). Access standards for electronic and information technology in the federal sector were issued under Section 508 of the Rehabilitation Act Amendments of 1998 "which requires that such technology be accessible when developed, procured, maintained, or used by a Federal agency" (Access Board, p. 1; available online at: http://www.access-board.gov/sec508/standards.htm)

Curb cut.

The Five Titles of the 1990 Americans With Disabilities Act and Enforcement Responsibilities

Title I, Employment, prohibits discrimination against qualified individuals with disabilities in such areas as job-application procedures, hiring, discharge, promotion, job training, and other conditions of employment. Employers must make "reasonable" accommodations for an individual's disabilities, unless to do so would cause hardship for the employer. Employers must also post notices that explain the act (Miller, 1992, p. 18). The Equal Employment Opportunity Commission (EEOC) is responsible for enforcement of Title I of the ADA. The EEOC is further responsible for issuing interpretative guidance.

Title II, Public Services, prohibits exclusion of persons with disabilities from benefits, services, or activities, including transportation, offered by federal, state, and local government in accordance with the requirements of section 504 of the Rehabilitation Act of 1973. This coverage now includes all services provided by state and local governments regardless of whether they receive federal money or are privately funded. Part A covers state and local government and part B covers transportation. Part A is enforceable as designated in 28 Code of Federal Regulations (CFR) 35.190 and individuals may also file a private lawsuit. Part B enforcing agency is the Department of Transportation. The Department of the Interior will enforce new guidelines for recreation areas under Title II.

Title III, Public Accommodations, guarantees persons with disabilities access to all public businesses and the programs and services of private, commercial and not-for-profit agencies. Also covered is public transportation provided by a private entity. The Department of Justice and the Department of Transportation are the enforcing agencies and they accept individual complaints. Individuals may also file complaints with the U.S. Attorney General and file private lawsuits with local courts. The Department of the Interior will serve as the enforcement entity for recreation areas under Title III of the ADA.

Title IV, Telecommunications, requires telephone companies to provide interstate and intrastate telecommunications relay service so that hearing-impaired and speech-impaired individuals can communicate with others (Miller, 1992, p. 18). Enforcement is the responsibility of the Federal Communication Commission, which does receive complaints from individuals.

Title V, Miscellaneous, refers to the administration and handling of complaints under the ADA. Administrative actions may include: awarding of reasonable attorney's fees in any proceeding under the ADA, prohibiting retaliation against, or coercion of any person who makes a charge, allowing insurers to continue to rely on actuarial procedures in underwriting risks, authorizing state governments to be sued under the ADA, providing that state laws offering greater or equal protection cannot be preempted, and, amending the Rehabilitation Act to conform its coverage of drug users to the provisions of ADA (Miller, 1992, p. 18).

Responsibility for enforcement of the ADA is shared by multiple government agencies based on each title of the law. While individuals can complain directly to federal agencies, it is preferred that they try to work through the dispute at the source of the problem. The Access Board suggests, "Where appropriate and to the extent authorized by law, the use of alternative means of dispute resolution is encouraged." Also, "The Department of Justice may not sue a party unless negotiations to settle the dispute have failed. The Department of Justice may file lawsuits in federal court to enforce the ADA, and courts may order compensatory damages and back pay to remedy discrimination if the Department prevails. Under title III, the Department of Justice may also obtain civil penalties of up to $55,000 for the first violation and $110,000 for any subsequent violation" (U.S. Department of Justice, p.1-2, available online at: http://www.ada.gov/julsep07.htm).

In order to research and/or stay current with enforcement activities, the Department of Justice publishes quarterly reports that include: ADA litigation, formal settlement agreements, other settlements, and mediation activities (available online:http://www.usdoj.gov/crt/ada/enforce.htm). Additionally, the Department of Justice provides technical assistance manuals and publications for state and local governments (available online: http://www.usdoj.gov/crt/ada/publicat.htm).

It was not the intent of the legislation to create an atmosphere of conflict around the accessibility needs of people with disabilities. A thoughtful, rational, and cooperative process that involves all parties will more effectively educate an entity on the needs of people with disabilities. Improved awareness, sensitivity, and knowledge will provide a basis for understanding the guidelines and valuing accessibility. This approach has greater potential to result in accessible facility designs that are optimally functional and relationships that will promote inclusion.

Striving for Inclusion: Accessible and Universal Design

It is important not to get drawn into the "standards game" when designing facilities that are accessible to people with disabilities. The ADA is not meant to be seen simply as a set of building codes. Its primary purpose is civil rights legislation that makes it illegal to discriminate against people with disabilities because of their disabilities. To assist in the implementation of these efforts, there are regulations to follow, including the ADAAG, UFAS, and applicable State and Municipal Accessibility Codes and guidelines. Designers then have a choice to either apply the existing minimum standards in an effort to comply with accessibility law or to incorporate the guidelines into a universal design approach.

While the design of sports and recreation facilities strives to meet aesthetic goals, the primary purpose is usually based on some desired experience for the users. Whether the facility is designed for specific or multipurpose use, there will typically be a variety of human interactions to plan for. Such interactions will likely occur during staff meetings, at the information desk, in activity/event spaces, in support areas (e.g., restrooms, water fountains, locker rooms, and concessions), etc. Universal design provides opportunities for these interactions to happen in both dignified and meaningful ways and create a foundation for full inclusion of all participants and staff.

Universal design has its roots in accessible design beginning with the ABA. As a result of early accessible design efforts, before the ADA, it became apparent that creating accessible facilities helped more than just people with disabilities. It helped everyone at different times and in different ways.

According to Salmen (1996), "Universal design uses accessibility standards as a starting point and goes further, to consider issues such as percep-

tion, social and environmental relationships, cost effectiveness, and aesthetics. The very nature of these issues puts them beyond the range of what could be mandated by minimum design criteria found in the accessibility codes, and squarely within the concerns of people in their everyday lives" (p.14).

In addition to accessibility, universal design embodies other important concepts that benefit all people. These concepts include:

Sample handicapped accessible ramp, Science Building, Indiana State University

- Providing a range of choices in how a space can be utilized or an activity can be experienced. People with and without disabilities can select from the same choices.
- Offering a range of challenge levels for everyone within those choices. Don't assume that similar individuals want similar challenge levels.
- Minimal use of signage that indicates special services or access features. By nature, universal design reduces the need for this type of signage because functional options are more apparent.
- Providing access and services in and through the same space for everyone. Do not use a design that sends different people to separate features.
- Go well beyond the minimum standards when providing accessible spaces and features such as more accessible restroom stalls, easier ramp grades, and wider doors and passageways.

Most people at some time in their lives will experience either temporary or permanent sensory impairment and/or physical disability. These range from broken bones to age-related changes in functioning. Approximately 51.2 million Americans live with a disability (representing 18% of the population (U.S. Census Bureau; available online: http://www.census.gov/PressRelease/www/releases/archives/facts_for_features_special_editions/010102.html), with countless others affected by them. While there are legal mandates to create accessible

Handicapped parking.

Retrofitted aquatic transfer seat, Indiana State University

facilities for all people, those of us in the leisure, recreation, and sport fields have a moral imperative to apply universal design strategies. It is during leisure-time experiences that our diverse society finds merge points between different classes, races, beliefs, and abilities. All people are capable of leisure, just as we are capable of creating universal facilities that serve the leisure needs of all people.

Accessibility and Public Accommodations

Like no other previous legislation, Title III of the ADA, Public Accommodation, covers private, for-profit businesses, and not-for-profit agencies. This casts a huge net covering most sports and recreation facilities, programs, and services. There are some situations allowed by the law that permit alternative and partial methods of compliance and those will be discussed in this section.

A place of public accommodation is defined as a facility, operated by a private entity, whose operations affect commerce and fall within at least one of the following 12 categories:

- Places of lodging. (see also the Fair Housing Amendments Act. In instances where such housing is "rented" to the public, e.g., students, etc.; there are specific accessibility requirements that must be met.)
- Establishments serving food or drink.
- Places of exhibition or entertainment (stadium) accessible parking.
- Places of public gathering (auditorium).
- Sales or rental establishments.
- Service establishments.
- Stations used for specified public transportation.
- Places of public display or collection.
- Places of recreation (park).
- Places of education.
- Social service center establishments.
- Places of exercise or recreational sports (gymnasium, health spa, bowling alley, golf course, or other place of exercise or recreation).

Public accommodation further refers to the private entity that owns, leases or leases to, or operates a place of public accommodation. Thus, the ADA establishes responsibility for compliance not with a physical location but with the individual or group that owns or otherwise operates the physical location (Cocco & Zimmerman, 1996, p. 46).

A public accommodation shall remove architectural barriers in existing facilities where such removal is readily achievable. Examples of barrier removal include:

- installing ramps over steps or adjacent to steps
- making curb cuts that access sidewalks or accessible routes

Removing architectural barriers for sinks

- repositioning telephones within accessible reach ranges
- adding raised markings on elevator control buttons
- installing flashing alarm lights
- widening doors
- lowering a section of counter top that provides customer service, information, or equipment check-out
- bypassing a turnstile by providing an adjacent accessible alternative
- installing door hardware that provides accessible entry/egress
- installing grab bars in toilet stalls
- rearranging toilet partitions to increase maneuvering space
- repositioning a paper towel dispenser, soap dispenser, and mirror in a bathroom
- installing an accessible paper cup dispenser, at existing inaccessible water fountains
- removing high-pile, low-density carpeting
- lowering high doorway thresholds
- ramping indoor grade/level changes

A public accommodation is urged to take measures to comply with barrier removal in accordance with the following order of priorities:

- Provide access to a place of public accommodation from public sidewalks, parking, or public transportation, which includes accessible parking spaces, accessible routes to facilities, installing an entrance ramp if necessary and widening entrances.
- Provide access within places of public accommodation where goods and services are made available to the public; including aisles that access merchandise, dressing/changing areas, ticket booths, information/registration counters or facilities, food purchases, eating areas and checkout counters.
- Provide access to restrooms throughout the facility, including staff/employee areas.
- Take any other measures necessary to provide access to the goods, services, privileges, advantages, or accommodations of a place of public accommodation.

The ADA is designed to allow an otherwise-covered public accommodation to limit or "customize" its compliance using auxiliary aids and services or alternative means of providing equal goods, services, facilities, privileges, advantage, or accommodations. This is only required if those methods are readily achievable (ADA, 1990). In rare cases, due to concerns with an undue burden or a fundamental alteration in the nature of the service, program, or activity, it may be that a covered entity will not be required to provide accessible facilities and/or access to equal services. Language within the ADA that guides these decisions is explained in the following.

**Removing architectural barriers
for drinking fountains.**

Though not clearly defined in the ADA, *undue burden* is understood to mean that the actions needed to comply will require significant difficulty or expense. Determination of undue burden considers a number of factors, including an employer's size, the financial resources of the entity, and/or the nature and structure of the operation (Miller, 1990).

In the process of meeting the needs of individuals with disabilities, public entities are required to make reasonable accommodations. Should it be determined that the accommodation will drastically change (i.e., fundamentally alter) the service, program, or activity, the accommodation may not be required. A formal legal procedure is required to evaluate and substantiate this defense.

Similar to the standard of undue burden is the consideration of whether or not an accommodation is readily achievable. To be *readily achievable* means that the accommodation is easily accomplishable and able to be carried out without much difficulty or expense. While using identical determining factors as undue burden, the readily achievable standard is a lower standard than undue burden (Cocco & Zimmerman, 1996). In determining whether an action is readily achievable, the following factors are to be considered:

- The nature and cost of the action needed under the Act.
- The overall financial resources of the facility or facilities

**Removing architectural
barriers in the shower.**

**Handicapped aquatic ramp,
YMCA, Murfreesboro, TN.**

involved in the action, the number of persons employed at such facility, the effect on expenses and resources, or the impact otherwise of such action upon the operation of the facility.

• The overall financial resources of the covered entity; the overall size of the business or the covered entity with respect to the number of its employees; and the number, type, and location of its facilities.

—For example, corporations that own locally operated enterprises are responsible for complying with the ADA, and are deemed capable of affording accommodations based on the financial assets of the corporation. This is true also for state-funded entities, such as universities.

• The type of operation or operations of the covered entity, including the composition, structure, and functions of the work force of such entity; the geographic separateness, administrative or fiscal relationship of the facility or facilities in question to the covered entity (ADA, 1990).

Short- and long-range strategic planning is an integral part of an organization's stated intention to comply with federal accessibility regulations. These plans should include specific actions and timelines for compliance. If an organization claims "undue burden" to avoid financial strife, it will only provide short-term relief. Planning to permanently discriminate against people with disabilities is not an option. It is important to note that the ADA itself is not static legislation. It will continue to evolve, increasing in scope and degrees of accessibility. Waiting to comply when it is convenient for the organization is an ill-advised strategy. It is imperative that organizations plan ahead, take advantage of federal tax incentives, and strive to at least meet, and where possible, exceed current accessibility legislation.

Compliance with public accommodation accessibility regulations is required with all new construction, with most remodeling projects, and when offering programs and services to the public.

Removing architectural barriers for toilets.

All elements of new recreation and sports buildings, parking facilities, and site development must be accessible. Where specific guidelines are not available for new facilities, then the best information available should be used. All remodeling of facilities and developed areas must meet applicable standards and guidelines with consideration being given to concerns of undue burden and impact on the essential nature of the service or experience (Quarve-Peterson, 1996).

To assist with ADA compliance, it is suggested that state and local building oversight agencies pursue certification of their codes. Under Title III of the ADA, the DOJ is authorized to certify state and local accessibility building standards/requirements indicating that they meet or exceed ADA requirements. Certification promotes voluntary compliance while providing oversight through plan approval and building inspection. This approach can also save substantial costs by identifying design or compliance problems during the planning stages. The certification of building codes for the purpose of compliance with the ADA is also encouraged by President G.W. Bush's New Freedom Initiative.

A good example of an accessible drinking fountain.

Making programs and services accessible will range from relatively simple to complicated. Modifying seating, installing a wheelchair lift on a van, widening a racquetball court door, and providing large print literature are examples of accommodations that will allow participants with disabilities access to the same program or service available to all other participants. In some cases, however, it will be necessary to create equitable alternatives in order to provide program access. Usually there will be a variety of ways to provide accessible options. In these situations it is suggested that people with disabilities and technical experts be consulted to help identify the "best and most cost-effective option" (Peterson, 1996, p.46).

ELECTRICAL, MECHANICAL, AND ENERGY MANAGEMENT

5

Richard J. LaRue, University of New England
Thomas H. Sawyer, Indiana State University

At its best, technology should conform to the way we work, the way we play, and the way we live. Through electrical and mechanical engineering, we have an opportunity to create extraordinary environments through the manipulation of basic components: lighting, sound, and other electronic technologies; heating, ventilation, air-conditioning, and refrigeration (HVAC-R); and humidity and air quality control. Advancements in engineering these technologies, in both indoor and outdoor spaces, require planners to understand the basics and expect unlimited potential for new technologies. Planners must avoid setting limits on how far ahead they look. Only a few years ago, the computer was a luxury. Now computers are a necessity of everyday life, operating everything from membership systems to the building automation and HVAC systems of "intelligent buildings" (Myers, 1997, p. 53). Today's engineering must be about providing for the way we will work, the way we will play, and the way we will live.

Lighting is an important factor when selecting facility surfaces. With increased efforts to manage aesthetics, as well as participant and spectator satisfaction, lighting should be addressed in the planning phase of building construction. Indirect lighting is largely viewed as ideal for most competitive sports and recreational settings. Indirect lighting; however, is heavily influenced by its surroundings. Paint type (flat vs. gloss), paint color, shadows, HVAC-R systems, sprinkler pipes, and acoustical features can all impact lighting efforts (Cohen, 2002). As mentioned throughout this text, the efforts of the architect can have a significant impact on a variety of design elements within a facility.

Further, energy-efficient lighting retrofits can offer an extraordinary chance to cut operating costs and improve lighting quality. However, along with the opportunity for improvement comes the opportunity for costly mistakes. Table 5.1 outlines common lighting mistakes that should be avoided.

Table 5.1
Common Lighting Mistakes

1. Selecting the wrong project team
2. Conflicting change of command
3. Neglecting frontline people
4. Engaging experts too late
5. Underestimating the importance of an audit
6. Buying based on price
7. No "what-if" planning
8. Not testing thoroughly
9. Botching up installation
10. Falling for "bargain" products
11. Failing to thoroughly scrutinize proposals
12. Using average electricity rates to calculate savings
13. Falling in love with hardware
14. Overlooking opportunities

If the planners know how energy use breaks out, they will be able to better identify opportunities to save energy in buildings. Table 5.2 shows the common use of energy in a commercial buildings.

Table 5.2
Energy Use in
Commercial Buildings

Lighting	29%
Space heating	25%
Office Equipment	16%
Coolign	9%
Water heating	9%
Other	7%
Ventilatoin	5%

Electrical Engineering

A theoretical basis of electrical engineering includes an understanding of circuits, electronics, electromagnetics, energy conversion, and controls. Conceptually, when planners consider lighting and sound, they are also considering the broader areas of illumination and acoustics. Therefore, the planning basics of lighting, sound, and other electronic technologies, in this text includes information relevant to the design of electrical systems; which goes beyond electrical engineering in its strictest sense.

Basic Considerations in Lighting

Lighting is simply a means to illuminate or further brighten an object, individual(s), area or space. The two primary lighting options are energy-produced lighting and natural lighting. The product of lighting in combination with other variables, such as the level of darkness, the amount of reflective light (from surfaces), distortion, and the color of the lighting, results in illumination (good or bad).

Illumination is measured by the foot-candle. Brightness is the luminous intensity of any surface and is measured by the foot-lambert. Glare, which is an important consideration in physical education and sports facilities, is nothing more than excessively high or accentuated brightness.

The amount of light in any given area and the quality of light are of equal importance. Providing efficient illumination is complicated and challenging, and the services of an illumination engineer are recommended in order to obtain maximum lighting efficiency. Gymnasiums, classrooms, corridors, and other areas have specific and different lighting requirements. Planning for illumination requires that each area be considered relative to specific use.

The foot-candle is a measurement of light intensity at a given point. Light intensity, measured in foot-candles, is one vital factor in eye comfort and viewing efficiency; but, intensity must be considered in relation to the brightness balance of all light sources and reflective surfaces within the visual field.

The reflection factor is the percentage of light falling on a surface that is reflected by that surface. In order to maintain a brightness balance with a quantity and quality of light for good visibility, all surfaces within a room should be relatively light, with a matte rather than a glossy finish.

The foot-lambert is the product of the illumination in foot-candles and the reflection factor of the surface. For example, 40 foot-candles striking a surface with a reflection factor of 50% would produce a brightness of 20 foot-lamberts (40 x .50 = 20). These values are necessary when computing brightness differences in order to achieve a balanced visual field. Table 5.1 gives a relative indication as to a comparison of illuminations for specific indoor spaces.

Installation

Lights in arenas, gymnasiums, and other high-ceiling activity spaces need to be a minimum of 24 feet above the playing surface so they will not interfere with official clearance heights for indoor sports.

Indoor lighting systems are generally of two types: direct and indirect lighting. Direct lighting systems face directly down at the floor. Indirect lighting systems face in some direction other than the floor, such as sidewalls or ceiling, to reflect the beaming light in an effort to reduce glare. Indirect lighting is more expensive to operate, since with each reflection the light is diminished. Therefore, more energy is consumed with indirect lighting as compared to direct lighting, in order to obtain the same final illumination of an area.

Both lighting systems should meet the required level of foot-candles without causing glare or shadows on the playing surface. The type of lighting—incandescent, fluorescent, mercury-vapor, metal halide, quartz, or sodium-vapor—will likely depend upon the type of space and the way the space will be used (see Figure 5.3); as well as the projected cost of installation, operation, and maintenance. The style of fixture may have more to do with aesthetics than functionality, though the advantages and disadvantages of aesthetics versus functionality should always be considered.

Designed for Impact

In spaces where the play may involve hitting, kicking, or throwing balls, lighting fixtures should be designed to deflect or absorb impact. Lighting systems are available that include shock-absorbing characteristics. Perhaps more important is the additional protection these lights require in the event that they are struck and the bulb is broken. Fall-

Table 5.3
Levels of Illumination Recommended for Specific Indoor Spaces

Area	Foot-Candles on Tasks
Adapted physical education gymnasium	50
Auditorium	
Assembly only	15
Exhibitions	30 to 50
Social activities	5 to 15
Classrooms	
Laboratories	100
Lecture rooms	
Audience area	70
Demonstration area	150
Study halls	70
Corridors and stairways	20
Dance studio	5 to 50[2]
Field houses	80
First-aid rooms	
General	50
Examining table	125
Gymnasiums	
Exhibitions	50[2]
General exercise and recreation	35
Dances	5 to 50[2]
Locker and shower rooms	30
Gymnastics	50
Archery	
Shooting tee	50
Target area	70
Badminton	50[1]
Basketball	80[1]
Deck tennis	50
Fencing	70[1]
Handball	70[1]
Paddle tennis	70[1]
Rifle range	
Point area	50
Target area	70
Rowing practice area	50
Squash	70[1]
Tennis	70[1]
Volleyball	50
Weight-exercise room	50
Wrestling and personal defense room	50

continued

Table 5.3 continued
Levels of Illumination Recommended for Specific Indoor Spaces

Area	Foot-Candles on Tasks
Games room	70
Ice rink	100[2]
Library	
Study and notes	70
Ordinary reading	50 to 70
Lounges	
General	50
Reading books, magazines, and newspapers	50 to 70
Offices	
Accounting, auditing, tabulating, bookkeeping, and business-machine operation	150
Regular office work, active filing, index references, and mail sorting	100
Reading and transcribing handwriting in ink or medium pencil on good-quality paper, and intermittent filing	70
Reading high-contrast or well-printed material not involving critical or prolonged seeing, and conferring and interviewing	50
Parking areas	1
Storerooms	
Inactive	10
Active	
Rough bulky	15
Medium	30
Fine	60
Swimming pools	
General and overhead	50[3]
Underwater[3]	
Toilets and washrooms	30

These standards have been developed by a panel of experts on facilities for health, physical education, and recreation after careful consideration of the activities involved. In all instances, the standards in this table are equal to, or exceed, the standards that have been recommended by the Illumination Engineering Society, American Institute of Architects, and National Council on Schoolhouse Construction. [1]Care must be taken to achieve a brightness balance to eliminate extremes of brightness and glare. [2]Should be equipped with rheostats. [3]Must be balanced with overhead lighting and should provide 100 lamp lumens per square foot of pool surface.

Courtesy of Illuminating Engineering Society of North America.
The IESNA also provides educational publications, including: Sports and Recreational Area Lighting (available from the IESNA online): *http://www.iesna.org/shop/item-detail.cfm?ID = RP-6-01&storeid = 1.*

ing shards of glass from broken lights should be avoided at all costs.

Lights need to be covered with a transparent polycarbonate sheeting (a screen may not be enough) that will catch broken glass bulbs and also protect the bulbs from direct impact. The sheeting or cover should also keep softer, potentially flammable sports implements (e.g., tennis balls, shuttlecocks, and Nerf or wiffle-balls) from lodging within the fixture against a high-temperature bulb (Turner, 1993).

Lighting Types

The incandescent light is instantaneous, burns without sound, and is not affected by the number of times the light is turned on or off. Incandescent lights and fixtures are considerably cheaper in initial cost; are easier to change; and the lamp, within limits, may be varied in size within a given fixture.

Incandescent fixtures, however, have excessively high spot brightness and give off considerable heat; a problem when high levels of illumination are necessary.

In December 2007, H.R. 6, the Energy Independence and Security Act of 2007 was signed into law, and the incandescent lightbulb, as we know it, will be phased out in favor of more energy-efficient lamps. "The new devices include current products such as compact fluorescents and halogens, as well as emerging products such as light-emitting diodes and energy-saving incandescent bulbs" (Davidson, 2007, p. 1). Compact fluorescent bulbs costing approximately four times as much as incandescent, last about six times longer; therefore meeting the new standard established by the law. "Under the measure, all light bulbs must use 25% to 30% less energy than today's products by 2012 to 2014. The phase in will start with 100-watt bulbs in January

Figure 5.1

2012 and end with 40-watt bulbs in January 2014. By 2020, bulbs must be 70% more efficient" (Davidson, 2007, p. 1).

Fluorescent lamps also have the advantage of long life and give at least two and a half times the amount of light that incandescent lamps give for the same amount of electrical current used. They frequently are used in old buildings to raise the illumination level without installing new wiring.

Mercury-vapor lighting is expensive in terms of initial installation. The overall cost of mercury-vapor lighting, however, is cheaper than incandescent lighting. The primary objection to mercury-vapor lighting is its bluish color. However, when incandescent lighting is used in addition to mercury-vapor, a highly satisfactory lighting system results. Mercury-vapor lights are being phased out in favor of metal halide lights.

Metal halide lights do not last as long as mercury-vapor lights but give a better light output and operate more efficiently. Metal halide lights do not have the bluish tint of mercury-vapor lights. Quartz lights and high-pressure sodium lights are outdoor lights. It has been only over the past few years that these lights have been utilized indoors. Quartz lights are not much different than incandescent lights, except they have a slight bronze color and are slightly more efficient. High-pressure sodium lights might well be the indoor activity light of the future. They have long life expectancy; they are highly efficient and give the best light output of all the lights mentioned. The only problem with high-pressure sodium lights is the yellow-bronze hue associated with them.

Lighting Levels

A number of systems exist that allow different levels of lighting so that special events or lighting requirements can be met. The Jack Breslin Student Events Center at Michigan State University (opened in 1989) affords such variety using an intricate Holophane lighting system.

The lighting levels are turned up or down through a computerized control system, which is pre-programmed for different lighting and uniformity levels. On another control panel, a single button designated for one of eight different preprogrammed scenes can adjust the lights. For example, facility personnel can press one button to set the lighting for televised basketball games, another for non-televised games, another for pregame setup, and so forth (Rabin, 1993, p. 6).

When the Dan and Kathleen Hogan Sports Center at Colby-Sawyer College opened in 1991, the NCAA lighting standard for swimming was 60 foot-candles at the water's surface. Today 100 foot-candles of illumination are required for U.S. swimming and collegiate championship events. Because the planners decided upon a higher-than-minimum level for lighting the natatorium at the center, the facility continues to meet required lighting standards without any modification. However, now every light must be in working order to meet the newer NCAA standard.

Using Natural Lighting

Windows and other translucent materials allow natural light into a facility. Natural lighting can reduce operational costs and enhance the aesthetics of an indoor space. The major problem with windows is that it is very difficult to control the glare that they allow to enter. Avoid windows in any activity area where visual acuity is an important commodity for both learning activity skills and safety. However, other translucent building materials are available that do several things windows cannot:

- Provide higher values for insulation reducing both heat loss (during colder seasons) and/or heat gain (during warmer seasons).
- Diffuse the light that comes through, reducing glare.
- Provide greater resistance to breaking so they are safer to use in spaces where broken glass is a serious problem, and they are harder to break into from a security standpoint.

Translucent materials are not perfect. Translucent panels or blocks in a high-moisture area will still allow moisture to condense on the inside surface if it is colder outside; and, they do not allow clear images to transfer. Windows can also have movable shades, shutters, curtains, or blinds that assist with controlling glare and can improve insulating levels. Skylights are acceptable in "slow movement areas," and vertical skylights are recommended in order to keep both glare and leakage to a minimum. Regardless of the materials used, natural light seems a worthy goal when the facility is designed and used appropriately.

Maintenance

Planning must also take into account the need to change bulbs or replace fixtures. Unless there is a catwalk or crawl space in the ceiling, the lights will need to be changed from the floor using poles, ladders, scaffolding, or hydraulic hoists. Experience informs us that changing all the lights in a space at the same time is the most cost-effective approach to maintenance. However, if your lighting fails to meet required levels whenever a single fixture is out, you will be forced to change your bulbs more frequently. Consider adding a couple of fixtures more than are required in each space (e.g., if the space/activity standard calls for 50 foot-candles on task, you may wish to exceed this standard by four fixtures, so that you can lose up to four lamps and still meet the minimum). And when four bulbs are gone, it is probably time to replace all the bulbs in the space. As you plan for the need to change bulbs and replace fixtures, remember the characteristics of the space. Even telescoping poles need minimum clearance to get inside a space. Racquetball courts with standard-sized doors can allow the use of a small hydraulic hoist rather than a giant stepladder. Finally, direct-lighting bulbs can sometimes be changed using only a pole (standing on the floor), while indirect lighting can only be changed using a catwalk, crawlspace, or other more time-consuming approach. Therefore, when planning your lighting system maintenance, you should consider designs that will serve the facility without being labor intensive (which also influences cost).

Unique Lighting Settings and Issues

Unique settings in sports and recreational facilities require either special lighting systems, special fixtures, or carefully planned designs. In spaces with a higher level of moisture (pool areas, shower and toilet areas, locker rooms, etc.), vapor-proof lighting units are recommended. Remember that broken glass in any such area is a mini-disaster. If a bulb breaks in spaces where participants are often bare-footed, extensive cleanup will be required. Locker rooms and athletic training rooms are two examples of spaces where light placement will directly affect the quality of the environment. Fixtures should be placed to enhance the areas between lockers in locker rooms, to afford clear reflections at mirrors, and to brighten places where visibility is critical to the operational goals in athletic training rooms.

Aquatic Facilities

Lighting indoor swimming spaces has never been the easiest part of natatorium design, although frequently, and with regrettable results, it has been treated that way. With today's multipurpose aquatic centers frequently accommodating diverse programming activities in a shared environment, it has become an even greater creative challenge to get the light right. Natural light is an increasingly attractive option for indoor aquatic facilities. Large windows or open fenestration can be energy-efficient ways to supplement artificial heat and lighting, and they add interest for users and a much-appreciated connection to the outside for employees who work all day in an enclosed environment. With all its advantages, however, natural light can be accompanied by an undesirable partner—glare (Hunsaker, 1998, p.51).

If windows are used in aquatic areas, the glare trade-off must be addressed during the planning stages. Glare is not an exclusive problem of natural lighting. Glare can result from improperly located artificial lighting when the lights reflect off either the water surface or sidewalls. With safety a major consideration in aquatic facilities, every effort must be made to control for glare and/or the blind spots caused by glare. Underwater lighting can reduce some of the glare problem and can further enhance visibility in deeper water (underwater lighting is required in some jurisdictions). And in aquatic facilities, there are maintenance issues

related to the location of light fixtures over the pool (the preferred location for competitive facilities). The YMCA's Walter Schroeder Aquatic Center in Milwaukee, Wisconsin, was able to locate light fixtures directly over their 50-meter indoor pool after determining that by using the two movable bulkheads, a hoist could be positioned anywhere a fixture required re-lamping. This avoided the added construction expense of a catwalk or crawl space and the labor intensiveness of using a scaffolding setup in an empty pool to replace bulbs. Finally, artificial lighting in pool areas must consider the variability of water depth.

Outdoor Lighting

Outdoor lighting for sports fields can have some very specific requirements. "Sport lighting should provide a specified quantity and quality of light on the playing surface. For a football field, the quantity (level) of light is determined by the player's skill level, the number of spectators and any television requirements" (Rogers, 1994, p. 53). Although specific considerations apply when planning illumination of a specific-use field, for the purpose of this chapter, the discussion of outdoor lighting will focus on multipurpose installations.

Multipurpose sports fields are more complicated to light than single-purpose fields, but you will save money by combining activities on one field. Several issues need to be addressed when lighting a multipurpose field. Light levels and pole placement become big factors, and design decisions become critical. Controlling spill and glare is also very important. Lighting a multipurpose field is extremely cost-effective. By sharing poles and fixtures among several sports, initial costs can be reduced by 40% or more. At some point, making the decision to use the field for both sports increases the land's productivity, and so will the decision to give it light (Rogers, 1996, p. 51).

Planning steps include the following:

- "Determine the layout of the field and all its potential uses. The most common multipurpose fields combine football with soccer, or football or soccer with softball" (Rogers, 1996, p. 51).
- Determine the quantity (level) as well as the quality needed (Rogers, 1996). The Illuminating Engineering Society of North America (IESNA) publishes light-level guidelines for outdoor sports (see IESNA's Web site for further information: http://www.iesna.org).
- Determine the type of lamp desired (Rogers, 1996).
- Determine the number of luminaire assemblies (luminaire assemblies consist of lamp reflector, ballast mounting, crossarm and mounting hardware) and poles required to light the playing surfaces while avoiding spill and glare (Rogers, 1996).
- Decide on the type of poles to be used: wood, concrete, and steel are the standard options.

Each has advantages and disadvantages.

- Consider all aspects of safety. The lighting system must comply with the National Electric Code as well as state and local codes and use luminaire assemblies that have the Underwriters Laboratory (UL) approval (Rogers, 1996).
- Establish switching controls that allow for maximum flexibility and maximum efficiency.
- Recalling that some activities require more lighting than others; switches should afford higher and lower levels of illumination. "Switching capacity becomes even more important with overlapping fields" (Rogers, 1996, p. 54).

Outdoor sports lighting should be safe, simple, and efficient. Basic requirements include one transformer and a simple service entrance with a basic feeder and branch circuit. Grounding at the service center and at each pole is needed to ensure the safety of anyone who comes in contact with the pole or electrical equipment. Grounding for lighting protection should be designed and installed according to the National Fire Protection Association (NFPA) Code 780. Safety disconnects on each pole provide additional protection for service crews. Individual fusing of each fixture avoids gang failure of the lights, eliminating costly emergency repairs (Rogers, 1994, p. 56).

Finally, the planner should consider and compare the warranties offered by different manufacturers: the length of the warranty, the items included, and those not included. "Manufacturers that offer a multiyear warranty are making a strong statement of confidence in their product" (Rogers, 1994, p. 56).

Supplementary and Special Lighting Requirements

It is advisable to provide supplementary lighting on such areas as those containing goals or targets. Supplementary light sources should be shielded from the eyes of participants and spectators in order to provide the proper brightness balance. Other special lighting requirements include:

- Night lighting—lights that remain on 24 hours per day (can be the same circuit as the emergency lighting), lighting large spaces, lobbies, corridors, stairwells, and classrooms.
- Exit lighting—located at all exits (including exit-only locations), should be mounted according to local and state codes. Because these lights remain on 24 hours per day, cost savings can be realized if fluorescent bulbs are used instead of incandescent bulbs or LED (light-emitting diode) signs are used as both fluorescent bulbs or LED fixtures have much longer lives. All exit lighting should be on special circuits that will remain on, even if the power is lost.
- Emergency (white) lighting—should be provided for exits (including exterior open spaces to which exits lead). This lighting should be on

a special emergency circuit (battery powered) that will power up whenever normal power is lost.

Lighting Controls

When planning for lighting, the methods of control are also important to consider. The central light-switch box should be located at a major entrance area, and all teaching [or activity] spaces should have individual light switches. A relatively unusual approach to controlling illumination in spaces where lighting is only on as needed (e.g., individual racquetball or squash courts, rest rooms, etc.) is motion sensor or "occupancy sensors" switching. If the sensor detects no movement over a period of ten to 15 minutes, the lights automatically switch off. The lights come back on as soon as someone enters the room. Light-level sensors are also available for use indoors as well as outdoors. These sensors adjust the lighting level in response to the amount of natural lighting. Replacing the all-

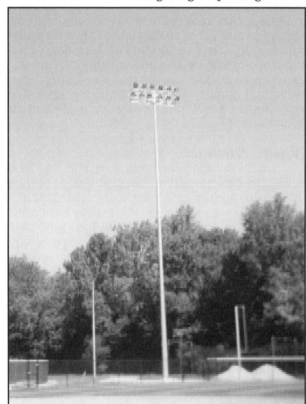

Outdoor lighting on metal poles.

or-nothing on/off switch in parking areas or skylit rooms can give just the right amount of artificial light needed as the natural light fades.

Trends in Lighting

On the horizon, if not already here, is the use of Circadian lighting systems in 24-hour operations. Circadian lights facilitate true physiological adaptation to working nights and sleeping during the day. These system installations have proven "entirely successful in providing a means in keeping the shift workers awake (industrial settings) and alert while on-shift, improving the safety of the commute home, improving the day sleep of the shift worker, and having a positive impact on family life" (Murphy, 1998, p. 1). In other words, Circadian lighting systems have proven to have a positive biological effect on users in a 24-hour, three-shift environment. More research will be needed to determine the possible use and effects of Circadian lighting in more traditional settings.

Basic Considerations in Sound and Acoustics

Sound

Sound is an important part of everyday life, and subsequently it is an important part of sports and recreation. From the public address system to the telemetric microphone, the ability to hear what is going on is almost as critical as seeing what is going on; as frequently, one sense will support another in completing the act of communication. From the sound quality we need in aerobic dance studios to the sound system required for a halftime show at the Super Bowl, technology is advancing the availability of high-resolution sound (Fenton, 1997).

For the sports or recreational facility, sound design starts with creating a suitable sound environment. Beginning in the lobby, where users first enter, several approaches can be utilized:

- Design a small audio/visual system that plays DVDs or other electronic media, with the audio portion of distributed to other areas as well.
- Building on the first approach, include a media wall in the workout area that receives the same transmission as the unit in the front lobby.
- Have your sound distribution originate in a workout space such as an aerobics studio, and then distribute this sound or allow it to "drift" to the lobby and/or other areas of the facility (Hall, 1993).

In strength-training spaces, the major sound considerations are: even distribution, the ability to overcome background noise, and low-fatigue factors. Correct selection and placement of appropriate speakers will provide even distribution, reduce the impact of background interference, and satisfy low-fatigue requirements. Wall-mounted speakers usually work best, although clubs that have a lot of tall equipment in rooms with low ceilings should use ceiling speakers. Whenever possible, include in your design a dedicated sound system for free-weight areas to increase your flexibility in sound sources and level control (Hall, 1993, p. 42).

In cardiovascular areas, "the most satisfactory approach for most clubs is to supply each exercise station with a headphone and flexibility in source selection, along with one or more video monitors visible to several stations at once" (Hall, 1993, p. 43).

The aerobics room is the one area where facility users most expect to hear sophisticated, high-quality sound. Achieving this in a room full of hard surfaces and highly active people is difficult. A well-designed and properly operated sound system will add precision and impact to your classes, establishing a sense of timing and inspiration without fatigue, stress, or hearing damage created by distortion and excessive volume levels (Hall, 1995, pp. 42-43).

Four categories of components have a very direct effect on these various factors (Hall, 1991, p. 40):

- speakers,
- CD or other electronic media players
- amplifier, receiver, and equalizer (soft limiter)
- wireless microphone and microphone mixer (Hall, 1991).

Selecting the correct components is easier when you understand the elements of a high-quality sound system. However, it is important to seek the advice of individuals and/or companies who are familiar with the specific needs of an aerobic studio when choosing components for your new studio or when upgrading your current system.

Acoustics

Because of the amount of noise and sound that emanates from the activities in physical education and sports, acoustics and sound are of paramount importance in building design. Acoustical treatments in building design are the domain of the acoustical engineer. An acoustical engineer should be consulted when dealing with absorption and reflection qualities of all surfaces within a facility.

Acoustical treatments must both enhance sound so that we can hear easily, and absorb sound. Background noise, basically unwanted sound that originates either in the teaching station itself or intrudes from another area, must be controlled. Internal background noise might consist of "squeaking" chairs sliding on a floor, reverberation or "echoing" of sound, and reflective sound. All sound travels spherically. When a space is to be acoustically treated, walls, ceilings, floors, and other surfaces within that space must be considered for appropriate materials.

Internal Treatments

There are four common modes of internal acoustical treatment of spaces. The use of walls and other barriers is one method of controlling sound. Air space itself is an acoustical treatment. The larger the space, and therefore the farther sound travels, the more it is absorbed. The use of soft acoustical materials on various surfaces is a major means of sound control. Acoustical clouds suspended over large, open arenas are yet another means of controlling sound. Extending walls beyond dropped ceilings can afford better acoustical control than stopping internal walls at the dropped ceiling height.

External Treatments

External background noise or unwanted sound from outside the teaching space also must be planned for acoustically. Unwanted sound or noise may be transmitted into the room by means of ventilating ducts, pipes, and spaces around pipe sleeves. The transmission of sound through ducts can be reduced by the use of baffles, or by lining the ducts with sound-absorbent, fire-resistant materials. The ducts also may be connected with canvas or rubberized material to interrupt the transmission through the metal in the ducts. Pipes can be covered with pipe covering, and spaces in the pipe sleeves can be filled.

Sound also can be transmitted through the walls, floors, and ceilings. This can be reduced to a desirable minimum by the proper structural design and materials. In conventional wall construction, alternate studs can support the sides of the wall in such a manner that there is no through connection from one wall surface to another. This sometimes is known as double-wall construction. The space inside the walls can be filled with sound-absorbing material to further decrease sound transmission. Sometimes three or four inches of sand inside the walls at the baseboard will cut down the transmission appreciably. Likewise, sound absorption blankets laid over the partitions in suspended ceiling construction frequently can reduce the sound from one room to another.

Machinery vibration or impact sounds can be reduced by use of the proper floor covering and/or by installing the machinery on floating or resilient mountings. "Sound locks," such as double walls or doors, are needed between noisy areas and adjoining quiet areas. Improper location of doors and windows can create noise problems. It is imperative to consider the location of the facility itself and also to consider the placement of internal areas of the facility for sound control. Placing physical education and sports facilities in a semi-isolated area of a school helps control acoustics. This same theory needs to be applied internally within the sports facility. The placement of "noisy" areas such as weight-training areas, aerobic areas, locker rooms, swimming pools, gymnasiums, and spectator areas must be planned for in relation to quiet areas such as classrooms and offices. It is not good acoustical planning to have a weight room above or next to a classroom. Care must be taken in the maintenance of acoustical materials. Oil-based paint reduces the sound-absorbent qualities of most materials. Surface treatment for different acoustical materials will vary. The most common treatment of acoustical-fiber tile is a light brush coat of water-based paint,

but most acoustical materials lose their efficiency after several applications of paint.

Exterior Treatments

Sometimes the exterior of a space or building must be acoustically treated. If a gym is located on the landing flight path of a local airport, or if it is located next to a fairly steep grade on a major truck thoroughfare, exterior acoustical treatment might be needed. Utilize the same acoustical principles as inside, with an exterior twist. Keep hard surfaces such as paved areas and parking lots to a minimum. Use shrubbery, trees, and grass wherever possible. Walls, solid fences, berms, and water are all good exterior acoustical items. It is important to plan for acoustics and sound control in a variety of ways. Think spherical, think internal, think external, and think exterior in order to best acoustically treat a facility.

Whitney and Foulkes indicated that "Many acoustical problems can be avoided from the start if sound transmission concepts are kept in mind at the initial planning stage of a recreational facility. Keeping noisy spaces separated from quiet areas is easy to achieve in the initial design phase; correcting problems due to improper space adjacencies is more difficult. Even the best sound-isolating construction techniques cannot completely solve the problems created by improper adjacencies. The final results will always be more acceptable if serious acoustical issues are solved in the schematic design" (1994, p. 58).

Other Electronic Technologies

Electronic Communication

The standard communication tools in sports and recreation facilities include an intercom system and two-way audio systems to various activity and office spaces. Additionally, telecommunication has advanced tremendously, allowing for the integration of telecommunications devices for the deaf (TDDs), text typewriters (TTS) or teletypewriters (TTYs), and faxing capabilities to standard telephone installations.

Audio and visual communication needs for the 21st century require many facilities to be integrated for computerization and satellite/cable television reception. Any space that might utilize a computer or video connection should be part of this integration. Fiber optics is the current standard for such integration. However, a thorough planning process will also consider future technologies. Minimally, appropriate conduits should be installed during facility construction to afford the broadest range of future choices.

Within spaces, especially those used for instruction, the planning process should also consider the electronic technologies required for distance education, such as two-way audio and visual communication tools (I see you—you see me, I hear you—you hear me), computer links for internet and computer presentation, conference-call telephones, digital and laser disc players, LCD overhead projectors, keypads for student responses, and so forth.

Scoreboards and Electronic Timing Systems

The science and technology of scoreboard design has changed the entire sports spectator experience. A scoreboard not only provides spectators with game data, but it can be configured with a giant video screen and message system and integrated with the facility's sound system (Bradley, 1994). Large indoor sports arenas are using giant four-sided scoreboards that literally pay for themselves with sponsor advertisement. If timing is your need, recent advances in video systems allow sports races to be judged fairly, regardless of the hundredths of seconds between finish times or the failure of conventional timing equipment (Goldman, 1995).

Elevators and Other Hydraulic Lifts

Elevators and other hydraulic lifts are necessary design features of many sports and recreational facilities. Besides offering users with disabilities federally mandated access to facilities, they enhance the ability of staff to move equipment (possibly reducing the potential for worker-related injury), and they facilitate deliveries. To determine if your facility is required to provide elevators and/or hydraulic lifts, refer to Chapter 4, Designing for Inclusion.

Security

Effective facility security begins with building designs that control access to the facility through a main-desk control area and egress-only doors that do not allow re-entry. A number of electronic technologies can further affect the security of a facility, including:

- Entrance/exit (access/egress) controls and alarms such as card systems; electronically controlled doors and gates, check points with metal detectors (magnetometers), and annunciators (egress door alarms). Card access can also be used to gather enlightening and useful data on the facility's clientele (Patton, 1997, p. 64).
- Closed-circuit television monitor systems
- Motion-sensor alarms for controlled areas such as pools (sensor detects water motion).

It is important to remember that as electronic technology is applied to security, any power failure will disrupt such systems unless they are backed up by battery or emergency generator systems.

Emergency Alarms

Facility safety begins with smoke and fire and emergency alarm systems that appropriately warn building users in the event of fire and warn facility staff in the event of a life-threatening emergency. Smoke and fire alarms include those that are user-activated, smoke- or heat-activated, and water pressure-activated (usually found in wet sprinkler systems). Special alarms for the pool or other exercise area have been designed to notify facility staff in the event of a life-threatening emergency; these are staff activated. Weather or disaster notification will usually utilize an existing intercom system to warn facility users. Emergency alarms, especially those that are designed to warn users, must also be backed up by battery or emergency generator systems.

Emergency Generators

With an increasing reliance upon some of the above electronic technologies and/or the use of arch-supported roofs for indoor sports spaces, power outages will require an emergency generator back-up to ensure the safety of facility users and the well-being of the facility. These generators need only provide minimum levels of power (to be determined by the specifications of the facility) to be effective tools. However, where electric energy is at a premium, it is possible that some sports or recreational facilities will plan on a bank of generators to provide unrestricted energy service.

Trends in Electronic Technologies

Illuminated game lines on sports courts and underwater pace lights in swimming pools are two of the more innovative uses of electronic technology. And, with laser technology, it is only a matter of time before distances in field events are determined using a laser rather than a tape measure.

Web-to-telephone calling combines the convenience of IP telephony (IP telephony is the use of an IP network to transmit voice, video, and data) with the flexibility of traditional calling. The Web-to-phone interface works via a Web browser plug-in that can be downloaded from a Web site. There is no software to buy. Once call center components are in place, people browsing a company's Web page can use the Web-to-phone plug-in to speak over the Internet directly with someone (Dresner, 1998, p. 42).

Finally, Cable Microcell Integrators (CMIs) are in the news, turning terrestrial television cable systems into communications networks for overcrowded cellular systems. A unique characteristic of CMI technology is the independence of signal coverage from the number of base transceiver stations. In other words, service providers need not build excess capacity to handle occasional, but regular, surges in demand. "Fans and reporters who clog a professional football stadium eight Sundays out of the year might require an additional cell tower/base station to use their telephones, but a CMI system can handle this demand surge without an additional physical plant" (Ackerman, 1997, p. 21). Facility planners may well consider checking with area wireless communication companies to see if a CMI installation is appropriate for their facility. It is fair to say that as technology continues to develop in the 21st century, new ideas will result in wonderful advances.

Basic Considerations in HVAC-R

Sports and recreational buildings incorporate a wide variety of HVAC systems. The principal goal of an energy management program is to maximize the efficiency of all systems. Efficiency is a term that describes the relationship between energy input and usable energy output (ASHRAE, 1994).

Air-Handling Systems

Air-handling systems consist of air-handling units and distribution equipment such as ductwork, dampers, and air diffusers. The typical air-handling unit refers to a ventilation device that, when installed in a building, may serve a number of purposes. The system should be providing an airflow with adequate pressure and speed to reach all areas served by the unit; filtering and conditioning the air with cooling, heating, and dehumidification processes; and mixing a measured quantity of fresh air with re-circulated air. A typical air-handling unit may contain some or all of the following components: fan(s), filters; heating, cooling, and dehumidification coils; humidifier; dampers to control the direction of the airflow and the mixing of outside and re-circulated air; and control devices to regulate temperature and humidity of the airflow.

Conditioning the Air

Conditioning of the incoming air is generally limited to dehumidification and heating. A room thermostat generally controls the amount of heat required to maintain room comfort. Desiccant systems and heat pipes dry air far more efficiently than causing condensation by super-cooling air. Using a desiccant dehumidifier dries air without cooling it, causing the water to absorb to the surface of the desiccant. The desiccant is recharged using either waste heat from the boiler, from a solar collector, or with gas heat that is returned to the space.

The components of an air-exhaust system include an exhaust fan, ductwork and grilles, and hoods to capture contaminated air as close as possible to the source. In addition, most exhaust systems incorporate a series of controls to regulate the operation of the fan and its accessories, such as a motorized damper. Energy management action for exhaust systems will depend in part on the area being exhausted.

Fans that exhaust air from locker rooms normally need to operate continuously, especially when athletic equipment needs dried. If this is not the case, then these exhaust fans can be run only when the rooms are occupied.

Heat-recovery potential is present in most air-handling systems. However, the use of the recovered heat by a system must be economically justifiable. Return of the recovered heat to the process from which it came should be the first priority, since such systems usually require less control and are less expensive to install.

The hot water-heating plant of a building incorporates a number of components that individually are responsible for some form of heat transfer and therefore have their own particular efficiency. Heating systems are made up of three principal components: supply equipment (e.g., boiler); distribution equipment (e.g., supply and return piping); and end-use equipment (e.g., heaters and associated controls).

Boiler efficiency is indicated directly from temperature and composition of flue gases. The latter indicates the air/fuel ratio at the burner, which is the most important parameter affecting combustion efficiency. Maintaining boiler water quality is essential to maintaining high system efficiency. In the generation of steam in a boiler, certain impurities (solids) in the water must be purged from the system on a continual basis via an adjustable blow-down valve. Proper adjustment of the blow-down valve must be maintained at all times. Furthermore, ensuring the regular maintenance of distribution piping can minimize energy losses in the heating system. Regular maintenance includes an inventory of the system components and documentation of their condition.

End-use equipment in heating systems includes steam and hot water radiators, and heating coils in ventilation units. Conditions that result in excessive energy use in these components include valves that leak or are stuck open and faulty controls. These conditions are often associated with comfort problems in the space that is heated. Proper maintenance will avoid excessive energy use by end-use equipment.

Air Conditioning

All air-conditioning equipment requires regular, planned maintenance to ensure energy-efficient operation. Cooling system maintenance should include periodic inspection of cooling coils (chilled water or direct expansion) for icing or dirt accumulation on the coil. Both will reduce heat transfer rates, reduce airflow to the space, make it difficult to maintain comfort, and waste energy. Cooling system valves and controls should also be inspected periodically to ensure efficient system operation.

Ventilation Systems

Ventilation systems can be large energy users and energy wasters—both directly and indirectly (Energy Ideas, Nov. 92). Energy is used directly in operating fans. Indirect energy use takes place in heating or cooling and dehumidifying the fresh air brought in from outside. Damper condition should be checked periodically, because damper efficiency and general condition are directly affected by frequency of use. A damper assembly generally controls the damper unit. A motor mounted at one end of the assembly will control damper positioning. The damper controls how much air is brought in from the outside.

Filter Maintenance

Filter maintenance is another factor that is important in ensuring the energy-efficient operation of air-handling systems. Filter replacement or cleaning should occur on a regular basis according to the rate of the dirt buildup. Clogging of filters does not increase energy use directly. However, a pressure drop increase across a filter, due to dirt buildup, will result in an airflow reduction and fan power increase. The system cannot operate efficiently with dirty filters.

Other Considerations

Other operating and maintenance energy considerations are:

- Dehumidifier Maintenance—Improperly maintained dehumidifiers can increase energy use by maintaining a humidity level higher than required.
- Water Treatment of HVAC-R Systems—An effective water treatment program should maintain a clean system, free of any hard-water deposits or any corrosion products. A water distribution system that is fouled with deposits has a much lower rate of heat exchange and will reduce the energy efficiency of the entire distribution system.
- Cooling Tower Condenser Water—The most expensive part of an HVAC-R system to treat is the condenser cooling tower system. A cooling tower has high water losses due to evaporative cooling and requires water make-up to prevent water deposits from forming on the condenser tubes of the chiller. Proper water treatment procedures require the use of water scale control chemicals and corrosion inhibitors.
- Domestic Hot Water Systems—Domestic hot water temperatures should be closely monitored to reduce excessive scaling. Systems can be flushed and de-scaled at regularly scheduled intervals to improve heat transfer at the heat exchanger.

Environmental Climate Control

Environmental climate controls related to HVAC-R affect the quality of our work and play environments. Sports and recreational facilities, specifically, must provide an environment where fresh air is exchanged and effectively circulated, where air temperature and humidity are controlled in a manner that promotes good health, and where the air quality is safe.

There are four factors that, when combined, give an optimal thermal environment:

- radiant temperature where surface and air temperatures are balanced
- air temperature between 64° and 72°F
- humidity between 40 and 60%
- constant air movement of 20 to 40 linear feet per minute at a sitting height

These factors must all be considered to achieve an optimal thermal environment. However, they are only part of the planning that must go into providing indoor environments that are technically sophisticated and also enhance user effectiveness, communication, and overall user satisfaction—the best definition of an "intelligent building" (Tarricone, 1995). Intelligent buildings link such technologies as "HVAC, fire detection and alarm, access, security, elevator, and communication systems to one computer . . ." (Tarricone, 1995). Although this section deals specifically with HVAC-R, it is important to consider the advantages of creating the intelligent building with a single computer control. This concept has been implemented in both new designs and retrofits. The key is planning ahead.

Additionally, a number of building design characteristics directly impact the optimal thermal environment in buildings. These interior and exterior characteristics include:

- building envelopes that reduce heat loss and gain through insulation, barriers, and thermal mass
- moisture control through vapor barriers and external shading devices
- properly glazed windows that have good insulating and glare-reduction properties
- double- or triple-paned glazed windows that prevent condensation on windows
- adequately sized [facilities], ventilated, cooled, and designed for easy access, future growth, and reconfiguration; and passive heating, cooling, and lighting methods (Myers, 1997, p. 52)

And when considering building automation and HVAC-R systems, there are additional choices to make, including:

- centralized or decentralized HVAC-R systems; heating systems (such as boilers) and cooling systems (such as chillers and cooling towers); ventilation systems; substation sensing; humidification and dehumidification control; facility energy management programs such as Night Cycle, Night Purge... (Myers, 1997, p. 53)

All of this does not negate the need for design planning that includes the choice of heat or energy source: fossil fuels (coal and heating oil), and heat or energy alternatives (propane/natural gas, wood, electricity, below-grade heat pumps, and solar or wind energy). Factors in these choices include geographic location and heat and energy resource availability. Additionally, the start-up or installation costs of some systems are more expensive, but cost less to operate and/or maintain over the long term, and vice-versa for installation of other systems. If the facility is located in a rural area with clean extended air, make sure that windows can be opened (double hung, slider, hopper, awning, or casement). In polluted environments, such as urban areas, single-hung windows are acceptable.

Propane/natural gas, solar, wind, heat pump, and nuclear power are all considered "clean" sources of heat or energy and are worth thinking about, considering the depletion of ozone in our atmosphere from the use of fossil fuels. These sources of heat or energy may ultimately reduce operating costs, including the "scrubbing" of exhausted air from your building. Finally, the actual selection and type of HVAC-R should consider the economy of operation, flexibility of control, quietness of operation, and capacity to provide desirable thermal conditions.

Air Quality

Facility ventilation is directly tied to the indoor air quality (IAQ). The IAQ is a product of the quality of the fresh air introduced into the ventilation system and the quality of the existing indoor air that is recycled.

Typically, HVAC-R systems re-circulate as much conditioned air (warm or cooled) as is allowed by health and building codes in order to maximize energy efficiency and reduce the size of mechanical and electrical equipment. In facilities where health and indoor air-quality issues are paramount (or in facilities where no energy-recovery system exists) as much as 100% of the conditioned air may be exhausted. Such facilities in climates with significant indoor/outdoor temperature differentials in winter and summer can exhaust otherwise reclaimable energy.

Energy recovery in HVAC-R systems involves transferring heat from one air stream to another. In summer months, intake air at a higher temperature rejects heat to cooler exhaust air prior to being mechanically cooled by the chilled-water or direct-expansion coil (of the air-conditioning process). Conversely, during the winter, intake air is warmed by transferring heat from exhaust air. Approximately 60% to 65% of the available sensible heat may be recovered; latent heat is not recovered (Fabel, 1996, p. 36).

The air-quality issue in sports and recreational buildings has developed into a significant concern for today's building owners and operators. The public now has greater awareness of health-related concerns, and there is increased research documenting these issues. On the other hand, heating and cooling systems that use excess fresh air also require more energy. To compound this problem, there is no single, accurate method of measuring

air quality, and solutions to air-quality problems tend to be building- and site-specific. The challenge for building managers is to find the optimum levels of fresh air to maintain comfort conditions. Good air quality and energy conservation should be complementary. One should not be achieved at the expense of the other.

Air quality is an evolving issue. Standards and guidelines for air quality in buildings have developed along with an evolving understanding of human requirements for fresh air to support health and of the major air-related contaminants and their effects. The American Society of Heating Refrigerating and Air-Conditioning Engineers, Inc. (ASHRAE) was one of the first organizations to establish guidelines for air quality. ASHRAE's research has led to the publication of minimum ventilation rates to maintain the indoor environment within a key range of guidelines.

Air quality is a complex issue that affects occupant comfort, health, productivity, and acceptance of energy conservation measures. Modern building materials contain many new chemicals that can give off gases or vapors such as formaldehyde and radon. Other organic and inorganic chemicals are introduced to recreation buildings through paints, solvents, and photocopiers. Allergens from airborne particles and dust are also present in these environments.

HVAC-R designers and building managers in existing buildings have reduced outside air ventilation rates to lower levels in keeping with energy conservation guidelines. Moreover, outside air quality has generally deteriorated in our major cities due to pollution from industrial plants, automobiles, and other combustion-type processes.

Variable air-volume systems used in many large spectator facilities often have decreased air-circulation rates compared to conventional constant-volume systems. Air-circulation rates affect the purging of local contaminants, such as cigarette smoke and heat from the activity and spectator areas. Many older buildings are undergoing major retrofits to HVAC-R systems to reduce energy costs. Fans are being modified and generally operated for fewer hours each day. New control strategies call for the conversion from outside air systems to recirculation-type systems with less outside air delivered to the space. This is especially helpful in settings where the outside air is of poor quality.

In older or poorly designed HVAC-R systems that merely re-circulate conditioned air without exhausting enough air and/or introducing enough fresh air, the IAQ can become compromised. Indoor air quality can be managed, even in older systems, if a proactive approach is used to address the IAQ issues. This includes controlling pollution at its source, from both indoor and outdoor sources.

One low-cost way to prevent IAQ problems is to stop potential sources of indoor air pollution where they originate. Known as source control, this process manages pollutants by removing them from the building, isolating them from people by using physical barriers, and controlling when they are used (Anonymous, 1998, p. A10). The National Institute of Health (NIH) and ASHRAE have been busy funding research related to IAQ and controlling pollutants at the source. Specifically, the NIH recently funded a study of the CREON2000™ Disinfection Unit. The CREON2000™ uses ultraviolet light to destroy harmful microbes causing allergy, asthma, and illness. Another such disinfecting unit, designed to be placed directly into building ventilation systems, is the Sanuvox™ UV Air Purifier. In one documented application, the Sanuvox™ UV Air Purifier reduced air contaminants by 66% in a southern California classroom. In this case, the UV unit picked up where vacuuming, HVAC-R maintenance and fresh-air ventilation left off, stripping contaminants in the air such as mold spores, bacteria, mildew, formaldehyde, solvents, and viruses (Author, 2003).

In 2003, ASHRAE approved funding for eight research projects in the areas of indoor air quality, comfort and health, energy conservation, operating and maintenance tools, and environmentally safe materials and design tools (ASHRAE, 2003).

Generally, comfort is perceived when physical, chemical, and biological stresses are at a minimum. Quality of air and the perception of air quality can be quite different. The major components influencing each are common and are listed below:

- physical—physical contaminants in the air
- chemical—chemical contaminants in the air
- biological—biological contaminants in the air
- thermal factors—air temperature and relative humidity, air velocity

Physical Contaminants

Some of the major physical contaminants are listed below:

Contaminant	Source
Dust particles	Outdoor air
Tobacco smoke (particulates & vapor)	Cigarettes
Asbestos fibers	Asbestos building products
Metallic dust	Building materials
Wood particles	Building materials

The particles of smoke, dust, pollen, and other physical contaminants enter the indoor environment either from outside by infiltration or from activities and processes in the building. The amount of material entering the building from outdoors will depend on the wind velocity and the amount of infiltration. Particles can be generated indoors by smoking, other indoor combustion processes, and existing building materials.

Chemical Contaminants

A number of chemical contaminants can be found in the indoor air of a typical sport or recreation building. These include the products of combustion, namely, carbon monoxide (CO), carbon dioxide (CO_2), oxides of nitrogen (NO_x), and sulphur dioxide (SO_2). These chemicals, in some concentrations, can be found in the indoor air whenever a combustion source is within the building. Ice resurfacers and edgers in ice arenas, carpet cleaning, and forklifts on indoor soccer and field houses, and vacuum systems for cleaning seating capacity venues can contaminate the air with carbon monoxide and nitrogen dioxide fumes. Ozone concentrations can increase due to photocopiers and other sources, such as aerosol spray cans. Cleaning agents can give off toxic fumes. Building materials such as paints and particleboards can add to formaldehyde and other hydrocarbon concentrations.

Biological Contaminants

Biological contaminants are microorganisms that can spread through a facility and be inhaled. Constant temperature levels between 60 and 120 degrees in stagnant pools of water provide ideal conditions for the growth of microorganisms. These conditions are found in humidifiers, dehumidifiers, and cooling towers, where there is sufficient moisture and appropriate temperature for the growth of bacteria algae and microorganisms. Examples of bacteria-related building epidemics, such as Legionnaires' disease and humidifier fever, have been cited in literature on air quality.

Finding the best solution to an air-quality problem in a specific facility requires knowledge of the building and its mechanical systems as well as its environment and occupancy conditions. As detailed earlier, the design and construction of the building envelope will determine the infiltration rate, that is the rate of uncontrolled air leakage into the building. In some buildings, infiltration is depended on as a source of supply for makeup air to replace air removed by exhaust appliances. Any change to the air tightness of the envelope will affect the infiltration rate and the amount of fresh air available to the building.

Thermal Factors

Thermal factors affect air quality in two ways. The human perception of air-quality control is related to factors such as air temperature, as well as the actual composition of the air. For example, too high a temperature or lack of air movement may create a sensation of stuffiness. Secondly, the thermal characteristics of the air will affect the actions of contaminants in the environment. For example, excessive humidity will promote the growth of microorganisms. A thermally acceptable environment will minimize physical stress.

- Air temperature—The temperature set by building operation can vary considerably due to temperature stratification within the space, and such variations can affect occupant comfort.
- Air velocity—Air-distribution systems may create the sensation of drafts or conversely of stuffiness.
- Relative humidity—Relative humidity expressed as a percentage varies in the range of 20% to 80% for most buildings. Relative humidity below 20% will result in discomfort for some people.
- Static electricity—Static buildup can also occur with low relative humidity. Testing has shown that most people link dryness or perception of humidity level to air temperature.

Air-Quality Checklist

There is no single method for improving indoor air quality. A general checklist follows that will serve as a reference for air-quality troubleshooting. As a first step, it is always useful to check air temperatures and comfort criteria in problem areas.

Exhaust Re-intake
- Check for recirculation of exhaust air into outside air intake.
- Check outside air intakes at ground level to ensure automobile exhaust or other contaminants are not introduced into outside air intake. Since many sports teams travel by bus, it is important to park the buses away from the facility. Motor fumes can be easily sucked into the building by the air-handling systems.
- Check exhaust air systems to ensure toilet exhaust is not re-circulated to return to air systems.

Avoid Exhaust Air Opening Near Outside Air Intakes
- Check proximity of cooling tower to outside air intake. Ensure biological water treatment of cooling tower, especially in summer months.
- Avoid having stagnant pools of water on roof or near outside air intakes.
- Check humidifier pans and sprayed cooling coils for biological contaminants or growths.

Ensure Proper Water Treatment of Spray Systems
- Check fan coil units for stagnant water in drip pans. Ensure drip pans drain properly.
- Check flooded carpet areas for biological contamination. Change carpet in contaminated areas.
- Check fan rooms for solvents and other chemicals to ensure chemical contamination is not spread by the air-handling system.

- Check chemicals used for rug cleaning and review concentration of cleaning agents used on rugs and floors.

Exhaust at Source
- Check for exhaust from high-humidity locations, smoking rooms, kitchens, photocopy rooms, and other process applications.

Dilution
- Check minimum outside air setting and calibrate for normal occupancy.
- Check ambient air concentrations for CO_2 and other contaminants.
- Adjust fan hours of operation and schedule to suit occupancy.
- Check supply air distribution patterns to ensure adequate flushing of occupied space.
- Check for vertical temperature stratification as evidence of poor air distribution.

Planning for the Future

When planning for the future, an essential component leading to quality HVAC-R is the integrity of the building envelope. Integrity in a building envelope is accomplished when the designer creates a space that is protected from the outdoor elements and is free of challenges, such as roof leaks, moisture that seeps in through the walls or up through the floors, and so on. The integrity of the building envelope is then further guaranteed when building materials are used that will ensure the space's envelope will not be breached. Because facilities are generally intended to last for many years, the envelope materials should be capable of withstanding the stresses of time and/or be readily maintainable/replaceable when needed.

Experience with sick building syndrome is establishing poor envelope design, poor materials, and/or improper maintenance as the leading causes for poor IAQ. An elementary school in Saco, Maine, was recently deemed useless because of mold. Clearly, over time, this building's envelope failed to keep out moisture, and undetected mold began to grow in parts of the building. Only after a period of time, when staff and students began to get sick, was the mold established as the cause of the illnesses. And, there was no doubt that the flat roof design and perhaps unforeseen/unattended

Jim Moravek (1996) has further challenged future decision making with the concept that technologies no longer outlast buildings:

> Designing for flexibility in buildings rather than for specific technologies is the best way to overcome obsolescence of the structure in the future. Buildings often outlast the most current technologies, and new consideration must be given to making buildings and

technologies work together. Flexible design has both structural and system components. Buildings require ample space—both vertically and horizontally—so old systems can be removed and new systems installed quickly, without affecting structure, exits, or life-safety systems. Heating, ventilating, and air-conditioning (HVAC) and power-distribution systems need the capacity to service existing loads and the ability to respond to future requirements (p. 28).

However, no project can be considered without planning for HVAC-R. And this planning should be done by an engineering professional and based upon the technical data and procedures of ASHRAE and appropriate federal regulations.

These standards are on various changes in technologies and government regulations. The ASHRAE also issues position statements, such as the Indoor Air Quality Position Statement (approved by ASHRAE Board of Directors, February 2, 1989). This ASHRAE document states the importance of indoor air quality and energy conservation and its impacts, with the belief that "indoor air quality should be maintained at levels expected to protect occupants from adverse effects and discomfort" (p. 1).

Challenges and Future Trends in HVAC-R

Sick building syndrome is the result of poor indoor air quality. The basics of IAQ seem to minimally require that potential indoor pollutants are controlled at the source and that the building's HVAC-R system—including all the equipment used to ventilate, heat and cool; the ductwork to deliver air; and the filters to clear air—are well maintained (Anonymous, 1998).

The challenge of HVAC-R is clearly to increase energy savings without compromising indoor air quality. Future trends in HVAC-R involve continued research in evaporation cooling and the compliance with ever-changing federal and ASHRAE standards.

Mechanical and Electrical Summary

The technologies of mechanical and electrical engineering are constantly changing. However, facility planners should become familiar with concepts related to the function of HVAC-R, sound, and lighting. Each of these technologies has professional organizations that support ongoing research and publish commercial and consumer information online. Before facility planners make the final decision to accept a solution and purchase and install equipment; they need to do their homework and seek out the best solutions for their situations.

Basic Considerations in Energy Management

Over the last decade, energy management has moved from being a one-time activity to an ongoing and essential part of facility planning and management. Furthermore, energy management has become a widely known applied science with new measures, technologies, and analytic approaches. The importance of energy management to facility planning cannot be overemphasized, especially in sports and recreation facilities that consume large amounts of energy.

The long-range forecasts for the world's energy supplies and prices indicate that it is wise to design systems to reduce consumption of energy during periods of shortage and rapidly escalating prices. New technologies and improved heating and air conditioning equipment show that further savings are possible, even during periods of lower fuel prices.

Next to staffing, utilities normally are the second-highest cost of operating sports and recreational facilities. This section will provide an overview of energy management and outline specific aspects of energy management in the building envelope; building operations and maintenance; heating, cooling, and air-handling systems. We will look at how domestic hot water and air quality affect energy consumption and the impact that lighting and building automation systems have on energy management opportunities. Energy management will be addressed, looking at planning and construction issues as well as maintenance and operating criteria. Finally, the chapter provides reference sources and Web sources for the further study of energy management.

In the planning and construction process for sports and recreation facilities, whether for a new building, a building addition, or major renovation, there are thousands of issues that must be resolved by the owner, the architect, and the construction contractors. Many of these issues deal with design, selection, and integration of facilities energy systems (the HVAC-R systems, lighting, and other energy-consuming equipment). Oftentimes, these issues get very little attention in the design process and end up being serious and costly mistakes, because over the life of the facility, the energy costs will exceed the initial cost of all the energy systems.

Because many of these issues are quite technical and involve parts of the facility no one usually sees, energy questions may be mishandled in the design process. This results from design professionals designing the building envelope, HVAC-R, lighting, and other energy-consuming systems independently and, to protect themselves from liability or complaints, typically over-engineering these systems. Energy-efficient buildings should be designed by an integrated design approach in which all of the design professionals work together with energy efficiency as one of their goals.

A second reason that energy issues are mishandled in design is the fact that almost everyone makes decisions on the basis of initial cost or first cost rather than on life-cycle costs that take into account the initial cost and all of the costs associated with operating and maintaining the facility during its useful life. The most cost-effective time to incorporate energy efficiency into a sports and recreational facility is during construction, when the energy savings need only pay back the incremental cost difference between a "regular" system and a more efficient one. Unless the design team evaluates alternative options on a life-cycle cost basis, sound decisions cannot be made.

Energy Management as a Process

Initially, energy management was viewed as a one-time application of conservation principles to the building envelope and mechanical systems. Experience has shown that greater savings may be obtained and sustained when energy management is considered to be an ongoing process. It is a process that involves a number of key elements such as:

- an assessment of the building and its operating systems
- a list of appropriate energy conservation measures based on the assessment
- careful, planned implementation
- regular review of actual energy savings

Once started, energy management is an ongoing process that is integrated with building maintenance and operation and with any changes in building occupancy, envelope, or mechanical equipment. Sports and recreation facilities have major changes in occupancy loads during varying periods of the day and seasons of the year, and understanding these impacts on the mechanical system is a critical step to designing systems. Moreover, these facilities are normally large spaces with big building envelopes containing glass entrances and large roofing structures. Under normal circumstances, these characteristics do not lend themselves to being energy efficient.

Energy management as a process also recognizes that buildings are not static. Occupancy changes can affect internal space allocations and patterns of building use, which affect the demands on and performance of mechanical systems. Occupancy codes require a certain number of air changes per hour to satisfy the fresh air needs of the participants as well as the spectators. These requirements directly affect the HVAC-R systems.

The three major steps involved in energy management are: conduct an energy audit and analysis, implementation of a strategy, and monitoring of the results.

Energy Audit and Analysis

While a simple walk-through audit will often reveal many opportunities for savings, it is recommended that a full energy audit be undertaken. This will serve as the foundation of the implementation program and as a reference point for partial studies that may be required in future years owing to major changes in building occupancy, envelope, or mechanical systems.

A full energy audit is a complete assessment of the building and its energy use patterns. The physical characteristics of the building shell (e.g., walls, windows and doors, roof, floor, etc.) and the various electrical and mechanical systems (e.g., HVAC-R equipment, lights, water heaters, etc.) are inspected (*Energy Ideas*, Feb. 93). Utility bills are reviewed to determine actual energy use. If possible, energy use is allocated to each building system separately.

The energy audit also provides the necessary information for designing an implementation program. A list of energy conservation measures is developed based on the energy analysis and target energy use. The list is usually divided into no-cost housekeeping measures, low-cost maintenance, and upgrading and major retrofit or upgrading projects involving considerable capital expenditure. Capital costs and estimated savings for each measure are summarized in the energy audit report. With the deregulation of electricity, there are numerous energy audit companies available to work with sports and recreation professionals to design conservation plans for facilities.

Implementation of Strategy

In addition to the building information and recommended measures from the building energy audit, many other practical concerns should be considered in the development of the implementation plan. These include: existing maintenance program for envelope and mechanical system, existing repair and upgrading program for envelope and mechanical system, projected plans for changes in building occupancy, projected plans for major repairs or renovations; available funds, and available staff resources for implementation and program management. Implementation of specific energy management measures will proceed according to the implementation program. Some key steps in the program are: allocating of capital funds and staff resources, obtaining estimates and selecting consultants for measures that require professional assistance, assigning a project manager or energy manager responsibility for program implementation and monitoring results, and selecting contractors and/or internal staff to

Monitoring of Results

Monitoring an energy management program is essential in order to measure results and to steer the program with progressive feedback. The simplest monitoring technique involves reviewing energy bills on a monthly and annual basis and comparing them to a previous reference year. However, a more complete monitoring program will include keeping records of factors that affect energy usage. A sample list of the components of a complete monitoring program is noted below:

- measuring energy/usage and costs
- logging building system performance through indicators such as supply air temperature and boiler efficiency
- logging weather conditions
- recording any additions or modifications to the building, patterns of building occupancy and use, and occupant comments on comfort
- recording any changes in occupancy patterns and use
- recording energy management measures as they are implemented
- logging maintenance of building equipment and systems

Energy Accounting

Energy accounting is defined as the systematic tracking and analysis of energy costs and consumption in order to better manage and control energy in buildings (*Energy Ideas*, Feb 93). In energy accounting, the information gathered through monitoring is used to report on the progress of the energy management program. It involves determining where, how much, and why energy is used.

Many factors affect building energy use. These include: weather conditions at the building site; design, quality, and condition of the building envelope; insulation value of walls and roof; number and size of windows; quality and type of windows; air leakage around windows, doors, and other openings; building mechanical systems; HVAC-R systems and their operation; process activities inside the building such as lighting, hot water and appliances; maintenance of building equipment and systems; efficiency of systems and components; and patterns of building occupancy and use.

A good energy accounting system can provide tangible benefits that pay for the cost of the system many times over (Goldberger & Jessop, 1994). Some of the most attractive benefits include: verifies monthly invoices, pinpoints problem areas, helps manage budgets, monitors energy management programs, justifies energy conservation investments, provides reports to senior management, and provides financing options for energy.

Energy management programs can be financed using a number of options:

- Operating Funds—Many low-cost/no-cost measures can be funded from existing operating budgets. Energy is an operating expenditure, and energy cost savings can be used to purchase energy retrofits.
- Capital Budgets—Energy management retrofit programs can be funded from capital budgets.
- Leases—Leases can be used to purchase energy management equipment. Lease payments can be designed to be less than the projected energy cost savings.
- Energy Service Agreement—An energy service agreement is a performance contract in which a private company offers to execute efficiency capital improvements in exchange for a portion of the energy cost savings that accrue. Typically, a company enters into a long-term contract and, at its expense, designs, installs, and manages or co-manages an energy efficiency system for the facility.

It is important to evaluate the cost and payback period for each measure as it relates to a particular building. What may be a low-cost measure for a large sports facility would represent a substantial investment for a smaller recreation operation. Each situation has to be looked at separately.

Building Envelope

The building envelope consists of the roof, floor, walls, windows, and doors—all parts of the building that enclose the interior building space and separate it from the outdoor climate. The envelope performs several functions. It provides shelter from the elements, lighting (windows), and in some cases, air changes through natural ventilation (windows), and infiltration. The envelope's success in performing these functions is dependent on the building design, quality of construction, and maintenance of the envelope components.

A building's shape and size will greatly affect its heating and cooling loads. Compact facilities generally require less energy than large seating capacity sports venues that ramble and sprawl all over the site. Proper choice of architectural form and orientation can often reduce energy cost. Large sports facilities should respect the path of the sun and be oriented east–west to minimize solar gain in the summer and maximize solar gain in the winter. Reduced air infiltration and proper analysis for optimum insulation is also critical to study early in the design process.

The role of the mechanical systems and purchased energy is to make up the difference between that which the envelope can provide in occupant comfort and what is required (Energy *Ideas*, Oct 92). The quality of the envelope, then, is a major factor in determining energy used for heating, cooling, lighting, and ventilation. Improvements to the envelope can significantly reduce energy demand.

Uncontrolled air leakage through the building envelope is often associated with moisture damage to building components. An added benefit of energy management attention to the envelope is the resolution and prevention of problems affecting the service life of envelope components. It is important to understand the causes of heat loss through the building envelope and to understand the strategies for upgrading the thermal performance of the building envelope.

Energy to heat interior spaces (in winter) or to cool interior spaces (in summer) is lost through heat transfer and infiltration/ex-filtration. Heat transfer refers to the movement of heat through walls, windows, doors, roof, or floors whenever there is a difference between the exterior temperature and the interior temperature. Heat transfer occurs through three natural processes: convection, conduction, and radiation.

Convection is the transfer of heat by the movement of a fluid such as air. For example, cool air moving over a warmer surface picks up heat, carries it, and transfers it to a cooler surface. *Conduction* is the transfer of heat directly through a solid (e.g., wood, brick, drywall, etc.). *Radiation* is the transfer of heat from a surface by electromagnetic waves.

The temperature difference and thermal resistance factored against the square foot area of the envelope determines the amount of heat transferred. Poor thermal performance of the envelope puts greater demand on the mechanical systems for heating and cooling. In addition, cold surfaces or excessive solar gain can create comfort problems and decrease the efficient use of the space. Building elements with poor thermal performance such as single-glazed windows can be the site of condensation that can cause deterioration of surrounding finishes. Thermal weak points in the envelope can also contribute to the defacement and/or deterioration of building components.

During cold weather, warm air rises to upper levels, where it leaks out to colder outside air (ex-filtration). The air lost at the top is replaced by cold air leaking into the building at the bottom (infiltration). The building mechanical systems can affect the pattern of infiltration/ex-filtration through requirements for the combustion and draft air and by operation of ventilation systems.

There are two basic approaches to saving energy through modifications to the building shell. Infiltration/ex-filtration may be reduced by air sealing cracks, air barriers, weather-stripping, or adding better-fitting windows and doors. Thermal performance may be improved by adding insulation to the roof, walls, or floor, or by adding double- or triple-glazed windows. Insulated windows, either aerogel or multiple-paned, can prevent conduction of heat through the glass. Low-emissivity (low-E) windows and window films allow windows to reflect heat rather than transmit it, keeping rooms cool in the summer and warm in the winter (Energy Ideas, 1998).

In general, air sealing and other measures that reduce air infiltration/ex-filtration should be implemented before adding insulation. The major areas and extent of air leakage can be determined by means of a complete building audit. The techniques used may include: a walk-through building audit, a fan-depressurization test, an infrared thermograph scan, and a smoke pencil test. Normally, infiltration and ex-filtration should be checked at building joints, windows and doors, mechanical penetration areas, and at the top of buildings where the roof structure attaches to the walls. Since sports and recreation facilities are large buildings with roofs spanning long distances, these are important areas to have sealed.

Upgrading the thermal performance of the building envelope can lower demand for heating and cooling. It can also improve occupant comfort and use of space by eliminating uncomfortable drafts and cold spots. Energy conservation measures may also provide effective solutions to serious building damage by correcting thermal weak points that can cause deterioration of building components. A complete energy audit of the building will present a "thermal picture" of the envelope. Furthermore, this will indicate areas of greatest heat loss and cooling load. A thermal picture will be determined by the size and shape of the building, its age, and type of construction. Each part of the building envelope offers unique opportunities and constraints regarding thermal upgrading. The best time to address the thermal performance of a sports facility is during the design phase.

Operation and Maintenance

Proper maintenance is essential to conserving energy in the long term. The building should be designed with future maintenance in mind. Easy access to equipment, having major components of the mechanical and electrical systems labeled and as-built drawings provided are good first steps to making maintenance easier to perform. A manual containing operating instructions and information on all of the components of the mechanical and electrical systems should be turned over to the owner when the systems are commissioned.

A thorough and well-managed maintenance program will directly contribute to reducing energy costs. Equipment that is well maintained operates more efficiently and consumes less energy. If maintenance of HVAC-R, or electrical systems is neglected, costs will increase in the long term. This includes the cost of equipment downtime, emergency repair costs, and the increased energy cost to operate the equipment. Energy costs will also increase, owing to poor operating efficiencies resulting from neglect.

Good operational and maintenance procedures can complement a well-designed energy management program, specifically as they relate to the following systems: heating, cooling, ventilation, water treatment, and lighting. Energy management must become part of daily operations to be effective. All operating procedures should be energy efficient. Operations logs and well-documented operating procedures are essential ingredients of energy management. Keeping operational logs is one activity that is part of the standard operating procedure for a building. Operating logs perform several functions: they provide a permanent historical record of system performance, ensure that systems are inspected frequently, identify problems by providing historical records of changes in operation and/or energy performance, and provide a base for evaluating new energy efficient

Heat Pumps

A heat pump is essentially a refrigeration cycle where the heat rejected at the condenser is used for heating purposes. The total heat delivered to the condenser is the sum of the heat extracted in the evaporator and the heat from the compressor work necessary to compress the refrigerant.

The heat pump must have a source of heat to be cooled in order to work. In residential applications, the source of heat is usually outside air, water, or the ground. In large buildings, the source of heat can be waste heat from lighting in interior building areas or heat from computers. The heating requirement must occur at the same time as the cooling requirement if the heat source is inside the building or thermal storage must be used to transfer the heat to another time period.

Domestic Hot Water

A hot water plant may include one or several hot water boilers, a heat exchanger to produce domestic hot water, circulating pumps, and control devices. A hot water distribution system, sometimes called a hydronic system, is used to circulate hot water between a boiler and the heat transfer equipment located in the various heated areas of the building. A steam distribution system is used to convey steam from a boiler to the heat transfer equipment (Energy Ideas, March 93).

Domestic hot water systems provide potable water for hand washing, showers, swimming pools, ice resurfacing, and cleaning. Most sports and recreation buildings incorporate some form of domestic hot water heating system. The domestic hot water system is similar to hot water heating systems, except that the heated water is potable and cannot be chemically treated. Cold water is supplied as make-up to this system from the local water utility.

Domestic hot water systems can be subdivided into unitary and central systems. Unitary systems are point-of-use systems with no distribution piping to serve multiple points of use. Unitary systems, or instantaneous water heaters, eliminate long pipe runs and associated line losses. Central systems are more common in sports facilities and incorporate distribution piping to serve more than one point of use. A central domestic hot water system generally includes: a hot water generator heated by steam, by natural gas, or by an electric element; a storage tank (frequently integrated with the hot water generator); piping (usually copper pipes); re-circulating pump(s); plumbing fixtures

such as faucets and showerheads; and control devices that regulate the water temperature and occasionally the water flow to the appliances.

The key energy management measures related to various components of the above systems include:

- Hot water consumption can be reduced through the use of restricted water flow showerheads.
- Consider use of separate boiler for domestic hot water heating if domestic hot water is the only summer load for a large boiler.
- Stopping circulating pumps one hour after occupied periods end can reduce piping losses. Restart the re-circulation pumps not more than one hour before occupancy periods begin. Computerized energy management systems can be programmed to accomplish these functions based on the activities scheduled in the facility.
- Reduce tank losses of the water heater when hot water will not be used for a period of 72 hours or more. Tanks and lines should be insulated to avoid unnecessary losses.

Water, like energy, is an increasingly scarce and expensive commodity whose use has enormous environmental repercussions. Unfortunately, the prices most users pay for clean water do not come close to covering the real cost (Chernushenko, 1994). Moves are afoot in a number of areas; however, to develop pricing mechanisms that transfer the real cost of water to the consumer. Since price can only go up, the sports facility that has taken steps to reduce its water consumption may be only marginally affected.

Large volumes of water are typically consumed by sports facilities for indoor pools, landscaping, and turf maintenance. Artificial snowmaking is another major water consumer. Below are some effective general steps.

Indoor Water Use

The principal areas of indoor water consumption are washrooms, showers, and laundry rooms. Steps to improve water conservation in these areas are:

- Instruct and remind washroom and shower users to shut off taps fully.
- Repair drips and leaks promptly.
- For automatic flushing systems, check that timing cycles are appropriate for the frequency of urinal use. Shut them down entirely after hours.
- Install low-flow aerators and automatic shutoff valves on tapes.
- Retrofit toilets to reduce water consumption.

Outdoor Water Use

Facilities such as golf courses and playing fields spend heavily on keeping their turf healthy and green. Watering during dry spells actually works against the health of the ecosystem as a whole by depleting water reserves elsewhere. Sports facilities can reduce demand for irrigation by helping encourage an evolution in the attitudes of users to the point where turf, which is less than forest green, is acceptable.

Steps to reduce outdoor water consumption are:

- Plant only native vegetation or species suited to the climate.
- Limit watering of turf to playing surfaces that receive heavy use.
- .Water only during the evening and overnight to reduce evaporation.
- Use trickle or soaker hoses rather than aerial sprinklers.
- Design parking lots and roadways to allow rainwater to return to the soil, streams, and ground water.

Lighting

Lighting costs in sports and recreation facilities can account for 30 to 50% of total energy costs (Energy Ideas, March 93). Until recently, electrical costs were low and little thought was given in building design to the operational costs of lighting systems. Rather, the selection and design of lighting systems were often based on minimizing capital cost. As a result, there exists a wide range of opportunities to reduce lighting energy use in most buildings.

Lighting systems in sports and recreation facilities serve five distinct purposes: to provide sufficient illumination to enable occupants to see and play in a safe manner; to illuminate safe pathways for the movement of persons in and out of the building; to complement the architectural and interior design by providing a comfortable and pleasant environment; to deter vandalism (outside lighting); and, to enhance or highlight a product or display. A lighting system with higher levels than necessary results in higher first cost and operating expenses.

A well-designed lighting system should provide adequate and safe levels of light for the activities carried out in a space. Often, when a system is designed, the quantity (illuminance) of light is used as the only criterion for providing suitable lighting. However, recent studies have now found that the quality of light installed is also a very important factor to consider when designing or upgrading a lighting system.

Occupant visual comfort and productivity are directly related to the amount of lighting and the way it is provided. Opportunities for reducing lighting energy usage should also be looked upon as opportunities to improve the quality of lighting.

Before developing an energy management plan or program for a building's lighting system, an analysis of the existing facilities should be undertaken. Information should be collected that relates to: the amount of light provided in each area; the type of fixtures and their energy consumption; and the occupant activity for specific lighting areas, including the time period in use.

Once this information is collected, lighting levels can be compared to recommended levels for the activities involved. Opportunities for energy savings can then be identified. They may include: reducing power consumption of fixtures through modification or replacement of fixtures or through reduced lighting levels and reducing the operating period of fixtures based on occupant activity. The quality of lighting depends on the following factors as well as the actual level of illumination: geometry of the space to be illuminated; mounting height of lighting fixtures; light-reflecting properties of the ceiling, walls and floor; and color rendering of the particular light type under consideration.

Maintaining adequate illumination levels requires effective lighting system maintenance. An effective maintenance program comprises not only lamp replacement but also routine, planned cleaning of lighting fixtures and room surfaces. A regular cleaning and relamping program has definite long-term benefits: more light is delivered per unit cost of electricity, lower-wattage lamps can be installed, fewer luminaries can be installed, and overall labor costs are reduced.

A final factor to be considered before embarking on a lighting energy management program, particularly for large sports and recreation buildings, is the effect of lighting on the HVAC-R systems. The lighting–HVAC-R effect refers to the impact of lighting on the heating and cooling load of a building.

Effectively, all of the energy consumed for lighting ultimately ends up as heat. This heat can become a significant part of the cooling load of an air-conditioned space. The energy required to air-condition an interior space includes the energy used by the refrigerating equipment (central chiller or rooftop air conditioners). It may also include pump energy to deliver chilled water to the space, and fan energy to deliver cool air. All of these components can be reduced in size if heat output from lights is reduced. Conversely, reducing the energy use of lights increases the heating load of a space in winter, since the heating effect of lights is reduced. This lighting–HVAC-R effect in heating and cooling must be calculated when planning lighting measures.

Building Automation Systems

Building automation systems can be included in energy management plans both in the planning and design phases of new facilities and with the renovation of older facilities with operating problems, owing to antiquated control systems. Installing a building automation system not only saves money by reducing unnecessary energy consumption, but it can also increase comfort significantly.

The features of an automated control system that can be utilized in conjunction with an energy management program are: sensors to measure the environment, controllers to regulate equipment, and operating equipment. An example of a sensor is a temperature sensor that sends a pneumatic or electronic signal proportional to the temperature back to a controller. Controllers are designed to received sensor inputs, compare the input to a set-point, and send a signal output to a controlled device. The operating equipment is any device connected to and operated by the controller.

Building automation systems include systems that control energy-management functions as well as systems that control other building-management functions, such as security (Cohen, 2000). Building automation systems can be classified by: the number of control points, the means of control, and the type of data communication used between the controller and the control points.

There are a number of reasons why a building operator or manager might want to incorporate an automated control system into a building: to improve building operation and comfort; to increase building safety or security; to reduce operating costs, including energy costs; or to provide more efficient building management. Below is a brief description of the various control options that can be incorporated into a computer-controlled, automated system:

- Programmed Start/Stop—Programmed start/stop is a software-based function that permits the user to schedule starting and stopping of equipment according to a predetermined schedule. In sports facilities when specific occupancy scenarios are known, air-handling equipment can be programmed to increase air volumes when spectators are scheduled in the facility and reduce the volumes during non-use periods. Furthermore, hot water circulating pumps can be programmed to deliver hot water when users are expected to take showers and be turned off otherwise.
- Alarms/Monitoring—This type of software-based function signals an alarm or initiates a particular action when an upper or lower limit has been exceeded. Sports and recreation facilities have many entry and exit doors to monitor and control. This type of system can be used to signal an unauthorized entry into a space.
- Energy Monitoring—This function allows the recording and accumulation of fuel and electricity consumption data, allowing for improved

analysis of the consumption rate of fuel and electricity.
- Demand Control—This software feature reduces electrical power demand by stopping or delaying the operation of certain pieces of nonessential electrical equipment during peak demand periods. Utilities charge a premium to users who consume a lot of electricity at peak periods of time. Staying below this demand level will cut electrical costs all year long, since one high-use period sets the rate for the entire year.
- Duty Cycling—This software executes the stop/start cycles for equipment. One can therefore avoid the simultaneous operation of several loads that do not require continuous operation and limit the energy consumption of all the controlled equipment.
- Optimized Stop/Start—This type of program function calculates the best time to initiate pre-heating or pre-cooling of the building.
- Optimized Ventilation—This software is used to optimize the blending of outside air and return air based on the enthalpy of the two air streams.
- Optimization of Supply Air Temperature—This software allows the adjustment of supply air temperature as a function of the heating and cooling loads of the building.
- Chiller/Boiler Optimization—When the cooling system comprises several chillers, this type of function operates the minimum chilling capacity to satisfy the load.
- Supply Water Temperature Optimization—This type of control can regulate the chilled water and hot water supply temperatures of the cooling/heating systems as a function of the actual demand of the building.
- Temperature Setback/Setup—Temperature setback/setup type of controls provide scheduling of building space temperatures during unoccupied periods.

Other control options available with building automation systems include: controls for exterior and/or interior lighting and security; domestic hot water optimization; cistern flow optimization that modulates water flow to cistern-operated urinals; and options for specialized applications, such as swimming pools and ice arenas. As the technology improves, these systems will change to reflect the additional energy and cost savings available.

ANCILLARY AREAS 6

Jeffrey C. Petersen, Ball State University
Rick Gonzalez, University of Wisconsin–Eau Claire

The primary purpose of any facility constructed for health, fitness, physical activity, recreation, or sport is for users to engage in the activity or event itself. However, the actual use of the gymnasium, weight room, pool, or other activity space is typically dependent upon additional support spaces such as locker rooms, administrative offices, storage spaces, restrooms, and others. In fact, the effective use of any activity space can be greatly impacted by the design, quality, and condition of such ancillary spaces. As such, it is vital that these ancillary spaces be properly designed and constructed to enhance the primary use of the overall facility. Actual ancillary space design recommendations for specific facility situations will not be presented in this chapter, because each physical activity facility will have unique needs that should be considered by the professional planning/design team. However, the chapter will include key information and analytical guidelines that can guide the planning process for each of these important common support spaces.

According to the *Dictionary of Architecture and Construction* (2006), ancillary space is defined as a space having a secondary or dependent use. In architectural design circles, building code requirements are essential components to ensure the safety of building occupants. Within building codes, the appropriate term that expresses the same thought is known as accessory use.

In a building of any type, there will typically be a primary use associated with that building. The concept of primary usage is important as it determines how a building needs to be constructed and who will be allowed to legally occupy and use that building. For example, a simple basketball court without viewing areas would not need fire resistant construction or sprinkler system to protect the occupants. The introduction of bleachers and the capacity of those bleachers could require fire resistive construction and/or fire sprinklers as well. The primary use, the facility area, and the capacity of the occupants are major inputs in determining how a building must be constructed and how it may be utilized.

It is also possible to have mixed-use facilities. Mixed-use facilities are facilities that contain more than one primary use. An example of a mixed-use facility is a secondary school facility that includes classrooms for teaching activities, offices for the educators, which also has an attached gymnasium for spectator viewing. In building code terms, this is mixing an educational occupancy, business occupancy, and assembly occupancy. It is also possible to have additional mixed uses other than these in the same facility.

Mixed-use facilities are ideal to share common areas and place more activities under one roof rather than building separate facilities for each use. It can utilize available land more readily and reduce construction costs. Whether the facility in question has one or more primary use, it will always require some accessory use spaces. Even dedicated-use facilities such as professional sports facilities can be classified as being of mixed use. These types of facilities can have a combination of other occupancy uses due to the large size and occupancy capacity of the facility.

From a building code perspective (International Building Code, 2006), the occupancy possibilities include the following:

- Assembly group—the use of a building or structure, or a portion thereof, for the gathering of persons for purposes such as civic, social, or religious functions: recreation, food, or drink consumption; or awaiting transportation.
- Business group—the use of a building or structure, or a portion thereof, for office, professional, or service-type transactions, including storage of records and accounts. Educational occupancies for students above the twelfth grade are also included in this group.
- Educational group—the use of a building or structure, or a portion thereof, by six or more persons at any time for educational purposes through the twelfth grade.
- Factory group—the use of a building or structure, or a portion thereof, for assembling, disassembling,

fabricating, finishing, manufacturing, packaging, repair, or processing operations that are not classified as a high-hazard group or a storage group.

- High-hazard group—the use of a building or structure, or a portion thereof, that involves the manufacturing, processing, generation, or storage of materials that constitute a physical or health hazard in quantities in excess of those allowed in control areas constructed and located as required.
- Institutional group—the use of a building or structure, or a portion thereof, in which people are cared for or live in a supervised environment, having physical limitations because of health or age are harbored for medical treatment or other care or treatment, or in which people are detained for penal or correctional purposes or in which the liberty of the occupants is restricted.
- Mercantile group—the use of a building or structure, or a portion thereof, for the display and sale of merchandise, and involves stocks of goods, wares, or merchandise incidental to such purposes and accessible to the public.
- Residential group—the use of a building or structure, or a portion thereof, for sleeping purposes when not classified as an institutional group use.
- Storage group—the use of a building or structure, or a portion thereof, for storage that is not classified as a high-hazard group.
- Utility and miscellaneous group—the use of a building or structure, or a portion thereof, not classified in any specific occupancy group.

From the above list, it is important to note that a building used for health, sport, recreation, fitness, and physical activities can potentially have several of the occupancy classifications in large enough areas to warrant the need to be classified as a mixed-use facility. When it comes to facilities that are either new or scheduled to be remodeled, members of the design team should be tasked to review the potential implications of various occupancy types and give the owner potential options to reduce construction costs.

There are building code exceptions that may at times shift an occupancy group from one of the above categories into another category. For example, educational facilities above the twelfth grade are classified under the business group rather than the educational group. A competent design professional or designated code official can best determine how different uses can be accurately classified. These different occupancies are extremely important because it can very much impact project costs, how the facility functions, and the safety and risk management aspects of the facility.

Despite the fact that a building may have a designated primary usage, it is important to note that any health, sport, recreation, fitness, and physical activity building will require ancillary spaces in order to function appropriately. For example, a health club or fitness center may require spaces of different types in order to meet the needs and expectations of its customers. This may include but are not limited to the following:

- Entrance lobbies
- Waiting areas
- Locker rooms
- Massage space
- Athletic training rooms
- Treatment rooms
- Storage area
- Office space
- Meeting rooms
- File storage
- Mail room
- Maintenance shops
- Laundry room
- Circulation spaces
- Corridors
- Janitor's closet
- Chemical storage
- Trash and recycling areas
- Employee lounge
- Retail Elements (such as juice bars, concession stands, pro shops, team stores, etc.)

These ancillary spaces are in addition to the primary use spaces that may include but are not limited to the following:

- Aerobic dance rooms
- Weight rooms
- Aerobic exercise machine areas
- Stretching areas
- Swimming pools
- Gymnasium multipurpose court areas
- Racquetball/Squash courts
- Tennis courts

In this example, any possible combination of primary use spaces and ancillary use spaces could be selected in order to create an ideal building. No two facilities are ever exactly alike, as they should always be designed based upon the needs of the users and the goals to be achieved within the facility. The ancillary space requirements for a private health club will differ from the requirements of a college student recreation center or a cardiac rehabilitation facility. The important thing to remember is that the primary activity use will require ancillary space in order to fully support the primary activities. Minimizing the importance of that ancillary space in the planning process can sharply reduce the overall effectiveness of any facility.

It is easier to plan in the types of spaces when a project is in the design phase rather than later. Adding space after a project is complete and in use can be very difficult and can be very costly. Sometimes there may be no choice but to deal with space issues after the fact because of less than optimal planning and design.

Within studies of physical activity facilities, ancillary areas have typically been grouped together as the service areas. In 1962, the National Facilities Conference established eleven distinct categories of ancillary space which included: dressing rooms, shower rooms, toweling rooms, equipment drying rooms, storage rooms, toilets, first aid rooms, laundry rooms, custodial areas, kitchenettes, and staff/faculty areas. Strand (1988) grouped and categorized the ancillary areas into seven distinct categories in his research involving member schools of the Big Ten Conference. These categories included: locker rooms, classrooms, offices, secretarial spaces, storage, laboratories, and training rooms. Petersen (1997, 2007) found that the application of ancillary space categories to high school settings had only six primary categories (locker rooms, classrooms, offices, secretarial spaces, storage, and training rooms), as the need for laboratory space was not applicable at the secondary education level.

In order to consider the design and planning of ancillary spaces, the most common and key ancillary space components will be identified and examined. For the purposes of this chapter, it will include locker rooms, offices, meeting rooms, storage areas, laundry areas, and janitorial/maintenance areas. Athletic training rooms are an ancillary facility component, but this will be covered specifically in chapter 23. Further consideration

for customizing ancillary spaces toward the specific needs of projects in several specialties will be considered including: athletics, physical education, fitness clubs, recreation centers, and multipurpose facilities.

Locker Rooms

In most physical activity-based facilities, the locker room will be the largest and most complex of the ancillary spaces. The locker room is much more than just a room full of lockers. The locker room fulfills a number of functions related to dressing, storage, personal grooming, social interaction, instruction, safety, and privacy. The most basic of components for all locker rooms include: lockers, toilets, showers, and grooming stations. Key design factors include the location of the locker room in relation to the activity spaces as well as arrangement of the locker-room components. Whenever a pool or other aquatic venue is a part of the activity spaces, the locker room should be on the same floor level. Figures 6.1, 6.2, and 6.3 demonstrate three basic locker-room layouts.

Locker rooms typically fall into three design categories based upon cost, finishes, and features: low, medium, and high end. The low-end locker room typically will include sealed concrete floors, standard metal lockers, basic lighting, non-finished ceilings, and gang showers. The mid-level locker

Figure 6.1-3
Locker-Room Concepts

Figure 6.1.
Concept A

Figure 6.2.
Concept B

Figure 6.3.
Concept C

room might upgrade to customized metal lockers, integrated bench systems, showers with tile floors and walls, and finished ceilings. The high-end locker room tends to feature custom wooden lockers, completely tiled floors and walls, carpeted areas, individual showers, solid surface countertops (stone, Corian, etc.), and extra amenities like saunas, steam rooms, or whirlpools, lounge spaces and televisions (Fickes, 1999). Regardless of the design category and cost, all locker rooms have common basic components that all need to be carefully planned for an effective locker-room design.

As per Ramsey, Sleeper, & Packard (2004), locker-room essentials can include the following:

- Fixed benches
- Lockers with raised base
- Locker numbering system
- Provisions for hair dryers (ground fault circuit interrupters)
- Mirrors for dressing, shaving, make-up, etc.
- Shelving for towels, personal storage, etc.
- Drinking fountains
- Bulletin board
- Dressing booths
- Clock
- Door and exit signage
- Sound system
- Adequate lighting
- Adequate ventilation
- Natural light
- Visual supervision as required
- ADA accessible benches, lockers, showers, and toilet facilities

Lockers

The lockers themselves are a primary component of the locker room. The lockers provide secure personalized storage space for personal athletic uniforms and gear as well as street clothes. Historically, the primary locker materials were steel or wood, with more recent innovations of plastic laminate and phenolic resin products now in the locker

market. Steel lockers still dominate the market at about 70-80%, but many have new features such as improved ventilation panels (louvers or mesh designs), anti-microbial treatments, custom and graffiti resistant paints, and all-welded construction that add to their value (Brown, 2008). Wood lockers are still the choice for high-cost custom locker applications. The wood is less durable but provides a luxurious appearance. Any type of wood can be used from exotics to oak, but the level of care for wood lockers is much higher. Plastic lockers now available are much more resistant to rust and water damage than the wood and metal materials, and some models are even constructed of recycled materials. Plastic has an advantage over metal lockers in the sound level created during use.

Regardless of the locker material selected the size and configuration of the lockers have a myriad of options. Depending on the sport or needs of the user the locker may need to be very large for equipment (football, hockey, lacrosse) or it may have more modest space requirements (physical education or soccer). Large single-tier locker systems may be 12-33 inches wide by 12-24 inches deep and 60-72 inches high in standard mass-produced models with 30 inches being the most typical width of an athletic locker (Dahnert & Pack, 2007). These large, stadium-style lockers often include an integrated seat with storage below, clothing and equipment hooks and hanging bars in the main compartment with storage shelf and possible locking compartments above. Locker configurations may also divide their tiers vertically into two to nine compartments to provide additional locker units in smaller sizes.

New trends in locker designs include Z-lockers that take a two-tier or half-locker and notch the dividing panel in the center to provide eight to 24 inches of additional space for hanging clothes such as sport coats, jackets, or longer garments without folding for each of the two stacked half-lockers (Dymecki & Stevens, 2007). Extremely small lockers are also available for small items such as wallets, keys, and jewelry. These often come in four-foot-square grids with compartment sizes as

Figure 6.4
Typical Locker Door Sizes and Configurations

(Ramsey, Sleeper, and Packard, 2007)

small as three to four inches square. These units are useful in applications where facility users are already attired for participation and need minimal secure storage space. In instances where security is of lesser concern lockers units without doors or cubbies can be used for storage in locker room facilities.

In Figure 6.4, typical locker sizes and most of the possible configurations for doors are indicated. Even though there are many available locker configurations, there are only two basic types of lockers: those used for storage and those used for dressing. Locking systems for the lockers can vary from the traditional portable combination lock, to built-in keyed/combination systems, to keyless systems like keypad systems or swipe card systems (Brown, 2008). Each locking system has its own distinct advantages and disadvantages that should be considered by the planning team.

The determination of the total number of lockers to be provided in the locker room is vital to the planning and design process. A peak load of facility users should be determined or projected in order to provide adequate numbers of lockers for all users. Where total space is limited this may require a mix of locker sizes and configurations in order to meet user demand. However, locker sizes must still be able to fully accommodate the storage needs of clothing and equipment for the users. Ideally, the number of lockers should exceed the current peak use in order to accommodate for program growth without the need for immediate facility renovation.

Final selection of lockers should take into consideration a number of factors including: cost, appearance requirements, durability, and abuse resistance, corrosion resistance, locking systems, size and configuration options, and installation requirements. Lockers should be selected early in the design process to help ensure that they are not overlooked and underfunded at the end of the design and building process. Additionally, the specifications for each locker model installation are important in the planning process. Locker selection and locker-room design should also take into account that at least 5% of each type of locker must be accessible to persons with disabilities that includes easy to operate handles or latches that do not require pinching or grasping to operate and a maximum 54" side reach height (Howard, 2001).

Showers

A second primary element in the locker room is the showers. The number of showers provided in the locker room and the corresponding capacity of the water heating system are critical to the functionality of the locker room. Cold showers or long waiting lines for shower use will create a very negative experience for any facility user.

The determination of the appropriate number of showers within a locker facility is not an easy task. If usage patterns are known or can be easily projected, then the number of showering stations should be set to meet the peak user demand. The generally accepted ratio of one shower per 20 lockers can at times greatly overestimate or underestimate the true need (Lavoie, 2005). According to the Architectural Graphic Standards, shower facilities located in an area where people have significant time constraints should be sized so there are ten showers for the first thirty persons and one shower for each additional person. Once a projected peak load and shower number is determined, this information can provide mechanical engineers with the necessary information to determine flow rate and hot-water generation capacities needed to properly operate the shower facilities. Innovations such as on-demand tankless water heaters can reduce the total costs in providing hot water as well as reduce or eliminate the dreaded cold shower.

The shower control valve and showerhead are both key elements of shower operation and aesthetic appearance. Water conservation can be attained through the installation of electronic metering valves. These valves can be programmed to set running times from a short number of seconds to a set number of minutes. All shower valves should include thermostatic mixing to control water temperature and prevent scalding (Pfund, 2006). Architectural Graphic Standards recommends tempering water so that the maximum water temperature cannot exceed 110 degrees F. The showerheads determine the spray patterns provided and also can impact the water usage. Ultralow-flow misting showerheads use little water but also may require longer showering times to remove soaps. High-flow showerheads may provide a luxurious shower experience, but they will cost more in both water and water-heating expenses. Regardless of the shower valve and head selected the plumbing for the shower should remain accessible for maintenance and repairs without damaging the walls via service panels.

Another key consideration in shower design is the level of privacy desired. The most private of settings may include private individual showers combined with individual drying/dressing areas. A second privacy option would be individual shower with an open drying area. Gang showers provide no privacy for the users but allow many more showerheads or showering stations within a given area. The gang shower may be configured with either wall showers, pedestal showers, or a combination of both. A modification of the gang shower to provide a higher level of privacy is to add partitions or modesty modules. These modesty modules are similar to toilet partitions only shorter. They are added around a prefabricated shower fixture for a lower cost space saving alternative to full-walled individual shower units (Bonney, 2004). Figure 6.5 displays several possible shower design layouts.

Figure 6.5
Shower Room Sizing

Other important considerations in shower planning include the following:

- Providing a drying area(s) adjacent to the showers
- Installing a flush mount hose bib in the shower area for cleaning
- Creating water resistant ceilings with tile or epoxy paint finishes
- Setting shower head heights according to anticipated users with men 6'-8" to 7'-0", women 6'-2" to 6'-6', and children 5'-6" (from floor to shower head)
- Providing a minimum of 30" for each gang shower station
- Creating sloped floors in shower and drying areas to center or perimeter drains

- Installing shower walls and floors that are impervious to water and easily cleaned and maintained such as ceramic tile, stone, or etched terrazzo
- Consideration of shower amenities such as towel distribution and collection, soap and shampoo dispensers, shelving, benches, and hooks (Lavoie, 2005).

Toilets

The location and total number of locker-room toilets must be carefully considered. One primary consideration is the wet toilet. If the facility includes aquatic elements then it is likely that wet patrons will use some toilets. As such, wet area toilets should be provided either in a wet area of the locker room or in a restroom directly connected to the aquatic facility. If wet toilet use is anticipated within the locker room, then it is important to also provide dry toilets in another area of the locker room. Mixing of traffic between wet and dry toilets should be avoided for several reasons. First, no dry person would enjoy sitting on a wet toilet. Second, street shoes in a wet toilet area can lead to slips and falls, and wet bare feet on wet floors soiled by dirt from street shoes is both unpleasant and unsanitary.

The number of fixtures (both water closets and urinals) should be designed to meet the peak demands within a locker-room facility. A commonly accepted standard of one water closet per 60 lockers may be adequate for many applications; however, this ratio should be modified as needed to specific needs of facility users (Lavoie, 2005). All toilets should provide privacy for the user; this is typically done with partitions. Selection of partition materials should take into account that most locker rooms have a more corrosive environment than a typical restroom. A growing trend in locker-room construction is the creation of individual full-walled toilet rooms for added privacy, each with their own ventilation system (Kufahl, 2003).

ADA requirements call for at least one toilet and shower facility per gender that meets these requirements. The required number can increase based on the total number of occupants for a given facility. The primary difference between accessibility standards for lavatories and for vanities is the need for forward approach clearance with knee space. Accessibility standards include requirements for faucets, mirror height, and pipe protection (Architectural Graphic Standards, 2007). The number of specifications that can adequately describe ADA requirements for any facility are extensive and could not be fully presented in this chapter. Additional information is provided in chapter 4, and it is highly recommended that the reader fully research ADA requirements to the level of detail that this fully deserves.

Grooming Stations/Lavatories

The provision of grooming stations in the locker room complex is the final of the four basic locker-room components. These grooming stations may also be referred to as vanities or lavatories. The grooming station will provide users with a location to dry hair, comb hair, brush teeth, shave, apply makeup, wash hands, and other related tasks. At a minimum, the dry grooming station will have a mirror, a ground fault interrupter (GFI) electrical receptacle, and a counter or shelf area. A wet grooming station will include a hot and cold water sink, in addition to the dry station elements. A number of additional embellishment options can be added to the grooming stations, such as handheld hair dryers, wall-mounted hand/hair dryers, soap and lotion dispensers, paper towel dispensers, tissue dispensers, waste receptacles, make-up mirrors, scales, and other related items.

Key considerations for the grooming station planning and design should include:

- number of stations analyzed according to user needs with typical grooming stations equal to or slightly less than the shower count location along a seam between the wet and dry areas of the locker room not too far removed from locker and changing areas lighting to illumine both sides of the face and to provide natural coloration such as warm-white fluorescent or incandescent bulbs
- addition of at least one full-length wall-mounted mirror
- vanity/counter heights of approximately 36" for standing use, 42" for stool seating, 30" for chair seating (Lavoie, 2005).

Figure 6.6
Wet Facilities and Drying Areas

WET TOILET AREA   DRYING AREA   (Ramsey, Sleeper, and Packard, 2007)

Wet/Dry Considerations

The high levels of moisture and water in the locker-room areas create a unique layout challenge. The water and humidity can affect the mechanical systems, structural systems, electrical fixtures, and floor and wall finishes. Proper ventilation systems that create negative air pressure in wet areas are one way to combat moisture issues. Secondly, locker rooms must be designed to minimize the movement between wet and dry areas (Cohen, 1998). Distinctly wet areas of the locker room include the showers, drying areas, and any wet amenities like whirlpools or steam rooms. These wet areas ideally should have a separation or transition area to dry components of the locker room. Drying areas placed between the fully wet areas and the dry areas is one design element to separate the wet and dry locker-room elements. The use of sloped floors with floor drains is another method to prevent excess water from building up and being tracked into the dry areas. However, the separation of wet and dry areas should not rely upon raised curbs as this will not comply with Americans with Disabilities Act (ADA) accessibility standards. Figure 6.6 depicts wet toilet facilities that have been integrated into the shower drying area.

Drying areas should be sized to be as large as the shower area that it supports. This area should have sufficient drainage, have adequate towel hooks or bars, be constructed of the same water resistant materials, and be designed to contain water from the main locker area.

The mix of wet and dry area concerns makes flooring selection of great importance for the locker room. One key factor in flooring selection is slip resistance. A wet area of the locker room must provide enough traction to reduce or eliminate slips and falls. However, there is a balance to be maintained in creating high-traction floors. As a floor surface is made more textured for anti-slip purposes, this rougher surface becomes more difficult to keep clean and can be more uncomfortable to bare feet. Primary floor choices in the locker room include lower cost options like coated concrete and flow-through interlocking tiles, mid-priced options like ceramic tile and poured epoxy, and higher end options like high-grade carpet, porcelain, slate, or marble tile (Popke, 2006). Figure 6.7 depicts one option for flooring in a shower or drying area.

Size Considerations

The overall size of a locker room must be determined in relation to the number of expected facility users, as well as the additional amenities that may be required by the users. The typical range for locker-room square footage accounts for 35-60% of total ancillary space within the facility. The determination of the space need for the locker rooms should be based upon the peak load expected within the activity areas of the facility. Occupancy levels can be estimated in most applications from the activity area sizes as follows:

- Gymnasiums: 12 people per game court
- Racquetball/Squash courts: two people per court
- Tennis courts: four people per court
- Lap Pools: four people per lane
- Therapy/Exercise Pools: one person per 50 square feet
- Group Exercise Rooms: one person per 45 square feet
- Fitness Floors: one person per 65 square feet
- Walking/Jogging Tracks: one person per 25 linear feet (Lavoie, 2005).

Figure 6.7
Locker-Room Flooring Option

12" x 12" PERFORATED, RESILIENT INTERLOCKING TILES (3/4" THICK, TYP.)

BEVELED BORDER NOSING

FLOOR DRAIN

INTERLOCKING TAB

(Ramsey, Sleeper, and Packard, 2007)

Figure 6.8
Locker-Room Aisle Sizing

(Ramsey, Sleeper, and Packard, 2007)

An additional allowance of 25-45% of the above load should be considered to account for users waiting to participate and those finished with activity and are using shower and dressing areas. The number of lockers provided should meet this predicted demand. For each locker space planned a total of seven to 15 square feet should be allocated in the locker room area (Lavoie, 2005). In most instances, the size of the locker rooms for both men and women should be the same, and this is vital in educational institutions where Title IX is applicable.

Traffic-Flow Considerations

Traffic flow in the locker-room complex has two key considerations; first, movement into and out of the locker room, and second, movement within the locker room. The locker room should be located within the facility in an area with direct contact to the activity spaces whenever possible. When both men's and women's facilities can be located in adjacent areas, the mechanical, janitorial, and special service areas can often be combined. The number and size of entrances and exits will be impacted by building codes, but typically the number of open entrances to the locker-room facilities is minimized for security purposes. Main access corridors and doors should be large enough to handle heavy two-way traffic with patrons carrying bags and equipment. When possible the primary access doors should be held in an open position with door stops or code-approved electromagnetic devices if required for fire suppression measures (Lavoie, 2005). According to the *Interior Graphic Standards* (2004), locker-room entrance and exit doors should

have vision barriers. Heavy-duty moisture resistant doors at locker-room entrances and exits should be of sufficient size to handle the traffic flow and form natural vision barriers. Entrance and exit doors for the locker-room area should be equipped with corrosion resistant hardware.

In Figure 6.8, dimension A should be no less than 36", and Dimension C should be no less than 42". Increases in both dimensions need to be based on the capacity of the locker rooms. Traffic breaks between benches should occur at least every 12 feet. ADA-accessible benches when required tend to be at least 42 inches long, and be from 20" – 24" deep, and be from 17" to 19" high. These need to have back support or be affixed to a wall. These benches also need to have a clear floor space for a parallel approach to the end of the bench (*Architectural Graphic Standards*, 2007).

The movement of facility patrons within the locker room is another major consideration in planning the layout of any locker room. The location of key elements (lockers, showers, toilets, grooming stations, and special amenities) in relation to one another becomes critical to a smooth-operating locker room. The spaces for passage within the locker room whether in open areas or in corridors must allow for free and unencumbered movement. Additional consideration for persons with disabilities requires that all passageways be a minimum of 36 inches wide to provide full access (Howard, 2001).

The layout of the lockers themselves and their associated benches for changing is a great starting point in locker-room traffic flow considerations. Areas for changing clothes should be located out of the main areas of traffic flow within the locker room. Therefore, many locker areas are designed with numerous alcoves to create separate dressing zones and to create additional space for lockers.

Points of access, such as doors or corridors to the locker room, must carefully consider sight lines. Anyone passing by the outside of the locker room must not have a direct view into any portion of the locker room. Planners should not consider a door alone as sufficient to provide privacy in a locker room setting, as high traffic into and out of the facility limits it effectiveness as a sight barrier. In many instances, locker-room doors are maintained in an open position during regular business hours. Typically, a full or partial wall partition is included near all access and egress points within the locker room that will block the view of passers-by from the outside.

Locker-Room Amenities

Many upscale locker rooms are designed with special amenities to provide additional services to the facility users, such as saunas, steam rooms, whirlpools, or massage areas.

The sauna is typically a small facility designed to provide dry heat at high temperatures. This Finnish form of sweat bathing is used primarily to soothe and relax tired muscles. It has become a popular addition to many locker rooms. As such, the special design considerations for saunas include:

- Wood-lined walls, floors, and seats, as wood provides less heat conduction than tile or metal for the high temperatures (ranging from 150° to 190° F).
- Use of light woods such as spruce, Western red cedar, hemlock, redwood, and aspen reduces sweat staining if combined with regular cleaning and required towel.
- Use two linear feet of bench per person with a typical minimum of 100 square feet for a group sauna.
- A door that opens swinging out with wooden handles to prevent burns and a glass panel to allow for supervision.
- Temperature controls maintained in lock box or secure area.
- A self-priming floor drain as the high heat can cause the trap to dry out, allowing sewer gases to enter (Patton, Grantham, Gerson, & Gettman, 1989).

A steam room, sometimes also referred to as a Turkish bath, is a small high-humidity heat facility. The steam room is typically at a much lower temperature than a sauna (110° to 120° F) but at 100% humidity. The high humidity levels of the steam bath make these small facilities costly to properly build and maintain. Special considerations for steam baths include:

- Two to 2.2 linear feet of bench space per person or 12 square feet per person with a steam generator with appropriate capacity for the room volume.

- Slope the steam room interior ceiling at 1:12 slope to a side wall or space in the room where users will not be dripped upon by condensing droplets.
- Walls, floors, and ceilings must all have a totally waterproof membrane, as the high humidity can permeate grout, cement board, and moisture resistant drywall.
- Interior surfaces should be ceramic tile or stone set with thin-set mortar.
- All fixtures (hinges, lights, frames, fasteners) must be corrosion resistant.
- Door (preferably glass) should swing out and into an area that will not be damaged by exposure to steam-laden air.
- Maintenance access to the steam generator should be accessible from a mixed gender corridor so the frequent maintenance will not require closing of the locker room (Carter, 2008).

The whirlpool is a small communal body of water with a hot temperature (typically 100° to 104° F) along with air and water jets to create a massage effect for the immersed bather. Roy Jacuzzi invented the whirlpool bath in the 1960s, and it has grown in popularity as a locker-room feature. The addition of commercial-grade whirlpools to the locker-room areas has become common in many health clubs and fitness centers. The free-standing fiberglass whirlpools designed for residential use are not recommended for application in the facility types included in this text. The consideration of adding a whirlpool to a locker room should take into account the following:

- Approximately 10 to 15 square feet per person within the whirlpool for space planning.
- Interior tub surfaces of tile or stainless steel are most desirable.
- Exterior surfaces in the areas surrounding the whirlpool of tile, stone, aluminum, plastic, or glass will help reduce the corrosion from the chlorinated vapors and humidity.
- Air-handling systems that will create a negative pressure to surrounding areas to prevent the spread of the corrosive vapors and odors to other areas of the facility are a necessity.
- At least two sides of the whirlpool must be surrounded by non-slip deck space at least four feet wide (Lavoie, 2005).

The provision of a post-exercise massage has become a desired amenity at many clubs and spas. A dedicated space for massage directly within or adjacent to the locker-room complex is desirable. The massage area should allow for total privacy, as the massage recipient will often only be draped with a towel or sheet. The room should be large enough to include a massage table and have sufficient space for the masseuse to move around all sides of the table. About 80-100 square feet should be allocated for a massage area with one station (Patton, Grantham, Gerson, & Gettman, 1989).

Rheostat controlled lighting that may be adjusted or dimmed is desirable, along with adequate ventilation if aromatherapy is combined with the massage. Separate massage areas may be provided for each gender, but if only one massage area is to be included, it would be desirable to have an access door to the massage area from both the men's and women's locker room with controls for the sight lines into each locker room.

In addition to these primary locker-room amenities described above, many locker-room designs may include other auxiliary spaces to meet specific user needs. For example, social lounge space within the locker room, attendant services such as towel service, laundry service or shoe shine, tanning beds or booths, facial rooms, herbal wrap rooms, loofah baths, and private dressing booths all have been found within locker-room facilities. The facility-planning team should thoroughly consider the rationale for inclusion or exclusion of each locker-room amenity.

Specialty Locker Rooms

Family Locker Rooms

The family locker-room concept is a small locker-room space that allows simultaneous access to both genders with special needs such as:

Mothers with a young son too old to enter the women's locker room but too young to be unsupervised in the men's locker room.

Fathers with young daughters too old to enter the men's locker room but too young to be unsupervised in the women's locker room.

An individual with a disability that requires the assistance of an opposite gender care giver in the locker-room setting.

An individual with special privacy needs due to a surgical scar, deformity, or personal preference (Lavoie, 2005).

Family locker rooms have the same basic components as a traditional locker room, but their design has been changing rapidly over the past 20 years (Bynum, 2004). The family locker-room basic elements include private changing rooms, lockers, sinks, toilets, and showers. They may be as simple as single room with all these elements or more complex with multiple private changing and shower, toilet, and lavatory areas with common co-ed locker storage areas or other combinations of these components.

Other considerations and features for the family locker room are:

- Inclusion of Americans with Disabilities Act (ADA) compliant toilet, shower, sink, and locker.
- Addition of toddler-sized toilets and a grooming station with a lower sink /counter height.
- Inclusion of a diaper-changing station or area.
- Direct access to any aquatic attractions within the facility.

The growing popularity of the family locker-room concept even has some designers and architects pushing for facilities with a single co-ed only locker room. These types of facilities have common locker areas with multiple private shower and changing areas and gender separate restrooms (Bynum, 2004). In many respects it is essentially

Figure 6.9
Family Locker-Room Sample Design

FAMILY CHANGING ROOMS

C. = CHANGING ROOM WITH BENCH
H. = ADA CHANGING ROOM W/TOILET, SHOWER AND SINK
T. = ADA POOL TOILET

an oversized family locker room. A typical family locker-room design is displayed in Figure 6.9.

Staff Locker Rooms

Those involved in teaching or coaching in the physical activity setting also have need for locker-room facilities. In some instances, staff locker storage, shower, toilet, and lavatory/grooming station can be included as a component of the office area, and in other instances, a small separate locker-room facility may be needed. In the commercial fitness club setting, staff changing within the main locker rooms can actually displace paying customers. The additional cost for separate staff locker-room facilities must receive due consideration in the planning process. One effective solution to the staff locker room is the creation of a co-ed staff lounge (with kitchenette, basic furnishings, and storage lockers) that has a pair of private adjacent unisex changing, shower, and restroom compartments.

Officials Locker Rooms

Venues designed to host athletic competitions should include a space available for contest officials. Game officials will need a secure area in close proximity to the playing court or field. The official's locker room should include enough space to accommodate the entire officiating crew, so consider the number of officials required for the sports hosted and the number of contests that may be held in a given session. This facility should provide a space for changing from street clothes to officials' uniforms, storage for clothing and personal items, showers, toilets, and a grooming area with a lavatory. Ideally this space should also allow space for the officials to sit prior to the contest and a secure place to rest during game intermissions. This area should also be capable of being secured from coaches, players, or fans. Additionally, the growing trend of mixed-gender officiating crews may require an additional space for official changing, showering, and grooming.

Table 6.1
Considerations for Development of Workstation Standards

Consideration	Standard
Job Classification or Function	Workstation user and job function: executive, manager, supervisor, professional, or technical, clerical
Work Surface Area	Number and size of work surfaces: primary, secondary, tertiary
Machine use	Amount, types, and sizes of electronic equipment: VDT, PC, printer
Workstation Area	Amount of spaces to be allocated for the individual task
Conference Requirements	Number of guest chairs required
Storage Requirements	Amount and type or unit size of the material to be stored, and storage locations (under counter or overhead): letter or legal files, computer printouts, binders, bulk
Configuration	Configuration of work surfaces, primary orientation, and opening for the workstation
Wire Management	Type and location of wire management components: baseline wireway, beltline wireway, grommet locations, clips or trays
Accessories	Type and number of accessories: tack surfaces, pencil drawers

Table 6.2
Work Styles of Americans

	BOOMERS	GEN X	GEN Y
Schooling style/work style	Work alone Structured Unstructured, unsupervised: play with others	Group projects Discussion Team sports for women Mothers worked Computer as a tool	Care-free Need it now Have to be stimulated Can't amuse themselves Multitask
Thought Process	Pen and paper	Personal digital assistant (PDA)	Computer
How they get information	Individual research	Internet	Internet, inquiry
What they do with information	"Power is knowledge"; can be knowledge hoarders	Share info across team and individuals	Team comes first; knowledge resides with the team
What they do if they don't like something	Protest, whine	Drop out, withdraw	Circumvent the rules
How they handle interruptions or noise	Close the door	Put on headset	Not bothered by interruptions-"just one more thing"
Expectations for their work environment	Offices is status symbol; need desk, credenza, conference table, view	Quick access; not isolated; comfort; community space; like to change environments, people, locations	Do not need to own space; need stimulation
Work hours	8- to 12-hour days	Leave when the job is done	Flexible 24 hours

Express Locker Rooms

According to an informal fitness center study, there was a 40% rise from 1996 to 2003 in the number of peak-hour users arriving to the facility already dressed and ready to work out (Kufahl, 2003). This growing trend of reduced locker-room use in both fitness centers and campus recreational facilities has led to the development of the express locker room. Patrons of express lockers are not in need of shower and changing facilities, but only need a place to store personal belongings (keys, wallet, cell phone), and perhaps a coat and a change of shoes. Express lockers are typically co-ed, and include small lockers (half, quarter-sized or smaller) for storage and benches. These express lockers are often located outside of the main locker room to reduce the main locker-room traffic and increase the privacy for the patrons there. A good express locker-room location will often be along or close to a traffic pattern between main points of access and primary activity areas. In some settings, the express lockers may be coin-key or swipe card-key operated to provide additional revenue, and to avoid the need for user provided locks.

Offices

The design of commercial office space serves to function appropriately, extend human capacity, and enhance productivity. Office space also serves as an aesthetic image of the company's mission (Interior Graphic Standards, 2004). Offices, regardless of type, must be functional; otherwise, the spaces will not operate as required. It is important to understand how people work, so spaces can be designed to meet those operational needs. Table 6.1 identifies a number of key considerations and standards related to office space development. It is also important to take into account ergonomics. It is always best to avoid situations that could result in time off for on the job injuries and costly claims.

The age of the workforce will have an impact on the habits of those workers. It will also impact the quality of the workplace expectations as well. Understanding who will most likely work within organizations should also play a part in how the spaces are designed and furnished. Generational trends and its impact in office structure is detailed in Table 6.2.

Interaction and autonomy are the two key factors that must be considered together when under-

Figure 6.10
Workspace Layout Options

PATTERN OF WORK: GROUP PROCESS
PROCESS TEAMS TACKLE STRAIGHTFORWARD GROUP WORK THAT
REQUIRES A CHANGING BALANCE OF DIFFERENT, INDEPENDENT SKILLS.

TYPE OF SPACE LAYOUT: DEN
OPEN AND SHARED. GROUP SPACES WITH A MEDIUM AMOUNT
OF STORAGE. COMPLEX AND CONTINUOUS SPACES INCORPORATE
MEETING SPACES AND WORKSPACES.

USE OF IT
PERSONAL COMPUTERS AND SOME SHARED
SPECIALIZED GROUP EQUIPMENT.

PATTERN OF WORK: TRANSACTIONAL KNOWLEDGE
HIGH-PERFORMANCE TEAMS MADE UP OF SELF-DIRECTED INDIVIDUALS WORK
BOTH COLLABORATIVELY AND INDEPENDENTLY AS WORK PROCESSES ARE
CONSTANTLY BEING REDESIGNED.

TYPE OF SPACE LAYOUT: CLUB
OPEN, CLOSED, AND SHARED. DIVERSE, COMPLEX, AND MANIPUTABLE SPACES
WITH A RANGE OF SETTINGS THAT SUPPORT A WIDE VARIETY OF TASKS.

USE OF IT
VARIETY OF INDIVIDUAL PERSONAL COMPUTERS ON NETWORKS
AND WIDESPREAD USE OF LAPTOPS.

INTERACTION IS THE PERSONAL, FACE-TO-FACE CONTACT THAT IS NECESSARY TO CARRY OUT OFFICE TASKS.

DEN

CLUB

HIVE

CELL

AUTONOMY IS THE DEGREE OF CONTROL, RESPONSIBILITY, AND DISCRETION EACH WORKER HAS OVER THE CONTENT, METHOD, LOCATION, AND TOOLS OF THE WORK PROCESS.

PATTERN OF WORK: INDIVIDUAL PROCESS
DIRECTED CONTRIBUTORS PROCESS WORK THAT HAS BEEN BROKEN DOWN
INTO DISCRETE TASKS USING INSTRUCTIONS WITH LITTLE DISCRETION.

TYPE OF SPACE LAYOUT: HIVE
OPEN. CLUSTERED WORK SETTINGS WITH MINIMAL PARTITIONS,
MAXIMUM FILING AND IMPOSED SIMPLE SPACE STANDARDS.

USE OF IT
SIMPLE, "DUMB" TERMINALS OR NETWORKED PERSONAL COMPUTERS.

PATTERN OF WORK: CONCENTRATED STUDY
INDEPENDENT AGENTS PERFORM ISOLATED, SELF-DIRECTED WORK.

TYPE OF SPACE LAYOUT: CELL
CLOSED. PRIVATE WORKSPACES, SUCH AS ENCLOSED OFFICES OR
INDIVIDUALLY USED, OPEN WORKSTATIONS WITH SCREENS OR PARTITIONS.

USE OF IT
VARIETY OF INDIVIDUAL PERSONAL COMPUTERS ON NETWORKS
AND WIDESPREAD USE OF LAPTOPS.

standing an organization's work processes. Space plans have a powerful effect on work processes. Performance is enhanced when space layouts support levels of interaction and autonomy (Interior Graphic Standards, 2004). Figure 6.10 depicts four workspace layout options with the implications of the design related to the workers and tasks.

Back Office v Front Office

In sport and recreation facilities, it is not uncommon to have front- and back-office arrangements. Front offices may be used for security or for sales operations. These front-office operations are not to be confused with professional sports' front-office operation, which generally refers to the management of a team or league. Back-office operations tend to be those that are not intended to be as visual. These offices may be where the real work takes place. File storage, cash handling, IT operations, human resources, accounting, and other activities that are not intended to be visible could occur in these offices. Front offices may be more lavish and attractive than back-office spaces.

Administrative and Support Staff

In all office situations, there will be a need for space for key administrative and support personnel. These people handle the day-to-day filing of records, answering phones, greeting guests, copying, mail services, ordering supplies, etc. Sometimes these are to be very visible activities in order to prevent duplication of space. Careful planning must allow for adequate administrative and support space with sufficient space for required storage and for office equipment. These types of spaces may require more power and communication outlets than a typical office space. Photocopiers, fax machines, computers, with modems, phones with multiple lines, and other equipment needs will stress the need for greater connectivity.

Allow sufficient space for copiers. Today, most copiers are leased, and the space allowed for today's leased copier may not sufficient for the copiers of tomorrow. Larger copy machines may also require 220 volt electrical supply in lieu of the standard 120 volt. Fax machines typically operate with analog phone lines. This is an important thing to note, as many offices are being wired for Voice Over Internet Protocol (VOIP). VOIP lines are digital and allow for much greater information and communication capacities.

Office Design Considerations

Offices require three basic but very important utilities in order to function. The first is power, which is required in the right amount and location. The second is lighting. Lighting should be designed to be suitable for the task at hand. Tasks that involve great detail and precision require higher lumens to support that task. Lastly, a space must be adequately ventilated. People are capable of reacting to poor power and lighting situations much easier that to conditions of poor ventilation. Ventilation is the key to good indoor air quality and cannot be minimized.

People can be very particular about their office requirements. Some people may insist on an outside window, or being located away from the front door to avoid drafts, or away from high-traffic areas to avoid unnecessary noise. It is always a good objective to give people what they want, because if they are happy, it may affect their productivity, but it may not always be possible to be so accommodating. Each building only has so many windows, separate temperature control, offices near the back door, and private office spaces. Situating people will always be a challenge. The best one can probably do is situate people so the size, configuration, location, and furnishing reflect the contribution that those persons make.

All office space should be sized and furnished based on who will occupy the space and what that person does. High-level administration may require a large office to conduct important business. That important business may include hosting small- to medium-sized meetings. Figure 6.11 depicts a more spacious middle-management type of office that uses 225 square feet, while Figure 6.12 depicts a much smaller office for a lower-level worker who functions in 100 square feet. It is certainly possible

Figure 6.11
Office Concept A

(Ramsey, Sleeper & Packard, 2007)

Figure 6.12
Office Concept B

(Ramsey, Sleeper & Packard, 2007)

Figure 6.13
Office Space Dimensions

OFFICE SPACE DIMENSIONS

(Ramsey, Sleeper & Packard, 2007)

Table 16.3
Legend for Figure 16.13

Value	Dimension
A	30" to 40"
B	60" to 84"
C	18" to 28"
D	24" to 30"
E	23" to 29"
F	36" minimum
G	96" to 126"
H	30" to 45"
I	30" to 44"
J	10" to 14"
K	20" to 30"
L	4" to 16"
M	20" to 30"
N	8" to 16"

to exceed the size of the middle-management type office for a much senior executive, and it is also possible to have useable offices in as little as 64 square feet. Important office dimensions are detailed in Figure 6.13 and Table 6.3.

Special consideration should be given to noise control. Offices where confidential information is discussed should be designed to minimize noise transfer. This can be achieved through many different methods. Walls can be insulated, double-pane windows with shades can be installed, ceilings can be insulated, and walls can extend to the underside of the above roof structure. Not all of these are necessary in the same wall; each method is a way to achieve low sound transmission. Control-

ling sound transmission is not important just for new construction. Existing walls and ceilings can be modified to easily achieve this goal.

Meeting Rooms

According to the *Interior Graphic Standards* (2004), there are multiple types of meeting, conference, and training (not athletic training) rooms. How rooms of this type are designed should reflect the activities that each room will support. In general, rooms should be designed and furnished to allow for maximum flexibility, so the end user is not constrained in how to best utilize the room. Well-designed training rooms can enhance business operations in dynamic environment, increase work-

Table 6.4
Conference Room Seating Standards

	THEATER STYLE EXECUTIVE SETUP[1]	THEATER STYLE MAXIMUM SETUP[2]	CLASSROOM STYLE EXECUTIVE SETUP	MAXIMUM SETUP	HOLLOW SQUARE SETUP	U-SHAPED SETUP	CONFER-ENCE SETUP	BAN-QUET SETUP
Ballroom	14 (1.5)	11 (1.0)	22 (2.0)	18 (1.7)	N/A	N/A	N/A	14 (1.3)
Large Conference	16 (1.5)	13 (1.2)	24 (2.2)	20 (1.9)	40-45 (3.7-4.2)	50-55 (4.7-5.1)	N/A	N/A
Medium Conference	18 (1.7)	15 (1.4)	26(2.4)	22 (2.0)	34 (3.2)	42 (3.9)	40 (3.7)	N/A
Small Conference	20 (1.9)	15 (1.4)	30 (2.8)	24 (2.2)	32 (3.0)	38 (3.5)	35 (3.3)	N/A
Breakout Room	N/A	N/A	N/A	N/A	N/A	N/A	25 (2.3)	N/A
Boardroom	N/A	N/A	N/A	N/A	32 (3.0)	N/A	40 (3.7)	N/A
Ampitheater	N/A	N/A	25 (2.3)	N/A	N/A	N/A	N/A	N/A

*Figures represent optimum square feet (square meters) per person.
[1]Executive setup includes executive conference chairs and 24- to 30-in.- (610- to 760-mm-) wide tables.
[2]Maximum setup includes stacking banquet chairs and 18-in.- (457-mm-) wide tables.
Adapted From: Penner, 1991, p 213.

place diversity, support technology advancements, and help organizations be more competitive. The room types are as follows:

- Auditorium—large capacity with fixed seating for one hundred fifty or more
- Amphitheater—with built-in work surfaces
- Ballroom—a large capacity meeting room with the potential to serve food
- Boardroom—an upgraded version of a conference room with higher grade finishes and furnishings and seating capacity of 16 to 24
- Large conference room—typically greater than 1,500 square feet in size and used for formal presentations requiring little audience participation
- Medium conference room—typically 1,000 to 1,500 square feet in size and used for interactive group programs
- Small conference room—typically 300 to 1,000 square feet in size and used for interactive group programs and small discussion groups
- Breakout room—small discussion area or informal meeting space
- Classroom/training room—varies in size but generally between 300 and 800 square feet in size
- Computer training room—workstation configuration
- Intensive strategy rooms—smaller specialty rooms with high technology requirements and computer capability
- Seating standards for these types of meeting rooms are summarized in Table 6.4.

Key design issues that need to be considered when planning meeting rooms should include the following:

- Adjacencies required
- Traffic flow and circulation
- Will a lobby or reception area be required?
- A/V or other presentation requirements
- Will lounge and breakout areas be required?
- Are there any food service requirements?

Storage needs

Room usage, number of occupants, and furniture layout will determine the required room dimensions. Certain dimension or clearances may be required for specific uses. Consider room accessories that will add functionality. These could include the following:

- Whiteboards
- Projection equipment
- Projection screens
- Hanging rails systems
- Shelving
- Clocks
- Easels
- Lecterns
- Equipment cabinets
- Serving counters

Seating comfort for meetings of long duration is critical. Conference room seating types may differ depending on the type of room and function. A related or compatible series of seating will unify the image of the conference facility. Consider the following when selecting seating for meetings and conferences:

- Ergonomics
- Upholstered seat and back cushions

Table 6.5
Video Conference Room Sizes

CAPACITY	ROOM SIZE FT (MM)	APPLICATIONS
1-2	Workstation or desk	Informal meetings Interviews Research Development
2-3	9 x 12 (2,745 x 3,660)	General business meetings Interviews Progress meetings
3-5	11 x 16 (3,550 x 4,880)	General business meetings New business development Group sales meetings Product demonstrations
6-8	15 x 17 (4,570 x 5,180)	General business meetings Branch site meetings Capabilities demonstrations

- Chair shape and adjustment features
- Lightweight chairs
- Five Caster design
- Select upholstery to match the chair usage and room ambiance

Meeting rooms often can be modified to function for video conferencing in addition to in-person meetings. Table 16.5 present basic specifications and applications for video conferencing space.

Team Rooms

Within the athletic realm, team rooms often are multifunction spaces that combine athletics and academics. Used as a lounge, bonding place, "second home," or even as a kind of classroom, the team room should provide comfortable seating for individuals and groups, including cable television, a VCR and DVD player, study area with Internet access (often wireless), and storage for reference books and videotapes. Many times, the team room/lounge is used for smaller group meetings, and the locker room is used for larger group meetings.

Both the team room and locker room are key places to use branding, with the logo and team colors on finishes and objects, and appropriate storage and lighting for displays of photographs, awards, memorabilia, and inspirational signs and posters.

Today, there are few, if any, differences between women's and men's locker rooms and team rooms, other than those required by a particular sport. The provision of a small private drying/changing space adjoining each shower stall in the women's locker room is becoming a more common amenity in men's facilities as well (Dahnert & Pack, 2007).

Storage

The storage space necessary for supplies and equipment is often one of the most overlooked areas in the facility planning process. An examination of the programs operating within a facility can help to determine the storage needs. It is important to gather input from those administrators, teachers, managers, coaches, and others who will have to deal with the storage of equipment and supplies.

The arrangement of the storage space should also be considered. One option is to have one large, centralized storage area. This type of storage is advantageous to large-scale programs that may have a full-time equipment manager and staff. With this arrangement, it may be easier to control the issuing, returning, and maintenance of equipment and supplies. One possible problem with the creation of a large centralized storage area is that it may become a target for renovation into a classroom, lab, office space, or other possible uses.

Storage space must be suited for the intended purpose. The storage requirements for boxed files are quite a bit different than the requirements for large two-person kayaks. Sport and recreation activities could require multiple spaces with each space designed for a specific purpose. Figure 6.14 depicts a very basic storage configuration that would be suitable for towels, uniforms, files, or any other small- to medium-sized item that can be easily boxed or stacked. Never underestimate the need for storage.

Figure 6.14
Basic Storage Room Concept

(Ramsey, Sleeper, & Packard, 2007)

A second option is to have small, separate storage areas. These storage spaces would be located near the individual team or program activity spaces. An advantage of this system is that individual coaches or program leaders would control their own access to equipment. This arrangement may allow equipment to be stored closer to its point of use. The disadvantage to this system is that control of access to the multiple areas can be difficult to monitor.

In many instances, facilities do not have enough storage space or have outgrown their existing storage space. Utilization of just-in-time purchasing and delivery is one option to reduce the amount of storage space required. For example, rather than ordering and receiving your facility cleaning supplies in bulk for the year, the items could be purchased in bulk but delivered on a monthly or bi-monthly schedule. This would reduce the amount of storage space that would need to be dedicated to these types of supplies. This form of purchasing, however, does not work well with large equipment or non-consumable items.

Regardless of whether the storage space is arranged in a large centralized space or in smaller point-of use areas, the total amount of space available must be adequate for the proper storage equipment and supplies. Proper storage would include keeping equipment secure and protecting it from inappropriate use or theft. Proper storage is also necessary to reduce liability for the facility operators and owners. In fact, the American College of Sports Medicine (ACSM) *Guidelines for Health/Fitness Facility Design and Construction* call for separate spaces from activity areas for operational storage (Tharrett, McInnis, & Peterson, 2007). In addition, proper storage should include adequate temperature and humidity controls for equipment that could be adversely impacted by environmental extremes. The use of overhead roll-up doors or oversized double doors also can help maximize use and access of storage space.

How much storage space for equipment is enough? That is a question with no simple answer, but there have been a number of facility studies conducted over time that have tried to approach

Table 6.6
Equipment Storage Space Recommendations: A selected chronology

Date	Researcher(s)	Recommendation	Source & Level
1938	Evenden, Strayer, & Englehardt	400-square-foot apparatus storage room	Expert panel for collegiate facilities
1961	Sapora & Kenney	40% of total activiity space dedicated to all ancillary areas including lockers, showers, drying areas, equipment storage, supply rooms, & offices	Research of Big 10 Conference
1967	National Facilities Conference	35% of activity area for all ancillary areas including lockers, showers, drying areas, equipment storage, supply rooms, & offices	Expert panel for collegiate facilities
1968	*College & University Facilities Guide*	250-330 square feet of storage space for each exercise area	Expert panel for collegiate facilities
1969	Berryhill	35% of activity area space for all ancillary areas including lockers, showers, drying areas, equipment storage, supply rooms, & offices	Research of 1 high school with expert panel input
1988	Strand	20-30% of all ancillary space within the facility	Research of Big 10 Conference Universities
1989	Walker	20-22% of all ancillary space within the facility	Research of 18 small colleges from two conferences
1997	Petersen	20-22% of all ancillary space within the facility	Research of 40 high schools
2007	Petersen	18-22% of all ancillary space within the facility	Research of 60 high schools

(Adapted from Walker & Seidler, 1993)

this question in a systematic manner. Some of these studies have relied on the opinions of expert panels, while others have relied upon data collection from selected facilities and input from facility administrators. Table 6.6 traces the development of these recommendations over a period spanning more than 70 years. These recommendations provide an excellent starting point for consideration of storage space needs. Once an appropriate guideline has been selected for the proper level and facility, then the recommendation for storage space can be tested with the actual and projected needs specific to the programs to be served by the storage.

Laundry

Onsite laundry services can prove to be very cost effective if well thought out. Before building an onsite laundry capacity, one should consider many questions that should include the following:

• Who will operate the equipment?
• How much capacity is required?
• What special construction details will this operation require?
• Will residential equipment suffice, or will commercial equipment be required?

Determining the capacity requirement is an important issue, as it will also lead the operator to the conclusion of whether or not to purchase residential or commercial grade equipment. All washers and dryers are sized by the dry weight capacity of the unit. A washer may be sized to hold 25 pounds of soiled towels and linens, but some items may be too bulky to meet the units' actual capacity. Dryer capacity is based on the wet weight of processed items. Because of this, it is typically recommended that the dryer capacity be sized to process about 1.5 times that of the washer(s).

In sizing equipment, it is important to estimate the desired level of laundry service, the amount of items that require processing, the amount of each item type, which items can be mixed together, how many hours a day and how many days a week one plans to operate the laundry. Back-up towels or other fabric items should be planned for, so one does not run out at the wrong time. If it is preferred not to operate the laundry over weekends or during peak operating hours, then size the inventory accordingly.

Except for commercial operations, it is unlikely that an operation will actually weigh soiled items to achieve maximum water and power consumption efficiencies, but an operation should initially develop rules of thumb for each subsequent operator. Useful rules of thumb could include how many towels of a certain size approximate the load capacity of the washer. These useful rules of thumb can then be posted for other operators to read and simplify the process.

Commercial equipment requires many construction details that residential units do not require. Heavy-duty washer/extractors spin at very high g-forces and can vibrate so much that normal concrete would be pulverized in a short period of time. These high g forces are necessary to remove as much water from the washed linens and towels in order to reduce the required drying time. Reinforced concrete floors with a high design strength can be constructed in new or existing buildings. These washer/extractors also release high volumes of water in very short periods of time, so such equipment can easily overwhelm normal-sized waste-water piping. High-capacity trenches tied to a recessed floor drain allow these high volumes of water from rinse cycles to be released without causing backflows and flooding. The actual size of these trenches is based on the amount of water that the washing equipment will release in a given period of time. Commercial dryers can generate more heat than residential dryers and can thus be greater fire hazards. Commercial equipment require greater air ventilation to offset the increased heat generation and internal humidity levels. In addition to gas and electrically operated, commercial equipment may also have the ability to operate using fuel oil and steam, if such sources are available. For drying, commercial-grade gas-fired equipment can process about a third more product than steam and twice as much as electric.

Depending on geographic location and the general water quality, water softening may also be required. It may also be necessary to supply compressed air for certain commercial equipment.

Commercial equipment has the ability to process more loads and at a higher capacity per hour than residential equipment. Residential equipment is typically not designed as heavy duty as commer-

Figure 6.15
Single Washer and Dryer Laundry Room Concept

OPEN STORAGE SHELVES

TUMBLER

CONCRETE PAD 4" ABOVE FLOOR; SLOPE TO DRAIN

WASHER EXTRACTOR

TRENCH DRAIN

2'-6" x 8'-0" TABLE

CART SPACE

ROOM SIZE 15'-0" x 19'-0"

50 LB

25 LB

(Ramsey, Sleeper & Packard, 2007)

Figure 6.16
Multiple Heavy Duty Residential Style Equipment
Laundry Room Concept

SERVICE SPACE

FOLDING TABLE

THREE DRYERS

BAR FOR HANGER

WASH TUB

SEATING

THREE WASHERS

TRENCH DRAIN

ROOM SIZE
15'-0" x 19'-0"

FOLDING TABLE

(Ramsey, Sleeper & Packard, 2007)

cial units. Using any type of residential equipment may also void any manufacturers' warranties, so always check before purchase.

Initial design should plan for maintenance in the laundry area, as significant amounts of lint and other debris can be generated. This can clog exhaust vent piping and waste drains. Removable catch baskets in drains and access hatches in exhaust vent piping should be included in the design. The number of turns in both types of piping should be minimized, and try to prevent any turns that approach 90 degrees. Allow for easy access around equipment for service and maintenance.

In addition to the laundry equipment, it is important to plan for other needs as well. These needs can include areas for folding, cart storage, linen storage, chemical storage, bulletin boards, back-up towels and linens, operating instructions, and emergency information. Sample laundry room designs are displayed in Figures 6.15 and 6.16.

There can be great advantages to having an in-house laundry facility, but it will come at a high cost for space, initial cost for equipment, annual cost to operate, and to staff the equipment. Planners and administrators should carefully analyze their operations to determine whether it is cost effective to make such a long-term investment.

Janitorial and Maintenance

An effective area for an important duty such as cleaning is typically overlooked in most facilities. Ideally, janitors' closets should be situated in a convenient location, be easily accessible, and sized to store all required items that can include the following:

- Chemicals—some that may require separation for safety purposes
- Tools
- Equipment—such as ladders, floor scrubbers, carpet extractors, backpack and upright vacuums, floor buffers, or burnishers, etc.
- Mobile equipment such as man lifts for high ceilings, carts, mobile trash bins
- Recycling bins and storage
- Supplies such as paper towels, toilet tissue, soap, toilet seat covers, etc.
- Counter space with electrical supply for battery charging

Designing a space for work can substantially increase the desired end result in quality. Users of sport and recreation facilities expect a high level of cleanliness in their facilities. Janitorial and maintenance spaces are generally not good candidates for shared use.

Specialization in Ancillary Spaces

Effective space planning is essential in the development of support facilities for athletics, recreation, or physical education. Optimal flow of participants between the activity or sport venues, locker rooms, offices, meeting rooms, and other support spaces is crucial. There is no universally accepted layout of these spaces; instead the ancillary spaces must be laid out in response to the culture of the institution, the user needs, and the existing facility and funding constraints (Dahnert & Pack, 2007). The specialized type of use may also greatly impact design considerations whether dealing with athletics, physical education, health and fitness clubs, recreational facilities, or any combination of the uses within a given facility.

Athletic Facilities

At the collegiate level, the locker room and other ancillary spaces like team meeting rooms and training rooms play a significant role in the recruiting process. The design of many athletic locker rooms resemble the high scale health club locker room and more with plush carpeting featuring team logos, customized wooden lockers, video screen, sound systems, and other amenities. This is especially evident in the major revenue sports of football and basketball at the large college level. Now many NCAA Division III schools are beginning to follow this trend (Fickes, 1999). Smaller teams may use their locker-room facility as a team meeting area, while larger sport programs will often utilize a separate meeting room (Dahnert

& Pack, 2007). In the interscholastic and intercollegiate athletic realm, Title IX requires not only equitable athletic opportunities, but also equitable locker space and shower-room facilities. In order to maximize locker-room multiuse and efficiency, many new locker rooms are designed with fewer differences for males and females, so that they can be used interchangeably based upon the needs of the sport season or competition schedule (Rittner-Heir, 2001).

Sport teams such as football, ice hockey, field hockey, basketball, and lacrosse have special locker-room requirements. First, the locker sizes for these sports are typically large, stadium-style lockers to accommodate all the necessary equipment. The flooring must also be selected to handle the rigors of the footwear requirements. Metal-tipped cleats and skate blades require special surfaces for the safety of the athletes and well as for the durability of the facility (Cohen, 1998). In some instances, direct outside field access from the athletic locker room is desirable, rather than requiring movement of the athletes within halls or corridors to access the locker room.

Physical Education Facilities

Special considerations for school-based physical education focus primarily on the locker room. Physical education locker rooms often included a high traffic flow within the school day and require a high number of lockers or combinations of storage lockers and changing locker systems. Additionally, the school physical education locker room requires a high degree of supervision by the teachers. The layout of lockers and dressing areas and showers

Table 6.7
Summary of Ancillary Space Component Allocations

	Strand (1988) Large College	Walker (1989) Small College	Petersen (1997) NM High Schools	Petersen (2007) IN High Schools
Locker Rooms	35-40%	45 -50%	55-57%	54-60%
Class Rooms/ Team Rooms	5-8%	10-12%	5-7%	5-10%
Faculty/Coaching Offices	15-20%	10-12%	10-12%	10-12%
Support Staff Offices	5-8%	2-4%	0-1%	N/A
Storage	20-30%	20-22%	20-22%	18-22%
Laboratory/Research Space	5-15%	2-4%	N/A	N/A
Athletic Training Rooms	1-5%	4-6%	4-5%	N/A

should avoid hidden areas where mischief could occur. Teacher offices should include easy access to both locker rooms and activity areas, and ideally provide for visual supervision via windows or doors. An additional physical education need is ample-sized and secure storage areas for equipment that is quickly accessible from the activity spaces.

In many secondary-level schools, post-participation showering is not always mandated, and as such, many showers are underutilized and at times not used at all during a typical school day. Due to this factor, the number of showers provided in the physical education locker room should be carefully scrutinized by the planning team so as not to provide an excess number of showers if the space and funds might be better allocated for other uses.

The determination of the amount of space provided for the ancillary facilities should be carefully considered in the physical education setting. Factors such as the overall school enrollment, the number of required and elective physical education classes offered, the size of the teaching staff, amount and types of equipment used, and the peak load of physical education students should all be taken into consideration in the planning process. Several studies regarding space allocation have recommended ancillary space guidelines in relation to the percentage of total ancillary space (Strand, 1988; Walker, 1989; Petersen, 1997; and Petersen, 2007). A summary of these ancillary-space allocations are provided in Table 6.7.

Fitness Clubs

For-profit health clubs, racquet clubs, and fitness centers must maintain a tremendous focus on the overall quality of their facilities in a competitive market. The ability to provide the best activity spaces, ancillary spaces, and customer service in this industry is crucial. Many clubs look to upgrade and provide as many amenities as possible within the ancillary spaces. In some cases, multiple types of locker rooms may be constructed within a fitness club based upon services provided. One type is providing more basic services compared with a second executive or elite level providing maximal levels of amenities and services for a higher membership rate. Depending upon the clientele of the clubs, some facilities may also choose to add an express locker room for those requiring minimal storage and service for the members' activities.

Administrative office space in the fitness setting forms a significant portion of ancillary space. This is due to the various professional staff members included in the fitness setting such as: membership sales, fitness programming, management, accounting, human resources, and food/beverage services. In addition to these types of professional office spaces, a front-desk check-in area for all members is required for both management and security purposes. The front-desk area should separate the open public spaces from the membership only area, provide for check-in and validation of membership credentials, control access to the facility and convey information about programming and facility/service reservations.

The addition of child-care ancillary space has become a common element in the health club and fitness center. This space provides an area for the care of small children while allowing patrons to utilize the facilities. These areas should include activity space for the children, diaper-changing stations, a restroom for supervised used, and an audio/video system.

Recreational Facilities

The most common recreational facility applications are campus recreation centers in the collegiate setting, and community recreation centers in the municipal setting operated in a not-for-profit manner whether by a city or by a group such as the YMCA/YWCA or similar organization. The recreation center ancillary space needs are similar in many ways to the for-profit fitness centers and health clubs. However, the level of finishes and amenities provided in most recreational facilities are not as high compared to typical private clubs. Access control within recreational facilities remains important and can be accomplished via a front-desk check-in area. The number of lockers typically required can be determined by a ratio of one full-sized day use locker for every ten members in most recreation and fitness settings (Lavoie, 2005).

Multipurpose Facilities

In many instances a sport, recreation, or physical activity facility is developed with multiple uses, and when this is the case the support space design must accommodate the needs of multipurpose use. For example, a high school facility may be used for physical education during the school day, for athletic team use in the after-school hours and open for community recreation use in the before-school hours. These diverse user groups may require different or additional support areas. The locker-room needs for a physical education class of 40 students may be far different from the football team of 60 athletes. With proper scheduling there may not be an overlap of activity space (gyms, courts, fields etc.) use, but often, additional support spaces are required in multipurpose facilities. There may be economic advantages to these multipurpose facilities in that the facilities are in use for a greater period of time each day, and in the fact that activity spaces are not duplicated. However, in any multipurpose facility conflicts for space and time are inevitable. The two areas most common for multipurpose use are secondary level schools and colleges and universities. In order to best plan the ancillary spaces for a multipurpose facility the needs of each user group constituency must be represented in the facility planning, curriculum planning, and scheduling processes. Then the full complement of needed ancillary spaces can be determined before the construction process begins.

GRAPHICS AND SIGNAGE

7

Michael G. Hypes, Morehead State University

Signs and signage have been a part of facilities for years. Until recently, signage, or environmental graphics, had been relegated to a back seat in terms of facility planning. Today's large and complex facilities, great numbers of sports facility users, guidelines developed through the Americans With Disabilities Act (ADA) and Occupational Safety and Health Administration (OSHA), and a litigation-oriented society, are all moving signage to the forefront when planning a new facility. Increasing use of computer technology, the use of electronic signs, and architectural signage will be the basic areas to rapidly develop in the near future.

Planning for Signs and Graphics

Have you ever visited an arena, stadium, or convention center for the first time and found that the signs were too small, hard to read, lacking, or obstructed from view? People in that situation experience a high level of frustration, become lost, and eventually stop looking for their destination.

Clear, informative graphics and signs are essential for conveying directional, instructional, or general information to the public. This is especially true in arenas, stadiums, or convention centers that house a wide range of events and attract large crowds.

Townsend (2004) suggests, when thinking through graphics and signs for a facility, the planners should consider the following key questions during the design phase:

- What will the sign be used for?
- How long will it be used?
- What image is the graphic or sign to depict?
- What is the target audience for the graphic or sign?
- What is the viewing distance for the graphic or sign and the length of time it will take for viewers to read it?
- Where will the graphic or sign be placed and how will it be installed?

- What is the budget for the graphic or sign project?
- Are there permits required or restrictions imposed on the sign?
- What other graphics or signs does the facility need?
- When is the graphic or sign needed?

Importance of Signs

Signs are an essential part of a facility and should be an integral part of the planning process in a new facility. Signs have come a long way in the last decade. New materials, colors, and graphics have changed the signage world. Many architectural firms now refer to a signage system as the environmental graphics of a facility. All sports and recreation facilities include a wide variety of signs. It is important to identify facility entrances and to direct individuals to concourse levels and seating sections. Restrooms, concession areas, first aid stations, information centers, locker areas, security areas, and exits must be clearly designated. Information concerning parking area locations must be located near the exits. Traffic-flow information must be imparted by external facility signage. The parking area, if large, will need to be sectioned off by effective signs. Elevator and room designation signs must have raised-letter markings for users with visual impairments. The centers of these signs should be placed 60 inches above the floor. Other facility signs should also have raised letters, even though at this time this is not an ADA requirement (see Figure 7.1). Where diverse populations exist, signs must be designed in multiple languages. The use of international graphics (or pictograms) can also help in designing signage for multiple languages.

Many sports facilities are large, sprawling, one- or two-floor facilities. If the facilities have been around for a number of years, there is a good chance that additions have enhanced them. Add-ons can create logistic nightmares, and signs become paramount to direct individuals through a

Figure 7.1
Guidelines for ADA Signage

- Pictograms must be placed on a background with a height of at least six inches. Pictograms must have a text counterpart.
- Raised characters must be at a minimum of 5/8 inch and a maximum of two inches.
- There are character proportions as well. Letters and numbers must have a ratio of width to height of between 3:5 and 1:1, and a stroke width-to-height ratio of between 1:5 and 1:10.
- Braille and raised characters have to be raised 1/32 inch, and the font must be either upper-case sans serif or simple sans serif. The font must be accompanied with Braille grade 2.
- There are requirements for the finish and contrast of the characters. The contrast must be at least 70%, and the colors of the background and characters must either be matte, eggshell, or some other nonglare finish.
- Signage must be mounted at least 60 inches above the floor to the center line of the sign.
- Signage must be mounted and installed on a wall that is adjacent to the door's latch side. But, if there is no space for that, then the signage needs to be installed on the nearest adjacent wall. Individuals must be able to approach the signage within three inches without any protrusions, such as the door swinging or any nearby objects.

facility. It is not uncommon to find sports facilities with interiors of more than 200,000 square feet. Sports facilities are also among the most heavily used facilities on campuses and related sites. Large sports facilities, such as arenas and stadiums with large numbers of users, call for a well-planned signage system.

Types of Signs

The basic purpose of any sign is to impart information. This information varies with the type of sign used. Five categories of signs are identified for use in facilities. These categories are:

- warning, danger, caution, and emergency signs
- notice and standard operational signs
- directional signs
- rules and regulations
- sign graphics

Handicap-accessible signage

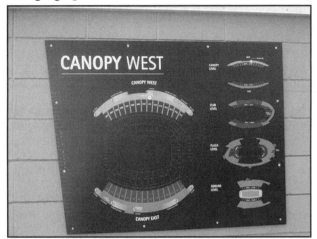

**Stadium seating signage,
Paul Brown University**

Even though signage is divided into five distinct categories, the groups overlap. A sign could fall into just one category, or it might fall into two or three categories, depending on its purpose and the type of information it is conveying.

When developing signage for a facility or a specific area within the facility, special consideration should be given to the purpose of the signage and the eventual audience for the information. OSHA identified the following issues regarding the communication of hazardous conditions:

- comprehensibility
- readability
- standard phrases

Comprehensibility refers to the ability of the individual reading a sign to understand the information sufficiently to take the desired action. Comprehensibility is different from *readability,* in

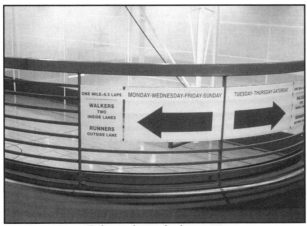

Directional signage

that the latter is simply a measure of the grade level of the written information, while the former is a measure of how well the receiver of the information understood it.

Standard phrases refers to the use of "signal words" in signage. The use of the word *danger* indicates an imminently hazardous situation, which, if not avoided, may result in death or serious injury.

This signal word should be limited to the most extreme situations. *Warning* indicates a potentially hazardous situation, which, if not avoided, could result in death or serious injury. *Caution* indicates a potentially hazardous situation, which, if not avoided, may result in minor or moderate injury. It may also be used to alert against unsafe practices.

An example of repetitive signage

The population at large may not share the importance that professionals attach to signal words. Many organizations (e.g., American National Standards Institute, U.S. Military) have guidelines for the determination of what signal words are to be used with specific hazards, and these are usually unknown to the public. The arousal effects of signal words and accepted organizational guidelines need to be incorporated into the design of effective signage.

Designing Signs

If at all possible, design your signs during the planning process of your building and its surroundings. If you are renovating or making additions to an existing facility, this is a prime time to plan for all new environmental graphics in your complex. Make your signs an aesthetically pleasing part of your facility.

Signs need to be simple and understandable, and they need to attract the facility user's attention. Placement, size, shape, repetitiveness, color, and graphics are all important in designing simple, understandable signs that attract user attention.

Placement

Signs must attract the facility user's attention. A well-placed sign maximizes its effect on the facility user. Signs need to be placed in the appropriate area and need to be placed at the appropriate place and height to have the greatest impact on the user. For instance, a sign stating "No Skateboards Allowed in the Building" will not make its point in the interior of the building. This sign needs to be placed at all building entrances so that it can be seen before one enters the building with a skateboard. On the other hand, the sign "No Food or Drink in the Weight Area" needs to be posted outside the weight area as well as inside the weight area.

It is also important to place signs in normal sight lines. Placing signs too high, too low, or off to the side makes them less visible. It is important to remember that sight lines vary according to the user's height. Signs for young users, six to eight years of age, should be placed lower than signs for adults. Individuals in wheelchairs need signs placed in their sight lines.

Signs may be on a wall, a ceiling, a floor, suspended, freestanding, on columns, or on doors. In some instances, a sign may be on two or more surfaces. It may be partially on a wall and continue onto an adjacent wall or floor. The effect of a sign

**Scoreboard signage,
Paul Brown Stadium**

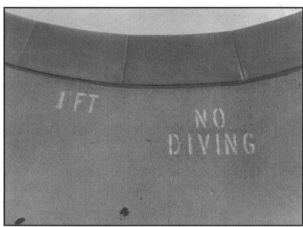

**Example of signage found
in swimming areas**

on multiple surfaces is eye-catching, thus attracting attention to it.

At times, signs must be repetitive within a facility. An example of repetitive signage is in an indoor racquet court battery. If there are eight courts, some signs will need to be repeated eight times, once at each court. An example of repetitive signage is: "Eye Guards Are Mandatory!"

Materials

Signs may be an integral part of the facility as a permanent part of the structure (painted on walls or other surfaces or tiles of different colors that make a sign) or they can be attached to surfaces by a frame or brackets. Architectural or permanent signs are recommended whenever possible. These signs not only impart information, but they are also an aesthetically pleasing part of the structure of your facility. If architectural signage is used and planned for carefully, few signs will need to be added to your facility. It is paramount to plan in advance for successful architectural signage. If mistakes are made in the planning process, they become permanent mistakes, or, at the least, costly mistakes to overcome. Even with the greatest of planning of architectural signage, some signs will have to be non-permanent, and some signs will have to be late additions. As time and facility use change, signs need to be changed and updated, even though some architectural signage will never need to be changed. Architectural signs are usually made of "like" building material. For instance, a painted wall has a painted sign or an asphalt tile floor has different size, texture, or color inset tiles to form a sign. Signs may be made of wood, metal, tile, paper, glass, paint, and plastic or any combination of the aforementioned items. Signs may be electrified such as lighted signs, billboards, scoreboards, or "running" sign boards. Electrical signs are more expensive than non-electrical signs. An electrified sign, on the other hand, stands out and attracts attention to it. Electrical signs must be in a secured location because they are easily broken

and are expensive to repair. If electrical signs are to be used, one must plan carefully for electrical outlets or electrical hookups directly in relation to sign placement. Extension cords running from signs to an electrical power source are unaesthetic, unsafe, and unacceptable.

Shape, Color, Size, and Graphics

Signs do not have to be rectangular in shape. Rectangular signs do afford maximum use of space if the signs contain only words. Other sign shapes have the ability to be eye-catching and/or informational. Take the eight-sided red sign at the end of the street, attached to a metal post, located on the right hand side of the street. This does not need to be read—the octagonal shape, location, and color indicate *stop*. Explicitly shaped signs, for specific information, can be used in facilities to impart information by using sign shape. Example: all pentagonal signs indicate classrooms, all circular signs indicate laboratories, and all diamond-shaped signs indicate offices.

An X-shaped sign in facilities immediately signals not to do something ("No Diving," "Do Not Run") just by the shape of the sign itself. The idea of effective sign shapes follows a recent international trend toward standard pictorial signs. Facility signs now must take on and convey a universal message to many ethnic populations. A sign featuring graphics will not alienate a facility's foreign users as much as a sign in English might.

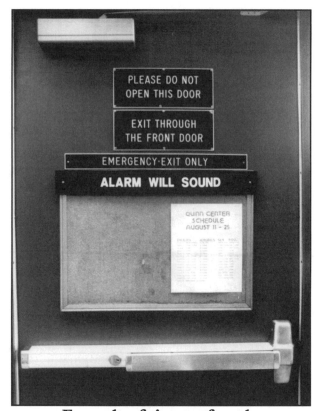

**Example of signage found
in swimming areas**

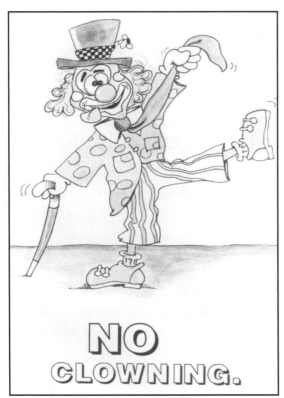

Using humor to relay information.

Color, as the red in stop signs, can also be an important aspect of signage design. All signs of one color can indicate storage and housekeeping areas. Color in signs can be used to attract the attention of facility users. Bright-colored signs on a bland wall surface, in most instances, attract attention. A colored sign will attract a user's attention better than a black and white sign. Incorporate color in your signage theme.

Signs vary in size. The size of a sign, in itself, is a method of drawing the attention of facility users. A very small sign indicating *exit* is easily seen suspended from the ceiling or wall. Sometimes a large sign is needed to house important information and to draw the facility user's attention. "No

Lifeguard on Duty—Swim at Your Own Risk" is effective as a large sign. Vary the size of your signs depending upon the information to be imparted and make use of sign size to attract attention.

The size of a sign's images and print also are instrumental in how the information is relayed. Words and graphics that are too small make the reader work harder and can result in the sign being ignored. Just as some signs can be too wordy or hard to comprehend, too many signs posted in a small area also create problems. An overabundance of signs may cause the reader to miss a certain sign that has been lumped together in the busy array of other signs. Separating and isolating signs is important to their overall effectiveness (Turner, 1994).

The content and message of a sign must be designed for the educational level(s) of the individuals using the facility. Content of a sign for a university will read differently than the content of the same sign for an elementary school. In all cases, it is important to keep signs as simple as possible. The simpler a sign, the easier it is to read and understand its content, thus making the sign more effective.

The old adage that a picture or graphic is worth a thousand words is still accurate for sign design. Using a clown figure to enhance a "No Clowning" sign in a weight area attracts attention to the sign. A facility user's attention is drawn to

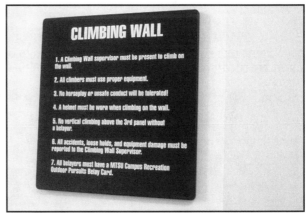

Information signage.

attractive signs and adding graphics to signs makes them more attractive. A little humor about a serious matter can help to impart important information to facility users.

Signage and the Three Groups It Serves

Though most signage will be directed at facility users, there are two other groups for whom signage is vital: facility employees and emergency personnel. The litigious society that we live in has placed an increased importance on proper and effective signage in our facilities. Effective signage may prevent an injury from occurring or it may be important in one's defense during a trial. Think of

Bengal seating, Paul Brown Stadium

effective signage as both a money and stress saver when it comes to litigation.

Information contained in signage is important not only to the facility users but also to the facility staff. Signs help facility staff acclimate quicker and more safely to their jobs. Good location, direction, and rules signs help new employees adapt more quickly to a new environment.

Hazardous materials are found in many facility laboratories and swimming pools. Staff must handle biohazardous waste, toxic chemicals and gases, and nuclear contaminants routinely. Signage is paramount in these areas. Signs should first indicate the hazard and secondly inform the employee how to work safely with the hazard. Containers for hazardous material and waste need effective signage in the form of visible labels. Signage should also be placed in break room and workroom areas to inform employees of various performance and safety requirements. Emergency personnel are the third group of individuals for whom signage must be well planned. Signs must be planned so that emergency personnel can find their way easily in a complex facility to save lives or deter additional injuries to facility occupants. Emergency personnel should not have to wander around a building before they can complete their jobs. Clear and effective signage in laboratories and pools indicating specifically what hazardous materials were present when an injury occurred can save a life.

Signage Maintenance

Signs placed throughout the facility need to be maintained. If you have electrical signs, you will

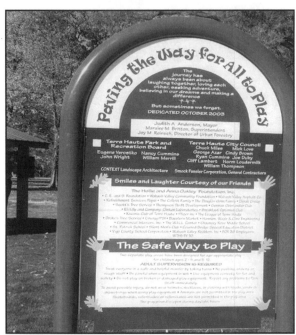

A good example of an entrance sign leading into a universally accessible playground

have to replace bulbs and other electronic components. Most of these signs can be maintained from the front; however, there are some electrical signs that need to be maintained from the rear or from the top. If the electrical signs are small, they are easy to remove and repair. If the electrical signs are large, heavy, and cumbersome, one needs to plan for this in sign placement. A large, rear-entry sign can be placed over a planned opening in a wall so that there is easy access for repair work to the rear of the sign without having to remove the sign.

Signs can break. Breakage of signs may be accidental or intentional. Signs in sports complexes take much abuse. Balls hit them, rackets and bats hit them. When there are too many signs, they need to be protected. If possible, place signs out of abuse range. Placing signs higher and in areas away from projectiles and hitting devices will help to prolong sign life and reduce maintenance costs. Some signs must be placed in harm's way. Polycarbonate sheeting works best for signs that need to be encased or covered with a clear material. Be careful, though, because the glossy finish of the sign or its covering can create glare problems and take away from the effectiveness of the sign, as well as provide an unwelcome distraction.

Wire mesh (the kind that sometimes covers clocks in school gymnasiums) works as an effective cover on signs whose faces would not be sufficiently protected by plastic sheeting, such as signs that are in the path of balls and other flying objects. If a sign must be covered with a mesh cage, make sure it can still be seen well enough to convey its message (Turner, 1994).

Signs can also be defaced. By placing signs out of reach, one can avoid some defacing. Use materials in the construction and covering of signs that deter defacing. The use of polycarbonate sheeting and other slick surfaces will help keep sign defacing at a minimum.

Signs need to be cleaned on a regular basis. Fingerprints, smudges, dust, and other airborne particles need to be removed from signage as a regular routine. Electronic signs need special attention and regular cleaning to ensure that they function at an optimal level. Soiled signage of any type can curtail the amount of information imparted by the sign. Set up a regular cleaning schedule for signage.

Miscellaneous Considerations

Signage cost will vary with materials, size, number of signs, and whether or not the sign is electrical. It is suggested to figure your signage cost as a part of your facility construction cost. In some cases, parts of construction costs are bid separately and signage may be bid after the facility is built. This is not recommended. Repetitive signs will reduce costs since more of the same product reduces the cost per sign. The geographic location of your facility will also be a factor in signage cost. It is suggested to purchase high-quality products,

**Examples of use of graphics
(above and below)**

even though initially these products may be more costly than low-quality products. Over the lifetime of facility signage, quality products cost less.

The geographic location of the sports complex will dictate which and how many languages will be used in signs. Locations of multiple ethnic populations will dictate signage languages. Signs can be affixed to surfaces either permanently or semi-permanently. The method of affixing will depend on the philosophy of the design and use of the facility. It will also depend on the longevity of the signage. "Exit" signs, for example, are rather permanent, whereas rules and regulation signs may change over time. Signs may be attached flat onto a surface or they may extend out perpendicularly or horizontally from a surface.

Protruding signs are sometimes needed for visibility and code adherence. One of the problems with protruding signs is that they are more susceptible to breakage than flush-mounted signs. Keep in mind that the size and shape of some signs might be dictated by local, state, and federal regulations. Check local fire and building codes to be certain that a particular facility includes all the required signs. Additionally, check with state and national offices for signage needed to meet ADA and OSHA requirements.

In some instances, a one-sided, flush-mounted sign is not sufficient. Signs suspended from the ceiling may impart information on two, three, or four sides. Protruding signs usually give information on two or three sides. As signage is designed, always consider using signs with multiple sides. Some signs will need to be freestanding in order to be moved from one area to another area of the facility. An example of a free-standing sign would be, "Caution: Wet Floor." Freestanding signs can take any shape or form; however, the most common is a two-sided pyramid shape.

Sponsorship in sports complexes is common. Sharing a sign with a sponsor is common in athletics (e.g., rolling sponsorship signs). Scoreboards and other signs are either purchased by the sponsor or rented by the sponsor so they can advertise on the sign. This concept of sponsorship can be used for signage in other areas—not just for athletics. Sponsorship or sharing of signage is an important concept and should be studied carefully for all signage in a facility. In any case, sign sponsors and sports complex directors can both obtain mutual benefits by this partnership (Turner, 1994).

A rather new area in signage design is the use of art graphics in a sports complex. These art graphics or permanently painted or inset materials are designed as integral parts of the facility. Various images can be placed on surfaces in the form of sports art, murals, or basic signage.

These images are color coordinated with the color scheme of the facility. The images can bring life, motion, brightness, and attractiveness to an otherwise plain and dull facility. Currently, there are a number of companies that do art graphic work for sports complexes. Computer imagery is now enhancing the appearance of sports art, graphics, and murals.

INDOOR SURFACES

8

Hal Walker, Elon University
Tony Weaver, Elon University

Although discussions about indoor surface materials seldom elicit excitement, interest, or enthusiasm among sport and recreation consumers, choices made in the facility planning and construction process are integral to "facility success"—from any perspective. All facets of facility appearance, utility, maintenance, cost, safety, and functionality are impacted by the nature of the surfaces in a given facility. Three main categories of indoor surfacing include floors, walls, and ceilings. These surfaces have far-reaching and profound effects on numerous aspects of facility utilization and care. This chapter will provide useful information to assist in the process of outlining the types of materials available for these surfaces, along with some advantages and disadvantages based on use in specific areas. The importance of planning in the selection of surface materials, along with a consideration of individual needs, cost, maintenance, safety, acoustics, and aesthetics will be addressed in this chapter.

Indoor facility surfaces are generally divided into three distinct areas. These areas are the service/ancillary areas, the main floor, and office/administrative areas. Planning for, and the selection of, appropriate indoor surface materials, along with proper installation and maintenance over the facility life span, can profoundly impact facility use and costs. Making informed surface choices allows for optimal facility use, enhanced user satisfaction, and reduced incidence of injuries. Surface options, however, provide a vast and confusing array of choices, with numerous companies touting state-of-the-art textures, materials, colors, and performance characteristics. Yet, of the hundreds of products currently offered on the market, few surfaces are ideal for all of the activities a typical facility plans to offer. This situation leads to countless errors in the decision-making process, as it is rare that facility planning takes place with equal participation among all players impacted by this process: owner/funding source, facility manager, maintenance staff, and the end users. There really is no perfect surface—as the needs and desires of each of these groups can be vastly different. Communication, however, is critical to the selection of facility surfaces that effectively meet the demands of the various planning constituents. Available budget, planned activity offerings, life expectancy, maintenance costs, risk management, foundation, and climate are but a few of the factors that must be considered when making informed facility surface choices.

Selection of Indoor Surface Materials

Indoor surface materials must be chosen carefully, considering the nature of the facility and the activities that are planned. As mentioned above, the primary surfaces addressed in this section are floors, walls, and ceilings. "When viewed as an essential piece of equipment in a sports facility, the sports floor is the point where the athlete and the activity merge" (Cooper, 2004, p. 4). The following text will outline the types of materials available for these surfaces, their characteristics, along with factors to consider when going through the planning and decision-making process.

Generally speaking, the planned activity in a given area should dictate the type of flooring surface utilized. Many, if not all surfaces, however, are utilized for more than a single purpose. There are three distinct areas of consideration in facilities currently being built. The first of these areas are the service/ancillary areas such as locker rooms, shower rooms and bathrooms. These areas require surfaces that take into account heavy moisture content as well as slip and fall concerns. The second area is the main arena or activity center of the facility. This area tends to encompass the majority of time spent on the decision-making process; however, each area should warrant considerable thought and planning. These central activity areas typically require either a hardwood floor or a resilient synthetic material. Offices, administrative areas, and classrooms account for the third facility location. Special areas require different materials, layouts, and treatments. For example, basketball courts should be of a non-slip nature, while a dance area should have a finished treatment that allows individuals to slide across the floor. Safety, hardness, absorption, resilience, and lateral foot support are each critical in the selection of surfaces for dance floors (http://www.stagestep.com/).

Durability, flexibility, and cost are three considerations that have allowed synthetic floors to challenge traditional hardwood flooring. Synthetic surfaces take the form of grass or non-grass surfaces. The two most popular synthetic surfacing materials are polyvinyl chlorides (PVCs) and polyurethane. Polyurethane is either poured in place or produced in prefabricated sheets that are adhered on the site, while PVCs are typically prefabricated. The general perception is that polyurethane possesses most of the desirable characteristics sought in a multipurpose facility surface (Popke, 2001).

Multipurpose approaches are common for many facilities as a variety of activities take place on the same court. Multipurpose courts often "include hardwood, synthetic sheet goods poured urethane products and suspended interlocking plastic tiles" (Popke, 2001, p. 47). No surface meets the specific needs of each activity; however, finding the right surface that meets a majority of the user needs is the goal of most facility managers (Kollie, 2004).

It is essential to understand that there are countless types of wooden floors, many floor manufacturers, and the costs can vary dramatically (Dahlgren, 2000). Costs also vary extensively among other surface alternatives, such as synthetics and carpets. Varying costs often depend on the materials used, the thickness of the surface selected, and the condition of the existing surface. Thicker synthetic surfaces, for example, although they may absorb more shock and offer greater resilience, are generally more expensive. Once again, the planned use should be the central factor directing all facility surface decisions.

In the past, the third area—administrative offices and classrooms—has been satisfactorily covered with some type of tile that may include vinyl, asphalt, rubber, or linoleum. Many believe consideration should be given to using carpet in some of these spaces. Hard maple floors are generally the most expensive when looking at initial installation; however, over a long period of time these flooring options become more than competitive when compared with most synthetic surfaces (Neuman, 2003). Unfortunately, many decisions are made based on available finances during initial facility construction, rather than the "best" and most economical surface for the long term. The cheapest flooring surface option is generally viewed as indoor-outdoor carpeting.

Floors

Flooring choices are influenced by many factors. Initial cost, maintenance, performance features, aesthetics, and longevity are examples. According to Kroll (2002), flooring choices should be made on the basis of "a facility's design, function and budget." With ever-advancing technology and a variety of factors that contribute to flooring decisions, the large number of options only tend to make this decision more complicated (Piper, 2003; Steinbach, 2002). According to Piper (2000), flooring choices tend to be made by individuals responsible for design and construction aspects of a project, rather than those ensuring that the surface meets the needs of the end users. The maintenance and operational costs is often overlooked by concerns over the initial financial outlay (Piper, 2003; Piper, 2000).

Understandably, flooring choices are often made by financial rather than practical purposes. Floors are often repaired, rather than tearing out a damaged or worn surface and installing a new floor. Cost management factors often force facility managers "to take the low bid or a Band-Aid approach" to facility flooring repairs and updates (Popke, 2007, p. 57). One should carefully consider this decision, as properly installed and maintained floors can have a healthy life expectancy, influencing the real cost of flooring alternatives.

Before analyzing factors related to flooring choices, various issues need to be considered. Sport flooring surfaces, according to Viklund (1995), are categorized as *point-elastic* or *area-elastic*. Point-elastic surfaces maintain impact effects at the immediate point of contact on the floor, with the ball, object, or individual. Area-elastic surfaces allow for dispersion of impact, where a bouncing object, or an individual jumping, can be felt approximately 20 inches around the point of impact. *Hardness* is another term that is utilized to describe the nature of a flooring surface and its ability to react to surface contact. The term hardness is defined readily in the fields of mineralogy, metallurgy, and engineering. In mineralogy hardness is defined as the ability of the surface to resist scratching—with a softer surface obviously scratching more easily. This is measured by the Mohs scale, after Friedrich Mohs, a German mineralogist. In metallurgy and engineering, hardness is determined by pressing a hard material on a given surface, and the size of the indentation made is measured to report the "hardness" of a substance. This is called the Brinel test, named after a Swedish engineer, Johann Brinel (Williams, 2005, p. 9).

Another internationally recognized standard for sport flooring surfaces is known as Deutsches Institut für Normans (DIN) (see Appendix H). This standard was developed by a testing lab in Germany, establishing minimum standards for flooring (Cohen, 1998; Killie, 2004; Bynum, 2004).

"The DIN standard was embraced by manufacturers of wood athletic floors and quickly became the industry-wide benchmark against which all indoor sports floors would be—and still are—judged" (Bynum, 2004, p. 86). DIN standards are available for minimum levels of shock absorption, ball bounce, deflection, surface friction, and rolling load. These standards suggest a floor must meet the following: i) shock absorption—flooring needs to absorb at least 53% of an object's impact; ii) ball bounce—balls must maintain 90% of their bounce if on concrete; iii) deflection—the point of impact must be a minimum of 3/32nds of an inch, and 20 inches from the point of floor impact, the floor must measure 15% or less than the original point of impact; iv) surface friction—these standards vary depending on the nature of the activity; and v) rolling load—floors need to withstand 367.7 pounds of weight (Cohen, 1998). A complete listing of DIN requirements (1991), and the differences between DIN Standard (1991) and Pre-Standard (2001), area-elastic floors are shown in Tables 8.1 and 8.2 below (Bynum, July 2004, p. 88)

Viklund (1995) discusses the concept of *resilience* when analyzing performance characteristics of various flooring options. Resilience is the shock-absorption ability of a floor based on the amount of force applied to the surface area. For comparison, concrete is a base value, with no resiliency (zero percent). Point-elastic surfaces (synthetics) have a low-absorption level (10 to 50 percent), with most in the 25- to 35-percent range. Resilience is influenced by both the thickness and the hardness of the floor material, as well as the sub-flooring under the surface (Viklund, 1995). When considering carpeting as a surface choice, the quality of the underlay also has a significant impact on the carpet performance as well as the carpet life. According to Driscoll (2000, p. 54), "the use of a quality underlay can prolong the life of a carpet from 50 to 75 percent."

Facility surface choices must also consider the influence of the sub-flooring material. Flooring characteristics on porous or "floating" surfaces will react very differently than others placed on concrete. Flooring choices, in fact, should be carefully

Table 8.1
DIN 18032-2 (1991) REQUIREMENTS

	Area-Elastic	Point-Elastic	Combination
Force Reduction (min.)	53%	51%	58%
Ball Rebound (min.)	90%	90%	90%
Vertical Deflection	Minimum 2.3 mm	Minimum 3.0 mm	3.0-5.0 mm
Area Indentation (max.)	15%	—	5%
Direction I	No limit	No limit	No limit
Direction II	No limit	No limit	No limit
Rolling Load	1,500 N	1,000 N	1,500 N
Slip Resistance	0.5-0.7 mm	0.5-0.7 mm	0.5-0.7 mm

(N = 1 Newton, or the amount of force that causes an object with a mass of 1 kg to accelerate at 1 m/s.)

Table 8.2
DIFFERENCES BETWEEN DIN 18032-2 STANDARD (1991) AND 18032-2 PRE-STANDARD (2001), AREA-ELASTIC FLOORS

Criteria	DIN 18032-2 Standard (1991)	DIN 18032-2 Pre-Standard (2001)
Vertical Deflection		
Average (Each Point)	No limit	Minimum 2.3 mm
Area Indentation		
Average (Each Point)	No limit	Maximum 15%
Direction I	No limit	Maximum of 20%
Direction II	No limit	Maximum of 20%
Direction III	Not measured	Maximum of 20%
Direction IV	Not measured	Maximum of 20%
Force Reduction		
Average (Each Point)	No limit	Minimum 53%
Ball Rebound		
Average (Each Point)	No limit	Minimum 90%
Slip Resistance	0.5-0.7 mm	0.4-0.6 mm

considered based on the sub-flooring material that is present. The condition of this sub-flooring can also influence the cost of the project, as this surface may need special preparation for the chosen surface materials to be placed on top. According to Dahlgren (2000), shock-absorption characteristics of wood floors may be more heavily influenced by the sub-flooring than the actual surface material itself.

Area-elastic floors also need to be evaluated based on activities planned for the space. *Area of deflection* must be considered with regard to the primary use of the facility surface. Area deflection is the amount of impact that is felt in the vicinity around the points of contact. With area-elastic flooring, it must be decided that the area of deflection will not adversely impact the activities of other individuals concurrently on the surface. According to Viklund (1995), area of deflection is not a major concern for recreational use; however, it could be a major consideration for competitive or varsity play.

Another important consideration for most organizations in making flooring choices is a concept known as the "rolling load." Rolling load is the capacity of a floor to withstand damage from external forces such as bleacher movement, equipment transport, or similar activities (Viklund, 1995). Any surface utilized for multipurpose activities must be able to withstand the movement of equipment or materials over the surface area during transition from one activity to another. Related to this concept are the "walk-off" areas that experience heavy use. Even the most durable surfaces, over time, will undergo rapid deterioration under heavy pedestrian or equipment traffic. Mats, padding, or varied traffic patterns can be established by the careful planning of equipment storage areas to extend the life of most facility surfaces. The choices made for the planning of *tare space*, or areas that are not developed for primary activities, might also influence the wear and tear on a floor over the life of the facility surface. Decisions for the storage and transport of equipment should not be viewed as unimportant in the facility surface decision process, as this can directly influence the deterioration of a surface with heavy equipment and pedestrian traffic.

Life-cycle costs of a surface are also important to consider when making various flooring choices. Piper (August, 2000), suggests that hardwood flooring is rated for 25 years, as is terrazzo, followed by 15 years for vinyl tile, and approximately ten years for most carpets. It is stressed, however, that these suggested guidelines might not necessarily match individual expectations. A product's *life cycle* may describe how long a product will withstand expected use; however, the aesthetic appearance is also valued by most organizations. For this concept, a product's *attractive life* describes how long a surface will remain acceptable based on the product's appearance, not its functionality. As a result, organizations should consider the amount of *churn*, which describes the general wear and tear on a given surface, given the expectations for a given location (Piper, August 2000). If extensive *churn* is predicted for a given area, it may not be sensible to place a long-term, high-quality surface, that will not remain aesthetic for the *life cycle* of the product, when compared with its *attractive life*.

There are a variety of floor surface options that can be used successfully as a main gym floor. Once again, this important surface choice is normally dictated by the primary activity planned for the space. Options for indoor sports flooring are generally broken down into two categories: wood and synthetic. Each surface option has strengths and weaknesses. According to Bishop (1997), wood flooring with proper maintenance can last 50 years, compared with 20 years for a synthetic surface and 15 years for a vinyl tile. Table 8.3 illustrates initial cost, life expectancy, and annual maintenance cost for vinyl tile, synthetic surface, and wood flooring for a 5,000 sq. foot gymnasium (Bishop, 1997).

Initial cost, life expectancy, and annual maintenance cost for vinyl tile, synthetic surface, and wood flooring for a 5,000 sq. foot gymnasium

Vinyl tile floors have a life expectancy of approximately ten to fifteen years but begin to show their wear after the first few years (Bishop, 1997). Recent technology, however, has significantly improved the quality of sheet vinyl and vinyl composition tile, making this flooring choice both more aesthetic as well as more durable (Hasenkamp & Lutz, 2001). Vinyl floors, however, tend to be very hard and have poor absorption qualities. These characteristics can also lead to athletic injuries if high humidity levels are prevalent, or if water spills are not managed properly. Unlike other sport surfaces, which require only washing and damp mopping, a vinyl tile floor must be stripped, sealed, and waxed at least three times annually. In contrast, synthetic floors also require regular cleaning, but may require line repainting or a touch-up every five years (Bishop, 1997).

An updated lifecycle cost analysis of indoor sports flooring is offered for wood and synthetic flooring options in Table 8.4. Installations as well as daily, biweekly, quarterly, annual, and major maintenance factors are utilized to comprise an annual cost for each flooring option (Bynum, November 2004, p. 133).

Hardwood floors are generally designed with intricate sub-flooring to provide shock absorption and can be expected to last the life of the school. Wooden floors must always be kept clean to provide proper traction. They must also have the lines repainted or touched up and should be sanded down and refinished every three years. Synthetic floors do not allow for as much sliding as hardwood floors. As a result, if the activities on the floor involve sliding actions, a wood floor is the better choice. Wood floors can also be designed in a number of ways, including sub-floor systems, cushioned systems, and spring systems.

Table 8.3
Initial cost, life expectancy, and annual maintenance cost for vinyl tile, synthetic surface, and wood flooring for a 5,000 sq. foot gymnasium

Type of Flooring	Life Expectancy	Initial Cost
Vinyl Tile	15 years	$15,000
Synthetic Surface	20 years	$40,000
Wood Flooring	50 years	$65,000

Initial Cost/Life Expectancy	Maintenance Cost Annually	Total Cost Annually
$1,000/yr (vinyl)	$1,210	$2,210
$2,000/yr (synthetic)	$2,000	$4,000
$1,300/yr (wood)	$2,666	$3,966

Table 8.4
INDOOR SPORTS FLOORING LIFECYCLE COST ANALYSIS

CATEGORY	WOOD		SYNTHETIC					
Type	Maple	Pre-finished Engineered	Linoleum	PVC	Rubber	Tile	Full-pour Urethane	Pad-and-pour Urethane
Installation costs*	$3,200	$2,368	$1,600-$3,000	$2,600	$2,333-$2,833	$2,750	$3,333-$4,667	$4,333-$5,667
Daily maintenance costs**	$2,088	$2,088	$2,088	$2,088	$2,088	$2,088	$2,088	$2,088
Biweekly maintenance costs**	—	—	$1,800	$1,800	$1,800	$1,800	$1,800	$1,800
Quarterly maintenance costs**	—	—	$1,300	$1,300	$1,300	$1,300	$1,300	$1,300
Annual maintenance costs	$2,800	—	—	—	—	—	—	—
Major maintenance costs***	$1,070	$420	—	$500	—	$250	$350	$350
Life Expectancy (yrs.)	38	38	15-50	25	30	20	15	15
Total annual cost	$9,158	$4,876	$6,788-$8,188	$8,288	$7,521-$8,021	$8,188	$8,871-$10,205	$9,871-$11,205

All surfaces are assumed to be 10,000 square feet.
*Installation costs have been amortized over the expected life span of each surface.   **Figures for daily, biweekly and quarterly maintenance represent annual totals, including the cost of labor ($12 per hour) and materials. ***Major maintenance costs have been amortized over the span of 10 years.
Sources: Athletic Business research, Maple Flooring Manufacturers Association

A process to assist with estimating both annual and lifecycle costs for a maple strip, PVC sheet, and poured urethane sport floor is offered in the worksheet on p. 107. According to Bynum (November 2004, p. 133), although these costs were published in 1994, the Maple Flooring Manufacturers Association (MFMA) reports the information is valid today, with the possible exception of installation costs.

As mentioned above, the nature of the subflooring can often be a more significant factor than the actual surface material chosen for a floor (Dahlgren, 2000; & Holzrichter, 2001). Kroll (December, 2002) suggests that cost-cutting processes during

Lifecycle Cost Comparison Worksheet

THE FOLLOWING CHART HAS BEEN DESIGNED TO HELP YOU ESTIMATE ANNUAL AND LIFECYCLE COSTS FOR A MAPLE STRIP, PVC SHEET GOODS OR POURED URETHANE SPORTS FLOOR IN ANY FACILITY, BASED ON SQUARE FOOTAGE. TO COMPUTE THE ESTIMATED LIFECYCLE COST COMPARISON OF A SPORTS FLOOR:

1. Enter the square footage of the floor on line one.

2. On lines two through seven, compute the annual costs for each component by multiplying the annual per-square-foot cost by the square footage of your floor.

3. For a total annual cost, add lines two through seven.

4. For a lifecycle cost, multiply line eight by line nine.

	MAPLE STRIP	PVC SHEET GOODS	POURED URETHANE
1. Your floor's square footage	_____ sf	_____ sf	_____ sf
2. Installed cost	x $0.32 = ____	x $0.26 = ____	x $0.33-$0.57 = ____
3. Daily maintenance	x $0.21 = ____	x $0.21 = ____	x $0.21 = ____
4. Bi-weekly maintenance	x $0.00 = ____	x $0.18 = ____	x $0.18 = ____
5. Quarterly maintenance	x $0.00 = ____	x $0.13 = ____	x $0.13 = ____
6. Annual maintenance	x $0.28 = ____	x $0.00 = ____	x $0.00 = ____
7. Refinish/resurface	x $0.11 = ____	x $0.00 = ____	x $0.04 = ____
8. Total estimated annual cost for your floor	_____	_____	_____
9. Life expectancy	x 38 years	x 25 years	x 15 years
10. Estimated lifecycle cost for your floor	= _____	= _____	= _____

the planning phase of building development often alter the sub-flooring preparation intended for a given flooring option. This in turn may extensively alter the actual performance and longevity characteristics of chosen surface.

Generally, there are three types of recommended sub-floor constructions. The first is a suspension floor, which is made out of either plywood, foam rubber, or some other type of synthetic material, available in a variety of patterns. The finished floor rests on top of the sub-floor material. The second type of sub-floor construction is a spring floor. This involves coiled metal springs, covered by a plywood sub-floor, with the finished floor resting on the plywood. The third type is referred to as a padded floor. Padded materials, such as foam or other synthetic or porous materials, are laid over concrete or plywood and then covered with the finished floor (Stoll & Beller, 1989). As technology and testing procedures for various flooring options continue to develop, manufacturers pay increasing attention to various floor performance characteristics (Steinbach, July 2002). Steinbach describes an approach where "strips of foam, as opposed to one solid sheet, can effectively soften a floor" (p. 82). Any number of variables can be altered, resulting in subtle or profound changes in the ultimate performance of the floor. Naturally, the more materials needed, along with the cost of these materials, impact the cost of the flooring choice. Safety is yet another consideration that should also be considered throughout the decision-making process. In any instance, it is important to be familiar with all these factors such that everyone is aware of the factors involved and their impact on performance, cost, appearance and life expectancy of the surface chosen.

Synthetic floors remain a popular choice, and they tend to be much softer than wood floors and perform much better acoustically. Wood floors, depending on the effectiveness of their suspension systems, can also have dead spots. Dead spots are areas on the floor that can cause objects impacting the floor surface to perform inconsistently. An example would be a basketball that would have a variable bounce due to a change in the characteristics of the floor. Synthetic floors are evenly laid and are less likely to have dead spots, although inconsistent ball performance can still occur. Quality installation will maximize optimal surface performance with any surface choice. Upkeep of all gym floors calls for constant maintenance. Rubberized synthetic floors, although popular, tend to have higher maintenance costs when compared with wooden floors.

There are many different floor-covering options related to sport and recreational activities in today's market. Some examples include ceramic tile, cushioned wood flooring, and rubber compound flooring. The selection criteria for certain flooring materials should include:

1) Economic feasibility with initial outlay and lifecycle costs. Floor-covering choices entail much more than the initial up-front cost. Many now realize that the initial cost for materials and installation is only a small component of the total investment needed. Life-cycle cost considerations not only include the initial expense and installation, but the number of years the flooring is expected to last, cost for removal or disposal of the floor, lost revenues during remodeling or replacement periods, and maintenance costs

over the course of the surface life (Hard Questions, Critical Answers, 1998).

2) Ease of maintenance and replacement.
3) Potential performance capabilities for both intended and possible use.
4) Overall compatibility in appearance according to surrounding surfaces and equipment in the facility (Barkley, 1997; & Dahlgren, 2000).

An important factor that is often overlooked when considering floor options, concerns the planned events within the facility. Access to electrical outlets, placement of equipment securing devices (floor plates for volleyball uprights), and tare space necessary for intended spectator traffic and equipment movement are each important considerations. If floor plates are to be utilized, they should taken into consideration early in the process, as well as covered, for ease of maintenance, access, and safety factors. In particular, electrical outlets should be installed in the floor, covered and flush with the floor's surface, as they are commonly associated with safety issues related to traffic flow. Also to be taken into consideration is the time spent in preparing a facility for various activities. Greater planning for both functional and safety factors can save time (equipment set-up and tear-down), reduce costs (tape and mats to cover electrical and media system cords), and reduce accidents (tripping over exposed wires and cords).

When selecting a surface, it is a wise choice to consult other facilities that have similar need and use patterns to explore all flooring options based on performance characteristics. It is also important to consult with individuals who work with and maintain these facilities (i.e., maintenance personnel, students, athletes, publics, etc.), since they will likely have a different perspective regarding the suitability of various facility surfaces. The ultimate choice is made by the planning team; however, all factors should be considered to make optimal surface decisions.

Although cost tends to be perceived as the over-riding factor that drives a facility surface choice, aesthetic factors are being increasingly considered in the decision-making process. Wood flooring, for example, tends to be chosen based on the quality or grade of the actual wood. Quality is categorized into first, second, and third grades. First-grade wood has the fewest number of defects and deficiencies when inspected prior to sale. "First grade allows for a very modern, clean, and, in some minds, sterile look because it is fairly defect-free. You don't see dark blemishes or a lot of graining" (Dahlgren, 2000, p. 78).

Wood flooring choices are also made based on color, which once again is influenced by visual appeal. Maple tends to be the industry standard and offers good durability due to a "tight grain and density"; however, the light color also supports its popularity (Dahlgren, 2000). Second- and third-grade woods tend to offer a darker, more grainy, and warmer appearance; however, this choice once again boils down to personal or committee preference. Also a consideration that should not be overlooked is the impact of the floor color or aesthetics on the participant as well as the spectator. A dark or grainy floor, although more appealing to the eye, may be a distraction to the participant. As far as performance is concerned, according to Hamar, president of the Maple Flooring Manufacturers Association, "you could blindfold a person and have them dribble a ball on a first-grade floor, a second-grade floor and a third-grade floor, and he or she would never know the difference" (Hamar, 2000, p. 84).

A final consideration in the quest for enhancing the visual appeal of a floor surface is achieved by creative efforts with paint, patterns, colors, and contrast. Tiled flooring can easily be created in various patterns and designs that are very appealing to the eye; however, during the reconditioning process of a wood floor, alterations in surface applications can create a new look with the same old floor. Again, all these issues need to be addressed by communicating with other facility management personnel and discovering the strengths and weaknesses of the numerous options available before an ultimate decision is made for any facility.

Surface Selection Process

As stated earlier, choosing the appropriate flooring surface is a major decision in either the initial design or the renovation process. Floor materials and maintenance patterns can greatly impact athletic performance, determine how well multiple uses are served, and impact the incidence of sport injuries. Floor surfaces come in innumerable materials, textures, colors, and performance characteristics (see Figure 8.1). Yet, of the hundreds of products on the market, no one surface is perfect for all uses, and there is plenty of room to make the wrong choice (Viklund, 1995; Kollie, 2004).

A logical and systematic approach should be followed in conducting a search for the appropriate surface. These guidelines will assist in the decision-making process. According to Viklund (1995, p. 46), the steps in the following flooring checklist are recommended:

- Select the room or space to be considered
- Prioritize the sports/activities that will occur within the space
- Decide whether the preferred floor should be area elastic or point elastic
- Review the performance criteria for the selected floor type
- Test flooring options by reviewing samples and comparing costs
- Compare life-cycle costs for flooring options
- Play on the different surfaces
- Check the manufacturers' referenced projects
- Make the final decision

Figure 8.1. Attributes of Various Floor Surfaces

Legend:
- ● = Above Average
- ◗ = Average
- ○ = Below Average
- V = Variable
- D = Daily
- W = Weekly
- M = Monthly
- Y = Yearly
- P = Periodically
- S = Semiannually in high traffic areas or yearly in average traffic areas

Material	Strength	Durability	Thermal Insulation	Moisture, oil, chemical resistance	Stain Resistance	Abrasions Resistance	Wearability	Mildew Resistance	Heat Absorption	Limited Application Locations	Sweeping or dust mopping	Vacuuming	Damp mopping	Wet mopping	Scrubbing	Stripping	Dry Cleaning (Chemicals)	Hot water extraction	Waxing	Buffing	Resealing	Regrouting	Sanding & refinishing	Overall Maintenance Ranking
Hard — Ceramic Tile (6"x6"x1/2") Mortar and Grout	●	●	●	V	◗	●	●	●	○	x	D	x	D	x	S	S	x	x	M	M	x	x	x	High
Ceramic Tile (6"x6"x1/2") Mastic and Grout	●	◗	●	V	◗	●	●	●	○	x	D	x	D	x	Y	Y	x	x	M	M	x	x	x	High
Quarry Tile Mortar and Grout	●	●	●	●	●	●	●	●	○	x	D	x	D	x	x	x	x	x	Y	Y	x	x	x	Medium
Exposed Concrete Sealant (2 coats)	●	●	○	○	◗	●	◗		●	✓	D	x	W	Y	x	x	x	x	Y	x	x	x	x	Medium
Terrazzo (1 3/4")	●	●	◗	●	●	●	●	●	◗	x	D	x	W	x	Y	x	x	x	x	x	x	P	x	Low
Epoxy resin	◗	○	●	●	●	◗	●	●	○	x	D	x	W	x	Y	x	x	x	x	x	x	P	x	Low
Laminated wood (synthetic core) Vapor barrier & adhesive	◗	◗	●	◗	◗	◗	●	◗		x	D	x	W	x	Y	x	x	x	x	x	x	P	x	Low
Wood plank (2 1/4")	●	◗	●	◗	◗	◗	◗	●	◗	x	x	D	x	x	x	x	x	S	S	x	x	x	x	Medium
Resilient — Bamboo flooring Vapor barrier & adhesive	●	◗	●	○	◗	●	●	●	◗	x	x	D	x	x	x	x	x	S	S	x	x	x	x	Medium
Linoleum (.125")	◗	●	●	◗	◗	●	●	●	○	x	x	D	x	x	x	x	x	S	S	x	x	x	x	Medium
Vinyl Composisiton Tile (VCT) Vapor barrier & adhesive	◗	◗	●	○	V	◗	○	○		x	D	x	D	x	x	x	x	x	x	x	Y	x	x	Low
Vinyl Sheet Vapor barrier and adhesive	◗	◗	●	○	V	◗	○	○		x	D	x	W	x	M	x	x	x	x	x	P	x	x	Medium
Rubber Sheet (1/8") - Adhesive	●	○	●	●	◗	●	◗	◗		x	D	x	W	x	M	x	x	x	Y	Y	x	x	x	Medium
Cork (1/8") - Adhesive	○	○	●	◗	○	○	○	◗	○	x	D	x	W	x	M	x	x	x	x	x	x	x	x	Low
Soft — Carpet tile (18" x 18", 20 oz/syd) Hard back	◗	◗	●	◗	●	◗	◗	●		✓	D	x	D	x	x	x	x	x	x	x	x	P	x	P · Low
Carpet tile (18" x 18", 20 oz/syd) Cushion back	◗	●	●	◗	●	◗	◗	●		✓	D	x	D	x	x	x	x	x	x	x	x	x	x	Low
Carpet (Nylon loop pile 40 oz/syd) Adhesive	◗	◗	●	◗	●	◗	◗	●		✓	D	x	D	x	x	x	x	x	x	x	x	x	P	Low

It is recommended that the following steps be considered when selecting a surface:

- **Definition**. Define the characteristics required to meet specified needs (i.e., bounce characteristics, sunlight effects, etc.). Many of these questions are addressed by manufacturers in their literature.

- **Solicitation**. Cost should not be a limitation for one's initial research and review of possible flooring systems. One should request as much information from as many manufacturers as deemed reasonable. The review of this information will allow for a broader knowledge of different systems and a basis for comparison. Material estimates and project costs should be obtained from various manufacturers. Manufacturers should also provide references, a list of installers, and the location of like facilities for comparative analysis.

- **Comparison**. After reviewing manufacturer materials and comparing all possible systems, a categorization of all materials should be performed. Categorize information by type and desirable qualities, i.e., natural vs. synthetic, resiliency, initial cost, longevity, safety, aesthetics, and any additional factors significant to your decision-making process. A table that compares the various positive and negative attributes of each surface option is generally deemed helpful in making the right surface choice for your facility.

- **Visitation**. After the field of choices has been narrowed down based on established criteria, a site visit for each of the facility surfaces being considered should be performed. A closer inspection and discussion with personnel at each facility is also likely to be helpful in making the best choice for your facility. Performance as well as maintenance factors must be explored, as initial cost and utility are only two of the numerous factors in making a wise surface choice.

- **Selection**. At this point, select a system based on upon all research efforts. Take into consideration all performance criteria and always keep in mind that

Wood floor protective coverings.

surface choices are a significant factor in the overall success of a facility.

- **Quality**. A specific surface may be selected; however, there are numerous levels of quality among any number of surface options. Once more, take into consideration the quality of the materials, workmanship, guarantees, facility use factors, and any other significant considerations when making this important decision.
- **Manufacturer**. Choosing a manufacturer is also important. How long have they been in business? What type of technical support do they provide? What are their methods of quality control, both in the manufacturing process and in the field? What is their reputation? How soon can they provide you with the requested materials? What guarantees do they provide? Many questions should be compiled and asked of each company being considered. Always remember that references are important to obtain; however, be careful to do your homework in the inquiry process. One should never rely too heavily on references provided by the company being considered, as they will obviously be more than willing to provide positive references for their own work history. Unsolicited references should be sought for all finalists in the bidding process followed. It is common in the industry that manufacturers will provide products to clients in exchange for positive reviews.
- **Installer**. An installer should be recommended by the manufacturer to help insure that they are familiar with installation of the manufacturer's product. The installer should be asked questions similar to those asked of the manufacturer. Another key

piece of information is the time frame required for completing the installation. Many jobs are started on time; however, seek guarantees for job completion, or factor this item into a reduction in cost for jobs not finished when promised. Facility visits and communication with other clients will once again be helpful in deciding upon an installation company.

- **Maintenance**. Maintenance is a considerable portion of the operating budget, and it is important to define exactly what is involved. What type of maintenance is required? How often will the surface need to be refinished, covered, lacquered, replaced, etc.? Facility planners should not underestimate the expense of properly maintaining facility surfaces, and figure this expense into the overall surface cost and flooring choice.

Kennedy (2000) recommends that maintenance staff should have a thorough knowledge of the various floor surfaces they are maintaining. Piper suggests the maintenance and cleaning costs can "typically account for more than 50 percent of the total cost of ownership" (Piper, August 2000, p. 4). Cleaning approaches can also vary based on the intended use of the surface. Recent research by Agron (2001), describes an overall reduction in expenditures for both maintenance and operations in elementary and secondary schools in recent years. This same author, however, reports an increase in spending for maintenance and operations budgets in higher education facilities. In either case, this concept needs to be factored into the flooring decision process. A less expensive floor may have a very limited life span without proper care. The same can be stated for more expensive flooring that requires more specialized care to attain maximal life-cycle utilization.

Moussatche, Languell-Urquhart & Woodson (2000) provide information that relates life-cycle costs with operations and maintenance considerations for hard flooring, resilient flooring, and soft flooring options. As mentioned earlier, the actual cost of the initial flooring is only a portion of the life-cycle flooring expense. "Life-cycle cost analysis allows the evaluator to fully examine each alternative and the true service life cost of the material" (p. 20).

- **Initial Cost**. What is the total initial cost of the system? Make sure there are no hidden costs that will arise later. If two systems are considered similar, yet one is more costly than the other, why? Is it the quality of the system, materials, or both? Sometimes product name or reputation is a reason for cost inflation.
- **Life-Cycle Cost**. This comparative analysis considers the initial cost, operational costs, maintenance costs, and if necessary, replacement costs during the estimated life cycle. These figures will generate the anticipated total costs. Generally, a higher initial cost system will be comparable in the long run, with less expensive systems when all factors are considered.

- **Bidding**. When bidding is required, attention should be directed toward written specifications to ensure the product and installation methods are accurately described to avoid misunderstandings.
- **Installation**. It is in the owner's interest to require the manufacturer to perform periodic on-site supervision of the installer. This will help insure compliance with the manufacturer's specifications.

Risk Management and Safety Considerations

Flooring surface choices clearly need to be assessed based on facility use expectations, however, with liability concerns, surface choices need to be made with extensive consideration of various safety factors. Resiliency, slip, traction, absorption, foot support, activities planned for the space, and the age and ability of the intended users are some of the considerations when deciding upon a flooring choice. Literature supports the notion that a lack of effective communication exists within the process of deciding upon a flooring choice; however, all parties should be concerned about the impact of this choice on risk-management outcomes. "Health considerations and their accordant legal and financial liabilities are influencing the selection of sports surfacing" (Cooper, 2004, p. 2). Another author states "the distance between the recreation and maintenance professions" is a key factor (Cohen, November 2002, p. 106). In this article, the author discusses the fact that recreation management professionals often have little input into maintenance functions. Maintenance functions are stated as being "dominated by longtime city employees, refugees from other businesses, volunteers, and seasonal and part-time workers" (Cohen, November 2002, p. 106). Piper (December 2003, p. 3) states that flooring choices are frequently chosen based on aesthetic appearance when new, compared with how they will last through their service life, as well as their resistance to gouging, indentations, stains, rolling loads, acoustics, and slip-resistance characteristics.

A device recognized by the American Society of Testing and Materials (ASTM), called a tribometer, establishes the slip resistance of various flooring surfaces and footwear (Di Pilla, 2001). Knowing exactly how slippery each floor surface is enables a determination of appropriate activities for this space, possible shoe requirements, as well as cleaning schedules. A simple change in cleaning materials or application method can impact how slippery the surface will be. Although a comprehensive risk-management program can address some of these factors, this issue needs to be considered in the planning process to avoid the resultant risks from slips and falls.

Repairs to surface materials need also consider the impact on end users, as well as the effect on initial manufacturing warranties. Although some repairs may be made by custodial and maintenance staff, surface repairs may need to be made by industry professionals to maintain the initial integrity of the facility surface. Facility surface repairs tend not to be repairs that can go on a list of things to do later—as the utilization of the facility is dependent on a quick solution. According to Cohen (2000, p. 46), "each player . . . is just one misstep from finding that hole, breaking an ankle, and suing you for negligence."

Walls and Ceilings

Walls serve a greater function than providing a divider, or perimeter, for specific activity areas. Walls function as barriers to sound, heat, light, and moisture. Depending on the location and intended use of the facility, the selection of wall surfaces should be given careful consideration for the acoustical properties of the material as well. Generally speaking, moisture-resistant walls with sound acoustical properties are ideal.

Perhaps one of the most common characteristics of a typical gym is the inability of the various surfaces to absorb sound (Holzrichter, 2001). The acoustical treatments utilized on walls or within the overhead structures should be high enough so they will not impede the utilization of wall space, the travel of objects, and will not be easily damaged by users. As mentioned earlier with flooring, there remains a trend toward greater aesthetic pursuits on walls and ceilings in the utilization of colors, pictures, and graphics on these surfaces. Banners, sound panels, and other porous materials can be utilized to improve acoustical sound properties of a typical gymnasium. Tasteful color schemes can also have a positive psychological value on the participant or spectator, along with making the environment more aesthetically pleasing (Flynn, 1993; Hasenkamp & Lutz, 2001).

Another wall consideration that has evolved in recent years is that of padding: how much, how high, how thick, and what material? With lawsuit numbers increasing, the performance of wall padding has earned greater concern by facility architects, planners, and managers. Not only the fact that wall padding is necessary in specific facility locations, but also the effectiveness of this padding in preventing serious injury upon contact. An additional factor is how extensive should efforts be to pad all possible contact zones? Steinbach (March 2004) describes a 1997 accident where an eighth-grade student collided with a padded gym wall during a basketball tryout, resulting in the eventual death of the child. Steinbach continues, describing current efforts to establish recognizable standards for wall padding—thickness, material, and location.

Walls in the main gym or activity area should have a minimum height of eight feet and should always be padded for safety reasons. Electrical outlets should be provided every fifty feet and should also be protected by padding. Small inserts can be cut out of the padding and affixed with fasteners for easy removal and replacement, for access to electrical outlets. All padding should be checked with regularity, as it can wear and harden with age and contribute to significant injury upon contact. Keep in mind that some unobstructed flat wall space may need to be kept available as appropriate, for teaching and/or lecture space. In some cases all walls should be kept unobstructed, however, this would be based on the specific activities planned for the space (i.e., indoor soccer).

Roof design, local building codes, and the nature of the planned activities should determine ceiling construction. Ceilings should be insulated to prevent condensation and be the appropriate height to accommodate all planned and future activities. Painting ceilings can also improve the physical look of the facility, as well as enhance light reflection. Bright white ceilings are strongly advised against in areas where light colored objects are utilized, i.e., shuttlecocks and volleyballs. It is difficult to visually follow these objects against a bright white ceiling background. A light color is still recommended for ceilings, however, and most facilities find an *off-white* color to work best. A twenty-four-foot minimum distance (lowest suspended object) is required in any teaching station designed for a variety of activities (Flynn, 1993). Cohen (April 2003), suggests 25 feet; however, he also states that volleyball has a minimum ceiling requirement of 12.5 meters (37.5 feet), as well as the impact of other planned facility uses, which may force planners to create greater ceiling heights to accommodate activities such as commencements and concerts. Whenever possible, facility planners should attempt to exceed minimum ceiling heights, as minimum heights can still contribute to game interference, equipment lodging (i.e., shuttlecocks), and greater ceiling fixture expenses as a result of occasional contact with equipment (i.e., volleyballs).

Ceiling height may also impact factors not initially considered when making such choices. Planning for high ceilings may result in alterations of original equipment plans, as "high ceilings might render ceiling-hung basketball standards impractical, necessitating greater storage to accommodate portable backstops" (Cohen, April 2003, p. 72).

Acoustical ceiling materials are needed in instructional spaces and areas with many planned activities. Dropped ceiling panels will require considerable maintenance because they are susceptible to damage by objects or individuals. Since most acoustical instruments are not necessarily made out of the hardest materials, they need to be placed out of range of flying objects. In some cases where there are low-ceiling activity areas, dropped ceilings may be equipped with spring-loaded clips that will return the acoustical panel back into place after contact. It should be noted that false ceilings with catwalks above them have been effectively constructed to allow for easier maintenance, and the repair of lighting and ventilation arrangements.

As mentioned earlier, the ceiling should have a minimum height of 24 feet to the lowest obstacle with an off-white color usually being appropriate. A clear-span ceiling design without minimum support pillars and substructure girders should be investigated for safety, viewing, aesthetics, and more open and usable space. If one chooses to mount or store equipment in the ceiling area, structural reinforcement may become necessary at these sites. It is very important to consider all necessary factors when constructing or remodeling the primary features of a facility.

Once again, the planned usage of a given area should guide all planning and material requirements. "The ceiling is the primary acoustical treatment in the office" (Moeller, in Roberts, September 2000, p. 2). According to Roberts (September 2000) and Kroll (December 2003), Noise Reduction Coefficient (NRC), is the capability of a ceiling to absorb noise. An additional consideration is the Sound Transmission Class (STC). This concept measures the effectiveness of a wall or ceiling in blocking sound between offices. Kroll (December 2003) continues, elaborating on the increased demand for sound reduction within many facilities, based on privacy concerns. With the passage of the Health Insurance Portability and Accountability Act (HIPAA), health care providers must make reasonable efforts to respect the privacy of clients. This is particularly true within medical facilities, where sensitive material is shared and the ability of a surface to minimize sound deflection is important.

Figure 8.2 provides a guide for floor, wall and ceiling choices for a variety of rooms within your facility.

Windows

The use and aesthetic value of windows are often overlooked in the planning of indoor facilities, as well as within the process of making surface choices. Windows can provide durable and attractive enclosures, as well as divisions of space within a facility. Facility planners must keep in mind, however, that windows may face daily exposure to the elements along with frequent contact with objects utilized in the activities planned for the space (Johnson & Patterson, 1997). Climate is also a consideration when deciding on window placement and use, as it can enhance warming features due to sunlight, which can obviously be a benefit or a detriment, depending on the facility's geographical location. Windows can also create glare problems; however, with appropriate placement (northern exposure), can greatly enhance the aesthetic quality and appeal of indoor surfaces (Holzrichter, 2001). Fenestration is the technical term for the natural lighting created by windows.

The selection process for windows, according to Piper (1998), is based on a number of factors, some of which include: 1) Lighting: the three most common ways for controlling the light passing through windows are tinted glazing, heat-absorbing

Figure 8.2 Suggested Indoor Surface Materials

ROOMS	FLOORS							LOWER WALLS								UPPER WALLS						CEILINGS			
	Carpeting	Synthetics	Tile, asphalt, rubber, linoleum	Cement: abrasive, non-abrasive	Maple, hard	Terrazzo, abrasive	Tile, ceramic	Brick	Brick, glazed	Cinder Block	Concrete	Plaster	Tile, ceramic	Wood Panel	Moistureproof	Brick	Brick, glazed	Cinder Block	Plaster	Acoustic	Moisture-resistant	Concrete or Structure Tile	Plaster	Tile, acoustic	Moisture-resistant
Apparatus Storage Room				1		2		1				2	1	C											
Classrooms		2			1						2	1	2						2	1		C	C	1	
Clubroom		2			1						2	1	2						2	1		C	C	1	
Corrective Room	1					2				2	1	2					2	2	1	2				1	
Custodial Supply Room				1						2															
Dance Studio					1																	C	C	1	
Drying Room (equip.)				1				2	2	1	2	1	1				1		1						
Gymnasium		1			1						2		1		2		2	2	1	2	*	C	C	1	
Health-Service Unit			1				1				2	1	2						2	1				1	
Laundry Room			2						1	2	1	2	2		1	C					*	*		*	*
Locker Rooms		3	3					2	1		1	2	2	3	1	*	1		1	2				C	1
Natatorium							2		1	2	1	3	2		1	*	2	2	1	*	*	C	C	1	*
Offices	1	3	2								2	1	1						2					1	
Recreation Room		2			1			2			2	1		1			2		1	2	*		C	1	
Shower Rooms			3					2	1		1	2	1			*	2	1	2	2	*			1	*
Special-activity Room		2			1					2		1	1				1		1	1			C	1	
Team Room	1		3					2	1	2	1	2	2	3	1	*	1		1	2				C	1
Toilet Room			3					2	1		1	2	2	2	1	*	1		1	1				1	
Toweling-Drying Room			3					2	1		1	2	1			*	2	1	2	2	*			1	*

Note: The numbers in the table indicate first, second, and third choices. "C" indicates the material as being contrary to good practice. An * indicates desirable quality.

glazing, and low-emissivity coatings; 2) Keeping the elements out; 3) Heat loss; 4) Aesthetics; 5) Security; and 6) View. Windows are often overlooked when making wall surface choices; however, they should be incorporated into the overall building's aesthetic plan, the regional location of the facility, as well as incorporated into the activities scheduled within the facility. Windows also add to the construction costs; however, apart from the impact they may have on the activities planned for the space, they can add extensively to the aesthetic appeal of most facilities.

Lighting

Although not always considered when making surface choices, lighting is an important factor when selecting facility surfaces. With increased efforts to address aesthetics, as well as participant and spectator satisfaction, lighting should be addressed in the planning phase of building construction. Indirect lighting is largely viewed as ideal for most competitive sport and recreational settings. Indirect lighting, however, is heavily influenced by its surroundings. Paint type (flat vs. gloss), paint color, shadows, HVAC, sprinkler pipes, acoustic strips, all impact lighting efforts (Cohen, May 2002). As mentioned numerous times previously, the efforts of the architect can have a significant impact on a variety of design elements within a facility.

Photo by Hal Walker.

Photo by Hal Walker.

Photo by Hal Walker.

Additional Floor, Wall, and Ceiling Considerations

Floor considerations include:

- an adequate number of floor drains in the proper locations
- proper floor sloping for adequate drainage (if necessary)
- water-resistant, rounded base, where the flooring and wall meet in any locker or shower area
- floor plates are flush-mounted and placed where they are needed
- provision of non-skid, slip resistant flooring in all wet areas (i.e., pool, shower, etc.)
- lines painted as appropriate, prior to any sealers being applied (Patton et al., 1989)

Wall considerations include:

- an adequate number of drinking fountains, fully recessed into the walls
- a minimum of one wall of any exercise room with full-length mirrors
- all "corners" in the shower and locker room areas are rounded
- all wall coverings be aesthetically pleasing, as well as matching the decor and color scheme of the facility
- electrical outlets placed strategically within the wall (or floor), firmly attached, and accessible, if the wall is protected with padding
- in wet or humid areas, materials should be easy to clean and impervious to moisture (Patton et al, 1989).

Ceiling considerations include:

- ensure the provision of adequate ceiling heights for all planned facility activities
- all ceilings, except storage areas, are acoustically treated with sound-absorbent materials
- ceilings and access areas are easily accessible for purposes of routine repair and maintenance
- use acoustical materials that are impervious to moisture when they will be used in moisture-dense areas (Patton et al., 1989).

Service and Ancillary Areas

Locker and Shower Areas

There are numerous options for cost-effective, safe, and easy to maintain locker and shower areas. Although the surface choices for these areas haven't changed much in the past twenty years, greater emphasis is being placed on voluntary standards such as the LEED Green Building Rating System®. This represents "a measurement of green design developed and administered by the United States Green Building Council" (Popke, 2006, p. 76). For obvious reasons, locker and shower areas require surfaces that are slip resistant. Slip-resistant surfaces by nature tend to be more difficult to clean. Areas that are more difficult to clean tend to require more chemicals, which opposes the efforts of most environmentally-concerned facility operators. Tile, poured epoxy, coated concrete, rubber/vinyl/acrylic, carpet, flow-through tile, and exposed concrete and punched surfaces comprise the most common wet-area floor options, along with various "emerging LEED-compliant possibilities" (Popke, 2006, p. 77).

Locker-area surfaces should possess a combination of maintenance ease along with a strong consideration of hygiene factors. All surfaces should be durable and able to withstand excessive moisture and humidity, as well as the accumulation of dirt. Aesthetic appeal once again remains a central issue in facility design within locker-room areas, as many participants base their attitudes and opinions about the facility as a whole, on their likes and dislikes within the locker-room environment. This idea is espoused by Huddleston (November 2001, p. 63) in stating "careful attention to the design and maintenance of locker rooms can greatly enhance a facility's image and contain its odor."

Locker-room areas should contain hot and humid/wet areas, as well as dry dressing areas, typically within close proximity. Floors in wet areas should always be designed with safety, aesthetics, and maintenance in mind. For obvious reasons, non-slip tile is the best surface for these floors. Since soap and dirt often have a tendency to build up, a beige or brown-colored grout is recommended to keep the tile clean. Some facilities have stopped providing soap as the resultant slips and falls can create legal problems. Frequently wet areas, such as locker rooms, require greater risk-management efforts to readily notice problem areas and reduce potential risks (Di Pilla, 2001).

All wet-area floors within locker rooms should be pitched away from the dry areas and directed toward a drain. Some alternative sources include epoxy sealants over waterproof sheet rock or, concrete block. These surfaces have proven in the past to work satisfactorily in the dressing room, sink, and common areas. It should also be noted that all corners of these areas should be rounded so moisture cannot penetrate the seams (Patton et al., 1989). Although many facilities make decisions to avoid carpeted surfaces within locker rooms, the right carpeting is better equipped to handle moisture than people think, in particular in change areas (Huddleston, November 2001). Carpeting is not particularly advised in heavy water areas near showers; however, flow-through flooring has been known to handle heavy water areas. Flow-through flooring allows excessive water to pass through the surface area to the subflooring below, before it passes to the floor drains. As long as this process allows for air circulation and drying of the subfloor system, this helps maintain a dry surface and can reduce slip and fall occurrences (Huddleston, November 2001; Popke, 2006).

Moisture is clearly the enemy in any building and even more so where humid or wet areas exist. Precautions during the design process as well as the life span of the facility are important to minimize negative outcomes resulting from humidity, moisture, and microbe growth. Migration of moisture into contiguous areas must also be controlled. Measures must also be taken during the construction process to ensure that all building materials are not moisture damaged prior to installation. An effective and efficient heating, ventilation, and air control system (HVAC) must maintain a balance between humidity control and energy savings (Straus & Kirihara, 1996).

Prevention is the key in controlling microbiological gardens from growing in your building.

Clearly, the most eminent hazard is moisture. Moisture can range from large pools of water from roof leaks, or broken water pipes, to invisible rain that is absorbed into building materials, or moisture that condenses on facility surfaces. Dust also serves as a nutrient source for microbial growth. Although chemicals are a common method to combat these problems, moisture is the real culprit and should be the primary focus of effective and routine maintenance procedures (Straus & Kirihara, 1996).

In drier areas of the locker room, the floor is a major concern for interior decorators and designers. Mildew and mold are constant problems, and the materials should be able to withstand long periods of moist conditions and show little or no signs of delaminating. A one hundred percent nylon carpet is recommended for flooring material in a health and fitness setting. The carpeting provides an aesthetically pleasing appearance and is easily maintained with daily vacuuming and periodic shampooing. It should also be noted that the nylon carpets will have a longer life and will be more easily maintained if they are mildew resistant and Scotch-guarded (Patton et al., 1989). Wear tests have also concluded that appropriate cushioning beneath the carpet surface can greatly enhance carpet life, as well as comfort for the participant (Goodman, 2000).

Wall coverings in locker-room areas usually consist of epoxy-coated paint, vinyl, or wallpaper. The chosen material should be strong and not show dirt. There should also be consideration given to the corners and wall-to-wall moldings to reduce the amount of black marks and cuts that often appear, typically with heavy use. Ceilings are typically finished with moisture-proof hand-finished paint. As mentioned earlier, acoustical materials should also be used in conjunction with paint, to reduce the noise levels that occur in locker rooms (Patton et al., 1989).

Steam Rooms

Steam rooms require specialized knowledge for construction and care. Building materials utilized and the planned methods of application are critical to minimizing the maintenance efforts in steam rooms. It is highly recommended to hire a contractor with previous experience in the construction of wet areas, when considering steam room construction. The floor surface of a steam room should be covered with a liquid rubber material and applied over a concrete slab. A layer of fiberglass fabric is laid over the rubber material, followed with an additional coat of liquid rubber. The floor should also slope toward the drain for proper water drainage. This system both protects against water leaks and expands with floor movement (Patton et al., 1989).

Steam room walls and ceilings should be covered with a cement building board and fiberglass tape. This wall surface should also be placed on galvanized metal studs or womanized lumber. It is important to remember to slope ceilings as well, to enable moisture to run-off rather than drip-off. This system has proven to be durable and helps to prevent against rot and mildew. As with other wet areas, the selected tile should be both attractive and durable. A textured non-slip tile should be used on the floors, whereas many choose to use glazed ceramic tile for the walls and ceilings (Patton et al., 1989).

Aerobic/Exercise Facilities

As aerobic exercise and other impact activities remain popular in fitness, recreational, and athletic centers across the nation, the effort to reduce impact-related injuries continues. Spring-loaded or "floating" hardwood floors are the most popular surfaces, followed closely by heavily padded carpet surfaces that are sealed and plastic-laminate-bonded to inhibit moisture leaks into the pile textures. This type of flooring allows for regular steam cleaning and avoids the hygiene problems from accumulated perspiration, as with a carpeted and/or padded area. Important considerations are compliance (shock absorption), foot stability, surface traction, and resiliency (energy return). Furthermore, there are synthetic and specially made floors that may be used as alternatives (Patton et al., 1989). Research on various flooring types should be available from most manufacturers that address the specific needs and demands of the activity you plan to offer.

Finding a balance between all facility surface areas is a considerable challenge for the facility planning team. For example, one of the best shock-absorbing floorings is any type of thick sponge pad. Regular foam may develop dips after prolonged use, but some new synthetics have been specially developed to hold their shape. One such surface is microcell foam, which is available at one-fourth the cost of wood, but it should be noted some difficulties may arise with the interlocking sections. These types of synthetic floors are usually soft enough that individual mats are not needed for floor exercises. It should be noted that cleaning may also present unique problems with these floor types. Bacteria growth may also be a problem, in particular if the surface is textured or not properly maintained (Walker & Stotlar, 1997).

Although the quality of polyurethane surfaces continues to improve, these surfaces are not considered resilient enough by some because they are simply poured directly over concrete. The testing results of a surface may meet all the necessary industry standards; however, the surface hardness may still be inappropriate for many activities, again due to the nature of the sub-flooring material. This point was made earlier; however, it is imperative to consider the sub-flooring material just as vital to the qualities and characteristics of use, as the visible surface that is applied, laid, or poured on top. Maintenance issues remain a significant factor, as these surfaces are often plagued with cracking and peeling with age. The life cycle of these surfaces are also much shorter than wood.

Carpeting is relatively easy to install and newer sport varieties have special shock-absorption properties. These should always be used with foam cushioning and never be applied directly over concrete surfaces. Carpet is versatile, inexpensive, and works well, especially in multipurpose areas. It should be noted, however, that carpets are highly susceptible to staining, can be easily discolored or stretched, as well as retain odors. The expected life span of most carpets is two to four years depending on the use, cleaning methods, and quality of the materials.

Historically, wood floors remain a popular choice. Wood is aesthetically pleasing and provides a high degree of flexibility within most multipurpose activity areas. Wood floors, however, depending on the sub-flooring utilized, are often extremely hard, not resilient enough for high-energy exercise, and excessive humidity can cause the wood to warp (Walker & Stotlar, 1997).

Strength Training Areas

Another area of continued popularity is the strength training room. The dark and dingy weight rooms of the past are now replaced with colorful new flooring options and light, airy, and open spaces (Steinbach, January 2002). The type of flooring sought depends largely on the nature of the equipment selected, however, the aesthetic appeal is increasingly becoming important in this decision-making process. If a weight area is primarily equipped with machines (Nautilus, Universal, etc.), an easily maintained durable carpet is sufficient. If the room is dominated by free weights, a resilient rubber surface is recommended—tiled, poured, or pre-fabricated. Pre-fabricated options come in the form of sheets or tiles and are simply glued on top of the existing surface or concrete slab.

The desired appearance of the strength training room is an important consideration when selecting a flooring material. The level of supervision over these areas is also a factor, as observed participants tend to be less likely to treat equipment roughly and purposely damage equipment or flooring surfaces. Once again, aesthetic appeal is becoming more important, and creative and attractive options are not necessarily more expensive, however, they do take more planning (Hasenkamp & Lutz, 2001). The color schemes of the walls, equipment upholstery, and flooring must all be coordinated to appeal to the user. Assistance in this area can be provided by consultants or interior designers and seeking the assistance of these individuals is becoming more popular (Steinbach, January 2002; Patton, et al., 1989).

Racquetball Courts

The overall playing surface for a racquetball court requires 800 square feet. Traditionally, racquetball courts are covered with a wood floor surface. Maple floors are attractive, provide favorable ball bounce, and absorb shock to the feet, but there is one disadvantage. When moisture enters the wood, it will buckle the system and cause a swelling in the floor. This becomes an important factor to note if subterranean facilities are built in areas with porous soil. The only other viable system is a synthetic one. New polyurethane materials have been implemented with satisfactory results. These floors are poured and trawled over the concrete floor slab (Patton et al., 1989).

The most popular wall systems to choose from are reinforced fiberglass concrete, plaster, panels, poured-in-place cement slab, and shatterproof glass. Before deciding on a wall system, one should consider the following: material cost, land considerations (moisture and stability), overall appearance, maintenance, and ball action. Plaster is often viewed as a mainstay as it has been around for years; however, maintenance costs usually prove to be expensive. Poured-in-place concrete slabs have not been used very often. The cost is prohibitive, and obtaining a straight wall from a slab that is poured on the ground and then erected, is difficult to accomplish. Reinforced fiberglass concrete has a promising future, but many applications have proven inconsistent. Plexiglas walls provide an aesthetic appeal but are too costly for some facilities. Lastly, the floor system with perhaps the best reputation is a panel system designed from compressed wood. The quality of panel systems varies widely, so facility-planning members must be careful in selecting a system with a satisfactory quality-to-price ratio (Patton et al., 1989).

Racquetball court ceilings are often constructed from the same materials used for the walls. A popular alternative involves a combination of the wall material for the front half of the ceiling and acoustical tile for the back half. The acoustical tile has been found to be successful in deadening the sound of the ball. Another alternative is the use of sheet rock covered by paint or a glazed material (Patton et al., 1989).

LANDSCAPE DESIGN, SPORTS TURF, AND PARKING LOTS

9

Richard J. LaRue, University of New England
David A. LaRue, Landscape Architect
Thomas H. Sawyer, Indiana State University

When planning the outdoor spaces of sports and recreation facilities, adjacent transitional space, and/or sports fields, the process must include individuals who can lend their understanding and expertise to the process. From a design standpoint, a licensed landscape architect or experienced landscape designer should be employed. If a sports field is the focus of, or is included in, the plan, then an experienced sports turf manager is important to the process. Finally, as all outdoor facilities and spaces will require maintenance, a logical planning resource will be the maintenance director and/or an experienced representative of the maintenance staff.

Perhaps the most important individual in the early stages of the planning process is the landscape professional. This person will be invaluable when making decisions related to site selection for the facility and utilization of all adjacent outdoor spaces.

More than any of the other major environmental design professions, landscape architecture is a profession on the move. It is comprehensive by definition—no less than the art and science of analysis, planning design, management, preservation, and rehabilitation of the land. In providing well-managed design and development plans, landscape architects offer an essential array of services and expertise that reduce costs and add long-term value to a project. A landscape architect has a working knowledge of architecture, civil engineering, and urban planning and takes elements from each of these fields to design aesthetic and practical relationships with the land. Members of the profession have a special commitment to improving the quality of life through the best design of places for people and other living things (ASLA, 1998, on-line).

Sports fields are truly special facilities. When natural turf is selected, a sports turf specialist is needed to oversee the development of a total field management program (Lewis, 1994). Lewis suggests that a comprehensive program should include the following: 1) selecting an adapted grass for the locality; 2) mowing this selected grass at proper height and frequency; 3) fertilizing at the proper time and rate according to the turfgrass growth; 4) irrigating as needed to encourage establishment and to reduce stress periods; 5) aerifying to relieve compaction or dethatching according to the turf and the amount of play; and 6) using the appropriate pre-emergence and post-emergence herbicides. The goal is to first produce a vigorous turf that will be competitive to the weeds (p. 28).

Such a program will be served by the design of the field, including irrigation and drainage, the choice of grass, and so on. Careful consideration involves knowing the grass and soil makeup, need for aeration, fertilization, top dressing, seeding, and later, weed control (Mazzola, 1998).

Parking lot design is a related part of the planning process. A successful parking facility can present an important and positive first image to visitors to the recreation or sports facility.

Finally, as the ultimate success of the facility planning process is often measured years later, it is important to consider those aspects of groundskeeping and parking that will be predetermined in the design of the fields and other outdoor spaces. Specifically, the labor and equipment required to maintain these spaces can be controlled with a carefully prepared design. Additionally, the life expectancy of the green and hard goods is directly related to the level of quality afforded. Management of money and resources (capital expenditures, debt load, salaries and wages, existing equipment vs. new equipment, etc.) begins with the planning process and the investment decisions made prior to plan implementation (Hughes Jr., 1996).

In summary, the planning process must include consideration of both the facility and the adjacent outside or transitional space. Further, the planning process will benefit from the expertise of a registered landscape architect or experienced landscape designer, an experienced sports turf specialist (if planning a formal play space), an experienced parking lot consultant, and a representative of the facilities maintenance staff. The quality of the planning process will be measured against the ability of the facility and all aspects of the plan to meet the goals described in the facility's case statement or building program document.

Landscape Design: Aesthetics, Function, and Safety

Frequently, when money is tight and/or the facility costs are exceeding expectations, careful development of the adjacent outdoor space is readily ignored. Experience has demonstrated that this is shortsighted, as there are essential components that must be considered exclusive of the site selection of a facility. The design of this transitional space, whether for an indoor or outdoor facility, should consider the following characteristics:

- the aesthetics of the space relative to all adjacent facilities
- the functional characteristics of the space relative to adjacent facilities
- the safety of users (including accessibility) within the space and relative to adjacent facilities

Aesthetics

The basics of aesthetics in landscape design are sight lines that bring focus to important features of a facility or space, the use of space (especially spatial relationships), and the ability of the finished product to enhance the quality of the experience for all users.

Annuals Commonly Used in Landscaping

A good landscape needs anchor plants: trees, shrubs, and perennials that keep providing color year after year. However, to keep the landscape lively, you need to mix in new, different annuals each season.

The annuals need to be selected for sun or shade, cool or hot weather, and humid dry conditions. The top 10 annuals for landscaping are (Atchison, 2003):

- impatiens (shade)
- petunia (sunny)
- angelonia or summer snapdragon (full sun)
- geranium (sunny)
- vinca (sunny)
- pentas or star cluster (sunny)
- viola (sunny, cool)
- begonia (shade)
- ornamental millet (sunny)
- marigold (sunny)

Function

There are critical components to a comprehensive design related to function. The way the implemented design reacts to natural and man-made stresses is indicative of the time and resources

invested in the planning process. Further, the long-term demand for maintenance will be affected by the design. And the way the design serves the facility program and user needs is a direct result of the planning process.

Photo by Meghan Rosselli
Sample use of lighting, bench, and garbage can.

In addition to the characteristics described above, site selection is an important part of function for an outdoor facility and should also include consideration of

- the orientation of play spaces with respect to the sun angle and predominant wind direction,
- the topography of the developed and undeveloped outdoor space,
- the existing and necessary surface and subsurface irrigation and drainage,
- the appropriate use of natural and man-made barriers,
- environmental concerns, and
- the minimization of normal wear and vandalism (Macomber, 1993).

Safety

It is critical that the planning process for safety results in a landscape design that manages the risk of all adjacent outdoor spaces so that all foreseeable user accidents or injuries can be avoided. This planning for safety and security should include:

- signage in large lettering that clearly identifies pedestrian and vehicular paths, facilities, right-of-way, accessible parking, no parking and fire zones, and any other user-friendly restrictions or expectations,

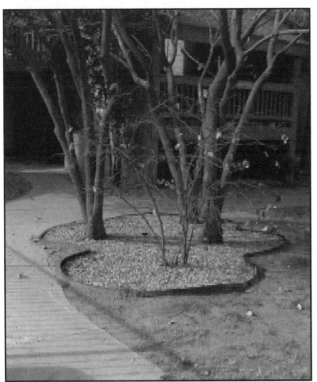

Photo by Meghan Rosselli

Tree-lined sidewalks (above and below).

- perimeter fencing or appropriate use of natural barriers,
- programmable and/or light-sensitive night lighting,
- pedestrian and vehicular circulation that is easy to maintain and has reasonable and unobstructed views of cross traffic at every intersection,
- smooth (yet skid-resistant) pavements and other path or road surfaces,
- bollards (permanent and removable barriers) restricting vehicular travel on pedestrian paths; and
- surveillance.

Surface and Subsurface Irrigation and Drainage

An effective landscape design will consider the operation of surface and subsurface irrigation and drainage. Not having enough moisture can be deadly to your grass and plants. Too much moisture and no way for the water to drain can also drown your plants and fields. When rain does not come, appropriate irrigation must be available. Irrigation planning is both an art and a science. There are extraordinary examples of how, after large amounts of rain and subsequent flooding, the drainage of a sports field has allowed a contest to be held in an amazingly short time (Smith, 1998; Tracinski, 1998).

Irrigation

The principle of "deep and infrequent" watering remains the norm. This practice over the years has proven to be effective. The physical properties of the soil must be considered in planning any watering program. For example, a clay soil will not accept as much water as a sandy soil and will require lighter, more frequent irrigation.

Most turfgrasses need as much as 1 to 1.5 inches of water per week during the growing season to support turf growth (Puhalla et al., 1999, p. 82). The best time to irrigate turf is in the early morning hours, just prior to or after sunrise. This eliminates interference with use, reduces disease incidence, and increases the amount of water placed in the soil for plant use.

There are two basic types of irrigation systems available for use—portable and installed irrigation. Portable irrigation systems include traveling irrigators (i.e., rotating sprinkler attached to a hose, propelling itself along a wire), quick coupler systems (i.e., systems are comprised of a series of underground pipes with quick couplers permanently installed flush with the ground), and rain guns (i.e., a huge impact-type sprinkler that is used to irrigate a large turf area).

The price for installed systems is decreasing, while the reliability of operation is increasing. Automatic systems save maintenance labor costs when compared to portable systems and the even distribution of water is improved.

Photo by Meghan Rosselli

Drainage

Whether designing a drainage system for a new field or for an existing field, certain questions need to be answered, including:

- How quickly should the field be returned to playable condition after a rainstorm?
- In what climate is the field located?
- Is the field designed for amateur or professional use?
- What kind of flexibility will there be in rescheduling?

Photo by Tom Sawyer

Example of a culvert.

- Will the field have a crown or will it be flat but sloped?
- Will the field have a dense, clay-like soil or a sand soil?
- Will the collection system be shallow or deep?
- Will there be a single- or multi-layered filter system?

Most landscape architects will use the following rule of thumb relative to drainage: whether designing a single field or a multi-field complex, keep in mind that each field should be designed and constructed as an individual drainage unit. A well-designed drainage plan will install interceptor drains to isolate water, cuts and fills, catch basins, swales, and French drains.

Further, Puhalla et al. (1999) suggest field designs for surface drainage fall into one of two categories—crowned or flat. The typical percentage of slope for a sports field runs between 1% and 1.75%.

The most common type of crowned field has been a football field (see Figure 9.1). However, now that many football fields are also used for soccer, they have become flat fields because the soccer field overlaps the football field. Most soccer fields are often designed using a lower percentage of slope and installed drain systems are usually added (see Figure 9.2).

Most flat fields need an installed parallel or grid drainage pattern while crowned fields typically have a herringbone pattern (Breems, 2001). In either case the drainage pattern should extend at least 15 feet beyond the playing surface on all sides. Be certain that the field records indicate it is a flat, sloped, or a crowned field. Otherwise, 10 years after initial construction, some well-meaning person might try to "recrown" the field, causing a real mess. The collection system should be located near the surface of the field. The deeper the collectors are located, the slower the drainage will be. The system that is submerged six inches with sand located above and around the collectors is fast and efficient (Breems, 2001).

Finally, a multilayered filter system protects the collectors from failure due to binding and guarantees a long life. A fabric filter prevents the core from filling with fine sand and silt. A 3.5- to 4-ounce needle punched geo-synthetic fabric does a fine job. An inch or two of very course sand surrounding the fabric will prevent the fabric from blocking. As the water passes through, the sand particles of clay and silt are arrested before they reach the fabric filter (Breems, 2001).

Trends and New Technologies in Landscape Design

Finally, the planning process will consider new trends or cutting-edge technologies when designing outdoor spaces. Consider making a significant investment in all aspects of the planning process to reduce short- and long-term mistakes. Once the plan is implemented, the success of the planning process will be easily measured in its ability to meet the needs of the facility program. Include the right people in the planning process. The experts are easy to remember. However, user input is also critical to promote inclusion and a sense of ownership in the process. Users include the people who will manage the facility and outdoor spaces as well as those who will participate in facility programs. An appropriate number of such people will help build goodwill and, more importantly, should serve the planning process effectively because of their unique "user" viewpoint. The long-term reality of maintenance and the cost of labor, materials, and equipment demand that landscape designs provide for minimal maintenance. A landscape architect or experienced landscape designer as well as a representative member of the groundskeeping staff should provide the expertise to design minimal maintenance into the outdoor spaces. Finally, the planning process should consider future implementation of the design when it comes to the level of quality selected in green and hard goods. Experience tells us that when purchasing such goods, the better the quality, the better the satisfaction.

Photo by Tom Sawyer

Example of a drainage ditch.

Figure 9.1
Grid Drainage Plan for Sports Field Drainage

Trends and new technologies in turf management are often made available by academics who are committed to this aspect of venue design and management. An excellent source of such information can be found at http://turfgrass.hort.iastate.edu/extension. Articles specific to athletic fields and made available by Dr. David Minner of Iowa State University at this internet site include:

- Infield Skin Testing
- Athletic Field Generic Football Field Maintenance
- Athletic Field Procedure for Selecting a Sand Rootzone
- Athletic Field Coring and Topdressing Table
- Athletic Field Poa Annua Control
- Athletic Field Safety and Maintenance Checklist

- Athletic Field Evaluation and Traffic Survey
- Athletic Field Construction, Renovation, and Maintenance Costs
- Athletic Field Management—Tips for a Limited Budget
- Athletic Field Gypsum?
- Athletic Field Liability Signage
- Athletic Field Care Tips
- Athletic Field—Selecting Bluegrass Varieties
- Athletic Field Pre-germinated Divot Mix
- Athletic Field Seeding Schedule
- Athletic Field End of Season Practices
- Grass System Response to Traffic and Recovery

Additionally, and at this same site, Dr. Minner includes a couple of scholarly articles related to turfgrass and golf courses.

Figure 9.2
Herringbone Drainage Plan for Sports Field Drainage

Sports Grasses and Turfs

Characteristics of Turfgrasses Commonly Used for Sports Turfs

Puhalla, Krans, and Goatley (1999) suggest there are 11 grasses commonly used as turfgrasses. However, of these species, only five are widely used in sports turf situations: Bermuda grass, Kentucky bluegrass, tall fescue, perennial ryegrass, and creeping bentgrass. There are two other grasses that are sometimes used: buffalo grass and zoysiagrass.

Further, Puhalla et al. (1999) indicate Bermuda grass (monostand) is planted and maintained alone except when overseeded with perennial and annual ryegrass for winter play. Tall fescue, perennial ryegrass, and Kentucky bluegrass are planted and maintained as either monostands or in combination with other cultivars (polystands). Creeping bentgrass is usually planted as a monostand.

Turfgrass selection is usually based upon weather zones (i.e., warm, transitional, or cool).

In warm-weather zones (Southern states across the United States), sports turf is generally dominated by Bermuda grass, because it flourishes in the hot summers and mild winters and can withstand occasional summer dryness without damage. In the transitional zone, fields are dominated by tall fescues and specifically developed Bermuda grass. Finally, in cold zones (Northern states across the United States), Kentucky bluegrass and perennial ryegrass predominate and a mixture of those species is probably the most popular sports turf (Puhalla et al., 1999). "Both types tolerate the cold northern winters adequately, and the mixture allows for the aggressive spreading and recovery characteristic of Kentucky bluegrass, along with the stability and wear resistance of perennial ryegrass" (p. 8).

In some very dry climates where pure water is not available or can't be used to irrigate turf fields, some turfgrasses have been designed to tolerate a blend of saline and fresh water. For example in Dubai, UAE the five primary sport clubs have turf

Photo by Tom Sawyer

Example of French drain.

fields that are maintained in excellent condition using partially saline water and a carefully managed selection of turfgrasses, throughout the dormant (summer) and growing seasons (fall-spring). The balance is likely an annual ryegrass overseeded in the late spring for the summer months (hottest and driest); and when the fall comes, the annual ryegrass dies, making way for the overseeding of Bermudagrass or Seashore Paspalum.

The National Turfgrass Evaluation Program (NTEP) tests hundreds of commercially available cultivars and experimental entries of turfgrass annually. Researchers conduct these tests at universities in 40 states and a few Canadian provinces. Data from each year are summarized and published on a Web site (http://www.ntep.org) and also in CD-ROM format. Go to the Web site and read the disclaimer at the bottom of that page, then click enter. This will take you to the main page (http:www.ntep.org/ contents2.shtml). To find a grass species, simply click on the link in the yellow box "All NTEP Reports—Select a Turfgrass Species."

Portable Grass

During the '90s, Popke (2000) indicated a number of natural-grass suppliers (e.g., Green-Tech® Inc-ITM turf modules, Hummer Turfgrass Systems Inc.-Grasstiles™, the Motz Group-TS-II™, Desso DLW Sports International-DD GrassMaster, SportGrass® Inc-SportGrass system, Southern Turf Nurseries-STN 2000, Thomas Brothers Grass, a division of Turf-Grass America Co-SquAyers, Southwest Recreational Industries Inc.-AstroGrass® became responsive to facilities' needs for a more durable natural grass product.

The suppliers began to use (1) portable grass that unrolls as a cover for concrete floors and parking lots, (2) grass tiles with roots that are reinforced and stabilized with synthetic fibers, and (3) systems that mix grass with synthetic fibers woven or stitched into a backing. These renewed processes allow sections of worn surface (e.g., golf tee-boxes, areas in front of a soccer goal, middle sections of

football fields) to be replaced without tearing up the entire area and the entire surface can usually be removed or installed in less than 24 hours. All of the systems claim to be able to better reinforce the root zone and extend usage.

Often, with these portable systems, grass is grown in trays that allow for drainage and air movement. Synthetic reinforcements play a role in several portable grass surfaces and are considered 100 percent natural by their suppliers. This can be said because the majority of the additional synthetic material is inserted below the grass surface for root reinforcement and additional wear resistance. However, a better term might be *hybrid*.

Some of the hybrid systems are a combination of sand-filled, fibrillated synthetic tufts, and a dual component backing of biodegradable fibers and plastic mesh. The matrix shelters the vegetative parts of the grass plant that are essential to rapid growth and recuperation while the grass roots intertwine with the tufts and grow down through the plastic mesh. If the turf canopy wears away, the sand-filled synthetic matrix continues to provide a consistent playing surface. There are a few systems that do not use a cloth backing. Instead, they train the roots to grow on top of a plastic barrier, similar to roots in a potted plant.

A Kinder, Gentler Synthetic Turf

Popke (2000) describes three new kinder, gentler synthetic turfs—Astroplay®, Fieldturf™, and Sofsport™. These synthetic surfaces have been designed to reduce injuries to players. The new synthetic surfaces blend and tuft polyethylene and polypropylene fibers into a permeable surface backing. Each synthetic grass fiber is placed so as to create a pattern of natural grass. The fill is made from sand and ground rubber, which surround each fiber much like soil holds a blade of grass. One supplier does not use sand, but rather uses

Photo by Rick LaRue

**Al Ahli Sport Club, Dubai,
United Arab Emirates**

a combination of rubber and nylon fibers mixed with longer polyolefin strands. This combination enhances drainage, reduces compaction, and adds resilience.

On July 30, 2008, the Consumer Product Safety Commission released its evaluation of various synthetic turf fields with regard to lead exposure. "CPSC staff evaluation showed that newer fields had no lead or generally had the lowest lead levels. Although small amounts of lead were detected on the surface of some older fields, none of these tested fields released amounts of lead that would be harmful to children" (CPCS, 2008).

Though the bottom line is the amount of lead exposure that older artificial turf fields may release was not found to be significant; older fields may need to be tested and participants should wash their hands, etc. after playing on these fields.

Another caution regarding artificial turf (and perhaps turfgrass fields as well); any fields that have been flooded due to a combination of rain and sewer systems, should be tested for coli form and other bacteria. Especially on artificial turf fields, coli form can be a hazard to players who suffer skin abrasions. Under these circumstances, the field may need to be cleaned and retested to ensure the safety of all participants.

Groundskeeping: Management, Maintenance, and Equipment Planning Responsibilities

Appropriate to the review of groundskeeping management, maintenance, and equipment are three concepts related to success in these areas: time management, money and resource management, and machinery and equipment management (Hughes, 1996, pp. 2-3). The responsibility for planning related to groundskeeping should be shared by a seasoned member of the groundskeeping staff. Efficient use of staff time can be facilitated in a properly planned landscape design. A significant aspect of the plan will be the reduction of labor as it relates to maintenance. If, by design, you reduce the employee labor required, you are managing time more efficiently. Secondly, if you demand quality green goods when installing your landscape design, then the money and resources for your project will be managed more efficiently. Finally, if your planning process includes a design that can be maintained with existing equipment, you are taking responsibility for the future without ignoring the reality of the present. Groundskeeping management must be considered when designing your landscape. And few people can better assist you with this planning than a knowledgeable representative of your groundskeeping staff.

Topdressing a Baseball Softball Field

Topdressing describes the application of a structural material to the top layer of turf. According to Wilkinson (2002), a structural material is one that is not solubilized rapidly in water (e.g., soil conditioners, sand, and soil). Topdressing benefits the field in three ways: 1) improves the quality of the turf surface, 2) protects the turf crowns, and 3) improves the soil's porosity and reduces the organic thatch. Most baseball and softball fields can be improved by topdressing. Both the skinned and turf areas can benefit.

The skinned area of a baseball or softball field is often built using heavy-textured clay and a soil clay amendment is worked into the top few inches to achieve a desired surface (Wilkinson, 2002). The surface of the skinned area should be almost 100 percent soil clay amendment. The surface should be topdressed once or twice a month, depending on usage. The soil amendment should be spread uniformly and raked into the top inch of the soil. The use of ceramic conditioners will dry out the skinned area and cause it to harden and crack. A great deal of water will need to be used to achieve a great playing surface.

Topdressing a baseball or softball turf can help the turf and produce a great playing surface. A turf area should not be topdressed with a structural material containing more than 40% ceramic conditioner (Wilkinson, 2002). The more clay soil amendment added, the greater the chance of stressing the turf. The recommended mixture for a topdressing is 30% or less ceramic conditioner to 70% or more the natural soil the turf is growing in. If the field was built with sand, then add 30% soil amendment to the same kind of sand. For single application of topdressing, add enough to achieve a layer 1/8 inch thick or less (Wilkinson, 2002).

How to Select a Field Cover

Field covers keep fields dry, reduce the risk of rainouts, increase turf enhancement, and lend themselves to great advertising and sponsorship arrangements. The advertising dollars should be spent on the cover for the tarp when it is rolled up. More people will see the advertisement, and it is easier to place logos on the cover for the rolled-up tarp than it is to place logos on the actual tarp material. The color of covers can play an important role in turf management. Tests conducted by several turf specialists found that certain colors of covers can have a positive effect on turf development. For example:

- White/silver combination with white side exposed to the sun, on average, has 14°F less heat build-up under the cover than other color combinations. This color combination would be appropriate for southern climates.
- Black/silver combination with black side exposed to the sun draws more heat to the turf surface. This combination would work well in northern climates.
- Orange/white combination allows light penetration and enhances turf development. This

combination would be appropriate for northern and southern climates.

Both woven polyethylene and vinyl provide a good cover. The common differences between polyethylene and vinyl are outlined in Table 9.1.

Field Traffic

A frequent concern for turf managers relates to field traffic (number of events per field, per year). Minner (2004) has been collecting field-use data (by hours and user group) over the past four years, relating field use to field performance.

On average, an individual field is receiving 125 events per year. A field receiving over 79 events should not be able to recover to an acceptable level. Most turf managers feel they could maintain an acceptable field if the annual event schedule were less than 64 events (p. 38).

However, this is not a definite maximum. Some programs cannot even tolerate 64 events, while others because of proper management have tolerated many more. There are a number of variables regarding field tolerance, including: "warm/cool season climate, soil type, grass selection, irrigation, cultivation, seeding/sodding renovation, etc." (p. 38).

Minner (2004) recommends that turf managers begin collecting their own data (specific information reflecting field activity and performance) to use when making important field-use and planning decisions. "Without this type of data, it will be difficult to limit field-use or to plan the appropriate number of fields when building for future growth" (p. 38). You can review *Minner's Athletic Field Traffic Survey and Quality Assessment* at http://www.hort.iastate.edu/turfgrass/extension/EGtrafficsurvey.pdf

Combining field performance information with accurate field use records on a person/hour or field/hour basis will give the turf manager the best decision-making data from which to work. When organizations do not allow for reasonable field usage, Minner (2004) suggests that, an appropriate amount of funding must be channeled to grounds management to offset field damages from high use. In cases of extreme field activity there may be no level of funding that will keep the fields from wearing out and your only recourse is to close the fields for revegetation (p. 38).

Rotational Field: A Relatively New Concept

As the interest in team sports, such as soccer, continues to grow at all levels, the demand for time on traditional playing fields has escalated. Daily team practices, eight- to ten-game weekend schedules, and pick-up games when the fields are not in use are becoming quite common. Bob Stienhaus, president of Pioneer Fields (Pittsburgh) and fellow founder Matthew Butch have come up with a practical solution for preserving natural turf fields that requires less maintenance and provides for safer, year-round play. The concept is a rotational athletic field.

The design concept incorporates a rectangular athletic playing field fitted within a substantially circular turf area. The uniquely graded circular area can essentially be scaled to fit any size rectangular playing field (e.g., football, field hockey, lacrosse, or soccer) with some buffer space. The playing field rotates at select times throughout the season of play to limit the amount of play in high traffic areas or to avoid damage or unsafe turf. The rotation schedule can range from daily, such as following a rough game in heavy rains, to just three times a year for seasonal play and seasonal turf repairs (Saunders, 2001).

Chemical Handling and Storage, Legal Aspects, and Recommendations

Besides the Chemical Hazards Act managed under the Occupational Safety and Health Administration (OSHA), both state and federal regulations govern the handling of many of the chemicals used in weed control, insect management, and fertilization. The Chemical Hazards Act requires the employer to properly warn and protect employees using such chemicals. All chemical manufacturers must ship hazardous chemicals with Material Safety Data Sheets (MSDS), which should be kept

Table 9.1
Comparison of Polyethylene and Vinyl Covers

Characteristic	Polyethylene	Vinyl
Weight	1/3 lighter	1/3 heavier
Price	1/2 less in cost	1/2 more in cost
Color	fewer choices	greater choices
Snow removal	not as durable	more durable
Wind	less effective	more effective
Joining sections	Velcro®	plastic zipper

on file for employees and specifically outline the guidelines for proper use of their products. Other government regulations require groundskeeping staff to be certified in the proper application and handling of chemicals. It is the responsibility of the groundskeeping staff to be knowledgeable in the use and handling of these chemicals and associated equipment. With a knowledgeable resource on the planning committee, the facility can provide for proper storage of chemicals and clean up of chemical application equipment used in groundskeeping.

Lining Athletic Fields

Steinbach (2000) suggests the primary concern when marking grass fields is to keep the turf in good growing condition. Water-based paints are the preferred choice. Chalk (e.g., limestone or marble) is less friendly to turf due to the accumulated build-up that blocks water's movement to the grass root system. The best paint contains a higher concentration (one to two pounds per gallon) of titanium oxide (TiO_2), which brightens the paint. The other common ingredient is calcium carbonate ($CaCO_2$), a paint filler. Colored paints will have a higher amount of calcium carbonate. White paint can be diluted up to 9:1, but colored paints can only be diluted to 1:1 ratio. Too much calcium carbonate makes playing fields abrasive, and it can kill the turf grass.

The following are a few painting tips provided by Mike Hebrard, owner, Athletic Field Design:

- Grid method—make an enlargement of the logo to be painted, then draw a series of lines in a graph format on the logo at a workable uniform spacing. Lay out the size of the logo, converting inches to feet, and mark dots on the grass at the edges of the design. Use an inverted spray chalk or blue to do the initial layout. Repeat the graph, using string and long nails, going back and forth until the graph is completed. By looking at the drawing, note where each line crosses a grid and duplicate it on the grass by painting a line, gradually connecting the shape of the logo. Use inverted aerosol cans to differentiate colors and features. Once the logo has been completed, you can brighten it using an airless sprayer.
- The most popular method of painting on athletic turf is the stencil on a heavy plastic sheet or tarp. These are readily available from most athletic paint suppliers. After use, fold up the stencil and put into a marked duffle bag to store and identify its contents.
- The key to painting dirt is to have it moist enough to take the paint, much like staining wood. If it is too wet, the paint will bleed into the other colors. If it is too dry, the paint will not be very bright and will wear off quickly.

Parking Lot Design

Facilities managers are being challenged to 1) develop fair and customer-focused parking strategies, 2) prioritize the use of decreasing parking resources, 3) understand the explosion in parking technology, 4) provide cost-effective parking solutions while catching up with deferred maintenance, 5) address the widely held perception that safe and convenient parking can only be provided next to the front door, and 6) provide adequate handicapped spaces for the size of the lot (see Table 9.2).

The traditional parking paradigm must be expanded in order to meet the planning challenge. In the past, planning focused on the number of vehicles within given parking parameters. However, as the number of available sites decreases and the cost to develop and operate parking facilities increases, communities are demanding more cost-effective solutions.

Ideally, the parking design should be incorporated into the overall landscape and building design, especially in terms of aesthetics, function, and safety. However, there are some additional

Table 9.2
Number of Accessible Parking Spaces Required under Federal Law

Total Parking in Lot	Required Minimum Number of Accessible Spaces
1 – 25	1
26 – 50	2
51 – 75	3
76 – 100	4
101 - 150	5
151 – 200	6
201 – 300	7
301 – 400	8
401 – 500	9
501 – 100	2% of total
1001 – over	20 plus 1 for each 100 over 1000

Photo by Meghan Rosselli

Parking lot security monitors.

design options to be considered including function, aesthetics, and safety.

Function

Will parking discriminate against users who arrive later in the day? Do plans include large and visible signage in order that users understand all allowances and restrictions? Is there adequate parking?

Will the facility require a parking garage? Can users exit the parking areas in a timely fashion? In the past, planning focused on the number of vehicles within given parking parameters. The new focus should be on consumer needs. Planners and facilities managers should move away from the traditional parking paradigm to one that is consumer oriented.

The Traditional Parking Paradigm

Considerable energy has been focused on the management of vehicles and pedestrians within the boundaries of parking areas. Traditional parking technology contributed to this planning focus, with the "pay-on-foot" approach in parking structures, central pay stations in surface lots, "smart cards," debit cards, proximity cards, and so on. Planners are bombarded with issues, concerns, and solutions within the parking space boundaries.

Photo by Meghan Rosselli

Toll parking entrance and exit.

Traditional master planning guidelines for sports and recreation venues have also contributed to this planning focus.

Kirkpatrick (1997) suggests that many planners have successfully implemented a pedestrian orientation to the recreation and sport environment, resulting in parking located at perimeter or off-site locations. Typically with this approach, the need for transportation has correspondingly increased (p. 950).

Yet, the planning focus has remained within the boundaries of the parking areas as planners have attempted to match and manage the vehicle demand to the space available. Over the years, many strategies have been developed to manage the increasing demand for limited parking space.

Parking planners have matched various forms and combinations of reserved parking, zoned parking, and open parking to the specific community culture. But the planning focus remained directed at single-occupant vehicles within designated parking boundaries. Regardless of the system that is used to manage vehicles within designated parking boundaries at perimeter locations, customer dissatisfaction with parking systems increased dramatically. Customers lamented that convenient parking space was not available and that the cost of parking was rising. At the same time, many facility managers were faced with deferred maintenance, escalating costs to operate and maintain a parking system, and increasing customer demand for a decreasing supply of parking.

The following factors contribute to the increasing customer and administration dissatisfaction with parking systems that traditionally were perceived as successful:

- New parking structures are costly to build.
- Costs to maintain structures are escalating.
- Surface lots are costly to build.
- Costs to maintain core area surface lots are escalating.
- Deferred maintenance is adding up for many older structures and surface lots where security, aesthetics, and quality construction may not have been a priority in the past.

Thus, it can be seen that costs to build, repair, and maintain parking structures and surface parking lots are escalating. At the same time, customers are not willing to absorb these additional costs by paying higher parking rates, especially when a perceived value may not be present.

A Parking Paradigm Shift: Customer-Oriented Parking

Planning that traditionally started once a vehicle reached a parking area now encompasses options for getting from home to the sports and recreation venue. This has become necessary because

- many sports and recreation venues cannot cost-effectively operate and maintain the traditional expansion of surface lot and structure parking,
- the customer or participant is typically not willing to pay the increasing cost, and
- the traditional parking planning focus of one vehicle per person no longer meets the diverse needs of all customers.

The customer-oriented parking paradigm requires that planners understand and know the customers so as to meet their needs and provide a better service. The parking menu should reflect choices in terms of cost to convenience. For example, the following parking options may be included:

- Reserved space or parking area.
- Core area parking.
- Perimeter area parking.
- Designated motorcycle parking in the preceding four areas if demand requires.
- Carpool/vanpool parking in the first four areas above if demand requires it.
- Bicycle parking, which might include bicycle storage lockers and the traditional hoop.
- Shared parking resources with the surrounding community, such as with park-and-ride programs.
- Economic incentives provided to promote shared bus services with the surrounding community.
- Walking may be a parking option that needs only to be promoted. Typically, the implementation of many sports and recreation venue master plans has resulted in a pedestrian orientation to the venue where special attention has been focused on providing appropriately placed sidewalks (seven or eight feet wide for snow removal, which is also a good width for group walking) with excellent lighting, an effective emergency telephone system, and beautiful grounds.

Kirkpatrick (1997) indicates that:

The key to implementing a successful menu of parking options, based on the match of

Photo by Meghan Rosselli

Parking garage.

cost to convenience, is an understanding of customers' needs and their perceptions of solutions, as well as a willingness by all involved to be receptive to trying new ideas (p. 953).

Another key to success is the flexibility of a parking system to provide multiple options to fit diverse life-styles.

Parking Systems

Parking administrators have matched various forms and combinations of reserved parking, zoned parking, and open parking to their specific recreation and sports and cultures. The following are advantages and disadvantages of each form:

- Reserved parking is typically the most expensive, with the lowest occupancy. As space constraints continue to grow with the projected decrease in core area parking, it may be increasingly difficult to provide reserved parking for large numbers of people.
- Zoned parking typically restricts parkers to an area close to their work site. The occupancy rate is generally higher than that for reserved parking. As core area parking space continues to decline, the demand will typically exceed the supply.
- Open parking, commonly referred to as "hunting license" parking, provides a system of parking on a first-come basis and has the highest occupancy rate. However, as the demand for parking increases, the level of frustration grows as customers perceive wasted time in hunting for a parking space.

Parking Options

The following menu of seven parking options is listed, in order, from the most expensive to the least expensive:

- Reserved space or area. This option is usually the most expensive and has the lowest occupancy rate. If the demand exceeds the supply, the challenge may be to develop criteria for eligibility that customers perceive to be fair.
- Core area parking. This option typically provides parking within a reasonably short walking distance to most recreation or sports activities.
- Perimeter parking. This option generally provides parking that requires a longer walk or a short bus ride to most recreation or sports activities.
- Motorcycle programs. Space that typically cannot be used for vehicle parking may be promoted for motorcycle parking. Because less space is required for motorcycles than for cars, a lower rate could be charged, whether in a reserved area, core area, or perimeter area parking location.

- Carpool/vanpool programs. This is a cost-effective approach for those who are willing to contend with the perceived inconvenience of organizing. Payment choices could be offered depending on whether reserved, core area, or perimeter parking is used.
- Bicycle parking. A choice of bicycle parking could be offered, from the traditional hoops to bicycle lockers. Because many bicycles are expensive, the provision of lockers may promote the use of bicycles over vehicles. Attended bike corrals are also becoming more available.
- Park-and-ride parking. This option may provide an opportunity to share resources with the surrounding community, to reduce operating costs, to take advantage of parking space that may be underused, and to address a unique need of commuting participants.

Finally, flexibility must be built into the parking system to provide customers with easy access to multiple parking options based on their own unique needs.

Parking Technology

Like many fields of endeavor, the parking industry is experiencing an explosion in technology. Extensive amounts of data may be tracked and monitored. However, implementation of such technology may be costly. The initial task is to identify the information that is essential to manage a successful parking system. The typical challenge is to fund only the hardware and software that are actually needed but with expansion capabilities for future growth. Effective strategic planning, together with a total quality management approach, will help to identify the likely future direction for use of emerging parking technologies.

The following are examples of parking technologies that are available:

- Equipment to monitor parking structure activity Typically this involves a chip in a card or on a permit or sensors installed in the pavement. For enforcement purposes, gate equipment may be used. Types of information that may be monitored are as follows:
  - —Number and time of entry/exit.
  - —Occupancy trends.
  - —Use by permit type such as student, client with disability, or guest.
  - —Amount of parking used per parker.
  - —Identification of maintenance needs such as a gate remaining open.
  - —The system may include a "Parking Available/Full" sign at the entrance for customers' convenience. If the system operates close to full occupancy on a daily basis, all structures may be networked so that if a particular structure is full, a message sign will direct customers to the next closest structures that have parking available.
- Central pay stations may be used in structures or surface lots. Individual parking meters are eliminated and customers are directed to a central location to pay. Advantages for the customer are that a parking receipt is provided and dollar bills may be used, eliminating the need to carry a large number of coins. Advantages operationally are that 1) enforcement will pull a tape at the central pay station to quickly identify vehicles whose time has expired, 2) collection time is saved because collection occurs at one location, and 3) audit control is simplified because a tape is provided that identifies the amount of revenue being collected. If multiple locations are added, central pay stations may be networked to an administrative location for on-time identification of all activity in total or per lot. For example, data could include occupancy, percentage of illegal parkers, and/or revenue collected.
- Debit card systems. These systems allow the parker to add value to a card from a central location or multiple locations and pay only for actual time parked. Debit card capability may be added to many systems such as central pay stations or individual parking meters. The key advantage to the customer is convenience (i.e., not having to carry change). Advantages operationally are that revenue is collected up front, collection costs are reduced, and audit control is simplified.

Referencing the above examples, astute questions must be asked to determine the minimal level of hardware and software needed to operate an effective parking system; however, there must be an understanding of future directions to ensure that the system can be expanded.

For example, in monitoring structure activity, is it necessary to know parking use per customer, or is overall occupancy and identification of peak use enough information to operate a parking system successfully? Networking parking structures with a message sign may be costly. Is the cost worth the customer service? Networking multiple central pay station locations provides extensive information at a glance. Does the need for quick information justify the cost of networking and staff time to track and monitor data? Debit cards are a customer convenience. Careful planning must be done to determine whether one solution is better than other options.

Aesthetics

The first experience people have at the facility will likely come when they park their vehicle and approach the facility on foot. What are the sight lines, the use of space, and the placement of parking to the facility that make this experience inviting? Can parking be distributed in a way that avoids a large "car-lot" look? Are there natural and man-made barriers that can enhance the aesthetics of the parking space(s) without compromising safety?

Image of the Parking Facility

The parking environment can influence a visitor's first impression of the facility. Many factors will contribute to a positive image. Key factors are the level of maintenance, lighting, signage, and the perception of safety.

Level of Maintenance

An appropriate level of maintenance must be established in the following areas:

- landscape care
- striping
- miscellaneous painting such as pavement arrows, objects of caution, structure railing, stairwells, and lobby areas
- sweeping
- pavement cleaning, such as of oil spills
- relamping and cleaning of light fixtures
- pavement care such as repair of potholes and cracks
- replacement of faded, damaged, or missing signs
- structure window washing
- trash removal
- snow removal

Ideally, maintenance should be scheduled during times of low occupancy. However, when this is not possible, prior notification of any closure should be provided for good public relations.

Lighting

Many customers associate safety with lighting level. Incorrect lighting, particularly in parking structures, can create a variety of problems including shadow zones, sense of insecurity, reduced visibility, loss of direction, and even a sense of claustrophobia. Planners have to be sensitive to the correct illumination, uniformity, color of light, surface colors, and reflectance.

Signage

Most successful signage systems are those that provide as little overall signage as possible. The following ten guidelines will contribute to a successful system:

- Letter size and wording should be standardized throughout the system.
- Warm and fuzzy wording will contribute to a friendly image. For example, "Please Drive Slowly," rather than "Drive Slowly," may go a long way toward achieving customer cooperation.

- Sign locations should be standardized as much as possible. Customers typically learn where to look for directional signage.
- Signage should be coordinated with lighting locations to further enhance signage visibility.
- High-pressure sodium lighting will distort many colors. If color coding is used as a level indicator, colors should be selected that will not be distorted. For example, red will appear brown, but yellow will not change in appearance.
- Typically, a successful directional system will incorporate multiple approaches. For example, some customers will remember colors better than the printed word. A level or area indicator sign may include the number "2" above the written word "TWO" against a blue background. Such a sign includes numerical and written identifiers as well as color coding.
- Traditional colors such as red, brown, yellow, and blue will probably have a higher recognition level than trendy colors such as mauve, taupe, coral, and cinnamon. Some customers may not know the name of such colors to use when asking for directions.
- Signage located around the perimeter of a surface lot rather than within the parking lot will provide ease of snow removal and sweeping.
- Information panels, campus directories, and "you-are-here" maps should be clustered in pedestrian areas such as structure elevator lobbies and bus pullouts.
- Standardizing signage, maintaining an inventory, and fabricating and installing in-house typically will provide faster service and a more cost-effective approach.

Funding of the Parking System

Ideally, a parking system should be self-supporting. Typical funding sources are as follows:

- permits
- metered parking
- designated visitor parking
- parking for special events
- parking tickets

Budget for the Parking System

Assuming that the parking system is self-supporting, rates should be set to fund the following components annually:

- administration
- maintenance
- repair and renovation
- deferred maintenance
- new construction
- a reserve for new construction
- alternate transportation options

As the annual budget is itemized for projected expenses and revenue, it is helpful to attach an explanation for each item. For example, why is permit revenue expected to increase/decrease or why are utility costs expected to increase/decrease? This information may be invaluable in the future for projecting trends.

Safety

The safety and security of users are the most important characteristics of parking design. Will facility users circulate between the facility and parking areas secure in the knowledge that they will be safe and their vehicle will remain intact? Will the location of the parking areas mandate use of perimeter fencing? Can pedestrian paths be designed that allow users to avoid walking in vehicular areas in the parking lot? Are permanent or removable bollards required to manage vehicular traffic on pedestrian paths? Is lighting adequate for user safety and security at night? How will surveillance in the parking areas be managed: using closed-circuit cameras or parking attendant(s)? Will the parking areas have emergency telephone towers or call stations? And, if the lot is gated, will the entrance use pedestrian-safe, one-way traffic controllers with below-grade spikes?

The parking area should be controlled and monitored for safety. This will require a number of important decisions to be made, including:

- type of parking systems (e.g., ticket and ticketless—magnetic stripe, microwave, etc.)
- type of dispensers (e.g., machines, meters, cards, or tags)
- using a van or shuttle system

Additional action may be needed to combat a past stereotype that parking structures or areas are not safe. The following strategies may have to be considered:
- installing an emergency telephone system, highly visible, in standard locations
- adding of glass panels in stairwells to increase visibility
- installing video cameras
- adding parking attendants during evening hours
- providing security personnel walking or driving through the structure
- increasing lighting level
- publishing procedures to enhance safety awareness
- establishing safety programs such as escort services

SECTION II

FIELD AND COURT SPECIFICATIONS

INDOOR AND OUTDOOR COURTS 10

Bernie Goldfine, Kennesaw State University

Indoor and outdoor courts are popular competition and recreation venues. These venues are continually being modernized and improved. In this chapter, a discussion of 14 of the most popular courts will outline important considerations for planners developing new facilities.

Tennis Courts

Layout, Orientation, Dimensions, and Fencing

Tennis was first played in the United States during the mid-1870s. At that time, the game was slow-paced and was played on the grass lawns of houses and parks. The game has now changed to a fast-paced athletic sport. As tennis has changed, so too have the courts on which it is played. Today's outdoor courts are laid out in a manner that minimizes the effects of wind, sun, background vision, and the lay of the land. Tennis courts are constructed of grass, clay, soft and hard composition, asphalt, concrete, and various synthetic materials. Many other features such as accessibility, storage, parking, lighting, and fencing need to be carefully planned for indoor tennis court construction.

In constructing outdoor tennis courts, prevailing winds must be taken into account in the planning process. If prevailing winds exist, courts should be placed near natural barriers, such as woods or hills that act as windbreaks. If no existing barriers are in the area of court construction, a thick stand of staggered trees can be planted to serve as a barrier.

Alternatively, if existing buildings are near the construction site, they may be used as a wind barrier. Visual background must be planned for in the layout of tennis courts. The background at both ends of the courts should be natural grass, shrubs, woods, or other natural landscaping. Roads, parking areas, and pedestrian high-traffic areas are not acceptable at the ends of tennis courts. Too many objects moving in front of the tennis player causes lapses in concentration and makes play more difficult. If the busy areas must coexist with tennis courts, they should be at the sides of the courts. Furthermore, tennis complexes should not be placed too far from the remainder of the sports complex or center campus. The more removed the courts are, the more difficult user access will be. Court layout must also meet Americans With Disabilities Act (ADA) requirements (see chapter 4) for all users with disabilities.

The contour of the land for proposed tennis court construction also needs careful thought. It is much cheaper to construct tennis courts on flat land than on rolling terrain; it is less expensive in terms of both earth-moving and drainage concerns. If courts must be on rolling terrain, they should be laid out with the minimum of cost for earth moving and drainage. Also, hills should serve as natural barriers whenever possible.

Outdoor tennis court planning must also include the sun, which can create visual problems for the tennis player. If tennis courts are to be used mostly between April and October, they should be aligned north to south on the long axis of the court. If courts are to be used year round, the long axis should be northwest to southeast at 22° off true north. These orientations minimize the amount of sun-related visual problems for tennis players (USTA, 1997).

If courts are nonporous, provisions must be made for the drainage of water off the courts. Courts may be sloped from 0.5% to 1.5% depending on the type of surface. Any slope greater than 1.5% can be visually detected by the players and is not acceptable. Courts may be sloped side-to-side, end-to-end, center-to-end, or end-to-center. If only one individual court is constructed, either a side-to-side or an end-to-end slope works well. If a battery of courts is being constructed, the slope should be dictated by the fastest way to drain the most courts as quickly as possible. For example, if five courts were built side by side, an end-to-end slope would be best, since all courts would drain and dry simultaneously. If a side-to-side slope were used, the courts on the upper end of the slope would dry quickly; but, the last few courts would retain water for a much longer period of time since the water from the upper end-slope courts would have to drain across the courts at the lower end of the slope (USTA, 1997).

Center-to-end and end-to-center slopes are least desirable. When these types of slopes are used, the water remains on the court and court perimeter-playing surface much longer than when side-to-side or end-to-end slopes are used. Additionally, an end-to-center slope requires drains at or near the net. Drains on the court itself are not desirable.

When planning to use slope, natural drainage basins should be used whenever possible. Thus, if a small creek basin or lower land is adjacent to the court area, it is worthwhile to slope courts to these areas to limit artificial drainage and minimize drainage costs.

As outdoor tennis courts are planned, the size of the courts as well as the perimeter space around the court need careful attention. A singles court is 78 feet long and 36 feet wide. Including perimeter space, the minimum size for one doubles court

would be 122 feet by 66 feet. These dimensions give minimum safety between the court and the fencing on both the sides and the ends of the court (USTA, 1997).

The minimum distance between side-by-side courts is 12 feet. The minimum distance between the court sideline and the side fence is 15 feet. Finally, the minimum distance between the court baseline and the end fence is 24 feet (USTA, 1997). The shortest distance is between courts since a player has open space (the adjacent court) to run to in order to retrieve a ball. There is more distance between the sideline and the side fence since players can run into the fence. Finally, the baseline distance is the greatest since this area is essentially a part of the playing area, even though it is not a part of the actual court. Figure 10.1 illustrates these minimum distances as well as the dimensions of a tennis court. Tennis courts should be enclosed with chain-link fence. The fence can be either 10 or 12 feet high.

Figure 10.1
Tennis Court Diagram and Dimensions

The 12-foot-high fence is more expensive than the 10-foot-high fence; however, those additional 2 feet of fencing keep in a significantly greater percentage of balls (USTA, 1997). Chain-link fence comes in a No. 6 or No. 9 gauge. The No. 6 gauge is thicker and thus more costly.

Either gauge is acceptable. Fence is also available with a polyvinyl chloride (PVC) plastic coating (most often green). Coated fencing is more expensive; however, in addition to its aesthetic qualities, it does not rust as will galvanized fencing.

Line posts that hold the fencing must be no farther than 10 feet apart and all corner and gateposts should be stabilized by cross braces. All line posts should be embedded at least 3 feet into the ground. If a wind/visual screen is attached to the fence, all line posts should be embedded in a concrete footer.

Adequate gates should be placed throughout the tennis court complex. These gates need to meet the needs of both instructors and players. Each set of courts in a complex must have an external gate and internal gates. Gates are expensive; but compromising on the number of gates will compromise accessibility to the courts, both internally and externally.

Types of Courts

Courts are classified as either porous (those that allow water to filter and drain through the court surface itself) or nonporous (those that do not allow water to penetrate the surface). The sloping as previously mentioned is for nonporous courts but is sometimes used in porous courts to carry penetrated water into the subsurface drainage system. Clay, grass, soft composition (fast dry), porous concrete, and various synthetics are porous courts. Concrete, asphalt (cushioned and non-cushioned), hard composition (liquid applied synthetic), and various synthetics are nonporous courts. As a group, asphalt courts are composed of (1) asphalt plant mix, (2) emulsified asphalt mix, (3) plant and emulsified mix, (4) asphalt penetration mix, and (5) asphalt bound system (cushioned) (USTA, 1997).

In 2000, the International Tennis Federation (ITF) launched the Court Classification Scheme, through which courts are assessed in terms of their surface pace rating. Each surface receives a pace rating that categorizes it as slow (Category 1), medium (Category 2), or fast (Category 3). This classification also aids tournament organizers in determining whether to use fast-pace (Type 1) or slow-pace balls (Type 2). This ITF Court Surface Classification is valid for a period of three years (http://www.itftennis.com/technical/equipment/courts/class.asp).

Numerous items must be considered when selecting the appropriate type of court. Initial cost, cost of upkeep, amount of use, area of country, maintenance personnel needed, type of players, level of competition, and age of players must be factored in when determining the type of court to be selected.

Clay, grass, and soft composition courts are much easier on the legs of players and allow for a much slower ball bounce than other courts. These courts are superior for young players, beginning players, and older players. However, they need a high level of maintenance, which is costly in both materials and personnel. Clay courts must be leveled, must have clay added periodically, require watering, and must be kept free of vegetation. Soft composition courts must be rolled, require watering, and need to have screen and base components added often. Grass courts are similar to golf greens and need daily maintenance.

Additionally, grass courts that receive heavy use should be alternated daily. That is, a court used on Monday should not be used again until Wednesday. Consequently, more court space is necessary for heavily used grass courts. Grass courts give a skidding ball bounce, and sometimes an erratic bounce, because of small divots, excessive wear, and taped lines. Overall, clay, grass, and soft composition courts are recommended for commercial clubs where the cost of upkeep can be packaged into member fees.

They are not recommended for schools and recreation programs because of upkeep costs.

Asphalt, concrete, and hard composition courts need less maintenance but provide a faster ball bounce and cause more stress on the legs of players. Of the three types, asphalt courts are the most inexpensive to construct, and hard composition courts are the most costly. Hard composition courts take a few months to cure and harden, and they should not be used until they cure completely. Hard composition courts can be constructed with multiple layers of cushioning material. The more layers in the courts, the greater the resiliency of the surface will be; however, each additional layer of cushioning increases the cost. Hard composition courts are smoother than concrete or asphalt, therefore they cause less wear and tear on balls, shoes, and rackets. Asphalt, concrete, and hard composition courts are recommended for schools and recreation programs. Hard composition is the optimum choice of the three.

Numerous synthetic court surfaces are available. If synthetic outdoor courts are to be constructed, users should be consulted to determine the advantages and disadvantages of such courts for both players and owners. Also, product descriptions of the material should be studied carefully to help determine which synthetic surface best meets the specific needs of the court under construction.

Regardless of the type of court surface, it is paramount that a tennis court construction firm be employed to build the court(s). A local construction firm with no tennis court-building experience should not be permitted to construct the courts. Typically, a builder inexperienced in tennis court construction does not have the expertise to properly build tennis courts. This lack of expertise results in the use of poor construction techniques; more importantly, it ultimately results in premature (and costly) repairs and renovations.

Costs for an outdoor court surface and base vary depending upon the number of courts being built, the geographic location, and the amount of grading and drainage required, ranging from $25,000 to $50,000 for an asphalt court (Lavallee & Westervelt, 2004). Clay courts usually run about $10,000, whereas synthetic courts range from $40,000 to $50,000. These costs do not include fencing ($5,000 to $10,000 per court) or lighting ($5,000 to $10,000 per court). Without a doubt, tennis courts are expensive (USTA, 1997).

All tennis courts should have sufficient secured storage areas constructed on a concrete base adjacent to the court complex. The size of the storage area is dictated by the amount and type of equipment to be stored in it. Consider ball hoppers, tennis rackets, fanny packs, ball-throwing machines, and other teaching equipment. The storage area must be waterproof and include shelving, bins, racks, and hook.

If maintenance equipment is needed at the courts, a separate storage area must be built for appropriate machines, rakes, hoses, screens, and materials. Parking areas need to be built in close proximity to the court complex. The size of the parking area is dictated by the maximum number of user vehicles for the complex in addition to sufficient space for spectator parking. If the tennis complex is lighted, the parking area should be illuminated with high-pressure sodium lights.

Night outdoor tennis is popular in many areas of the country. The recommended surface lighting level for recreational tennis is 38 foot-candles and 63 foot-candles for tournament tennis. Lighting tennis courts is a necessity in some areas. Information as to the number of light standards and how much light will be needed for the complex can be obtained by consulting the local electric company and a manufacturer (e.g., General Electric). A number of outdoor sports lighting companies install quality tennis court lighting systems. If the cost of ongoing high electric use is of concern, coin-operated light boxes can be installed to defray the electricity cost (USTA, 1997).

Although lighting may be optional, water must be provided at each court complex. One water fountain (refrigerated) and one hose connector are recommended for each set of four courts. Electrical outlets must be provided for each court and for any electrical maintenance equipment. All outlets should be located in the fence area and at the storage areas.

Benches need to be provided outside the fencing for those awaiting an empty court. Unobstructed spectator seating should be provided as close to the courts as possible if tournaments or instruction are to be provided on the courts. Courts used for tournaments and high-level competition also require scoring equipment, officials' seating, tables, benches, concession areas, and a protected area for videotaping.

Finally, court surfaces can be a variety of colors. Synthetics can be found in any color whereas most nonporous tennis courts use a contrasting red and green color scheme. Several factors should be considered when deciding on court colors including the effect of a color on perception of the ball, how well a color scheme masks or highlights wear and stains, and the color's compatibility with its surroundings (Jones, 1990). Considering ball perspective, single-colored courts are easiest on participants' eyes due to the fact that multicolored courts promote eye fatigue as one's vision changes focus from light to dark areas. A subtle difference between actual court coloring (within the lines) and surrounding court coloring (e.g., light green inside the lines, surrounded by dark green) allows for similar reflectivity level and subsequently less eye fatigue. As far as a court's ability to hide stains or wear marks, darker colors are advantageous. It should be noted that a variety of colors are available for tennis courts from traditional green to the much-publicized purple courts the Association of Tennis Professionals (ATP) experimented with during the Men's Tour of 2000. Choosing a color that is in harmony with the surrounding vegetation (e.g., green courts in an area surrounding by lush green vegetation) provides a nice aesthetic appeal (Jones, 1990).

Indoor Tennis Courts

Indoor courts can be practical for tennis. Since the weather can affect the ability to play, tennis is a seasonal sport in many parts of the country. Consequently, indoor courts meet a specific need in certain regions.

The number of courts to be enclosed depends on the number of users and the amount of money available for construction. The type of enclosure varies greatly from complex to complex. Prefabricated steel buildings, air structures, tension membrane structures, and standard brick-and-mortar buildings have all been employed successfully. The use of combination structures has some advantages. A translucent tension membrane that allows light onto the courts combined with a turnkey or one standard structure can save roofing costs as well as electricity costs during the day. The following is a cost comparison of three four-court structures (USTA, 1997):

- sports frame metal building—$561,000 ($140,250 per court)
- tension structure—$422,495 ($105,624 per court)
- air structure—$366,000 ($91,500 per court)

Lighting should be indirect, so that the tennis ball is not lost in the glare of lights. The background at the end of the courts should be plain. Traffic patterns need careful planning to ensure they do not conflict with play on the courts. Netting must be used between courts, since fencing does not exist, and the ceiling height needs to be a minimum of 30 feet. Most indoor court surfaces are synthetic. As with outdoor courts, planning should include storage, parking, water fountains, electrical outlets, seating, concessions, officials' needs, videotaping, and locker and shower facilities.

Paddle Tennis

Dimensions

Paddle tennis courts are 50 feet long by 20 feet wide. The safety space or unobstructed area should be a minimum of 15 feet behind each baseline and 10 feet from each sideline or between each adjacent court. As Figure 10.2 shows, service lines for each side of the court run the entire width of the court, parallel to and three feet inside each baseline. The center service line extends from the service end line, down the middle of the court. The service boxes, therefore, are 22 feet long by 10 feet wide (USPTA, 1996).

Paddle Tennis Web

An optional restraint line extends the width of the court, 12 feet from the net. These restraint lines are used in doubles play only. All dimensions for paddle tennis court markings are to the outside of the lines with the exception of the center service line, which is divided equally between service courts.

Miscellaneous Considerations

Paddle tennis net posts are located 18 inches outside of each sideline and are 31 inches in height. Unlike tennis courts, the net is strung taut so that the height measures the same (31 inches) at each post and in the middle of the court. Court surfaces are concrete or asphalt, although competition can also take place on hard-packed sand (USPTA, 1996).

If construction of stand-alone paddle tennis courts is not an option, paddle tennis court markings can be superimposed on a regulation tennis court by using chalk or tape or by painting lighter colored lines and the net can be lowered to the proper height.

Figure 10.2
Paddle Tennis Court Dimensions With Restraint Line

Paddle Tennis Web

U.S.P.T.A. OFFICIAL
COURT DIMENSIONS
(with Restraint Line)

Paddle

Dimensions

The sport of paddle has recently been introduced in the United States and is played in approximately 15 countries. A paddle court is 65 feet, 7 7/16 inches (20 meters) long by 32 feet, 9 3/4 inches (10 meters) wide with a plus or minus 1% tolerance level. The net, which divides the court in half, extends to the perimeter fence where it is anchored to the two center posts of this fencing or to an independent anchoring system. Regardless of the anchoring system, the net must coincide with the perimeter fence.

The net measures 37 7/16 inches (0.95 meters) at the posts and is two inches lower at the center of the court (35 7/16 inches or 0.90 meters) where it is held down at the center by a central belt that is two inches wide (APA, 1996).

The service lines for each side of the court run parallel to the net and are placed 22 feet, 9 1/2 inches (6.95 meters) from the net. A central service line, two inches wide, runs perpendicular to the net. This line bisects the court, dividing it into equal service zones on both sides of the net. Each service zone measures 22 feet, 9 1/2 inches long by 16 feet, 4 7/8 inches wide. All measurements for the court markings are made from the net or center of the central, perpendicular service line (APA, 1996).

The paddle court (Figure 10.3) is completely enclosed by back walls, sidewalls, and fencing on the remaining sideline areas. The back walls at the end of each court measure the width of the court (32 feet, 9 3/4 inches) and are between nine feet, 10 1/8 inches (three meters) and 13 feet, 1 1/2 inches (four meters) in height. The partial side or "wing walls" extend 13 feet, 1 1/2 inches (four meters) from the back walls. The wing walls decrease in height from nine feet, 10 1/8 inches (three meters) to five feet (1.5 meters) beginning at the wing wall's midpoint (six feet, 6 3/4 inches, that is, two meters from the junction of the back and wing walls) to the end of the wall. This decrease in height on the wing wall should be at approximately a 38-degree angle. The remainder of the court perimeter is enclosed with a wire fence measuring 13 feet, 1 1/2 inches (four meters) in height from the court surface (APA, 1996).

Miscellaneous Considerations

Paddle court surfaces vary from hard courts to artificial grass. The sport can be played on outdoor as well as indoor courts. If played indoors, however, courts must have a minimum ceiling clearance of 25 feet.

Back walls and partial sidewalls consist of stucco, concrete, or glass and/or a blindex material that provides for optimum spectator viewing of the court from all surrounding areas.

Figure 10.3
Paddle Court

Portable courts (not inclusive of surfacing) are available for purchase for approximately $25,000.

Platform Tennis

Dimensions

A platform tennis court is 44 feet long by 20 feet wide. The entire platform surface is 60 feet by 30 feet, which allows for 8 feet of space beyond each baseline and five feet of space between each doubles sideline and the fencing. All court markings are two inches wide and measurements are to the outside of the lines except for the center service line, which is equally divided between the right and left service courts. Service lines running parallel to the net are 12 feet from the net, and doubles alleys are two feet wide.

Net posts are located 18 inches outside of the doubles sidelines and the net height is 37 inches at the posts and 34 inches at the center of the court. Fencing, which measures 12 feet in height, is 16-gauge hexagonal, galvanized, one-inch flat wire mesh fabric.

Miscellaneous Considerations

The total area needed for construction of a platform tennis court is 2,584 square feet (68 feet by 38 feet). This allows for the foundation beams at the corners and at the locations of the uprights (Figure 10.4). Specifications for a platform tennis court

typically call for four-inch-by-six-inch foundation beams across the base of the platform. It is recommended that wood beams be waterproofed with creosote. Each beam rests on four evenly spaced concrete blocks; the blocks should be placed such that the beams rest four feet apart (measured from center to center). The foundation beams at the corners and at the locations of the uprights must project far enough to afford a base for the outer support of the uprights. The deck surface should be constructed of Douglas fir planks measuring two feet by six feet. The planks should be laid 1/8 inch to 1/4 inch apart to allow for drainage. The corner uprights and the intermediate uprights must measure 12 feet from their base (i.e., the deck surface) to their top. The corner uprights should be constructed of four-inch-by-four-inch beams; the intermediate uprights should measure two inches by four inches.

The construction of the backstop is a detailed procedure. Top rails are bolted horizontally to the insides of the tops of the uprights and measure two inches by four inches along the sides. Therefore, the rails to which the wire fabric is attached project inside the uprights by four inches at the ends and two inches at the sides. All of the space around the platform is covered by wire except 12-foot openings in the center of each side, at least one of which is closed with either netting. This closure is for containing errant balls. All wiring should be attached vertically on the insides of the uprights

Figure 10.4
Platform Tennis Court

ISOMETRIC SHOWING FENCE (TYPICAL WOOD CONSTRUCTION)

Platform tennis layout.

and stretched in six-foot widths from the top down to the tension rail below.

Badminton

Dimensions

A badminton doubles court (Figure 10.5) is 44 feet in length by 20 feet wide; a singles court is the same length (44 feet), but three feet narrower (17 feet). All court markings including the center service line, short service lines, and doubles long service lines are marked in yellow or white and measure 1.5 inches in width. All dimensions are measured from the outside of the court lines except for the center service line, which is equally divided between service courts.

A net that is exactly five feet above the ground at the center of the court and five feet, one inch at the net posts bisects the court laterally. The net posts are placed directly on the doubles sidelines. However, when it is not possible to have the posts over the sidelines, this boundary should be marked with a thin post or strips of material attached to the sideline and rising to the net cord. The safety distance or unobstructed space behind the back boundary line should measure eight feet behind and four to five feet outside of each sideline or between courts.

Miscellaneous Considerations

Ideally, ceiling clearance for indoor badminton should be no less than 30 feet over the entire full-court area. This is the standard for international play. However, a 25-foot clearance is the recommended minimum and is sufficient for other levels of play.

Basketball

Dimensions

Indoor and outdoor basketball courts vary in size depending upon the level of competitive play. It is recommended that courts for junior high, high school, and recreational play be 50 feet wide by 84 feet long. Competitive collegiate and professional basketball requires a 50-foot-by-94-foot court. Regardless of the level of play, a 10-foot unobstructed or safety space is highly recommended, especially considering today's game and the increased size of the players. However, the collegiate (NCAA) and high school (NFHS) rule books require a minimum of three-foot safety buffer and suggest preferably it be 10-foot (see Chapter 2). However, if a court is constructed with less than 10-feet of safety space, wall padding should be installed the entire distance of the wall that parallels the end line. Another important safety consideration concerns any glass or windows that are part of the surrounding basketball gymnasium. All glass and windows should be shatterproof safety glass. Finally, in a gymnasium setting, especially where other sports can be played, a height clearance of 30 feet is strongly recommended, but a minimum clearance of 23 feet is imperative. Appendix A

Figure 10.5
Badminton Court

provides a detailed display of basketball court markings (NCAA, 2000).

Concerning the size and colors of the lines, several guidelines should be kept in mind:

- All lines must be two inches wide, except for the neutral zones.
- The color of the boundary lines should match the midcourt markings.
- The color of the lane space and neutral zone markings should contrast with the color of the boundary lines (NCAA, 2000).

The three-point arch measures 19 feet, 9 inches from the center of the basket for high school and women's collegiate competition. However, starting in the 2008-2009 NCAA Collegiate basketball season, the college men's three-point line is being moved back one foot from this 19 feet, 9 inch standard to 20 feet, 9 inches. This decision was the first modification of the three-point shot since it was first established in the 1986-1987 season. Considering that the women's three-point line will remain the same, the men's new three-point line will have to be painted a contrasting color (http://sports.espn.go.com/ncb/news/story?id=2882740).

Miscellaneous Considerations

Collegiate competition requires backboards that are transparent and measure six feet horizontally by four feet vertically. The backboard should have a two-inch white-lined target centered behind the goal. This target should measure 24 inches horizontally by 18 inches vertically. The backboard should also have two-inch-thick gray padding on the bottom and up the sides for the players' protection (Head-Summit & Jennings, 1996). Attached to the backboard is an 18-inch (inner diameter) bright orange ring mounted parallel to and 10 feet above the floor. Although the standard height for a basketball goal (from rim to floor) is 10 feet, adjustable standards that allow the rim to be set at the standard height or lower (i.e., as low as 8 feet) provide opportunities for young children to practice shooting at a goal that is more age-appropriate (NCAA, 2000).

The gymnasium flooring is an important consideration. It is imperative that the flooring provides sliding characteristics (the surface friction of a finished floor) and shock absorption that conform to criteria established by the Deutches Institut für Normung (DIN) standards (see Appendix H) to help minimize the possibility of participant injury. Also, the flooring should provide adequate ball bounce or deflection as prescribed under the DIN standards. A final consideration is the placement of padding in appropriate areas, such as the wall directly behind each basketball backboard, especially if the distance between the backboard and wall is less than 10 feet.

Outdoor basketball courts should run lengthwise in approximately a north-south direction. Proper drainage can be insured by slanting courts from one side to the other allowing "one inch of slant for every 10 feet of court." If a backboard is mounted on an in-ground pole, the pole should be padded. Additionally, the pole should be off the playing court and the backboard should be extended at least four feet onto the court. The buffer or safety zone (unobstructed areas) should be 10-feet at the ends and three to 10 feet on the sides. Fencing is not a necessity; however, if finances allow, anodized aluminum chain-link should be used. The fence height should be a minimum of 10 feet. The fence posts should be placed 6 inches to one foot inside the hard surface and the fence fabric should be affixed on the inside of these supporting posts. Posts should be mounted in concrete such that 35% to 40% of the length of the pole is above the surface. Gates or fences should be constructed large enough to allow maintenance equipment to be brought into the court areas.

Volleyball

Dimensions

Although volleyball courts within the United States traditionally measure 30 feet in width by 60 feet in length, the United States Volleyball Rules (which are those of the International Volleyball Federation) call for the court to measure 59 feet by 29.5 feet (18 meters by nine meters) (Figure 10.6). Notably, all court dimensions are measured from the outside edge of the lines and all court lines should be two inches (five centimeters) wide (Sanford, 1997).

A minimum of 6 feet, 6 inches of safety or unobstructed space should surround an indoor court; however, the ideal situation is to provide at least 10 feet from the sidelines and 13 feet from the end lines (NCAA, 1997).

Ceiling clearance is a critical issue. Although United States Volleyball Rules call for "a minimum or 23 feet (seven meters) of unobstructed space as measured from the floor, 30 feet of overhead clearance is highly recommended" (Neville, 1994, p. 6). Figure 10.6 provides a detailed display of volleyball floor markings. Notably, in recent years, the service zone has been extended the full width of the court as a result of a rule change permitting players to serve anywhere behind the end line.

Net Height

The volleyball net height is 7 feet, 11 5/8 inches (2.43 meters) for men's competition and 7 feet, 4 1/8 inches (2.24 meters) for women's competition, as measured at the center of the playing court. The two ends of the net, directly over the sidelines, must be the same height from the playing surface and may not exceed the official height by 3/4 inch (although a constant height is far more

Figure 10.6
Volleyball Court Dimensions

The Playing Court

Design of the Net

Design of the Net

Age Groups	Females/ Reverse Mixed 6	Males/ Mixed 6
70 years and above	7'0" (2.13 m)	7'6" (2.29 m)
60 years and above	7'0" (2.1 3m)	7'9 5/8" (2.38 m)
55 years and above	7"2 1/8" (2.19 m)	7'9 5/8" (2.38 m)
45 years and above	7' 2 1/8" (2.19 m)	7' 11 5/8" (2.43 m)
15 to 18 years of age	7' 4 1/8" (2.24 m)	7' 11 5/8" (2.43 m)
13 to 14 years of age	7' 4 1/8" (2.24 m)	7' 4 1/8" (2.24 m)
11 to 12 years of age	7' 0" (2.13 m)	7' 0" (2.13 m)
10 years and under	6' 6" (1.98 m)	7' 0" (2.13 m)

desirable). The net height may be varied for specific age groups in the following ways (*USVA Rule Book*, 2007-2008, p. 10):

The net itself is 39 inches wide and a minimum of 32 feet long. The posts (supporting standards) are fixed to the playing surface at least 19 1/2 inches to 39 inches from each sideline. Two white side bands, two inches wide and 39 inches long, are fastened around the net vertically and placed perpendicularly over each sideline. Six-foot-long antennas are attached at the outer edge of each side band and extend 32 inches above the height of the net (USVA, 1997).

Miscellaneous Considerations

One of the most important safety factors is to provide poles that are sunk directly below floor level in sleeves or that telescope up from below the floor. Volleyball standards/poles that are on mounted or weighted bases are extremely hazardous. Likewise, volleyball net systems that rely on guy wires are not desirable. If wires are part of an existing volleyball net system, they should be clearly identified and padded. Furthermore, volleyball posts should be padded to a minimum height of six feet and all official stands should be padded.

Ideally, in a facility built primarily for volleyball, the walls (particularly those behind each end line) should be painted a color that provides some contrast to the color of volleyballs, which are generally white. This contrast in color allows participants to more easily track the flight of the ball during play.

Additionally, the ceiling color should be off-white or another light color that provides a contrasting background for players attempting to follow the flight path of the volleyball.

Light fixtures need to be placed at least as high as the lowest ceiling obstructions to avoid any shadowing effects. Also, lighting needs to be bright (a minimum of 27.9 foot-candles, measured at one meter above the playing surface). The lights, however, should not be closely grouped such that they would create a blinding effect for participants (USVA, 1997).

Outdoor Sand Volleyball Court Guidelines

The dimensions for an outdoor sand court are identical to indoor volleyball court dimensions (i.e., 59 feet [18 meters] long by 29 feet, 6 inches [9 meters] wide, as measured from the outer edge of the boundary lines). It should be noted that the Federation Internationale de Volleyball (FIVB), the world governing body, approved the reduction of the dimensions of the two-person outdoor sand volleyball court from 16 meters in length to eight meters in width. In non-metric measurements, this particular professional court is six feet shorter and three feet narrower than the traditional measurements.

Ideally, the court should be constructed with the net running in an east-west direction so that the morning and evening sun does not face directly into the eyes of one team. Outdoor courts should provide a minimum of 9 feet, 10 inches or three meters of free space, composed of sand, surrounding the court area.

In other words, the complete sand area should measure a minimum of 80 feet long by 50 feet wide. For professional competitions, the court should be centered on an area 93 feet long by 57 feet wide. Standard net heights are the same as for the indoor game: 7 feet, 11 5/8 inches (2.43 meters) for men's and coed play and 7 feet, 4 1/8 inches for women's and reverse coed play. Children ages 10 to 16 may have the net height adjusted according to the standards listed above regarding indoor volleyball net adjustments (Sandorfi, 1995).

Boundary lines are brightly colored 1/4-inch rope or 1 1/2-inch webbing tied to the four corners with buried deadpan anchors. No centerline is required for outdoor play but approximately 14 feet of rope will be needed, beyond the 177 feet total necessary for court lines, to anchor the corners (Sandorfi, 1995).

Net supports should be made of metal, wood, or other material that will withstand tension. The supports should be about 14 feet long and should be buried five feet deep using a concrete footing unless the soil is solid, in which case packing in and washing the soil should suffice. These support standards should be set 39 inches (one meter) from the boundary of the court. Any less space will leave insufficient room for the full net and adjusting cables (Sandorfi, 1995).

Suggested specifications for different net supports are as follows. Metal net supports should be four-inch, diameter schedule 40, galvanized steel pipes. Round wood poles should measure eight inches in diameter and should be made of treated, weather-resistant wood. Square wood supports are not recommended, because of the potential for participant injury on corner edges. In all instances, padding the support poles is an important safety measure. If the support does not have equal sides, the narrower side should be the net anchor side (facing the court) (Sandorfi, 1995).

Hooks, hook-and-eye hardware, and any winch hardware (padded) are necessary to attach the net to the standards. One way to provide for total adjustability of net height is to have four metal collars made that have loops for attaching the net (i.e., the top and the bottom of the net on both sides) that can slide up and down the poles. Holes can be drilled into the collars and set screws inserted which can be tightened with an Allen wrench. Finally, the net should be 10 meters in length with a cable top, although strong rope such as Kevlar also works well. However, the effort of fashioning this system can be avoided by purchasing outdoor standards now available from a variety of vendors.

Actual sand court construction should start with the excavation of the area with a front-end loader. The court area should be excavated between two and three feet in depth. In low-lying areas, such as the shoreline areas of Florida, the court should be excavated only six to eight inches. This will yield an elevated court rather than one that is flush with the ground. Also, the dirt that is excavated should be used to create a slight slope up to the court.

The court perimeter edges can be contained to keep dirt and grass from leaking into the court. Lawn edging material or rubber handrail material from escalator companies seated atop two-inch-by-six-inch wooden boundaries is a good method of providing perimeter boundaries. If railroad ties or similar materials are used, the top edges should be padded to minimize injury potential (Sandorfi, 1995).

Drainage of the court under the sand is important. The installation of leaching pipe on the standards with a slant of 14 degrees is highly recommended for a good permanent court. Perforated pipe (approximately two rolls of 250 feet) can be laid perforated side down with the open end at the low point of the court. Each section of the pipe should be wrapped with a flex wrap or "handicap wrap," which can be purchased at plumbing supply houses. This wrap prevents sand from filling up the pipes. Finally, the drainage points should lead away from the court at the lowest point (Sandorfi, 1995).

The next step is to set the standards in concrete. Poles should be set at a slight angle outward from the court to allow for any bending caused by eventual net tension. To allow for ease of maintenance or replacement, steel poles should be seated in steel sleeves so that they can be easily removed.

Small. pea-sized gravel used for drainage (#56, #57, #2, or #3) should then be placed over the drainage pipe to a depth of about one foot. Approximately 2,600 cubic feet (110 tons) of this gravel is necessary. Plastic landscaping or ground stabilization filter fabric (a woven polyblend that will not deteriorate easily) is placed over the gravel to prevent the sand from washing through (Sandorfi, 1995).

The final step in sand court construction is depositing the sand. A good court requires an investment in good sand. Sand comes in a variety of grades; some types are very "dirty" and unsuitable for a court. Washed beach (dune), washed plaster, washed masonry, or washed river sand are the most desirable types of court sand. The most highly recommended sand is silica sand regionally available by contacting Best Sand at 1-800-237-4986. This sand should be deposited and raked level around the court; it should measure one to two feet in depth. The minimum recommended depth of the sand is 19 1/2 inches. In essence, a sand court requires approximately 5,200 cubic feet (205 tons of washed sand). The final price tag for the construction of a good sand volleyball court will range anywhere from $6,000 to $10,000 (Sandorfi, 1995).

Racquetball, Handball, and Squash Courts

Dimensions and Design Considerations

Four-wall courts for squash and handball have been in sports facilities for over three-quarters of a century. Originally, these courts were made from Portland cement with smaller than normal doors.

Paddleball and racquetball were first played on these courts in the late 1950s and early 1960s. Today's courts are designed for racquetball, handball, and squash, even though other activities may also be played in these enclosed four-wall courts (such as walleyball and Bi-Rakits). Today's state-of-the-art courts are constructed of laminated panels and/or tempered glass. In the planning of four-wall courts, teaching, competition, accessibility, and amenities need to be considered (AARA, 1997).

Figure 10.7
Four-Wall Handball and Racquetball Courts and Dimensions

The recommended four-wall racquetball/handball court is 40 feet long and 20 feet wide with a front wall and ceiling height of 20 feet and a back wall at least 14 feet high (Figure 10.7). The lower back wall provides a space for a viewing or for an instructional gallery, which may be open with a three- to four-foot-high railing. Clear polycarbonate sheeting should be placed under the railing for seated viewing purposes and safety. The gallery may be totally enclosed with clear polycarbonate sheeting and a small four-foot-square open window. An open gallery is recommended for communication purposes between instructors/officials and the players. However, an open gallery poses the risk of spectators being hit by a ball, therefore appropriate signage should be posted to indicate this hazard. Squash is becoming very popular in some regions of the United States. The international singles squash court is 21 feet wide and 32 feet long (Figure 10.9). The old North American standard of an 18 foot, 6 inches-wide singles squash court is no longer acceptable and should be avoided (Figure 10.10).

Figure 10.8
North American Doubles Squash Court

North American doubles squash is played on a larger court measuring 25 feet wide and 45 feet long (Figure 10.8). Squash court wall heights vary compared to the standard 20-foot racquetball/handball wall heights (USSRA, 1997).

When more than a single battery of courts is to be constructed, the batteries should be arranged so a corridor approximately 10 feet wide and 12 feet high separates the back walls of each. Courts should be located in the same area of the facility rather than being spread out. Courts should be placed on adjacent walls rather than on opposite walls in order to achieve close proximity, thereby aiding in quality instructional time. Corridors and galleries should be illuminated with indirect light. The minimum number of courts for schools should be dictated by maximum class size and total student enrollment. Normally, no fewer than six to eight courts are recommended, which can adequately handle 15 to 20 students at a time. The number of courts for clubs and private usage is determined by the number of users and by the popularity of racquetball, handball, and squash in any given area.

Walls may be constructed of hard plaster, Portland cement, wood, laminated panels, or tempered glass. Laminated panels and tempered glass are recommended. The panels are four-by-eight-foot particleboard or resin-impregnated Kraft papers covered with a melamine sheet. The panels come in different thicknesses, from 13/16 to 1 1/8 inches. The thicker the panel is, the truer the rebound action of the ball will be; however, the thicker panel is also more expensive. Panels are mounted on aluminum channels or metal studs. Screws that hold them to the wall superstructure are inset and covered with a plug.

This creates a monolithic surface for the walls.

Figure 10.9
International Singles Squash Court

The panels have a high life expectancy and are easily maintained. Glass walls of 0.5-inch-thick tempered, heat-soaked glass is ideal but expensive. All courts are recommended to have the minimum of glass back walls, and one court should have an additional glass sidewall. This will offer good instructional and spectator viewing (Figure 10.11). Finally, one-way glass, which provides spectator viewing but appears to be a solid surface to participants within the court, is a relatively new innovation.

If glass walls are utilized, spectator and instructional viewing areas should be planned for carefully. These areas usually are stepped with carpeted risers along the sidewall or back wall of the court. A built-in, two-way audio system should be utilized for this court. Carpet color should not be totally dark and definitely should not be blue or green, since ball visibility through the glass walls is obscured with dark colors as a background. Courts with two glass sidewalls, those with glass sidewalls and a glass back wall, and all glass-wall

courts are superior to other courts; however, their cost is prohibitive in most facilities.

Doors are standard size and are placed in the middle of the back wall, not in the corners of the court. The corners are crucial real estate in intermediate and advanced racquet sports, so doors that can cause "untrue" bounces should not be placed there. Door handles should be small and recessed, and all door framing should be flush on the inside of the court. Doors should open into the court and there should be no thresholds under the doors.

Floors should be hardwood, as in standard gymnasium construction. The more sophisticated the floor system is, the more costly it will be. Resilient wood floors play differently than more rigid system wood floors, but they are more expensive. Any good hard maple floor system is acceptable. Floors should be flush with sidewalls so that no joint is evident. Joints collect dirt, dust, and debris and are a maintenance nightmare. Floors should be resurfaced as needed with a high-grade finish. When floors need refinishing, they become slip-

Figure 10.10

pery and can be very dangerous. The amount of use, the types of shoes worn during play, and the amount of dirt and grit brought into the courts on shoes will dictate how often refinishing is needed. Floors should be cleaned with a treated mop daily or as needed. Synthetic floors should not be used in racquet courts because they create too much friction and do not allow feet to slide, which is needed for effective and safe racquet sports.

Court line markings should be a lighter color, rather than a dark color like blue or black, which helps the participants' visual acuity in following a dark ball across lighter lines. Off-white, light pastel yellow, or light gray lines are best. Squash lines are red.

For racquetball and handball courts, the first 12 feet of the ceiling from the front wall should be devoid of any heat or ventilating ducts. This portion of the ceiling must be hard and compatible to the wall surfaces for ball rebounding. Lighting and any other fixtures in the ceiling must be totally flush. The rear 8 feet of the ceiling is not as crucial since this part of the ceiling is used very seldom in play.

The ceiling is not used in squash, but it should still be made of an impact-resistant material in case errant balls hit it. Panels or Portland cement would be good for the front 12 feet of the ceiling. If walleyball is to be played in the court, the ceiling must be strong enough to absorb the impact of the volleyball. Panels, but not Portland cement, work well in courts.

Lighting, Acoustics, and Ventilation

All lighting must be flush with the ceiling. Lights should illuminate all portions of the court equally; therefore, they should be spread throughout the ceiling. Shadows and low-light areas are not acceptable in these courts. Light accessibility for changing bulbs must be planned carefully. Since there is normally a battery of courts, the chore of changing light bulbs is magnified by the number of courts needing a bulb-changing system. The best light bulb-changing method for courts is to have a crawl space above the ceiling. This enables maintenance personnel to change bulbs from above. This system eliminates the need to use cumbersome hydraulic lifts and/or A-frame ladders (AARA, 1997).

A metal halide system of lighting is recommended. Metal halide lights give the most light at the least cost. Metal halide bulbs also have a long life expectancy. However, to garner cost savings and longevity, the court lights must be on at all times. Turning these lights off and on causes a delay (about six to eight minutes) for the bulbs to obtain full brightness. Turning halide lights off and on also increases the cost of lighting and decreases bulb life expectancy. Metal halide lights should be controlled from a central console, not at each court.

If single courts are not used often, a recommended method of turning the lights on and off is to install switches that are activated by opening or closing the door to the court. This method requires a metal halide lighting system. When the door is closed, lights in the court will turn on.

When the door is opened, the lights will turn off automatically, leaving only the night light to burn continuously. Usually, a two- to three-minute delay occurs before the lights go off after the door has been opened preventing a disruption of lighting during the brief time it takes for players to exit or exchange the court.

A relatively new concept utilizes an annunciator (an electrically controlled signal board) to indicate to the building reservation/control center which courts are occupied at any time. Lights on the signal board are activated by the trip switch on each door as it opens or closes. When lights are continually turned off and on, incandescent bulbs work fairly well. Fluorescent lights should not be used in racquet courts, because they tend to flicker and can cause visual acuity problems during play. If walleyball is to be played in the court, stronger light shields and light fixtures will be needed to absorb the impact of a volleyball.

Court walls and floors are hard surfaces, and much sound reverberates in the courts. For non-glass court surfaces, acoustical treatment is important within the surfaces. Insulation in the walls and ceiling will help to buffer sound within a court and also between courts. The rear eight feet of the ceiling should be constructed of acoustical tiles, because this area is seldom used in racquetball and handball and never used in squash. Although these tiles provide minimal acoustical treatment, it is very important to attempt to control sound and they should be considered in each court. If walleyball is played in a court, soft acoustical treatment cannot be installed on the ceiling.

Ventilation should be provided by air-conditioning. The ventilation of each court is very important so that moisture does not build on wall surfaces and make the courts unplayable. Ample air-circulation and air dehumidification are major concerns in the ventilation of the courts. Only air-conditioning can provide circulation, cooling, and dehumidification. To minimize the potential for moisture, courts should not be built underground with walls exposed to external moisture. Moisture and/or condensation can easily intrude to the interior wall surfaces of the courts. If courts must be built underground, extra waterproofing needs to be completed in this portion of the facility.

All vents for air circulation should be located in the back eight feet of the ceiling for racquetball and handball (Turner, 1992), but squash courts may have vents anywhere in the ceiling. The temperature of each court should be controlled by an individual, jar-proof, flush thermostat that is preset and tamper-proof.

Miscellaneous Considerations

Small storage boxes should be built flush with wall surfaces into sidewalls near the back wall of each court to house valuables and extra balls. The door to this storage box should be constructed of clear polycarbonate sheeting. Storage areas for students' coats, books, and other gear should be provided in an area near the courts. Extra storage must be provided for rain gear and winter gear where applicable.

Secured storage for racquetball rackets, handball gloves, squash rackets, eye guards, and balls should be provided near the court area.

All courts should have joints, seams, doors, vents, lights, and corners flush with the surrounding surface. Any unevenness in a court will cause untrue ball rebounds, which are unacceptable in court games. Each court should be equipped with a two-way audio system. Access to this system should be housed in the central console. This audio system can be used to make announcements, provide music, and facilitate instructional purposes between the court user and the instructor.

Effective external signage is important for all courts. Signs for court rules need to be posted near each court entrance. Rule signs such as "Eye guards are mandatory" and "Only non-marking athletic shoes may be worn in courts" are typical for racquet courts. Other signage includes the designation of a challenge court(s) with rules and a daily sign-up sheet. Courts also must be numbered and a visible wall clock near the courts is important.

Courts and galleries should be accessible to individuals with disabilities. Doors should be wide enough for wheelchair passage and have no barriers such as thresholds or steps at access points. Additionally, the court's location within the sports facility and a route from adjacent parking areas must be free of barriers.

University courts should be built at a location with easy access from all points on campus and ample parking in close proximity of the courts should be carefully planned. Within the sports complex, the courts should be located near the console control area.

In any facility, all courts need to be situated near refrigerated water fountains. In a commercial court complex, an area close to the courts must be designated for a pro shop. This area needs to be large enough to accommodate the types of equipment and apparel to be sold. The pro shop area must also be able to be secured by either lockable doors or a metal mesh gate, since it will not be staffed during all operation hours of the court area.

If there is a hallway access to courts and/or galleries, the hallway must have a ceiling height of 12 feet. A lower ceiling height lends itself to damage from individuals jumping up and hitting it with their rackets. Light shields in these hallways should be flush with the ceiling to deter breakage. Skylights above the court ceiling height, in gallery areas only, add a nice aesthetic touch. The use of a translucent glass or polycarbonate sheeting in skylights will alleviate glare problems.

Movable metal "telltales" can be installed across the front of handball and racquetball courts for use in squash instruction. However, the courts are racquetball size, not squash size. The floors, walls, ceilings, lighting, heating, and ventilation of squash courts are similar to those of four-wall racquetball and handball courts.

One court at any instructional facility should be a permanent teaching court. There should be a three-foot-by-three-foot front wall viewing and videotaping square. This "window" should be covered with a single sheet of clear polycarbonate sheeting. The window should be three or four feet high from the floor and closer to one side or the other of the front wall. Access to this window from outside the court must be provided. There should be a small lockable area behind the viewing window, preferably five feet by five feet with a ceiling height of eight feet. An adjustable-height table and chair need to be in this small room and a small area for storage of a portable video camera, videotapes, and speed gun should be provided there as well.

The teaching court also needs two flush, covered, electrical outlets for power sources. A multimedia projector and a video camera should be mounted within the back wall. Both projector and camera need to be protected with a clear polycarbonate sheet. A lockable, flush console should be built into a sidewall to house a laptop computer and VCR. This setup allows for slides, videotapes, television, and computer viewing. None of this high-tech equipment ever needs to be moved into or around the courts.

Polycarbonate mirrors, each section measuring six feet long by six feet high, should be placed flush on two adjacent walls. The back wall and a sidewall work best for the mirrors. Mirrors are great instructional tools, because they allow the students to view themselves.

Foot templates for various movement patterns should be permanently placed on the floor. Different colors may be utilized along with arrows to indicate foot movement direction. Ball-flight path patterns should be painted on the floor and flight paths for a down-the-wall passing shot and/or a cross-court passing shot should actually be templated onto the floor. Again, different colors should be used for different ball paths. An elliptical circle six feet wide and four feet deep should be painted and labeled "center court" in the center area of the court. An area three feet square also needs to be painted and labeled in each back corner. The back corners and center court are the two most important areas in racquet courts.

Targets of varying size and height should be placed on both the front wall and sidewalls to serve as aiming points for various shots. A few targets also need to be placed on the ceiling near the front wall as ceiling shot templates for racquetball and handball. Skill templates such as "Be Patient and Play the Ball Low" and "Culminate All Sources of Power at Ball-Racquet Impact" should be placed in a few selected areas of the court. These become constant visual educational reminders for students.

Figure 10.11
Racquetball Teaching Court

Ideally, the teaching court should have one glass sidewall and a glass back wall. A glass back wall alone will suffice. A two-way communication system must be in place for the instructor when in the court to be able to talk to students out of the court and vice-versa (see Figure 10.11).

Good court construction is paramount for teaching, competition, safety, and maintenance. All court surfaces must be flush. The activity that is played in the court will be a determining factor in both the size of the court and the materials used in court construction.

Shuffleboard

Dimensions

The actual playing area of a shuffleboard court is 39 feet long and 6 feet wide (Figure 10.12). However, the area outside the court markings includes a six-foot, six-inch standing area at both ends of the court and a two-foot area adjacent to the sideline boundaries. Thus, the entire area for a shuffleboard court should measure 52 feet in length and 10 feet in width.

Lines painted with a black dye, white road paint, or white acrylic stain mark off the shuffleboard court. The lines measure from 3/4 to 1 inch in width. The base lines are extended to adjoining courts or two feet beyond the sides of the court.

The separation triangle in the 10/off area measures three inches at the base and extends to form a point in the direction of the scoring area. The outline of the legs of this triangle is 1/4-inch wide, with a clearance of 1/2 inch at both the point and base. Finally, the base of the separation triangle is not marked.

Miscellaneous Considerations

Outdoor shuffleboard courts should be oriented north-south and must be constructed on a level area. A smooth playing surface is essential; therefore, the surface of an outdoor court is typically concrete or asphalt. Furthermore, the courts should be developed over a well-drained area. For proper drainage, a depressed alley should be installed between and at the sides of all courts. The alley must be 24 inches wide and must slope from both baselines toward the center of the court. To ensure proper flow of rainwater, the alley should descend one inch in depth during the first six inches in length (moving along the alley from each baseline toward the center of the court) and gradually increase in depth to at least four inches at mid-court where a suitable drain should be installed. The court can be lit using a 20-inch hinged pole with a 1,500-watt quartzite floodlight. This pole should be erected outside the courts next to the scoreboard or benches at the base of the courts. Overhead lighting is also an option in recreational areas. Frequently, two-inch-by-two-inch backstops are installed (in a loose fashion) to prevent discs from rebounding back onto the court.

Figure 10.12
Shuffleboard Court

Indoor shuffleboard courts must also be constructed in a level area. Reinforced concrete or any reasonably smooth surface is sufficient. Also, portable courts are available from vendors.

Croquet

Dimensions

The two most common forms of American croquet are six-wicket croquet (Figure 10.13) and nine-wicket croquet (Figure 10.14). Dimensions, configurations, and layouts are different for each game and are described separately.

The standard croquet court for American six-wicket croquet is a rectangle measuring 105 feet (35 yards) long by 84 feet (28 yards) wide. Boundary lines should be clearly marked, the inside edge of this border being the actual court boundary. If the area is too small to accommodate a standard court, a modified court may be laid out in accordance with the same proportions as a standard court (i.e., five units long by four units wide; for example, a court could be 50 feet long by 40 feet wide). In fact, in instances where the grass is cut high or beginners are competing, a smaller court

such as a 50-foot-by-40-foot court is more desirable (USCA, 1997).

The stake is set in the center of the court (see Figure 10.13). On a standard full court, the wickets are set parallel to the north and south boundaries, the centers of the two inner wickets are set 21 feet to the north and south of the stake, and the centers of the four outer wickets are set 21 feet from their adjacent boundaries. On a smaller modified 50-foot-by-40-foot court, the corner wickets are 10 feet from their adjacent boundaries, and the center wickets are 10 feet in each direction from the stake (USCA, 1997).

American nine-wicket croquet is played on a rectangular court that is 100 feet long by 50 feet wide with boundaries, although marked boundaries are optional. However, a court may be reduced to fit the size and shape of the available play space. If the court is reduced, a six-foot separation should be maintained between the starting/turning stake and the adjacent wickets (USCA, 1997).

Miscellaneous Considerations

For further information regarding the construction of courts, rules, or equipment, contact the

Figure 10.13
Six-Wicket Croquet Layout

Figure 10.14
Nine-Wicket Croquet Layout

United States Croquet Association. Their contact information can be found at http://www.croquetamerica.com.

Fencing

Dimensions

The fencing court (Figure 10.15) is referred to as the foil strip or piste and is constructed of wood, rubber, cork, linoleum, or synthetic material such as plastic. The strip is from five feet, 10 inches (1.8 meters) wide to six feet, seven inches (two meters) wide and 45 feet, 11 inches (14 meters) long. The strip markings include seven lines that cross the width of the entire strip: one center line; two on-guard lines, one drawn six feet, seven inches (two meters) from each side of the center line; two end lines at the rear limit of the strip; and two warning lines marked three feet, three inches (one meter) in front of the end lines. Portable strips are also an option for those wishing to avoid permanent floor markings. Finally, ceiling clearance should be a minimum of 12 feet.

Miscellaneous Considerations

For electric foil and epee, a metallic piste must cover the entire length of the strip, including the extension areas. Electrical outlets and jacks should be located at the ends of the strips to provide power for electrical equipment. For safety, any rackets for mounting fencing targets should be either recessed flush with the wall or fastened to the wall at least as high as seven feet.

Figure 10.15
Fencing Court

NOTE: The width of the strip shall be a minimum of 1.8 meters (5'10'')
and a maximum of 2 meters (6'7''). The length of the retreat zone shall
be a minimum of 1.5 meters (4'11'') and a maximum of 2 meters (6'7'').
For Foil and Epee, the metallic surface of the strip shall cover the entire retreat zone.

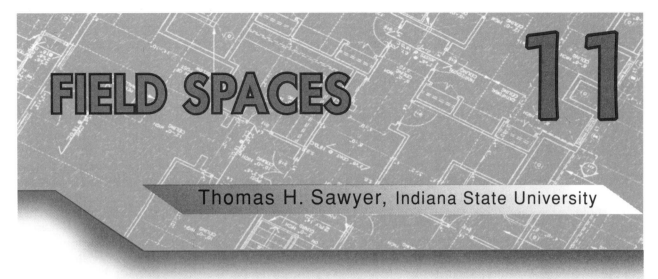

FIELD SPACES

11

Thomas H. Sawyer, Indiana State University

Sports fields generally require the largest amount of space in an outdoor complex. The activities that can be conducted are varied and require a variety of sizes. Additional acreage is required for spectators, officials, service personnel, and service areas (e.g., concessions, restrooms, equipment storage, score boards, and press box).

The usability of the areas, particularly at night and after inclement weather, often requires substantial support utilities, such as communication, drainage, irrigation, lighting, security, and sewer systems. Further, the surface material, synthetic or natural, and its substructure systems are also critical.

The various sports field venues that will be highlighted in this chapter include baseball and softball, boccie, cricket, croquet, field hockey, football, lacrosse, lawn badminton, lawn bowling, lawn volleyball, rugby, soccer, and team handball. The beginning of the chapter will highlight common planning challenges for all fields, and the latter portion will cover specific needs for the various fields.

All fields must have adequate seating for spectators. Numerous types of seating are available, from concrete stands to steel or wood bleachers of various heights, to portable aluminum bleachers. The seating has changed from 18 inches wide to 20 inches to accommodate the spectators' larger backsides. Many of the seats are fiberglass rather than wood, and some are aluminum. The seats are contoured for greater comfort and some areas have soft theater seating. The choice comes down to the size of the purchaser's pocketbook.

The planners need to consider the following safety suggestions when developing seating for spectators for outdoor events: 1) conforming to Americans With Disabilities Act (ADA) guidelines (see Chapter 4); 2) conforming to Consumer Product Safety Commission guidelines to providing railings for each side and the top row to prevent falls; 3) closing areas under each row of seats to prevent children from falling through or climbing; 4) enclosing the structure to gain space for storage, concessions, or restrooms and at the same time preventing children from playing under the bleachers; and 5) providing aisles with railings for ease of accessing seating.

Safety and Fields

The owner of a potential sports field property must apply the sound and proven guidelines for planning a facility that are outlined in this textbook to reduce the athletes' exposure to risks (see Chapter 2). The planning process should include an analysis of the causation of injuries.

The size of the field area is critical. Neither athletes nor spectators should be exposed to any of the following hazards, and planners need to consider each concern when selecting a location for a field:

- Streets should not be located any closer than 100 yards to a facility and should be fenced off.
- Railroad tracks, like streets, should not be any closer than 100 yards to a facility and should be fenced off.
- Watercourses, man-made culverts, or natural stream ways can contain deep, fast-moving water that can trap or entangle people who slip, walk, or slide into them. They should not be any closer than 100 yards to a facility and should be fenced off.
- Trenches or gulleys can be hazards that hold deep muck, hidden snakes, other reptiles, or rodents or that contain wires, quicksand, or reinforcing rods that can pierce or entrap a person. They should not be any closer than 100 yards to a facility and should be fenced off.
- Settlement ponds or basins can contain toxic liquids, silt, or flammable materials and should not be any closer than 100 yards to a facility and should be fenced off.
- Storage yards, with old concrete or other culvert pipes that can roll and crush; junk cars and machinery that can cut or pierce; old wood and metal junk piles; and hazardous drums of liquids (e.g., lead paint, paints, sealants) or acids that

can explode or burn should not be any closer than 100 yards to a facility and should be fenced off.

- Climatic noise, odors, smoke, and dust should be avoided.
- The protective perimeter of the area should consist of fencing to keep spectators away from the area of play and to keep players within the play area.
- The area must not consist of soils that are toxic, poor draining, decaying, or of poor structure. They should be free of debris and glass.
- The field space should be located in an area that has no other activity spaces in close proximity in order to protect the athletes and spectators.
- The visibility of the entire area should accommodate foot and vehicle security.
- The area should be illuminated at critical times to facilitate supervision and security.
- The multipurpose fields that are used for baseball or softball as well as soccer, field hockey, or football should not have ruts that create dangerous high-speed bounces of the ball on the playing surface.
- The games of baseball and softball have three major concerns for spectators and parking areas—foul balls, home runs, and overthrows as well as overruns which are likely in all field sports.
- The participants' age, gender, skill levels, and/or experience must be considered in creating facilities for all participants.
- The area must be accessible to participants and spectators with disabilities.
- Concealment areas caused by shrubbery or tree canopy or adjacent structures should be eliminated to deter improper activity.
- The public comfort for players and spectators must include restroom facilities close to supervised areas, properly designed and positioned litter containers, benches, drinking fountains, and walkways.
- The safety or buffer zone around the field and its appurtenance and equipment must be large enough to keep players from hitting stationary objects along its perimeter and if existing, such objects should be padded.
- The padding or other accepted, proven safety precautions, such as releasable or yieldable devices for outfield fences, stanchions, barriers, and other perimeter containments must be used and/or sufficient buffered perimeter areas should be used.
- The safety glazing of nearby windows, observation panels, and doors is a necessity.
- The relationship of fields and appurtenance among facilities should be harmonious and complementary in encouraging and facilitating play.

- The traffic flow of users from one field or appurtenance to another should be designed to be safe.
- The durability and maintainability of the types of appurtenances within and adjacent to the field must be considered.
- The pedestrian, player, and spectator traffic around the activity field is important. The field must be located so that there is no interference with the traffic of people, buses, automobiles, service vehicles, vendors, and bicycles. Pedestrian traffic should be routed to have easy access to comfort stations, security, refreshments, lockers, and other related facilities.
- The automotive and service (e.g., lawn mowers, maintenance vehicles) driveways should not bisect or parallel open play or human access areas.
- Immovable barriers should be installed to separate any automotive traffic routes from all activity areas.
- Maintenance vehicle access to fields should have the correct sub-base and surface materials installed so as to limit wear and irregular surfaces.
- The utility lines, above, on, or below ground should be positioned so as not interfere with players, the game, or spectators, or to be accessible to contact with any person.
- Storm drains are frequent hazards, often within the field limits or directly adjacent to them. Players can have their feet entrapped by such street-sized drains. They should be located at least five yards from the play line.
- Irrigation heads for pop-up or quick-couple sprinklers can cause tripping if not designed properly. They should be recessed as per manufacturers' guidelines.
- Relocatable aluminum irrigation pipes and sports equipment left on the field are also hazardous and should be properly stored and secured.
- Power lines, poles, transformers, and control panels must not be in proximity to playing and/or spectator areas. They should be in remote and inaccessible, secure locations.
- Fire hydrants, hose bibs, and drinking fountains must not be placed in the vicinity of the area of play.
- The buffer/safety zone for outdoor fields should be 10 yards. When there are multiple fields in a field complex, the distance between parallel fields should not be less than 10 yards on each side of the field. Bleachers should not be any closer than 10 yards from the sideline or end zone.

The types of turf that are used on sports fields are synthetic and natural turf. (See Chapter 9 for a complete discussion on natural turf.) In the 1960s to the late 1980s, many natural turf fields were converted to synthetic turf fields. The conversions were intended to reduce the cost of maintenance and to provide flexibility to sports schedules without concern about the wear and tear that occurred on natural-turf fields being used by numerous sports teams. Conversions back to natural turf through the 1980s and 1990s were prompted by the increase in athletic injury related to synthetic turf. In 1988, the next generation of synthetic turfs, which replicate a natural grass surface, began to appear. This product is durable, cost efficient, and consists of a sand and rubber infield system that has reduced sports injuries related to synthetic fields.

Type of Surfaces

Bioengineered Surface

Synthetic materials can be soft or firm. They can be piled, turfed, graveled, or smoothed. They can be rolled or poured, paneled, or sprayed. The ingredients of the turf can be rubber, polymer, pigment, polyvinyl chloride (PVC), thermoset, thermoplastic, and a host of other new high-tech materials. Synthetic products have substrates that are also of varied ingredients.

Synthetic turf is attractive to players for a number of reasons, including that the surface and footwear interact well for better footing, the surface stays in place, it is resilient, balls bounce well, the surface dries rapidly, and it has a cooling effect. It also has distractions for players, including that the surface has little resiliency, balls respond inconsistently, the surface affects the speed of the ball (making it faster), and the surface is very hot on hot days.

Attractions for operators include that the surface is repairable, picturesque, portable, durable, stable, paintable, and it drains rapidly. However, the greatest detraction of synthetic surfaces for the operator is life of the surface, which is approximately 15 years.

Sports Field Lighting

Lighting (illumination) is critical to safety and revenue generation (see Chapter 5 for detailed information). The illumination level for baseball and softball is 20 foot-candles for the outfield and 30 for the infield. The lighting for other team sport fields (e.g., field hockey, football, lacrosse, rugby, and soccer) requires a minimum of 30 foot-candles. If sporting events are to be televised, the lighting requirement will be much different. However, if this happens only occasionally, portable lighting companies can be hired to provide additional lighting requirements. The air should be monitored for contaminants that can cause the reflector surface to change by increasing diffusion and decreasing total reflection. This results in less total light energy leaving the face of the light, with less lumens. There should be no shadows on the field that create

unsafe catching, nor should there be any glare or irregular bright patches. All stanchions or poles must be outside the field of play.

Sports Field Orientation

There are various thoughts about the orientation of baseball and softball fields. It depends on where the field is and the time games are to be held. One school of thought is that the back of home plate should be set to point south to southwest or have the baseline from home plate to first base run in an easterly direction. The theory is for the batter to look into the sun, which implies the catcher as well. Another thought is for the batter to look away from the sun. Presently, the orientation is probably the least of the safety problems. However, since batter and catcher or pitcher are in the most hazardous positions, they still require consideration. A line through these positions would be the axis for orientation for either position. After locating the axis, locate the sun's position at sunrise, early morning, late afternoon, and sunset. Establish an orientation for the field that avoids the batter and catcher or pitcher from facing directly into the early morning or late afternoon sun.

Photo by Tom Sawyer

All other fields should run north to south to avoid the direct movement of the sun from east to west. However, if all contests are played in the evening after sundown, the sun does not become a factor.

Sports Field Fencing

Generally speaking, fields should be fenced to protect the field, athletes, and spectators. The height of the fence ranges from four feet for youth fields to eight feet for interscholastic, intercollegiate, and professional fields. A number of fields have six-foot fences, which is acceptable but not ideal. All fences less than eight feet high should be covered with a brightly colored vinyl protector with or without padding. The fence should be sturdy enough to withstand an athlete's weight as well as serve as a windscreen.

Photo by Tom Sawyer

Baseball and Softball Fields

The fence height should start at eight feet as it leaves the backstop around the circumference of the field, including in front of the dugouts. The fencing should be attached on the field side of the poles, with all attachments and prongs on the outside of the fence. The fence should be stretched down from the top to the tension rail on the bottom. The fence is meant to protect players as well as spectators. It should be no closer than 30 feet to the sidelines or foul lines but preferably will be 50 to 75 feet away.

Sports Field Drainage and Irrigation

A properly constructed sports field has a good drainage system (see Chapter 9), so that play can resume after a short waiting period, and the turf is not destroyed when played upon in a wet condition. Turf that is too wet or too dry will be compromised. The subsoil of the field should be composed of sand (80 to 90% sand base) to improve the speed of drainage. The playing field should be crowned to allow the heavy rainwater that cannot be absorbed to drain to the sidelines. The slope on either side of the crown should not exceed 1/4 inch per foot toward the side-line drainage area. The sideline drainage area should be at least 5 yards from the playing field, contoured and,

Photo by Tom Sawyer

sloped to catch the runoff to direct it to large drains that are approximately 20 yards apart along the sidelines. These drains should be approximately 15 to 20 feet deep with a 3- to 5-foot diameter filled with gravel and covered with a metal grate. Marketers always say the key to sales is "location, location, location." The key to a great field is drainage, drainage, drainage.

The irrigation of a field is very important in dry climates. There are basically three types of irrigation systems available for fields, including underground with sprinkler heads throughout the field space, underground with sprinkler heads on the perimeter of the field, and above ground with portable piping and sprinkler heads or hoses. The latter option is very labor intensive and requires a lot of equipment storage. The other options are the most convenient and least labor intensive.

The planners of the irrigation system need to consider the following: 1) the safety of the participants (i.e., perimeter or within-field sprinkler layout), 2) type of sprinkler heads, 3) the watering pattern layout (i.e., the number of overlapping zones needed, based on the available water pressure, to reach all areas of the field evenly), 4) the source of water (i.e., wells with a pumping system or government or private water company), 5) a timing system, 6) a plan for winterizing in climates that have temperatures below freezing, 7) tie-ins for drinking fountains and hose bibs, and 8) the possibility of a liquid fertilization option.

Sports Field Service Areas

Sports field service areas include concessions areas, press box, restrooms, scoreboards, and storage. These areas are very important to spectators and support staff. If the service areas are well designed and maintained, they will increase fan loyalty.

Concessions Area

The concessions area should be centralized ideally behind home plate, especially in multifield complexes as shown in Figure 11.1. The area can be constructed from wood or concrete block. It should have plenty of counter space for preparation of products and to service the patrons. The floor should be concrete with numerous drains. There should be at least one double sink and ample cabinet space for storage. The area should have numerous electrical outlets and ground fault interruption (GFI) outlets near water sources. The lighting should be florescent. The equipment in the area should include refrigerator, freezer, stove top with at least four cooking elements, microwave, popcorn popper, hot dog cooker/warmer, coffee maker, soda fountain, ceiling fans, shelving for merchandise, sign board for advertising, and cash register.

Figure 11.1
Diagram of a Multi-Field Arrangement

Photo by Tom Sawyer

Scoreboards can be simple or very complex in nature. The planners need to consider what they want the scoreboard to depict before determining the type of scoreboard to be purchased. The choices include 1) score; 2) periods or innings; 3) injury time or penalty time remaining; 4) times and places by lanes; 5) diving score by judge, degree of difficulty, total points scored, ranking after "x" number of dives; 6) balls, strikes, outs; 7) roster; 8) players vital statistics; 9) advertising; 10) PA system; 11) multiple functions for various sports using the field complex; 12) close-ups of players and spectators; 13) time of day; 14) scores from other games; and much more depending on the planner's imagination.

Press Box

The press box is important for the press, scouts, scoreboard operator, and those filming games. The press box should be located higher than the highest part of the bleachers. The size will be dependent upon the number of users. It should have an unobstructed view of the playing field. The following should be available for the press: 1) table to write on or broadcast from; 2) comfortable chairs; 3) phone hookups; 4) computer hook-ups; 5) electrical outlets; 6) refrigerator; 7) coffee maker; 8) separate areas for press, radio announcers, scorekeeper, public address (PA) announcer, coaches, and scouts; and 9) an area above the press area exclusively for filming games. These facilities are generally constructed of wood with fluorescent lighting.

Restrooms

There need to be numerous restrooms provided, preferably not portable. The number of facilities for women should be twice as many as that provided for men. Each restroom should provide changing areas for babies, with adjacent waste disposal units. Each restroom area should be handicapped-accessible, or at least an appropriate number of restrooms need to be handicapped-accessible and so labeled. These facilities are generally constructed of concrete block with concrete floors with drains for cleaning. The lighting should be fluorescent. The rooms should be adequately ventilated.

Scoreboards

There are a number of reliable scoreboard companies. The planners need to consider first what the function of the scoreboard will be—to depict score and time remaining only or to provide entertainment and information as well.

Storage

As is true with indoor facilities, there is never enough storage. The planners need to consider what items need to be stored. These include, but are not limited to: 1) various types of riding lawn mowers; 2) push mowers; 3) tillers; 4) weed eaters; 5) shovels, rakes, and hoes; 6) utility vehicles; 7) irrigation pipes; 8) hoses and sprinkler heads; 9) field liners; 10) goals; 11) field flags; 12) benches; 13) waste containers; 14) protection screens; 15) pitching machines; 16) tarps; 17) fertilizers, insecticides, and talc; 18) paint; 19) chains, yard

Photo by Tom Sawyer

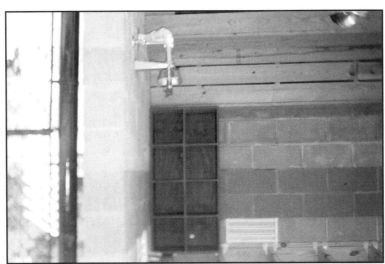

Photo by Tom Sawyer

markers, and padding for goal post for football; and much more.

Storage areas generally are constructed out of concrete blocks with concrete floors and an appropriate number of drains for cleaning. The space should have fluorescent lighting with an adequate number of electrical outlets. There should be a separate work area with a workbench and adequate amount of storage with shelving. The entrance should be an automatic roll-up door at least eight feet high. The ceiling height should be at least 10 feet. The voids under bleachers should be enclosed (these spaces make inexpensive storage areas). The space for chemical storage must meet OSHA guidelines.

Baseball and Softball Fields

Baseball and softball facilities are important aspects of sport in public schools (grades 5 to 12), colleges and universities (varsity competition as well as recreation), community recreation programs, Babe Ruth Leagues, Little Leagues, Miss Softball Leagues, corporate recreation programs, and military recreation programs. The space requirements for these spaces varies (see Table 11.1)

Due to the alarming number of injuries reported to the CPSC, safety is a principal concern. This concern places pressure on field operators, turf managers, maintenance managers, and others to have a safe playing field. A "field of dreams" is created from a consistent set of proven guidelines and safety standards to ensure consistency around the country. It is important for the planners to be aware of the field specifications described in the various rules books that govern these two sports (e.g., National Federation of High School Activities

Association, National Collegiate Athletic Association, National Intercollegiate Athletic Association, National Junior College Athletic Association, Softball USA, International Softball Federation, National Association for Girls and Women's Sports, Little League Association, etc.). These rulebooks are the gospel in regard to the specific dimensions for the fields, and most rulebooks are revised annually.

Common Design Errors with Possible Solutions

There are four common design errors that planners need to avoid when designing baseball and softball fields, including (1) incorrect field contours, (2) failure to isolate fields as drainage units, (3) insufficient clearance around the field, and (4) failure to provide sufficient access. Each of these will be discussed below with possible solutions offered.

Sports field contours are expressed as percentage of slope. Incorrect field contours are those that are less than 1% or more than 2% except for infields, which should have a .5% slope. The preferred slope, according to Puhalla, Krans, and Goatley (2003), for grass sport fields is 1.25%-1.75%. The optimal slope for skinned areas should be .5% - 1.75%. The infields of a baseball and softball field should be the highest point to enhance surface drainage. Finally, a field with a 1.5% slope should be graded evenly with a 1½ ft. differences in grade over a span of 100 ft.

No field should be expected to drain away more water that which falls on it. Planners need to be careful not to isolate fields as drainage units. Even if a field is built with correct contours, water

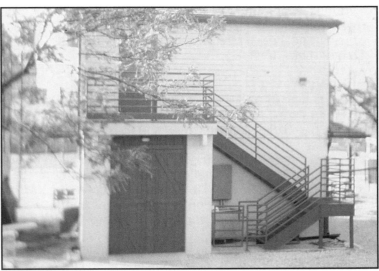

Photo by Tom Sawyer

Table 11.1
Space Requirements

Type of Field	Distance to Center Field Fence (ft)	Acres	SqFt
Baseball:			
90 ft Bases	400	4.5	195,000
80 ft Bases	315	2.8	123,000
70 ft Bases	75	2	90,000
60 ft Bases	215	1.5	64,000
Softball:			
65 ft Bases	75	2.4	105,000
60 ft Bases	200	1.4	60,000

Puhalla, J., Krans, J., & Goatley, M. (2003). *Baseball and softball fields.* Hoboken, NJ: J.W. Wiley, 4.

running onto the field from another field or an adjacent area can seriously compromise playability in rainy conditions, according to Puhulla, Krans, and Goatley (2003). The preferred design isolates each field as an individual drainage unit by using swales and/or catch basins around the field, or by making the field higher than its surroundings.

Fields that are designed or constructed with insufficient clearance, according to Puhulla, Krans, and Goatley (2003), will have inherent problems: out-of-bounds areas may be too small for the safety of players, spectator areas may be cramped or unsafe, and surface drainage around a field may not work as intended. The designers should consider space requirements in the planning stages. Making sure there is enough space around each field before construction begins will prevent it from being locked in by other fields, parking lots, roads, buildings, and the like.

A well-designed sports field, according to Puhulla, Krans, and Goatley, includes access roadways for players, spectators, maintenance equipment, and heavier renovation equipment (e.g., large trucks, tractors).

Bases

The base areas must be level, with all irregularities eliminated. The type of base used in either baseball or softball varies, and the rulebooks stipulate what types are permissible. The planner should contact the American Society of Testing and Materials (ASTM) for detailed information regarding the appropriate standards for bases. Presently, the ASTM F-8 Committee on Sports Equipment and Facilities is establishing standards and classifications for bases.

Bases are intended to be a reference point on a baseball or softball field. They are an integral part of the game. There are four types of base designs used, including permanent or stationary bases, modified stationary bases, release-type bases, and throw-down bases. The type of base usually refers to how the base is secured to the playing field, or its function.

Stationary Base

This base uses a ground anchor permanently installed in the playing field. The anchor measures either 1 or 1 1/2 inches, installed a minimum of 1 inch below the playing surface. The base is designed with a stem that fits into or over the ground anchor and holds the base securely in place.

The base should be constructed of permanently white material, which can be rubber, polyvinyl, polyurethane, or other synthetic material to increase service life. The base top should have a molded tread pattern to increase player traction and reduce slippage. Base size and color should conform to individual governing organizations.

Permanent or stationary bases can be used on fields by players with more advanced or higher skill levels only after 1) the players have been thoroughly warned that they can be seriously injured for life if they make a mistake in judgment or miscalculation, and 2) they have been made thoroughly aware of other options (e.g., the tapered side base or low silhouette which tapers to the ground eliminating impact of a sliding player against a vertical surface and uses that momentum to slide over the base). Bases are the number-one cause of injuries to ankles and other body parts, especially stationary, modified-stationary, and poorly designed release-type bases.

Modified Stationary Bases

The flexible base is a one-piece base that uses a fixed-anchor system for secure placement. It is constructed with interdependent ribs that allow the base to compress and absorb energy generated by a sliding player. The cover flexes inward and downward but does not release.

The strap-down base or tie-down base must be held in place by four spikes inserted into the ground. Straps attached to the base are inserted through loops in the spike head and tightened down. The base is constructed of vinyl-coated nylon or canvas filled with a foam or other resilient material. If installed properly, a portion of the base will remain somewhat stable. However, it has a tendency during play to loosen and move. This style is low cost relative to other base styles, which accounts for its popularity.

Release-Type Base

The release-type base is designed to reduce the chance of injury to a sliding player by releasing from its anchor system on the impact of a hard lateral slide. The release base must use a permanent ground anchor securely positioned below ground for installation. There are two-piece and three-piece designs. The release-type must not expose hidden secondary hazards after the primary above ground base portion releases.

Throw-Down Base

This base is a thin square, sometimes using a waffle design on the bottom, usually constructed of canvas or synthetic material with little or no padding. It is not physically attached to the playing surface, and therefore is dangerously subject to moving when a player steps on or rounds a base. Throw-down bases are not recommended for teaching basic skills in a gym, such as in a physical education class.

Specialized Bases

The flush or recessed base (except home plate, which is mounted flush with the playing field) is usually not considered for the following reasons: 1) difficulty in keeping the base visible and clean, 2) difficulty for umpire in making a call at the base when the base is not visible, 3) the change in the nature of the game, and 4) the fact that it is not widely used.

Double First Base

The double first base uses a securely positioned ground anchor system. The base is designed to reduce or eliminate the contact between the first baseman and base runner. It is a unit equal in size to two bases side by side, one-half white and mounted in the normal first base position, and one-half colored, and mounted in foul territory.

Home Plate

The home plate, batter's box, and catcher box and their correct dimensional size and positioning must conform to the game and the rules of the appropriate governing body. The area should be well compacted, properly tapered, and level, with no irregularities. The plate must be firmly anchored and any undermining or ruts corrected before play begins.

The home plate is a reference point on the playing field. It establishes the horizontal limits of the strike zone used by the umpire in calling balls and strikes. It is imperative that all home plates have a white surface that measures 17 by 8 1/2 by 8 1/2 by 12 by 12 inches flush with the surrounding playing surface. Further, all home plates must have a peripheral black bevel that does not exceed 35 degrees. The outermost edge of the bevel must be sufficiently below the playing surface. It does not matter how the plates are field mounted as long as they remain flat and flush with surrounding playing surfaces with no sharp corners or sharp nails exposed.

There are four styles of home plate, including buried, staked, anchored, and throw down.

Buried. A rubber or synthetic plate 2 inches or more thick is buried, and the uppermost white surface is installed flush with the playing surface. It can be mounted in a concrete sub-base to provide greater leveling stability.

Staked. A rubber or synthetic plate 3/4 to 1 inch thick has an installed white surface flush to the playing surface. It can be mounted in a concrete sub-base for better anchoring.

Anchored. A rubber or synthetic plate has a stem built into the bottom that fits into a permanent ground anchor. The uppermost white surface must be installed flush with the playing surface.

Throw down. A rubber or synthetic thin mat sometimes using a waffle design on the bottom is laid down on the playing surface and is not mechanically held in place. Throw-down home plates are not recommended for teaching basic skills in a gym, such as in a physical education class.

Skinned Infield

With an eye to player safety, begin the outfield slope 20 feet back into the outfield, lessening the transition from the infield to outfield (this is for both synthetic and natural fields). The infield slope should be established at 0.5%, and the outfield slope at 1.3% all the way around to further speed drainage. The infield should be a 80:20 premixed sand to clay material at a depth of three inches. The demarcation between skinned area and turf must be smooth and firm. The skinned areas must maintain the proper pitch to eliminate puddling and erosion. Irregular clumps of turf, uneven edges, and undermining of skinned materials are among some of the causes of ankle and leg injuries in the game.

Skinned areas could be just cutouts around the bases, home plate, and pitchers mound or include baselines or the entire infield area. In all cases, the skinned areas must be continuously inspected and groomed. All irregularities must be eliminated, particularly around bases where sliding groves the area.

Clay is most often used for a skinned area; however, other materials and mix of materials have been used depending upon local sources and preference. Most fields should be designed to be playable within 15 to 20 minutes after rain. A higher percentage of sand may be needed to achieve that without underground drainage.

Turf Infield and Outfield

Chapter 9 contains a discussion regarding natural turf as well as irrigation concerns. However, it needs to be noted here that natural turf in the infield and outfield should be Tifway™ Bermuda grass. It should be overseeded (see Base Paths) with Topflite™ perennial ryegrass. Table 11.2 displays the square footage of the skinned area and the grass area for common-size baseball and softball fields, including foul territory

Pitchers Mound

The pitchers mound and its plate must meet the requirements of the game's governing body. The height of the plate, the pitch of the slope within the circle toward home plate, the radius of the circle, the level plate length and width size are all critical to safety in any type of designated and designed fields and must be checked and maintained before any game.

Base Paths

A regular maintenance concern is the rutting of the base path. Like the infield, the base path should be free of ruts and irregularities in the surface. Periodically hand rake the base paths between first and second and second and third to identify any low spots. The base paths between home and first and first and third can be composed of clay and sand like the infield, or natural turf or synthetic material. If the base path is composed of natural turf, it should be over-seeded with Topflight™ perennial ryegrass prior to the season, periodically during the season, and at the conclusion of the season, as well as in early fall.

Prior to over-seeding in the early spring and early fall the area should be aerated, then de-thatched to provide good seed-to-soil contact. The seeded area should be fertilized first with 10-10-10 fertilizer, and one month later with a slow-release 30-16-10.

Warning Track

The warning track should encircle the entire playing field and provide noticeable surface variations in feel and sound to provide ample warning to players chasing a fly ball who are unaware of the perimeter and any obstacles. The track can be made of clay or crushed (M-10) granite or brick. The crushed brick will add color for enhanced TV coverage. The warning track and/or buffer zone should be equal in width to 5% of the distance

Table 11.2
Square Footage of Skinned Area and Grass Area

Type of Field	Distance to Center Field Fence (ft)	Skinned Area (sqft)	Grass Area (sqft)
Baseball:			
90 ft Bases-95ft Arc			
With Grass Infield	400	11,500	120,500
With Skinned Infield	400	8,300	113,700
80 ft Bases-80 ft Arc			
With Grass Infield	315	8,400	74,500
With Skinned Infield	315	13,650	69,250
70 ft Bases-70 ft Arc			
With Grass Infield	275	6,800	53,550
With Skinned Infield	275	10,700	49,650
60 ft Bases-60 ft Arc			
With Grass Infield	215	3,850	39,500
With Skinned Infield	215	6,700	36,650
Softball: (Skinned Infield)			
65 ft Bases-65 ft Arc	275	9,300	61,450
60 ft Bases-60 ft Arc	200	8,350	31,500

Puhalla, J., Krans, J., & Goatley, M. (2003). *Baseball and softball fields.* Hoboken, NJ: J.W. Wiley, 5.

from home plate to the deepest part of the playing field and completely encircle the field (see Table 11.3). Care should be taken that any edge between the track and the turf be smooth and even.

Backstop

The backstop is a key element of a field for safeguarding the players and spectators. The basic purposes of backstop include 1) keeping the ball within the playing area, 2) protecting the spectator, 3) safeguarding others involved in the game (e.g., batters in the on-deck circle, bat persons), and 4) protecting nearby activities from conflict with pop-ups (e.g., adjacent ball fields, concessions areas, rest-rooms, parking areas).

When designing the backstop, the planners should consider the following: 1) using small mesh to discourage people from climbing the structure; 2) ensuring the parking and traffic areas are not close; 3) installing a double mesh to prevent fingers, faces, and other body parts of spectators from being crushed by errant balls or thrown bats; 4) keeping the mesh free from any barbs or penetrating parts to ensure safety for players and spectators; 5) ensuring the distance between home plate and the backstop is not less than 25 feet but preferably 60 feet to ensure player safety; 6) using ground materials of either turf with an appropriate warning track composed of clay or crushed granite (M-10) or crushed brick, or no turf with either clay or crushed granite (M-10) or crushed brick; and 7) ensuring the height of the backstop is at least 18 feet, preferably 20 feet, with a four- to six-foot overhang at the top with a 45-degree angle.

The most frequently used backstop consists of three 12-feet wide panels that are 18 to 20 feet high covered with a 1 1/2-inch galvanized wire mesh material. These panels can be made of steel, aluminum, or wood. One panel is placed directly behind home plate and the other two on each side flaring at 30 degrees with the center panel. The fencing on either side of the side panels should gradually taper down to eight feet behind the players' bench area to provide greater protection for the spectators in bleachers on the other side of the fence. The top of the backstop will have three panels, four to six feet by 12 feet, attached to the upright panels and positioned at a 45-degree angle to contain errant balls. This overhang will be covered with the same material as the uprights.

Players' Bench Area

There are two types of players' bench areas commonly constructed for baseball and softball. These areas are the dugouts and field-level shelters. The safer of the two is the dugout, but it is also the most expensive to construct. The dugout is usually four feet deep, constructed of poured concrete and concrete blocks with drains to remove water quickly. It has an elevated players' bench area, entrance to locker rooms (if in a stadium complex), drinking fountain, communication system, bat rack, other storage space, lights, and electrical outlets. Recently, to better safeguard the players, either shatter-proof plastic or wire mesh has been installed to repel errant balls and bats. The roof is constructed so as to discourage people from sitting or climbing on it.

The field-level shelter is at field level with a poured concrete floor and concrete block walls. It has a wire mesh fence at least six feet high to repel errant balls or bats. The space should have a bat rack, communication system, a drinking fountain, additional storage, lights, and electrical outlets. The roof should be constructed to discourage sitting and climbing.

Batting Cage

The batting cage should be located outside the fenced playing field. It should be constructed of steel, aluminum, or wood. The minimum size for one batter should be 10 feet wide, 100 feet long, and 10 feet high. If more than one batter is going to be hitting, then the cage needs to be wider

Table 11.3
Recommended Warning Track Dimensions

Distance from Home Plate to Backstop (a)	Recommended Warning Track Width	
	Foul Territory (b)	Outfield Fence
25 ft	8 ft	12 ft
30 ft	10 ft	12 ft
40 ft	12 ft	15 ft
50 ft	15 ft	15 ft
60 ft	15 ft	15 ft

(a)   The distance from the foul lines to the dugout is the same.
(b)   Includes backstop fence and foul line fence.

Puhalla, J., Krans, J., & Goatley, M. (2003). *Baseball and softball fields*. Hoboken, NJ: J.W. Wiley, 18.

(i.e., 10 feet wider for each batter) with a separating mesh curtain. The space must be completely covered by mesh netting to protect other players and spectators. There needs to be a source of electricity and numerous GFI electrical outlets. The floor surface should be similar to home plate for the batters and natural mounds for the pitchers.

Bullpen

The bullpens should be located either down the first- and third-base lines into the outfield area or in right and left center fields. These areas should be protected from errant balls and the spectators. The area behind the catcher should have a protective fence to protect the spectators. The pitching mounds should be exact replicas of the actual playing field mound. There should also be a home plate area. Finally, there should be benches available for the players.

Photo by Tom Sawyer

Photo by Tom Sawyer

Field Size

The area required for a baseball or softball field will vary from 260 to 460 feet, depending on the level of play anticipated. Since baseball and softball are now often scheduled on the same fields, the age group and type of activity govern the field size. It is recommended that if multiple age groups are to play on a field, it should be sized for the optimum use. Many fields have been planned for a size for high school play, only to have young adults scheduled for the same field. This creates numerous incidents with players colliding with obstacles or other players. Ideally, if funding is available, there should be separate facilities for the various age groups.

It is common to see multifield complexes for baseball, softball, and combination baseball and softball. The most common multifield complex contains four fields. If one were to view the complex from an airplane, it would resemble a wheel with four spokes coming from a central hub.

The central hub (See Figure 11.1) would contain a two-story building with each side facing a different backstop and field. The first floor would contain a concession area, restrooms, storage for game and maintenance equipment, and a first-aid space. The second floor would have four large screened windows, four scorer tables, four scoreboard controls, a communication center, and field light controls. The pathways leading to the various fields would contain either crushed granite (M-10) or crushed brick. The parking area would be located at least 100 yards from the nearest outfield fence. All fields would be lighted.

Field Hockey, Football, Lacrosse, Rugby, and Soccer Fields

Fields for field hockey, football, lacrosse, rugby, and soccer have a number of common requirements. For example, a drinking fountain should be available for each team to use near the team benches. A utility structure should be placed at midfield, set back from the field 25 feet, to store equipment and house the scorer and controls for the field lights and score board. Shade must be available for the teams at halftime, preferably from a deciduous tree grove at either end or side of the field and about 25 yards away from the playing field.

Field Hockey

This sport needs sleeves in the ground for corner flags and goal posts. The actual field dimensions are similar to those in Appendix A. Official rulebooks can be purchased from the NCAA or National Association for Girls and Women in Sport (NAGWS); rules are revised annually.

Football

There should be sleeves in the ground for the end zone flags. The goal posts (usually a single pole with uprights) need to be centered and secured at the end line. Actual field dimensions are similar to the ones in Appendix A. Official rulebooks can be purchased from the NCAA; rules are revised annually. Planners should review carefully the ASTM publication *Safety in Football*.

Lacrosse

There should be sleeves in the ground to hold the goals. Actual field dimensions are similar to the ones in Appendix A. Official rulebooks can be purchased from the NCAA or NAGWS; rules are revised annually.

Rugby

There should be sleeves in the ground for the end flags and the goal posts. Actual field dimensions are similar to the ones in Appendix A. Official rulebooks can be purchased from the United States Rugby Association; rules are revised annually.

Soccer

Sleeves in the ground are needed for the flags for the corner kick area, substitute area, and the goal posts on the end line. Tie-down hooks should be inserted at least one foot into the ground for securing the nets to the ground. There should be a drinking fountain available for each team to use near the team benches. Actual field dimensions are similar to the ones in Appendix A. Official rulebooks can be purchased from the NCAA; rules are revised annually.

Planning Checklist for Fields

The following is a checklist to be used by field planners when designing field spaces:

- Define the use of the field complex (i.e., single- or multiple-sport users; youth, adolescent, or adult; amateur or professional).
- Pay careful attention to slope on fields to encourage proper and adequate pitch for drainage.
- Ensure sub-drainage requirements are met, the type as well as placement of drainage outlets is well out of the playing area, and swales are beyond safety or buffer zones.
- Make sure fences on the perimeter are offset beyond safety or buffer zones. The height of the fence should be consistent with the ASTM standard (i.e., at least eight feet) for the type of activity. Fences should be flexible, resilient, and padded. Further, ensure that fences are placed in front of players (i.e., dugouts and field-level shelters) and spectators. The fence should be sturdy enough to attach a wind screen or sunscreen. Finally, the mesh on the fences should be of a size to discourage climbing and the top should have knuckled mesh.
- Provide gates for security and for service of different practice areas and game areas.
- Design warning tracks to provide advanced warning of perimeter barriers and ensure they are wide enough and of appropriate material to meet ASTM standards.
- Ensure that light poles, fence poles, and foul poles are not in the field of play and are padded.
- Plan that mowing or maintenance strips along fences are provided so they are not hazardous.
- Place all shrubs and tree plantings well outside the playing area.
- Ensure that the turf (artificial or natural) is suitable for different weather conditions (i.e., hot, cold, dry, or wet).
- Install the scoreboard well outside the playing area and its fence line.
- Design the irrigation system so that it will not interfere with play and that all valves, distribution boxes, and other fixtures are well outside the field of play.
- Make sure that vehicular and pedestrian traffic-flow patterns prevent conflict and interference, and that bike and vehicle parking is marked and controlled.
- Ensure that emergency call stations are placed at strategic locations and emergency vehicle access is available for immediate response to all areas.
- Plan the field area so that hazards are not nearby (e.g., major highways, railroad tracks, waterways, culverts, ravines, industries, woods, uncut roughs, and utility lines).
- Create the field area so that security vehicles have easy access and surveillance during game time as well as other times.
- Understand the importance of field orientation relative to the movement of the sun and prevailing wind patterns.
- Configure spectator seating to ensure the best viewing of the game as well as easy access and exit.
- Ensure each activity space has the appropriate safety or buffer zones.
- Review the plan to ensure that the field dimensions are accurate and meet the specified association rules for the level of play.
- Configure all field spaces to include metal sleeves for goalpost, goals, and flags.
- Encourage the owners to ensure that regular maintenance and inspections are done to elimi-

nate ruts, ridges, and depressions in the fields after use; remove debris and rocks from the playing area as well as safety zones; ensure all hooks on goalposts, foul line posts, and fencing are recessed; eliminate all sharp edges on posts, rails, and welds; and make sure benches, seats, and bleachers are protected by screening or barriers.

- Create backstops that protect players, spectators, and other game personnel from injury from errant balls or bats.

BLEACHERS

Michael G. Hypes, Morehead State University

Bleachers and grandstands are part of almost every sports facility. It has been estimated that there are approximately 60,000 facilities with bleachers in the United States. This number includes school facilities, sports facilities, state and local parks, and fitness and recreation centers. Providing safe bleachers and grandstands has prompted the passage of the Minnesota Bleacher Safety Act and the development of the Consumer Product Safety Commission's (CPSC) Guidelines for Retro-fitting Bleachers.

Type of Bleachers

Bleachers are structures designed to provide tiered or stepped seating and are available in various sizes and configurations. The bleacher system normally consists of a series of seat boards and footboards, generally without any type of backrest. A grandstand is nothing more than a bleacher with a roof attached. The type and number of bleacher components are dependent upon the activity, space requirements, number of spectators, and available financial resources. Bleachers can be classified into one of four basic categories:

- permanent or stationary bleachers
- portable or movable bleacher
- telescopic or folding bleachers
- temporary bleachers

Permanent or stationary bleachers are typically large units that will remain in the same location for the life of the facility. Permanent bleachers can be made of metal or concrete and are usually secured to the ground by an anchor.

If they are made of metal, exposure to the sun can create extremely hot conditions, which could cause burns.

Portable bleachers are usually smaller units and are constructed of lightweight materials. Such bleachers will have skids or a wheel system that makes them easy to relocate from one site to another.

Telescopic bleachers are typically found in gymnasiums where space is at a minimum. These bleachers can either be pushed in or pulled out for spectator seating. When closed, this type of system

Photo by Tom Sawyer

takes up relatively little space and can function as a divider.

Temporary bleachers are typically stored in pieces or sections and then constructed together for use during special events (e.g., golf tournaments, parades, circuses, inaugurations). After the event, the bleachers are then disassembled and stored until needed the next time.

Bleacher Components

As mentioned above, a bleacher system has some common elements. These common elements include

- footboards
- seat boards
- risers
- guardrails railings

Photo by Tom Sawyer

Bleachers usually come in four- to 52-row systems. Local and state building codes should be consulted when planning bleachers. Table 12.1 provides generalized seating capacity for various types of bleachers. Telescopic or pull-out bleachers should have a wheel or channel system to prevent damage to the floor surface. In addition, these systems are best utilized if they are automated. Electrical systems allow the telescopic bleachers to open or close with the turn of a key. This type of system allows the user to open entirely or partially a section of bleachers without having the section get out of line or damaged. With any mechanical system, a manual override is suggested. For bleachers already installed that do not have an automated system, there is equipment (such as a portable power system) that is easily handled for convenient movement of bleachers.

Rails are used as a safety feature. They provide security while entering or exiting the bleachers. There are a variety of styles that will minimize the exposure to injury. Folding rails are ideal for recessed areas and other obstacles. Rails should be lightweight for easy setup and takedown, yet strong enough to provide adequate support. Guardrails should extend 42 inches above the lowest surface of the leading edge of the bleacher component (i.e., footboard, seat board, or aisle). Risers and footboards are typically aluminum and should be weather resistant for outdoor use. Seat boards can be aluminum or vinyl-covered metal. Indoor bleachers may have risers, footboards, and seat boards made of wood. It is desirable to mark the edges of treads so that they can be distinguished.

When planning bleachers, it is important to consider any gaps or openings that will be in the final product. Any opening between the components in the seating, such as between the footboard, seat board, and riser, should prevent passage of a four-inch sphere where the footboard is 30 inches or more above the ground and where the opening would permit a fall of 30 inches or more.

Photo by Tom Sawyer

The power or automated system:

- provides the ability to open and close bleacher systems quickly and correctly,
- omits and/or reduces maintenance costs,
- solves the problem of broken board ends from manual operation,
- adds stability to the gym bleachers by attaching all sections together to operate as one system,
- omits manual operation by unauthorized personnel, and
- reduces liability exposure on your gym bleacher equipment.

Codes and Regulations

There are several agencies/organizations that have developed codes and/or standards for the construction of bleachers. These organizations include:

- International Building Code (IBC) of the International Code Council (ICC)

Photo by Tom Sawyer

Photo by Tom Sawyer

- National Building Code (NBC) of the Building Officials and Code Administrators (BOCA)
- Standard Building Code (SBC) of the Southern Building Code Congress International (SBCCI)
- Uniform Building Code (UBC) of the International Conference of Building Officials (ICBO)
- National Fire Protection Association (NFPA)

Table 12.2 provides a summary of current industry codes and standard requirements for guardrails and openings in bleachers. In addition, state and local codes adopt and modify these codes to develop policy for constructing new bleachers. The local building inspector

Table 12.1
Sample Number of Bleacher Seats Based on Length and Number of Rows

Length in Feet	4 Rows	7 Rows	10 Rows	13 Rows	16 Rows
18	48	84	120	156	192
36	96	168	240	312	384
54	104	252	360	468	676
72	192	336	480	624	768
90	240	420	600	780	960
108	288	504	720	936	1,152
126	336	588	840	1,092	1,344
144	384	672	960	1,248	1,536
162	432	756	1,080	1,404	1,728
180	480	840	1,200	1,560	1,920
198	528	924	1,320	1,716	2,112
216	576	1,008	1,440	1,872	2,304
234	624	1,092	1,560	2,028	2,496
252	672	1,176	1,680	2,184	2,688
270	720	1,260	1,800	2,340	2,880
288	768	1,344	1,920	2,496	3,072
306	816	1,428	2,040	2,652	3,264

Length in Feet	19 Rows	22 Rows	25 Rows	28 Rows	31 Rows
18	228				
36	456				
54	684	792	900		1,008
72	912	1,056	1,200	1,344	1,488
90	1,140	1,320	1,500	1,680	1,860
108	1,386	1,584	1,800	2,016	2,232
126	1,596	1,848	2,100	2,352	2,604
144	1,824	2,112	2,400	2,688	2,976
162	2,052	2,376	2,700	3,024	3,348
180	2,280	2,649	3,000	3,360	3,720
198	2,508	2,904	3,300	3,696	4,092
216	2,736	3,168	3,600	4,032	4,464
234	2,964	3,432	3,900	4,368	4,836
252	3,192	3,696	4,200	4,704	5,208
270	3,420	3,960	4,500	5,040	5,580
288	3,648	4,224	4,800	5,376	5,952
306	3,876	4,488	5,100	5,712	6,324

Table 12.2
Overview of Code and Standard Requirements

2000 International Building Code (IBC) of the International Code Council (ICC)

Guardrails
- Required on open sides more than 30 inches above grade.
- Guardrails must be at least 42 inches high, vertically measured from leading edge.
- Guardrails shall have balusters to prevent passage of four-inch sphere through any opening up to a height of 34 inches.
- From a height of 34 to 42 inches, should prevent passage of an eight-inch sphere.

Openings
- Where footboards are more than 30 inches above grade, openings between seat and footboard shall not allow passage of a sphere greater than four inches.
- Horizontal gaps shall not exceed .25 inch between footboards and seatboards.
- At aisles, horizontal gaps shall not exceed .25 inch between footboards.

1999 National Building Code (NBC) of the Building Officials and Code Administrators (BOCA)

Guardrails
- Required along open-sided surfaces located more than 15.5 inches above grade.
- Guardrails should be at least 42 inches in height measured vertically above leading edge.
- Open guardrails shall have balusters of solid material that prevents passage of four-inch sphere through any opening.
- Guardrails shall not have an ornamental pattern that would have a ladder effect.

Openings
- Openings between footboards and seat boards should prevent passage of four-inch sphere when openings are located more than 30 inches above grade.
- Horizontal gaps between footboards and seat boards shall not exceed .25 inches.

1997 Standard Building Code (SBC) of the Southern Building Code Congress International (SBCCI)

Guardrails
- Located along open-sided walking surfaces and elevated seating facilities that are located more than 30 inches above grade.
- Guardrails shall not be less than 42 inches vertically from leading edge.
- Open guardrails shall have intermediate rails or ornamental pattern to prevent passage of four-inch sphere through any opening.

Openings
- There shall be no horizontal gaps exceeding .25 inch between footboards and seat boards.
- At aisles, no horizontal gaps should exceed .25 inch between footboards.

1997 Uniform Building Code (UBC) of the International Conference of Building Officials (ICBO)

Guardrails
- Perimeter guardrails shall be provided for all portions of elevated seating more than 30 inches above grade.
- Guardrails shall be 42 inches above the rear of a seatboard or 42 inches above the rear of the steps in an aisle.
- Open guardrails shall have intermediate rails or ornamental pattern to prevent passage of a four-inch sphere.

Continued

Table 12.2 cont.
Overview of Code and Standard Requirements

Openings
- The open vertical space between footboards and seats shall not exceed nine inches when footboards are more than 30 inches above grade.

2000 National Fire Protection Association (NFPA) 101 Life Safety Code
Guardrails (applies to both new construction and existing installations)
- Guardrails are required on open sides more than 48 inches above adjacent ground.
- Guardrails must be at least 42 inches above the aisle or footboard or at least 36 inches above the seat board.
- Guardrail is exempted where an adjacent wall or fence affords an equivalent safeguard.
- Openings in guardrails cannot allow passage of four-inch diameter sphere.

Openings (applies to both new construction and existing installations)
- Vertical openings between footboards and seat boards cannot allow passage of four-inch diameter sphere where footboards are more than 30 inches above grade.
- Openings in footboards cannot allow passage of .5-inch diameter sphere.

Inspections (existing installations)
- Annual inspection and maintenance of bleacher/grandstand or folding/telescopic seating required to be provided by owner to ensure safe conditions.
- Biennially, the inspection is to be performed by a professional engineer, registered architect, or individual certified by the manufacturer.
- Owner required to provide certification that such inspection has been performed as required by authority having jurisdiction.

Modified from U.S. Consumer Product Safety Commission, Guidelines for Retrofitting Bleachers.

Photo by Tom Sawyer

should be consulted early in the planning phase to avoid expensive and time-consuming errors in the construction of a bleacher system.

2001 Minnesota Building Codes and Standards Division Requirements

States (such as Minnesota) develop their own policies regarding construction. The Minnesota Building Codes and Standards Division reviewed the Uniform Building Code, International Building Code, and the National Fire Protection Association Life Safety Code in developing Policy PR-04 (3/00). Under Minnesota law, reviewing stands, grandstands, bleachers, and folding/telescopic seating, whether indoors or out, must be designed, constructed, and installed in accordance with the applicable provisions contained in the Minnesota State Building Code (Minnesota, 2001).

This policy addresses the following areas of concern with regard to bleachers and grandstands:

- press box construction
- number of seats to an aisle
- required plumbing fixtures
- aisle width

- accessibility
- foundations
- use of space below bleachers/grandstands

Press Box Construction

According to UBC Section 303.2.2.3, combustible non-rated A-4 occupancies are limited to a height of 20 feet above grade. Except for the press box located on top of most school grandstands serving ball fields, most grandstands are built of noncombustible construction. These noncombustible bleacher structures are permitted to be at least 40 feet in height. However, press boxes are typically built with combustible construction materials (wood framing). This results in classifying the entire structure as combustible, and, therefore, severely limiting the maximum permitted height of noncombustible grandstands with combustible press boxes to 20 feet (Minnesota, 2001). Minnesota derived the following alternative to part of UBC Section 303.2.2.3. Press boxes located atop open-air bleachers may be built of combustible construction as long as other components of the bleacher system are of noncombustible construction.

Number of Seats to an Aisle

Prior to the 1997 edition of the *Uniform Building Code*, the number of seats without backrests between any seat and an aisle could not be greater than 20, for a total of 42 seats in a row with aisles at each end. In general, this is what the bleacher seating industry has used as a standard for the manufacture of their products for years. Now both the 1997 UBC and 2000 IBC only permit a maximum of 14 seats per row with the typical 12-inch wide aisle accessway. In contrast, for indoor bleachers the 1997 UBC permits nine seats between any seat and an aisle, for a total of 20 seats in a row. This is less restrictive than that permitted outdoors. The maximum number of seats permitted between furthest seat and an aisle in bleachers is 20 in outdoor bleacher seating (Minnesota, 2001).

Required Plumbing Fixtures

Minimum numbers of water closets and lavatories are to be provided for all buildings and structures including exterior assembly areas, such as bleachers and grandstands. The Standards Division recognizes either of the following to satisfy this requirement:

- permanent fixtures located either on site or available in an adjacent building
- portable temporary fixtures that are available on site when the bleachers are in use

The use of portable fixtures as acceptable modifications is based on the concept that outdoor bleachers are seasonal in nature. Lastly, the ratio of water closets for women to the total of water closets and urinals provided for men must be at least 3:2 in accordance with the Minnesota Building Code (1300.3900).

Aisle Width

The Standards Division identified two methods for determining aisle width. Method A identifies that aisles are not required to be more than 66 inches in width, nor does one have to be considered a dead-end aisle when the following are satisfied:

- The seating is composed entirely of bleachers.
- The row-to-row dimension is 28 inches or less.
- Front egress is not limited.

Method B is based on IBC Section 1008.5.3. The clear width in inches of aisles shall be not less than the total occupant load served by the egress element multiplied by 0.08 where egress is by aisles and/or stairs. The multiplier is 0.06 where egress is by ramps, tunnels, corridors or vomitories (Minnesota, 2001).

Accessibility

Bleacher seating structures complying with the Minnesota Accessibility Code require:

- Access—Exterior access to elevated seating areas in exterior bleachers must be accessible by a route having a slope not exceeding one in 20 and a width not less than 48 inches.
- Wheelchair locations are to be provided in the number and location required.
- Alterations to an existing area containing a primary function will not apply if alterations to existing bleacher seating facilities only address compliance with the Minnesota Bleacher Safety Act (Minnesota, 2001).

Foundations

"A foundation plan must be prepared by a Minnesota Licensed Engineer for all open-air bleacher and grandstand facilities. This does not apply to 'portable' bleachers of five rows or less" (Minnesota, 2001).

Use of Space Below Bleachers or Grandstands

Spaces under a grandstand or bleacher shall be kept free of flammable or combustible material. Storage is permitted under bleachers, provided it is separated with fire-resistive construction (Minnesota, 2001).

U.S. Consumer Product Safety Commission Guidelines

The U.S. Consumer Product Safety Commission (CPSC) has developed Guidelines for Retrofitting Bleachers as a result of a petition by Representatives Luther and Ramstad of Minnesota in 1999. This petition led to the adoption of the first bleacher safety law at the state level. A summary of the CPSC's retrofit recommendations is found in Table 12.3.

Table 12.3
Summary of Retrofit Recommendations

- Guardrails should be present on the backs and portions of the open ends of bleachers where the footboard, seat board, or aisle is 30 inches or more above the floor or ground below.
- The top surface of the guardrail should be at least 42 inches above the leading edge of the footboard, seat board, or aisle, whichever is adjacent.
- When bleachers are used adjacent to a wall that is as high as the recommended guardrail height, the guardrail is not needed if a four-inch diameter sphere fails to pass between the bleachers and the wall.
- Any opening between components of the guardrail should prevent passage of a four-inch sphere.
- Any opening between the components in the seating should prevent passage of a four-inch sphere where the footboard is 30 inches or more above the ground.
- The preferable guardrail design uses only vertical members as in-fill between the top and bottom rails. Openings in the in-fill should be limited to a maximum of 1.75 inches. If chain-link fencing is used on guardrails, it should have a mesh size of 1.25-inch square or less.
- Aisles, handrails, nonskid surfaces, and other items that assist in access and egress on bleachers should be incorporated into any retrofit project where feasible.
- The option of replacing as opposed to retrofitting should be considered.
- Retrofitting materials and methods should prevent the introduction of new hazards, such as bleacher tip-over, bleacher collapse, guardrail collapse, or contact/tripping hazards.
- Bleachers should be thoroughly inspected at least quarterly by trained personnel and problems should be corrected immediately. Maintain records of these actions.
- Bleachers should be inspected at least every two years and written certification should be obtained that the bleachers are fit for use. A licensed professional engineer, registered architect, or company that is qualified to provide bleacher products and services should conduct inspections.
- Keep records of all incidents and injuries.

Modified from U.S. Consumer Product Safety Commission, Guidelines for Retrofitting Bleachers.

SECTION III

RECREATIONAL SPACES

AQUATIC FACILITIES 13

Leland Yarger, Ball State University
Steven Dalcher, Ball State University

Strong human interest in aquatic-related facilities is often traced back to the Roman Empire. In the Roman society, aquatic recreation and therapy were frequent and popular pastimes. The Romans developed specialized aquatic facilities for both hot and cold water therapy and were the first documented cases of a plumbed water supply for the population. Plato regarded anyone unable to swim to be "uneducated." The Greeks dismissed people who did not know how to swim (AI 2003, July/Aug.).

The first city pool in the United States was established in 1887 at Brookline, Massachusetts (*Swimming Pools*, 1987 Human Kinetics). The early pools were referred to as "baths." These early public pools were simply filled with water and periodically drained. The baths were not sanitized or filtered as now required. Today, the professional aquatic community does exceptional work in maintaining water quality and keeping the water safe. Disease transmission is rare in the properly planned, designed, and managed aquatic facility.

In this chapter, we discuss a brief history of aquatic facilities and how planning, construction, and operations specifically affect aquatic facility design. There is a collection of aquatic books identified throughout this chapter that provides additional information. As with any profession, this text is just one of the many resources that the supervisors of aquatic assets must utilize. This chapter will enhance the manager's ability to limit personal and organizational liability, create a cost effective facility, and keep patrons and staff safe.

History and Trends

From the late 1800s to the early 1950s, pools gained popularity so that by the end of this period, there were approximately 184,200 pools in the United States of America (AI 2003, July Aug.). In the 1920s, this country saw a surge in aquatic recreation activities and the use of naturally occurring springs as resort spas. These resort spas were widely visited and renowned. Like the early baths, the spas were not sanitized and did not have a process of mechanical water exchange. Subsequently, there were health issues and cases of disease transmission. Once the Great Depression hit, like other areas of society, most of these American resorts went into financial ruin.

Years after the Great Depression, growth in swimming and pools continued. After World War II, there was an industrial boom in the United States. This boom in growth was not limited to industry, substantial increases in public pool construction happened as well. The standard swimming pool, both in residential and public facilities, was the typical "box" of water. These boxes of water were typically rectangular shaped, shallow, and three feet deep to about 10 foot deep in the pool basin. Pool decks were generally small and recreational activities sparse. Pools were a place to simply cool off or swim laps. In 1975, the White House added a swimming pool; similar to many locations today, aquatic facilities represent status of well-to-do communities and families (AI 2003, July Aug.).

Many of the standard "box" pools are still in use today at community centers, YMCAs, YWCAs, parks and recreation departments, in schools and universities. These pools are of significant note because they are nearing the end of their useful life, and in many cases have become maintenance nightmares for the owners. These early pools had 50-year life expectancies; often, new construction companies will only plan to build for a 20-year life expectancy for aquatic facilities. Considering the capital expense involved, this short-sighted planning is foolhardy.

As more was learned about the potential for disease transmission in pool water, the practice of unfiltered swimming pools gave way to chemically treating and mechanically filtering the swimming pool to clean the water. Proper planning, design, and management currently includes understanding the demands placed upon the facilities water and insuring that filtration, sanitation, and monitoring happen 24/7.

Generally, pool water is extremely safe; take a moment to reflect upon other bodies of water like oceans, lakes, rivers, and ponds that people enjoy. Consider all of the creatures that live in and around these waters. The children's book *Everybody Poops* comes to mind when the authors think about water quality in these locations. Rarely, we hear of massive outbreaks of sickness or even death in these waters. Because we do not control the open bodies of water the way that we can control the water in pool basins, this simple fact goes unnoticed. Pool water should meet higher standards for obvious reasons; however, pool management frequently is poorly understood and often overlooked, especially in seasonal community pools. Consider the fact that water venues are visited about 360 million times per year. During an 18-year period, the Centers for Disease Control (CDC) reports that the most common Recreational Water Illnesses (RWI) resulted in 19,000 people becoming ill. This equates to one illness in 341,232 visits (*Journal of Environmental Health*, 2006).

In recent years, swimming has consistently ranked second only to fitness walking as the most attended physical activity / sport according to the National Sporting Goods Association (http://www.nsga.org/i4a/pages/index.cfm?pageid=3346). With the high volume of people seeking water relief and recreation, aquatic facilities must ensure that sanitation of their facilities is consistently at the highest level. The implications for unkempt facilities due to poor design or management can be costly to owners and operators. Health depart-

ments are the common enforcement group that inspect and investigate facilities and water quality.

In the late 1970s, theme parks joined in on water attractions starting the waterpark craze. These facilities had high-energy water rides and attractions that drew patrons from hundreds of miles. The water parks created a new vacation activity, and some waterparks can take many days to experience all of the attractions. Water parks are popular today, and the parks are creating new attractions that even defy gravity; uphill water slides have gained popularity recently. During the period from 2000 to 2006, the research shows that the indoor waterpark industry grew eightfold (Inter, F. (Fall 2007) Waterpark resorts today).

In the 1990s, municipalities, hotels, and smaller organizations with pools have decided to cash in on the theme-style water attractions. The potential revenue from providing mini-vacations to regional residents has become very popular. Aquatic facilities in some locales have morphed into mini-waterparks/leisure facilities that boast multiple smaller attractions. Instead of the five-story-tall water-park water slide, smaller versions of these types of slides are placed indoors. Some slides have music and visual displays in the slides to further entertain riders. This trend is still growing today, and planners have limitless ideas for rides and interactive structures.

There are in excess of 6.6 million pools in the United States today (AI 2003, July/Aug.). Granted, many of the pools are at residential properties. Public pools are under more pressure to provide recreational, educational, and athletic opportunities to offset operational costs. As such, aquatic professionals are hired to manage public facilities to help reduce risks to the organization. Organizations that have had serious incidents understand that significant financial and human losses are possible due to negligence. The aquatic professional must be involved with the aquatic facility design and policy development. Aquatic operations have specific education and certifications requirements. A professional with this knowledge can provide an aquatic facility growth in a safe and successful process.

Planning

What Kind of Facility?

The first step is to decide what you wish to use the facility for. What services and programs do you intend to offer? What staff training must be conducted at the facility? All of these questions must be understood and answered prior to the facility design process.

Today, across the nation, we find aquatic facilities that represent a whole range of assets. Examples of typical indoor and outdoor traditional pools as defined earlier in this chapter, water theme parks, splash pads, wave pools, flumes / water

Children enjoying leisure pool activities.

treadmills, water slides, rehabilitation pools, spas/ hot tubs, water playgrounds, diving wells, Olympic style competition facilities, simulated waterfronts, wave/surf machines, lazy rivers, rapids, water rides similar to roller coasters, and a variety of interactive attractions based around water attractions.

Always remember that the facility's ability to be functional must always precede its looks. Often, architects come up with very unique designs for facilities to become area landmarks. That is great as long as the facility can serve the organizational mission.

Of course, a major question is choosing an indoor or outdoor facility. This answer depends upon facility use, climate, and obviously the cost to build the facility. Facility types are broken into general groups in the following paragraphs to help you determine what you need and what specific design/operational considerations should be understood.

Competition

Lap Pools

The standard competitive lap pool is designed with a standard length of 25 yards, 25 meters, or 50 meters, depending upon the sanctioning body that you wish to compete in. The sanctioning bodies define pool depth, lane widths, starting block specifications, as well a host of other specifications including lighting, markings, and stanchions to name a few.

Diving Wells

As with competitive pools, diving wells have very specific dimensional requirements set forth by sanctioning bodies. You must also consider bathing code requirements and specialty equipment that often sanctioning bodies do not discuss. These include bubbler systems, rope and harness systems, trampolines, and land-based springboards with crash pits. A bubbler system allows divers in

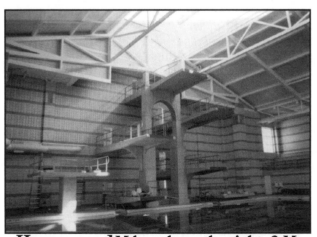

Here we see 1M boards on the right, 3 M boards on the left and 3, 5, 7.5 and 10 M platforms in the center for competitive diving.

training a softer water entry because the bubbles break the waters surface tension. Rope and harness systems allow a diver to be belayed by an assistant to arrest his or her fall over the water, over a trampoline or over a crash pit when the diver attempts new complicated skills during training sessions.

Springboards

Commonly referred to as diving boards, the springboard is common to many facilities and generally is considered safer than a water slide. Not only should bathing codes be reviewed for proper installation, but guidelines produced by the National Collegiate Athletic Association (NCAA), USA swimming and diving, as well as Federal Internationale de Natation (FINA) must be considered. Commonly, 12 feet of water depth is needed under the one-meter diving board, but this is not a mutually exclusive requirement. Many state laws vary from this requirement. The owner must decide what the springboard's purpose will be—high school competition, recreational, instructional, state, or international competition.

Many details for diving boards and diving standards are required to be observed especially for competitive use. A useful text, *Official Swimming Pool Design Compendium* provides regulations from governing competitive bodies that include design drawings (1997).

For springboards, the fulcrum or pivot point should be locked in the full forward position during recreation use times. The fulcrum provides trained divers the ability to generate great amounts of lift when they press the board during the approach of the dive. Inexperienced recreation divers can easily hurt themselves by using the springboard with the fulcrum in the rear position.

If a pool is considered that does not have a separate diving well that can maintain a warmer water temperature, a hot tub dedicated for competitive divers should be considered in the facility design.

Competitive swimming and diving pool resources:

Local / State High School Athletic Association, Amateur Athletic Union (AAU), NCAA, USA Swimming, and FINA.

Recreational

The recreational facility's primary focus is on family and individual recreation opportunities. Thirty years ago, this meant open swim, often with one- or two-lap swim lanes. The children would play in the shallow water or off the diving boards while the adults often talked or swam laps.

Today, with the advent of many interactive aquatic assets, the recreational facility can provide attractions for all ages, such as:

- Age-appropriate water playgrounds
- Diving boards

- Water slides
- Bubble benches
- Climbing structures
- Wave pools
- Zero-depth entry pools/simulated beaches
- Surf machines
- Water basketball
- Water volleyball
- Water obstacle/confidence courses
- Water polo
- Various land activities
- Group spas or baths
- Tanning booths
- Individual hot tubs
- Moveable bulkheads
- Moveable floors

Many items on this list require very specific design considerations dealing with additional space and construction depth. The simple ability to make the water temperature comfortable may be a costly challenge.

Special attention should be given to the sanitation and filtration systems of warm water (85 + degrees F.) basins. For example, a typical small hot tub with minimal users has a sanitation load similar to a normal-size pool at maximum capacity. Any hot tub or spa installed for use in aquatic facilities should be specifically designed for commercial use and operation. Failure in oversight here can lead to severe illness and or disease transmission to many patrons.

Recreational facilities are attractive to parks and recreation departments, YMCAs, hotels, resorts, and private clubs. Park departments and hotels are cashing in on the mini-water park concept. Nation wide, mini-water parks provide mini-vacation opportunities with high-excitement attractions like water slides and wave pools. The

This picture shows a typical water playground

following organizations provide guidelines for many of the areas listed in this section.

Recreational pool references: National Swimming Pool Foundation (NSPF), YMCA of the USA, National Recreation and Parks Association (NRPA), National Intramural Recreational Sports Association (NIRSA), Association of Pool & Spa Professionals (APSP)

Health and Fitness

Traditional water fitness is often viewed as simply lap swimming and water exercise. If the primary users are health and fitness clients, the facility may also have large areas of chest-deep water and large deck areas. Both of these areas may have equipment similar to what is found in the traditional land fitness room. There may be multiple workout stations and a staff of personal fitness trainers as well as water aerobic instructors. Depending on the age, flexibility, and health conditions of the clients, things like water depth, water temperature, and the types of pool access fixtures will vary. Arthritic participants generally need stairs or ramps into warm water (88-plus degrees) pools. Newer aquatic fitness facilities sometimes include flumes and water treadmills. The flume allows a relatively small area for the individual to swim in place against a pump-generated current. This allows trainers to evaluate the swimmer's cardio, respiratory, and physical techniques while controlling the speed of the water and thus the swimmer's exertion. The water treadmill (like a land treadmill) is diagnostically similar to the flume in that the water resistance while using the treadmill allows trainers to closely monitor land athletes in a therapeutic warm water environment.

Multipurpose Facilities

Today, the multipurpose aquatic facility allows for a host of recreational, instructional, and athletic activities to take place in the same facility. Sometimes, a variety of activities can even take place at the same time. The purpose of this section is to look specifically at multipurpose aquatic facilities versus the multipurpose recreation center.

Pool temperature and sanitation are the two biggest problems if a one-basin multipurpose facility is considered. The sanitation problem for a single body of water comes primarily from accidental fecal release by a child. The treatment process is lengthy and thus closes the body of water to all patrons. This can literally bring your facility operations to a complete halt. Multiple basins and sanitation systems are a better choice. If there is a fecal accident in one basin, it can be closed and treated while other pools can still be used as long as they have independent sanitation and filtration systems.

Pool temperature on a one-basin multipurpose facility will create the most complaints and safety issues. The water temperature varies dramatically for different programs. For example, recreational swimmers and learn to swim participants enjoy water close to 85 degrees, therapy and rehabilitation patrons use water temperature of 88 + degrees, while competitive swimmers need 77-79 degree water so that they do not experience heat exhaustion.

It is not realistic or cost effective to raise and lower the water temperature for each group using the facility. Separate pool basins are the solutions to these problems. Many facilities also worry about closure due to equipment wear. These facilities often install redundant systems for heating, water circulation, and filtration. This will allow an operator to fix the problem without closing the facility.

This facility will have to close if there is a fecal accident.

There is a growing trend to include recreation aspects into all facilities. This helps to provide new facilities with a multipurpose aspect and hopefully, for the owner's higher usage and revenue opportunities. Current high-excitement trends include stationary wave generators to surf or body board in place, a variety of interactive attractions and play structures, slides of many shapes with the ability to even ascend similar to theme park roller coasters. Some of these high-excitement fixtures require significant floor space, vertical clearance, as well

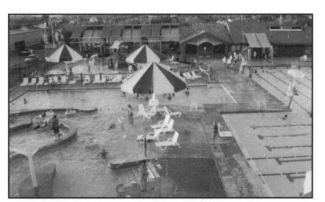

**This is a better design because there are separate basins so the water from one does not go into the other areaas.
A fecal incident will close one but not the entire facility.**

as extra staff. The typical high bather loads may require additional filtration and sanitation system capacity due to state laws. One result of the new facility concepts include mechanical spaces that are far larger than the typical '50s to '70s rectangular pools.

When designing the multipurpose aquatic facility, you must consider organizations and groups that provide guidance in these areas. The ensuing list provides some suggestions for the types of assets considered.

- Water Slides: World Waterpark Association (WWA).
- Hot Tubs/Spas: NSPF, YMCA of the USA, NRPA. Training/education
- Lifeguard Training: ARC, American Safety and Health Institute (ASHI), Ellis & Associates, National Aquatic Safety Company (NASCO), United States Lifesaving Association (USLA), YMCA of the USA.
- Swimming Lessons: ARC, YMCA of the USA, Ellis, Starfish Aquatics.
- Canoe and Kayak: American Canoeing Association (ACA), ARC.
- SCUBA: National Association of Underwater Instructors (NAUI), Professional Association of Diving Instructors (PADI), SCUBA Schools International (SSI), SCUBA Diving Institute (SDI), Handicapped SCUBA Association (HAS), International Association of Nitrox and Technical Divers (IANTD).
- Pool Operations: NRPA Aquatic Facility Operator (AFO), NSPF Certified Pool-Spa Operator (CPO), YMCA Pool Operator On Location (POOL).

There are many documents and texts produced by the groups listed above that should be reviewed for compliance. The depth and scope of the recommendations from these groups is comprehensive and should be given lengthy study.

Instructional

For structured activity classes, it is crucial to understand the training requirements for courses. For some swim instructor classes, there are swim tests with standard pool lengths. The height of participants must also be accounted for; adults generally see shallow water as four feet deep or less. Children in four feet of water may have the water line at their eyes. Anyone standing with the water at their eye level and just learning how to swim will be uncomfortable; therefore, this would be a poor learning environment.

Facilities designed for the educational focus must pay attention to training agency standards and curricular requirements to be fully functional. Agencies that offer certification based programs must comply with the training standards or risk serious liability consequences. Aquatic facilities can offer a host of educational opportunities including:

- Learn to swim (all ages)
- CPR and first aid courses
- Lifeguard training
- Junior lifeguard courses
- Canoeing
- Kayaking
- Competitive swimming
- SCUBA diving
- Springboard or platform diving
- Synchronized swimming
- Water aerobics
- Water survival
- Biomechanics of swimming and diving
- Fitness swimming
- Water Rehab/ / therapy instruction
- Swimming instructor class
- Watercraft safety
- Residential pool safety
- Pool operations / Facility management
- Water Polo

Athletic

Many of the educational activities offered above translate into athletic opportunities. Competitive swimming opportunities from youth age group swim and diving teams, Masters teams, to high school and collegiate swim teams. Depending upon local demand, synchronized swimming and water polo provide additional athletic opportunities.

Figure 13.1
Bulkhead Design

Legal Considerations

Federal Law

Recently, a new federal law, titled the Virginia Graeme Baker Pool and Spa Safety Act, (H.R. 6-303 to 309, Title XIV – Pool and Spa Safety) passed. This law impacts existing and new aquatic facilities. The law requires that all public pools must have a main drain cover that complies with ASME/ANSI A112.19.8 (Robledo & Kozen, 2008). The intention of this law is to prevent entrapment of body parts by the suction created by circulation or feature pumps. This is the first federal law of its kind that specifically addresses design and operational safety for aquatic facilities. Past cases of entrapment have included drowning by the suction holding persons underwater and evisceration from the suction forces created.

Basin Accessibility

Compliance with **Americans with Disabilities Act** (ADA) *Accessibility Guidelines* is recognized at non-aquatic facilities but frequently overlooked at aquatic facilities in the early stages of planning. ADA requirements are enforced through the Department of Justice (DOJ). Most construction codes for pools require, at a minimum, vertical pool ladders to enter and exit the pools, these do not meet accessibility guidelines. These vertical ladders are not user friendly to many pool participants. If your facility has an older population, heavier weight population, arthritic participants, physical disabilities, or the very young, consider some of these alternatives:

Stairs: Stairs into pools are probably the most common accessible entry fixtures and have been built into basins during the last 20 years. Stairs must have handrails, and the step surfaces must be slip resistant with one-inch tile or other non-slip surfaces.

Transfer Tiers: The use of transfer tiers can help many participants in wheelchairs enter the pool by themselves or with minimal assistance. A transfer tier is simply a seat or high fixed step that a participant can roll up to on the deck next to the side of the pool. When the participant is seated in his chair, he can slide over onto the tier and swing his legs into the waters edge from the tier.

Zero-depth entry: The typical gradual beachfront entry closely resembles the zero-depth entry pool. The typical depth change at the zero depth entry point is one-inch depth for every 12 to 20 inches of distance. Some state codes specify the minimum change in depth for zero-depth entry points.

Ramps: Portable and fixed pool ramps may also enhance accessibility and provide new freedom to participants with limited mobility.

Lift Chairs: Both fixed and portable lift chairs can provide access to the pool basin and often require manual, hydraulic, or electrical input for operations.

State and Local Law

Most states have some construction code that is required for swimming facilities. Again, the aquatic professional will provide valuable insight for planning to meet the state construction requirements. Along with construction code, most states have some type of bathing or operational code for public pools. These laws mandate everything from lighting requirements to staff required at the facility.

Specific examples of state operational requirements that affect the design and operation of aquatic facilities include:

- Indiana specifies that one lifeguard is required for each public pool that has a pool surface area that exceeds 2,000 square feet. Additionally, there must be one lifeguard on duty for every 75 people and additional guards for each additional 75 bathers (IAC 410).
- Florida specifies that a certified pool operator must be on duty whenever the pool is open (FDOH, Chapter 64E-9).

If the state has no requirements, then the supervisor must rely on other codes, industry standards, and recommendations. Additional codes include county and municipal requirements that are often more rigorous than state codes. Other standards often come from building construction codes and requirements from a variety of groups that include but are not limited to American National Standards Institute (ANSI), American Society of Mechanical Engineers (ASME), American Society for Testing and Materials (ASTM), National Fire Protection Association (NFPA), National Electrical Code (NEC), National Science Foundation (NSF), and Underwriters Laboratories (UL). Recommendations also come from a variety of sources like the APSP, NSPF, YMCA, Centers for Disease Control (CDC), Consumer Product Safety Commission (CPSC), ARC, and a variety of professional texts. Owners have professional responsibility to follow standards recognized for safe operations of certain types of facilities to protect patrons. If laws in your state do not address professional standards, then refer to texts including, but not limited to *Aquatic Facility Management*, the second edition of *The Complete Swimming Pool Reference*, the *NIRSA Aquatic Directors Handbook*, *Swimming Pools*, *YMCA Aquatic Management*, as well as a variety of pool operations and lifeguard certification texts. This collection of material constitutes knowledge that is commonly referred to as professional standards or practices.

Industry Practice

The aquatic professional will be a great asset in the design and construction phases. Consideration should also be for delays that occur in construction. When construction is delayed for weather or other issues, the aquatic professional can work on the Standard Operating Procedures (SOPs) and Emergency Action Procedures (EAPs). This prior planning is crucial for the opening of any new facility.

Industry practice also refers to common procedures that veteran aquatic professionals have learned over the years that may not be reflected in industry literature. This knowledge and experience is invaluable when setting up a new facility. It may limit the potential for negligence and thus reduce financial losses.

Training agencies for some programs have very specific facility design requirements for certain certification programs. If the facility is built ignoring these facts, it may create an operational nightmare. For example, there are pool depth requirements to train and certify lifeguards by some agencies, such as the American Red Cross (ARC), which requires seven to 10 feet of water depth to retrieve a 10 lb. diving brick during a swim test (ARC 2007). If the facility does not meet these requirements, it may have to go elsewhere to find qualified trained guards instead of training your own staff on site.

Training agencies often have additional mandates that affect staffing at facilities. All major lifeguard training agencies in the United States require that two lifeguards perform spinal injury rescues in the water and also require two persons be utilized for victim removal from the water. A facility planned for one lifeguard only operations will clearly violate this standard and thus creates an unsafe position for the guard and patron care is sacrificed to save a few dollars. A single basin with few swimmers may warrant only one guard actively watching the swimmers, but a second guard must be immediately accessible with a moments notice in an emergency.

Facility owners rarely wish to spend the time learning a new profession, and therefore hire an aquatic professional to understand the legal obligations that the facility should follow to prevent negligent actions or inactions at their facility. Ignorance of laws or professional standards will not protect you from negligence-based lawsuits.

Emergency Management Design Considerations

Designed for Immediate Emergency Care for Patrons

Lifeguards are considered by most training agencies as first responders. As such, the lifeguards need immediate access to the tools that they are trained to provide care with, including automated external defibrillators (AEDs) and emergency oxygen. The facility must be well planned to house these items along with other equipment, so that rapid access can be provided to the victim in need of care. Research tells us that if an AED is utilized for a cardiac victim within the first minute of arrest that there is about an 85% rate of survival (Law-Heitzman 1998). On-scene emergency oxygen is recognized by many training agencies as beneficial to patients for almost every emergency care situation. Emergency oxygen care has a long, confirmed useful history in the SCUBA diving community. In January of 2003, the YMCA of the USA mandated that lifeguards must have emergency oxygen certification prior to being hired at all YMCAs (YMCA of the USA, 2001, 2003). The use of both AEDs and oxygen can significantly aid in the favorable resuscitation of near-drowning victims. AEDs and oxygen both require scheduled maintenance and record keeping. AED batteries and defibrillation pads have expiration dates. Oxygen tanks must be verified each shift as being full and ready to use. AEDs are electronic; operational tests vary from each of the manufacturers. These checks are critical if the units are to be functional when they are needed.

Medical Emergencies

Along with on-scene care, the design team must consider EMS provider access to a patron in need. There must be a point of rapid access to the victim who needs EMS care. Careful planning and

AED and pads on the left and complete oxygen kit including tank, regulator/flow-meter, BVM, non-rebreather mask, and nasal cannula on the right

design can save time that the victim desperately needs for treatment in emergency care. When the facility is being planned, consider dedicated pool area emergency evacuation points. This consideration is generally automatic for fire concerns but often forgotten when it comes to emergency medical care. If a patron has a heart attack, how will you get them to an arriving ambulance quickly? Can the ambulance come to you? What does the local EMS service recommend? What can our staff do on site to enhance victim care? This should be discussed in planning and operational meetings early on.

The most common care provided at aquatic facilities is general first aid. Often, scrapes, cuts, and bruises happen even in well-managed facilities. Therefore, the facility must insure that it has all of the emergency care equipment and supplies the lifeguards are trained to use. A dedicated area or room for these activities can greatly influence patron care and provide some privacy for the injured person.

Fire Emergencies

Aquatic facilities, like other facilities, are required to take into account fire emergencies. The construction and operational codes dictate fire alarms, extinguishers, signage, and exits. Typically the NFPA (National Fire Protection Association) standards guide these codes.

Specific fire concerns that often get overlooked are the specific chemicals to be stored at the facility for water balance and treatment. The chemical rooms should display hazardous material placards that assist first responders in the evacuation and control of chemical related emergencies. It should be noted that some chemicals can react violently with organic materials.

Patron care by facility staff and equipment assets can make the difference between life and death. These considerations must be planned for in the initial design and construction. Proper planning and coordination with the local fire department representatives can enhance the facility response in fire emergencies.

Lightning and Severe Weather Planning

Both indoor and outdoor facilities should consider the risks involved with lightning. The National Lightning Safety Institute says that pools should be cleared for 30 minutes from the sight or sound of lightning. Some state laws are very specific to the legal requirements for the operation of public pools when lightning is in the area. Some codes require pool closure for lightning even at indoor facilities.

There are now lightning predictors available that can alert the facility to atmospheric conditions that are conducive for producing lightning. This investment especially at outdoor facilities can save lives and take the guesswork out of facility closure criteria.

Due to current safety concerns for staff and patrons, a large reinforced interior "safe" room on the first floor or below grade should be considered for the immediate cover for facility users. The safe room may also be useful in the event that a person threatens violence; those seeking a secure location may be able to quickly flee to this location in such an emergency. This room can also double for a training/meeting area or reserved space for events or parties.

Construction Issues

There are many important construction issues for swimming pools, and the requirements often vary from state to state. This section will identify specific issues that are significant to all aquatic facilities.

Preconstruction through Operation

Proper planning and anticipated growth for future needs during the planning phase can greatly reduce costs to expand later or correct preventable problems. The single largest impact for aquatic facility design lies with understanding the operational requirements for the facility. Having the input of an aquatic professional that is looking out for the

This multipurpose indoor facility should be evacuated during severe weather due to the patron exposure from all of the windows.

organizations interests is critical. What you plan to do with the facility once it is completed drives the design and construction. The aquatic professional understands construction and operational codes as well as the industry standards. What appear to simply be management concerns prior to facility construction are in fact paramount to the lawful, successful, and cost-effective operations of the aquatic facility.

Operations that significantly affect annual budgets include staffing, heating, cooling, chemicals, and electrical costs. Poor planning can easily double or triple the expenses of any one or all of

these areas. The aquatic professional should be one of the project managers during the aquatic planning, design, and construction phases to reduce the potential for major problems later. This professional should have experience ranging from programming, operations, and obviously construction of swimming facilities. The initial cost to hire this individual is minimal in the long run. This person should report to your organization and not be tied to the consultants, engineering firm, construction company, or be in any way related to the company building the facility.

Facility Longevity

The new aquatic facility is a substantial investment, and the construction methods should represent a 50-year-plus lifespan for the facility. Contractors who do not plan for these terms should be avoided, or substantial maintenance costs could be realized.

In the planning phase, determine what the organizational goals are for the facility. There may be primary users and then secondary users. After all, you have constant costs, so schedule the facility use as close to 24/7 as possible to get more bang for your operational buck. These constant financial costs include filtration, electrical, chemicals, and heating.

What do you have to have from the facility, and what would you like to have? Can you afford it? Calculate costs and revenue projections, and then maybe the items wanted will increase your revenue to justify them in the main project. Failure to plan for the 50-year lifespan can significantly reduce revenue and lead to added annual expenses due to renovation costs within the first couple of decades.

You must specify exactly what you want in the scope of work for the bidding process. Failure to specifically identify things like basin dimensions and depth can leave you with a facility of limited use. Oversight in this area can limit your programming, create safety hazards, and prohibit you from conducting staff certification training. If you simply plan for next year or the next five years, you will be disappointed with your facility shortly after construction is finished. Never build to minimum standards; seek out preferred standards so that your facility does not become immediately obsolete.

Site Survey

Evaluation of the future site of the pool basin is important because of the depth of excavation needed for pools. Core samples must be taken so that building cost can be estimated accurately. This is because excavation of soft soil is much easier and less expensive than digging through rock. Oversight here leads to additional cost and longer construction time for the project.

Another critical aspect for the site is locating the site away from major streets and highways. Children commonly trek to the pool and play around the facility; speeding traffic and children playing is a combination for disaster.

The site elevation should be analyzed to verify that the facility will not flood with regular precipitation. If the facility is prone to flooding, plan for frequent pool closures. It can take weeks to get the pool chemically re-balanced once dirty run-off or ground water enters the basin.

Compaction of Soil

Another site preparation concern specific to aquatic facilities is the importance of proper soil compaction prior to the placement of footers, floors, and walls. Consider the weight of the structures and then consider the volume of water to the basins. At 8.3 pounds per gallon of water, consider that the typical 25 yard, three- to ten-foot-deep competition pool holds about 150,000 gallons or 1,245,000 pounds of water. This weight on improperly compacted ground can lead to subsidence or the sinking of the basin. This sinking can lead to structural damage, broken plumbing, and leaking water from the basin.

Basin Construction

There are many choices for pool basins, included are the traditional concrete/reinforcing bar, metal (aluminum and pvc laminated stainless steel), and reinforced fiberglass. Often a concrete basin will be lined with tile, gunite, stone aggregate, pvc, painted with epoxy or polyurethane coatings.

Depending upon the pool use, some surfaces can be very expensive to install. For example, a competitive lane line on the pool bottom is easy to install in both pvc and tile, but a stone aggregate would be more expensive. This is also true for the basic cost of the materials. A painted concrete basin is often the least expensive but also has the shortest life span. Concrete, tile-surfaced basins are expensive but generally give the longest life. Aggregates are typically the most expensive but provide better durability than painted surfaces.

Most bathing codes require a gutter system for pool water surface skimming. Like pool basins, there are many types of gutter designs available in materials as listed under basins. You can select a gutter system that is flush and virtually unseen by patrons or traditional open gutters with a variety of volume capacities. Often gutters will also perform overflow duties similar to that of a surge or balance tank. This is so that water displaced by swimmers is not lost but relocated until the swimmers leave the pool basin.

As pools age and repeatedly flex, some basins require painting, grouting, or sealer. If you need to paint, insure that appropriate surfaces are non-skid and that epoxy or polyurethane base paints are used. These paints cost more but are more resistant to chemicals and are less likely to flake off in only one season.

Hydrostatic Pressure

Hydrostatic pressure is simply water pressure exerted upon an object. The installation of hydro-static pressure relief valves must be mandated during initial basin construction or verified as present and operational during basin repairs and renovations. The valves are placed in the deepest main drain sump or sumps in each basin. These valves automatically relieve water pressure that can be under the pool due to a shallow water table or flooding. If you drain the pool without operational hydrostatic relief valves, the pool can literally float out of the ground like a boat. Many home pools and a few public pools have been destroyed when the pool was drained due to this hydrostatic pressure. This damage arises from a lack of relief valves or the failure of the valves. The pressure can become so great that the basin floats, breaking pipes and damaging the foundation soil. Once this happens there is no putting the pool back together.

Deck Surfaces

There are a variety of construction materials available for pool deck construction. The absolute best non-slip, attractive, and long-lasting surface is one-inch-by-one-inch tile. These small tiles are expensive but satisfy so many desired needs. The state and local bathing and construction codes must be reviewed so that you do not select colors that are prohibited by law.

If selecting some other deck or basin materials, the planner should seek out solid references and warranties for the product being considered. A less expensive alternative is not less expensive if you have to repair it frequently or replace it all together in a few years.

Broomed concrete is often chosen at outdoor pools because it is inexpensive. When the deck is poured, the surface is broomed or power troweled to leave striations in the concrete surface to act as an non-skid surface. Be aware that after a season of operation, the concrete may need to be resurfaced or it will be extremely slippery.

Tiles larger than one inch by one inch should be avoided due to the limited contact resistance from larger tile with the bottom of your wet feet. Slip and fall injuries can lead to serious legal problems. Other deck surfaces include pvc liners or removable plastic walkways that sit on top of concrete decks.

Facility Sanitation

Planning for the long-term maintenance of the facility is important to keep operational costs manageable and patrons safe. Anything that is on the deck typically ends up in the pool. This includes algae that grows in puddles in the parking lot, sidewalks, pool decks, and locker areas. Of even more concern is the variety of bacteria and viruses that can live and multiply in water. The big three for pools include: E-Coli, Giardia, and Cryptosporidium. Failure to conduct normal maintenance can result in costly repairs or worse, growth of a variety contaminates. Due to this growth, locker and bathroom decks must be sanitized with a 5%

This end wall structure clearly shows 1" x 1" tile on the face.

bleach to a gallon of water solution daily. (YMCA, 2003) This solution must be made fresh before each use. The pool deck should be hosed off daily and sanitized weekly. This practice reduces the spread of bacteria and viruses and allows the pool sanitizers to work more effectively providing better water quality. The pictures below show a scum line in a pool gutter. This is similar to a dirt and oil ring found after taking a bath in a tub. Enforcing that all patrons take showers and daily deck sanitation will reduce this deposit.

A big part of pool sanitation involves not allowing street shoes on deck. Consider shower entry points that prevent people from entering the pool deck dry; showers with automatic motion sensors can help insure that anyone entering the pool is showered. This will reduce the amount of body debris introduced into the pool as well as a deterrent to street clothes on deck. Showers placed with these sensors will also reduce water consumption and heating costs for the water.

Water Quality

The water quality of the pool is a direct result of the proper design, planning, management, and dedication by staff at the facility. Water quality must comply with federal, state, and local guidelines. In addition to these laws, the industry has commonly accepted practices that can be found in texts/certification programs such as the National Swimming Pool Foundations Certified Pool Operator (CPO), National Recreation and Parks Association Aquatic Facility Operator (AFO), and YMCA of the USA Pool Operator On Location (POOL). These three programs account for the vast majority of pool operators trained and certified in the United States. Proper water chemistry is so very important that some states require certified pool operators to be at the facility at all times when public pools are in operations. In our opinion, having a qualified pool operator on staff should be required.

The physical treatment of pool water happens through circulation, filtration, and sanitation. These systems must be designed to operate 24/7.

The circulation/filtration systems most commonly found in commercial pools are pressure or vacuum sand or diatomaceous earth (DE) combinations. DE has the ability to filter down to about four microns, where the best sand filters down to about 25 microns. Thus, if filming or other photography will be a regular part of the facility operations, DE filters should be considered carefully for crystal-clear water quality.

The sanitation or treatment of pool water is possible through many methods. With the proper planning and appropriate staff training, all are safe. Chemical treatment is the most common method for water treatment in pools. The four dominant chemicals used are tablet chlorine, gas chlorine, liquid chlorine, and bromine. Bromine is preferred for high water temperature applications like hot tubs. Tablet chlorine comes in many compositions, the most commonly used being Calcium hypochlorite at about 65% chlorine. Chlorine gas is the most potent form at 99%, but many municipal codes may forbid its use. Liquid chlorine is very common but degrades rapidly, and even at its most concentrated, fresh solution is only about 15% chlorine.

Other methods of treatment of pool water during the past 15 years include ultraviolet light chambers (UV), ozone generators, chlorine generators, and non-chlorine sanitizers. Codes vary from state to state and some methods may not be recognized by your state. Both UV and ozone systems primarily treat the water in the circulation system plumbing, but have limited or no affect on the water in the basin. Chlorine generators make your own chlorine on site in the pool system. In low bather load pools, the chlorine generators work well, but often are not correctly sized for heavy-load situations and may need alternate methods of treatment if not properly planned for. Some facilities have started to use non-chlorine chemicals like potassium monopersulfate with their chlorination systems to help reduce combined chlorine levels. Other non-chlorine oxidizers include sodium percarbonate and hydrogen peroxide.

Chemical Control and Feeding Systems

Water management systems are commonly installed and in some codes, certain automated systems are required to add chemicals to the pool while swimmers are present. Today technology provides the owners the ability to monitor and make changes to the water quality off site. Some of the automated systems also retain electronic reports of minute-by-minute water samples allowing owners to validate proper water quality around the clock.

It is foolhardy to ignore these systems. The alternative to these systems means hiring someone to test, analyze, and adjust the water quality every moment that the facility is open. To do so is akin to having central air in your home with no thermostat and attempting to keep the house at exactly 78 degrees.

The most rudimentary systems allow the monitoring and automatic adjustment of pH and chlorine. Advanced systems can include monitoring of alkalinity, hardness, temperature, combined chlorine, and the saturation index.

Dangerous Rooms

Insure that chemical and mechanical rooms are secured whenever staff are not in those areas. This prevents wet patrons from finding themselves in a room with many high-voltage items. Additionally, pool chemicals that are unsecured may make a tempting invitation to young children, as some chemicals can look like little white mints. If ingested, the result could be fatal.

Pool Design Supervision Issues

Designed for Direct Supervision

The direct supervision of patrons in the facility is a key factor to reducing submersion (drowning) incidents. To do this effectively, guards need training on how to watch patrons, and a variety of techniques must be employed by supervisors. Facilities must also consider this job during the design and planning phase. If a large basin is designed, then elevated lifeguard stations should be considered. The elevated station allows guards to see the bottom of the pool without their view being obscured by the viewing angle or glare from the water surface. The elevated station also enhances their perceived authority over the facility. The guard stands must have an unobstructed view of the area supervised. Support columns for the roof must not be placed where the guards view prevents observation.

Facilities both indoor and outdoor must carefully consider the position of the facility in relationship to the sun. The ability for staff to properly supervise the patrons in the water attractions can be seriously impacted by glare from the sun. In outdoor pools this means pools shape and guard towers must be carefully planned so that glare is to a minimum or staff have multiple stations to select from during the course of the day. Indoor pools should consider ways to limit direct sunlight. Use reflected lighting methods to both reduce lighting costs but also maintain an observable body of water.

Lighting

Planners should consult their state and local bathing and construction codes because often, lighting requirements are very specific for pools. Like external natural light, the selection of artificial pool lighting is a serious proposition. Lighting fixtures and replacement bulbs are not inexpensive; so, you must consider things like bulb placement, operational hours, replacement costs, and effects of water or humidity on the system.

Bulb life may help you determine long-term costs, and if you can access a burned-out bulb easily or will you have to bring in special equipment to replace them? Determine how long will the bulb provide x number of lumens or candle feet of light when new? How about after 1,000 hours of operation? What is the kilowatt-hour electrical consumption for the proposed systems?

Also, decide if you need underwater basin lights or if overhead systems are sufficient for your facility. Do you have an emergency lighting plan if

This is a good example of glare on the water surface because of window location.

there is sudden power loss to the facility? Again, the bathing code for your area must be addressed before any decision is made.

Drowning Prevention

Drowning prevention must be designed into the facility to help your staff provide a safe environment. Currently, there are new technologies that maybe able to assist your facility staff though drowning detection systems. One system named Poseidon is about a decade old and has a proven

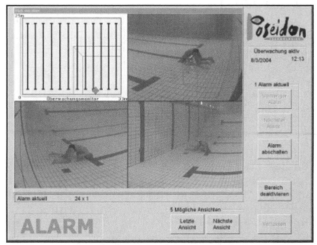

track record to help save lives at indoor facilities. This computer-based system uses a series of cameras to evaluate swimmers and determine when someone might be in trouble. This system does not replace lifeguards; it does provide another set of "eyes" (cameras) on the water, so to speak.

Access Points

When new aquatic facilities are designed, a simple oversight can lead to tragedy. The placement of entry points to the pool deck in relation to where the deep water of the pool is located is very important. Locker rooms that enter the pool area next to a diving well or water deeper than the average swimmers height are "asking" for patrons to immediately enter water over their heads and those with poor swimming skills find themselves in trouble. Make sure that pool deck entrances are at a shallow area of the pool basin.

Physical Security and Safety

The organization should give special consideration for the security of the facility outside of operational hours. The design can help staff quickly determine that the facility is secure and that no person can gain easy access at closing or during the night. All windows, doors, gates, and vents should be verified as secure at closing each day and an alarm system should be considered to prevent unauthorized entry and use. Trespassers should be prosecuted immediately. A swift punishment may be a deterrent to others thinking about breaking into the facility. Failure to prosecute may help make a case against your facility as an attractive nuisance. By building an inviting facility with little thought for securing it, your organization may find itself in legal difficulty.

Operational Security

Facilities should consider single points of access to the facility for normal operations. This will limit the staff needed to control facility use and observation. Systems like floor-to-ceiling turnstiles with swipe card readers should be considered to control access and speed patron entry and egress for the facility. The theft of both facility items and patron property may be reduced by the use of turn styles. A main operational desk can be located in the lobby just prior to the turn styles allowing for monitoring of patron entry. This also means that "one-stop shopping" can happen in this location. From program registration, to memberships, both concessions and pro-shop sales, this location can control it all. With a limited number of staff, security and services can happen from this central location.

Fences

Fencing is often used as an inexpensive barrier device when long distances must be covered, especially at outdoor facilities. Consider how the fence will be used and pay close attention to insuring that climbable opportunities are not created by the design. This situation happens at 90-degree corners; the fence becomes an easy way in, due

The fence in the foreground is decorative and may prevent toddlers from entering the pool areas but adults can easily circumvent it

to the corner support poles. Consider sweeping, rounded corners to make turns in the fence.

Ideally, the fence itself should be the ???inch hole, non-climbable type and at least eight feet tall. Consider the fence around tennis courts; it has two-inch holes, is 10 feet tall, and is used to keep balls in the court. Is it more important to keep a ball in a tennis court or keep children out of an outdoor pool after hours?

Other Aquatic Design and Operation Concerns

Air Quality

The air quality at indoor pools has a serious effect on the water quality, staff health, patron health, and facility structural longevity. Air quality is not just heating and cooling; it also includes dehumidification and the reduction of chloramines in the air.

Notice that even with this small pool area, two guards are clearly seen.

The air temperature at indoor pools should be three to five degrees higher than the water temperature for bather comfort. If people complain about the water temperature being too cold, they typically are uncomfortable because the air temp is too warm; thus, the water feels colder. Do not regularly change the water temperature; it will not solve the problem and it will cost you dearly in heating expenses.

Staff will see the consequences of poor air quality when they contract breathing problems like lifeguard lung, which is common to pools with poor air quality. Worse yet, staff or patrons who have mild asthma may have elevated effects because of the poor air quality. This could mean increased EMS visits to your facility when people fall ill.

By doing serious research and consultation about aquatic facility air quality, your facility can have a long life and your patrons will have enjoyable use of the attractions.

Rooms at the Facility

The following usable spaces should be considered for every well-designed aquatic facility:

- Guard Office: This office will be the area that staff store rescue equipment, records/reports, and their on duty personal items like uniforms, pocket masks, whistles, eye and skin protection. Other testing and monitoring equipment may also be kept within this area.
- Main office: This room will be the central point of access for entry and information for the facility and should include the pro shop and concession activities.
- Pool mechanical room: This room will house the circulation, filtration, and pool water heating systems. Sufficient room is need around each piece of equipment to monitor and maintain the equipment. Computer control systems for chemicals should also be in this room for a longer operational life.
- Chemical Feed room: This room will have only the chemical feed systems due to the caustic nature of pool chemical. Only pool chemicals should be stored here, no mechanical equipment except the chemical feeders.
- Electrical room: A dedicated electrical room that feeds the electricity to the facility will be distributed from this point.
- Custodial room: This room should provide the needed area to store cleaning equipment and supplies to maintain the facility.
- Locker rooms: The locker rooms should provide a changing area, toilets, and showers typical to any bathing facility.
- Storage: There is never enough storage, so anticipate future programs and operational storage needs for this space.
- Class/meeting room: To conduct staff training, classes with land-based components (such as

CPR and First Aid) as well as a room for pool parties or other programming should be considered.

Pool Utilities and Being Greener

Like any facility being considered, heating, ventilation, and air conditioning (HVAC) the facility is a common issue. In aquatic facilities, heating, cooling, and dehumidification become critically important for both patron comfort and facility longevity. There is substantial cost in proper aquatic facility air quality and control systems, of course, shortened facility longevity due to ignoring these issues is costly, too.

Serious consideration must be given to not only the purchase price of air-quality systems, but also to operational and maintenance expenses. These systems must effectively control the pool area humidity but also account for fresh air exchange and the reduction of off gassing pool chemicals into the air. Failure to consider these issues can result in a non-functional facility that has a dramatically shortened useful lifespan. The American Society of Heating, Refrigerating and Air Conditioning Engineers (ASHRAE) creates standards in this area and should not be overlooked.

Today, more than ever, people and facilities must consider "green" facilities. Solar heating can supplement pool heating but cannot be consistently relied upon to bring the water temperature to the ideal range by itself. Solar heat can reduce the amount spent on electrical or gas heating. Another option to help reduce the heating expenses is geothermal heating. Geothermal heating allows the facility to use the warmer ground temperature to cold tap water and bring it to ground temperature prior to electric or gas heating to the desired level. This works in the reverse in the summer; you can actually cool the water in the summer months as needed. Wind and photovoltaic electrical generation can off set some of the facilities costs as well. Large wind generators, similar to windmills of the past, in some regions of the country may be able to generate more power than the facility can use. Photovoltaic cells may be placed on the roof of the pool area along with solar thermal heating plumbing to reduce both electrical and heating expenses.

Simple solutions like the color of the exterior roof surface, i.e., a light color versus a dark color, can reduce cooling costs dramatically. Exterior AC units should be a light color, preferably shaded, protected, and regularly inspected for damage and debris. Insulate all exterior ceilings, walls, as well as pool walls if a gallery is present. The gallery or hallway/crawl space under the deck that surrounds the pool allows for easy plumbing repairs and provides access for underwater filming/instruction. In the pictures below a gallery shows the plumbing, a video camera, and underwater windows. Also note the insulation on the ceiling, this facility has radiant deck heating in the concrete just under the tile pool deck surface. The insulation helps keep the heat in the deck as warm water heats the deck and the facility is heated by the rising warm air in contact with the deck surface.

Outdoor pools should all have pool covers to reduce water loss through evaporation. The covers can also retain heat on cool nights, thus reducing heating costs. Pool cover auto retracting systems can be built into the design of the basin during construction. External units can be purchased after construction but wear can be excessive if staff do not receive proper training on cover handling.

PLAYGROUNDS 14

Donna Thompson, University of Northern Iowa
Susan Hudson, University of Northern Iowa

Playgrounds are an essential part of children's play. These play sites can be found in a variety of settings, including public parks, schools, child care centers, apartment complexes, churches, and commercial establishments. Whatever their settings, all playgrounds should have certain things in common. These include:

- the fostering of a child's physical, emotional, social, and intellectual development; and
- the provision of age-appropriate equipment to meet children's needs.

The use of the word *playgrounds* for this chapter refers to designated areas where stationary and manipulative play equipment is located to facilitate a child's physical, emotional, social, and intellectual development. These areas employ:

- the use of proper surfacing under and around equipment,
- the placement of equipment that allows for easy supervision by adults, and
- the regular maintenance of the equipment and the environment.

This chapter will review trends in playground design; general planning considerations; specific planning steps; installation of the equipment and the surfacing; and ongoing maintenance, repair, and inspection procedures.

General Planning Considerations

Playground Guidelines and Standards

During the 1970s, in response to consumer interest and complaints, the United States Consumer Product Safety Commission (CPSC) initiated a process to develop safety guidelines for playgrounds. The first guidelines were produced in 1981. The guidelines came in two handbooks—one designed to give general information to the public, the other to give technical assistance to the manufacturers of playground equipment. These guidelines were revised in 1991 and merged into one handbook for use by the public. In 1988, the American Society for Testing and Materials (ASTM) accepted responsibility for creating a standard based on the refinement of the technical specifications for playground equipment.

The CPSC has maintained its involvement with the technical standards for public use by assisting the ASTM with further development and refinement of these specifications. As a result of these efforts, the first voluntary standard for the playground industry was developed in 1993. This standard, known as F-1487-93 (Standard Consumer Safety Performance Specification for Playground Equipment for Public Use), provided technical specifications for playground equipment, use zones, prevention of entrapments, and maintenance. The standard was revised in 1995, 1997, 2001, and 2007. A surfacing standard was created in 1991 (F-1292-91). This standard provides for the testing of the impact attenuation of playground surfacing. Specifically, it provides the methodology to assess the amount of surfacing necessary under and around playground equipment to prevent fatal head injuries of children who may fall to the surface off the equipment. This standard has been revised four times (1993, 1995, 1996, and 2004).

Both the ASTM standards and the CPSC guidelines (which were revised again in 1994, 1997 and 2008) have been instrumental in creating safer play environments for children by providing design criteria for surfacing and equipment. Together, they are essential documents needed for designing playgrounds.

A third guideline now influencing the playground design comes from the United States Access Board. In November 2000, the U.S. Justice Department published the Access Board's guidelines regarding the interpretation of the Americans With Disabilities Act (ADA) and public playgrounds. These guidelines address issues of accessibility to and from play equipment as well as the use of the play equipment by children with disabilities. All new public playgrounds, including those found in schools and community parks, should conform to these guidelines. If major renovation is done on existing playgrounds, then they also need to comply with the guidelines. In addition, whether new or old, all public use playgrounds need to provide access to and from the play equipment as mandated in the ADA regulations passed in 1991.

In order to design safe playgrounds, four major elements must be considered:

- the placement of equipment and support structures (e.g., benches), which facilitate the supervision of children in the play area
- the proper positioning of age-appropriate equipment to promote positive play behavior
- the selection of appropriate surfacing that will absorb the impact of children falling from the equipment
- the consideration of equipment and surface maintenance issues that contribute to the development of safe playground environments

Supervision Design Considerations

Supervision requires individuals to be able to see and move through the playground area; therefore, design considerations for supervision include age separation of equipment, use of signs, open sight lines, and zones for play.

Age Separation

It is important to divide the playground area into sections appropriate for different ages of the users. A new ASTM standard f-2373 was developed in 2005 for children ages six months to 23 months. Therefore, play equipment found in the play area should be separated into three distinct zones for children ages six months to 23 months, ages two to five, and ages five to 12.

Mixing the three distinct types of equipment means that the supervisor will have a difficult time guiding children to use the equipment appropriate for their developmental age level. (A more complete discussion of this can be found in Age-Appropriate Design Considerations on next page).

Use of Signs

Signs can provide information to adults concerning both the age separation of equipment and the need for supervision. The use of signs provides adults with a clear indication as to which age group should be on the equipment. It also reminds adults that the equipment will not supervise the children. This is an important consideration for schools whose playgrounds are used before and after the organized school day and in public parks where no formalized supervision is in place. It provides a "good faith" attempt by a sponsoring agency to promote safe supervision practices.

Open Sight Lines

Open sight lines refer to several angles of visual access for the supervisor. Sight lines must occur through equipment and through natural vegetation. Further, sight lines for play structures should allow visual access to all points of the age-appropriate design—older structures from at least two directions at any one elementary children using point of observation on the play site the overhead ladder. (Bowers, 1988, p. 42). Essentially, the ability to respond to emergencies is dependent upon ". . . the ability of the supervisor to approach the structure and get to all the events to provide assistance" using the routes implied by the sight lines (Bruya & Wood, 1997).

Zones for Play

Play sites should also be divided into zones for different activity types. Two types of zones that the designer should pay attention to are activity zones and use zones. Activity zones describe the type of play behavior that children might engage in given the space and equipment that is present. Examples of activity zones include areas for social/dramatic play, fine-motor play, gross-motor play, and quiet play.

Use zones refer to the safe areas around equipment that need appropriate surfacing. Use zones will be further discussed in Considerations for Proper Surfacing on next page.

Age-Appropriate Design Considerations

Playgrounds should be designed according to the characteristics of the intended user. Therefore, age-appropriate design considerations include selection of the correct size of equipment for children, developmental needs of children, and the physical layout of equipment to support positive play activities.

Correct Size of Equipment

Size of equipment refers to its height, width, and bulk. The *height* of the equipment includes the overall distance from the top of the equipment piece to the surface. It also includes the space between various components, such as steps and platforms. Since 70% of reported playground injuries involve falls to surfaces, the height of the equipment becomes a critical factor in designing a safe playground. Experts suggest that equipment for preschool children be no taller than children can reach. Maximum height for most equipment for school-age children should be eight feet (Thompson & Hudson, 1996).

Width of platforms should also allow children to make decisions about how to get on and off equipment safely. A child standing on top of a six-foot slide should have sufficient room to turn around and climb back down the ladder if that child decides not to slide down.

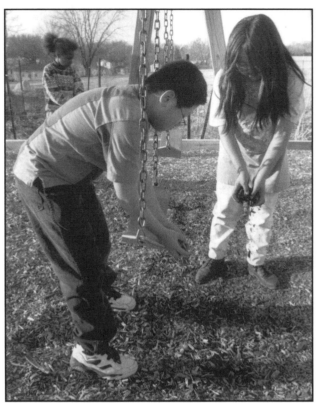

Falls to surfaces—children replacing appropriate surfacing so the depth is proper for the next class.

Bulk is the relationship between the thickness of the material and the grip size of a child's hand. All handrails, rungs, and other components that children grasp should be between 1 and 1 1/2 inches in diameter.

Developmental Needs

Developmental needs of children are also a factor in age-appropriate design. Children grow and develop by stages. The thinking ability of a three-year-old is much different from a seven-year-old. Preschoolers are physically smaller than school-aged children. It is important to consider the developmental needs and abilities of children in planning and designing age-appropriate playgrounds. These needs and abilities include:

- physical (i.e., strength, grip, height, and weight)
- emotional (i.e., risk-taking and exploration)
- social (i.e., cooperation, sharing, and accepting)
- intellectual (i.e., decision-making, inquisitiveness, and creativity)
- accessibility (i.e., mobility)

These needs and abilities apply to all children. As previously mentioned, even children with limited physical, emotional, social, and intellectual capacities, and/or mobility have the legal right to use public play areas. Thus, the designer needs to design for the composite "typical/atypical" child if the playground is to be one where all children can interact successfully.

Physical Layout of Equipment

The physical layout of the playground pieces can limit or enhance the play value and safety for children. An interconnected play area is one in which easy movement throughout the play structure is developed through the inclusion of alternate routes of travel (Bowers, 1998). Shaw (1976) investigated interconnection between parts of the structure, which he came to call the "unified play structure." As a result of the Creative Learning Project, he determined that overall use patterns decreased for separate play modules when compared to the "unified" play space. Thus, by unifying or interconnecting play elements in a play space, overall complexity was increased. In a 2004 study by the National Program for Playground Safety, it was found that over 95% of all school and park playgrounds now have composite structures.

While composite structures help to increase the complexity of the play space, it also can cause a safety problem if not carefully thought out. Over 84% of park playgrounds now have composite structures that they claim are appropriate for ages two to 12 (Hudson, Olsen, & Thompson, 2004). What this means is that the interconnections of these structures are allowing two-year-olds up to heights and on equipment not designed for their developmental abilities. Planners need to understand that one size does not fit all. If composite structures are used, they should be clearly labeled for the age group that they are designed for—either two to five or five to 12. Having a composite structure for ages two to 12 is inappropriate and goes against the ASTM standards and CPSC guidelines.

Considerations for Proper Surfacing

Surfacing is the third important general design element. Factors that need to be considered include how much fall protection is required, accessibility, maintenance, management requirements, and costs.

Adequate Fall Protection?

For the prevention of life-threatening injuries, adequate fall protection needs to be present. The National Program for Playground Safety (NPPS) has developed a safe surface decision-making model to help individuals determine whether or not a playground surface will meet the criteria of adequate fall protection. As can be seen in the model outlined in Figure 14.1, there are four decisions that are involved in the selection of surfaces that will provide adequate fall protection. These include the selection of suitable materials, the height of the equipment, the depth of the materials, and adequate coverage in the use zone.

Selection of Suitable Materials

According to the Consumer Product Safety Commission (CPSC, 1997), there are a number of materials that help to reduce the risk of life-threatening injuries. Acceptable materials include sand, gravel, wood chips, engineered wood fibers, shredded rubber, and synthetic surfaces. Hard materials, such as asphalt and concrete, are unacceptable surfaces under playground equipment. Similarly, earth surfaces such as dirt, soil, grass, and turf are unacceptable, because their shock-absorbing properties vary depending on wear and climatic conditions (CPSC, p. 4).

Height of the Equipment

Equipment height affects the choice of shock-absorbent surfacing in two ways. First, some surfaces, such as pea gravel, provide shock absorbency protection for limited heights (e.g., six feet in the case of pea gravel). Second, currently no surface over 12 feet has been laboratory tested. Thus, to date, no one can guarantee the shock-absorbency characteristics for equipment over the height of 12 feet. Because research studies indicate that equipment over six feet in height has doubled the injury rate of equipment under six feet, the NPPS recommends that the height of playground equipment should not exceed eight feet for school-age children and five feet for preschool children.

The CPSC recommendations for the fall heights for various pieces of playground equipment are as follows:

- Climbers and horizontal ladders—the maximum height of the structure.
- Elevated platforms including slide platforms—the height of the platform.
- Merry-go-rounds—the height above the ground of any part at the perimeter on which a child may sit or stand.
- Seesaws—the maximum height attainable by any part of the seesaw.
- Spring rockers—the maximum height above the ground of the seat or designated play surface.
- Swings—since children may fall from a swing seat at its maximum attainable angle (assumed to be 90 degrees from "at rest" position), the fall height of a swing structure is the height of the pivot point where the swing's suspending elements connect to the supporting structure.
- Slides—CPSC has no recommendations concerning slide height. Research has shown that equipment higher than six feet has double the injury rate than equipment at lower heights.

It should be noted that equipment that requires a child to be standing or sitting at ground level during play is not expected to follow the recommendations for resilient surfacing. Examples of such equipment are sandboxes, activity walls, playhouses, or any other equipment that has no elevated designated playing surface.

If the surface does not meet minimum standards for shock absorbency, then it should not be used. Minimum standards are determined through testing procedures as stated in the ASTM F-1292 standard for Playground Surfacing. However, because of time and cost constraints, many consumers cannot afford to perform this testing. Consequently, as a public surface the NPPS conducted testing of five common loose-fill materials: pea gravel, sand, wood chips, shredded rubber, and engineered wood fiber. The results are provided in Table 14.1. The chart reports the heights at which a life-threatening head injury would not be expected to occur for compressed loose fill materials at three different depths. As can be seen in Table 14.1, 12 inches of compressed sand, wood chips, shredded rubber, and engineered wood fiber can provide shock absorbency for equipment up to eight feet in height. In contrast, the maximum height for 12 inches of pea gravel is six feet. The depth of any loose-fill material could be reduced during use, resulting in different shock-absorbing properties. For this reason, a margin of safety should be considered in selecting a type and depth of material for a specific use. When loose-fill materials are used, it is recommended that there be sections of containment around the perimeter of the use zone (CPSC, 1997) (See Table 14.1).

Coverage in the Use Zone

The final element that helps decide if the appropriate surface is present is the determination of the placement of the surfacing under and around playground equipment. *The Consumer Products and Safety Commission Handbook for Public Playground Safety* defines these areas as use zones. Table 14.2 presents the requirements for use zones as outlined in the CSPC handbook.

The basic use zone is six feet. However, because children move off swings and slides in different ways than onto another piece of equipment, the use zone is expanded to provide a larger safety zone. For instance, if a swing beam is eight feet high, then the use zone extends 16 feet in front and 16 feet in back of the swing beam to accommodate children who might jump out of the swing seat while in motion.

Accessibility

The second characteristic that needs to be considered in the selection of surfacing is that of accessibility. According to the previously mentioned Americans With Disabilities Act of 1991, discrimination on the basis of disability in public accommodations is prohibited. While the entire playground area does not have to be accessible, there must be an accessible pathway to accessible playground equipment. Therefore, a pathway made of an accessible surface material must be provided.

Figure 14.1
Safe Surfacing Decision-Making Model

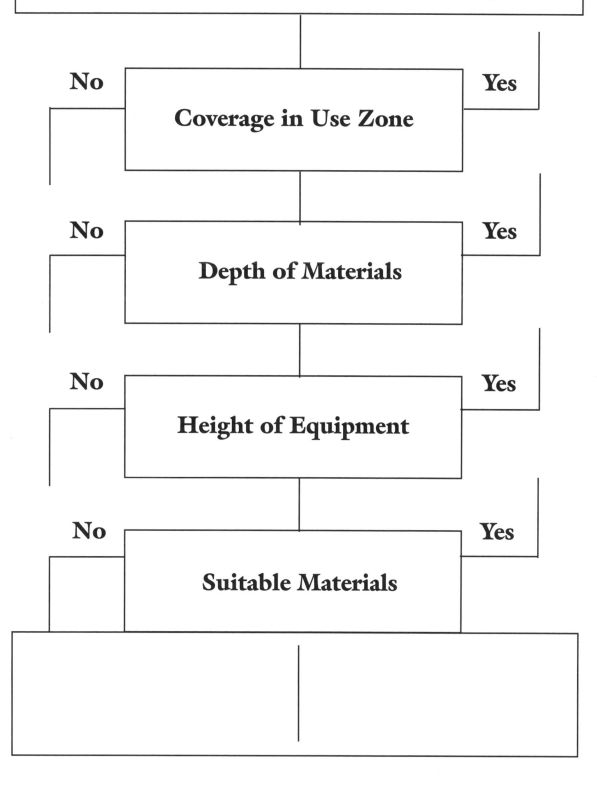

Table 14.1
Playground Surface Materials

Height of Equipment	Pea gravel			Sand			Wood Chips			Shredded Rubber			Engineered Wood Fiber		
	6"	9"	12"	6"	9"	12"	6"	9"	12"	6"	9"	12"	6"	9"	12'
1'	Y	Y	Y	Y	Y	Y	Y	Y	Y	Y	Y	Y	Y	Y	
2'	Y	Y	Y	Y	Y	Y	Y	Y	Y	Y	Y	Y	Y	Y	
3'	Y	Y	Y	Y	Y	Y	Y	Y	Y	Y	Y	Y	Y	Y	
4'	Y	Y	Y	Y	Y	Y	Y	Y	Y	Y	Y	Y	Y	Y	
5'	N	Y	Y	Y	Y	Y	Y	Y	Y	Y	Y	Y	Y	Y	
6'	N	N	Y	Y	Y	Y	Y	Y	Y	Y	Y	Y	Y	Y	
7'	N	N	N	Y	Y	Y	N	Y	Y	Y	Y	Y	Y	Y	
8'	N	N	N	Y	Y	Y	N	Y	Y	Y	Y	Y	N	Y	Y

*Based on depth test results conducted by NPPS or manufacturers' literature.
Note that the loose-fill results are based on materials tested in a compressed state.

Y = Yes, it did meet CPSC recommendations for this critical height.
N = No, it did not meet CPSC recommendations for this critical height.

At this time, the testing of loose fill materials for accessibility is still in process. However, it is well accepted that sand and pea gravel are not accessible surfaces. Until more testing is done, the only materials that are generally considered accessible under certain conditions are wood fibers and unitary materials, all of which are commercially available. According to a U.S. Department of the Interior advisory, uniform wood fibers tend to knit together to form an accessible surface while other wood materials (e.g., wood chips, bark, mulch, etc.) do not (McCroy, 1994).

Maintenance

The third characteristic, which is often ignored during the selection process, is the maintenance re-quirements that various surfaces need in order that the shock-absorbency characteristics are properly retained. Three elements that should be considered in this area include environmental conditions, soil conditions, and management requirements.

Environmental Conditions

Environmental conditions such as strong winds, rainy weather, high humidity, freezing temperatures, and so forth may influence the appropriateness of the type of surfacing selected. For example, strong winds can erode organic loose-fill materials and sand so that they must be replenished often. Wind and dirt tend to form a hard pan or crust in pea gravel that needs to be broken up periodically. When wet, sand tends to stick together

Table 14.2
Use Zones for Equipment

Equipment	Use Zone Requirement
Stationary equipment	Six feet on all sides of the equipment.
Slides	Six feet on all sides. Four feet plus the height of slide in front of slide chute.
Swings	Six feet on each side. Twice the height of the swing beam in front and back of swing.

A piece of playground equipment that needs maintenance.

and becomes almost rigid. Some types of unitary materials are susceptible to frost damage. Thus, the climatic conditions of the playground must be considered when selecting a surface material (Mack, Hudson, & Thompson, 1997).

Soil Conditions

Playgrounds located over poor soil will not drain well, causing pooling of water under equipment. In some areas of the country, the shrink/swell characteristics of clay soil can loosen the foundation of play equipment. Shrink/swell conditions can also cause sinkholes under playground surfaces. This problem can easily destroy a poured-in-place or other unitary surface. One should check with the local soil conservation district or a county extension agent to check the suitability of the soil for playground development.

Finally, the designer must pay attention to the drainage of the site. Normally, one would want water to run down away from the playground. This might mean that the area around the equipment will need to be slightly raised. Since drainage is also dependent on soil type, as mentioned above, the soil composition should be checked prior to the installation of equipment. One should also be aware of what might drain into the playground area. For instance, if a parking lot is located above the play area, grease, oils, and even gasoline may be washed into the play area during a rainstorm. Be certain that there is good drainage at and around the site to avoid problems.

Management Requirements

Consideration must be given to how the area will be managed. A site that will have high traffic use will require a surface that will be durable without frequent maintenance. Rubber tiles or poured-in-place surfaces, although initially high in cost, may be more appropriate for these types of areas. Loose-fill materials would be more easily displaced, which would have an impact on the overall safety of the site.

However, in areas that have controlled use, loose-fill materials may be appropriate. Maintenance costs and the needs of surfacing materials vary greatly, with loose-fill materials tending to have much higher maintenance needs. In high-use areas, loose materials may need to be raked daily to replace materials that have been pushed or kicked away. Loose-fill materials need to be regularly inspected for protruding and sharp objects such as glass, pop tops, sharp rocks, and metal objects. These surface materials may also have to be tilled periodically to loosen compaction. Sand should periodically be turned over, loosened, and cleaned. Additionally, loads of loose material may need to be added on an annual or semiannual basis to keep the surface at an appropriate depth.

While not as time-consuming, unitary materials such as rubber mats, tiles, and poured-in-place surfaces also have maintenance needs. Repairs may need to be made to gouges, burns, and loose areas. Unitary materials may also need to be swept frequently to prevent sand, dirt, rocks, or other loose materials from becoming a slip hazard. Finally, rubber surfaces must be washed occasionally to remove spilled beverages, animal excrement, and other foreign matter.

Costs

Cost factors of the surfacing material should be prorated over the life expectancy of the playground. Materials with low initial cost include sand, pea gravel, wood chips, and bark mulch. However, one should also consider the replenishment costs of these materials along with the initial purchase price. In addition, some method of containment is needed and the materials cannot be installed over existing hard surfaces such as concrete and asphalt.

Materials with medium initial cost include wood fiber and shredded rubber. Some of these materials are easily installed while others require professional installation. They may also require a drainage system. Like other loose-fill materials, some type of containment is required, and they cannot be installed over concrete or asphalt.

Unitary materials such as poured-in-place surfaces, rubber tiles, and rubber mats have a high initial cost when compared to low-cost loose-fill materials. Poured-in-place surfaces are usually the most expensive with a cost 10 to 15 times higher than common loose-fill surfaces. Rubber mats and tiles typically cost six to 12 times that of the cheaper materials. Installation and site preparation costs should also be considered, because these materials must be professionally installed. Unitary materials also require a hard base. If the existing surface is not concrete or asphalt, then a subsurface must be installed prior to the rubber surface. However, if the current surface is concrete or asphalt, installing a rubber surface will avoid the costs of excavating and removing the existing surface.

Equipment and Maintenance Considerations

Considerations about maintenance have to be part of the initial planning process. A poorly built playground is difficult to maintain. Providing good upkeep for a safe play environment begins with planning the playground site. Factors that need to be considered regarding this area include preplanning, materials, inspection, maintenance, and environment.

Prior to any installation of equipment and surfaces, a proper site analysis needs to be conducted. A site analysis addresses natural, manufactured, and aesthetic elements that may affect playgrounds. All of these items will be discussed in greater detail in the next section.

Materials

There is no perfect material for playground equipment. Without good maintenance, wood will splinter, metal will rust, and plastic will crack. Any good maintenance plan should be based on:

- instructions received from the designer/manufacturer,
- materials used for equipment and surfaces,
- age of the equipment and surfaces,
- given frequency of use on the equipment and surfaces, and
- environmental factors at a specific location.

Be certain that all instructions from the designer/manufacturer are retained in a file and that the schedule of maintenance is followed. Remember, any modification, deviation, or change from these instructions means that liability issues will reside with the agency, not the designer/manufacturer.

Inspection

Inspect all materials prior to installation. Wood products are aesthetically pleasing but will weather faster than metal or plastic. Plastic materials may not be appropriate in areas of great temperature extremes. Metal materials also tend to absorb heat and cold, which can cause problems in hot and cold climates.

Even newly installed playgrounds should be inspected for hazards. Just because a playground is new does not mean that problems cannot oc-

cur. This is especially true if the equipment was installed improperly or the overall design and placement of equipment is faulty. On the other hand, older playgrounds do need more regular inspections simply because parts may wear out due to age.

Maintenance Schedule

A well-used playground will need more frequent maintenance than one that is used less often. This is especially true with playgrounds that have loose-fill materials as the surface under and around playground equipment. An agency that schedules only one refilling of these materials a year may find that over half its playgrounds are unsafe due to the high usage. Each play area may have its own use cycle and the maintenance schedule should reflect this.

Environmental Factors

Finally, the environmental factors at a specific location are going to determine the required frequency of maintenance. A playground that is located near a shady grove of trees may need to be inspected more frequently because of materials left on the surfacing (e.g., leaves) or other hazards (e.g., overhanging limbs). A playground that is in a wide-open area and exposed to the elements may also experience greater maintenance needs.

It is evident that to maintain a safe playground environment, maintenance practices and procedures need to be thought about at the beginning of the design process. It is also important that these practices and procedures be continually revised and improved.

Specific Planning Steps

The actual planning and design of a playground is accomplished in four distinct phases. They are: site analysis, preliminary design, equipment and material selection, and final design.

Site Analysis

Site analysis involves the gathering of information and data about the playground site and adjacent properties. "The purpose of site analysis is to find a place for a particular use or find a use for a particular place" (Molnar & Rutledge, 1986). One of the first steps that should be taken during the site analysis is an on-site visitation. Personal site visits enable one to see how the area is used and how it relates to surrounding land uses (IPRA, 1995). It allows the planner to mentally visualize the space available for the project. During the site analysis, step information about environmental elements, manufactured elements, and hazardous conditions is gathered and analyzed.

Environmental Characteristics

Environmental characteristics that should be considered during the site analysis includes soils and geology, drainage, topography, vegetation, and any other physical characteristics that may have an impact on the development process.

Soils and Geology

Soil type is important because it is directly related to drainage. The playground should be constructed on well-drained soils. A playground constructed on poor soil will be subject to water pooling or standing. It will also tend to erode the foundations of the equipment and cause other problems of equipment stability.

Drainage

In general, water should drain away from the playground. As mentioned earlier, the play area may need to be slightly elevated to accomplish this. One needs to remember that construction of the playground and/or surrounding areas may alter the water movement patterns on the site. If there are questions about preventing or solving water problems, a good source is the local office of the Soil Conservation Service (SCS).

Topography is concerned with the general lay of the land. Playground developments work best within a range of slopes. As a general rule, slopes around and beneath playgrounds should conform to the following guidelines (IPRA, 1995):

- Slopes between 1% and 4% are most suitable for playgrounds (a 1% slope falls one foot for every 100 linear feet).
- Slopes less than 1% may result in drainage problems.
- Slopes greater than 4% may require site modifications to install and level the equipment.

In addition, slope is an important consideration in providing equal access into the playground for everyone regardless of physical capabilities. The accessible route into the playground must have a maximum slope of 5% (one foot of fall for every 20 linear feet) and a maximum cross slope of 2%.

Vegetation

Vegetation is another environmental consideration in playground design. Shade should be an essential ingredient for every playground. If trees are not present, it may be necessary to provide man-made shade, such as the placement of shelters. While trees planted along a western and southern exposure may provide the necessary shade, caution must be taken to ensure that overhanging limbs do not interfere with play activities. "In particular, trees planted inside the playground must be carefully located because they may be used for climbing" (IPRA, p.13). In addition, one should avoid planting trees and shrubs, which are messy or likely to attract stinging insects such as bees.

Other Considerations

Other environmental considerations include sun orientation, wind patterns, climate, and animal control. Slide surfaces that tend to absorb heat should avoid being placed on a western exposure. The best orientation is north. However, if this is not possible, then natural or manufactured shade needs to be provided.

The direction of the prevailing winds should also be determined. If at all possible, the playground should be located downwind from open fields, farms, or areas like unpaved roads where dust from these sites will blow directly into the play area. In addition, if an area is susceptible to strong winds on a routine basis, some type of windbreak should be created (Thompson, Hudson, & Olsen, 2007).

Climatic conditions that affect playground equipment and surfaces include heat and cold, humidity, and precipitation. As mentioned earlier, temperature extremes have a direct influence on different materials used for equipment and surfacing. In addition, humidity may affect certain loose-fill surfaces, as well as cause the surfaces of equipment to become slippery and hazardous. An area that has constant precipitation may need to have a cover over the equipment as well as excellent drainage.

Manufactured Elements

The second factor to consider in the site analysis is manufactured elements. These include utilities, roads, buildings, adjacent land use, accessibility, and anything else that could affect or be affected by the playground.

Utilities

As a general rule, playgrounds should not be constructed under utility lines. One needs also to pay attention to unused utility easements. There might be a temptation to use these seemingly open areas, but nothing can stop a utility from using the easement at a later date for power lines. Another utility consideration is the support structures that may be found near the playground site. Power poles and towers can constitute an attractive nuisance in the play area. In addition, guidewires or other supporting cables on these utility structures can create a hazard for children in the area.

Roads

The playground should be located far enough away from roads and parking lots that moving vehicles do not pose a hazard for children. A barrier surrounding the playground is recommended if children may inadvertently run into a street. If fences are used for such barriers, it is recommended that they conform to applicable local building codes (CSPC, 1997). In addition, ASTM has developed a specific standard for fencing around playgrounds (ASTM 300).

Buildings

Proper use zones need to be maintained in relation to any buildings or structures that may be present on the site. For example, a school playground should be located far enough away from the school buildings so that a child on a climbing structure would be in no danger of falling off the play equipment into the building. In addition, close proximity of the playground to windows may encourage vandalism problems.

Adjacent Land Use

Neighboring land uses need to be considered because they may affect or be affected by the playground (Hudson, Thompson & Olsen, 2008). Railroads, freeways, landfills, streams, and rivers may all contribute to a hazardous environment for children. The long-term effects of some of these items (e.g., waste dumps) may not be determined for years. On the other hand, the location of the playground itself may be seen as a less-than-desirable element within the neighborhood environment. Some people may be upset by the perceived increase of noise, vandalism, and traffic they assume a playground will attract.

Accessibility

Accessibility to and from the site is also a consideration. How will project users get to the playground site? Will it involve children arriving on bicycles, walking, or being brought by cars? The answers to these questions will determine the need for bicycle racks, pathways, and parking lots.

Other Considerations

Other considerations may include sources of noise such as airports, railroad lines, roadways, heavy machinery, and factories that can detract from the recreational experiences of playground users. Odors from factories, sewage treatment facilities, and stagnant ponds can have the same effect. Locating a playground adjacent to such detractors should be avoided (Hudson, Thompson & Olsen, 2008).

Hazardous Conditions

A variety of hazardous conditions must be considered before determining the site location of the playground. These include visibility and security, crossings, water, and mixed recreation use zones.

Visibility and Security

Visibility and security are primary considerations. Large shrubs (above four feet in height) should not be planted around a playground since they inhibit the ability to observe children at play. In addition, as already mentioned, low tree branches (below a height of seven feet) should be removed to prevent climbing. Any trees that will be seriously affected by the development of the playground should also be removed before they create a hazardous situation.

Crossings

Children should not be required to use unprotected crossings to reach playgrounds. Railroad tracks are a similar hazard. Fencing or natural barriers may be necessary if alternative solutions are not feasible (Hudson, Thompson, & Olsen, 2008). Another traffic consideration can occur around schools and child care centers where delivery truck routes may pose a potential hazard for children going to and from the play area. Special care should be given to be certain that these routes do not intersect the play area and are not located nearby.

Water

Water is another site element that may pose a hazardous situation. Children are attracted to ponds, streams, and drainage ditches. Cement culverts or ditches are especially dangerous, since their smooth sides may not allow a child easy escape in case of a flash flood. Signage alone will not stop children from trying to incorporate these areas into their play behavior.

Mixed Recreation Use Zones

Mixed recreation use zones can also produce hazardous situations. A soccer field or baseball diamond located too close to a playground is a safety concern because of the chance that errant balls may enter the play area and injure playground users. Locating a playground adjacent to basketball courts, tennis courts, and other similar recreation facilities can also create conflicting access patterns and users.

Preliminary Design

The preliminary design phase is where information about the activity, user, site, and necessary support factors are analyzed and alternative solutions evaluated. At the end of this step, the actual schematic plans will be developed.

Activity Information

What is the purpose of the playground? This fundamental question needs to be answered in terms of performance objectives rather than physical objectives. For instance, if one answers this question by saying the purpose of the playground is to provide slides, swings, and climbing apparatus, then one will limit the possibilities of the play behavior of children. On the other hand, if one answers this question by looking at what children should be able to do, then a different design may result. The philosophical basis for the existence of the play areas must be reflected in the answer to this question. For example, in a school setting, the purpose of the playground should be tied to the educational goals of the total curriculum. Thus, the playground may be designed so that it contributes to a child's understanding of math, language arts, science, and physical education. In a park setting, the playground may reflect the extension of school goals as well as emphasize the physical, emotional, social, and intellectual development of a child. In a child care setting, the play areas should reflect the growth and development of the different ages of young children (Hudson, Thompson, & Olsen, 2008).

Once the philosophical question about the purpose of the playground is answered, the next step is to decide what experience opportunities should be provided. Experience opportunities are ways that the child will participate in the playground experience. Four different experience opportunities are usually present in the playground environment:

- basic ability level
- skill improvement
- program participation
- unstructured participation

Basic Ability

This is especially important in planning play environments for young children. Children do develop in different stages. For instance, in terms of access on play equipment, ramps provide the easiest way for a small child to get onto equipment, followed by stairways, stepladders, rung ladders, and climbers. Thus, if one wanted to provide basic skill level opportunities, the design of the play structures would incorporate a variety of ramps and small stairways as well as be built fairly low to the ground.

Skill Improvement

This allows for children to develop their abilities in incremental steps. For instance, at the age of six, children don't automatically have the upper-body strength to control their bodies on overhead ladders. Some intermediate type of equipment is needed between a six-foot-long and a 20-foot-long overhead ladder where a child can build up the muscle strength and endurance needed to master the higher and longer apparatus without the fear of falling.

Program Participation

A playground developed on a school site should be designed to complement the academic offerings of the curriculum. Thus, the design of this playground should have specific equipment pieces and shapes that would supplement the academic program (math, science, art, etc.).

Unstructured Participation

This means an area where children are free to roam, explore, discover, and play. Again, this type of experience opportunity demands some specific design considerations including placement of equipment, open sight lines, and easy access.

Not all playgrounds have to emphasize the same experience opportunities. However, if the designer/planner fails to recognize which opportunities should be present, the playground may become only an area where equipment is randomly placed.

User Information

A brief profile of the intended users is an important aspect of the planning process. Such a profile should include the age distribution of the intended users, developmental and skill levels, known disabilities, and participation time patterns. In addition, information about participation rates per activity period is necessary to determine the design load of the area in terms of needed equipment units, support areas, and services. Seasonal, monthly, and weekly peak participation periods may be additional planning factors in terms of maintenance and operational considerations.

Site Factors

A third consideration in this preliminary design stage is the resource and facility factors that are directly related to the site development. Special requirements, such as the spatial size for the playground area, need to be noted. Preliminary layout of equipment on a grid will allow the planner to visualize traffic flow on and off equipment, relationships of equipment pieces with one another, and space requirements for use zones (Hudson, Thompson, & Olsen, 2008). Other special requirements may be the location of items such as tree limbs, power lines, and telephone wires that can infringe on air space and cause a hazardous situation.

The solar orientation of the space in relation to the placement of equipment is also an important factor. The primary consideration should be to minimize glare and sun blindness during play and avoid hot surfaces on the equipment.

Necessary Support Factors

Items that are auxiliary to the playground but support the area also need to be considered during this preliminary design stage. These items help enhance the overall aesthetic appearance of the area, contribute to the safety of the children, and provide amenities that create an overall positive experience. Trees, bushes, and other vegetation may need to be planted to help provide shade and/or avoid a stark appearance of the playground site. Fencing may be added to keep children safe during play and keep out unwanted animals and others during other times of the day. Benches, water fountains, and shelter areas may provide children and adults with areas to relax and refresh during their visit to the playground. These support factors and others such as bicycle racks, trash and recycling cans, and security lighting will not suddenly appear unless they are planned for in the preliminary design stage. Furthermore, if they are added later, their placement may not be in congruence with the overall design of the area.

Equipment and Material Selection

Equipment for playgrounds should be designed for public use; be durable; and meet requirements for insurance, standards, warranty, age appropriateness, and use. Any equipment purchased should conform to both CPSC guidelines and ASTM Standard F-1487 and 2373.

Product Compliance

Always require a certificate of compliance with the CPSC guidelines and ASTM Standard from the manufacturer prior to the purchase of the equipment. The same type of compliance with ASTM F-1292 should be secured for any surfacing material. If a manufacturer is unable to produce such documentation or will only provide oral assurances as to compliance, purchase equipment elsewhere (Thompson, Hudson, & Olsen, 2007). In addition, be certain that any equipment purchased for public-use playgrounds is designed for that purpose. Many times, people with good intentions but limited funds will purchase equipment intended for home use and place it in a public setting. This equipment is neither durable nor strong enough to withstand the constant, heavy use that is found in public sites. In addition, the standard for home-use equipment is quite different from that for public-use equipment.

Product Materials

Playground equipment is usually made out of one of four types of materials: wood, steel, aluminum, or plastic. Each material has its own advantages and disadvantages.

Wood must be treated to prevent rotting by weather or insects. This is especially true when wood is in direct contact with the ground. Any chemical wood preservative used must be approved for contact with humans. Wood is also subject to splitting and checking, which may eventually weaken the structure. Watch out for evidence of splitting in new wood, especially pieces used as support beams and poles. Sanding and other treatments may be required to avoid injuries from splinters. Although aesthetically pleasing, wooden pieces usually have a life span of only 10 years (Thompson, Hudson, & Olsen, 2007).

Steel equipment pieces should be galvanized and have a protective coating that inhibits rust such as powder coating and painting. Any paint used should not have lead as a component. It should also be noted that scratches and construction defects are subject to rust. Steel also can heat up to dangerous levels with direct exposure to sunlight. On the other hand, steel equipment pieces are very durable and have a long life span.

Aluminum components are rust resistant and offer lightweight installation. Aluminum is sometimes more costly at purchase; however, the reduced maintenance is often worth the extra cost.

Shipping charges will be reduced because of the lighter weight. Like steel, aluminum can heat up with direct exposure to sunlight.

Plastic can be molded, cut, or formed into a wide variety of shapes for playground use. Because of this, it is a favorite material that is used by many playground manufacturers. However, most plastics do not have the strength of natural lumbers and metals and can sag and bend. It is recommended that ultraviolet (UV) light inhibitors be added to the plastic to extend the life expectancy and color. Plastic components must meet safety standards (Hudson, Thompson, & Olsen, 2008).

Purchase Factors

One should consider at least five factors prior to purchasing any equipment or surface materials. These include product liability insurance, compliance with standards, product warranty, age appropriateness, and public-use equipment. Product liability insurance protects the buyer against any accident caused by the design of the equipment. However, if the buyer makes any alteration or modification or fails to maintain the equipment properly, the insurance will not cover the agency. The equipment vendor should furnish the agency with certificates of insurance and original endorsements affecting the coverage. As with all documentation, be certain the insurance coverage is in writing and on file.

Compliance with standards should also be documented and on file. Do not buy equipment that does not meet CPSC guidelines and ASTM standards F-1292 for surfacing and F-1487 and 2373 for equipment. In addition, a certification of proper installation should be obtained from the manufacturer or his or her representative following the final inspection. Once the manufacturer agrees that the playground is in conformance with its installation recommendations, ask for a sign-off letter stating the date of inspection. Make sure that you keep this document on file. It is extremely important should an injury occur due to improper design or installation.

Product warranty simply provides the buyer with the length of time for which any products are protected against defects. Many times, the product warranty is a good indication of the product's life expectancy. Again, any modification or repair made without conformance to the manufacturer's guidelines will nullify most warranties.

Age appropriateness of the equipment has already been covered. However, you should notify the manufacturer in writing what the ages of the intended users are to ensure that they have provided you with age-appropriate equipment at the time of purchase.

Public-use equipment is the last item to consider. Not all pieces of equipment are recommended for use in a public playground. The following is a list of equipment to avoid primarily because it fails to meet safety guidelines:

- spinning equipment without speed governors
- tire swings that do not meet requirements for clearance
- seesaws that do not meet current safety standards
- heavy swings (metal, wood, animal-type)
- ropes/cables that are not attached at both ends
- swinging exercise rings and trapeze bars
- multiple occupancy swings
- trampolines
- homemade equipment

Final Design

At this stage, one is ready to put all the components together in a scaled schematic drawing that shows layout, use zones, site amenities, access points, and other construction details. Also, one needs to insure that accessible routes to the equipment are present.

The easiest way to begin this process is to use cutouts or round bubbles to represent the actual equipment and place these items on a scale grid plan. In this way, one can visualize how the equipment pieces fit together and where potential conflicts of use may arise. Any moving equipment, including swings, should be located away from other structures, preferably at the edge or corner of anticipated traffic patterns. In addition, be certain to separate infants (six months to 23 months) from preschool (ages two to five) from school age (five to 12) equipment.

All equipment has space requirements. By moving the cutouts or squares around, one can make sure that the use zones of the various equipment pieces do not overlap. Remember that these use zones are minimum guidelines. The authors have seen several instances where slide exits were placed directly in front of swing sets. Although the proper use zone was in place, exuberant children who jumped out of the swings landed directly in front or to the side of the slide. Of course, the best way to avoid this situation is not to place these two activities across from one another in the first place.

As mentioned earlier, site amenities should be part of the planning stage. Make sure that the scaled drawings include the placement of benches, bicycle racks, trash cans, and so forth. If these items are not in the drawings, they will be haphazardly provided later, perhaps at inappropriate spots.

Before finalizing the drawings, be certain that you have considered traffic flow patterns on and off equipment and general access to the area. Every playground should have at least one accessible route to the equipment that will permit children with disabilities the opportunity to be in the playground area and interact with others. Although the final ADA regulations have not been finalized, it is important to understand that just getting to the equipment will not be enough to satisfy the law. Once at the equipment, some type of accommodation should be made to allow children on at least some of the equipment as well as to interact with their nondisabled counterparts. Consult the U.S. Access Board for further information on this subject.

Installation

Installation of equipment is an important part of the overall planning process. If equipment and surfacing are installed improperly, the safety of the total play environment will be jeopardized. When dealing with the installation of equipment and surfacing, there are three factors to consider:

- planning of the installation
- actual installation of the equipment and surfacing
- liability issues related to the installation

Planning of the Installation

Five items need to be considered during the planning of the installation process:

- the manufacturer of the equipment
- the manufacturer of the surfacing
- the materials needed
- who will perform the installation
- budgetary factors

The Manufacturer of the Equipment

This business must be selected carefully. The decision about which manufacturer to use should be made on the basis of the planning committee's criteria. It is critical that the manufacturer decided upon produces equipment that meets the ASTM F-1487 or F-2373 current standards and the *CPSC Handbook for Public Playground Safety Guidelines*. After the tentative selection of the manufacturer has been made, the planning committee should talk with others who have purchased equipment from the potential vendor and check the company's competency. The committee should also find out whether the equipment installation process was understandable and reasonable, and most importantly, how the equipment held up after being installed.

The Manufacturer of the Surfacing

As with the equipment manufacturer, the surfacing manufacturer should also be selected with care. Again, any decision should be based on the criteria established by the planning committee. The surfacing manufacturer must be able to provide testing data from an independent laboratory to show the depth of the product needed proportionate to the height of the equipment purchased. The testing procedure used must be based on the ASTM F-1292 current standard. In addition, it is a good idea to talk with others who have dealt with the prospective manufacturer to determine the company's competency and service record.

Materials Needed

A third item that needs to be considered in the planning process for installation is the materials needed. It is easier to obtain materials in some areas of the country than in others. This will affect their costs. Weather factors have been previously discussed; however, the time of year that installation will occur also needs to be considered. This is especially critical in relation to surfacing and the setting of cement for footings. It also is a consideration for the drying time of preservatives on wood products.

Who Will Perform the Installation

The determination of the actual installer(s) is the fourth factor. It is possible to use an installer recommended by the company. If that is the decision, the installer should be trained by the company or be a certified installer recommended by the company. A trained installer adds to the overall cost of the equipment. Thus, many times, in an effort to reduce cost, the purchaser will decide to use in-house agency personnel to install the equipment and surface. If this method of installation is selected, it is important for liability protection to have a company representative observe the actual installation process or direct the process. Either way, an agency should have the company sign off that the installation process has met the company's specifications (Hudson, Thompson, & Olsen, 2008).

Budgetary Factors

The budget for installation is the last item that needs attention. The budget will be determined by the cost factors associated with who does the installation, the materials needed, and the time it takes to perform the installation. Cutting costs on installation is many times a shortsighted cost savings. As mentioned before, if the equipment is not properly installed or poor materials are used, the playground will cost the agency more money due to increased maintenance and liability issues.

Installing the Equipment and Surfacing

Four factors should be considered in relation to the actual installation of the equipment and surfacing:

- manufacturer's instructions
- coordination of the installation
- time needed for installation
- manufacturer sign-off

The Manufacturer's Instructions

According to ASTM F-1487, the manufacturer or designer must provide clear and concise instructions and procedures for the installation of each structure provided and a complete parts list (ASTM-F-1487-07, 2007 or F-2373-05, 2005). It is important that these procedures be followed during the installation process. In addition, these instructions should be filed in case any liability issues arise concerning the proper installation of equipment (Thompson, Hudson, & Olsen, 2007).

Coordination of the Installation

The next step is to coordinate the installation process. Four potential groups need to interact with one another during installation. These groups include the manufacturer, the owner of the site, the organizer for the personnel who will perform the installation, and the vendors from whom products will be purchased.

Time Needed for Installation

Time is also an important issue that needs to be considered. In particular, the amount of time needed for the installation will influence the number of people involved in the actual installation process. One needs to determine whether or not the community will tolerate weekend installation, or if the work must be done during usual work hours or in the evenings. If installation takes a period of time, protecting children from using partially built structures is a priority.

Manufacturer Sign-Off

After the installation is completed, the agency should have the manufacturer of the equipment and surfacing sign off that both items were installed according to specifications. This ensures that the structures and the surfacing are safe for children to use (Hudson, Thompson, & Olsen, 2008).

Liability Issues

Since we live in a litigious society, it is important to protect the agency from being sued. Following appropriate procedures will not prevent lawsuits, but it may reduce the amount of financial responsibility that is imposed if a suit is upheld. However, the most important item to remember about following proper installation instructions is not the liability issue, but the safety issue. By following manufacturer's instructions, the agency is being proactive in trying to reduce the potential for children being injured on the playgrounds.

An agency should be concerned with four liability issues regarding the installation of equipment. According to Clement (1988) these are:

- manufacturer's specifications,
- manufacturer's recommendations,
- the posting of manufacturer's warnings, and
- the importance of following manufacturer's instructions.

Manufacturer's Specifications

It is critical that the agency is certain that the installer has followed the manufacturer's specifications for installation. The responsibility for this falls on the manufacturer, if the company performs the installation. If the agency does the actual installation, it assumes the liability and the burden of proof regarding the following of proper procedures.

Manufacturer's Recommendations

Any recommendations by the manufacturer must also be followed. For example, in order to properly deal with the impact attenuation of a surface, it may be recommended that pea gravel be separated from a wood product by use of a fabric. Once installed, it is the agency's responsibility to see that such a separation is continued. Other recommendations may include that bushings on swings be checked annually for wear or that wood products be covered with a preservative on an annual basis. In each of these cases, it is imperative that the agency follow the recommendations of the manufacturer (Thompson, Hudson, and Olsen, 2007).

Posting of Manufacturer's Warnings

The agency must post any manufacturer's warnings that are included with materials. Many manufacturers now place labels on equipment that suggest ages for which the equipment is designed or the proper depth for loose-fill surface materials. In cases where warnings accompany playground equipment, the agency is responsible for replacing the warnings if they become illegible, destroyed, or removed. Diligence on the part of the agency in regard to the posting of the warning label will inform adults about ways to prevent a child from being injured.

Following Manufacturer's Instructions

Last, following manufacturer's instructions is extremely important in the installation of equipment. These instructions should include the proper use-zone placement of equipment, the installation of the equipment at the proper depths, the correct method of mixing adhesives for surfacing materials, mixing cement in correct proportions with water, and the use of proper tools to lock joints of structures. The agency may need to be able to provide evidence that such procedures were followed. As adults work with installation, they can conclude that they are dealing literally with the dirt of responsibility, the grit of reality, and the grind of responsibility.

Ongoing Maintenance, Repair, and Inspections

The playground area should be perceived as an environment for play that contains many elements including playground equipment (Hendy, 1997). Parking lots, sidewalks, field areas, seating, shelters, and restroom facilities are only a few of the amenities that complement many playground areas. These amenities require maintenance as well. To insure proper long-term maintenance, a comprehensive program must include the total playground environment, not just the equipment.

The basic function of maintenance is to ensure the safety of users by keeping the playground area and equipment in a safe condition. Maintenance also keeps the equipment functioning efficiently and effectively. A track ride is not much fun if the bearings are worn and the mechanism won't glide easily. Maintenance is also performed to keep the area hygienically clean. By keeping an area well maintained, it remains aesthetically pleasing.

A safety audit should be performed when new equipment is purchased and installed to verify that the equipment and installation are consistent with the Standard of Care set forth by the agency and the manufacturer. The audit will not need to be repeated unless the Standard of Care changes, the equipment is heavily vandalized, or a natural disaster impacts the equipment.

Inspections

There are basically two types of maintenance inspections that are performed on playground equipment: seasonal (periodic) and daily (high frequency). A seasonal or periodic inspection is one performed two to three times a year. This is an in-depth type of inspection to evaluate the general wear and tear on the equipment. A daily or high frequency inspection is done routinely to identify rapidly changing conditions due to weather, vandalism, and sudden breakage. It also identifies surfacing problems typically associated with loose-fill surfacing materials.

There is no magic formula for determining the frequency necessary to perform each type of maintenance inspection. How often the playground is used and by what age group are two of the common considerations that will determine frequency of inspection. The vandalism rate in an area will also dictate the timetable chosen to inspect the playground.

The nature of the area and the environment will influence the need for playground maintenance. The soil type and drainage conditions as well as other geographic and climatic conditions will also influence inspection frequency.

Record Keeping

Documentation of inspections, repairs, and maintenance should be recorded regularly. In addition, the agency must establish a system of work requests that will enable maintenance staff to expedite the ordering of replacement parts and repair services. As part of the overall comprehensive program of playground maintenance, it is important to document all inspections and maintenance procedures. A fail-proof system of follow-up must be established that enables a supervisor to review the inspection forms, noting:

- who performed the inspection;
- items that were corrected on site at the time of inspection;
- hazards that need to be corrected;
- work orders that were issued;
- purchase orders for equipment services or replacement parts;
- when equipment, parts, or services were supplied or rendered;
- when repair work was completed;
- who performed the repair work and
- final approval from the supervisor.

DESIGNING FACILITIES FOR PARKS AND RECREATION

15

Kimberly J. Bodey, Indiana State University
Thomas H. Sawyer, Indiana State University

Park and recreation departments aim to build communities and connect citizens with leisure, fitness, and education opportunities. Recreation centers improve the quality of life for the patrons they serve as well as lure new businesses, provide jobs, and build local communities. Park and recreation facilities are experiencing a multitude of trends that are impacting the planning process. Planning principles are not typically subject to change. However, inputs to the process are undergoing substantial change.

The last decade may be characterized by a variety of trends:

- Changing participation rates in existing recreation and leisure activities.
- Expanding new recreation activities, especially in adventure recreation and exer-gaming.
- Changes in the stability of employment and in the workplace as the baby boomer generation begins to retire and new generations enter the workforce.
- A greater recognition of how cultural and ethnic background impacts the type of recreation and recreation facilities.
- A greater understanding and recognition of women's needs in recreation.
- A changing population and household composition.
- Marked advances in medical care.
- Dramatic innovations in leisure equipment technology.
- Impact of computers, electronic media, and burgeoning electronic marketplace.
- Changes in world energy and growing green movement.
- Changes in regional economies.
- Unstable political environments.
- The slowdown of the economy and resultant impact on recreation facility development and construction.

Facilities and open spaces must clearly be conceptualized and designed to accommodate the dramatic changes occurring in America. The planning process will continue to need the involvement of the varied public to be served.

General Planning Issues

A Master-Plan Concept

The planning process, regardless of the size of the community involved, typically occurs at three levels. First, there must be a master plan conceptualized at the policy-making level. Second, there is a concept plan which concerns physical matters in that it is site-specific and incorporates factors associated with landscaping, layout, facility mix, and construction. Third is the planning stage, which has a focus on operation and maintenance for facilities, parks, and open spaces. All three levels are critical to sound planning (see Chapters 3 and 4); however, the master plan level is the most important since it is at the policy-making level where critical initial decisions are made that guide and control all future decisions at the second and third levels of planning.

Community Involvement

In developing plans for new recreation, park, and open spaces and in proposing improvements to existing facilities and areas, all planning, as suggested within the master plan concept, must reflect the wants and needs of the community. Public co-operation and involvement in the initial planning stages will serve to strengthen community interest, both actively and financially. There are many ways to involve the public in the planning process. One is the public meeting. Although time-consuming, a series of well-organized public meetings is an effective means of presenting proposed plans. While the public meeting has been a marginally successful method in the past and should not be discarded, it cannot be the only method. Public meetings are effective in bringing large groups of people together although even the best planned meetings cannot bring large crowds out. In many communities, large crowds are brought about by controversy over proposed planning. Other methods of involving the public are also effective and may provide more detailed and useful information. These include focus groups (small groups of eight to 12 people), individual interviews, presentations to service clubs and special interest groups, and the like.

A survey of leisure behavior and attitudes can be useful in determining the needs and desires of the people within the planning area. Surveys can be conducted by mail, telephone, internet, or through the newspaper. Conducting a successful survey requires a carefully constructed process, and even then many people have become wary of responding. Surveys can be costly and, if not well constructed, might not provide effective information for the agency. Use of consultants or university personnel in the process is strongly encouraged.

Today, in most of America, far more taxpayers do not have children in public school than do have children in public schools. It is important to engage this large tax-paying population in any recreation and park project. They need to see that the project will benefit them as well as the rest of the community.

One of the methods used to strengthen proposals is through interagency agreements for shared use and funding of facilities. Also, cooperation between community agencies and organized groups facilitates planning, promotes financial considerations, and assures community involvement.

Rebuild, Renovate, or Reinvest?

Facility planners are increasingly faced with the question of whether to rebuild, renovate, or reinvest in older recreation space, infrastructure, and design. Decision-making is largely based on an assessment of what the community wants to see changed. Consider two types of obsolescence: physical and functional. Physical obsolescence pertains to problems related to layout, ventilation, floors, and lighting, or meeting current standards and codes. Functional obsolescence simply means patrons do not enjoy what the facility has to offer. It is possible to renovate or reinvest in recreation spaces that is adequate from a structural perspective but is not very desirable. Thus, planners must ask the question: What can be done to increase the recreational values of this facility? To a large extent, the answer lies in understanding community demographics and preferences. There is no one size fits all design. Every facility must be tailored to fit the unique needs and wants of the intended users.

Planning Considerations for Urban Areas

Rapidly growing urban population centers have placed open space at a premium. This has led to a growing public concern about recreational facilities and services. The following factors must be considered when planning recreational facilities within congested urban areas:

- Declining availability of open space and limited economic resources make it essential that multi-jurisdiction government agencies cooperate in planning facilities areas. Recreation use of public housing facilities, the presence of social and health care programs in recreation centers, and parks and trails crossing multiple jurisdictions and jointly administered are a few examples of ways in which the public can maximize facility use.
- Multiple and not necessarily compatible uses of facilities, both public and private, should be considered. For example, the parking lot of an industrial plant can be used for recreation activities on evenings and weekends with little or no additional cost if properly planned.
- The mobility of people in dense urban areas is often restricted. Therefore, facilities must be easily accessible to the people by sidewalks, bike paths, bus and train routes, etc.
- All facilities need to meet the requirements of the Americans With Disabilities Act (1990).

Multiple-Use

Planning facilities for multiple use is a major consideration in the establishment of parks and recreation areas. Multiple-use facilities require space that can accommodate varied activities for all age groups during various times of the day, week, month, season, or year. The traditions of seasonal activities are lessening as technology allows most weather-dependent activities to be conducted year-round, and single sports have developed year-round training programs and participation. Facilities that are planned to accommodate a single use become an expensive investment if allowed to stand idle much of the year. Changing recreation preferences requires that indoor and outdoor areas not be restricted with permanent spatial and architectural fixtures designed for specific activities in a set period of time. There must be flexibility built into indoor and outdoor facilities.

The character and location of the population are constantly changing. The ethnic, socioeconomic, and demographic features such as age and family size can vary within neighborhoods. With today's mobile population, a community facility that is planned on the basis of a static population soon has many obsolete features. And yet, failing to plan for a neighborhood's ethnic and cultural foundations also means the use for the facilities may be nonexistent. Only in recent years have recreation and park planners come to a realization that recreation patterns are strongly affected by ethnic background and culture. Understanding these cultural impacts allows planners to develop facilities that meet specific ethnic needs and can be adapted for differing populations.

Eliminating Architectural Barriers

It is essential that all recreation facilities be designed to serve people with disabilities. Therapeutic recreation services for people with disabilities need to be considered in the planning process to ensure that activities and facilities will serve them. Guidelines for the elimination of architectural barriers are detailed in Chapter 4.

Green Design

According to the United States Green Building Council (USGBC) there are many positive outcomes related to green design. Green design protects the planet and reduces a facility's operating costs through energy efficiency and water conservation while promoting occupants health and productivity through improved air quality. Moreover, green design enhances a building's marketability and helps to create a sustainable community.

The USGBC's Leadership in Energy and Environmental Design (LEED) rating system is the known standard for designing, constructing, and operating green facilities. Specifically, being "green" means those design and construction practices that significantly reduce or eliminate the negative impact of buildings on the environment and occupants in five areas. These areas include sustainable site planning, safeguarding water and water efficiency, energy efficiency, and renewable energy, conservation of materials and resources, and indoor environmental quality. As with any facility plan, there is no one-size-fits-all approach to green design. Trade-offs exist that must be considered in relation to resource availability and community needs and wants. However, the capacity to select materials that meet LEED criteria is made easier by the availability of certification programs and online product directories administered by unbiased organizations.

Indoor Recreation and Community Centers

Neighborhoods, quadrants, communities, and cities form the basic units for planning programs, activities, and facilities. The park and recreation agency, in order to plan and manage its services properly, establishes its activities and facilities on the demands of its designated service populations. The larger the planning and managing agency, the broader the population groups with which it will be concerned.

Recreation and Community Center Types

There are different types of recreation centers based on community needs. Traditionally, the two main types have been neighborhood recreation centers and community recreation centers. Neighborhood recreation centers focus on serving neighborhood needs and are discussed in more detail below.

Neighborhood recreation centers are more common in large communities (500,000 or more) but are sometimes present in smaller cities. Community recreation centers serve a larger population base. Community centers are common in cities of various sizes. In smaller cities and communities they may be the only recreation centers available. In larger cities they supplement neighborhood centers and provide specialized services and programs.

There is a new type of recreation center, frequently referred to as a supercenter, which has a minimum of 80,000 square feet in size. Supercenters are a reflection of commercial trends of creating large, one-stop shopping super stores. The supercenter reflects an expectation by consumers to meet all of their recreational needs in one location. These supercenters can cost in excess of $20 million.

Authors and organizations have historically provided classifications for types of recreation facilities based on service areas. Some larger communities have created their own standards for recreation facilities. Yet there remains no commonly accepted standard for the number of people a recreation center should serve or what should be contained in a recreation center. Recreation planners have learned that communities have different expectations for services, and the cookie-cutter approach of the 1960s and 1970s has given way to unique facilities designed to meet community member desires. Even with this knowledge, some common terminologies for recreation centers can be suggested. Table 15.1 shows what types of facilities may be found based on community size.

Recreation centers should be planned to meet the needs and interests of all people in the neighborhood or community. They should provide a safe, healthful, and attractive atmosphere in which every person in the community or neighborhood may enjoy his or her leisure by participating in activities of a social, inspirational, cultural, or physical nature.

Recreation centers range from the simple picnic shelter to a multipurpose community recreation center with a variety of common and special service facilities. They vary in design from the rustic to the contemporary. Present-day buildings provide for adaptability and multiple uses. This change from the simple to the complex has stimulated the development of a variety of recreation centers. These are classified by function and then categorized by size. The size of a recreation center is usually based on the population to be served and the program to be conducted.

Table 15.1
Recreation Center Type and Frequency Based on Size

Type of Recreation Center	Large City (250,000 or More)	Medium City (100,000 to 250,000)	Small City (50,000 to 100,000)	Small Community (Less Than 50,000)
Neighborhood recreation center				
Community recreation center				
Supercenter				
Specialized facilities				

The Neighborhood Center

The facility that is, perhaps, closest to the grassroots service level is the neighborhood center. A neighborhood recreation center is designed to service a specific area of the city. Such a building encloses 15,000 to 30,000 square feet. The size will depend also on whether the building is a separate entity or part of a park-school complex where facilities are available in the school.

The neighborhood center usually includes the following facilities:

- multipurpose room or rooms
- gymnasium (if not available in neighborhood school [see Chapter 20])
- shower and locker rooms when a gymnasium is provided (see Chapter 6)
- arts and crafts room
- multimedia room and library
- fitness and aerobics room
- dance and aerobics room
- child care area
- kitchen
- restrooms
- lounge and lobby
- office
- large storage areas

The Community Center

The community recreation center functions beyond the primary purpose of serving a neighborhood. It is designed to meet the complete recreation needs of all the people in the community. The size of the building depends on (1) the number of people to be served, (2) the projected program plan, and (3) whether it is a part of a park-school site or a separate building. This building usually contains 20,000 to 75,000 square feet of space and is usually located in a major recreation area such as a park-school site or community park.

The community center usually includes the following facilities:

- multipurpose rooms that can be organized into one large room and multiple smaller rooms
- gymnasium (see Chapter 22)
- climbing apparatus and tower
- shower and locker rooms (see Chapter 6)
- stage and auditorium (sometimes combined with gymnasium)
- rooms for programs in the arts (art, dance, music, drama)
- game room
- kitchen
- restrooms
- lounge and lobby
- office and security station
- large storage areas
- clubs or classrooms
- seniors area
- fitness and exer-gaming areas
- dance, yoga, and aerobics room
- child care area
- multimedia room
- computer/technology room
- teen area
- possible specialized areas as program dictates (racquet courts, gymnastics, weight and exercise room, photography workshop
- picnic and barbeque areas

The Supercenter

The supercenter represents the newest trend in the development of recreation centers. As previously mentioned it ranges in size from 80,000 to well over 100,000 square feet and is designed to be a true one-stop recreation center. It serves a large metropolitan area or may serve several communities. It is usually not linked to a school park. The size of the facility allows for both indoor and outdoor facilities.

It might, for example, include a water park rather than a traditional swimming pool and have water play equipment, slides, a lazy river, and the like. It almost always has a large fitness, aerobics, and gymnasium area and an indoor track. It usually has many classrooms and specialized rooms such as pre-schools, arts and crafts rooms, teen areas, or a photography room. Most rooms are designed to be multiple-use. The use of folding walls allows rooms to be configured in different sizes so groups as small as 10 or 15 can be accommodated as well as groups of several hundred. The child care area allows the family to come to the center and leave their toddlers in a licensed day-care setting while the parents work out and the school age children attend classes such as fitness, martial arts, arts and crafts, or computers, or they have fun in the indoor water park. Many of the supercenters are supported with outdoor facilities such as golf courses, outdoor water parks, large park pavilions, and so forth. There is no single common design for a supercenter; however, the use of computers to track facility use, conduct registration, manage the facility, and track maintenance operations is mandatory. Many of the buildings are also wireless, encouraging residents to bring their laptops for use in the open spaces. Open space that is inviting and comfortable is essential. There is usually a single entry that has a front-desk monitored by knowledgeable staff that helps patrons find where they need to go, check for membership, take registration for classes, and monitor building use.

Specialized Rooms

Multipurpose Room

The multipurpose room should be designed to accommodate such activities as general meetings, social recreation, active table games, dancing, dramatics, music, concerts, banquets, and the like. The area of this room should be approximately 2,000 to 3,000 square feet. It should be rectangular in shape, with a minimum width of 40 feet. The minimum ceiling height should be 16 feet.

There are many types of flooring surfaces available. Wood flooring, usually maple, is always a favorite, but it requires considerable upkeep and does not respond well to some uses. Composite flooring such as a poured or rollout type of floor is as costly as a wood floor but is highly versatile. Participants can play basketball on it in the morn-ing, and it can be the shot-put area in the afternoon, then used for indoor soccer in the evening. The floor should have a nonskid surface to prevent many common accidents. It is recommended that the floor also be level to permit multiple-use for meetings, dancing, dramatic presentations, and so on.

Gymnasium

If only a single court is constructed then the structure should be at least 90 feet by 100 feet with a minimum height of 24 feet. This size will permit a basketball court of 50 feet by 84 feet with additional room for telescopic bleachers seating approximately 325 spectators on one side of the gymnasium (see also Chapter 22). Community centers and supercenters will have multiple courts side by side, typically with 12 feet between the courts and vinyl walls with netting that descends from the ceiling when desired.

Multiple-court gymnasiums will usually have seating for just one court, and it is retractable. Provision should be made for a mechanical ventilating system with air-conditioning considered where climate dictates. It is preferable to have no windows in the gymnasium. However, if desired, windows should be placed at right angles to the sun at a height of 12 feet or more and they should be equipped with protective guards. The wainscotting, or tile, in the gymnasium should provide clear, unobstructed wall space from the floor to a height of 12 feet. Many recreation centers are moving to portable basketball standards, thus removing the basketball areas from multiple use structures.

Floors with synthetic surfaces have become predominant in recreation gymnasiums. Maple flooring continues to be selected as a preferred alternative to a synthetic surface, usually when the floor will have limited conflicting use. If maple flooring is used, the cork spring clip or other type of expansion joint should be installed on all four sides. If suspended apparatus requiring wall attachments is used in the gymnasium, these attachments should be at least seven feet above floor level.

Recessed drinking fountains should be located where they will cause a minimum of interference. Fountains should be hand- or hand-and-foot operated with up-front spouts and controls. Protective floor covering or drainage at the base of the fountain should be considered to avoid floor damage.

Locker and Shower Rooms

Locker and shower rooms should be provided for physical activities, athletics, staff, and the like. When designing or remodeling a locker and shower room planners should focus on three basic considerations: durability, maintainability, and cleanliness (see Chapter 6). A recent trend is for recreation centers to have multiple locker rooms. Typically, facilities have space for adult women, adult men, and families. An additional option is to design spaces for female and male patrons between the ages of eight and 17 years.

Family-friendly spaces are characterized by their barrier-free entrances, privacy corridors, child-size sinks and toilets, and a sizable number of hooks and shelves for child-size gear. The cabana design is often used in the family area and is popular among senior patrons who appreciate the extra space and private changing areas.

Stage and Auditorium

A stage and related facilities were traditionally built in conjunction with the gymnasium or multipurpose room. Contemporary facilities are building separate stages or working with community groups that provide auditorium space. The stage proper should be about 20 feet in depth and the proscenium opening should be at least two-thirds the width of the crafts area.

The approach to the stage from the floor of the main room should be by inclined ramp with a nonskid surface to accommodate older persons and persons with disabilities and to facilitate movement of equipment. The room should be designed to allow for a portable public address system with matched speakers and be equipped with outlets for additional microphones and audiovisual equipment. When possible, a master control from the office of the building should be considered. All stage lighting should be modern and should be controlled from a dimmer-control cabinet equipped with a rheostat or professional lighting console.

The base and wall of the room should be equipped with electrical outlets to accommodate floor and table lamps, motion picture equipment, floodlights, and other electrical apparatus. A heavy-voltage line may be necessary. Computer cabling, video projection equipment built into the ceiling, and areas where computer equipment can be accessed and used are also desirable.

The entrance should contain double doors. Stage doors should be of sufficient width and height to facilitate the movement of scenery. It is desirable to have a door at the rear of the stage area to permit the handling of stage properties and scenery. Door frames and thresholds must be flush with the floor to permit transfer of large objects. Adequate exit doors should be provided and be equipped with panic hardware.

Space should be provided for the storage of chairs, tables, and portable staging. This space can be under the stage or in an adjacent storage room provided with dollies that have swivel ball-bearing fiber or rubber-covered casters.

Acoustics are an important factor in an auditorium and should be kept in mind in the selection of materials for walls and ceilings. Rigid acoustical materials for ceilings are more economical and discourage vandalism better than suspended acoustical tile.

The entrance to the auditorium should contain double doors and should be at the end opposite the stage. Each door should have a minimum unobstructed opening of at least 32 inches with a removable mullion.

Game Room

The game room, approximately 30 feet by 64 feet in size, is designed for a variety of games including pool, table tennis, foosball, video games, and computer games. The game room may also include tables for billiards, table tennis, and other popular table-top games. In planning this room, sufficient storage space should be provided for the various items of game equipment and supplies.

This room should be close to office supervision and should be acoustically treated. The choice of floor material should be carefully considered because of the heavy traffic anticipated in this room. Windows may be placed high in the walls to reduce glass breakage. A chair rail or wainscotting to prevent the marring of walls should be installed to a height of three feet above the floor. Whenever possible, noncontact (non-marring) furniture should be used.

Kitchen

A kitchen is desirable for most community and neighborhood recreation centers. There is a choice between having a warming kitchen where the food is prepared elsewhere and taken on-site and served or having a full-service kitchen. Warming kitchens have become very popular with food preparation done either by a vendor or in a centralized kitchen. All kitchens must meet the local and state health board requirements and are subject to regular inspections. The kitchen should be located near the multipurpose rooms and the gymnasium. The kitchen is sometimes placed between two multipurpose rooms and made available to both rooms by the use of aluminum roll-up doors.

Adequate storage space, cabinet space, and electrical outlets for such appliances as the refrigerator, range, microwave oven, dishwasher, and can openers should be provided. Exhaust fans should also be installed.

Arts and Crafts Room

A separate room for arts should conform to local health regulations and have an open floor space at least 54 inches wide. Ample storage cabinets, closets, or lockers should be included for the safe storage of craft materials, unfinished projects, and exhibit materials. Base and wall outlets should be provided in all club rooms for the operation of electric irons, sewing machines, power tools, movie projectors, and other equipment. If a kiln is used, it should be equipped with a heavy-duty 220-volt electrical outlet. Bulletin boards and exhibit cases may be used to display completed projects.

Computer Room

Many recreation centers have computer rooms. A computer room may have few or many computers and is open to the general public. The room is networked and ideally linked to a T1 line for fast Internet access. It is best to work with information technology (IT) experts to design and manage the network. Issues of security and keeping inappropriate material off the computers are a major concern for most IT managers and recreation staff. Many recreation centers are now organized for wireless access from anywhere in the building.

Information Desk, Lobby, and Community Area

The information desk and lobby is located at the entrance of the recreation center. The information desk is the first contact point for all recreation center users and should be positioned to provide staff a direct line of sight with the entrance area. The counter should be accessible by individuals with disabilities as well as individuals who are able-bodied. This area has computer terminals and is networked. It provides space for information distribution and registration.

Depending on the size of the center, season, and time of day it may be staffed by one to five individuals. The adjacent lobby is spacious, so when a number of people are present it does not feel crowded and provides a queue area when needed. It provides access to the remainder of the building. The community area should open off the lobby and, if possible, should be close to the central office and to other recreation center features.

The community area and lobby are often combined into one space. This area should be attractively lighted and should contain a wall-mounted and recessed drinking fountain, comfortable seating, television monitors, wireless access, and other amenities. Adequate space, preferably recessed, and electrical and water connections for automatic vending machines may be included.

Carpet floor covering is desirable; however, terrazzo, quarry tile, and patio tile are preferred when cigarette damage is a possibility in those facilities that allow smoking.

Office

The community center and supercenter provide offices for administrative, supervisory, and building staff. Each office area has a different function and should be so designed. The administrative area may be the primary office for the recreation and park department and should be separate from the entrance to the building. It will be in the same building but, because of the function, should not be in the main flow of traffic. Supervisory and building staff should be closer to the action. Building staff should be located so they can see the day-to-day operations of the facility. This places them in the flow of activities so that they are available to handle day-to-day challenges and needs. However, provision must be made to ensure privacy when dealing with disciplinary problems, small meetings, and the like. Secretarial and program offices should be adjacent to the director's office.

Storage Areas

One of the most common errors in planning recreation centers is lack of sufficient storage space for equipment, maintenance, and custodial purposes. An area adjacent to the gymnasium should be provided for such storage. It should have an eight-foot-wide roll-up door opening with flush, louvered doors and a flush threshold to permit passage of the most bulky equipment. The minimum size of the storage room should be approximately 800 to 1,200 square feet. Provision should be made for storage of inflated balls, bats, softballs, and other supplies, either in separate cabinets or a special closet. Appropriate bins, shelves, and racks are suggested. In addition, a recessed alcove for the storage of a piano is desirable. Storage rooms should be located strategically throughout the building to support specialized needs as well as to reduce the amount of time to move equipment into rooms.

The maintenance storage room varies in size depending on the adjacent outdoor space and the size of the building. The room is ordinarily located on the ground level adjacent to the outdoor areas. An outside entrance should be provided by means of a burglar-resistant door large enough to permit the passage of motorized maintenance equipment. Recessed wall shelving and cabinet storage should be provided for tools, supplies, and equipment. This space should contain hot and cold water, a slop sink, a lavatory, a water closet, and a clothes closet. The floor should be concrete and pitched to a central drain. The junction of the floor and wall should be covered. A supply closet equipped with a slop sink and space for mops, pails, brooms, and cleaning supplies should be centrally located on each floor level.

Meeting and Multipurpose Classrooms

Experience indicates the desirability of providing a minimum of 1,000 square feet of floor space per meeting room. For community recreation centers, at least three to five rooms should be provided for multiple use. At least one large club room should be located adjoining a kitchen or warming room. The rooms may use moveable walls to increase or decrease classroom size.

When windows in clubrooms and lounges are placed high in a wall, they are not broken as often as low windows and they also allow more space for furniture, bulletin boards, pegboards, chalkboards, and exhibits. Since broken window glass is a major problem, a non-breakable type of pane is preferred. Windows may be omitted and sky domes and vent domes used, thus eliminating the need for draperies, venetian blinds, and curtains—all items subject to vandalism.

A chair rail or wainscotting to prevent the marring of walls should be installed to a height of three feet above the floor. Whenever possible, non-contact (non-marring) furniture should be used. Floor-level radiant heat in rooms where programs for small children will be conducted should be considered.

Photography Room

A special room can be equipped as a darkroom. Ventilation should be provided through light-proof ventilators. Hot and cold running water, special light outlets (both wall and base), and photographic sinks for developing and washing prints should also be provided. A mixer is desirable to control the water temperatures accurately. A filter should also be provided if the water quality is not good. Doors must be light-proof.

Music Room

The size of the music room should be determined by the potential number in the choral or instrumental group using this facility at any given time. A guide commonly used is to allow 20 square feet for each participant. Provision should be made for the storage of music, instruments, band uniforms, and supplies. Cabinets and shelves that may be locked are commonly used to store music equipment.

Auxiliary Gymnasium

The auxiliary gymnasium (see also Chapter 22) is for such activities as wrestling, weight lifting, tumbling, gymnastics (see Figure 15.1), fencing, and apparatus work. Acoustical treatment for this room is desirable. The size of the room and height of the ceiling will depend on the various activities for which this facility will be used. The floor should be treated with material that will withstand the use of such equipment as heavy weights.

At least one well-ventilated storage room will be needed for equipment and supplies used in the auxiliary gymnasium. If the apparatus is to be cleared from this room, an additional apparatus storage room should be provided.

Specialized Recreation Centers

Many cities and communities provide recreation programs that require specialized facilities. While the construction of these facilities can be justified in the majority of cases, care must be taken to provide for maximum year-round use. The specialized centers should be centrally located to serve all the public.

Art Center

In recent years, many cities have constructed community art centers to satisfy the public demand for programs in the arts. The size of the facility will be determined by the number of people to be served and type of art programs to be conducted. Generally, art centers will include work areas for ceramics, sculpture, painting, and sketching. Depending on the interests in the community, a center may also include facilities for woodworking, lapidary, stonecutting, and other arts and crafts. Some art centers include facilities for dance, music, and drama classes and programs as well.

Preschool Center

Preschool centers for day care, Head Start, and nursery school programs are being built in some communities with the aid of grants or federal funds. These buildings are smaller than neighborhood center buildings, and the design scale is geared to preschool children. Generally, the centers include a large multipurpose room, small rooms for small-group activities, an office, a kitchen and eating area, and ample storage space. Special care should be taken to ensure good acoustic treatment in the center.

Senior Citizen Centers

Senior citizen centers are similar in design to neighborhood recreation centers. However, more emphasis is placed on facilities for the arts, areas for conversation, and rooms for passive games and wellness activities than for large-scale physical activities. While a gymnasium is seldom found in a senior citizen area, a large multi-purpose room is needed for square dancing, shuffleboard, and similar activities. The senior citizen center should be a single-floor building and special care should be taken to eliminate all hazards such as steps and protrusions on walls.

Aquatic Center (Natatorium)

Many neighborhoods and communities have a considerable interest in water activities and demand that an aquatic center (see also Chapter 13) be included as part of the recreation center. A combination of learn-to-swim and therapy spaces, lap lanes, wave pools, lazy rivers, and water playgrounds are becoming more common. As with any good design, several factors such as local competition, demographics, geography, and community expectations and backing must be considered. Mixing the types of aquatic attractions makes more effective use of available space and serves a larger clientele.

A recent trend in new facilities is to have separate systems to control different bodies of water. In a single system design, the entire facility may be such down for water treatment. In contrast, a separate system design allows for different water temperatures, shutting down low activity spaces, or treating contaminates spaces without closing the entire facility.

Figure 15.1
Free-standing Gymnastics Area

Teen Centers

While teen centers have been very popular and continue to be built, the trend today is to construct multiuse centers that will provide opportunities for teen programs along with other activities. For example, a teen office and lounge are provided in many community recreation centers.

When a separate teen center is desired, it could include:

- multipurpose meeting rooms
- gymnasium
- skatepark
- shower and locker rooms
- game room
- multimedia room
- music, art, and theatre areas
- conversation areas
- restrooms
- lounge and lobby
- office and security station

Other Specialized Spaces or Facilities

The planning of any specialized recreation center demands a precise and logical approach. Since a recreation center reflects the unique needs and interests of a neighborhood or community, the specific design will vary, but the preliminary considerations of planning objectives will be the same. Types of spaces include fitness rooms, weight rooms, running tracks, child care, aerobics, and a multimedia center. The successful incorporation of accepted planning objectives will ensure maximum use of the building. The initial functional/spatial specification and the continuous reevaluation of the architectural specifications of the building prior to its construction should be considered in terms of the following checklist for indoor recreation facilities:

- Has the most effective use of the entire structure been determined?
- Does the preliminary sketch include all the essential facilities necessary to fulfill the program objectives?
- Does the layout provide for flexibility in use and for future expansion?
- Does the floor plan permit convenient access to and facilitate circulation within the building?
- Does the floor plan provide for ease of supervision and administration of the building?
- Have individual rooms been located to encourage multiple use within safety limits?
- Has the building been designed to ensure opportunity for its use by all members of the community, including older persons and individuals with disabilities?
- Has the building been designed to minimize the impact on the environment and occupants?

- Does the design encompass accepted aesthetic qualities that relate harmoniously to the surroundings?
- Is the building designed to ensure cooperative use with other public or private agencies?
- Is the building designed to permit economy in construction and subsequent maintenance?

Outdoor Facilities and Open Spaces

Population growth projections suggest that few metropolitan areas in the United States have sufficient open space to meet the demands of the future. Based on these projections, it is imperative that planning boards and commissions on all levels of government review previous planning philosophies with the intent of revision or, when necessary, the development of new master plans.

As open space becomes more expensive and less available greater consideration must be given to multiple use of available lands and every measure taken to use them both efficiently and consistent with good environmental management. Municipal and school authorities should acquire, plan, and develop areas for joint use. This process calls for professional guidance in the fields of planning, designing, and engineering and for the advice and counsel of professionals in the fields of education, recreation, community development, and park planning.

The most efficient and successful planning is accomplished when everyone in the organization, particularly those who will be identified with the finished product, have an opportunity to participate in the planning. Those who are to be served also should have a voice in the planning through community meetings.

Standards

Various standards for the size, location, and number of educational and recreation areas and facilities (See Appendix H) have been proposed over the years by persons with a great deal of experience in the operation of such areas and facilities. These standards are formulated to make possible a program to serve the basic needs of people for physical education and recreation. However, they are not valid in prescribing specific activities or facilities for every neighborhood. While they are a useful guide in the acquisition and construction of a property, standards can seldom, if ever, be applied completely or without modification, because a typical or common situation is seldom found. Standards are formulated to provide a basis for the intelligent development of local plans. Therefore, the standards for areas and facilities should be reviewed and appraised for each planning unit and modified whenever changing conditions warrant revision.

Photo by Meghan Rosselli

Play apparatus

Standards for areas and facilities developed by private planning firms, public agencies, and service organizations at the local, state, and national levels have been widely endorsed throughout the United States and have provided the basis for recommendations in scores of long-range plans for school, park, and recreation systems. The proposal that at least one acre of recreation and park space be set aside by urban areas for every 100 members of the present and estimated future population has been more widely accepted than any other space standard. However, this standard does not relate to the demographic or physiographic character of particular locales and is becoming obsolete. Professional and governmental authorities, including the National Recreation and Park Association and the National Park Service, have previously suggested the desirability of providing an even higher ratio of land-to-population in towns and small cities.

Modification of this general standard has been suggested for all planning entities based upon local requirements for populated cities. Some municipal planning officials believe the development of large outlying properties owned by the municipality will help meet the recognized deficiency in the inner municipality. However, this proposal should be considered as a practicable substitute indicative not just of necessity, but also of feasibility.

Previous number standards related to the number of tennis courts or swimming pools per thousands of people and so forth. Such numbers do not take into consideration the land or people and the climatic and geographic locale of the planning entity. The specification and allocation of facilities per thousand are arbitrary. They neither reflect the requirements of the community or neighborhood nor are universally applicable. A planning process of interaction and participation by the public should determine the number of facilities from one end of town to the other.

Recreation acreage should be based on potential usage. Basing acreage and number of facilities on potential usage has

some serious deficiencies but remains the best possible approach. Marketing demand studies can suggest levels of use but do not account for changing recreation patterns, changes in the economy, unanticipated competition, and the like. Guidelines for acreage allocations for different park types are only illustrative. Every activity has a public demand. The demand for some activities is often met by the commercial, nonprofit, or volunteer sector. Ski lodges, tennis centers, and other corporations all conduct market studies to ascertain the leisure needs of and probable use by their clientele. Public agencies must conduct comparable studies to analyze demand. If the municipality can ascertain the probable use, turnover, capacity, and low/peak load for each activity, it can compute the number of activity stations and facilities for each activity group. The park acreage is then computed for actual facilities, for circulating paths and roads, for landscaping, and for other features.

Park and Recreation Areas

The types of outdoor recreation areas described here represent a variety of service units that may be used in leisure, physical education, and competitive or recreational sport programs. Local conditions will dictate to a large extent which types are to be used in any given locality. Hence, different combinations of areas and facilities will emerge as the solution to the problem of meeting the needs and interests of a particular locality.

There is some controversy over parkland aesthetics as measured by the terms active and passive recreation. Many individuals with inherent interest in recreation or leisure pursuits associated with nature denounce the intrusion into parklands by activities that alter the natural environment. Battles have been fought over ball diamond location, loss

Photo by Meghan Rosselli

Celebration Station

Additional examples of play equipment.

of wetlands, and elimination of native species. Obviously, these two groups have different attitudes about the character and purpose of parklands. Parklands can be designed for active or passive use, or both, without destroying their aesthetic values. The use of parklands should reflect the greatest good for the greatest number and the protection of the health, well-being, and safety of all. Parklands may be of multiple-use in many cases, but there are also strong cases for maintaining natural areas. The balance between the two is often difficult to agree upon, but there should be a commitment for both. Community involvement is essential in helping to make these determinations. In some instances, state and federal environmental standards may determine what can and cannot be accomplished.

If a community is split over use of parklands, a cost-benefit analysis should be made to ascertain the feasibility and costs of various options. There is no sense in preserving a swamp that was created artificially and lacks any ecological value, but a natural swamp might be found elsewhere and preserved to meet specific needs and interests. There are alternatives in every planning process and they should be considered.

Abandoned industrial sites such as strip mines, waste disposal areas, and sand and gravel pits offer unique possibilities for park and recreation development. In many cases, recreation use is not only the most beneficial but the most economic use of such sites. The cost of development of the sites can sometimes be born by the owner, by state or federal reclamation funds, or through previous court settlements. Brownfields, waste disposal sites, and other areas that have been adversely affected by previous use should be carefully assessed and tested before being accepted for recreation

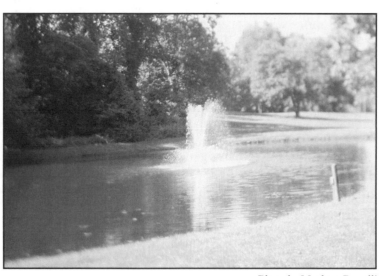

Fountain

and park use. The cost of environmental cleanup can easily run into the millions of dollars. The recreation planner must not overlook the possibility of obtaining these sites for public use. If possible, cooperative planning should be started while the site is still being used by industry so landscape features can be developed to make it more appealing for recreation use.

Playlot/Mini-Parks: Location, Size, and Features

A playlot/mini-park is a small recreational area designed for the safe play of preschool children. As an independent unit, the playlot/mini-

Example of an outdoor court.

Photo by Meghan Rosselli

A good example of park lighting.

park is most frequently developed in large housing projects or in other densely populated urban areas with high concentrations of preschool children. More often, it is incorporated as a feature of a larger recreation area. If a community is able to operate a neighborhood park within a one-quarter-mile zone of every home, playlots should be located at the playground sites. A location near a playground entrance close to restrooms and away from active game areas is best.

The playlot/mini-park should be enclosed with a low fence or solid planting to assist mothers or guardians in safeguarding their children. Thought should be given to placement of benches, with and without shade, for ease of supervision and comfort for parents and guardians. A drinking fountain with a step for tots will serve both children and adults. Playground equipment geared to the preschool child should combine attractive traditional play apparatus with creative, imaginative alternatives. Playground equipment should be marked with signs to designate the age group for which it is designed.

Neighborhood Parks

The neighborhood park is land set aside primarily for both active and passive recreation. Ideally, it gives the impression of being rural, sylvan, or national in its character. It emphasizes horticultural features with spacious turf areas bordered by trees, shrubs, and, sometimes, floral arrangements. It is essential in densely populated areas but not required where there is ample yard space at individual home sites.

A neighborhood park should be provided for each neighborhood. In many neighborhoods, it will be incorporated in the park-school site. A separate location is required if this combination is not feasible. A separately located neighborhood park normally requires three to five acres. As a measure of expediency; however, an isolated area as small as one or two acres may be used. Sometimes the functions of a neighborhood park can be satisfactorily included in a community or citywide park.

The neighborhood park plays an important role in setting standards for community aesthetics. Therefore, it should include open lawn areas, plantings, and walks. Sculpture forms, pools, and fountains should also be considered for ornamentation. Creative planning will employ contouring, contrasting surfaces, masonry, and other modern techniques to provide both eye appeal and utility.

Community Parks

The community park, like the neighborhood park, is designed primarily to provide facilities for a variety of types of organized recreation activities but it should also have the characteristics of a landscaped park. It should include passive recreation areas, provide visibility for security purposes, and have adequate lighting for night-time security. It usually serves as the playground for the children living in the immediate neighborhood but its primary service is to a much wider age group. Thus, it supplies a greater variety of facilities and more extensive service than can be justified at the neighborhood park. The school child, teenager, young adult, hobbyist, senior citizen, and family group all find attractive facilities at the well-developed community park and playfield. Because there is no school building at this area, some type of indoor facility is needed. In many cases, a multipurpose recreation center is provided to meet this need.

Citywide or District Parks

The citywide or district park serves a district of a large city or an entire smaller city. It should serve a population of 50,000 to 100,000 with a

Photo by Meghan Rosselli

Pagoda

wide variety of activities. The ideal location for this area is in combination with a high school as a park-school complex. Where this is not feasible, consideration should be given to placing the park as close as possible to the center of the population to be served.

The land available will be a determining factor in site selection. While the service zone will vary according to population density, a normal use zone is two to four miles. The size may range from 50 to 100 acres but is generally recommended to be in excess of 100 acres.

Depending on available acreage, topography, and natural features, the city-wide or district-park will contain a large number of different components. These would include, but not be limited to, the following:

- fields for baseball, football, soccer, and softball (see Chapter 11)
- tennis center (see Chapter 10)
- winter sports facilities (see Chapter 19)
- recreation or day-camp center
- accessible picnic areas (group and family) with barbeques
- pavilion with fireplace cycling paths or tracks
- swimming pool (see Chapter 13)
- water sports lake
- golf course (which requires considerably more acreage)
- walking trails with intermittent fitness equipment nature trails
- skateparks (see Chapter 19)
- multiple playgrounds for different age groups
- parking areas
- outdoor theater

The above facilities should be separated by large turf and landscaped areas. Natural areas and perimeter buffers should be provided.

Special-Use Areas and Facilities

Trails

Trails used by walkers and joggers have become very popular. In many locations in the United States, old, abandoned rail lines have been secured from the railroad companies. In some cases the companies have salvaged the rails and cross ties. In other cases they have donated the land, rails, and ties to the government. Once a trail has been established, it should easily blend into the environment. The planners need to consider the climate, flora and fauna, topography, local history, and available materials for the infrastructure.

The width of a walking trail should be between three and six feet. When developing a walking trail, the following points should

be considered: 1) local community input, 2) initial cost and long-term maintenance costs, 3) interesting attractions featured along the trail, 4) access to public transportation, 5) appropriate signage (e.g., names of plants and trees, distances, grades or elevations, direction of trail, trail layout and map, warnings of hazards, etc.), 6) surface preparation (e.g., asphalt, dirt, gravel, wood chips, saw dust, etc.), 7) fitness equipment along trail, and 8) loops and networks to provide options for the walkers. Many communities are developing city-wide trail systems that link together walking and bicycle paths with the park trails being the anchor for the system.

A walking trail requires some basic infrastructure: 1) handicapped accessibility (e.g., ramps, hand-rails); 2) adequate parking at the beginning of the trail and at select entry points along the trail; 3) rest stops with benches, drinking water, rest rooms, shelters, and picnic areas; and 4) a trail design to eliminate water drainage problems and minimize vandalism.

Bicycle Facilities and Pathways

Most of the recommended bicycle programs and facilities will require considerable investments of time and money to bring them to fruition. An alternative program might be considered. This program would develop bicycle-touring routes in and across the country using rural and low-volume vehicular routes. The only expenses involved in the creation of this system are for initial system planning, printing bikeway maps, and marking intersections. County and city governments together with schools and universities have implemented touring systems.

The steps in the development of bicycling facilities are:

Photo by Meghan Rosselli
Covered bridge

- Appoint a committee from interested groups of individuals, including representatives of educational institutions and the recreation department.
- Make a survey of county road maps and mark a conceptual bicycle system on a work map. One of the objectives is to create a roughly circular route. "Spoke" routes would radiate from central sites to the peripheral route. Select the safest possible routes. High-volume roads and intersections should be avoided. After the road map is finished, the committee should find that it has the framework for an adequate bicycling touring system.
- The next step involves field reconnaissance of the roads marked on the working map. Alternate routes may be selected if the original roads are not appropriate for bicycling. Actual travel by bicycle is recommended for the reconnaissance.
- Following the completion of the field reconnaissance, the next step is the drafting of the final bikeway map. Titles and safety information are also indicated on the map. The back of the map may be filled with a variety of safety tips and information about the local community. The bikeway should be marked, especially the abrupt turns. Paint distinctive symbols and arrows on the pavement of the road. Standard highway marking paint may be used and stencils for the symbols may be cut from heavy gauge linoleum.

Cycle trails require some additional planning beyond that needed for a walking or jogging trail. The planners need to include the following additional factors in the design: 1) minimum width of dual path should be 12 feet, 2) the path should have a safety zone on either side extending five feet clear of all vegetation, 3) the ideal surface material is asphalt for the path and small gravel or brick chips for the safety buffer, 4) appropriate sight lines will need to be determined for cyclists to avoid hitting walkers on corners, and 5) the cyclists may require bike racks at rest areas.

Bridle Paths and Rings

Horseback riding is popular with all age groups but is generally restricted to the larger park areas because of space requirements. Riding trails, sometimes called bridle paths, are usually a minimum of 10 feet wide to permit riders going in opposite directions to pass safely. Except on very steep terrain, very little is required in the way of construction. Clearing, a small amount of leveling, removal of large rocks and boulders, and trimming or removal of low-hanging tree limbs constitute the major items. Most small streams can be forded but an occasional bridge may be required as well as cross drainage on steep gradients. No special surfacing is required except that a gravel base may be needed in wet or boggy areas that cannot be avoided. Tanbark, cinders, and other materials are also used frequently on heavily used trails and in areas of concentrated use around hitching racks and in riding rings.

Stables and adjoining facilities such as feed racks, holding corrals, riding rings, and hitching racks should be located at least 500 feet from the nearest public-use area because of the fly and odor problem. The size of these facilities will depend on the number of horses. However, the stable will ordinarily contain a limited number of horse stalls, a feed storage room, a tack room, a small office, and restroom facilities. A fenced enclosure commonly called a holding corral or paddock into which the horses can be turned at the end of the day is required. A surfaced riding ring, sometimes encircled with a rail fence, is frequently provided for training novices in the fundamentals of riding.

Finally, horse riding trails are not compatible with walkers or cyclists. The horse trail cannot be of hard surface (e.g., asphalt or concrete) but rather a softer topsoil and clay mixture. The trail needs a good base in order to reduce maintenance costs. The tree limbs need to be cut close to the trunk. It is also necessary to provide good horizontal vegetation clearance (over six feet) and vertical vegetation clearance (over 10 feet).

Golf Courses

The design, construction, operation, and maintenance of golf courses is too vast a subject to be covered in detail in this publication. For general information and guidance, write the National Golf Foundation at 1150 South US Highway One, Suite 401, Jupiter, FL 33477 or The American Society of Golf Course Architects, 125 North Executive Drive, Suite 106, Brookfield, WI 53005.

The creation of new golf course facilities throughout the nation continued at a healthy pace during the first decade of the new century. As the popularity of the game continues to grow, there is an obvious need to increase the number of golf courses to keep up with demand.

Golf course construction costs vary greatly, but generally planners can count on spending at least $2.5 million. This does not include the cost of the land. A golf course construction budget might look like this in 2008 dollars:

- Construction of 18-hole course — $2.5 to $4.5 million*
- Maintenance equipment — $300,000 to $500,000
- Maintenance building — $125,000 to $450,000
- Clubhouse — $750,000 to $1.5 million
- Total — $3.9 to $6.95 million

* Includes basic golf course construction, clearing, grading, drainage, construction of tees, fairway and fairway features, greens, sand bunkers, irrigation system, seeding and grassing, shelters, bridges, and cart paths.

It must be emphasized that these cost figures are intended only as a rough guideline and do not include the cost of land, entry road, parking lot, other support facilities (e.g., restrooms, chemical storage areas, fuel storage, sand and topsoil storage areas, golf cart storage space, practice putting green, driving range, and tree nursery), golf course architect, and other necessary professional consulting fees. In addition, maintenance costs usually run between $250,000 and $650,000 annually, plus club operations and golf cart fleets.

Assuming the land is suitable for construction of a golf course, the following space requirements must be taken into consideration:

- For a standard 18-hole course—145 to 200 acres.
- For shorter executive courses—75 to 120 acres.
- For a standard 9-hole course—70 to 90 acres.
- For a 9-hole par three course (including a couple of par four holes)—45 to 60 acres.

Some of the most desirable features of the land to be used include rolling hills, interesting landscaping, ravines, creeks and ponds or lake sites, and irrigation resources. The more of these features that can be found on a piece of land, the less the overall construction cost will be. The planners need to also be concerned about environmental issues (e.g., wetlands, invasive plants and bugs), drainage, and quality of the soil. Other key components for site selection are the ease of utility connections and accessibility to the new project.

Marinas and Boat Ramps

America abounds in waterways. The myriad of inland lakes, the rivers and streams, the vast Great Lakes, and the thousands of miles of coastline invite America's citizens to take advantage of this natural resource. Today, boating commands more of the recreation dollar than baseball, fishing, golf, or any other single activity. There is a need for efficient, realistic, and functional planning for facilities to accommodate the present needs and the future growth that this recreation interest will precipitate. The launching, mooring, and storage of yachts and rowboats are the function of a marina that will serve the needs of the recreation boat owner.

It is suggested that knowledgeable and experienced personnel be engaged to study the number, types, and sizes of existing boats in the area, the number and size of existing berthing facilities, and the condition of such existing facilities. The survey should also include the potential population

Photo by Meghan Rosselli

Fishing deck

growth in the community and surrounding area to determine the future boat ownership. An accurate and comprehensive evaluation of such a study is the first step in planning a marina.

The study will determine the next important consideration in laying out a marina: selecting the correct number of slips of each size that will be required. Based on the needs of the community to be served, planners will determine the necessary number of slips to accommodate boats of various sizes.

Because marinas vary so greatly in their design, function, location, and capacity, it is virtually impossible to arrive at standard conclusions and judgments concerning a model marina. Each planner will be able to apply the general principles to his unique circumstances. From that point, however, he must adapt his marina to the peculiar needs and characteristics of a community.

A marina, since it is a parking lot for boats, will most likely be surrounded by a repair shop, fuel station, dry dock area, and general marine supply shop. Key planning issues include, but are not limited to: 1) environmental impact, 2) local politics, 3) waste management, 4) conservation, 5) quality of construction and compatibility with the environment, 6) financing (i.e., initial cost and long-term maintenance costs), 7) management and safety, 8) size of the project, and 9) monitoring of environmental problems.

A boat ramp is necessary for launching boats into a waterway. The initial task is to locate adequate, safe launching and retrieval facilities. Contrary to popular opinion, suitable locations for boat ramps are hard to find. Planners should consider the following when selecting a suitable location for a boat ramp: 1) protection from severe weather; 2) minimal impact on the surrounding environment; 3) large enough space to accommodate the ramp and trailer and vehicle parking as well as rigging and maneuvering of trailers; 4) accessibility to the proposed site by an all-weather road; 5) ancillary facilities such as restrooms, water supply, night lighting, telephone accessibility, wash down area, and waste disposal facility; 6) legal requirements (e.g., requirement for environmental impact study, zoning requirements, etc.); 7) local community input; 8) initial cost and long-term maintenance costs; and 9) water conditions (e.g., wave patterns and currents).

Curling

Curling is an ice sport popular in Canada and the northern United States. The advent of artificial ice has broadened the popularity of curling and extended its geographical interest zone. Sponsored by clubs and leagues, it is played with hand-propelled 42.5 pound stones, referred to as rocks. The curling sheet is a level ice area 146 feet long and between 14 feet 2 inches and 16 feet, 5 inches wide. A key aspect of the playing surface is the spraying of water droplets, called pebbles, on the ice. Friction between the stone and pebble cause the stone to "curl" that is, to turn inside or outside. The object is to slide one team's rocks nearest the center of a circle, called the house, at each end of the rink.

The house is a set of three concentric circles. The center of the house is formed by the intersection of two lines, center line and tee line, which divides the house into quarters. This is known as the button. The center line is drawn lengthwise down the center of the sheet. The tee line is drawn parallel to and 16 feet from the backboard. Two additional lines, the hoglines, are drawn parallel to and 37 feet from the backboard. The three rings that make up the button are set with diameters of four, eight, and 12 feet. Usually distinguished by color, the inner rings are used to determine which stone is closer to the center. The curler pushes off a traction device, called a hack, which is located 12 feet behind each button.

Performing Arts Areas

In the past few years there has been increased demand for suitable indoor and outdoor facilities for operas, plays, band and orchestral concerts, pageants, festivals, holiday programs, and civic celebrations. When performed outdoors, such activities usually require a stage or band shell with adjoining amphitheater capable of accommodating large numbers of spectators. Selection of the proper site for an outdoor theater is of primary importance. It should have good acoustical properties and be located in a quiet place away from the noise of traffic or of groups at play. A natural bowl or depression on a hillside with a slope of 10 to 20 degrees, preferably bordered by slopes or densely wooded areas, provides a fine location.

At some theaters, people sit on the slope of the amphitheater. At others, permanent seats are installed. Terraces with a turf surface are not recommended because they are too difficult to maintain. Sufficient level space should be provided at the rear of the seating area for the circulation of spectators, and aisles should be wide enough to facilitate the seating of large numbers in a short period of time.

Public comfort stations and refreshment facilities are usually provided near the entrance to the amphitheater. Provision for the nearby parking of automobiles is essential, but parking areas must be located where noises and car lights do not disturb the stage action.

The dimensions of the stage are determined by the proposed uses but rarely should a stage be less than 50 feet in width or 30 feet in depth. The rear of the stage may be a wall or high hedge, or even a planting of trees, and the wings may be formed by natural plant materials. The band or music shell, however, is more satisfactory for projecting voices and sound free from echoes and interference. A vertical rear wall with an inclined ceiling is not only the simplest and most economical to construct but affords excellent acoustical qualities.

The band shell usually contains dressing rooms, restrooms, storage space, and control centers for amplifying and lighting equipment, although sometimes these facilities are provided in separate structures near the back of the stage. An orchestra pit is generally located between the amphitheatre and the stage.

Mobile storage units with self-contained lighting and acoustical systems are becoming very popular, because they can be used in many parks instead of restricting programs to one permanent location. Equipped to serve as a band shell, stage, puppet theater, or platform for other performing arts, these mobile units can bring productions to audiences never exposed to such activities. Excellent units can be obtained at a cost less than that required for a permanent band shell.

Archery Range

This sport appeals to a sizable group in most communities. Sufficient space is needed to ensure the safety and enjoyment of the participants. An earth bunker or bales of hay and straw piled up to the top of the target may protect this space.

An archery range (see Chapter 24) should be fairly level. Orientation should be north and south so the archers will not be facing the sun. A fence enclosure is desirable, but not essential. The public should be controlled in some manner, however, so they do not walk through the range.

Bocce Ball

A bocce court is 91 feet by 13 feet. Many boccie courts are sunken, with retaining walls constructed out of pressure-treated landscaping timbers. When built above ground, a bocce court needs side and back walls. These can be constructed of wood, lattice, landscape stones, brick, or cinder block.

The bocce court area should include:

- shade trees
- flowers
- storage area for equipment
- lawn chairs and tables
- possibly lights for evening play.

Dog Parks

A dog park is a facility for dogs to exercise and play off leash in a controlled environment. A minimum area of 8,000 square feet of fenced perimeter is needed although a larger area of preferred. Dog parks vary in design and may contain some or all of the following elements:

- paved or gravel double-gated entry
- excrement pickup stations and trash cans
- hills or mounds
- swim area with pond or pool
- water spigot with bowl or flushable water boel system
- benches, tables, and covered shelters placed in shaded and unshaded areas
- granite, gravel, sand, or native plants and sturdy grasses
- gravel or paved warning track around the inside of the fence perimeter
- coat and leash rack near gate
- shy/small dog area
- time-out area for dogs who need to be contained (e.g., overexcited or aggressive, in heat, bleeding, etc.)

Areas for Outdoor Education and Recreation

Outdoor education is a term that refers to learning activities in, and for, the outdoors. Such activities can be provided in the curriculums of schools, colleges, and universities as well as in the programs of recreation; camping; and federal, state, and community agencies. Outdoor education is a means of curriculum extension and enrichment through outdoor experiences.

It is not a separate discipline with prescribed objectives, like science and mathematics; it is simply a learning climate that offers opportunities for direct laboratory experiences in identifying and resolving real-life problems, for acquiring skills with which to enjoy a lifetime of creative living, for building concepts and developing concern about humankind and the natural environment, and for getting people back in touch with those aspects of living where our roots were once firm and deep.

Outdoor education and outdoor recreation encompass a variety of activities, many of which can be conducted on a single, large tract of land. With careful planning, facilities, some in or near an urban area and others in more rural places, can be used. An outdoor-education complex on one piece of land or on several plots in close proximity has many advantages. Such a site lends itself

to wide community use with responsibilities for leadership and finances shared by several agencies. Obviously, the size and physical characteristics of an outdoor-education complex, and the resulting equipment and transportation needs, will depend on the geographic location and the topography of the land. Facilities and types of site treatment for a complex that would accommodate a broad program of outdoor education and outdoor recreation, and which would constitute an outdoor laboratory or field campus, are briefly described below. It is assumed that there will be many areas and facilities, public and private that can also be used in a comprehensive program.

Considerations in Selecting and Developing Park Sites

Size

The type of program planned should determine the size of the site. Size alone does not necessarily mean much except that it does affect the numbers of certain species of wildlife that might live in the area. A large area does not necessarily have a diversity of physical features. It may just be level land, harboring only a few species of trees, with no particularly outstanding features. Nevertheless, such an area could be made interesting from an educational point of view, provided good leadership and programming is available.

Many schools, recreation departments, and community agencies already have school sites, parks, and recreation areas that could be developed for outdoor programs. Schools, as well as other agencies, in some sections of the country, also have forest lands that could be developed and used in a broad educational and recreation program.

Site Characteristics

The type of program planned also determines the characteristics of the site. If plans call for a resident camp, many more requirements must be met than if the site will be used only on a daily

Photo by Meghan Rosselli

Picnic shelter

Photo by Meghan Rosselli

Picnic pavilion

basis. If the land and facilities are to contribute to all aspects of the educational curriculum, or if there is to be special emphasis on science, conservation, and outdoor skills, many characteristics will need to be considered, such as the following:

- A location to give some privacy and solitude.
- Year-round accessibility by road.
- A minimum of natural and manmade hazards.
- Interesting geologic features, such as rock outcroppings, open field, flat terrain, and a variety of soil types.
- A variety of native vegetation including woods.
- Wildlife that can be maintained with sound management.
- A pond, stream, seashore, or large body of water.
- Demonstration areas for conservation practices.
- Woods for practicing outdoor skills and use of native materials.
- Sanitary facilities including good drainage and good drinking water.
- Simple shelters in the event of inclement weather.
- Proximity to adequate medical and hospital services.

Special Features

Many kinds of developments are found in various types of outdoor education areas. Some of these are appropriate for camps, some for outdoor laboratories or nature centers, and some for outdoor recreation and sport centers. An outdoor education and outdoor recreation complex would include many site plans and facilities not possible in more limited areas. The adaptability of the area to the proposed program, the cost of construction, maintenance problems, aesthetic considerations, and available leadership are all factors in determining what facilities might be developed in a particular land area or cluster of acreages.

Listed below are some of the special developments that might be included in appropriate sites. Some of the features listed are discussed elsewhere in this text and are merely mentioned here. Others, not mentioned in other places, are discussed in more detail.

Grass, shrubs, and trees. They provide shade, prevent soil erosion, provide food and cover for wildlife, serve as windbreaks, mark the boundary of the property, act as a buffer zone to ensure privacy against an adjacent (presently or potentially) populated area, demonstrate principles of plant growth, serve as a resource for ecological studies, and give practice in forest management. A school forest offers many popular activities.

Soil-erosion demonstration areas. Such an area should be rich in vegetation, feature good conservation practices, be situated on inclined terrain, and be located next to a piece of land denuded of its vegetation and also located on an incline. Comparisons can then be made over a period of time to determine what happens to the quantity and quality of soil in both areas.

Wildlife sanctuary. Provide mixed plantings and construct birdhouses, feeders, and bird baths to attract a variety of birds.

Weather station. This is for the study of meteorology and should be located in an area that can be fenced off and locked.

Campfire ring. This facility provides a place for campfires, for conducting orientations before field trips, and for other special programs. The campfire ring should be located in a wooded area to ensure a feeling of isolation. Use logs for seats.

Nature trails. Develop, if space permits, a variety of trails with individual or multiple purposes. The use of trail markers, brochures, and naturalist-conducted programs can focus the trail use. One may be a geology trail winding its way through an area rich in geologic features. Another trail may emphasize the study of erosion while still another may lead to a historic spot.

Pioneer living area. Social studies lessons are vividly illustrated in such an area. Dramatize the life of the pioneer, including such activities as making dyes from plants, cooking outdoors, constructing shelters, learning to identify edible plants, and learning other survival practices.

Observation platform. This platform can be used for observing birds and for studying astronomy. It should be located on the highest point of the property.

Vegetable, bog, and native plant gardens. Each garden features a particular grouping of native plants found in the typical setting in which they normally grow.

Plant grafting. A demonstration area that provides interesting studies in genetics.

Animal-baiting area. Place a salt lick and some meat in a cleared area. Spread loose dirt around the baited spot, press it down with your feet, and smooth it out. Animals attracted to the area will leave their footprints, which can then be observed and studied.

Natural preserve. An area could be set aside in which no developments would be made. It would be given complete protection and would provide a spot for the observation of ecological aspects.

Orienteering courses. The development of several courses for map and compass use would stimulate educational and recreation use of the area.

Greenhouse. A place for the propagation of plants, some of which may be used for area improvement, is important. A greenhouse would make possible an acquaintance with plants and would be a means of providing projects for study during the off-season.

Winter sports area. Places for curling, skating, skiing, and coasting would be desirable in those parts of the country that have sufficient snow and cold weather to make these sports feasible.

Natural play area. An area set aside for children, containing such elements as climbing logs, ropes for swinging across low areas, sandbanks, and hide-and-seek areas, can provide play opportunities different from those found in the city.

Turtle pond. An attractive pond with water and plantings would make possible the study and observation of turtles and other amphibians.

Rifle and skeet ranges. Such an area will provide opportunities for instruction in gun safety as well as for participation in rifle and skeet shooting. These areas should be located away from high use areas and should have controls to monitor potential safety issues.

Casting and angling area. Developments for casting and angling would serve both instructional and recreation uses.

Amphitheater. For large-group programs, an amphitheater would be important. It could be used for lectures, drama, music, and a variety of demonstrations.

Astronomy area. A special area for astronomy may be developed on a large open area, waterfront, dock, or even a roof. Seating facilities are desirable and often a telescope is permanently mounted to facilitate observations.

Bird feeding station. A combination of seeds and syrups may posted to attract a variety of bird life.

Historical markers. Sites of old farms, early settlers' homes, Native American trails and village sites, and pioneer roads are illustrations of the kinds of historical sites that might be used for student projects.

Shelters. Adirondack or picnic shelters can serve day-camp and day-use groups during inclement weather.

Tree stump. Locate a fairly well-preserved tree stump. Make a sloping cut, smooth the top by sanding, and treat it with clear waterproofing material such as fiberglass resin. Much can be learned about tree growth from carefully studying a tree stump.

Herb garden. This garden features food seasoning and medicinal plants and serves as a useful teaching aid for a home economics class.

Photo by Meghan Rosselli

Horshoe pit

Photographic blind. Construct a blind near a bird-feeding station for taking pictures of wild birds.

Evergreen tree nursery. Trees can later be transplanted to desired areas.

Field archery. Targets are set up in wooded areas or fields to simulate actual hunting conditions.

Natural areas. Such areas are left relatively undisturbed and man-made modifications should be avoided as much as possible. These places serve as excellent resources for scientific studies of natural phenomena.

Picnic site. It is desirable to locate the picnic site on the periphery of the property.

Seashore areas. Communities adjacent to seashores may have areas set aside for study and observation. Developments might include ramps or walks to facilitate observation. Walkways through tidelands may be developed as nature trails. One of the national parks has an underwater nature trail.

Outdoor Laboratories

The term "outdoor laboratory" is used for a piece of land (including wetlands, lakes, and seashores) set aside by a school for learning experiences directly related to land and its resources. It may be located close to an individual school or it may serve a group of schools. It may be a part of the school grounds or a section of a park-school development. It may consist of only a few acres nearby or of several hundred acres many miles away. It may serve individual elementary schools, high schools, or universities or all of them jointly. Because outdoor laboratories are extremely varied in their site possibilities and their purposes, no rigid format for their development is possible.

The term "land for learning" has been applied to the school laboratory. It implies the opportunity of school groups to study, explore, and experiment with land and its resources. Outdoor study, field trips, and experiments with water, soil, plants, and animals constitute its major functions. Developments may range from nothing more than a few trails, with the area left natural, to nature trails, class and museum buildings, horticultural plots, developed ponds, forest plantations, gardens, and small-farm operations. The creativity of the teacher or outdoor education specialist, the potential of the available site, and funds available may be the only limiting factors in the development of program facilities.

If a laboratory is heavily used, water and restroom facilities might be essential. A storage building for tools and supplies might also be desirable.

Nature Centers

The term "nature center" is used to designate a particular type of development that will facilitate learning in the outdoors and the growth of recreation interests. The establishment of nature centers is being promoted extensively by several science- and nature-related organizations. Many centers exist across the United States. Children's museums may be considered a part of this development although some of these museums lack adjacent lands for outdoor education.

The Site

Some of the suggestions for the school outdoor education laboratory are applicable here. Nature trails, ponds, bogs, gardens, forest plantings, and the like may provide the variety essential for a rich outdoor education program.

The Building

The building should be designed in order to permit expansion as the program grows and as more funds become available. In its initial stage, the building should contain a minimum space of 2,500 square feet, which is large enough to adequately contain one program. The building should be designed according to the needs set by the program. The following general spaces are recommended:

- Office.
- Restrooms. Access should be provided to the outside as well as to the interior of the building.
- Large meeting room. The wall space can be utilized for exhibits. Low cabinets along the walls should be provided for storage of educational equipment and supplies. A long counter providing work and display space should be constructed on top of the cabinets.
- Classrooms. Moveable walls should be provided so that a class may be broken up into smaller groups if necessary.
- Workroom. This room would be used for constructing displays and for arts and crafts.
- Science laboratory. A room should be equipped with microscopes, soil- and mineral-testing equipment, and other materials necessary for

scientific studies. Inclusion of GPS and GIS technology has become more common.
- Library. The large meeting room can contain the library, which would occupy one section of the room. The library should contain reference material, field guides, magazines, and novels concerned with the outdoors.
- Storage room. Adequate space should be provided to store the instructional and janitorial equipment that are necessary for operating programs and facility.

It should be emphasized again that it is not essential for one center to have most of the spaces described here. Creative space management will allow a relatively small center with few amenities to provide a wide variety of programs.

Interpretive Centers

Although the name "interpretive centers" might well be applied to the outdoor laboratories and the nature centers mentioned earlier, it has a specific use in describing certain facilities of public parks offered as a service to the general public and, in some cases, to school groups. The National Park Service has the most extensive development of such centers. The United States Forest Service, Corps of Engineers, and Bureau of Land Management as well as other federal land managing agencies provide interpretive facilities. State parks and larger metropolitan parks have also developed interpretive centers.

The primary purpose of interpretive centers is to help visitors understand and appreciate the natural, historical, cultural, or archeological features of the areas in which the centers are located. Interpretation is tailored for each area. Facility developments are likewise varied and often unique to the site being interpreted.

Interpretive centers frequently contain a trailside museum or interpretive-center building. This may vary in size from 10 feet by 20 feet to a large, multi-focused structure. The size depends on the groups to be accommodated, the interpretive materials available, and the types of programs to be presented. A large building may contain some or all of the following:
- Museum-quality display rooms depicting cultural, historic, wildlife, and other exhibits
- Office space
- A laboratory for research and the preparation of display materials
- Theatre and meeting rooms for lectures, video, or computer presentations
- Restrooms
- Storage space for archived materials
- A counter for the sale of books and the distribution of pamphlets
- An outdoor amphitheater or campfire area for lectures and movies
- Trails to points of interest (often self-guiding nature trails)

- Parapets or other special observation points, often including mounted telescopes and pointers indicating places of interest
- Interpretive devices at points of interest.

School and Community Gardens, Farms, and Forests

Gardens, farms, and forests provide direct experiences with growing plants and, in some cases, with domestic animals. Schools, park and recreation agencies, and a few private agencies have been responsible for the development of facilities. Even when facilities are developed and operated by park and recreation departments or private agencies, some direct relationship with schools is often provided through an instructional program in which the school children are enrolled.

Display Gardens

Gardens of various kinds should be developed to provide for visual, cultural, and educational equipment. A formal garden may be composed entirely of one type of plant (such as roses), of various types of assorted plant materials, or of a series of individual gardens comprised of single types of plant units. Features such as a water fountain and statuary can be incorporated into the design. Informal gardens should have long, sweeping lawn areas to serve as a setting for plants and flower beds. Plants may include large specimen trees, flowering trees, shrubs, and vines. The flower borders can be of varied plants. All the plants should be of interest to the average homeowner and should be useful in helping him or her select plants for his or her own yard. Attempts should be made to keep abreast of the latest introductions and to display those types of plants that are hardy to the particular region in which the garden is located. This aspect of planting for the homeowner should be stressed in both formal and informal gardens, and demonstrations of plant cultural practice should be provided.

Naturalistic and native, or wildflower, gardens are established in a wilderness location where the plants native to the region can be assembled in one area so they are easily accessible to the citizens. Developers will probably need an area of varied topography—lowlands, highlands, and prairies—and an area with varied soil conditions—from alkaline to acid—to accommodate the various types of plants.

Tract Gardens

In a tract garden, which is the most common type of school or community garden, a piece of property ranging in size from one to 10 acres is divided into small tracts for the use of individuals. A typical plot size may be 10 feet by 20 feet, but adults and families can use larger gardens. A garden program with 25 plots can be set up on 1/4 acre of land although more space is desirable. Four acres of land can hold 100 gardeners with plots of varied size and community crops. This size allows space for a service building and activity area. It should be on rich, well-drained soil with water available. Garden programs may involve instruction, environmental projects, field trips, and science activities. Community projects may include novelty crops such as a pumpkin patch, gourds, Indian corn, and a Christmas tree farm. Gardening appeals to all ages and is an excellent program for families.

Some of the necessary or desirable features of the tract garden are the following:

- Garden building—either a small building for the storage of tools and equipment or a building large enough for class meetings and indoor activity during bad weather.
- Restroom facilities adequate to care for the maximum number of participants expected on the garden plot at one time.
- Greenhouse for plant propagation.
- Ready access to water, with spigots and hoses available for limited irrigation.
- Fencing for protection of the garden.
- Pathways and walkways to provide easy access to all plots.
- A demonstration home yard, with grass, flowers, and shrubs.
- Good landscaping.

Preferably, the tract garden should be located within walking distance of the homes of the participants. In many cases, gardens are developed on or adjacent to school grounds. Tract gardens for adults and families have been established in some communities. They are usually intended for people living in crowded urban centers or apartments who would not otherwise be able to garden. In some communities, these gardens are located some distance from homes with individuals responsible for their own transportation.

Farms

Community or school farms are becoming increasingly important, especially near metropolitan centers, and offer opportunities for a rich and varied program. Farm programs include animal care and training and traditional rural activities such as hay rides, picnics, and nature activities. Families who just want to walk through to see and pet the animals often use model farms. Simple barns and pens contain horses, cows, pigs, chickens, sheep, and other domestic animals, which children can help care for and feed. In an urban setting, it is essential that the facility be attractive and well maintained. An office, restrooms, drinking fountain, indoor and outdoor activity areas, and storage space are needed. There must be water, feed storage, and adequate exercise space for the animals.

In addition to the buildings that are generally found on a diversified farm, there are meeting places and exhibits that make it possible to carry on indoor instruction. Picnic areas, farm ponds, day-camp facilities, campfire circles, and hiking trails are often developed.

Working farms are sometimes adapted for recreational purposes. This type of facility actually produces a variety of products while city residents visit to learn, observe, take part in, and enjoy farming activities. Groups may use the farm on a day basis and overnight accommodations can be provided. In either case, a large room and open outdoor space are needed for activity and instruction.

Farm camps offer opportunities for a farm-oriented camping experience. The farm camp is a farm not worked for production but set up for resident programs in environmental education, farm activities, natural history, science, and other outdoor recreation. There may be a large farmhouse converted to a program building and farm buildings converted to cabins. Facilities needed are a kitchen, dining area, sleeping quarters, restrooms, large activity room, and ample storage space. Additionally, barns, farm equipment, and other facilities may be needed depending on the types of programs offered.

Forests

Numerous school and community forests can be found throughout the United States. Many of these were acquired from tax-delinquent land, through gifts, or through protection programs for community watersheds. Their use has followed diverse patterns. Some schools have carried on field trips, forest improvement projects, and other outdoor education activities. Many of these forests could be developed as outdoor educational laboratories. Some might be suitable sites for nature centers, day camps, or even resident camps. School and community forests may serve valuable purposes even without extensive development. Water, trails, and restrooms may be all the development needs to provide useful educational facilities. Such areas may serve their best function as places to study the ecological changes taking place over a period of years.

Outdoor Skills and Sports Areas

Outdoor skills or sport areas should be included in the outdoor education and recreation complex; however, it may be necessary to acquire special sites depending on the topography of the land. These areas should provide opportunities to learn and practice skills but they may also be used as outdoor laboratories.

The following are some of the specialized program facilities that might be included in the outdoor skills and sport area:

- Casting and angling—platforms and open, level spaces
- Outdoor shooting range (see Chapter 26)
- Climbing towers (see Chapter 18)
- Archery range—target field course, archery, golf, and other games (see Chapter 26)
- Camp craft skills area (see Chapter 20)
- Overnight camping area (see Chapter 20)
- Outpost camping—Adirondack shelters
- Facilities for water sports including swimming, canoeing, boating, sailing, skin diving, and waterskiing
- Area for crafts with native materials—carving, lapidary, weaving, and ceramics—with a simple structure to provide shelter in inclement weather and to house equipment
- Water sports—ski slopes and tow, ski shelter, tobogganing, and ice skating rinks.

Natural Areas

Natural areas are generally thought of as representative of native plants and animals of a locale. They may encompass a variety of habitats such as woodlands, deserts, swamps, bogs, wetlands, shorelines, or sand dunes. It is almost impossible today, even in the wilderness, to find undisturbed areas. Most places categorized as natural areas are protected lands that indicate the least disturbance and that, through protection, planting, and development, approximate the original characteristics.

It is characteristic of natural areas that they are protected from inharmonious developments and activities. Simple access trails, protective fencing, and simple interpretive developments such as entrance bulletin boards are usually acceptable. In designated natural areas, the enjoyment and study of the natural features are encouraged and uses that detract from the natural features are discouraged. Schools, parks, and camps are often the agencies that develop, maintain, and protect natural areas. Such areas are valuable assets in environmental education.

CAMPUS RECREATIONAL SPORTS CENTERS

Thomas H. Sawyer, Indiana State University

Over the past 20 years, a number of recreational sports centers have been constructed on campuses to meet the needs of the student body. These centers have been built for recreational purposes, not instructional or athletic ones. However, recently a number have been built with large aquatic areas (e.g., University of Toledo, Miami University of Ohio, University of Texas, Georgia Tech, University of Michigan, University of Minnesota, and Indiana University) to be used for both recreational and athletic purposes. These centers have been financed primarily with student fees and state and private funds. Most of the facilities include aquatic centers, entrance/lobby area, lounge areas, racquetball/wallyball courts, indoor and outdoor tennis courts, basketball courts, dance exercise areas, indoor running/jogging tracks, strength and cardiovascular training areas, climbing wall, locker rooms, indoor/outdoor in-line skating hockey court, indoor soccer area, administration area, proshops, concessions, and an area for equipment rental.

This chapter has been designed to provide the planner with an overview of the needs for a campus recreational sports center. The specifics relating to many of the spaces are found in other chapters in this book.

Planning for a New Recreational Sports Center

A common problem is how to secure these new facilities. The following can form the basis from which to justify requests for additional facilities. The initial step in the process of securing any new facility is defining the space requirements. This planning process uses three different types of space used in recreational, intramural, and informal sports programs. The three types, according to Mull, Bayless, Ross, and Jamieson (1977), are described below:

Type A space includes the following areas:

- Indoor teaching stations—space requirements: 8.5 to 9.5 square feet per student (total undergraduate enrollment) including

1) gym floors, mat areas, swimming pools, court areas, and so on; and
2) location adjacent to lockers and showers and within a 10-minute walking distance of academic classrooms (Mull et al., 1997).
- Uses—Recreational, intramural, and informal sports participation for student and faculty recreation.
- A1—Large gymnasium area with relatively high ceiling (22 feet minimum) for basketball, badminton, volleyball, and so on. (approximately 55% of Type A space).
- A2—Activity areas with relatively low ceiling (12 feet minimum) for combatives, therapeutic exercises, dancing, weight lifting, and so on. (approximately 30% of Type A space).
- A3—Indoor swimming and diving pools (approximately 15% of Type A space) (Mull et al., 1997).

Type B space includes the following areas:

- Outdoor teaching stations—space requirements including 1) sports fields of all types; and 2) location adjacent to locker and showers, and within a 10-minute walking distance of academic classrooms.
- Uses—Recreational, intramural, and informal sports participation for student and faculty recreation.
- B1—Sodded areas for soccer, touch football, softball, and so on (approximately 60% of Type B space).
- B2—Court type areas for tennis, volleyball, and so forth (approximately 15% of Type B space).
- B3—Specialized athletic areas for track and field, baseball, archery, varsity football, golf, camping demonstrations, and the like (approximately 25% of Type B space).
- B4—Swimming pools (included in B3 approximation) (Mull et al., 1997).

Type C spaces include the following:

- Sports fields and buildings, intramural and general outdoor recreation areas—space requirements, 120 to 140 square feet per student (total undergraduate enrollment) including playing fields and athletic buildings of all types, softball diamonds, tennis courts, field houses, and so on. Too far removed from student lockers, showers, living quarters and academic buildings for use as teaching stations.
- Uses—Recreation, intramural, and informal sports for student and faculty recreation.
- C1—Sodded areas for soccer, touch football, softball, and so on (approximately 40% of Type C space).
- C2—Court type areas for tennis, volleyball, and the like (approximately 10% of Type C space).
- C3—Specialized athletic area for track and field, baseball, archery, varsity football, golf, camping demonstrations, and so forth (approximately 45% of Type C space).
- C4—Swimming pools (included in C3 approximation).
- C5—Sports and intramural buildings providing lockers, showers, play space, office space, lounge rooms, and so on (approximately 5% of Type C space) (Mull et al., 1997).

Photo by Balthazar Korad, Ltd. courtesy of
TMP Associates, Inc.

**Multipurpose gym with rounded corners,
Central Michigan University.**

In order to compare a campus with the accepted standards, five steps should be followed: The first step involves the location of existing and potential areas within the boundaries of the campus. This is achieved by physically canvassing the campus and envisioning the potential of all areas. The initial phase of Step 1 should be the location and identification of all areas that are currently used by recreational, intramural, and informal sports.

The second phase is more difficult and requires more effort and imagination on the part of the observer. Potential areas of expansion are spaces (outdoor and indoor) that can be converted from whatever they are currently being used for to usable recreation areas. Costs of converting each area should be kept at a minimum to further enhance the attractiveness of securing new facilities (Mull et al., 1997). For example, the cost of converting a relatively small (50 feet by 100 feet) grassy area to an outdoor volleyball area would only include the installation of two poles and a net. If further funds were available and the sport popular, this area could be converted to a sand or beach volleyball court at a small additional cost. Providing alternatives or options also enhances the acceptability of the proposal.

Space for conversion should meet the general criteria for Type A, B, or C space before being considered for alteration (Mull et al., 1997). For example, an indoor area with an eight-foot ceiling should not be considered for conversion to gymnasium space; however, it could be converted to a dance studio or a karate practice room with the addition of mirrors and mats.

After all available and potential areas have been located, the next step requires computations

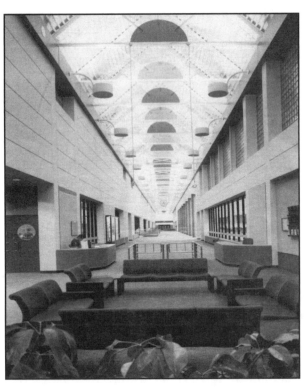

Photo by Balthazar Korad, Ltd. courtesy of
TMP Associates, Inc.

**Main Street, Student Recreation Center,
Central Michigan University**

of the area in square feet. For indoor areas, a tape measure is used; however, for large outdoor areas, a cross-country measuring wheel is most effective. When measuring any area, precautions should be taken to allow for a buffer zone of safety around any proposed playing area. An outdoor grassy area measuring 100 yards by 40 yards could theoretically accommodate an intramural football field, but if the boundaries are close to hazards such as chain-link fence poles, trees, or buildings, this area should be considered for some other recreational purpose.

The same precautions apply to indoor space. Most areas considered will be fairly easy to measure. Normally, spaces are either rectangular or square in shape. Odd-shaped areas should not be ignored and their areas should be estimated to the best of the measurer's ability while still allowing for the safety buffer zone. Odd-shaped areas are also sometimes ignored, because they do not fit the shape of a standard playing field. These areas may, however, accommodate a combination of two or more sports in that area. Any particular space should not be viewed as usable only for football or basketball, but leftover spaces could easily be used for a frisbee golf course or a single table tennis table.

The square footage for all areas considered should next be classified and totaled under one of the three types of spaces. This total figure of space classified according to type can now be compared with the recommended amount of space. Recommended space is computed by taking current enrollment figures and multiplying them by the median figure in the range of each type of space (Mull et al., 1997).

For example, a university with an enrollment of 15,000 students should have a recommended space requirement for Type A space of 135,000 square feet. The total amount of each type space is then compared with the actual amount to arrive at a figure illustrating the amount above or below recommended standards. A further breakdown of space within each type into the 12 sub classifications is required to determine the correct "mix" of facilities. This sub classification of space enables the director to specifically locate areas of deficiency.

When standards in terms of square feet per student are used as guides in college or university planning, it is natural to ask where the cut-off begins. Obviously, for a college of 200 students, nine square feet per student of indoor area for sports and athletics would be inadequate. It would not even provide one basketball court. A university or college meeting the space standards for 1,500 students represents the minimum physical recreation space needs of any college institution. As a college or university increases in size, these standards are applicable regardless of enrollment. Also, a ceiling effect applies to some sub classifications of space.

In the beginning phases of planning for recreational facilities, area standards must be developed.

A variety of standards relative to size, location, and development of school and recreation areas and facilities has been developed.

The standards provide a useful guide; however, standards can seldom, if ever, be applied completely or without modification. Because a typical or ideal situation is seldom found, standards simply indicate a basis for the intelligent development of local plans.

The third step involves a description of current and potential uses of each area. A description of current uses should be done first. It should include uses by physical education, recreation, intramural sports, and "outside" departments. If a particular area is not being used for any specific purpose, it should be so listed.

Potential uses (see Figures 16.1 and 16.2 for examples) should be as closely linked to the sub classifications as possible. It is in this phase of the process where the director must make responsible choices as to the development of any given area. A single area must have the potential to be developed into several different types of space. The director must refer to individual program needs and areas of deficiency to make informed decisions as to the development of that particular area. Again, it is important to provide campus planners with options. However, the director should limit the flexibility of the proposal to stay within the most urgent needs of his particular program.

The next step is to determine the cost of converting an area from its current use to its potential use. In some cases, the cost of conversion will be zero. This type of space should be accentuated in presenting the proposal before any board involved with campus planning. Often, cooperation between two departments regarding scheduling can vastly increase facilities available for recreational use at no cost to either program.

Obtaining other costs of conversion generally involves requesting estimates from the physical plant operations staff on campus or from outside contractors. These estimates should be obtained prior to presenting any proposal. Also, the estimates should enhance the flexibility built into the proposal. That is to say, each option should have its own separate estimate. This allows campus planning boards to examine all suggestions in the proposal independently of other suggestions in the proposal.

Finally, the last step involves defining the availability for use by the major users. If two or more users share facilities, the priority schedule for usage should also be listed. After all, a program may have access to a facility 40% of the total time available, but if those times are at undesirable hours, the facility is not meeting the needs of the program. If no consideration is given to the prime-time needs of students for recreational use, the percentage of availability may be misleading.

After information has been gathered, supporting documents for requesting new facilities

Figure 16.1
Indoor Recreational, Intramural, and Informal Sports Activities

The following is a partial listing of indoor recreational, intramural, and informal sports activities:

Single Function   **Specialized or Multipurpose Function**

Single Function	Country club	Gymnasium
Archery range	**Country club**	**Gymnasium**
Badminton court	Golf	Gymnastics
Basketball court	Swimming	Combatives
Billiards	Table sports	Basketball
Bowling alley	Strength training	Volleyball
Combatives room	Tennis	Badminton
Curling rink		Table tennis
Cardiovascular room		
Dance exercise room		
Diving pool		
Electronic games arcade	**Fieldhouse**	**Racquetball club**
Fencing salle	Basketball	Strength training
Gymnastics room	Track	Jogging
Handball	Soccer	
Ice rink	Lacrosse	**Recreation center**
In-line skating hockey rink	Jogging	Billiards
Racquetball court	Archery	Table sports
Rifle-pistol range		Table tennis
Roller skating rink	**Fitness center**	Swimming
Shuffleboard course	Swimming	Gymnasium
Squash court	Strength training	
Swimming pool	Cardiovascular training	
Table sports room	Jogging	
Table tennis room	Combatives	
Tennis court	Dance exercise	
Strength training room		
Wrestling room		
Volleyball court		

Indoor soccer/roller hockey

must be prepared. The proposal should contain five major parts. The first part should state clearly the objectives of the study. It should also list all areas and departments of the campus involved in conducting the study. Finally, it should include limitations or qualifications specific to the institution.

The second part should include brief historical developments of the sponsoring program from both a national and campus viewpoint.

The third section is a statement of the problem. In this section, all forces generating the study should be explained. All major problems affected by changing facility structures should be included as well as the majority of the information gathered in the aforementioned steps. Listing the standards with the organizations using them will lend national support to the proposal. The relationship between the standard and enrollment is

Figure 16.2
Outdoor Recreational, Intramural, and Informal Sports Activities

The following are common outdoor recreational, intramural, and sports activities:

Airfield	Hydro-slide
Baseball field	Ice rink
Basketball court	In-line skating hockey rink
Beach volleyball	Lacrosse field
Bike trail	Marina
Bicycle track	Miniature golf course
Boat launching ramp	Motocross course
Boccie ball course	Riding paddock
Bowling green	Rifle/pistol range
Cross-country course	Roller skating rink
Curling rink	Shuffleboard
Deck tennis	Skateboard/rollerblade course and ramp
Diving pool	Skeet and trap range
Field hockey field	Skiing course
Fishing pond/lake	Soccer field
Fitness trail (Par course)	Softball field
Football field	Speedball
Frisbee golf course	Swimming pool
Go-cart track	Speedball field
Golf course	Team handball field
Golf driving range	Tennis court
Handball court	Toboggan slope
Horseshoe pit	Volleyball

explained next. And, finally, the standards are applied to the specific campus in question. The comparison should emphasize those areas in which critical deficiencies exist, because the largest deficiencies are not always the most critical ones. Section three should conclude with a summary of the work completed on the study and a restatement of those problem areas.

Section four contains recommendations for immediate action and long-term improvements. Flexibility (options) within the overall goals of the organization should be the guiding principle when preparing this section.

Indoor track

Finally, appendices should be prepared to support the proposal. Participation figures may be used in this section; however, the major part of this section should contain a map of the campus with all areas clearly marked. The map should be accompanied by a list of all buildings and rooms investigated. The most precise way of presenting existing and potential areas is to list and explain each one according to the following seven-point formula:

- location
- area (structure footage)
- type of space
- current uses
- potential uses
- cost of conversion
- percentage of use

Indoor Facilities

In planning new facilities, it should be remembered that substandard facilities usually result in a substandard program. For this reason, official court and field dimensions should be used whenever possible. The following list identifies the types of areas that should be considered in planning indoor facilities for a campus recreational sports center:

- Main gymnasium—regulation basketball, badminton, tennis, and volleyball courts with mechanical divider nets. The divider nets should be constructed of solid vinyl for the first eight feet and the remainder of a mesh material.
- Auxiliary gymnasiums—regulation basketball, badminton, tennis, and volleyball courts, gymnastics area, in-line skating hockey rink, indoor soccer area, suspended track, fencing, batting cages, and dance exercise. The dance exercise area should have hidden mirrors to protect them when the space is used for other activities (e.g., basketball or volleyball), and a retractable instructor's platform. The planners might consider the possibility of locating two gymnasiums side by side with a storage area between to store equipment, an audio system, and retractable instructor's platforms. The storage area should be at least eight feet wide.
- Swimming pools—50-meter pool, diving pool, and/or instruction pool.
- Combative room—boxing, martial arts, and judo.
- Strength training area—progressive resistance-training equipment, free-weight equipment, and stretching area.
- Cardiovascular area.
- Handball/racquetball/walleyball courts.
- Golf room—sand trap, putting area, and driving nets.
- Archery/rifle/pistol range.
- Games room—billiards, table tennis, table games, shuffleboard.
- Administrative area—offices, storage, conference rooms, and audiovisual room.
- Lounge and lobby area—bulletin boards, trophy cases, control center, and artwork.
- Concessions, rental, and merchandise area—concession stand, seating area, rental shop, and pro shop.
- Training room—treatment area only.
- Locker rooms—student and faculty, gender-specific, shower rooms, drying areas, locker space, and common spa area (i.e., hydro-tube, sauna, and steam room).
- Equipment and storerooms.
- Climbing wall.

Outdoor Facilities

The following list identifies the types of areas that should be considered in planning outdoor facilities for a campus recreational sports center:

- Lighted fields—touch/flag football, soccer, field hockey, softball, baseball, handball, and rugby (see Chapter 11).
- Lighted courts—basketball, badminton, tennis, volleyball, handball/racquetball, and horseshoes (see Chapter 10).
- Lighted in-line skating hockey court (see Chapter 19).
- Lighted jogging/running/walking trails and/or track.
- Golf course and lighted driving range and practice green.
- Lighted skating rink.
- Swimming and diving pools (see Chapter 13).
- Boccie field and horseshoe pits.
- Storage building(s).
- Tennis practice boards and soccer kicking wall.
- Picnic areas with shelters (see Chapter 15).

Security Issues

The campus recreational sports center will quickly become the focus of campus interest. The center will be used heavily throughout the day and evening. The prime times will be 6 to 8 a.m., 11 a.m. to 1 p.m., 4 to 6 p.m., and 7 p.m. to midnight. The planners need to consider providing adequate security, including appropriate outside lighting at all sites, security cameras, alarmed doors (silent and audible), pool alarms, spa alarms, valuable lockers, fire alarms, sprinkling systems, and appropriate signage.

Outdoor recreation field at Indiana State University.

STRENGTH AND CARDIOVASCULAR TRAINING FACILITIES

17

Lawrence W. Judge, Ball State University

During the past 30 or so years, the popularity of resistance training has increased enormously. Weight-lifting facilities of yesteryear were a novelty, as most athletes were advised that serious resistance training might hurt their flexibility and athleticism. As the benefits of resistance training have been accepted by athletes, coaches, and the mainstream population, the demand for facilities has increased. Many school corporations, colleges, and universities and community organizations like the YMCA have developed multiuse strength and conditioning facilities.

Strength and cardiovascular training facilities (SCF) for use in physical education, recreation, athletics, and community wellness programs, have become larger and more sophisticated over the years. The growing use of these facilities, combined with the key administrative issues of equipping and staffing these facilities creates a need to better understand these facilities. Strength and cardiovascular training areas (commonly referred to as the fitness floor) are the lifeblood of any existing or future recreation/sport facility. When facilities motivate their members by captivating their attention and imagination and ensuring healthy activity by promoting safety, the facilities will sustain their existence even with the growing number of competing exercise facilities (Sawyer & Stowe, 2005).

Strength and cardiovascular facility coordinators must embrace the advances in technology and recognize the value of incorporating entertainment mediums as they embark upon developing or refining existing programs, refurbishing existing facilities, or planning for the expansion or construction of new facilities. The responsibilities of coordinators are demanding; however, when armed with the correct knowledge base, the facility creation will be an arduous process with a very successful outcome.

A strength and cardiovascular facility coordinator must be involved with every phase of the development process and continue to be heavily involved in day-to-day operations. From facility design concepts to choosing equipment to facility maintenance, the most successful planners immerse themselves in the process and understand the very last detailed information concerning strength and cardiovascular equipment and training. This chapter will take the reader on a journey through the full process of planning and operating the strength and cardiovascular training facilities.

Strength and Cardiovascular Training Facility Planning

Defining Objectives: Establishing Facility Goals

Accommodation of Membership

The program objectives of the organization, type, and availability of exercise equipment and size of the facility ultimately impact the clientele served. The clientele satisfaction can make or break the opening and continuing operation of a strength and cardiovascular training facility. The users of a facility are the financial support. So before even beginning to establish goals for the facility, make a commitment to fully understanding the population that will be the primary users (members) of the facility and make their needs facility needs. So it is time to ask questions: is the facility for sports performance like a collegiate football strength facility, is it a facility designed to serve the primarily the student body and faculty of a university, or does it have a variety of users/functions?

Team-Related Facilities

Facilities that focus upon preparation and conditioning of student-athletes for sports teams must devise strategic time schedules for them to use the facilities. The size of the respective team, the instructor-to-student ratio, and the program objectives also impact accommodation. Instructor ratios of 1:30 are acceptable; however, lower ratios are advisable for team sports that involve free weight and plyometric training. A performance-related facility will be equipped with lifting platforms, free weights, dumbbells, medicine balls, plyometric boxes, and a few machines.

General Population

Facilities that accommodate the general public, from teens to senior citizens, also have strategic issues of accommodation to be addressed. Many women are intimidated to use weight-training facilities because of the predominant number of men using the facilities. Providing cardiovascular and strength-training facilities strictly for women and seniors is highly recommended. It is advisable to lay out the facility so a number of different types of clientele can be accommodated. It is highly recommended to separate free weights, machines, and cardiovascular equipment. Doing so will increase member satisfaction and will reflect positively upon the organization in the desire to meet the unique needs of these populations.

Choosing Facility Goals

Before evaluating and/or constructing a facility, it is important that one has a clear understanding of the programmatic objectives and facility design vision. Equipment selection and allocation is an important issue for any strength and conditioning facility. Defining programmatic objectives is the first step to successfully planning a facility to meet the needs of the target population activity. What will be the necessary training philosophy for the target population: Olympic lifts, high-intensity training (HIT), machines, free weights (squat, bench press, incline bench press, military press, dead lift), trunk strength, posterior chain development, dumbbells? Do you need space for dynamic warm-ups, trunk strength and speed/agility/quickness training?

Decisions on the amount of free weight equipment, machines, and cardiovascular equipment are largely determined by the philosophy/priorities of the facilities. Facilities targeted primarily to-

Cardiovascular equipment has become part of secondary school facilities for use by physical education classes, community wellness, and athletics.

ward athletic use tend to have more free weights, Olympic lifting areas, and few machines. Physical Education/athletic facilities tend to have a mixture of free weights, dumbbells, and machines. Facilities designed to service athletics, physical education, and community wellness tend to include a mixture of free weights, Olympic lifting areas, lifting machines, and cardiovascular equipment. Advances in technology like the flat-screen television monitor have made the incorporation of sports performance analysis equipment and entertainment mediums part of the planning process.

After evaluating the membership, it is time to choose goals for the new or reinvented facility. To further analyze the target population, the planners of a strength and cardiovascular facility should answer a number of questions prior to initiating planning for the facility. The answers to these questions should be written down and become guidelines for construction, equipment selection and other planning requirements.

Demographics
- What is the demographic composition of clientele served: Children, teens, middle-aged persons, senior citizens?
- What is their gender?
- What is the size of the total membership or the membership registered to use the strength-training area?

Activities
- What are the specific training needs? (e.g., strength, endurance, circuits, and power)
- What specific activities or training functions will take place in the space?
- Will the spaces be used for team instruction, group programs, new member equipment orientations, and the like?
- Will the activities cater to individuals or small or large groups?
- What will be the size of classes?
- What equipment is needed to support the respective activities?
- What programs will be offered, for example, circuit training, free weights, cardiovascular training?
- What is the equipment preference (i.e., a mixture of free weights and machines, free weights only, machines only)?
- Is there a high demand for separate or co-ed areas?
- Has the equipment been chosen? If yes, who is the vendor, what are the specific dimensions of the equipment, and what is the proposed layout?

Limitations
- What are the financial constraints?
- What are the space limitations?

- What are the manpower constraints?
- What other limitations exist?

It is important for the planners to consider the desired outcomes of the completed facility. These outcomes should focus upon, but not be limited to: maximizing the use of existing or future space, assuring the safety of participants, achieving program objectives successfully, and increasing user satisfaction. So as the actual facility building process unfolds, not only the facility goals, but the facility design concepts and philosophy should guide the decision-making process.

General Facility Design Concepts and Philosophy

Defining programmatic objectives is the first step to successfully planning a facility to meet the needs of the target population activity. Before any further steps are taken, the facility planner must keep some global ideas in mind as each decision is made. These ideas will be referred to as facility design concepts and philosophies and are fundamentally important, because developing even the smallest facilities for the smallest populations can be a complicated process. It is important as one begins to pick equipment and plan facility layout to not lose focus on the global goals of the project. So as the planning process unfolds, always consider principles of maximization and minimization.

Maximization

One of the most important concepts to consider is space utility. Throughout each step of the facility planning process, the maximization of space must be well thought out. Understanding space utility maximization means having a vision and also entertaining many different types of ideas for layout. The process of idea trial and error can be arduous, but in many facility-planning instances, it may be the only way to ensure the best use of space. It is also crucial to keep an eye on the future; how can the facility grow with populace expansion? Meeting only minimum space standards does not allow for potential membership growth and facility expansion. When designing new facilities, attention should always focus upon how the facility can be expanded with some structural modifications such as removal of interior walls or exterior walls. Strategic facility design includes preparing for future growth. When considering membership in the facility layout process, use a simple rule of thumb: a minimum space requirement per lifter of 30 feet (2.8 m) and a maximum of 60 feet (5.6 m) (Greedwood, 2000).

It is best to always project larger at the beginning of a project. To figure square footage of room that is spacious and will meet future needs, an ideal number is 100 sq. feet per person. The floor plan of the room dimension (square, rectangle, L-shaped, round walls, and location of drinking fountains etc.) must be also considered.

The visual appeal of a facility significantly impacts the ability to attract and engage participants. It is important to design visually pleasing facilities that are easily maintained. The desired outcome is to create energy and to make the visit to the facility an "experience." If facility coordinators do not have a thorough understanding of the impact of interior design, the utilization of a professional interior designer to maximize the visual ambience is highly recommended.

Minimization

Liability will always be an issue for facility managers. Minimizing liability conflicts must begin at the very first conceptualization of the facility. All types of exercise equipment for both strength and cardiovascular exercise facilities will be a risk for participants if not set up and placed in activity areas in full accordance with the manufacturer's instructions, tolerances, and recommendations; and with accompanying safety signage, instruction placards, notices, and warnings posted or placed so as to be noticed by users prior to use. Safety in facility design is primarily achieved by providing sufficient walking space to keep members from inadvertently bumping into each other or when too many pieces of equipment are placed in a space that is inadequate. Also consider the inclusion of all populations for the facility. The facility manager is responsible for providing facilities, training, programs, services and related opportunities in accordance with all laws, regulations, and requirements mandating equal opportunity, access, and nondiscrimination. For example, all facilities must be planned in accordance with the Americans with Disabilities Act, requiring public facilities to provide appropriate services for the disabled.

From Scratch: the New Facility

The Building Design

Designing the new facility from scratch can seem like a daunting process. Since the design process can be complicated, it is all the more important to establish a set of detailed programmatic objectives and be well aware of the design concepts and philosophies. These will act as a guide as critical decisions are made. Each facility will have different needs; some may be additions to other facilities and others may be a complete stand-alone facility, but there are some general guidelines to follow in order to generate a successful facility. Table 17.1 represents an all-purpose checklist to help facility creators.

A successful facility begins with the assembling of qualified individuals. The construction of the facility is an exchange between facility planners and contractors. Starting with the facility planners, it is key to incorporate all of the management that will be involved with the facility. This may include athletic directors, a college administration, those in charge of the financial backing and even individuals that will be using the facility. It might also be beneficial to involve experienced professionals outside of the concerned administration. This could mean hiring someone well qualified, but depending on the project, it may be worth the security to have someone with experience to consult the project. In order to ensure that the planner vision comes to fruition, selecting a contractor and construction team with a reputable reputation is essential. Ask for and check numerous references from numerous contractors before reaching a decision. Maintain a solid relationship with the project supervisor and constantly review architectural drawings and process steps along the way.

Another crucial planning consideration is developing a realistic schedule and checklist for project completion. Making the checklist as detailed as possible will be a great aid during the process, especially as many tasks may be in progress at the same time. For a more complete idea of what to include as part of the facility checklist or project schedule, consult Table 17.1.

Table 17.1
Facility Design Checklist

General Features

✓ A comprehensive master plan has been prepared on the nature and scope of the program, and the special requirements for space, equipment, fixtures, and facilities have been dictated by the activities to be conducted (form follows function)

✓ The facility has been planned to meet the total requirements of the program, both present and future, as well as the special needs of those who are to be served. Any possible future additions or expansions are included in the present plans to permit economy of construction and costs.

✓ The plans and specifications meet the codes of all governmental agencies (city, county, state) whose approval is required by law.

✓ The plans of the facility conform to accepted standards and practices.

✓ The following factors have been considered for the proposed facility and site:

- feeder streets
- parking areas
- electrical supplies
- water supplies
- sewage lines
- gas lines
- storm drainage
- soil topography

✓ The selection of equipment and supplies has been based on a cost-per-use ratio, as well as on ongoing maintenance costs.

✓ Sufficient attention has been given to fire code, fire and security systems, and emergency escape routes.

✓ Window heights are appropriate for privacy, safety, maintenance and natural light

✓ Floor and wall surfaces have been selected according to the following criteria: year-round usage, multiple uses, dust and moisture resistance, stainlessness, inflammability, non-abrasiveness, durability, resiliency, safety, maintenance, and cost per use.

Indoor Facilities (General)

✓ All passageways are free of obstructions so two-way traffic can occur. Every effort has been made to eliminate hazards.

✓ Buildings, specialty areas, and facilities are clearly defined.

Table 17.1 Cont.

✓ Administrative offices, exercise rooms, and service facilities are properly interrelated. The same is true for medical, first-aid, and emergency rooms.

✓ Special needs of the physically disabled are met, including a ramp into the building at a major entrance.

✓ Storage rooms are of adequate size and are accessible to appropriate areas. All dead space is used, such as areas under stairwells.

✓ Low-cost maintenance features have been considered.

✓ All areas, courts, facilities, equipment, climate control, security, and the like conform rigidly to detailed standards and specifications.

✓ Drinking fountains are conveniently placed in the locker rooms and workout areas or immediately adjacent to them.

✓ Provision is made for repair, maintenance, replacement, and storage of equipment.

✓ Anti-panic hardware is used on doors as required by fire regulations.

✓ Properly placed hose bibs and drains are sufficient in size and quantity to permit flushing the entire wet area with a water hose.

✓ Space relationships and equipment are planned in accordance with the type and number of users.

✓ Warning signals, both visible and audible, are included in the plans.

✓ Ramps have a slope equal to or greater than a 1-foot rise in 12 feet.

✓ Minimum landings for ramps are 5 feet by 5 feet, they extend at least 1 foot beyond the swinging arc of a door, and they have at least a 6-foot clearance.

Climate Control

✓ There is climate control throughout the building (i.e., heating, ventilation, and air-conditioning or HVAC)

✓ HVAC systems are on both a zone control and an individual room control system.

✓ Temperature and humidity are specific to a particular area.

Electrical Control

✓ Lighting intensity meets approved standards

✓ An adequate number of electrical outlets are appropriately place throughout the facility. They should be 3 feet above the floor, unless otherwise specified.

✓ Service area lights are controlled by dimmer units.

✓ Natural light, when used, is controlled properly to reduce glare.

Walls

✓ Electrical wall plates are located within the wall where needed and are firmly attached.

Table 17.1 Cont.

✓ Materials that clean easily and are impervious to moisture are used where moisture is prevalent.

✓ Drinking fountains are provided in adequate number and are properly recessed in the wall.

✓ One wall (at least) of the aerobics room has full-length mirrors.

✓ Wall coverings are aesthetically pleasing and match the overall décor of the facility.

Ceilings

✓ The ceiling height is adequate for the activities to be performed in a given area.

✓ Ceiling support beams are designed and engineered to withstand stress.

✓ Acoustical materials impervious to moisture are used in moisture-prevalent areas.

✓ All ceilings except those in storage areas are acoustically treated with sound-absorbent materials.

✓ Skylights in exercise rooms are impractical and therefore are seldom used because of problems in waterproofing roofs and controlling sun rays.

✓ Ceiling and crawl spaces are easily accessible for maintenance and repair purposes.

Floors

✓ Floor plates placed where needed are flush mounted.

Storage and Issuance Rooms

✓ The storage areas conform to fire laws.

✓ The storage and issue areas are centrally located and are of sufficient number to handle peak periods effectively.

✓ The doors to storage areas are wide and do not have a riser. The storage areas have appropriate security.

✓ Storage areas have adequate ventilation.

Activity Areas

✓ The floor area and dimensions are determined by the activities to be conducted.

✓ Adequate space or buffer zones are provided between activity areas.

✓ Wall surfaces were selected to allow their use for activities, cleaning, and maintenance.

✓ The floor surface material has been selected to allow for a maximum variety of uses.

✓ Adequate storage rooms are conveniently located near activity areas.

✓ Acoustical standards are met for all rooms.

✓ Lighting quality meets all standards.

✓ There are provisions included for an emergency safety lighting system.

Table 17.1 Cont.

✓ There is a properly installed, high-quality public address system.

✓ There are provisions for an intercom system that may be connected with the public address system.

✓ There are adequate climate control systems.

✓ Floor plates have been installed.

✓ There are provisions included for repair, maintenance, and installation of ceiling fixtures.

✓ There are provisions included for proper and necessary signs, both illuminated and non-illuminated, pertaining to areas, exits, and participants.

✓ There is a suitable lock-key system for doors, storage rooms, light controls, sound system controls, intercom controls, climate controls, and public address systems.

Provisions for People with Disabilities

✓ Necessary provisions are present for parking, loading, and unloading areas and ramps are provided wherever necessary. (Elevators should also be considered.)

✓ All doorways and passageways are of sufficient width to accommodate wheelchairs. The feasibility of electrically operated doors has been considered.

✓ All thresholds are flush.

✓ All doorways or entryways to toilets, telephones areas, food and refreshment areas, locker rooms, and special rooms are sufficient to accommodate wheelchairs.

✓ Restroom facilities are provided for people with disabilities.

Physical Construction

The construction process will be in the hands of the project supervisor and contracted professionals. Before the construction begins, set and discuss realistic deadlines. It may also be advantageous to establish deadline penalties to prevent the already-long process from becoming not only drawn out, but out of control. A thriving facility planner will heavily involve him- or herself in the construction process with constant visits to the site, constant consultations with the project supervisor, and constant referrals to the programmatic objectives.

Staff Considerations

Hiring staff needs to be a deliberate, thoughtful process. Selecting staff members must comply with federal guidelines for hiring practices. Each position may require a different level of education or certification, so it is imperative to fully understand the position and hire accordingly. At this time, it may also be beneficial to set up in-house employee training. What will be the method for orientation to the facility? Also include, if applicable, continued-education programs.

Designing the Interior of a New or Existing Facility

Location and Access

One must keep in mind two important concepts when deciding where in the facility the exercise rooms should be. The equipment involved with strength and conditioning/cardiovascular fitness is very heavy and bulky, so for the easiest move, it is best to keep the location on the ground level. If this option is not possible, ensure that the flooring meets a load-bearing capacity of 100 lb/ft², or 488 kg/m² in order to completely compensate structurally for dropped equipment. If possible, allow for the construction of double doors in the facility or choose a room with double-door access. This will make it possible for wider or awkward equipment configurations to enter the facility easier. Sound is another issue: for customer comfort, make sure the room chosen for exercise is in a room with plenty of sound absorption. Location is also important when bearing in mind an office for supervisors or management. The office should be centralized with large windows in order to oversee the facility from within the office.

Before any equipment enters the facility, take careful measure developing the exits. All exits and emergency exits should be clearly marked. Entryways should meet a minimum width of 32 inches or 81 centimeters. The facility must be completely handicapped accessible; this includes doorways in and out of the facility, emergency exits, walkways, and ramps if necessary.

Ceilings and Floors

The ceiling height is an important factor when designing both a new facility and remodeling an existing facility. Especially in platform or power-lifting areas, the overhead clearance needs to be at least 12 to 14 feet high (3.7-4.3 m). When creating a new facility, keep in mind plans for ceiling fans, sprinkler systems, and other low-hanging items, and ensure that the lowest hanging item is still at least 12 to 14 feet high, making the actual ceiling itself higher. Consider your options carefully before including a drop ceiling in new facility plans. Suspended ceilings may allow for more design options, camouflage pipes, and provide sound absorption. But a suspended ceiling may restrict ceiling height and reduce the versatility of the facility. The higher ceiling provides more functionality to the facility for Olympic lifting and medicine ball work and gives the facility a greater sense of openness.

It is important for a facility to have the proper ceiling height for performing Olympic lifts.

The correct selection of flooring minimizes the potential of slips, falls, and other injuries. The selection of flooring is based on a number of factors, including facility usage, facility location, and sound reduction. There are many flooring options, and the option you choose may depend on the concrete base of the facility. You can choose a poured floor or a rolled one. A poured floor will not have any seams but is more difficult to repair down the road, and if damaged, the patchwork is never the same as the original. The concrete base under a poured floor must be smooth and fairly

level. Tile and rolled floors have seams, but they also have advantages. They can be moved to new space, can be replaced if damaged, and can be permanent depending on the adhesive used.

You can also choose square tiles or a puzzle lock-type system for covering just a part of a room. This is often a nice option for a dumbbell area. The industry standard for flooring is 3/8" thick for a resistance training area. Track surfacing companies like Mondo are now installing floors for (SFC) areas. Track surfacing companies are very experienced installing rubberized surfaces indoors and outdoors and may be very competitive in the bid process.

The Deutsche Institut für Normung (DIN) standards (see Appendix H) are ideally suited in the selection of the appropriate flooring for cardiovascular and strength training centers. The following DIN standards should be considered:

- *Shock absorption.* Without appropriate shock absorption, the potential for accruing an injury increases, specifically for ankle and knee joints. This is an essential component for aerobic and other group exercise spaces.
- *Standard vertical deformation/resilience.* Insufficient energy return in a floor causes sore ankles if a surface is too hard. Excessive energy return creates a trampoline effect.
- *Sliding characteristics/surface friction.* Side to side, lateral, rotating, and pivoting movements create strain on joints without the proper friction coefficient to minimize stress. "On a friction scale of 0.1 (ice) to 0.9 (fly paper), 0.5 to 0.7 is the DIN standard" (McPherson, 2004, p. 43).
- *Rolling load.* A floor's ability to withstand heavy weight without breaking or sustaining permanent damage.

Walls and Mirrors

The walls of the strength training and cardiovascular fitness facility can serve as facility dividers, acoustic control, and aesthetic value if done properly. Separate rooms for themed training will be discussed later in the chapter. Different types of exercise produce various loud noises; the facility manager should control for noise whenever possible. The substance chosen to for wall make-up will determine the amount of acoustical control, so it is important to select a durable material with acoustic value. Aesthetics are an underrated priority for gyms. The right décor can create a productive, happy atmosphere and can affect how a user feels. Options for wall decorations are limitless; some use posters or painted figures or pictures, but regardless, be deliberate with decoration. The design should reflect the aura of the organization and the users/membership. Patterned galvanized steel could also be mounted on the walls for protection as well as aesthetic value in high-traffic areas such as in free-weight areas where the numerous benches, bars, and Olympic plates may come in contact with the wall surfaces.

Mirrors should be positioned on the walls in various areas throughout the facility, especially in front of power lifting areas and squat racks. Mirrors will allow for personal trainers or strength and conditioning professionals to check lifting technique from various vantage points and also make the rooms seem more spacious. Be aware, however, that putting in too many mirrors may make certain individuals self-conscious. Mirrors should be placed at least 20 inches off the floor so that rolling equipment cannot hit or break them.

Signs

Keeping the proper signage in the strength-training and cardiovascular fitness areas means a safer facility. Signs will be divided into three categories: vendor, weight facility, and cardiovascular area. Vendor signs include the warnings for equipment use. These should be displayed on equipment in the line of vision at all times. Weight-facility signs refer to signs in the strength-training area while signs that belong near the cardiovascular equipment are termed cardiovascular area signage. Examples are displayed below.

Weight-Facility Signage
—Replace weights in their designated racks
—Do not drop the weights
—Children under the age of 14 must be accompanied by an adult
—The use of a spotter is advisable
—Clean equipment after use

Cardiovascular Area Signage
—Cease to use equipment if one feels light-headed or dizzy and notify a staff member immediately
—Report any equipment malfunctions to a designated staff member on duty
—Clean equipment after use

Electrical Service

A fitness facility requires special attention to electrical needs. To begin, because of electrical machines and the necessity for electrical cleaning equipment to operate throughout the facility, more outlets are essential. They should be placed, not only by the electrical equipment, but also around the room for cleaning. Grounded 100-V and 220-V outlets will be needed for larger cardiovascular machines. Lighting will also be an important issue for visual appeal and safety. The number of foot-candles designates lighting. Optimal lighting is considered 75 to 100 foot-candles, 50 at floor level. The facility should be void of any dark spots and equipment should be well illuminated. Lighting fixtures should be energy efficient and compliant with Green Seal Environmental Standards. Exit signs and hearing impaired signage should be illuminated and periodically inspected for burned out bulbs.

Environmental Factors

Air temperature should be kept constant between 72°F and 78°F (22°C and 26°C). If the room is too cold, athletes may become chilled after they finish warming up or between sets; if too hot, participants may become overheated or lose motivation to continue. Keeping constant facility temperature will also prevent condensation, damp floors, and equipment corrosion. Relative humidity should be at 60% or less. Air circulation should be at least eight to 12 air exchanges per hour. The result should be no detectable strong odors in the room and equipment free of slickness or rust due to high humidity. Lack of climate control can significantly reduce the life span of equipment, causing rust and moving pieces to corrode.

Color and Noise

Color is a significant dimension that contributes to the psychological, emotional, and physical response of participants. The coordination of equipment frame colors, upholstery colors, wall colors and textures, flooring patterns, use of lighting, ceiling heights, and window treatments are all factors that contribute to the overall visual appeal of the exercise experience. Facility enhancements may be as simple as painting accent colors on white walls for the purposes of creating a space that not only is visually appealing but also makes one feel good.

A significant amount of noise is generated with an exercise facility. Impact noise and vibrations occur from dropping of weights, members moving simultaneously during an aerobics class, and members' use of treadmills and other equipment, combined with high-volume music. Strategic placement of group exercise activities within the context of the actual center along with the inclusion of built-in acoustical controls will prevent these venues from negatively impacting other programs such as yoga classes. The strategies for addressing these issues ultimately depend upon whether a group is planning a new construction or trying to remedy an existing acoustical problem. Some weight rooms will provide music from a central system throughout the facility. Music volume should always be low enough so that trainers and members can easily speak. To ensure the music evenly fills the room or rooms, speakers should be placed at the high corners of the wall and ceiling.

Additional structural modification for new or existing venues provides multiple layers of drywall on both sides of studs when activities are going to be placed next to each other. Constructing floating wooden platform floors to support cardiovascular equipment is also another solution. Strength-training acoustical issues can be enhanced with the use of rubber flooring and rubber bumpers between weight plates on selected weight equipment. Addressing acoustical issues with the architect, engineer, and acoustical experts should be discussed early in the design phase of a new exercise facility. When having to remedy existing acoustical problems, they should be discussed before it negatively impacts the operation.

Selecting Equipment

Resistance Training Equipment

A comprehensive strength-training facility will include: Olympic benches, bars, and plates; weight trees; power racks that include adjustable spotter's bar for squats or bench-press purposes; adjustable benches for dumbbell activities; cable crossover and handle accessories; smith machine; assisted dip; hyperextension; and abdominal boards.

The number of Olympic benches and power racks is ultimately dependent upon the projected number of participants using the facility during peak hours of operation. Based on philosophy, a room is laid out based off the "meat and potatoes" of the program and fill in pieces of equipment that is easily programmable and try to avoid pieces that cause "bottle necking" (10-20 people waiting for one piece of equipment) in workouts.

Racks can range from half-racks for a smaller space to a full squat rack. A combination rack can be used for bench press and squatting at the same station. These are usually placed on a platform and have become very popular in performance-oriented facilities. The benches and power racks are generally manufactured with 7-11 gauge steel. The lower gauge rating (7 gauge) is desirable for heavy loads and tend to be more sturdy. There is a huge range in price based on the company, quality of equipment and where it is manufactured. Lifting platforms can have squat racks or be stand-alone stations for Olympic lifting. The selection of the appropriate Olympic bars is determined by the tensile strength. Bars used for squatting, Olympic lifts, and bench press ultimately require 1,500-pound test. It is generally recommended to have a bar that utilized for the squat and bench-press movements and a bar that is designed for Olympic lifting movements. The types of Olympic plates available are steel, rubber, or polyurethane-coated. The selected style is ultimately influenced by the budget and the desired aesthetic value that is to be achieved. Olympic plates and dumbbells can be monogrammed with the organization's logo to reinforce the organization's brand identity. It is important to determine if the plates and dumbbells should be purchased in kilos or pounds. Dumbbell sets generally range from 5 lbs. to 120 lbs. It is common for many strength facilities to have two to three full sets of dumbbells. The dumbbells range from simple plate-loaded bars, to molded cast iron, and the more expensive rubber-coated cast iron.

Selectorized or pin select machines have become a very important and effective tool for many types of fitness training and bodybuilding. Used in

The half rack is very versatile and can be used for squatting and pulling exercises.

conjunction with free weights and cardiovascular workouts, one can achieve goals for strength, weight loss, endurance, and toning. Selectorized weight systems offer a safe workout and an easy way of changing resistance for sets and workout partners. These types of machines work very well in a multiuse facility. Decisions on upholstery and padding on machines is another consideration. For example on glute hamstring machines, you can choose full pads or half-moon pads. Commercial strength equipment manufacturers include: Body Masters, Cybex, Flex, Hoist, Icarian, Life Fitness, Badger, Nautilus, and Paramount. One complete line of selectorized weight equipment should be included in the strength-training venue. Typically, a complete line (11 to 18 pieces) will accommodate all major muscle groups. Selectorized equipment is ideal for beginners, women, and seniors because of the elimination of the balance component and the reduction technical training associated with the use of free weight activities. Many of the selectorized pieces like the lat pull down will utilize a pulley system with cables. Pulley machines can be with or without seats. The pulleys can be cables or Kevlar belts. Cable pulley systems are a little easier to use but require a little more maintenance. Kevlar belts last a little longer but are sometimes difficult to install, not as smooth or as easy to use as cables. Cables must be constantly checked by the fitness staff for wear and tear.

Plate-loaded equipment has gained popularity in recent years. Plate-loaded machines are considered convenient to use because the need for coordination is minimal and the amount of resistance can be narrowly defined. There is a real range of users that this kind of machine can accommodate making it ideal for a multiuse strength and conditioning facility. Hammer Strength is the dominant manufacturer of plate-loaded equipment in the industry today.

The purchasing of exercise equipment is exciting; however, it is a time-consuming and involved process. There are many options one must consider when choosing equipment. With the numerous manufacturers of exercise equipment, the selection process is becoming much more difficult in trying to sort out which vendor to select. Purchases should be from reputable manufacturers that meet the fitness and industry standards for commercial equipment. Equipment for the home should never be considered for a public facility. There are events like trade shows to help guide these types of purchasing quandaries. Attend exercise equipment trade shows like Club Industry to learn about the different manufacturers. This allows for the prospective buyer to use equipment and compare equipment vendors all at the same location. It is also an opportune time to establish rapport with vendors, particularly when planning to do business with them in the future. Also, call other fitness facilities to determine their level of satisfaction pertaining to a brand of equipment being considered for purchase. What do they like or not like about the selected equipment? What common maintenance issues have they had to address? What was response time for making repairs and the quality of service? Keep in mind, not everyone does a complete room all at once due to the cost. A lot of schools do it in two- to three-year phases. Some are completely done by the booster club, a generous donation from someone in the community, PE grant, PE budget, athletic budgets, or a combination of all of these. The projected numbers in Table 17.2 are very attainable with a combination of the above-mentioned efforts and funds.

Aerobic Training Equipment

All equipment selected should reflect the needs of the clientele and the limitations of the facility. When making decisions, perform research and probe manufacturers to understand population needs and take inventory of facility electrical supply, budgetary considerations, and equipment warranties (two years for most). Consider questions like the number of patrons needed to be accommodated at one time. Consider a mixture of pieces (treadmills, ellipticals, recumbent bikes, spin bikes, upper body ergometer (UBE), stairsteppers,

Table 17.2
Cost Estimates for Secondary School SCFs

Small Schools

- 500 or Less Students
- 25-30 per class
- Flooring - 2,500 - 3,000 sq. ft. – $12,500 – $45,000
- Weight Equipment $60,000 – $150,000
- Cardio Equipment (10 pieces)- avg. $2,500 per piece $25,000
- Total to expect to pay = $97,500 – $220,000 Depending on Bells and Whistles

Medium Schools

- 501-999
- 35-45 per class
- Flooring - 3,500 – 4,500 sq. ft. – $17,500 – $67,500
- Weight Equipment – $90,000 – $180,000
- Cardio Equipment (15 Pieces) – avg. $2,500 per piece $37,500
- Total to expect to pay = $195,000 – $285,000 Depending on Bells and Whistles

Large Schools

- Over 1,000
- 50-70 per class
- Flooring – 5,000 – 7,000 sq. ft. $25,000 - $105,000
- Weight Equipment – $135,000 – $300,000
- Cardio Equipment (20 pieces) avg. $2,500 per piece $50,000
- Total to expect to pay = $210,000 – $455,000 Depending on Bells and Whistles

rowing machines). How many pieces need to be ADA compliant for handicapped individuals?

Are there any power restrictions (110 vs. 220) in the room that would not allow you to have certain pieces? After these ideas are properly reflected upon, it is possible with some vendors to engage in a trial period for equipment. This will allow members to give direct feedback. After receiving feedback from members and inspecting other venues; it is time to choose the appropriate pieces of equipment. Again, select a variety of equipment for the cardiovascular area including treadmills, mechanical stair-climbing machines, bicycle ergometers, computerized cycles, rowing ergometers, upper-body ergometers, and total-body conditioning machines.

Also include in the cardiovascular fitness area, at least one circuit of progressive resistance-training equipment, other than free weights, that includes either a machine or workout station for each of the following muscle groups: gluteus, quadriceps, hamstrings, calves, chest, upper back, lower back, shoulders, triceps, biceps, and abdomen. This area can be used for group exercise classes or circuit training.

With the growing popularity and variety of group exercise programs, the accessories associated with these activities are also expanding. Each class may have individual needs, and it is important to acquire the equipment with class number in mind. Storage of equipment is a significant priority when evaluating existing and planning future group exercise facilities. Avoiding the appearance of clutter and potential hazards can be eliminated with the installation of tiered shelving that can be rolled out and put into a storage closet after a respective activity is completed. Mirrors serve as a functional need in this area in order for the instructor to observe the participants' form and technique. So, along with the equipment for each individual class, plan for storage as well.

The facility requirements of the indoor cycling studio should complement the objectives associated with the activity, which is to enhance mental imagery of an outdoor riding experience. To a certain extent, this activity should be perceived as a theater production where the instructor can control the lighting and sound with dimmer controls, which contribute to the ambience and visual effect. The inclusion of DVD projection is also desirable. The group facilitator's bike should be placed on a platform for participants to observe the cadence, form, and technique of the instructor, as well as for the instructor to observe the participants. Self-contained heating, ventilating, and air-conditioning (HVAC) systems separate from the main facility are desirable, considering the intensity of the activity and the perspiration and heat that accrues. Ceiling fans should also be installed to circulate the air and keep the participants comfortable. The total space requirements are ultimately dependent upon the number of bikes to be included in the indoor cycling studio.

The International Health, Racquet, and Sport-club Association (IHRSA), NSCA, and the ACSM recommend that strength and cardiovascular training area planners should consider providing:

- A variety of types of equipment for the cardio-vascular area including treadmills, mechanical stair-climbing machines, bicycle ergometers, computerized cycles, rowing ergometers, upper-body ergometers, and total body-conditioning machines;
- At least one circuit of progressive resistance-training equipment (other than free weights) that includes either a machine or workout station for each of the following muscle groups: gluteus, quadriceps, hamstrings, calves, chest, upper back, lower back, shoulders, triceps, biceps, and abdomen; and
- A circuit for resistance training in a fashion that allows users to train the largest muscle groups first and then proceed to the smaller muscle groups. All compound movement machines should be placed in the circuit before isolated movement machines involving the same muscle(s).

The following considerations should be taken under advisement when making cardiovascular equipment selections:

- Age and condition of clientele served
- Available space in cardiovascular area
- Sufficient electrical supply to support equipment
- Budgetary considerations
- Maintenance requirements of selected equipment
- Proximity of equipment repair technicians to fitness facility
- Length of warranty (e.g., two years for most common equipment)

Stretching and Bodyweight Exercise Equipment

The designated space for stretching and core body training is ultimately dependent upon the scope and extent to which the following accessories are made available: stability balls, speed and agility training accessories, medicine balls, bands/tubing, plyometric training boxes, power wheels, functional training grids, balance and stabilization boards, and pads. Establishing systems to support the use and storage of accessories is essential. Will the area be used on an individual or formal group instructional basis? A minimum of at least 175 to 300 square feet is suggested for this space.

Delivery and Arrival

Proceed with the installation of equipment with caution and the utmost care. Establish a firm delivery date and time with the shipping company. Make an assessment to determine what entrance modifications, if any, need to be made to the facility when equipment arrives.

Questions to consider include: Should the facility be temporarily closed; is the removal of door jambs required; are pallet jacks or a four-wheel cart required; will additional staff to assist with set up and installation be required or is this service included in the delivery and set-up process?

Take pictures and write extensive notes pertaining to the condition of equipment upon arrival, specifically if it is damaged. Are upholstery colors and the models of equipment correct? Inventory the equipment immediately by securing the serial numbers from the delivery sheets or manually record the numbers off each piece of equipment. This is necessary because, when requesting future repairs, respective vendors will ask for serial numbers before processing equipment repair tickets. Sign off on deliveries, as long as items are acceptable. If equipment is not correct, an immediate call to the manufacturer or sales representative will determine the course of action to take, which may include the reloading of equipment onto the truck.

Organizing Equipment

Now that the equipment has been ordered, the next step is to organize the equipment within the facility. This process can seem complicated when one must consider placing many different types of equipment in sometimes-limited spaces. One suggestion to streamline this action is to decide first upon a unifying theme for the weight room. This means a careful look at the programmatic objectives and specific needs of the membership. One idea is to organize resistance-training machines according to the targeted body part and then designating specific areas for other themed activities, like cardiovascular exercise and stretching and bodyweight exercise. Some weight rooms will begin by first separating spaces for the different types of exercise and then organizing equipment within those designated areas. Regardless of the strategy, first deciding on a theme will guide the decision-making process.

Placing Equipment

Aside from designating specific areas for the three types of equipment, equipment placement should be used to affect the visual field and safety policy is a positive way. An exercise facility visual appeal depends on equipment placement. In order to increase the visual field within the facility, the tallest machinery, like squat racks and lat pull machines, should be placed against the walls, and for safety's sake, may need to be bolted to the floor. Smaller equipment should be placed toward the middle to not only increase vision, but also to promote easy motion across the room or rooms. On the same note, taller, more upright cardiovascular machines should be placed near the walls of the facility or towards the back of the cardiovascular fitness area with lower, seated cardiovascular machines toward the middle and front. To maintain safety, equipment should be at least six inches from mirrors, with power-lifting exercises placed significantly away from mirrors to avoid glass breakage and collisions. More specific measures to place equipment will be discussed in the next section.

Spacing Equipment

The following are the guidelines for equipment spacing suggested by the National Strength and Conditioning Association in Chapter 24 of the second edition of the *Essentials of Strength Training and Conditioning* (Greenwood, 2000). The National Strength and Conditioning Association establish many of the recommended standards for professionals in the field of strength and conditioning. This organization is a great resource when establishing policies and procedures for a SCF facility.

Facility Traffic Flow
—Traffic flow should be around the perimeter of resistance training and aerobic exercise machine areas. Different colors of flooring or carpet can be used to identify walkways through the facility.
—There should be at least one walkway that bisects the room to provide quick and easy access in and out of the facility in an emergency.
—An unobstructed pathway three feet (91 cm) wide should be maintained in the facility at all times as stipulated by federal, state, and local laws. Resistance-training machines and equipment and aerobic machines must not block or hinder traffic flow.
—Although ceiling height does not affect traffic flow on the floor, the ceiling should be free of low-hanging apparatus (beams, pipes, lighting, signs, etc.) and high enough to allow clients to perform overhead and jumping exercises. A minimum of 12 feet (3.7m) is recommended.

Body Weight Exercise, Flexibility and Medicine Ball Area
—A 49-square-ft (4.6-square-m) area (7 ft by 7 ft, or 2.1m by 2.1m) for each client should be allotted for stretching and warm-up activities.
—A larger area may be needed for medicine ball work and partner stretching.

Resistance-Training Machine Area
—All resistance-training machines and equipment must be space at least two feet (61cm), preferably three feet (91cm) apart. To effectively serve

Body weight excercise, flexibility, and medicine ball area must be planned space in the SCF facility.

clients who use wheelchairs, more than three feet (91cm) may be needed.
—If a free-weight exercise is performed in a resistance-training machine area, a three-foot (91cm) safety space cushion is needed between the ends of the barbell and all adjacent stations.
—More than three feet (91cm) of space is recommended between multistation machines and single-station machines. Multistation machines require more space than single-station machines.

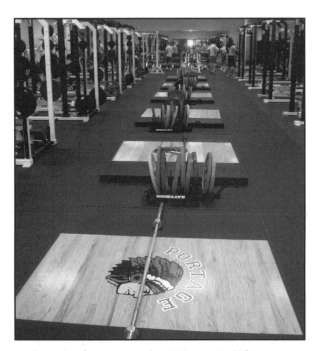

The platforms in the Olympic lifting area must be spaced for three to four people to work at each station.

Resistance Training Free Weight Area
—The ends of all Olympic bars should be spaced three feet (91cm) apart.
—The area designated for a free weight station should be able to accommodate three to four people.
—Racks holding fixed-weight barbells should have a minimum of three feet (91cm) between the ends of the bars.
—Weight trees should be placed in close proximity to plate-loaded equipment and benches, but not closer than three feet (91cm).

Olympic Lifting Area
—The dimensions of the Olympic lifting area should be at least 8' (2.43m) x 8' (2.43m) and accommodate three to four people.
—The walkway around an Olympic lifting platform should be three to four feet (91-122cm) wide.

Aerobic Exercise Area
—Ideally, a space cushion of three feet (91cm) should be provided on all sides of aerobic exercise machines (placement too close to walls should be avoided) for safety and to allow clients and supervising personal trainers easy access.
—It is suggested that each type of aerobic machine need its own spacing: 24 square feet (2.2 square m) for stationary bikes and stair machines, six square feet (0.6 square m) for rowing machines, and 45 square feet (4.2 square m) for treadmills. These recommendations include the needed space between machines.

Health Assessment and Testing Area
An organization truly having a vested interest in the physical well being of their membership will have a state-of-the-art fitness assessment, consultation, and educational seminar room (Sawyer & Stowe, 2005). This private area is used to obtain baseline measurements for future programming and personal training.

Programmatic Considerations
The members' achievement of their fitness goals requires that they have a baseline to measure their progress prior to beginning their exercise programs. The health-assessment process is an integral part in developing exercise plans. A determination must be made as to the scope of the health-assessment process and the extent that educational and lifestyle programs will be offered, because these dimensions will dictate the amount of facility space required. Most health assessments include body composition analysis, blood pressure screenings, muscular strength and flexibility testing, submaximal cardiovascular testing, cholesterol screenings, health history appraisals, and nutrition consultations.

The following are specific fitness-testing space and facility requirements:

- The scope of space required is ultimately dependent upon the scope of the health and fitness protocol completed. The fitness-testing space requires a minimum of 100 to 180 square feet, consultation room (90 to 120 square feet), and a seminar room (20 square feet per participant) all with a minimum of an eight-foot ceiling with suspended acoustical panels; wall construction comprised of dry wall and painted with epoxy paint.
- The electrical outlets need to be strategically located in proximity to the exercise testing equipment and should be ground fault interrupters (GFI). Fluorescent lighting within this area should be at least 50 foot-candles of illumination at the floor surface.
- A sink in the facility is required.
- The emergency response system should include emergency lighting and audible alarms. This is necessary for the purposes of warning other facility personnel of a medical emergency in the area.
- Because of the function of the space, adhering to these standards is essential. The HVAC mechanical systems must have a temperature environment of 68°-72°F (22° to 26°C), humidity control of 55 degrees, and ventilation (eight to 12 exchanges per hour with a ratio of 40 to 60 outside to inside air).
- Size: The testing area includes a fitness-testing space (100 to 180 square feet), counseling room (90 to 120 square feet), and seminar room (20 square feet per participant) all with an eight-foot ceiling (Peterson & Tharrett, 1997). There should be adequate space in this area to house two chairs, a desk, a file cabinet, a storage cabinet, a computer station, a bicycle ergometer, a flexibility tester, a treadmill, control console, crash cart, metabolic cart, 12-lead electrocardiogram (ECG), ECG defibrillator, cholesterol analyzer, examination table, double sink, spine board, and a storage cabinet for equipment such as skinfold calipers, stopwatches, and stethoscope(s).
- Walls: Simple drywall construction, epoxy painted with a pleasing color(s), appropriate graphics for the area, and a bulletin board.
- Floor: The floors should be carpeted with an antistatic and antifungal commercial-grade carpet, color coordinated with the walls and equipment in the room.
- Ceiling: A suspended acoustical panel ceiling is appropriate.
- Electrical: The electrical needs of the equipment in the room should be considered as well as the eventual location of the equipment. There should be numerous electrical outlets around the

perimeter of the room. The outlets near the sink should be GFI. The recommended lighting for this area is fluorescent units that will produce at least 50 foot-candles of illumination at the floor surface.
- Climate control: The mechanical considerations for this space include heating and cooling (68° to 72° F [22° to 26° C]), humidity control (55 degree), and ventilation (eight to 12 exchanges per hour with a ratio of 40:60 outside to inside air). Due to the activities in this room, careful consideration to cooling, humidity control, and ventilation are necessary.
- Plumbing: A facility should ensure that every fitness-testing space either has a sink or access to a sink.
- Security: There should be emergency lighting and an audible emergency alarm to alert other personnel to a medical emergency in the testing area.

Equipment for the Fitness-Testing Area

The NSCA and ACSM suggest that a facility should ensure that its fitness-testing area has the following equipment (Greenwood, 2000; Peterson & Tharrett, 1997):

- In the fitness-testing area—a bicycle ergometer, a treadmill or a fixed-step device (e.g., a bench) of a desired height, skinfold calipers or other body-composition measurement device, sit-and-reach bench on goniometer, tensiometer, or other device for measuring muscular strength and endurance, perceived exertion chart, clock, metronome, sphygmomanometer (blood pressure cuff), stethoscope, tape measure, scale, and first-aid kit.
- In the health promotion and wellness area—computer, overhead projector, video system, LCD projector, conference table, and chairs.
- In the fitness-testing, health promotion, and wellness area—a system that provides for and protects the complete confidentiality of all user records and meetings.

Operations

Scheduling and Staff-to-Member Ratios

Depending on the facility programmatic objectives, scheduling time in the facility can be a small or a large issue. Most SCFs, however, will need to schedule time in a section of the gym in one way or another: for personal training, aerobic classes, or for athletic teams. Improper scheduling can lead to crowdedness and dangerous staff-to-member ratios; both of these negative consequences can and should be avoided.

An important idea to understand before scheduling is the use of space and membership flow. Personal training, or one-on-one exercise consultation, should not be scheduled during peak hours unless the facility houses a special room for personal training. Aerobic or other themed exercise class should have their own room and therefore can be scheduled throughout the day according to staff limitations.

Scheduling becomes more complicated when facilities want to incorporate team sports, for example, varsity college weight rooms or facilities that accommodate youth sports or organized group activities. Typically, teams should be scheduled separately with in-season teams receiving time priority. Some small teams, however, in larger weight rooms can be scheduled together if equipment use does not overlap. For example, if a tennis team is working on plyometrics and agility drills, a power-lifting team may use the platforms at the same time. If one season is crowded with two or more teams, a rotating schedule of alternating days may work best to accommodate all athletes; one team can come in Monday-Wednesday-Friday, while the other team may come in Tuesday-Thursday-Saturday. Some bigger teams may not be able to be scheduled all at once for effective training, so it is important to consider the alternative and split the team into groups. The team may be split by position, a situation appropriate for football, or may be split by ability, sometimes appropriate for youth team sports especially those that include a range of different ages.

One critical variable to think about when scheduling is staff-to-member ratios. Because of the many different uses of the SCFs, it is important that traffic flow be monitored and investigated in relation to the presence of dedicated and/or certified professionals. Ideally, a higher number of dedicated strength and conditioning professionals should be used in those facilities with greater SCFs traffic flow and use levels (Armitage-Johnson, 1994). Having supervision from professionals is key to the safety and lifting technique of exercising members, but making sure the proper number of professionals is in the facility for any given activity is just as significant. A general rule to operate by is the younger and more inexperienced the athlete or member, the more professional supervision is needed. Here are some recommended guidelines: junior high athletes and members require a 1:10 staff-to-member ratio, high school age require a 1:15 ratio, and a 1:20 ratio is optimal for members older than the junior high or high school level. It is also recommended that facilities do not exceed a 1:50 staff-to-member ratio.

Maintenance

Proper maintenance of the facility and facility equipment means SCF longevity and safety. The type of maintenance necessary for facility upkeep demands an understanding of the types of materials and machines being dealt with. Maintenance is often a chore balanced between custodial, personal training, and gym supervising staff. Devising a maintenance schedule for both the facility and facility equipment can ensure appropriate, essential and regular upkeep.

Facility Maintenance

First check on the facility maintenance list is the flooring. No matter the type of flooring, the floor should be inspected regularly. Tile, resilient rubber, and carpet floors as well as mats must be either treated with an antibacterial and antifungal agent, or must contain these attributes. It is also important that mats and carpeting are nonabsorbent. Wood flooring demands extra attention to loose screws, nicks in boards, and other potentially hazardous problems. All types of flooring should be inspected for malfunctions daily with daily cleaning suggested.

Walls and wall hangings like mirrors and signs should be cleaned two to three times a week or as needed with special attention to high-traffic areas. Although the cleaning for walls is not as high maintenance as the flooring, be careful to ensure wall safety is maintained. Ceilings must also be cleaned and broken areas of the ceiling must be replaced as needed. Dust should not be allowed to accumulate anywhere in the facility. Regular inspection ensures that small problems never become big problems.

Equipment Maintenance

Stretching and bodyweight exercise areas usually comprise of a mat or another kind of skin-contact flooring and a variety of equipment such as medicine balls, individual mats, elastic cords, or physioballs. Because all of these items are in possible contact with membership skin, daily cleaning, and disinfectant is necessary. Signs and employees should also emphasize cleaning by the membership. Each individual should be encouraged to spray and wipe down equipment after each use; these items for cleaning should be multiple and available in well-seen areas. To ensure the longevity of the flooring in the area, equipment that could pierce or tear the floor or mat should be kept out of the area, and at the end of each day, all equipment should be inspected as it is replaced.

Resistance-training areas are comprised of machines, free weights, and sometimes Olympic-lifting areas. Each group has its own challenge for maintenance, but in general, each group will include upholstery in contact with skin. The upholstery needs to be cleaned and disinfected daily and should be free from tears and cracks. Resistance-training machines should be without any loose parts, including bolts, screws, cables, chains, or worn parts. Machines with guide rods should be cleaned and lubricated two to three times per week. Chains, cables, and pulleys should be checked and fixed when normal alignment is disrupted. Free weights include racks, benches, racks, weights, and dumbbells. Bench and rack welds should be inspected monthly or as needed. Dumbbells should be checked frequently for loose parts. In the Olympic lifting area, bar maintenance is critical: these bars require attention to the rotating areas to ensure the proper rotation, and should be free from chalk or other build up (Greenwood & Greenwood, 2000). Since the Olympic lifters will utilize various types of accessory equipment to lift, it is important to make sure leftover items are replaced to their original storage. If the area includes wooden platforms, check the platform for cracks and splinters weekly.

The aerobic exercise area can be a challenge for cleaning. These areas typically, after prolonged use, gather sweat from the user. Encourage users to disinfect the equipment after each use. The same types of cleaning materials provided in stretching and bodyweight exercise areas should also be present in the aerobic exercise areas. Machinery should also be maintained and no loose parts should exist. Check these monthly or as needed. To conclude the maintenance section, if a piece or pieces of a particular machine or weight is found to be broken, place a sign in the line of vision signifying the equipment is out of order.

Strength Training Equipment Maintenance Checklists

The following are the standard inspections that should be included in a comprehensive maintenance program:

- Inspection of weight stacks, cables, and attachments—are they appropriately secured?
- Inspection of snap hooks—clasps close appropriately?
- No worn or frayed cables on equipment?
- Chrome end caps on dumbbells are not becoming jagged or flaking shrapnel pieces?
- Dumbbells tightened and secured?
- Bolts appropriately tightened on all benches?

Keeping Records

Keeping both accurate and up-to-date records is an essential of a successful weight-training and aerobic facility. Two main categories of records must be a part of the venue documentation: clientele records and maintenance records. Clientele records include payments, workouts with hired trainers, complaints, and any other reports. One hopes to never be involved in a liability case, but if such a problem should occur, attaining a collection of records may be critical evidence. This point is one of the reasons why maintenance records are so important. Abiding by the suggested manufacturer's protocol not only ensures safety, but also prevents liability (Greenwood & Greenwood, 2000). Other records may include equipment purchase and warranty, schedules, and contractor receipts.

The Universal gym was one of the early pieces of exercise equipment in the SCF facilities of yesteryear.

Equipment Repair Work Order

Today's Date: _____

Name of Staff Member requesting repair: _____

Detailed Description of Item Broken: _____

Serial Number of the Product: _____

Organizational Inventory ID number (if used) _____

Was equipment taken out circulation or sign posted on equipment restricting use?
(Please Circle).
If no, describe what actions were taken!

_____

YES   NO

Date call was placed for repair? _____

Date Service was completed_____

Cost of Repair _____

Warranty of repair: 30   60   90   days.

ADVENTURE PROGRAMMING FACILITIES

18

Donald Rogers, Indiana State University

There are literally thousands of adventure programs in the U.S. conducted in schools, colleges, summer camps, recreation programs, commercial adventure enterprises, YMCAs, fitness clubs, and health-care settings. These programs offer individual and group experiences that are intended to provide recreation, education, personal growth, and enrichment, developmental and/or therapeutic benefits. Activities in these programs include adventure and cooperative games, group problem-solving initiatives, adventure-based recreation, leisure and sports, and climbing and challenge course-based experiences.

Adventure activities involve some degree of physical, psychological, emotional, and/or social risks. Programs can be generic in terms of who they serve, or they can be customized to meet the needs of specific individuals or groups. Typically these experiences foster trust and cooperation, improve problem solving and conflict-resolution skills, enhance self-image and confidence, improve physical skills, all in a fun and exciting context. From a facilities standpoint, the least resource-intensive programs involve the games and minimal-prop group initiative activities. These typically require an open space either indoors or outdoors that will allow for safe active movement, such as a gymnasium or open field. As programs seek to provide more complex and demanding adventure activities, the facilities necessary for the activities involved will require more in-depth planning and expertise.

Adventure-based recreation, leisure, and sports activities are traditional adventure-based recreation activities like mountain biking, kayaking, canoeing, hiking, skiing, and caving. All of these activities are appropriate experiences to meet adventure program goals; however, given that they tend to occur in minimally developed outdoor settings, these types of adventure activities have few facility requirements associated with them. Therefore, they will not be discussed in this chapter.

Climbing and challenge-course (ropes course) activities introduce risk that is often gauged by how high off the ground the participant is expected or is able to go. While there are other components of these adventure activities that involve psychological, intellectual, and social challenges, our useful fear of heights tends to frame the experience. There are also the physical demands of going vertical to consider. Fatigue is always a factor in climbing that impacts all the other challenges. The heights involved in these activities can range from a palpable one to three feet on low (teams) courses to a breathtaking 60 or 70 feet above the ground on the more extreme climbing towers and high-challenge courses. Of course, these extreme heights are not necessary to achieve most climbing-based program goals. Typical heights of towers, walls, and high-challenge courses range from 20 to 40 feet.

While there is tremendous variety in climbing-wall and challenge-course designs, each is guided by standards set by their respective professional associations. Indoor climbing facilities may be as simple as holds bolted to an existing wall, as elaborate as pre-molded replicas of famous rock-climbing routes, or low-bouldering faces that mostly involve lateral climbing. Outdoors there are freestanding towers framed on telephone poles or steel structures and walls attached to trees. All of these climbing facilities involve handholds, belay attachments, ropes, climbing hardware, and other safety equipment. Similarly, ropes courses utilize a variety of indoor and outdoor structural components, including roof trusses, girders, poles, and trees with additional features made of ropes, wires, lumber, pulleys, and extensive safety equipment. This chapter will provide an overview of the common steps in a facility-planning process, discuss the structures, equipment, and supporting materials needed for climbing walls and ropes courses, and identify safety and administrative considerations for those developing or conducting these types of adventure programs.

The Planning Process

The initial step in planning is to establish clear program goals and determine what type of facility is needed to achieve these goals. In most cases this will require a needs assessment of the populations to be served. It is a good idea to involve a representative group of stakeholders in the planning process. These stakeholders include other impacted units within the agency, existing customers/clients, potential customers/clients, and agencies that might partner on the project. It is also advisable to employ the services of an established, credible vendor who can provide expertise about types of facilities and consult with someone in your industry who is successfully operating a similar facility. Projects such as these require dedicated space for the wall or course, storage space for equipment, extra staffing, ongoing training, maintenance and inspection fees, and equipment replacement and upgrades. The initial costs can be in the tens of thousands of dollars, plus additional recurring costs.

Many agencies establish their programs with what they can afford and over time add components based on need and available resources. Of course, others will be able to afford a sizable state-of-the-art wall or comprehensive challenge course complex. Either way, it is critical to determine in the initial stages of planning that the addition of this adventure component is a good fit for the agency and its partners, it will serve the needs and interests of customers, and it is economically feasible. Many agencies have plunged into owning and operating adventure facilities because it seemed like an exciting idea that would surely appeal to customers, but found that the "build it and they will come" strategy worked better in the movies than in real life.

Once a general facility concept is developed, a detailed construction plan is needed. The facility may be designed and built in-house, or designed and built by an outside vendor, or a combination of the two. For example, installing a small bouldering wall (low climbing wall designed for lateral climbing) on an existing wall or as a free-standing unit can be done in-house with the help of maintenance or facilities staff, program staff, and volunteers, or climbing club members; however, building a large climbing wall or climbing tower is better left to professional climbing wall designers and builders. It is not unusual for them to involve agency volunteers in site preparation, general labor tasks, or even skilled tasks. It is helpful for designated agency staff to learn about the inner workings of the wall or course so they can perform periodic maintenance and minor repairs. There are some excellent references on the Internet that provide detailed information about building small-scale climbing and bouldering walls. For the more complex projects involving outside professional vendors, considerable planning and coordination will be required.

It is important to select a vendor who is willing to spend time getting to know the needs of the agency and its staff. There are many complex decisions to make in the planning and construction process that need to happen in collaboration between the vendor and agency. Ideally, the same vendor should also provide annual inspections, equipment replacement, major repairs, trainings, and consultation. This relationship could exist for many years, so finding a reliable, competent vendor will be a critical early decision. Again, the Internet is a good starting place to locate and research vendors. They should provide specific information about their qualifications and experience to do this kind of work. Look for a description of the services they offer to customers and be sure it includes the components of planning, design, construction, training, inspections, repairs, and consultation. Ask for references so you can speak directly with other programs similar to yours about the service they have received from that vendor. Check to be sure that they are a member in good standing with their professional trade organization and that they design and build according to current industry standards. A professional, experienced vendor should guide an agency through the planning, design and construction process, communicating the steps to be taken while anticipating and preparing to meet their future needs.

Today, adventure programs are widespread and operate in schools, universities, fitness clubs, commercial adventure program facilities, camps, and non-profit agencies. The growth of the climbing wall industry has been particularly extraordinary. Emerging in the mid-1980s as a training device for rock climbers, climbing walls have become centerpieces to draw prospective customers and provide recreation, competitive sport, and fitness opportunities for families, youth and adults alike. Examples of the climbing-wall phenomenon include the two large walls on the cruise ship Oasis of the Sea, the world's largest debuting in late 2009, owned by Royal Caribbean International; a wall in the new 65,000-sq. ft. military rehabilitation facility for wounded American soldiers; Goldman Sachs & Co. offers a climbing wall as part of an employee fitness center; and the fitness club chain Lifetime Fitness with 60 clubs, all with climbing walls or "caverns." Health/fitness centers and university student recreation centers are at the heart

Climbing on the Alpine Tower II

of the climbing-wall boom. They are no longer a secondary option for climbing real rock. The next section will address the design and management of climbing walls.

Climbing Walls

Planning Considerations

Climbing walls can be built indoors or outdoors. They can serve children and older adults. A climbing wall can be part of fitness, recreation, sport, education, and therapeutic programs. Their versatility is similar to challenge courses as a multifaceted adventure instrument. When deciding to include a climbing wall in a new facility or add one to an existing program, an organization has a number of questions to answer and options to consider.

Initial questions include where to locate the wall, how big will it be, and what kind of wall should it be? More technical questions would explore the safety systems, risk management, staffing, training, equipment, maintenance, and access control. Following are additional considerations provided by Sagar (2007):

- Who are your primary users and do they represent your desired target markets?
- What are your goals for the users' experience?
- Do those goals reflect the style of outdoor climbing popular in your region, as well as the progression of the sport?
- How do your facility's design and space limitations affect those goals? For example, are the walls too high for beginners? Are the routes not challenging enough to entice more experienced climbers?
- What does your facility offer that others in the area do not?
- Is the overall environment friendly and inviting to climbers of all skill levels?

- Do instructors communicate in a way that climbers understand and appreciate?
- Do business hours, and clinic and program schedules fit the needs of the wall's typical users?
- Do you provide related services (such as gear rental and sales) and customer service to climbers?
- Does the music played in the facility appeal to the typical climber?
- Does the facility's atmosphere encourage both performance and socialization?
- Is your building conveniently accessible both from the street and the parking lot?
- Is it easily identified as a climbing facility? (pg. 37).

It will help to do some initial research in climbing publications and Internet resources, particularly if no one in the organization has experience with climbing walls and adventure programs. At this point, another important question has to be answered, who will be our climbing wall vendor? A reputable vendor will be able to answer your questions and present options that stimulate your thinking about the function of a wall in your facility. Unless the plan calls for a small, inexpensive homemade wall, a professional climbing wall designer and builder with plenty of experience will be a necessity. There are numerous concerns around building codes, engineering, architectural and climbing features, matching program goals with designs, staff training, and long-term strategies that should not be left to chance.

Sagar (2007) encourages agencies to have a solid mission statement about the climbing-wall program. The mission statement should communicate who the program wants to serve, for example, climbers, families, or community. It should also indicate the desired outcomes of the program, such as fitness, skills, and/or fun. This information provides a guide for the design of the wall and the facilities around it, as well as the development of

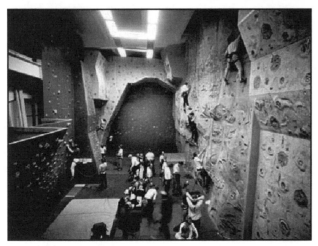

operating procedures, programming components, and staffing profiles.

Once an agency is clear about who it is serving and the desired outcomes, it is time to consider what kind of climbing wall and climbing experience is needed. The design concept should meet current needs and provide flexibility for future program growth and development.

The climbing-wall concept will vary greatly depending on how the climbing wall fits into the overall facility design. The type of wall designed for a commercial indoor climbing gym may be very different from a wall designed for an outdoor adventure program in a public school. Determining how the climbing wall will be integrated into other program and support facilities will also have an effect on the design concept. The location of the climbing wall in relation to entrances and exits, locker rooms, storage areas, offices, pro shops, water fountains, and other program areas, such as the ropes courses, gymnasiums, pools, fitness rooms, racquetball courts, and classrooms, will affect design concept decisions. Designers should consider general design criteria like visibility, control, and safety. Also, they need to decide if the climbing wall needs to be near to or isolated from any of the other features. Schematic drawings that show general size, location, and adjacencies will help refine concept development. More than one design option can be explored at this time.

Design Development

The design development phase is decision-making time. If more than one design concept was developed, whether on your own or with a vendor, a decision needs to be made on which design will go to full development. Full development requires decisions on:

- What is the scope of the project (including budget estimates, funding available, and space allocated for the climbing wall)?
- What heating, ventilation, and air-conditioning (HVAC) systems are needed?

- What features are needed for the walls, floor, and framework? (The wall, floor, and framework designs must meet climbing wall industry standards.)
- Which wall surface is desired (the real-rock look, seamless cement, prefabricated panels, wood, or doesn't matter)?
- How much wall height is desired (a nine- to 14-foot-high bouldering wall used primarily for horizontal climbing or a high top-roping or lead climbing wall)?
- Will a climbing treadmill meet program needs?
- What wall features are desired, especially the number, type, and location of handholds? Other surface features may be built into the wall, such as cracks, arêtes (corner), depressions, overhangs, caves, ledges, and so on.
- How much wall security is needed? (Will the climbing wall be in a self-contained, lockable area, or will the wall be in an open area and require some way to limit access to the climbing surface?)
- What type of landing surface is most appropriate? Bouldering walls and walls located in multipurpose locations like gymnasiums often have movable landing mats. Areas used exclusively for climbing usually have specially designed flooring such as thickly padded carpeting, six inches of rubber pieces, or six inches of gravel (consistent with ASTM International standard F 1292-04 regarding impact attenuation on playground surfaces). Most new facilities are using the heavily padded carpeting because it provides better protection, is easier to maintain, and is cleaner than gravel or rubber pieces. Current practice calls for protective flooring to extend six feet out from the furthest protrusion of the wall surface. In any case, the surface must not have gaps, needs to be secured in place, must cover all feasible landing surfaces, and must provide sufficient impact protection given the height of the fall, such as 12 feet on a bouldering wall.

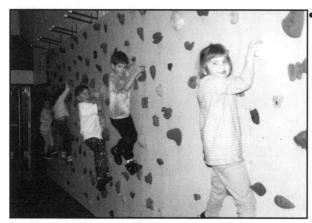

How much storage is required? A lot of equipment is required to operate a climbing program, ropes, climbing shoes, harnesses, helmets, and carabiners. The equipment needs to be located near the climbing wall so the storage areas for some of the newer climbing walls are built into the back or side of the wall.

Planning and Design Summary

Failure to adequately plan (do your homework) and develop a comprehensive project concept often results in a climbing facility that does not have the desired features or meet programming requirements. This may lead to a facility that is unpopular, unsafe, cannot compete locally, or prematurely obsolete.

Project planners must develop a comprehensive project concept that will guide specific design and operation decisions. Components of a comprehensive project concept for a climbing wall often address the following questions:

- Who are the target facility users? (Who will be climbing on the wall?) The design features for a bouldering facility to teach junior high school students will be very different from one designed to train lead-climbing mountain guides. Failing to identify the target facility users often results in an inefficient and ineffective climbing facility.
- Will the wall be a stand-alone entity, or will it be used with any other facilities? For example, part of a larger adventure or fitness program.
- What financial resources are available to fund the project?
- How many climbers will use the wall at any one time (peak load)?
- Is this a new build or retrofit of an existing area?
- How much space is available?
- How important are aesthetics? (Is a natural-rock look more important than having the maximum amount of climbing area?) This is an important consideration in situations where the wall will be the centerpiece within a facility or located in a prominent location. Creating a powerful aesthetic impact will likely require more expense with high-end flooring, wall materials, lighting, and access prevention.
- What type of flooring/landing surfaces will be best for the facility?
- Do the design features promote safety, minimize maintenance problems, and meet program needs?

Design Features

As you begin your research locating and identifying what is on the climbing wall market, the extensive array of designs, features, and options may amaze you. This is why you need to do the research and why it is important to employ a climbing-wall vendor early in the process. You want to get a sense for what is out there without wasting a lot of time trying to answer questions or make decisions that are not relevant. It's kind of like going fishing on a large, unfamiliar lake. There is so much to see and explore, and it is not like you don't enjoy that, but you also have limited time and gas, and you really want to catch some fish. After six hours of hunting for those apparently intelligent critters and nothing to show for your efforts, you are thinking, "Maybe hiring a guide wasn't such a bad idea."

Let's explore the types of climbing walls and the features that come with them. Remember that you are working toward an effective means of providing the kind of experiences your customers are anticipating. At the same time, try to be open minded about the ways this can be achieved and think in terms of providing options they may not have in mind and building in ways to expand and/or vary your program.

Climbing Wall Types

Before selecting individual features of a climbing wall, a decision must be made on what general type of climbing wall is desired. There are essentially two categories of walls, bouldering walls and tall walls (Stiehl & Ramsey, 2004). Bouldering walls will be between nine and 14 feet high, and shorter when used by youth or with overhangs. Consider not allowing pre-teens to boulder higher than nine feet. A rule of thumb is to not allow a fall that is greater than twice the height of the climber.

Tall walls, which have roped safety systems (belay systems) are generally 20 to 36 feet tall. Here is an overview of climbing wall types:

- Homemade—These are usually relatively simple walls made of framing lumber, plywood, paint, and handholds. Individual climbers build homemade walls for their personal use and institutions with limited resources build homemade climbing walls to support their program needs. An outdoor equipment store might build one in the facility to allow customers to try out climbing equipment or have a climbing club.
- Prefabricated panel system—Prefabricated panels are usually four feet by eight feet plywood or fiberglass panels with predrilled holes for handholds.
- Portable walls—There are three general types of portable walls: disassemble and reassemble, assembled walls on a trailer, and the portable treadmill-type wall.
- Steel structure wall systems—These systems are usually professionally designed and constructed walls with a structural steel frame and plywood surfaces. The surfaces may be coated with a cementitious materials, fiberglass, or blown synthetic material. Some of the cementitious surfaces have natural features like cracks, ledges, and indentations that are troweled in, while others replicate a real rock-style covering. Surfaces may also be precast or formed and replicate naturally occurring hand and foot holds (cracks, pockets, flakes, and grooves). Some vendors can offer replications of popular real rock climbing routes.
- Climbing towers—Towers are usually freestanding wooden towers built outside. They can be the only structure, or as is often the case, part of a larger adventure course. These structures utilize telephone poles and/or steel structure to support the climbing faces. The climbing faces are usually tongue and groove, pressure treated lumber with bolt on climbing holds; however, as the market is getting more competitive, elaborate precast faces are becoming more available.

Climbing Wall Features and Equipment

Most climbing walls have handholds that are attached to the wall using a T-nut or other comparable threaded anchor. These T-nut inserts may be installed by the contractor as part of the construction, purchased as part of pre-drilled wood or fiberglass panels, or added to climbing panels as part of a homemade project.

Handholds may be simple wood blocks fixed to the wall surface with epoxy glue, wood screws, T-nuts, or a combination of these, although wooden holds are rarely used in this era of custom walls. While wooden handholds are relatively inexpensive and can be formed into a wide variety of shapes and sizes, they can create splinters and split as they dry or respond to outdoor conditions. They still offer an option, however, for organizations that lack funding and want to construct an affordable program wall on site.

Most commercial handholds are designed for use with a T-nut system, but some can be attached to the wall with an epoxy process. There are literally thousands of different types, sizes, and shapes of handholds. Handhold packages are available that include handholds that replicate natural features in rocks and require climbers to use specific grip, foot, and protection techniques. Handhold color and texture can effectively duplicate natural rock, match the existing wall surface, or add color and flare to a climbing wall. Color-coded handholds may be used to designate specific climbing routes or difficulty levels. Colored or numbered tags can also be attached to the handholds to mark specific climbing routes. Incorporating movable or removable handholds provide options for changing routes, changing the size of a hold, or rotating the hold. It is a good idea to design in options for varying routes and difficulty levels in order to maintain climber interest and meet the needs of a range of climbers.

Climbing Equipment

Like challenge courses, climbing wall equipment is matched with the design of the wall and its intended purpose. While only a narrow range of equipment may be used on the wall on a regular basis, there is a tremendous selection of gear choices to be made at the outset. Numerous factors effect the decisions about climbing gear, such as nature of the program (e.g., competition, sport or real rock training), ages of the participants, how it will be belayed, and size and adaptability of the wall.

The decisions about specific gear choices and quantities of gear should be made in consultation with your vendor or consultant. Often the vendor has gear that they recommend based on their history with the equipment and a relationship that they have with the source of the gear. It is not unusual for the vendor to also be a retailer or distributor for specific brands of equipment. This should not be a cause for concern. Actually it presents benefits for the customer because they can bundle the equipment in the wall package for less than retail and provide discounts later when more or replacement gear is needed.

There are three bodies that determine standards for climbing equipment. These are Union of International Associations of Alpinists (UIAA), also known as The International Mountaineering and Climbing Federation and World Mountaineering and Climbing; the European Committee for Standardization (CEN), also the general equivalent for the European Union (EU); and the American Society for Test and Measurements (ASTM). Coding of CEN standards are written first with EN (European Norm) followed with a number, such as EN 892, which is the standard for dynamic mountaineering ropes. With climbing equipment, we are concerned with requirements and testing that address Personal Protective Equipment (PPE). The EU standards are legally binding in Europe. The new UIAA standards are based on these CEN standards, but in some cases have additional requirements.

The UIAA is recognized around the globe for climbing equipment standards, therefore purchasing UIAA-certified climbing equipment is a sound practice both in terms of real safety and legal liability. The specific selection criteria used to purchase equipment will vary with each application; however, the following are general selection criteria for standard pieces of climbing equipment. It is critically important that climbing equipment selection and use is done and supervised by someone competent to make those decisions. While certified climbing equipment has built-in margins of safety, these are assuming proper usage and care over time. Improper use or misused equipment can fail and a climber can be seriously injured or killed.

- *Ropes*—Most climbing programs use 11-millimeter dynamic kernmantle ropes (continuous parallel nylon fibers surrounded by a nylon sheath) as their primary climbing ropes. They

provide an excellent combination of strength, stretch, and suppleness. Kernmantle climbing protection ropes are classified as "dynamic ropes," ropes that stretch so they can absorb some of the shock if there is a fall.

- *Harnesses*—The harness secures the climber to the climbing rope. Commercial sit/seat harnesses are the standard in the industry. Some programs have used homemade harnesses in the past, but this is an unacceptable practice. Skilled climbers on real rock who need quick protection are able to safely fashion a harness for themselves and others, but this is outside the range of acceptable practice on climbing walls. Harnesses that are manufactured to meet CE/UIAA standards are the way to go. There are many different types of harnesses on the market with size, adjustability, gear loops, buckles, and other features to consider. If possible, try different harnesses to determine what will work best for your program and staff needs. Your vendor should be able to offer expert advice about harness selection.

- *Helmets*—Climbing helmets are essential pieces of safety equipment for many climbing and ropes course elements. Purchasing quality, UIAA certified adjustable helmets will provide an extra margin of safety, make adjustments easier, and prove to be good investments since they will last longer.

- *Belay system*—There are numerous types of belay systems, and all are designed to protect the participant from making an uncontrolled fall for a distance of more than six feet or less. Most belay systems are a top-rope design. This design has an approved anchor point at the top of the climb route that provides an attachment for a pulley or shear reduction device. The belay rope is threaded through this hardware and down to the climber's harness at one end and to the belayer/belay system at the other end. In some cases, a four- to six-inch diameter pipe securely welded in place provides the anchor and radius for the rope to go over. In cases where a pipe is used, be sure there is no way a participant can readily climb over the pipe. This would result in them being off belay.

- *Climbing shoes*—Serious climbing programs should have climbing shoes available. Tight-fitting climbing shoes with high-traction rubber soles facilitate good footwork. Climbing shoes clearly make for a better climbing experience, even when climbing on outdoor all-wood walls or when climbing on novice bouldering walls.

- *Carabiners*—Certainly one of the most recognized pieces of climbing equipment, carabiners come in a variety of shapes, sizes, colors, and materials. Usually these variations have functional implications and are not done to provide options for options' sake. Generally, a climbing-wall program will have a combination of aluminum (12mm) and steel (11mm) carabiners on hand. Most will be of the locking-gate variety. These tend to be either screw-to-lock or two-stage self-locking. In some lead-climbing situations, a swing or non-locking gate carabiner may be used, but this is a very technical application. Manufacturers will indicate the intended application of their carabiners. Using them in some other manner could result in a malfunction and full assumption of liability.

Purchasing, inspecting, and maintaining high-quality climbing gear designed for the intended use is very important in protecting climbers from injury and owners and operators from costly litigation.

Climbing Wall Standards

The Climbing Wall Industry Group (CWIG) and the Climbing Gym Association (CGA), both now disbanded organizations, were sub-groups of what was the Outdoor Recreation Coalition of America (ORCA). Replacing ORCA is the Outdoor Industry Association as the trade organization of outdoor industries in the U.S.

The Climbing Wall Association (CWA) is now the only trade association addressing the needs and interests of the climbing wall industry and operators. The CWA sets standards for the industry that guide the design, construction and operations of climbing walls (Zimmerman, 2008). As a trade organization, CWA can assist in locating qualified vendors, help answer questions about insurance coverage and provide continuing education and professional affiliation for your staff.

Some states are proposing to regulate climbing walls and challenge courses by bringing them under the umbrella of amusement rides, while others, such as Massachusetts and Missouri, have passed laws and adopted regulations governing climbing walls. Be sure to investigate the laws of your state when planning your facility, policies, and procedures. Local laws and regulations governing zoning, construction, and safety must also be reviewed to ensure compliance.

Climbing Facility Operation

Safety is always a work in progress, a process and outcome, and that is certainly true when operating climbing activities. Climbing is intended to challenge the participant in the context of an adventurous experience that is physically, psychologically, and intellectually demanding. It is an adventure, because there is no guarantee of success, you have to make the effort and expose yourself to the perceived and actual risks. The priority of owners and operators of climbing facilities is to protect the welfare of their customers/participants within acceptable parameters. In a comprehensive effort to meet this priority, it is necessary to fully understand the nature of the inherent risks and develop risk- and emergency-management policies and procedures that are based on professional standards. The staff must be knowledgeable of their responsibilities to manage the risks as specifically detailed in standard operating procedures and have the skills and abilities to implement such a program. In taking this approach, all parties are being protected which is a fair expectation. The Climbing Wall Association provides their members with comprehensive standards that address all aspects of owning and operating a climbing wall. These include Industry Standards, which cover areas such as ethics, informed consent, insurance coverage, accident reporting, risk management, record keeping, and a variety of programming concerns. They also provide standards that cover engineering and operations. Using the CWA standards, owners need to work with their vendor to create policies and procedures that work effectively at their facility.

What follows is a list of typical risk management and operating policy and procedure areas when conducting climbing and adventure programs. It is not a complete list and should only be used to generate initial discussions and planning.

- Explain to participants that climbing is a potentially dangerous activity and specifically what they are in danger of losing. This is related to the concept of informed consent. If they agree to participate knowing the risks, then they assume part of the liability in case of loss. This is determined greatly by individual state laws.
- Post appropriate signage with safety warnings, rules, policies, and procedures to be followed, emergency contact numbers, and any facility specific rules, such as "No Horseplay."
- Hire mature, responsible staff that are then well trained and stay current with their knowledge and skills.

- Conduct regular formal equipment and facility inspections and keep documented records of inspections made and corrective actions taken.
- Supervise all climbing activities with a qualified instructor.
- Secure the climbing area when not in use (access prevention).
- Purchase certified equipment designed for the specific application and keep it well maintained.
- Train and certify participant belayers.
- Maintain a written set of standard operating policies and procedures.
- Keep emergency equipment and supplies available.
- Maintain organized documentation of staff qualifications, inspections, maintenance/repairs, equipment retirement and purchases, accident/injury/incident reports, all participant forms/belay training, vendor communications, and meeting minutes.
- Warn participants about loose clothing or allowing long hair to hang loose, because it may become tangled in the ropes or hardware.
- Always make a final equipment check before beginning a climb. (A buddy check with verbal commands and visual checking is recommended.)
- Review communications procedures prior to starting a climb.
- Jewelry, including watches, should not be worn while climbing.

Challenge Course Adventures

This section of the chapter will define challenge courses, discuss the philosophy of challenge course programming, provide an overview of the industry, introduce the credentialing system implemented in 2007, describe some challenge course elements, provide strategies for how to include people with disabilities, and provide guidance on how to develop and maintain challenge course elements for an adventure program.

A challenge course, sometimes called a ropes course, "… is an experiential adventure program which offers groups and individuals the opportunity to participate in a series of activities involving mental, physical, and emotional risk taking. The ropes course consists of an aesthetically designed series of ropes, cables, and poles combined in such a way as to simulate challenges that might be found in a natural setting. Safety and cooperation, as well as individual achievement, are essential to the program" (Rohnke, Rogers, Wall, & Tait, 2007). There are three basic types of challenge courses that meet the above-mentioned objectives and those are teams courses, low-spotted courses, and high-belayed courses. These and other adventure activities, including climbing walls/towers, are usually used in combination to achieve program, group, and individual goals.

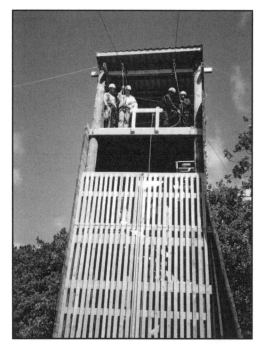

At the core of adventure is risk taking. On challenge courses, participants are faced with physical, psychological, emotional, and social risks. Of particular value with challenge courses is that the actual risk is low while the participant's perception of risk can be quite high. This is helpful in situations where groups want to build the skills necessary to face actual risks in other activities or situations. When people are being asked to take risks, they should have the opportunity to at least co-create those experiences and have the option to control how they participate. The concept of "Challenge by Choice" was introduced by Karl Rohnke (1989) to address this need for freedom of choice and self-determination within the challenge course adventure. It continues to be an important philosophical and programmatic guideline for most adventure programs.

The design of most challenge course programs fit within four categories:

- Adventure Recreation,
- Personal/Group Growth, Enrichment and Education,
- Developmental, and
- Treatment Services.

While a program will have a predetermined purpose within one of these categories, it is not unusual to draw on approaches used in the other categories depending on the needs of the group. In the fields of fitness/wellness, recreation, and sport, most programs will be designed as adventure recreation or personal/group growth, enrichment, education, or some combination of these. Mental and physical health treatment programs such as psychiatric centers, counseling programs, stress-care clinics, and physical rehabilitation centers will primarily utilize a combination of developmental and treatment approaches, while also blending in techniques as needed from the other categories. Challenge courses are often utilized to enhance team or group functioning. While using a team course, a team-building program would use design components found in all but the treatment services area.

In order to provide effective programs, it is necessary to assess client/participant needs. Determining outcome and process goals plus individual needs establishes the foundation for program design. In fact, knowing as much as possible about the kinds of groups that will use the courses and what they will expect from the experiences is critical to courses' design.

Outward Bound was the first non-military agency to utilize challenge courses with their participants. While the courses resembled the military confidence courses, Outward Bound tapped into the educational and personal growth potential of the experience. The first course was built at the Colorado Outward Bound School, using hemp rope, wood, and minimal safety systems (belays). Project Adventure (PA) was the next significant development in challenge course history. Attempting to reform traditional education methods, PA built its first course in a Massachusetts high school with a grant from the U.S. Department of Education (Prouty, 1999). This course was used primarily within the physical education program, but it led to applications in a wide range of settings, which today include schools, camps, community centers, organizational development, and therapeutic settings.

The Association for Challenge Course Technology (ACCT) is the professional organization dedicated to developing standards for challenge course programs. The ACCT has developed challenge course standards for materials, construction, inspection, operations, and ethical behavior. The ACCT began as an organization for vendors who design and build challenge courses. It has since evolved into a full-service organization that has an associate membership option for programmers, managers, and operators. The challenge courses business has evolved into full-service vendors who build courses, provide customer staff training, recommend equipment purchases, and conduct annual inspections. Though not directly involved in design and building standards, both the Association for Experiential Education (AEE) and the American Camping Association have accreditation standards that address challenge course staffing, programming, and risk management.

Design and Development of Challenge Courses

The design and development process for challenge courses is the same as described in the previous section on climbing walls. In an ideal situation, the vision of the desired facility and program would be clearly stated and agreed upon by all involved parties. There would be adequate funding to plan and build the challenge course plus provide the necessary staff training. To locate a reputable challenge course vendor, contact the ACCT via their Web site, http://www.acctinfo.org. This site provides a list of vendor-members, each of which has gone through a thorough screening process to determine the quality and reliability of their products and services.

Most organizations that want to build a challenge course do not have an ideal situation. They have to find a suitable location, struggle for adequate funding, promote the adventure facility and program, and search to find qualified people to staff the program. These are typical constraints that should not deter organizations from developing a course. There is considerable evidence that supports the value of using a challenge course. Challenge courses contribute to physical, emotional, and social development of the participants and are high-visibility features that may be beneficial for program marketing and public relations. A well-run program with a quality staff can also be a productive source of revenue.

In the past, agencies have built their own challenge courses. Copying existing courses and coming up with their own designs, they would either rely solely on internal resources, or bring in someone with building experience to guide the project.

While the in-house approach may seem like an affordable option, it is strongly recommended that only experienced and qualified challenge course builders direct the process and build these courses. The designs, materials, and standards have become so sophisticated that the do-it-yourself challenge course builder has gone the way of the wooden tennis racket. In addition to complex design and construction principles, there are substantial risk-management and legal liability issues to consider. It is unlikely that an insurance company will cover a program with a challenge course that is not built, annually inspected and maintained (major repairs) by a reputable ACCT vendor member. Insurance companies that provide coverage for challenge courses have very specific criteria to assess the construction, inspection, maintenance, administration, staff training, clientele, and other risk management concerns. Course builders or the ACCT will be able to identify insurance providers familiar with challenge course programs. In lieu of a fully build-it-yourself course, some builders allow user involvement with planning, design, and construction. Program staff may be able to assist with course design, layout, site preparation, basic carpentry, and physical labor. A collaborative approach is an effective way to foster staff buy-in and to help them learn about the course, how it works, maintenance needs, and programming potential.

For organizations with limited financing, it may be necessary to develop a multiyear challenge course building and funding strategy that begins with short-term attainable goals and a limited course facility. Additional support and funding may be forthcoming based on documented program success. With new ideas like a challenge course, decision makers and funders may be reluctant to commit resources until program benefits can be demonstrated. In this situation, starting with a small project, such as a team's course or a scaled-down complex, provides an affordable opportunity to demonstrate the viability of the program. Challenge course vendors can help with course planning and design that may easily be expanded in the future.

One of the first decisions is whether the challenge course will be an indoor course, an outdoor course, or a combination of the two. Many challenge course programs are part of a larger outdoor education program that may or may not have access to a multipurpose indoor facility. There are very creative designs available that utilize indoor spaces, both large and small.

Having an indoor component provides options for rainy days, winter programming, multiple groups, and possibly groups that would have difficulty using an outdoor course. Of course, agencies without outdoor space available will have no choice but to build indoors.

The next two decisions, site location and primary support structures, are often linked. A decision needs to be made whether the challenge course will be tree-based, using existing trees to support the challenge course; pole-based, which uses telephone type poles; a combination of trees and poles; or a climbing tower-based course, where a tower is used as part of the support structure of the challenge course. A tower-based course may also use natural trees, poles, or both for additional support points.

There are many new designs that combine these ideas with steel structures, tree houses, suspended yurts and gazebos, movable platforms, hydraulic systems, and elaborate prefabricated

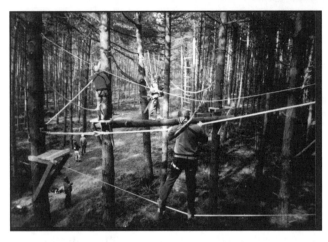

components. There is little to limit the types of designs that may be created.

The nature of the site available greatly influences the type of support structures used. If there are no healthy, appropriate trees at the proposed site, then poles or towers must be used. Other considerations include substrate composition, ground slope, erosion potential, and environmental sensitivity of the area. Using natural trees is less expensive than using poles or towers, so financial considerations may also be a factor in both site location and support structure. Visiting a challenge course program that is operating in a similar setting, observing the program in action, interviewing the staff, and reading the operating procedures are all helpful in the early stage of planning. Be certain that local zoning regulations and building specifications are checked before making the final site and support structure decisions.

Selecting Challenge Course Designs

A challenge course is a set of elements and activities that help programs and participants achieve goals. As presented previously, outcome goals will fall within the recreation, growth/enrichment/learning, developmental, and therapeutic categories. When providing adventure recreation, participants are given safe but challenging opportunities to solve group initiative problems and climb on the higher elements. There is very little briefing or debriefing of the experience. The emphasis is on participants having fun while they are being challenged physically and mentally. As program goals become more diverse, course design becomes more complicated. In order to meet the programming needs of diverse groups, highly versatile and flexible courses must be designed. A higher degree of design specificity can be employed if the course will only be used with a specified clientele.

Among the programming areas, there may be similar outcomes or benefits although the means and reasons may differ. The positive outcomes that are possible with challenge course programs are enhanced

- self-respect and respect for others,
- communication skills,

- sense of physical and emotional exhilaration,
- personal comfort zone,
- leadership skills,
- fears management,
- teamwork and cooperation,
- conflict-resolution strategies,
- problem-solving skills,
- safety awareness,
- planning and organization skills,
- caring and compassion,
- physical fitness and coordination, and
- stress-management skills.

Achieving goals with a challenge course requires skillful application of a well-conceived plan. When planning a challenge course, consider the

- course lay-out,
- program goals,
- actions of facilitators (program staff), and
- needs, desires, and past experience of the participants.

These four primary components are highly interrelated. Given the phenomenal nature of the experience, these factors could be described as having a synergistic relationship. In addition, factors such as environment, weather, and support facilities (restrooms, lodging) will have some influence on the process. The effectiveness of the course depends on the quality of the program and how skillfully it is administered. The course design is important, but it is just a means to an end within a dynamic cognitive, emotional, behavioral and social experience.

Any attempt to categorize challenge courses will be flawed in some way, because challenge courses are such versatile tools. Despite this limitation, courses tend to fall into three general types of courses, teams courses, low courses, and high courses. Some adventure facilities, by design, include multiple types of courses, which are called challenge course complexes. Combining course types in a complex may be done because there is limited space available, to be clustered together, or simply to provide program flexibility. There are situations in a complex where staff can overlap, allowing economy of staffing. Building all the course elements in one central location may reduce building costs by allowing for the sharing of poles or trees among courses/elements. From a programming standpoint, there are important questions to answer before deciding on a complex approach. Some of those questions include:

- Will participants on other course elements be distracted?
- When running multiple groups, will the visual and audible overlap be a problem?
- Does a complex format create safety concerns with some groups?

- Will being able to see other groups on the course have a negative effect on accomplishing desired outcome goals?

Complexes tend to offer more logistical, staffing, and economic benefits than programming benefits. Challenge course planners and designers must decide if the benefits of a challenge course complex outweigh the possible negative impacts on the intended program.

Teams Courses

As the name implies, teams courses are designed to provide group experiences. The height of a course element should not create unsafe situations for user groups. Keeping elements close to the ground (usually two feet or less) is the primary factor that allows these elements to be used by the entire group without employing ropes, harnesses, or extensive spotting when group members or staffs position themselves to provide support if someone falls. On teams course elements, spotting is provided as needed while the entire group negotiates the element.

Teams courses are designed to have groups work together to solve problems. These problems or initiatives have a variety of physical and mental challenges that the group must overcome. During the process of planning and implementing solutions, the participants interact in ways that generate valuable group dynamics. Teams courses are also called initiative courses, since they require the group to use a problem-solving approach to group learning and development.

Teams courses are relatively inexpensive, which makes them a good option for adventure programmers wanting a challenge course but have limited funds. They are also a good idea when space is an issue. Each element of a teams course is independent of the other, so it is easy to locate them in many different configurations. Decentralizing the elements (i.e., placing them away from each other, out of sight and hearing distance) is a good strategy. It limits the "Hey, I wonder how that one over there works?" distraction within the group. Decentralizing also allows for multiple group programming by rotating groups from element to element without them coming into contact with each other. Decentralizing course elements is only one of many strategies that can be considered. Challenge course builders sometimes provide design, operation, training, and maintenance consultation service to program personnel. Many of the well-known teams course elements are listed in *The Complete Ropes Course Manual* (Rohnke et al., 2003), which provides details about these and other challenge course elements.

Low-Challenge Course

A low-challenge course incorporates elements that are normally about two to five feet above the ground. Low-course elements are generally designed to present individual challenges within a group context. Individual group members negotiate the elements while the others provide spotting, performance feedback and encouragement. Since the elements are relatively low, participants perform most of the spotting and safety procedures without the aid of ropes and harnesses.

In recent years, there has been a trend to make low-course elements more team-oriented by creating situations where two people are on the element at the same time. These participants work together with the support of the rest of the group. Spotting is still provided by the group, though some incorporation of belay systems (a safety rope attached to the climber's seat harness) is being used. Having a belay system is very beneficial when programming with a diverse clientele. More information on programming for special populations is provided in the final section of this chapter, Accessible and Universal Designs.

No two low-challenge courses are exactly alike, but most have variations of common low-ropes elements. *The Complete Ropes Course Manual* is again a good resource to find examples of additional low-course elements.

High-Challenge Course

The high-challenge course has challenged many since it was first developed. Innovative design components include steel structures, hydraulic auto belay devices, moveable platforms, suspended yurts/gazebos, shock absorbing systems, multiple levels, and improved safety equipment. With these and other cutting-edge designs, high-challenge courses have become sophisticated, technical facilities. Elements on these courses range in height from between 20 and 60 feet. Additional safety systems and procedures are required for high-challenge courses. Each person negotiating the course must be connected to a belay system. There are variations to how these systems are set up, but generally they consist of a rope connected to a harness being worn by the participant. This rope is usually run through a pulley and then down to the ground, where another participant or staff member is prepared to prevent a fall.

Another approach is to employ a pair of short ropes that the climber clips onto cables or other approved anchor points. The ACCT has developed strict standards for belay system materials and construction.

Typically, a single participant negotiates his or her way through high-challenge course elements. Although this approach is still widely used, more programs are seeking designs that will allow multiple climbers or small groups on individual elements. Benefits are derived from the collaboration among participants on an element, sometimes called partner climbing. Partner climbing seems to more effectively capture and hold the attention of the group members who are on the ground observing. This also provides added value to the process with observers being supporters through encouragement and feedback.

High-challenge courses have administrative and financial factors to consider that are not as important for team and low courses. High-course planners, builders, and operators must consider:

- Increased staffing requirements—One facilitator can manage a group of 12 to 15 on team and low courses. On high courses, a minimum of two or three staff would be needed depending on the design of the course and the needs of the group.
- Additional equipment costs—Typically, all the necessary start-up climbing equipment is part of the course package. This equipment will need to be replaced on a three-to-five-year schedule depending on usage and environmental factors.
- Possible higher insurance payments—Although the high course is statistically safer than non-belayed courses, the majority of catastrophic injuries have occurred on high courses.
- Access control—Preventing unauthorized access to the high course can lead to an extra expense (fencing and other devices) and liability concerns.
- Staff training—Considerable staff training is needed to safely and effectively facilitate the high course. The safety of everyone on the course, including staff, depends on having knowledgeable and experienced facilitators running the program. A year-round staff training schedule is recommended to maintain reliable skills and operating procedures.

This list is not intended to discourage agencies from adding a high course to their program. To the contrary, a high course adds features to a challenge program that are not available with the other types of courses. These features include a heightened sense of perceived risk, greater physical challenges, greater awareness of individual effort and concerns, greater sense of individual accomplishment, a visually striking apparatus, and a greatly amplified wow factor. It also compliments other courses if available, by providing powerful individual challenges that serve to take the person's group-based learning to a higher level of commitment.

High-course elements are often similar to those included in low and teams courses. This provides a chance to apply newly learned skills under greater stress and by adapting skills learned on the lower courses. Again a more detailed description of many high-course elements can be found in *The Complete Ropes Course Manual* (Rohnke et al., 2007).

Universal and Accessible Design Considerations

For the past 10 years, finding ways to make challenge courses accessible to participants with disabilities has been an industry priority. There have consistently been sessions on this topic at Association for Experiential Education (AEE) and ACCT conferences. The ACCT has published a position statement that supports the inclusion of individuals with disabilities in challenge course experiences. Standards within both organizations address inclusion and challenge course vendors have been incorporating accessible and universal designs into many of their products and training.

In an ACCT general membership survey (unpublished, 2001), the ACCT tried to assess the status of inclusion in adventure challenge courses. Those responding indicated that 48% of the courses had design and program features to include participants with disabilities. This number has increased since the survey. Nearly 84% of the respondents agreed or strongly agreed that it is important to continue researching, advocating, and reporting challenge course designs that provide opportunities for people with disabilities. While only about half of the respondents' courses are designed to include participants with disabilities, a significant majority of respondents support accessible challenge course design. The challenge is to incorporate designs that create relevant participation opportunities for participants with a wide range of physical and mental functioning.

The Universal and Accessible Design Committee of the ACCT (www.acctinfo.org), *The Complete Ropes Course Manual* (4th Ed.) (Rohnke et al., 2007), and the National Center on Accessibility (www.ncaonline.org) are excellent resources for additional information on making challenge courses accessible. A partial checklist of concerns/considerations is included below:

- Environment
  —Are trail systems that lead to and link elements accessible? Planners need to consider slope, cross-slope, surface stability, and trail widths. Trail widths must be a minimum of 32 inches.
  —Are areas around individual challenge course elements level and firm with few obstructions?
  —Are drop-offs and steep embankments protected?
  —Are overhead clearances sufficient for participants with vision impairments?
- Elements
  —Is independent access available to each element?
  —Are platforms, decks, and elevated walkways large enough and at heights that are usable by all participants?

—Do transitions from element to element have options that consider the need for intermediate belay clip-ins and movement from one element to the other?

—Are hand- and footholds of various sizes and shapes used to include enough large holds to improve access?

—Are options for how individual elements can be negotiated (traversing, scooting, crawling, rolling, climbing) available?

—Are access ramps handicapped accessible (a slope of 12:1)? Ramps that are part of the element do not have to meet accessibility slope standards.

—Is edge protection used where participants with bony prominences might hit or have prolonged contact with a hard edge? Rounding edges and using foam to cushion edges and surfaces is recommended.

—Are belay systems and elements designed so there are options for participants with mobility or balance concerns?

- Equipment
  —Are mechanical advantage systems included to provide access to high courses? (A 3:1 or 4:1 pulley system is commonly used.)

  —Are full-body harnesses available and are course staff members trained to work with those who may need a harness? Many different harness configurations are available so handicapped climbers can minimize pain, support critical body parts, and make best of existing muscle function. Additional padding for harnesses may be needed when prolonged hanging in a harness is a concern. In most cases, no one should hang in a seat harness for more than 15 minutes. Harness suppliers will provide specific information on safe harness usage.

  —Are body protection systems available for participants with poor balance, diminished sensation or impaired muscle function? Areas to consider protecting include the head, elbows, hip-girdle, knees, and ankles. Padding used in other activities, such as skateboarding, works well in challenge course activities. Custom-fitting foam and other products to achieve a safe level of protection may be required.

  —Are hauling and counter-balance systems available to assist with access to high elements and climbing structures?

- Support facilities need to be accessible.
  —Do restroom facilities meet current accessibility standards?

  —Are storage facilities usable by all staff and participants?

  —Are debriefing areas, like the log circle, handicapped accessible?

When making decisions about how to make a challenge course experience accessible to participants with disabilities, it is important to understand that functioning levels and needs vary greatly. Conducting a needs and abilities assessment on each participant will help with activity selection and developing adaptations. When it is not clear how to include individuals with disabilities, it is best to ask them about their needs to assess their capabilities. Involving the individuals in the inclusion plan becomes a valuable part of the learning process. Providing a meaningful experience that maintains personal dignity for participants with disabilities may not be easy but with additional planning and a commitment to inclusion, challenge courses can provide exciting developmental experiences.

Challenge Course Operations, Administration, and Staffing

The overall safety record of challenge courses is impressive. They are among the safest of all physically demanding programs (Project Adventure, 2001). The ACCT has established safety and construction standards to provide guidelines for the safe and efficient operation of challenge courses. Even well-planned and -operated challenge courses are potentially dangerous; therefore, all participants need to be informed of the potential danger and should sign a waiver of liability (assumption of risk). Other challenge course operation considerations can be divided into administration and staff, equipment, and maintenance issues. An overview of these operations issues is provided below, but is by no means a complete list of all operational considerations. Additional operational guidance is available in the *ACCT Technical Operations and Inspection Standards*.

New to the challenge course industry is the certification of facilitators, managers, and trainers. This certification program was developed by the ACCT, its members and others across the industry. Vendor members of ACCT are implementing the program as individual certifying bodies based on their own training and evaluation methods. They will follow the certification guidelines of the ACCT and their certification program and practices are reviewed as part of vendor member accreditation. It is not necessary for all challenge course staff to be certified, though it is recommended that programs have a minimum of one certified practitioner. In large programs with numerous staff and extensive challenge course facilities, it may be necessary to have multiple certified staff and even a certified manager. As the certification program evolves and the industry is able to analyze the many aspects of its implementation and impact, we can expect changes. It is also likely that government regulations and the insurance industry will play a part in the future of challenge course credentialing. For complete information about certification, contact the ACCT via their web site or an ACCT Professional Vendor Member, also available through the ACCT site - http://www.acctinfo.org/.

Challenge Course Administration and Staffing

- Purchase and maintain liability insurance for the organization and the staff. Provide professional training for all staff members. Administrators must provide sufficient funding to ensure that staff members are up to date on current policies and operating procedures, including rescues and emergency response.
- Have a risk-management plan that clearly indicates actions and responsibilities. Be certain all staff members are up to date on their responsibilities by providing periodic training. Monitor staff credentials regarding current first aid and CPR certification.
- Keep accurate records of staff training, program operations and procedures, annual and periodic inspections, maintenance and repairs, liability forms, insurance, student training records, and accident reports.
- Maintain a comprehensive equipment inventory and use equipment sign-out sheets to maintain property accountability.

Challenge Course Maintenance

- Inspect the entire challenge course and the supporting equipment on a regular basis depending on use rates, environment, and nature of the equipment. An ACCT vendor-member inspector should conduct a comprehensive annual inspection, preferably.
- Use pressure-treated lumber for outdoor challenge courses. Weatherproof wood parts as needed. (Annually is best, if feasible.)
- Use only healthy trees with a solid root system as support trees. Before building in trees, consult a qualified arborist about the condition of the trees.
- Use wood chips or bark mulch around the base of trees to protect the soil from compaction. Provide for drainage under the chips or mulch.
- Immediately replace dead or insect-infected trees. Trees are susceptible to weather, insects, disease, rotting, ground impaction and need to be checked regularly. Trim and clear broken or overgrowing limbs. Remove splinters and rough edges on all wood parts. Replace and repair all rotten or cracked wood. Peen down sharp metal edges and pad protruding bolt or metal ends that are in participant traffic areas. Reset protruding nails as necessary.
- Check for rotting of the poles in the ground.

- Use only corrosion resistant bolts, cable, cable locks, rapid links, and other metal parts.
- Critical cables such as belays, zip wires, and most guy wires should be 3/8 inch diameter galvanized aircraft cable (GAC) that is 7 x 19 (seven strands with 19 wires per strand).
- Tighten nuts and bolts, turnbuckles, and clamps as required. Temporarily cover all frayed cable ends with tape until they can be re-fitted with a serving sleeve.
- Inspect cables for smoothness and rust. Cables need to be smooth if a participant's hands or feet will touch the cable.

Challenge Course Equipment

- Use UIAA or European Community Norm (CEN) certified climbing ropes and locking gate carabiners.
- Install only stainless steel or galvanized hardware on outdoor challenge courses.
- Have participants wear an adjustable harness. A full-body harness is used instead of the seat harness when there are concerns about distribution of forces such as with the pamper pole activity.
- On static or self-belayed courses, maintain constant vigilance to assure that participants are using their "lobster claws" correctly when they switch from element to element. (Two locking steel carabiners are attached to the participant by two shock-absorbing lanyards.) One carabiner is locked onto the next element's belay cable before the other carabiner is unclipped from the previous belay cable.
- Minimize rope wear and damage by using a shear-reduction device.
- Always have a first-aid kit available. Have a communication system in operation, such as two-way radios or cell phones, as part of an emergency response plan.
- Store equipment in a cool, dry place, preferably adjacent to the challenge course.
- Include lightning protection on high-challenge courses.
- Require helmets to be worn on high elements and whenever anyone is beneath an active high activity.
- Keep a rope log that tracks hours of usage and falls taken on each rope. Also inspect belay ropes regularly for wear, cuts, discoloration, glazing, stiffness, soft spots, and any other changes in specifications. If you are not sure about the integrity of a rope or its history, do not use it!

SKATEPARKS AND WINTER SPORTS AREAS 19

Thomas H. Sawyer, Indiana State University

In the new millennium, there continues to be a skateboarding renaissance. Facility development, equipment quality, skateboarders' techniques and abilities, and participant attitudes and maturity levels have all reached new peaks. High-performance facilities and equipment for every style of skating are available. The abilities of professional skaters visibly advance each month, seeing athletes (yes, athletes) literally reaching new heights.

Skaters have become less clique-oriented and more open-minded. All disciplines of skating are now respected.

These changes have made skating more accessible to many different people of varying ages. Presently, there are over 10 million skaters in the United States, making it the sixth largest sport (National Inline Hockey Association [NIHA], 2000). Skateboarding has become the third most popular sport among six- to 18-year-olds (International Association of Skateboard Companies [IASC], 2001). Further, one in 10 U.S. teenagers own a skateboard (IASC, 2001).

The popularity that skateboarding now enjoys is also reflected in the media. Skateboarding is regularly featured on major TV networks such as Fox, MTV, TSN, OLN, ESPN's notorious Extreme-Games (X-Games), and NBC's Gravity Games, thus bringing it into today's spotlight. Finally, this coverage, along with skating appearance in marketing campaigns for Nike, The Gap, The National Fluid Milk Processor Promotion Board, Coca-Cola, and Nintendo has seen skateboarding appear on billboards, in magazines, and on television. All this exposure has greatly expanded public acceptance of skaters and skating.

Skateparks

History of Skateboarding

In the 1950s, surfers created skateboarding in order to pass the time when the ocean was flat. Roller-skate mounts and wheels were innocently nailed to 254s. This was the birth of the "sidewalk surfer." The earlier skateboard parks in the '50s and '60s reflected the surfers' passion for fluid, wavelike forms, and smooth sensations.

In 1970, the urethane wheel was applied to the skateboard. Skateboard-specific trucks appeared in 1973, which were followed by precision bearings in 1975. Being of higher performance than their predecessors, these new products allowed for an easier, more enjoyable ride. These improvements encouraged advancements in maneuvers and more challenging facilities and spawned a skateboarding boom that supported massive private skateboard parks across the United States and in Europe. The parks perfected the backyard pools, drainage pipes, and ditches that skaters had taken to riding.

However, the demand for parks encouraged the development of poorly designed and constructed parks. This opened the door to insurance and liability problems. As a result, 80% of these parks were bulldozed in 1979, with the rest closing soon afterward. Some public parks remained, but basically skaters were left with nowhere to go, and many simply quit.

Yet during the '80s, the remaining dedicated and innovated skaters continued to push the value of the sport. Many changes took place in the design of facilities and equipment. The wooden backyard half-pipe ramps began their evolution, which led to today's modern half-pipes.

Presently, there is resurgence in building skateboard parks. This has occurred because of the demand to remove skaters from city streets and public spaces. Skaters took to the streets because most of the skateparks had closed during the '80s, and they developed the "street style" of skating creatively, adapting moves done in a pool or ramp in the defunct parks of the '70s to curbs, ledges, steps, handrails, and walls. Communities became concerned about the skaters and some considered them rebellious and a public nuisance.

Skateparks have come a long way from the early, unsafe private parks to the well-designed, safe public parks of today. The new facilities are larger and safer, and the skaters are using better-designed equipment and safety gear. Skateboarding is fast becoming a very safe and exciting sport for young (ages six to 18) males (74%) to spend their spare time perfecting their skills.

Liability

Liability is always a question when dealing with sports in general. Therefore, it is paramount that owners (public or private) carefully plan for a safe facility for participants and spectators. Today most insurance companies do not view skateparks as a high risk for governmental agencies. They are no more dangerous than swings and slides. Yet it is advisable to make sure the facility is covered with the same blanket plan as the city or town. (See Table 19.1 for a listing of insurance carriers)

It is further advisable that the agency seriously consider safety when planning the skatepark. Signs should be posted to indicate hours of operations, pad and helmet requirements, and that the park is used at the participant's risk. The public agency needs to also consider the level of supervision that it should provide. Current common practice with skateparks is to leave the park open to "free play" with no supervision (i.e., similar to playgrounds). This practice will decrease the agency's liability. However, the operator must be certain that the area is safe, free of hazards, inspected regularly, and well maintained (i.e., similar to swimming pools at motels/hotels, where legislation protects those who have proper and adequate signage, a fence around the pool, safety equipment available, and the pool is maintained regularly).

The passage of numerous pieces of state legislation has allowed local public agencies to build unsupervised skateparks and post signs requiring safety equipment to be worn while skating. Unsupervised skateparks are very popular with skaters, but care has to be taken to build them in safe locations. If you do not have an ideal location, you may want to consider supervising the park or partnering with a private skatepark or other youth group, such as a church, Boys and Girls Club, or YMCA.

Immunity for Extreme Sports Parks

The Indiana General Assembly provided in Senate Bill 0141 (2001) that public and private owners and operators of extreme sports parks or recreation areas are immune from civil damages for injuries caused by extreme sports if 1) the extreme sports park or recreation area is designed or maintained for the purpose of extreme sports use, 2) a set of rules governing the use of the facility is clearly posted at each entrance to the extreme sports park or recreation area, and 3) a warning concerning the hazards and dangers associated with the use of the facility is clearly posted at the entrance to the extreme sports park or recreation areas; and they are immune from civil damages for injuries if the extreme sports park or recreation area is closed and has a warning against entry posted at each entrance. Other states have similar statutes and it is important for planners to pay attention to the three provisions outlined above when planning a skate park.

Safety Statistics

In 1968, the U.S. Consumer Product Safety Commission (CPSC) ranked sports and recreation equipment on a mean severity index that ranged from 10 to 2,516 (10 being the least severe). Swimming pools were given 335, bicycles 70, and skateboarding 34. There have been three deaths involving skateboarders in the United States since 1970 and these incidents involved motor vehicles. Table 19.2 provides the results of a recent survey conducted by the United States National Electronic Injury Surveillance System.

Of those injured, 33% had been skating less than one week, 20% were people borrowing boards, and 95% received outpatient care. Most noteworthy is that 50% of the accidents occurred in unsafe areas where the skater struck an irregularity in the riding surface. Therefore, by providing and maintaining a professionally designed skate park instead of leaving these kids in the street, the above numbers would likely dramatically decrease.

General Planning Criteria

There are many sources of information on skateboard techniques and design of bowls, ramps, and other ancillary facilities. The following information is general in nature and provides the planners a place to begin this type of project.

Location

The planners should evaluate potential sites by considering the following issues: 1) potential

Table 19.1
Insurance Carriers

K&K Insurance Company	310-473-2522
Joint Powers of Insurance Agency	562-467-8720
Gelfand Newman Wasserman, General Liability, Participant, and Event Insurance	310-473-2522
Association of Bay Area Governments, Pooled Liability Assurance Network	510-464-7900
Association of Washington Cities, Risk Management Service Agency	360-753-4137
City Securities Corporation	800-800-2489
International Special Events and Recreation Association	801-321-1493

Table 19.2
Percentage of Injuries in Common Sports

Sport	Participants	Injuries	% of Injuries
Ice hockey	1,700,000	61,264	3.60
Football	14,700,000	409,206	2.78
Basketball	29,600,000	761,358	2.57
Soccer	10,300,000	146,000	1.42
Baseball	36,600,000	437,207	1.26
Volleyball	20,500,000	112,120	0.54
Skateboarding	6,200,000	27,718	0.49

usage of area (i.e., demographic analysis and a needs assessment), 2) size of site (i.e., how big is big enough), 3) access to public transportation, 4) drainage for the site, 5) access to public utilities, 6) noise pollution, 7) nuisance avoidance, 8) spectator seating, 9) parking, and 10) emergency access.

Safety

The following design features address safety issues that need to be considered by planners: 1) safe spectator areas, 2) low-maintenance site, 3) adequate sight lines of the area for supervision as well as viewing activities by spectators, 4) protective netting or barriers to guard against serious falls and to impede flying skateboards, 5) safety lighting, 6) emergency access, 7) exposure to environmental elements such as wind, rain, lightning, or sun, 8) shaded areas, and 9) drinking fountains.

Various ramps at the YMCA state park in Murfreesboro, Tennessee.

Other Considerations

The following are a few additional considerations for planners to think about in the design of the skatepark: 1) adequate lighting for night activities, 2) facilities for skateboarding are suitable for other disciplines such as in-line skating or roller blading (e.g., recreational speed skating, in-line hockey, and freestyle or aggressive skating) and BMX bikes, 3) noise and light intrusion on neighbors, and 4) north or south orientation rather than an east or west setting.

Consulting Services

The services that are normally provided by consultants (i.e., architect, landscape architect, skaters, and safety experts) in this area include:

- preparing a demographic survey of the local skate community,

- assisting in the site selection,
- determining designs and construction parameters (e.g., wood vs. concrete, size, budget [see Table 19.3 for costs associated with the various types of parks], amenities),
- acting as an intermediary between owners and local skaters,
- organizing and establishing a pro shop (e.g., contacting vendors, preparing initial orders, etc.),
- preparing drawings for public venues, and
- developing design specifications for either wood or concrete skateparks.

Design Services

Skateparks are designed of either concrete, steel, or wood. The designs are unique and customized to the specific site, wishes of the local skaters, and the needs of the owners. The park should be designed to provide the skaters with a fun and safe place to skate. Skateparks should include elements for all levels of skating ability,

Table 19.3
General Information on Skatepark Costs

Portable parks and wood parks—as little as $3,000 and up to $100,000 with the average park being 10,000 square feet and costing around $25,000; require regular maintenance; surfaces may be masonite, plywood, birch, skatelite, or skatelite pro.
Advantages—portable, movable, affordable.

Steel frame skateparks—steel frame with metal or skatelite surfaces; permanent parks; can be bolted to existing concrete pad; some maintenance; more expensive than wood, with a 10,000-square-foot park starting at around $30,000.
Advantages—park can be reconfigured, weatherproof, and affordable.

Concrete parks—concrete starting as low as $10 per square foot, averages $16 per square foot and can be as high as $20 per square foot depending on excavation, grading, drainage, irrigation, water table, and so on; average 10,000-square-foot park costs $140,000, you must work with qualified builders and designers and make sure the concrete crew is experienced with mistakes made in concrete which are expensive and permanent and are happening too often, two bowls ($132,000) were built and the concrete crew brushed the finish making them unskateable.
Advantages—are no maintenance, permanent park.

Figure 19.1
Skatepark Design

from beginner to advance with sufficient variety to challenge and keep them coming back for more. Elements are designed with the proper transitions and heights, and the layouts allow flow from one element to the next.

The designer of a skatepark should thoroughly understand skatepark design, site preparation (e.g., surveying, soil testing, etc.). The designer selected should be able to provide the following services:

- Conducting preliminary consulting services appropriate to design considerations.
- Preparing custom concept designs for wood, concrete, or combination of the two.
- Developing detailed construction drawings for wood skateparks.

Photo by Michael Hypes

Figure 19.2
Sample Ramps

Figure 19.3
Sample Ramps

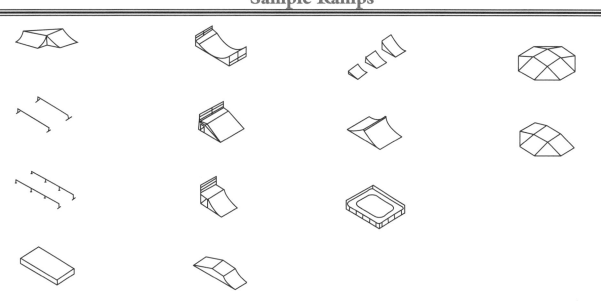

- Preparing detailed drawings for concrete parks.
- Providing budget estimates (see Appendix J).
- Preparing detailed specifications for wood park construction.
- Consulting with concrete and steel contractors on design elements.
- Producing drawings in various formats using the latest version of AutoCad (see Figure 19.1 for samples of skatepark designs from http://www.skatedesign.com).

Specific Design Features

Wood Ramp Construction

Wood ramps can withstand many years of abuse by both skaters and the weather. The critical factors are that wood ramps are designed properly, built by experienced carpenters, and constructed of the right materials. The advantages of wood parks are that they are relatively inexpensive, easily built, and can be placed on an existing concrete or as-

Photo by Tom Sawyer

Concrete skatepark in Greencastle, Indiana, above and below.

phalt pad. In addition, most wood equipment can be moved to change the configuration of the park to create new challenges for the skaters to enjoy. (See Figures 19.2 and 19.3 for types of ramps) Generally, specifications for outdoor wood parks include: (see also http://www.suburbanrails.com)

- All wood should be pressured treated.
- 3/4 plywood transition templates, on ends and every four feet or six feet.
- Two-inch x six-inch joists, spaced eight inches on center, four-foot spans/double joists every 24 inches.
- Two layers of 1/2-inch plywood subsurface.

- 3/8 polyboard, 1/4 Skatelite, or 12-gauge steel ramp surface.
- 12-gauge by 24-inch steel for all ramp bottoms.
- 1/4-inch polyboard on ramp decks.
- Coping, 1 1/2 or 2-inch schedule 40 pipe (2 or 2 1/2-inch OD).
- Ramp joists fastened with #8 by 3-inch galvanized deck screws.
- Each layer of plywood is fastened by rust-proof decking screws on a 12-inch pattern.
- Ramp surfaces and bottoms fastened with #10 by 3-inch sheet metal screws.

Figures 19.2 and 19.3 provide a few examples of ramps. They can be built with varying heights and widths. This list is far from comprehensive.

Concrete Skateparks

Permanent outdoor skateparks are constructed of concrete. The material is fluid and allows unlimited shapes to be integrated into the design. Objects can flow from one to another with no interruptions. Long, flowing designs that incorporate soft bumps as well as curbs, ledges, rails, and steps can be easily built to make interesting and challenging runs for skaters of all experience levels. If the owner has the budget, this is the way to go.

Concrete parks are built from the ground up. This allows for a more aesthetically pleasing park by incorporating varying elevations and by integrating grassy knolls, shade trees, flowers, and observation areas. Critical factors in concrete parks are the design and implementation of the transitions and placement of the coping. If a concrete park is poorly designed or built, the owner could be stuck with an area skaters will not skate.

Perfectly installed coping and forms will act as guides for templates. The templates then guide a blade, called a fresno, which precisely cuts the concrete to shape. The template is then moved to the end of the trimmed section and the process is repeated. The concrete used

Photo by Tom Sawyer

Photo by Michael Hypes

BMX bike on the YMCA skatepark in Murfreesboro, Tennessee.

is called shot-BMX bike on the YMCA skatepark concrete, which is also used for swimming pools.

A grey coat is recommended for bowls, pools, or anything with transition. Working steeply inclined concrete with floats and trowels makes the concrete slump and compresses the transition, forming a kink. Cutting the concrete, then putting a finish coat on later, allows more control to achieve a precise shape and smoother finish.

Lighting

Most outdoor skateparks require lighting. Chapter 5 provides a great deal of detail regarding exterior lighting. Lighting for the park serves two main functions: to provide light for night skateboarding and for security when the park is not in use.

Indoor Skateboard Park

There are many locations in the United States that have a combined indoor/outdoor park because of climate. The actual design of the park will be the same except it will be indoors rather than out. The other components of an indoor structure include heating, ventilation, air-conditioning, plumbing, electrical, and so on are found in other chapters of this book.

Skateparks are generally constructed of concrete and repairs are rarely needed. Those that have steel and wooden structures will require regular inspection and maintenance. The facilities are kept clean by the skateboarders themselves. They do not want to trip on soda cans or other rubbish. A major maintenance concern with steel is rust and loose bolts and screws. The wooden ramps also have problems with screws loosening and falling out. Weather can take a toll on both steel and wooden ramps.

The major concerns with concrete are cracks and pooling water areas. The cracks need to be properly filled prior to winter. Frost can be very destructive to concrete. Trees and other foliage enhance the visual beauty and provide shade for a park. However, trees require regular maintenance to keep them healthy. Areas around trees require regular cleaning to remove discarded limbs and leaves that could be a safety problem for the park. (See Chapter 9 for additional information regarding foliage, trees, and turf).

Other maintenance issues focus on cleaning restrooms, concession areas, offices, entrance and lobby areas, and the pro shop within the skate house. Further, exterior trash containers need to be regularly emptied and cleaned. Finally, the grass areas need to be mowed.

Winter Sports Areas

Sledding Areas

According to data provided by the CPSC, there were 115,000 emergency visits each year because

Photo by Tom Sawyer

Concrete skatepark in Green Castle, Indiana, above and below.

Photo by Tom Sawyer

of ski accidents but only 2.5% (3,750) are for head injuries. Sledding accidents account for 55,000 emergency room visits. Of those, 15% (8,250) are head injuries (CPSC, 2001). Most sledding accidents occur at a low speed between 10 and 20 mph.

Sledding Safety

Sledding is a great activity but results in many accidents each year, some of which are very serious and even fatal. The following safety recommendation should be considered when developing sledding areas:

- Avoid hills with trees, stumps, holes, fences, and rock walls.
- *Never* orient a sledding course toward a road, parking lot, pond, lake, river, railroad tracks, or raven.
- Allow for a sled return zone adjacent to the sledding course.
- Have all participants wear a helmet and mouth guard.

- Provide adult supervision.
- Pad all obstructions with hay bales.
- Use sleds that can be steered rather than snow discs.
- Do not allow participants to ride flat. Have the participants sit up and face forward.
- All participants should sled feet-first, never head-first.
- Do not allow inflatable tube sleds, they can bounce and throw children.
- Do not allow sitting or sliding on plastic sheets or other materials that can be pierced by objects on the ground.
- Be certain that the sledding area is well lighted during the evening hours.
- Post appropriate signage to warn participants of dangers of sledding and the do's of good sledding.

Designing a Safe Sledding Area

It is important to take into consideration the points made above when designing a safe sledding area

Figure 19.4
Sledding Course Design

for children. Sledding is a natural winter activity, and communities need to provide for safe sledding areas to protect the children.

A safe sledding area should include the following (see Figure 19.4):

- An entrance to the area.
- A wide, moderately sloped hill clear of stumps, trees, fences, and holes.
- The length should be between 50 to 150 yards.
- The runoff should be long and flat to accommodate deceleration of the sled.
- The sledding course should be clearly marked.
- The return alleys for the sledders should be clearly identified on either side of the sledding course.
- There should be a buffer/safety zone of at least 10 yards between the sledding course and return alleys.
- The end of the course should not be compromised by roads, ponds, lakes, rivers, or parking lots.
- All obstructions must be padded by hay or straw bales.
- Lighting should be provided if the area is to be used in the evening hours.
- A shelter should be provided at the top and bottom of the course for sledders to use during resting periods with restrooms nearby.
- There should be appropriate signage placed at the entrance and shelters outlining the safety recommendations for sledders.

Snow Sports

Ski and Snowboard Hills

Skiing has become very popular. If climatic conditions are suitable and desirable topographic features are available, a school or a park and recreation department might look into the possibility of developing the facilities needed to foster this sport. A variety of artificial surfaces simulating real snow have brought skiing instructional opportunities to all sections of the country independent of climate.

The provision of skiing in a school or public recreation system should be approached from an instructional standpoint, the theory being to give participants some basic instruction so they can enjoy it as a leisure-time activity in the resort areas that have more ideal facilities. If the park system contains ideal skiing hills with plenty of room, regular ski courses may be developed. Some of the basic facilities required for skiing instruction include proper topographical features, a headquarters building for rental of equipment, a refractory, and similar purposes, a ski tow, and various slopes for instructional purposes.

Normally, the series of classes is broken into three units—beginners, advanced, and expert. It is the opinion of ski instructors that the beginners' ski class is by far the most important for recreational skiing. Basic instruction in skiing may be conducted in classes not exceeding 25 to 30 beginners. For this group, a gentle and short slope with a relatively large, flat run-out area is desirable because it permits a beginner to have complete control of him- or herself and allows him to gain confidence in the use of his skis. In the advanced group, classes are much smaller, and in the expert group, instruction becomes almost individualized. For each successive group, hills become longer and a little steeper.

The following criteria are recommended for the selection of facilities for beginners' classes:

- Flat-top hill area, 50 square feet per skier, 25 skiers per class.
- Slope about 75 to 100 feet long, drop in grade of 15 feet, or 4:1 ratio.
- Starting line at top of slope, 100 feet wide.
- Run-out at bottom of slope either flat or uphill.
- Slope facing east or northeast.
- Instructional area free of stones, woods, and other impediments.
- Protective cover, such as trees or brush, around the area.

The following criteria are suggested for advanced classes:

- Top of hill about the same as for beginners.
- Slope is most important: ratio about 3:1 and length 100 to 150 feet.
- Width of hill or slope, minimum of 150 feet because of speed and space required for turning movements.

The following criteria are recommended for the selection of facilities for expert classes:

- Either the same hill as advanced classes or, preferably, a longer and steeper hill.
- Enough downhill length to permit a minimum of three turning movements—for example, 250 feet on a 3:1 slope.
- Greater width than that of slope for advanced classes.

Cross-Country Skiing

Cross-country skiing has a broad popularity across the northern United States. Cross-country skiing, also known as ski touring, has attracted many people who cannot afford to keep up with alpine or downhill skiing price tags or do not want to stand in long lines at the lifts.

One of the attractive features of cross-country skiing is that a successful program can be developed with limited facilities. Existing trails can be groomed in the winter using homemade or purchased equipment that is towed by a snowmobile.

Trail surfaces are best on a wood chip, grass, or gravel base. Asphalt bases do not work well. Trails can be carved out of almost any park area. If a golf course is used, the greens and tees should have a fence placed around them to keep skiers off of these sensitive areas. Trails should be signed with rules placed at starting points. The signs should indicate direction, distance, and level of difficulty.

Coasting and Tobogganing

Often a community has a hill or hills suitable for coasting, which become magnets after every snowfall for children with sleds, toboggans, and other coasting devices. In the absence of a natural coasting hill, some park and public works departments have built such a facility. These hills are usually located in a park safely guarded from the hazards of street traffic.

In developing local sledding (coasting) areas, care should be taken to incorporate adequate safety features. Sufficient space should be provided between sled runs, and up traffic should be isolated from the down traffic. The area should be as free as possible from hazards, such as nearby trees, grills, benches, or other park paraphernalia. Municipal risk managers will provide input into the safety of the area.

Communities with an extensive response to sledding or skiing may want to counter adverse weather with the use of artificial snow equipment or improve the activity with a ski lift. Communities where there are not available hills have created their own sledding hills. They typically serve as a sledding hill in the winter and as part of a park in the spring and summer where multiple activities can be programmed.

Tobogganing is a thrilling sport that requires designed space. Occasionally, natural slopes are used if they are free from obstructions and have a long bottom run-off. The common practice is to select a hillside with a reasonable steep and even grade. A chute is constructed using a wooden trough. It can be permanent or built in sections. Some communities have created artificial toboggan runs with refrigerated chutes. They are expensive to develop and maintain.

Ice Skating/Ice Hockey Rinks

Ice skating facilities are feeling the impact of modern technology in more and more communities each year. With the advent of mechanical freezing, the skating season has been extended from a 20- to 60-day average season to a 140-day season and, depending on climatic conditions, to as much as 240 days.

While natural ice rinks have not gone out of style, artificial rinks are replacing them as central or regional facilities. Natural ice rinks are continuing to serve as a supplemental neighborhood facility in many communities. A considerable number of skaters still prefer the rugged pleasure of an old-fashioned skating experience.

Ice Hockey

Ice hockey rinks may have a sports function as well as providing a recreation service. If ice hockey is to be part of the rink's activity schedule, goals will be needed and a four-foot-high solid fence, called the dasher, will have to be installed to enclose an area as near to 85 by 185 feet as possible. Dasher boards are heavily reinforced to stand the shock of players being pushed against them and are lined on the rink side with either wood or plastic. There is normally a chain link or clear plastic barrier another four to six feet on top of the dashers to enable spectators to view games safely. The dasher board enclosure should have round corners, because square corners present a hazard. A kickboard, six to eight inches high, is fastened at the base of the dasher boards and is replaced as often as necessary.

Because dasher boards reflect sunlight and cause melting of the ice, they should be painted a dark color. However, it is difficult to follow the puck if the dasher boards are too dark, so a shade of gray is recommended. If the hockey rink is indoors, the dasher boards can be painted a light color without causing a melting problem.

Typical Recreational Ice Floor Configuration

The following are the typical recreational ice hockey configuration:

- Full size hockey arena floor is normally 200' x 85'
- Olympic size hockey floor is 200' x 100'
- Curling sheets are 14' x 146' but are usually laid out at 15' x 150'
- Refrigeration Load can range from 45 to 300 tons for an arena

Cooling the Floor

The floor surface is occasionally constructed entirely with sand but this limits the use of the facility. More commonly the floor consists of a 5" or 6" cement pad reinforced with Rebar.

The brine is supplied to the floor via 6" to 10" headers. The headers are constructed of PVC or steel. The headers feed an in-floor-cooling grid consisting of 1" polyethylene or steel pipe spaced on 3" to 4" centers.

The cooling floor brine is usually a calcium chloride solution mixed to a freeze point of -5 to -10 deg. F. The pH should be maintained at a level of 7.5 to 8.5 The brine should be tested annually by a lab regularly engaged in testing arena brine samples.

Heating the Floor

The rejected waste heat from the refrigeration plant typically provides the heat source for the heating floor but boilers or electric resistance heaters are occasionally used as well.

The heated calcium is usually supplied to the heating floor via 4" brine mains. The mains in turn feed a 1" polyethylene grid spaced on 12" to 24" centers The heating floor is positioned approximately 1' under the cooling floor and is separated by insulation and a vapor barrier.

The heating floor brine should be kept at a freeze point of 10-15 deg. F. The pH should be maintained at a level of 7.5 to 8.5. The brine should be tested annually by a lab regularly engaged in testing arena samples.

Solving Humidity Problems in Ice Rinks

If you can control the humidity in your facility, you are one very large step toward creating the ideal ice skating environment. Humidity enters an ice rink with incoming ventilation air, the opening of doors, from the use of showers, and through the normal respiration of the people within the building.

If your facility is in a cold environment, such as Winnipeg, Manitoba, the incoming air can easily be 0F and 50% relative humidity during a typical winter day. If this entering cold air is warmed up to 400F, the humidity will now fall to less than 20% because warm air has the ability to hold more moisture. This lower humidity level poses little problem to the proper operation of the facility.

However, if your facility is in Los Angeles, California, the incoming air could easily be 650 F with a relative humidity of 65%. If this entering warm air is reduced to 500 F inside the skating rink the humidity will skyrocket to 100% relative humidity because the cold air will not hold as much moisture. At this point, there is only one place for the water vapor to go, it condenses into water droplets and the problems begin.

Just as a boiling kettle deposits moisture on a cold window on a winter's day, airborne moisture in an ice rink will also deposit on cold surfaces, and of course the coldest spot is very likely the ice surface itself. When this happens, the ice will cloud over, losing its desired sheen and will start to become sluggish to skate on. The glass around the ice surface will also fog over, obstructing the view of the audience.

In addition to the aesthetic inconveniences caused by excessive humidity the condensing moisture releases a tremendous amount of heat into the ice surface that must be removed at the expense of operating the refrigeration equipment longer than would normally be required. Condensation can permeate your building insulation, drastically reducing its effectiveness and of greater consequence, structural steel will start to rust and wood will start to rot, further reducing the integrity of your facility.

Luckily, with proper design, humidity can be controlled effectively and efficiently. The two commonly used styles of dehumidification systems are the mechanical dehumidifier and the desiccant dehumidifier.

Sand Floor versus Cement Floor

There are good reasons for installing both sand floors and cement floors in an ice skating facility. Hopefully the following should make your decision easier.

Sand floors are utilized to reduce the initial cost of an ice surface. A sand floor is generally used in a year round ice facility but can be installed in a seasonal facility with some precautions to prevent unwanted traffic on the piping system during the off-season.

A sand floor reduces the flexibility of the facility in that no off-season activities can be held directly on top of the sand. An ice covering can be used to facilitate light activities on top of the ice, but there is not enough support for rodeos, tractor pulls, etc. If for some reason the building must be sold, a sand floor will reduce the building's usefulness and resale value.

A cement floor for an NHL-size ice rink will cost between $50,000 and $125,000 more than a sand floor, depending on the floor strength, proximity of material, and a good super-flat contractor. A cement floor increases the flexibility of the facility in that dances, bingos, and trade shows can be held in the off-season. With a properly engineered floor, a circus or other heavy event can be held as well. As with a sand floor, the ice surface can be covered for non-ice events while the ice is in place.

In order to prevent puncturing the cooling pipes, additional care and attention is required during the initial stages of ice making with a sand floor. Before applying the first water, you must ensure that all of the pipes are in their chairs and the sand has been dressed out to its normal operating level.

In order to maintain a crisp, clean, efficient ice surface, all arenas should have the ice periodically removed to purge the buildup of solids and old paint that is deposited over time. On a sand floor, the residue tends to cake on the sand surface and can only removed by replacing the surface sand. This residue is easily washed away on a cement floor.

A cement floor is much easier to make ice on, especially with less experienced personnel. A sand floor requires gently misting the sand surface while avoiding puncturing the pipes until there is an ice layer thick enough to walk on and eventually drive a Zamboni on. When installed properly, a cement floor always ensures a precisely level surface to form the ice base. A sand floor can deviate over the years with use.

It is advisable to maintain 1 3/4" to 2 1/2" of ice on a sand floor to reduce the chance of puncturing pipe during ice events. Cement floors only require 2" of ice for safe use. Periodically measuring the ice surface thickness by drilling holes (ice taps) is much easier with a cement floor. With a sand floor, added attention must be taken to ensure that no pipes are punctured while edging or re-surfacing. This special care is not necessary on a cement floor.

Once the ice is in place, there can be a small amount of difference in energy consumption between a sand floor and a cement floor. The same amount of BTUs will enter the ice surface regardless of the style of floor. A well-designed cement floor will typically have 1" of cement cover and 1" of ice cover above the cooling pipes. A sand floor will typically have 2" of ice cover above the pipes. Ice has a K value of 1.3 and cement has a K value of 0.54. The K value is the rate a substance conducts heat with a higher K value conducting heat faster than a low K value. So, theoretically the cement floor would have to operate a little colder than the sand floor for the same amount of heat to be exchanged. However, in reality, many sand floors usually develop small hills and valleys over the years, which requires the ice level to be kept thicker in many areas, which reduces the efficiency.

Whichever way you choose to build your ice skating facility, rest assured that with proper care and attention, a great ice surface can be maintained on either a sand floor or a cement floor.

Calcium Chloride versus Glycol

On an indirect refrigeration system, a choice must be made between the type of secondary coolant that you select. Both Calcium Chloride and glycol have been successfully used over the years, and there are applications where both secondary coolants have an advantage. To a much lesser degree, other heat transfer mediums such as methyl alcohol have also been utilized in the ice rink industry.

In regard to energy efficiency, Calcium Chloride is the better choice. Its heat transfer coefficient is much better than glycol. This fact equates to smaller, less expensive chillers for the same heat transfer. The heat transfer in the floor piping system is also better. Due to the superior heat transfer characteristics, the brine pump can be smaller and the required pump horsepower and corresponding energy consumption is reduced with calcium chloride.

Calcium chloride is highly corrosive when not maintained properly. With proper system design and operation it is still the best choice for most ice rink applications. The system components must be selected specifically for the Calcium Chloride. Typically chillers are made out of carbon steel or cooper-nickle. Brine pump shafts and butterfly valve stems should be made out of stainless steel.

With a system utilizing Calcium Chloride, it is imperative that the system is kept full at all times and no air is allowed to come in contact with the internal components. A high-grade environmentally friendly rust inhibitor must be used to ensure equipment longevity. It is good practice to carry out routine in house brine tests to monitor brine

strength and pH on a semi annual basis and to request a lab report once a year.

In systems that are occasionally emptied and filled, such as a portable system, glycol can be a very good choice. Glycol will reduce the effects of corrosion in systems that are occasionally opened to the air. It is still important to use good-quality inhibited glycol, such as Dow SR-1, and to ensure that annual lab samples are taken to verify the integrity of the solution.

Should You Install a Heating Floor?

If an ice surface is in operation for more than seven months of the year, a heating floor is generally required. The purpose of the heating floor is to eliminate the buildup of an ice lens below the cooling floor, which can cause the floor to heave and buckle.

A high-quality insulation must be installed beneath the cooling floor, which will minimize the amount of heat loss from the soil below. It is considered good practice to install a double layer of 2" high density Styrofoam as well as a vapor barrier beneath the cooling floor (Total of 4" of insulation). In most installations, the insulation will slow the formation of ice but will not eliminate it unless you have approximately 11" of insulation. The cost of 11" of insulation is prohibitive, so it is more practical to install a heating floor.

Even if you are not planning on operating your facility more than seven months of the year, installing a heating floor in the beginning is prudent in case you change your mind later. The cost of a heating floor is typically from 7% to 15% of the refrigeration installation.

The result of a heaved floor can have disastrous consequences. An ice rink operating year round at 150 F without a heating floor will attract moisture from great distances much as a cold window in a humid house will. This steady accumulation of moisture has the potential of forming an ice lens 22' thick below the ice surface.

The first obvious result of a heaved floor is an ice surface that is out of level. There have been many ice surfaces over the years that have been more than 10" out of level as a result of frost heaves. The only way to level the playing surface is with the application of more ice on the low spots. The result is an inconsistent surface temperature over the entire plane and an ice plant that is operating overtime to accommodate the thick spots.

Of greater consequence is the structural damage that takes place. The cement floor can buckle and crack as a result of the heaves. Doors and gates can become impossible to open, and glass can fall out of its supports, causing bodily harm to the players and spectators. In some instances, the whole building can shift and sustain damage.

On many facilities with severe heaving problems, the only recourse is to totally remove the damaged floor and excavate the frozen material. The costs can be tremendous. For this reason, we always recommend a heating floor on all new installations.

Selecting a Primary Refrigerant

The objective of the primary refrigerant is to safely and efficiently remove the heat from the secondary coolant. There are several factors that must be taken into consideration when selecting a refrigerant: budget for construction, the cost of electricity, building design, availability of trained operators and technicians, and local codes and regulations.

Over the years, Ammonia and R-22 have been by far the most common refrigerants employed in the ice rink industry. With the future phase out of R-22, new alternatives are starting to appear on the market. The following is a brief description of some of the pros and cons of the regularly used refrigerants.

Ammonia

For energy efficiency and equipment first cost, ammonia is still by far the best choice. Ammonia has a significantly higher heat transfer coefficient then any of the other refrigerants. This can be exploited in two ways. Selecting a smaller chiller and condenser can reduce first costs. Alternatively, you can select components with the same heat transfer surface area and increase the total system efficiency by operating at lower discharge pressures and higher suction pressures. The higher BTU per pound of mass flow reduces the size of piping and valves. Ammonia's better thermodynamic properties reduce the cost of electrical consumption. An ammonia system requires less refrigerant than any of the alternatives, and the cost of ammonia per pound is approximately 1/5th of the other refrigerants.

Some facilities cannot use of ammonia for various code reasons. Due to its pungent odor and higher toxicity, special precautions must be taken in plant room and equipment design. The strong odor makes detection and leak prevention much easier than with the alternatives.

Ammonia systems are built with much higher construction standards than the alternative refrigerants, which results in a higher quality, longer lasting industrial grade system. With the recent improvements in compressor seals, limited charge chillers, leakproof valves and ammonia detection equipment, we feel that ammonia is still by far the best choice for an ice rink application.

R-22

Next to ammonia, R-22 is still the most efficient alternative. However, due to the .05 ozone depletion factor, R-22 is slated for total phase-out over the next 20 to 30 years. R-22 still is very reasonably priced in comparison to some of the new alternatives. Compressor sizing is slightly larger than ammonia, and the required horsepower per ton of refrigerant is approximately 8% higher. R-22 is still used in many new installations. Where possible, we suggest using components, piping, and valves so you leave the door open for an ammonia conversion if required.

AZ-50

AZ-50 has been used successfully as an alternative to R-22 since the mid-1990s. It is approximately 12% less efficient than R-22 on a reciprocating compressor application. This efficiency loss can be greatly reduced through some creative sub-cooling techniques. The mass flow of AZ-50 is greater, requiring larger line sizes and valves than R-22. The compressor size must be approximately 10% larger for the same refrigeration effect. AZ-50 requires the use of Polyolester oil, which is quite expensive. Discharge temperatures are significantly lower than R-22 or ammonia, which eliminates the need for any oil cooling. The lower operating temperature reduces equipment room exhaust fan run time. The cost of refrigerant is approximately double that of R-22. This price difference will reduce as R-22 phases out.

R-134a

Recently, R-134a has been used in a number of facilities. It is more expensive than R-22 and about 12% less efficient than R-22 on reciprocating compressor applications (20% less efficient than ammonia). The volume flow rate of R-134a is much higher than R-22, AZ-50, and ammonia, which means that the compressors must be approximately 60% larger to do the same job. This translates into higher first costs and maintenance costs.

Comparison of 1" Pipe in Cement Versus ½" Mat Style System

On floors with end headers, the 1" pipe permits higher glycol flow rates at lower pressure drops. This results in reduced temperature drops across the grid, faster temperature recovery, and superior temperature control. Better ice surface conditions are maintained during varying conditions. Equivalent flow rates can be achieved with the ½" mat style system if side headers are installed, but this will result in over 400% more mechanical joints and the corresponding potential for leaks.

The lower pressure drops in the large pipe system will result in reduced horsepower requirements per gallon of pumped glycol.

When the 1" pipes are imbedded in the cement floor, this design provides a very large thermal mass, which keeps temperature swings to a minimum further improving ice consistency.

The larger 1" pipes are less susceptible to fouling or blockage by foreign objects and have less mechanical connections, reducing the chance of leaks.

The 1" pipes, when imbedded in cement, require no further handling and do not deteriorate as rapidly as the ½" pipes that are rolled and unrolled over the years.

In order to provide sufficient pipe protection for the mat style system it is normal to operate with a thicker ice surface than is required with a cement floor.

A cement floor is easier to monitor ice thickness by drilling tap holes on a weekly basis. Consistent ice thickness means consistent ice temperature and reduced operating costs.

Set up and take down time is eliminated with the cement floor versus the mat style system that must be rolled up and put away if the ice is removed.

CAMPS AND CAMPING 20

Thomas H. Sawyer, Indiana State University

Historically, the word *camping* signified simple living outdoors and engaging in activities related primarily to the outdoors. Today, the term has broadened tremendously and encompasses a wide spectrum of developments for families and children. Resident centers, day camps, group camps, family camps, and wilderness camps are the common designations used for the various types of camps.

Camps have been developed by public agencies at all levels of government and by many voluntary youth-serving organizations. The rapidly increasing participation of children and adults in camping necessitates careful consideration of desirable areas and facilities.

Although most organized camping takes place on agency-owned or private property, public land is becoming increasingly involved. Public land is one of the major resources for school outdoor educational programs, and many resident centers have been constructed on public property or by public funds.

Schools use the facilities during the school year, and park and recreation agencies use them during the summer. The purposes of outdoor education, whether sponsored by park and recreation departments or by schools, are similar in many respects, and cooperative planning is not only necessary in order to get the most from the community dollar but imperative if suitable lands and sites are to be obtained. If adequate facilities are to be provided to meet the needs of both organized camping groups and schools, the facilities must be designed for year-round use.

Program Facilities:
What to Expect

Following are some of the facilities used for various camp programs. Specifications and construction details for most are found elsewhere in this book.

Water-related activities are among the most popular in summer camps. During the fall and spring, school groups and other groups may use developments for fishing, canoeing, and boating.

Lakes, ponds, streams, bays, and inlets offer many recreational opportunities. All should be studied in detail with regard to currents, eddies, depth, slope, shoreline, debris, and other factors.

Canoeing, boating, and sailing are activities that may be conducted on a lake, pond, river, reservoir, bay, or other body of water. The water area should have accessory facilities such as floats, docks, markers, or buoys. Various sizes of water bodies are required for different activities and events. For instance, canoe-racing courses are 100, 200, 440, and 880 yards, as well as one mile. Sailing requires a wider body of water, because the boats usually finish to windward. The different classes of sailboats, such as Sunfish and Sailfish, require different courses.

Casting is simulated rod-and-reel fishing. Practice casting on a playing field or in a gymnasium is possible year round. If a pond or lake is nearby, a beach or dock affords an excellent facility for the casting program.

In order to teach all phases of the activity, an area 300 by 100 feet is desirable. A football, soccer, hockey, or lacrosse field is ideal for class instruction.

Casting targets, which are 30 inches in diameter are easily constructed and can be an excellent project for any woodshop program. It is recommended that at least 10 targets be made. Others can be added as the program expands. Targets for use on the water are also 30 inches in diameter and are made of hollow metal tubing. They float and can be easily anchored.

Other facilities include campfire circles and council rings for which most camps develop centers for meetings and evening programs and craft centers, which can range from canvas-covered areas with provisions for storing tools to extensive and well-equipped craft shops.

Day Camps

A day camp is an area and facility intended to provide a program similar to that of the resident camp except that campers sleep at home. Many of the considerations of planning for resident camps apply to day camps. However, facility problems are simpler because day campers sleep at home and usually eat two of the day's meals at home. Provisions, however simple, must nonetheless be made for water, restrooms, rainy-day shelters, eating and cooking, refrigeration, first-aid and health, and program supplies. The focus of this section is that of selecting an appropriate day camp facility.

Abundant land for programs is extremely desirable, particularly when the emphasis is on outdoor-related activities. Reasonable isolation and a varied topography with outdoor program possibilities are essential. Natural parks, park-school areas, and community forests often lend themselves for use as day-camp sites. Some communities have developed special day-camp areas; others make appropriate picnic areas available for this special use.

Buses are often used to transport campers to the day camp. If more than half an hour is consumed in daily travel each way, the effectiveness of the program is reduced.

Day-camp groups are divided into units or counselor groups ranging from eight to 20 campers. Most day camps provide simple facilities for each unit, including a fireplace for cooking, storage cabinets, and tables. Some day camps serve a daily meal in a central dining hall to reduce or eliminate the need for unit cooking facilities.

Storage is needed for equipment, food, and program supplies. Some day camps use trailers or trucks for storage, hauling them back and forth each day. Also, a well-equipped first-aid station and a rest-area facility are necessary.

Group Camps

Many public agencies today provide special campsites for small groups such as scouts, church groups, and school classes. These sites generally accommodate from 10 to 40 persons.

Groups stay from one to five days. Small units in decentralized resident camps sometimes have facilities that can be used for group camping. Simple fireplaces for cooking, picnic shelters for use in bad weather, restrooms, and safe drinking water are necessities.

The increase in winter camping by small groups often necessitates special developments.

Some winter campers live completely outdoors in the cold, even in snow. Usually, however, winterized buildings are used for cooking, sleeping, and evening activities.

Campgrounds

Campgrounds are found in many types of settings and in many formats. Tent camping is the traditional form of camping, but the increase in motor homes, trailers, and pop-up trailers has changed the camping mix. Public campgrounds such as those found in federal, state, county, and municipal park systems have had to accommodate the changing camper. Traditional amenities have included water somewhere in the campground, restrooms, and maybe showers. In today's marketplace, these are called primitive conditions. Campgrounds desiring to attract motor homes and trailers now provide electrical (usually 110 and 220 volts), sewer, and water. Additional services can include cable television and telephone lines.

Campgrounds should be segregated, or at least partitioned. Motor homes, trailers, and pop-up trailers should be located in one section and tent camping in another. A natural segregation occurs by the designation of campgrounds as three hook-up, two hook-up, one hook-up, or primitive. The more hook-ups a section has, the more likely affluent campers will use it.

Roads need to be wide enough to handle a single motor home and most often are one way. Parking areas need to be hard stand, asphalt, or concrete and ideally long enough so a motor home can drive through the site, entering from one side and exiting from the other. This prevents potential problems with motor homes backing up and into other campers. Turns need to be casual enough to allow longer motor homes to make full turns without striking obstructions. The campground should include an entrance station to collect fees or provide information as necessary. Honor systems are available, but still require a ranger to manage the site.

Family Camps

Family resident camps offer complete meal and living accommodations for families or for adults only. The facilities may be similar to those of resident camps, except that some of the sleeping quarters may be adapted to families.

Most of the campgrounds in state or federal areas are destination camps. Campers generally stay more than one night and often for several weeks. In recent years, a great many resort camps have sprung up. These resorts, generally privately developed, are more or less complete vacationlands offering organized programs and facilities, including swimming pools, recreation centers, children's playgrounds, special game courts, marinas, and horseback riding trails.

Waterfronts

The use of waterfronts varies with the program offered. The type of program will determine the nature of the waterfront, and yet the environmental situation, such as ocean, stream, or lake, may influence the type and design of the facility. The following categories of use identify the specific areas of the aquatic program:

- Familiarization—Familiarization involves programs for acquainting the user with the water.
- Instruction—Instruction involves programs of teaching the user basic activities related to aquatics.

- Recreation—Recreation involves programs that are largely unstructured, for relaxing and refreshing the user, including participating in or watching special events such as synchronized swimming, water shows, and competitive swimming.
- Competition—Competition involves programs of training and competing in swimming and other aquatic activities. The user of a waterfront should be able to participate in a variety of aquatic activities in order to attain the desired objectives. This is especially true in the camp setting, where the camper participates in the constructive fulfillment of inherent attitudes and aptitudes.

Waterfronts for the conduct of aquatic activities are found in children's camps, parks, resorts, marinas, clubs, hotels, residential developments, and other recreational areas. The waterfront, whether it is a beach, floating crib, dock, pond, lake shore, pool deck, or some other area where aquatic programs take place, must be properly located and constructed to ensure the health and safety of the public using this facility. The post-World War II years have seen a tremendous development in children's camps in the United States, particularly day camps. Although many of the aspects of this chapter deal primarily with camps, most of the criteria may be applied to beachfront developments as well. In planning the location and construction of natural and artificial waterfront facilities, definite criteria should be established. These criteria should reflect not only the camp program, but also health and safety requirements.

Criteria for Natural Waterfronts

The natural waterfront site should have certain characteristics to make it desirable for aquatic program use. The recommended criteria for the selection of waterfront or beach sites are discussed below and helpful checklists have been provided for the planners.

Water Characteristics

The water content should be of a sanitary quality affording safe usage. The health conditions of a site are primarily judged by a careful examination of both its surrounding environment and the water content.

The first is accomplished by a careful field analysis, the second by a laboratory analysis. Both examinations can indicate the bacterial quality and physical clarity of the water.

Checklist:
- Surrounding water source
- Water quality (bacterial content)
- Water clarity (visibility test)

Water-Condition Characteristics

The circulation of the water through the potential waterfront site should be examined. Slow-moving water can produce swampy or built-up mud conditions, while fast-moving water can produce undercurrents and erosive conditions.

The ideal water temperature for swimming ranges from 72 to 78F, depending upon the air temperature. The American Public Health Association indicates that less than 500 gallons of additional water per bather per day is an insufficient diluting volume unless there is sufficient application of disinfection.

Checklist:
- rate of water flow
- rate of water turnover
- water-level fluctuation
- water constancy
- availability of water
- types of currents and undertow
- outlet for water
- eddies, floods, waves, or wash
- weeds, fungi, mold, or slime
- parasites, fish, animals
- debris, broken glass, and so on
- oil slick
- odor, color, tastes.

Bottom Characteristics

The waterfront bottom should be unobstructed and clear of debris, rock, muck, mulch, peat, and mud. The bottom should be of gravel, sand, or stable hard ground to afford firm and secure footing. The most desirable bottom is white sand with a gradual pitch sloping from the shallow to the deep end. The bottom should not be too steep or too shallow nor have holes, pots, channels, bars, or islands.

An investigation, by taking soundings in a boat and by making an actual underwater survey, should be undertaken before a final decision is made on the location of the waterfront. The waterfront should not be in an area where the channel shifts or silt builds up.

Checklist:
- bottom movement
- amount of holes, debris
- slope of subsurface
- amount of area
- condition of soil
- porosity of bottom
- average depth and various depths
- bottom color

Climatic Characteristics

Continuous dry spells or numerous rainy seasons may cause the site to have water-retention problems. Dangerous storms including tornadoes, lightning, hurricanes, and northeasters create extremely dangerous waterfront conditions. The severity of the winter can also affect the waterfront. Ice and ice movement can cause damage to waterfront amenities and bottom. A south-southeast orientation is ideal maximize the benefit from the sun and minimize exposure to the wind.

Checklist:
- number of storms and type
- prevailing winds
- amount of ice
- change of air temperature
- amount of precipitation
- fluctuation of temperature
- sun exposure

Environmental Characteristics

The locale of the waterfront should be carefully examined for all influences on its construction and utilization. Zoning regulations, building codes, insurance restrictions, health ordinances, title covenants, and a multitude of other legal restrictions by the Coast Guard, Conservation Department, Water Resources Commission, public works agencies, and Fire Department should be studied. The arrangement of land uses and their compatibility to the project, transportation, utilities, community facilities, population, and area economics should also be considered.

Checklist:
- ownership and riparian rights
- availability of water supply
- zoning and deed restrictions
- local, state, and federal regulations
- adjacent ownerships
- water patrol and a control agency

Program Characteristics

The waterfront should be situated so that it can be protected by a fence or other controlled access, particularly in a camp, marina, or other small area. It should be internally segregated (e.g., bathing from boating, boating from fishing, and so on). The site may have storage space for waterfront equipment, adequate spectator seating area during special events, a safety zone near the lifeguard station or post, and ready access to a road.

Checklist:
- distance of waterfront from other areas
- access road
- separation of waterfront activities
- area for unity of controls
- space available for adjunct activities

Access Characteristics

The waterfront facility must be accessible by transportation available to the user. There should always be a means of vehicular access for emergency or maintenance use. The site around the waterfront and along its approach should be free of poison ivy, sumac, poison oak, burdock thistle, and other irritating plants.

Checklist:
- location for access road
- area free of poisonous plants
- area accessible yet controllable

Area Characteristics

The waterfront bathing area should allow for at least 50 square feet for each user. There should be areas for instruction, recreation, and competition. The depth of the area to be used primarily for the instruction of non-swimmers should not exceed three feet. The area to be used for intermediate swimmers should not exceed 5 1/2 feet (primarily for competition). Smaller or larger swimming areas may be designed if users are divided differently.

The minimum recommended size for a camp swimming area is 60 feet by 30 feet and the desirable size is 75 feet by 45 feet providing a 25-yard short course.

Checklist:
- space for bathing
- capacity of waterfront
- water depths
- division of bathing area into stations
- size of boating area
- size of fishing area

Shore Characteristics

The shoreline for the waterfront facility should be free of irregular rocks, stumps, debris, or obstruction. It should be a minimum of 100 feet long for bathing in a camp area and can be many miles long in a park beach.

There should be trees adjacent to waterfront areas to provide shade and wind protection. Large, high trees should be eliminated because they attract lightning and moldy trees have many decayed overhanging branches. Too many trees of a deciduous nature create mucky shores and water bottoms because of their autumn leaves. There are fewer problems with coniferous trees.

Checklist:
- surrounding vegetation
- slope of the shore
- existing beach
- extent of clearing
- amount of debris

Criteria for Artificial Waterfronts

In locating and considering an artificial waterfront, most of the same characteristics as described for natural areas should be examined. Additional criteria that should be considered are outlined below.

Environmental Characteristics

If all available bodies of water are being utilized, then artificial waterfront facilities must be developed. In some cases, waterfront locations are unsatisfactory or unavailable for new camps or resorts. Thus, consideration must be given to utilizing undeveloped sites with sufficient watershed (runoff water), water table (underground water), and water bodies (surface water) for lakes, pools, or impondments.

Water Characteristics

Before any site is selected, the perculation rate and, in particular, the permeability of the soil should be carefully checked in order to be sure that water will be retained. The stability and structure of the soil must also be determined (from test borings and/or test pits) because of the various types of dams, pump houses, dikes, pools, berms, spillways, and other structures that must be built.

Water-Content Characteristics

Unlike natural bodies of water, the content of artificial bodies can be controlled by chlorination and filtration. Runoff water obtained from storms, and contained in a pond or lake, should be collected by diversion ditches and fed to a reservoir and chlorination plant. This water can then be recirculated until potable water is obtained.

Underground water that is obtained from wells or springs can also be contained in a pond. This type of artificial water body usually would have a continuous flow and thus would need only a simple filtration system plus chlorination.

Surface water that is obtained from running streams is usually contained in a bypass pond or in a pond in the stream itself. Both methods require the construction of a dam. These artificial water bodies have continuous running water. However, gate valves and floodgates are required, especially during storms when there is a large flow of water to control. Unless there is a constant turnover or supply of clean water, these impondments will require a filtration and chlorination system.

Climatic Characteristics

Climatic considerations are very important in developing artificial bodies of water and waterfronts. In most cases, natural bodies of water will fluctuate very little because of weather conditions. On the other hand, artificial bodies are solely dependent upon the climate because the water table, runoff, and stream flow depend on the amount and time of rainfall. All other climatic considerations mentioned for natural waterfronts generally apply to artificial waterfronts as well.

Drainage Characteristics

A low-lying area, regardless of its appeal, is not a good location for a pool or pond. Adequate drainage is essential so the surface and deck water will drain away from the water body and so the water body itself can be emptied without pumping. Groundwater and frost action resulting from improper drainage can undermine a foundation by causing it to heave and settle.

Construction Criteria for Natural Waterfronts

The natural waterfront facility should have features that make it both safe and usable. The following criteria are suggested as a basis for the construction of such a facility.

Bottom Characteristics

Most swimming facilities around natural bodies of water require the dragging and grading of the bottom sub-surfaces to eliminate hazards. In many cases, where definite improvement of the bottom is required, feed mat, mesh, or plastic sheets have to be laid down on top of muck and staked down. Once these sheets have been laid, sand must be spread over the mat surface. When the bottom is firm, sand can be spread six inches thick on top of ice in the crib area during winter. As the ice melts, the sand will fall fairly evenly over the bottom. This can only be accomplished, however, when the ice does not shift or break and float away.

Shore Characteristics

When a beach is constructed, a gentle slope of from six to 12 feet in 100 feet should be maintained. Where the waterfront requires a great deal of construction, a dock shoreline is recommended, rather than trying to maintain an unstable beach. The ground above the water can then be developed with turf, terraces, decks, and boardwalks, depending upon the nature of the project. When the bottom drops off very quickly, the shore can be dug out to the grade desired underwater. This forms a crescent-shaped waterfront with an excellent beach.

Access Characteristics

The owner should acquire access roads and streets around waterfront areas, if possible, to keep the area buffered from conflicting uses. These roads should be durable and be attractively maintained. Access roads should have clear horizontal and vertical vision so that pedestrian and vehicular conflict can be prevented.

Program Characteristics

The waterfront in small recreational areas such as camps or resorts should be completely enclosed by planting or fencing. There should be a central control for ingress and exit. Many facilities require the use of check in-out boards, tickets, and other similar devices for controlling the use of the area. The waterfront bathing, boating, and fishing facilities should be separated, each with its own control.

Construction Criteria for Artificial Waterfronts

Both artificial and natural waterfronts should have certain features that make them safe and usable. In improving and developing an artificial waterfront, most of the same considerations should be rendered as illustrated for the natural waterfront. The following criteria should be carefully considered in providing an artificial waterfront.

Bottom Characteristics

When constructing an artificial beach, the grade should be the same as that recommended for natural shores—six feet to 12 feet in 100 feet. For reservoirs and ponds, there should be a minimum of nine inches of large, crushed stone, then four inches of well-graded smooth gravel to fill in the voids, and then nine inches of washed medium sand. Where the sand beach terminates at a depth of approximately seven feet of water, it is recommended that rip-rapping be established to resist the tendency of the beach sand to move down the slope. The area above the beach should also be ditched where the natural slope of the ground exceeds that of the beach. Thus, the slopes of the beach should be approximately 6% percent below the water and 10% above. For areas in tidal waters, a maximum slope of five for 15 feet can be established for the bottom below-water line.

Shore Characteristics

In creating the shoreline for artificial bodies of water, there should be either a berm or dike if the water is to be confined. A steep slope to eliminate shallow areas is usually required to prevent weeds and other plant materials from growing in the water. If the soil conditions will not allow a steep slope underwater three feet deep to retard water-plant growth, then bulkheads or docks will be required, or only a limited beach can be provided.

Design and Construction of Camp Waterfronts

The camp waterfront is usually composed of either permanent docks or floats to provide safe swimming and boating areas.

Docks and Floats

Permanent structures are usually set on concrete, wood, or steel foundations, or pier piles. The decks should be made in sections of 10 to 20 feet for ease in removing for repairs or winter storage. The dock should be constructed with at least a one-foot air space between the deck and water. Underwater braces and other cross beams should be limited to prevent swimmers from becoming entangled in them.

When water levels change, allowances should be made for the piers to be outside the deck limits so the deck can move up and down on sleeves or brackets. Walkways or decks should be a minimum of six feet wide, preferably eight or 10 feet. They should be cross-planked so swimmers will avoid splinters. The planking should not be less than two inches thick by four to six inches wide. Boards should be spaced a maximum of 1/4 inch apart to prevent toe-stubbing. The deck should be treated with a non-creosote-based preservative, since creosote will burn feet, plus a plastic, non-lead paint that is not heat-absorbing.

The paint should be white with a blue or green tint to reduce the glare and aid in reflection. Flotation structures may be made of drums, balsa wood, cork, rigid polystyrene plastic, steel tanks, or other forms of flotation material. There are many innovations that have carried over from war days.

Pontoon decks, for example, are sometimes made from surplus bridge parts and 55-gallon plastic containers. All such materials should be treated with red lead after scraping, sanding, and repairing. A frame should be constructed of two-inch by eight-inch boards to fit over and contain the supporting units. The frame should fit securely, yet be removable at the close of the season. Some flotation materials or devices are just placed in the framing under the floats without any type of anchorage to the frame. Galvanized steel or aluminum straps of 1/8 inches by 1 1/2 inches under the floating units will save time and effort to prevent sinking when these units acquire a leak and fill with water. The various types of designs employed in waterfronts are shown in Figure 20.1. A typical camp waterfront is shown in Figure 20.2.

Waterfront Equipment

It is important to plan initially for all needed accessory equipment. The amount of equipment required will vary with the size of the waterfront. All necessary safety equipment must be located so as to afford immediate emergency use.

Lifeguard Station

Lifeguard chairs should be placed at a point where the location of beach equipment and sunbathing limit lines do not interfere with the guards' vision of the water areas. Chairs should be a minimum of six feet to a maximum of 10 feet above grade. Usually lifeguard chairs are made of galvanized pipe or wood.

Ladders

In all swimming cribs, there should be a ladder at least two feet in width placed at the sides in order not to interfere with persons swimming the length of the simulated pool.

Log Booms

Logs fastened end to end can form a continuous lifeline around bathing limits in rustic settings and, at the same time, provide the safety to swimmers so necessary at a waterfront.

Figure 20.1
Sample Waterfront Configurations

Lemmon Lines

Lemmon lines are small floats attached by a nylon or plastic rope or cable outlining and restricting swimming areas. They can be made of rounded wood, cork, or plastic.

Markers and Buoys

These are floats indicating the limits of areas or channels or for marking underwater obstructions, divers, moorings, and fishing nets. They are usually hollow cans or drums. They can also be flag buoys, a six-inch-square wood block with attached flag, a wooden cross of two inches by four inches with can on top, or a metal ballast with flag.

Rescue Craft

Boats should be of the round-bottom or dory type between 12 and 14 feet long. There should be lifesaving equipment in the boat at all times. The seats should be removable, and oarlocks should be of a permanent type. A catamaran, surfboards, and, in large beach waterfront facilities, helicopters supplement the lifeboat as a means of patrol.

Kick Rails

A rail for practicing and teaching swimming should be placed at water level. This can be made of galvanized pipe, wood rods, or rope.

Towel Racks

Racks for drying towels and bathing suits should be installed at or near the waterfront.

Miscellaneous Equipment

Life ring buoys should be spaced strategically around the waterfront on racks. These racks are usually in the form of a cross, with the ring suspended from the center and the rope wrapped around the ring from pegs protruding from each end of the cross. Torpedo buoys, bamboo poles, grappling irons, lifelines, shepherd's crooks, stretchers, blankets, microphones, and other such devices should be available to the lifeguards. Numbers indicating depths and the capacities of the crib and other swimming areas should be clearly visible. Kickboards should be available for practice as well as emergency use.

Figure 20.2
Sample Waterfront

SECTION IV

SPECIALTY AREAS

TRACK AND FIELD AND CROSS-COUNTRY FACILITIES

21

Lawrence W. Judge, Ball State University
Thomas H. Sawyer, Indiana State University

Fairness is a very important aspect of sport; how can athletes be tested against one another in competition if the competition is not regulated? When thinking of competition equality, most refer to the issues related to illegal substance abuse. It is important, however, to understand that many different factors including facility construction can contribute to fairness. Sport facilities must be properly designed in accordance with the rulebook to keep the playing field level for all competitors.

Track and field is one of the oldest sports in the United States, dating from the 1860s. In 1878, the sport of cross country was introduced as the sport served mainly as training for summer track and field athletes. Nine years later, cross-country running became a formal sport in the United States. Today track and field or athletics and cross country are governed by

International Athletics Association Federation (IAAF) at the international level, by United States Track and Field (USATF) at the domestic professional level, by the National Association of Intercollegiate Athletics (NCAA), at the collegiate level and by the National Federation of High Schools (NFHS) at the high school level.

Each national governing body (NGB) level has specific regulations for facility design and construction. Many of these are very similar and some are different. Please consult the rulebook for each organization before beginning a facility construction project.

Facilities in cross country and track and field are regulated to great detail to ensure fairness between high schools, colleges, and professional athletes in championships. Facility construction is not covered much in the mainstream media, but it is of extreme importance to track and field in many ways, not just in keeping competitions fair. The safety of participants and the liability of the facility site are completely dependent on meeting the regulations imposed by governing bodies. On the other hand, indoor and outdoor tracks are important to the general aesthetics of the campus facility and important to collegiate recruiting. When considering these different types of variables

dependent upon venue construction, an aspect that is sometimes forgotten in track and field suddenly becomes very critical to sport. A track and field competition complex is complicated at best when compared to other outdoor or indoor sports spaces such as an indoor basketball or volleyball court or a baseball, football, or soccer field. The track and field complex includes areas such as throwing, jumping, running, relaxation and warm-up, spectator, timing and recording, storage, and officials' dressing room. A cross-country course requires appropriate planning to service girls, women, boys, and men. The distances differ for genders and level of competition (e.g., interscholastic and intercollegiate).

The following chapter is a guide from start to finish in cross country and track and field facility design. The text in this chapter is based on the NCAA Track and Field/Cross Country Men's and Women's rules.

Coordinating Site Selection and General Facility Layout

Planning the Outdoor Track

Location Considerations

Picking a proper outdoor site is critical to the success of an outdoor track and field facility. A track will require a site of no less than five acres, a minimum of 600 feet long by 300 feet wide. Additional area must be allowed for grading, curbs, and drainage and for amenities such as grandstands, bleachers, lighting, walkways, and fencing. The site should also be reasonably level. While the track will be sloped slightly for drainage, for all practical purposes, the track must be level in the running direction. Water should drain away from the track. It is best to locate a track on a relatively level plain, higher than surrounding areas. Additional filling or drainage work required by a low site may add substantially to construction costs. Even under the best site conditions, tracks should be constructed with a perimeter drain on the inside of the track to remove storm water that has drained from the track and playing field. Even the type of soil matters to construction. Poor soil conditions often lead to excessive settling, heaving caused by freeze/thaw action, and drainage problems. The best soil is hard, well drained, and non-heaving. Locations with peat, clay, topsoil, shear sand, or other organic materials at a depth of eight to 12 inches should be avoided. It is also important to consider underground utilities. While the finished facility will require utility service, it is better to avoid constructing the track over underground utilities. No expense should be spared in developing a good, solid base for the running surface.

Wind is also a consideration. Straightaways should be parallel to prevailing winds, which is especially important for dashes and hurdle races. For athlete safety, jumping events should also take place with the wind since crosswinds can be particularly dangerous. Multiple-jump runways should be considered because of the addition of the women's pole vault and time constraints when there is only one runway for men and women for the long jump and triple jump. Throwing events should be located so that participants are throwing into the wind. Likewise, for safety reasons, it is essential that high-jump and pole-vault runways be located so that the athlete does not have to look into the sun or artificial lighting.

General Plan Considerations

The first stage in the construction of a running track is selecting a site and designing a track to fit the site. In calculating the accuracy of a finished 400-meter track, no minus tolerance is acceptable, and a plus tolerance must be no more than 1/2 inch in any lane. These very small tolerances and the numerous design and site factors to be considered make track design extremely complex and demanding. The construction of track and field areas will follow the International Amateur Athletic Federation rules with respect to grade or slope: "The maximum inclination permitted for tracks, runways, circles, and landing areas for throwing events shall not exceed 1:100 in a lateral direction and 1:1000 in the running and throwing direction." Owners should begin by deciding what size and shape of track is needed. A 400-meter, six- or nine-lane track is the standard for high school and college competition, although a few high school tracks and many large college tracks are 10 lanes wide.

Will the track be built around playing fields? Many tracks are built around football or soccer fields. In addition to allowing space for the field itself, space must be allowed for player seating, walkways, and other associated facilities. Artificial turf fields require additional space for anchoring detail at the perimeter. Tracks are designed in two basic shapes. An equal-quadrant track has two 100-meter straightaways and two 100-meter curves, while a non-equal quadrant track has two

straightaways of one length and two curves of another length totaling 400m. In the latter case, the result is a track with either a slightly stretched or compressed oval shape. Recently, a third design, nicknamed the broken-back track, has come into use. This design features a squarer track with shorter straightaways and rounded ends made of double curves. This design creates a larger infield that is large enough for an NCAA soccer field (which neither of the two more common designs can accommodate) and is useful for sites where one of the more common track designs will not work. Generally, an equal quadrant track is desirable, but site factors will determine which design is most feasible.

Will the construction project include field events? Most track projects built today include construction of a high-jump pad, long-jump runway and pit, pole-vault runway and landing area, shot put, discus, and hammer-throwing pads and landing areas, and sometimes a javelin runway and a triple-jump runway and landing pit. It is more economical to construct field event areas at the same time as the track. It is during the design phase that the design team must consider where the field events will be located. Placing the field events in the infield of the track may facilitate spectator viewing but may mean more traffic over the runways.

Planning the Indoor Track

Location Considerations

Designing the new facility from scratch can seem like a daunting process. Since deciding on a location can be a daunting process, it is all the more important to establish a set of detailed programmatic objectives and be well aware of the design concepts and philosophies. These will act as a guide as critical decisions are made. Each facility will have different needs; some may be additions to other facilities, and others may be a complete stand-alone facility, but there are some general guidelines to follow in order to generate a successful facility.

A successful facility begins with the assembling of qualified individuals. The construction of the facility is an exchange between facility planners and contractors. Starting with the facility planners, it is key to incorporate all of the management that will be involved with the facility. This may include athletic directors, a college administration, those in charge of the financial backing, and even individuals who will be using the facility. It might also be beneficial to involve experienced professionals outside of the concerned administration. This could mean hiring someone well qualified, but depending on the project, it may be worth the security to have someone with experience to consult the project. In order to ensure that the planner vision comes to fruition, selecting a contractor and construction team with a reputable reputation is essential. Ask for and check numerous references from numerous contractors before reaching a decision. Maintain a solid relationship with the project supervisor and constantly review architectural drawings and process steps along the way.

Another crucial planning consideration is developing a realistic schedule and checklist for project completion. Making the checklist as detailed as possible will be a great aid during the process, especially as many tasks may be in progress at the same time. For the indoor track and field facility, weather is not the main issue. Available land to support the full building will be the most critical variable facility planners will face.

General Plan Considerations

Many challenges exist for the indoor track and field facility planner. When considering strictly track and field purposes, one of the biggest obstacles is organizing all events and traffic flow to coexist without obstruction. This means an incredible attention to facility layout including plenty of space for equipment storage. This would be hard enough without the fact that most indoor track facilities are field houses shared with other sports. Coordinating the space to function for more than one sport adds additional issues and usually additional headaches. The design of the entire facility needs to be studied to allow adequate safety, based on the amount of land available, and planned from the meet management perspective—how all events will be run efficiently. This may require tradeoffs, with an understanding that if a greater number of events need to overlap in areas, the scheduling and length of meets will be affected.

Indoor venues pose a number of safety issues, such as the heights of ceilings and any hangings, projections from walls, nearness of walls to event locations and placement of throwing nets. Typically, the pole vaults are laid out in the center of the infield, or below the ceiling's highest point, to provide enough clearance. Other uses such as football or volleyball may require their own ceiling specifications, which must be considered in the context of field events. To function for track and field, the facility must be able to accommodate a 200m track complete with safety zones behind the starting line and beyond the finish line. There must be a minimum of 3m clear distance behind the starting line, and a minimum of 10m beyond the finish line, although 20m is the recommendation. The indoor throwing events present a problem because of the necessary space required and safety issues. To that end, many colleges and universities plan dedicated throwing areas outside the infield as part of their field houses. Typically, the throwing area is a double-height space in the range of 3,000 square feet that opens to the larger volume and may be separated with a fence for spectator safety.

Indoor weight throw/shot put area.

Merging Concepts

While planning the indoor and outdoor track and field facilities, two concepts merge: maximization and minimization. When constructing the site, the director of the project must maximize the use of the space with a clean organization of facility components and also must maximize the aesthetics of the facility. The project director must also minimize safety concerns and liability. Through each stage of the facility planning, keeping these concepts in mind will prevent mistakes in the plan and eventual construction. This will be a difficult task with the constraints of the land available.

Specifics for Outdoor Facility Components

Within the outdoor track and field facility are many different types of components that are very different and have very different uses, but at the same time, must coordinate and fit together in the specified space. It is important to have a full understanding of each of the components necessary to hold the track meet before constructing the facility. The next step after construction is correctly marking the facility with lines, flags, and circles where necessary. This section of the chapter will discuss these aspects of the outdoor track and field facility.

The Outdoor Running Track

When beginning to understand the precise measurements for the outdoor track facility, it is important to first dedicate the project to the metric system. For the facility to be considered official and to comply with NCAA rules, all measurements must be in metric. All measurements included in this section are from the *2009 Men's & Women's Cross Country & Track & Field Rules*. The measurements given are minimums to hold an intercollegiate track meet.

The standard outdoor running track should be 400m in length and no less than 6.42 meters in width in a circular shape with two parallel straights and two semicircular curves of equal design. The track should be bordered on the inside by a rounded curb of suitable material such as concrete, wood or aluminum approximately 5cm in height and a minimum of 5cm in width. The track must hold at least six hurdle lanes of 1.07m each marked by white lines 5cm wide numbered starting with lane one on the innermost section of the track. Lanes should be of the same width, at least 1.067m wide to accommodate hurdles; this measurement includes the white line to the right. The maximum width is 1.22m. (NCAA, 2009)

It is obviously important for race distances on the track to be exact. Lane one, and all race distances not run in lanes should be measured 30cm outward from the inner edge of the track when a regulation curb is included; when a curb is not in place, lane one should be measured 20cm from the left-hand lane line. A curb or cones, however, must be in place for race times to be official championship qualifying and also international and national record-setting times. Races run strictly on a straightaway should be measured in a straight line from start to finish. For races run in lanes around the track one or multiple times, the distance to be run in each lane should be measured 20cm from the outer edge of the lane line that is on the runner's left. This does not include lane one, which has already been specified earlier (NCAA, 2009).

The colored markings used on the track are there for a reason: to standardize tracks internationally. The following is the official color code for both the outdoor and indoor track facilities:

- Starting line (white): 55/60m, 55-/60-m hurdles, 100m, 100-/110-m hurdles, 200m, 300m, 400m, 1500m, mile, 3000m, steeplechase, 5000m, 10,000m
- Starting line (white with green insert): 800m, one-turn stagger
- Starting line (white with red insert): 800m relay, four-turn stagger
- Starting line (white with blue insert): 1600m relay, three-turn stagger
- Multiple waterfall starting lines (white)
- Finish line (white): all races
- Relay exchange zones: 400m relay (yellow), 800m relay (red), 1600m relay (blue)
- Hurdle locations: 100m (yellow), 110m (blue), 400m (green), steeplechase (black)
- Break line (green)

Visible Starting Line and Finish Line

The visible starting line, 5.08 centimeters (two inches) wide, is marked on the track just within the measured distance so that its near edge is identical with the exactly measured and true starting line. The starting line for all races not run in lanes (except the 800 meters) is curved so that all competitors run the same distance going into the curve (Figure 21.1).

The visible finish line, 5.08 centimeters (two inches) wide, is marked on the track just outside the measured distance so that its edge nearer that start is identical with the exactly measured and true finish line. Lane numbers of reasonable size should be placed at least 15.24 centimeters (six inches) beyond the common finish line and positioned to face the timing device. The intersection of each lane line and the finish line is painted black in accordance with Figure 21.2. Finally, a common finish line is recommended for all races. Lines in the finish area should be kept to a minimum. If additional lines are necessary, they should be of a less conspicuous color than the finish line so as not to cause confusion.

Figure 21.1
Track Measurements

Figure 21.2
Finish-Line Intersections

The break line will be the mark designating the point in the 800m race and second leg of the 1600m relay when athletes will be able to leave starting lanes and run in the innermost lane for the remainder of the race. This line should also be 5cm and will arc to ensure that each athlete in each lane will travel the same distance to the innermost lane. The line will be positioned at the entry of the back straightaway.

Relays involve baton exchanges within certain zones. To delegate these zones, the proper track markings are needed. The baton exchange must occur within a 20m zone; lines must be drawn 10m on each side of the measured centerline. In some cases, track designers will further designate the limits of the zone with boxes or triangles. These also must exist within the 20m zone. For races that allow for an international zone, a short mark 10m before the passing zone will designate the position on the track where runners can begin running before receiving the baton in 20m relay zone.

The unique event coined the steeplechase presents a challenge to track and field project managers (Figure 21.3). The standard distance for the steeplechase is 3,000 meters with 28 hurdle jumps and seven water jumps. The water jump should be

**The Water Jump at
Indiana State University**

the fourth jump in each lap. If necessary, the finish line should be moved to accommodate this rule. The following measurements are given as a guide and lengthening or shortening the distance at the starting point of the race shall make any adjustments necessary. The chart below assumes that a lap of 400 meters or 440 yards has been shortened 10 meters by constructing the water jump inside the track. If possible, the approach to and exit from the water-jump hurdle should be straight for approximately 7 m.

The hurdles, including the water jump, should be placed on the track so that 30 centimeters of the top bar measured from the inside edge of the track will be inside the track. It is recommended that the first hurdle be at least 5m in width, and that all hurdles weigh at least 80 kilograms.

The water jump should be 3.66 m in length and width. The water should be a minimum of 70 m in depth immediately after the hurdle and the pit should have a constant upward slope from a point 30 cm past the water-jump hurdle to the level of the track at the far end. It is recommended that the water jump be placed on the inside of the track. The landing surface inside the water jump should be composed of a nonskid, shock-absorbent material. The area between the vertical uprights of the water-jump hurdle should be sealed with a solid, rigid material or lattice work to provide safety and to aid the athlete with depth perception. A water source needs to be installed to fill the water jump and a drain installed to drain the water jump after use.

Outdoor Jumping Facilities

High Jump

It is recommended that the approach be an octagon or square with a surface of at least 21 m. The minimum length provided should be 15 m. The length of the approach run is unlimited. The takeoff area is the semicircle enclosed by a 3m radius whose center point is directly under the

Figure 21.3
Steeplechase Hurdles

Hurdle

Hurdle

Water jump hurdle

center of the crossbar. For a record to be approved officially, no point within this area may be higher than the tolerances.

Pole Vault

The pole vault event requires two components that must be built-in fixtures of the track and field facility: the vaulting box and the runway. The vaulting box is where the pole-vaulting athlete plants the pole to jump. It should be constructed of wood, metal, or other suitable sturdy materials and also should be painted white so that it is noticeable from the runway. The box should also be immovable and all of its upper edges should remain flush with the take off area. The angle between the bottom of the box and the stopboard should be 105 degrees (Figure 21.4).

The vaulting runway should have a minimum length of 40m with a width of 1.22m (Figure 21.5). The runway also needs to be marked. The full length of the runway may be permanently marked with lines on or touching the edge that are no more than 2cm wide by 5cm long to indicate the distance from the back of the vaulting box. The center of the runway should be marked with seven permanent lines. Each line is 5cm in width and 30cm from an adjacent line. Each short line is 30cm in length. The long line should be 90cm in length and centered with three short lines on either side. The distance from the edge of the long line furthest from the landing pit to the point where

the back of the vaulting box meets the runway is 3.70m. (NCAA, 2009).

Long Jump and Triple Jump

The long-jump and triple-jump events can be run on the same runway and landing pit, although track facilities usually have two jump runways with pits at either end of both runways to accommodate the wind. The minimum length for the runway for both events should be 40m from the edge nearest the pit of each event's takeoff board and the runway material should extend past the takeoff board into the beginning of the pit. Runway width should be 1.22m. If the runway blends with the general track background, the runway should be bordered by lines 5cm in width from the start of the nearer edge of the landing pit. Markers no more than 2cm wide and 5cm long may be permanently displayed on the runway to indicate the distance from the foul line. An important piece of the runway is the takeoff board (Figure 21.6). The board should be a rigid material, for example, wood. The board should be 20cm wide, 1.22m long at minimum, and no more than 10cm thick. The board should also be level with the runway surface and distinguishable from the runway, painted white. In the absence of a takeoff board, the takeoff area should be the same dimensions as a board and also distinguishable (NCAA, 2009).

The landing area should be no less than 2.75 or more than 3m in width, and filled with damp

Figure 21.4
Pole Vault Box

Figure 21.5
Pole Vault Runway Markings

sand leveled with the takeoff board (Figure 21.7). This next point concerning the distance between the takeoff board and the nearest edge of the landing area or pit is where the two events will differ. For long jump, the distance should be no less than 1m and no greater than 3m. For triple jump, the distance should be at least 11m from the foul line for men and 8.5m for women. Distances of 12.5m and 11m are recommended. Also for the long jump, the distance between the foul line and the farther edge of the landing area should be at least 10m (NCAA, 2009).

Outdoor Throwing Facilities

The outdoor track and field events include shot put, discus, hammer, and the javelin. The shot put, discus, and hammer are thrown out of circles of various sizes, while the javelin is thrown from a runway. Within each throwing event area construction are similarities and then specific differences corresponding to each event. This section will discuss similarities like the circle and the sector, and then describe the details unique to each event construction.

The Circle

As stated previously, three of the four outdoor throwing events are contested from a circle. The circles are very similar in construction, so it is important to begin the throwing facility assembly discussion with the circle. The actual circle or boundary encasing the throwing area should be made of a band of metal or suitable material 6mm in thickness and 19 (+/-6) mm in height; the outside of the circle should be flush with concrete. The interior of the circle should be of concrete or similar material and should be 19 (+/-6) mm lower than the surface outside the circle. The inside diameters of the shot put and hammer throw circles should be 2.135 (+/- 0.005) m and the diameter of the discus circle should be 2.500 (+/- 0.005) m.

The Sector

Throws made in competition are only valid or legal throws if they land within a specified sector. If the throws land outside the sector, they do not count for the competition. The rules for NCAA throwing events stipulate that the sector will be specified by radial lines 5 cm in width forming a

Figure 21.6
Long Jump and Triple Jump Takeoff Board and Foul Marker

Figure 21.7
Control of the Sand Level in Long Jump and Triple Jump

34.92-degree angle extended from the center of the circle. The inside edge of the lines will mark the sector. For the discus and the hammer-throwing events, sector flags should be available to mark the ends of the lines and the sector shall be centered within the enclosure. The level of the surface within the landing area should be the same as the level of the surface of the throwing circle.

Shot Put

One particular aspect of shot putting that is different from all other throwing events is the stopboard, commonly referred to as the "toeboard." The stopboard is an arc made of wood or other rigid materials. It should be painted white and firmly fixed so that its inner edge coincides with the inner edge of the shot put circle. The measurements are as follows: 1.21 (+/- 0.01) m in length along the chord between the endpoints, 112 mm and increasing to 300 mm in width, and 100 (+/- 2) mm in height (Figure 21.9).

Hammer and Discus Areas

The circles and sectors for these throwing events have been discussed (Figure 21.12). Because these events involve throwing weighted imple-

Figure 21.8
Establishing the Sector

a (meters)	b (meters)
5	3
10	6
15	9
20	12
25	15
50	30
75	45

ments a long distance, safety is a critical issue. As stated previously, sector flags will mark the end of the throwing and landing areas, encouraging spectators and passing athletes, coaches, and officials to be aware of staying beyond the sector boundaries. A cage-like structure surrounding the circle is set up to keep hammers and discs that are released in directions outside the sector from hitting anyone standing near the circle area or outside the sector boundaries.

The cage should be centered around the circle, while the sector should be centered on the

Figure 21.9
The Shot Put Circle

non-movable cage. The specifications for a discus ring and cage are listed in Figure 21.10 and 21.11.

The IAAF has recently passed new rules for the construction of hammer cages that will dramatically reduce the danger zone for hammer throwing. The IAAF considered the need for new cage designs to be urgent; past specifications did not provide enough safety. The problem with earlier hammer cage specifications and design is that implements could still land on the track front and back straight away even when the cage gates were operated correctly. In the new design modifications were made to augment safety by increasing the length (3.2m) and height (10m) of the gates as well as decreasing the opening between the front posts (8m) to accommodate the new throwing sector of 34.92 degrees. But keep in mind the NCAA specifications for hammer cages are different than the IAAF. The NCAA recommendations are far below the IAAF standards for safety.

The following are NCAA specifications for the hammer or discus cage thrown either outside the

Figure 21.10
The Discus Ring

stadium or thrown inside the stadium while other events are in progress:

- The throwing circle shall be surrounded by a cage made with suitable material, hung from and between rigid posts, sufficient to withstand and absorb an impact from the implement so that the implement will not escape over or through, and to reduce the possibility of the implement ricocheting or rebounding back toward the competitor. The purpose of the cage is to contain, but not interfere with, the flight path of the implement.
- Rigid posts, approximately six in number, positioned in line with and to the rear of the front edge of the throwing circle, should be approxi-

Figure 21.11
The Discus Cage

mately 4m from the center of the circle and allow for panels of suitable material between 2.74m and 2.90m in width that are at least 3.50m from the center of the circle. The height of these panels for the hammer shall be at least 5m.
- Panels of suitable material between 2.74m and 2.90m in width and at least 6.15m in height, should be hung between each of the two rigid posts in line with the front edge of the throwing circle and each of the two additional rigid posts toward the throwing sector that are not less than 2.85m away from the sector line. The location of these posts will be approximately 6m from the center of the throwing circle and provide a total fixed cage opening of between 8m and 9m.
- When used for throwing the hammer, movable panels of suitable material not less than 4.20m in length and not less than 6.15m in height, should be affixed to the rigid posts furthest from the circle toward the landing area. For a right-handed thrower (counter-clockwise throwing rotation),

The NCAA hammer cage

Figure 21.12
The Hammer Circle

the right movable panel is to be open so that it is parallel to the sector line on the right side and maintains the minimum 2.85-meter distance from the sector line. For a right-handed thrower, the left movable panel is placed in a position so that its non-pivot end is as perpendicular to the sector line as possible and is not greater than 1.5m into the sector and not less than 6m away from the center of the circle. For a left-handed thrower (clockwise throwing rotation), the movable panel configuration is reversed.

Even with the cage, spectators, officials, coaches, and athletes should be warned that they are not completely protected. The height of the panels surrounding the cage should be increased

whenever possible. If the discus and hammer are contested inside the track while other events are in action, the movable panel that is normally parallel to the sector line should be positioned closer to the sector line. Changes to the cage positioning that differ from the minimum requirements should be agreed upon by all participating coaches (Figure 21.13).

Figure 21.13
Construction of the Hammer Cage

Screen	Width	Height
(a)	2.74m	5m
(b)	2.74m	6.15m
(c)	4.35m	6.15m

Figure 21.14
The Javelin Runway

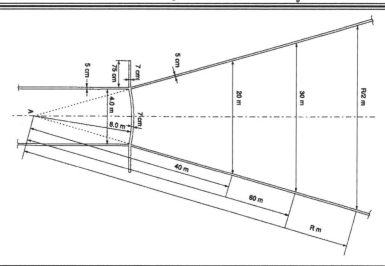

Javelin

The javelin event defies the norm of throwing events. It is thrown from a running start on a runway, and the competitor must stay behind the foul line for the completion of the throw instead of remaining in a circle. Throwing into a sector to mark fair throws is a part of the javelin throw, but where the sector begins differs from the other throwing events. The runway should be a minimum of 33.5m and a maximum of 36.5m in length, marked by two parallel white lines 5cm in width (Figure 21.14). The width of the runway should be 4m from the inside of each white line. If artificial material is used for the construction of the runway, it is important for the runway to extend at least 1m beyond the competition foul line. The foul line should be a 7cm-wide white line in the shape of an arc drawn with a radius of 8m. The distance between its extremities should be 4m, measured straight across from end to end. At right angles to the parallel lines marking the runway, lines 75cm in length and 7cm wide should be drawn from the extremities. The sector angle, sector line width and sector color are the same as the other throwing events but will be drawn from the middle of the imaginary circle created by the arc of the foul line. Because the javelin is a long-range event, flags should mark the end of the sector.

Combining Hammer and Discus Circles in Limited Space

Finding enough field space to hold the sectors for all throwing events may pose a challenge depending on the location of the track facility. The hammer throw and discus event require large landing sectors and both are thrown from circles; it makes sense to combine the two throwing areas into one. The problem with this idea is that the circles for both events are different sizes. The solution is an insert to convert a throwing circle from a 2.5-m diameter to a 2.135-m diameter. This insert should be metal or a suitable rigid material and be flush with the throwing surface. The height of the insert should be 19 (+ /-6) mm. Although rubber inserts are available and easier to manipulate, this material is not rigid enough.

Other Structures/Facilities: Finish Line Towers/Press Box

Towers

The finish line is the control center for running events. The finish line tower should be directly across from the finish line. There should be up to three towers on a track, one at either end of the straightaway, and another diagonally across from the main tower at the 200-meter start position.

Tower A should be a two-story enclosed structure, 20 feet by 40 feet square with eight-foot ceilings and a roof designed as a deck with railings. The first-floor area will contain space for restrooms,

The University of Florida Press Box and Spectator Seating Area

a storage area (for hurdles, etc.) with a small roll-up door, and concessions. The second floor will have picture windows facing the finish line. The second floor area will have space for the press, announcer, and the automatic timer, computers, and cameras.

Tower B will be a duplicate of Tower A except the first floor will be dedicated to the storage of hurdles, implements, and pads. The first-floor storage area will have a large roll-up door to accommodate the large landing pads. Both towers should have hot and cold water, sewer connection, communications lines (i.e., telephone, computer, and television), electricity, and appropriate ventilation.

Lighting

The track and field area should be lighted for security at a minimum, but serious consideration should be given to lighting the area for evening competition.

Fencing

The entire facility should be fenced so it can be secured when not in use. The fence should be at least eight feet high, plastic or vinyl coated, and painted to match the surrounding paint patterns. The fence should have gates in appropriate locations for entrance of athletes, officials, spectators, and maintenance vehicles.

Fences need to be installed to protect athletes and officials from throwing areas (e.g., discus, hammer, and javelin). These fences need to be at least six feet high. They should also be constructed with plastic- or vinyl-coated material.

Spectator Seating

Spectator seating is a necessity. The planners should design seating for both sides of the track. The running track will have two finish lines going in opposite directions. Depending on the prevailing wind, a decision will be made as to which direction the races will be run. Therefore, it is necessary to provide seating on both sides of the track for spectators. (See Chapter 12 for standards relative to new bleachers or retrofitting old bleachers.)

The total number of seats should be based on historical data regarding spectator involvement over the past five years. The seating can either be permanent; constructed of metal, wood, or other appropriate materials; or be portable aluminum bleachers. The higher the bleachers, the greater the liability concerns. If money is not a problem, construct concrete seating large enough to incorporate storage areas underneath the seats and a press box on the upper level.

Starting System

Modern timing systems are connected to the starter's gun. Therefore, the hard wiring that is required should be placed underground and junction boxes made available at the various starting lines for the races. These junction boxes should be at least four feet off the ground with a storage container for cable to be used by the starter crew.

Landscaping

There should be an irrigation system designed to provide water to all grass areas, shrubbery, and flowers. When planning the irrigation system, careful consideration needs to be given to providing additional water to drinking fountains throughout the complex and water for the water jump. The track and field area should be large enough to provide at least a half-acre of shaded area for athletes between events spread around the facility. The areas at the ends of the straightaways should have trees to provide a wind break for the athletes.

Track and Field Equipment

Starting Blocks

Starting blocks must be made without devices that could provide artificial aid in starting. They may be adjustable but must be constructed entirely of rigid materials.

Hurdles

Hurdles should be constructed of metal, wood, or other suitable material. The hurdles should consist of two bases and two uprights supporting a rectangular frame reinforced by one or more crossbars. The top crossbar should be wood or other suitable material with beveled edges and a height of 70 millimeters (2.76 inches). The center of the crossbar should be directly over the end of the base. The surface facing the starting line should be white in color with two vertical or diagonal stripes. A center chevron should be added to help contestants determine the center of the lane (see Figure 21.15) (NCAA, 2009).

Pull-over force refers to the 3.6 kilograms (eight pounds) of steady pulling force required to overturn a hurdle when applied to the center of the uppermost edge of the top crossbar and in the direction of the finish line. If the weights cannot be adjusted to the required overturning force, it is recommended that the next greater setting be used, since records will not be allowed when the overturning force or the weight of the hurdle is less than the required minimum (NCAA, 2009).

When no definite counterweight setting for intermediate hurdles has been made by the manufacturer, it is sometimes possible to attain the correct adjustment by setting one weight as for the 106.7-centimeter (42-inch) height and the other weight as for 76.2-centimeter (30-inch) height. A difference of three millimeters (0.12 inch) above or below the required height will be tolerated (NCAA, 2009).

Steeplechase Hurdles

Hurdles should be constructed of metal, wood, or other suitable material. The hurdles

Figure 21.15
The Hurdle

shall consist of a base and two uprights supporting a rectangular frame with a single crossbar. The crossbar shall be of wood or other suitable material without sharp edges or with a 6.35 millimeter (0.25 inch) bevel and have a height of 127 millimeters (5 inch) square. The crossbar shall be white in color with stripes of one distinctive contrasting color. The ends of the crossbar shall be smooth and not be covered with rubber or any other material that has the effect of increasing the friction between the surface of the crossbar and the supports. The diameter of the crossbar must be at least 29 millimeters but not more than 31 millimeters (1.14 to 1.22 inches). The crossbar should be between 4.48 and 4.52 meters (14.7 to 14.83 feet) in length. The maximum weight shall be 2.25 kilograms (4.96 pounds). For the purpose of placing the bar on the supports of the uprights, the ends of the crossbar should be constructed in such a way that a flat surface of 29 to 35 millimeters (1.14 to 1.38 inches) by 200 millimeters (7.87 inches) is provided (NCAA, 2009).

Other Accessory Equipment

The following pieces of equipment will be very useful for both indoor and outdoor track and field facilities (NCAA, 2009):

- pole vault standards base protection pads
- countdown timer
- wind gauge—now required for all collegiate 100, 200, 110, 110 hurdles, long jump, and high jump
- implement certification unit
- aluminum water jump
- foundation tray
- blanking lid
- take-off board with plasticine insert
- long jump/triple jump aluminum pit covers
- throwing rings
- toe boards
- concentric circles
- stainless steel or aluminum pole-vault box
- pole-vault covers

- finish post
- aluminum track curbing
- rotating track gate
- hammer cage
- discus cage
- indoor throwing event cage
- lane markers
- distance marker boxes
- long jump/triple jump distance indicator
- performance boards
- lap counter
- wind display
- awards stand
- judge's stand
- starter's rostrum
- hurdle carts
- platform cart
- starting block caddy
- implement carts—shotput cart, hammer cart, javelin cart, discus cart, combo cart

Specifics for Indoor Facility Components

The indoor track and field facility will follow similar general guidelines as the outdoor track and field facility. Differences, however, exist and make understanding the construction a separate project altogether. Not only is the track indoors, but indoor track and field involves a smaller-sized track involving a separate list of track events and a different set of throwing events.

The Indoor Running Track

The standard NCAA indoor track should be 200m with two horizontal straights and two curves that may be banked. As of January 1, 2004, no track constructed after the date exceeding 300m will be considered an indoor track. The inside radius of the curves on a 200m track should be no less than 18m and no more than 21m. The curves should be bordered by a curb similar to outdoor tracks, 5cm high and 5cm wide. In indoor facilities, the edge of the track may simply be marked with a 5cm white line. Cones at least 15cm high should be placed

The University of Illinois Indoor Track

near the white line to designate the boundaries of the track visually. The cones should be placed at distances not exceeding 2m on the curves and 10m on the straightaways. Tracks, runways, and takeoff areas should be covered with synthetic material or have a wooden surface with uniform resilience where possible. These surfaces should be able to accept 6mm (1/4 in) spikes for synthetic surfaces and 3mm spikes (1/8 in) for wood.

The track should have a minimum of six lanes. Lanes should be separated on both sides by 5cm wide white lines and a minimum of 1.067m and a maximum of 1.22m in width including the white line to the right. The indoor track lanes are numbered in the same way as the outdoor facility with the innermost lane labeled lane one. The intersection of each lane line and the finish line should be painted black. Behind the start line, 3m of space without obstruction is needed. Beyond the finish line, at least 10m of space free of obstruction should be the minimum with a recommended space of at least 20m.

For tracks that are banked on the curves, the angle of banking should not exceed 18 degrees for a 200m track. The angle may vary for different sized tracks. An inclination toward the inside lane shall not exceed 1:1000, and any facility that exceeds this inclination will be considered a banked track.

Other measuring distances and track markings follow the direction of the outdoor facilities. Consult the previous section for color codes, start and finish lines, break lines, relay zones and other particulars. One detail, however, that is not a problem for outdoor facilities, but is a concern for indoor facilities is overhead clearance. From the lowest point of the ceiling including lights and beams, the overhead clearance should be at minimum 9.14m.

Indoor Jumping Facilities

The high jump, triple jump, long jump, and pole vault are all contested indoors as well as outdoors. These events indoors also need the same dimensional requirements as outdoors. Consult the earlier Outdoor Jumping Facilities section depicting the layout for these events.

Indoor Throwing Facilities

The indoor throwing schedule differs greatly from the outdoor throwing schedule. Outdoor throwing events include the shot put, hammer, discus, and javelin, while indoor events consist of two: shot put and the weight throw. The throwing facility (typically because the facility is enclosed indoors there is only one circle), however, will remain similar to the outdoor shot put facilities with a few notable differences.

Shot Put

The requirements for the shot put facility are the same as the outdoor shot put facilities mentioned earlier in the chapter. Because the indoor implements roll farther and faster on the indoor surface, stop barriers should be used at the end of the sector. Stop barriers can be of any suitable height and material and should be placed at least 5m back from the personal best of the farthest thrower in the competition.

Weight Throw

Although the weight throw is specifically an indoor track or winter season event, the event may be contested outside. The event construction should follow the same rules when contested indoors and outdoors. All weight throws should be made from a circle and sector with the same specifications as the indoor shot put event with the exception of the removal of the toe board. The cage surrounding the weight throw event should comply with the safety provisions for the outdoor hammer throw. Differences specific to the weight throw include the rigid posts surrounding the circle and two movable panels at the front of the circle. The rigid posts should allow for panels of suitable material approximately 1.91m in width, at least 3.66m in height and at least 2.5m from the center of the circle. The two movable panels cannot be less than 1.30m in width and at least 3.66m in height. The sector should be about 90 feet long and there should be barriers at the end of the sectors to keep the shot puts and weights from rolling.

Indoor and Outdoor Track Facility Certification

All tracks hosting intercollegiate track meets must be officially surveyed. This certification must be maintained throughout the entire use of the track and is made available upon request of the NCAA. Permanent facilities must be certified after construction and reconstruction while temporary indoor tracks must be surveyed before the first competition of the season. A certification involves the exact measurements for the following facility components:

- Levels of the track, runways, approaches and landing surfaces
- Permanent track measurements
- Start and finish line
- Track lanes
- Baton-passing zones
- Steeplechase water-jump pit
- Hurdle placements
- Throwing surfaces and all sectors (NCAA, 2009)

Cross-country Facility Design

Planning the Course and Course Layout

Properly measuring the cross-country course is paramount; the distance of the course should be measured along the shortest possible route that a runner may take. Men and women cross-country competitors at the collegiate level race at different race lengths. A male cross-country course should be from 8,000m to 10,000m and a female course should be 5,000m. For women and men of the high school age, the race should be 3,000m to 5,000m and 5,000m. If race officials, the games committee, or coaches mutually agree to alter the length of the race, it is within the rules to vary from the specified distances. At the high school level, some variations are found between state associations.

The main concern when considering the course layout is participant safety. Confine the course to fields, woods, and grasslands. Dangerous ascents or descents, undergrowth, deep ditches, and in general, any hindrance detrimental to the contestants must be avoided. Narrow gaps must be no less than 2 and preferably 5m in width for non-championship courses. Obstacles and other hindrances should be avoided for the first 600 to 800m as well as the last 200 to 300m of the race. Championship courses must be at least 10m wide at all points. Continuous traversing of roadways should be avoided. All turns must be gradual.

Marking the Course

The course should also be properly marked so that competitors are easily guided through the course as they compete. The course must be marked clearly by at least two of the following methods presented in order of preference:

- Sign posts not less than seven feet high with large directional arrows on boards fastened to the tops of the posts so that the arrows will be visible plainly at a distance to competitors approaching the posts. The posts must be placed at every point where the course turns, on the side of the direction of the turn, and wherever there is any doubt as to the direction of travel.
- A single white or colored line for directional purposes only—not to be assumed as the measured line or two lines that mark the outside borders of the course, one on the measured course marking its shortest perimeter and the second such that runners cannot vary from the proper course. In addition, these two lines serve as restraining lines for spectators. Lines on the turns must vary in color from the color of lines approaching the turn.
- Flags, sign posts, or stakes that meet the following conditions:
    —markers at least seven feet above the ground level
    —a turn to the left marked by a red flag or arrow of direction on a sign post or stake
    —a turn to the right marked by a yellow flag or arrow of direction on a sign post or stake
    —a course continuing straight marked by a blue flag or arrow of direction on a sign post or stake
    —all flags, sign posts, or stakes marking the shortest perimeter of the course

Finally, all of the above course-marking devices must be placed on the edge of the measured line when lines and flags, sign posts, or stakes are used to mark the course.

The Start Area

In cross country, many competitors and full teams may be competing at the same time. The starting area for a championship course should be wide enough for at least 50 teams. The area should be flat and well drained. At either side of the starting line there should be permanent elevated (eight to 10 feet high) recall starter stands with steps to the platform and a roof over the platform to protect the recall starter during inclement weather. The lower portion of the platform should be enclosed and used as a storage area. Two more stands should be constructed across from each other at the 100-meter mark for the second set of recall starters, and one more at the 200-meter mark. Finally, the starter should be on a raised platform in the center, 100 meters from the start line. The platform should be covered in case of inclement weather. There should be a public address system attached to the platform. The platform should be at least six feet tall and padded to protect runners.

Figure 21.16
LaVern Gibson Championship Cross-Country Course

LaVERN GIBSON CHAMPIONSHIP CROSS COUNTRY COURSE

at the Bird-Gibson Recreational Facility
Terre Haute, Indiana

Women's 5K Race -- Start to 'Inner Loop 1"
to 'Inner Loop 2" past start to Finish Line.

Men's 10K Race -- Two 5K loops plus "Inner Loop 3"
past start to Finish Line.

There should be a fence (six to eight feet high) at the end of the starting area to separate the runners from the spectators. Behind the fence should be the official staging area for the athletes and portable toilets. An elevated permanent starter stand should be located in the center of the course. The tower should be equipped with a public address system and communications system to the finish line. The stand platform should be at least eight feet high with a ladder for the starter to climb to reach the platform.

Track press box and control center, Indiana State University.

The Finish Area

The finish area for a championship course should have an arched entrance with a digital clock embedded into the arch. The finish area should also be 15 to 20 feet wide with a face (six feet) along each side. The fenced area should extend for at least 30 yards. The actual finish line should be a concrete pad (20 by 20 feet) on which the timing pads can be placed. Directly adjacent to the concrete pad should be a timing booth to house the timing equipment and personnel. This booth should be covered to protect the equipment from inclement weather conditions. The booth area should have communication linkages to the starter tower and electricity. The final 300m of the course should have fencing (six feet) along both sides to keep spectators off the course as the athletes finish. This fencing may stretch from the starting area to the finish area if the course overlaps these two areas.

Control Center Building

The control center building for a championship course is used as a press box and for spectator seating. The building will be a two-story structure near the finish line. The lower portion of the building should be enclosed and used for storage of equipment, mowing equipment and utility vehicles. The second story will be the press box area. Above the press box will be spectator seating. The press box should be complete with electricity, heating, and communication linkages to the finish and starting lines.

Photo by Meghan Rosselli   *Photo by Meghan Rosselli*

Cross-country control center, Indiana State University

DESIGNING FACILITIES FOR K-12 HEALTH, PHYSICAL EDUCATION, AND DRIVER EDUCATION

22

Thomas H. Sawyer, Indiana State University

In a public school building, the unit of primary importance is the room or space where teaching occurs. All other parts of the school plant are, in a real sense, secondary. In physical education, therefore, the determination of the number and character of the teaching stations is basic to the planning process. Further, it is important to locate these facilities in a separate wing for a number of reasons, including, but not limited to, noise, evening and weekend use, and non-school-sponsored uses.

The term "teaching station" is used to identify any room or space where one teacher can instruct or supervise the learning experience of a class or group of students. For instance, a gymnasium would constitute a teaching station and, if divided, could provide two or more teaching stations. Swimming pools, auxiliary physical education teaching stations, and dance rooms are examples of other types of teaching stations. The number of students accommodated by a teaching station is controlled by the nature of the specific activity, the size of the facility, whether the facility is indoors or out, and accessibility concerns.

The number of teaching stations required is dictated by enrollment, policies pertaining to instructional physical education, average class size, diversity of program, number of periods in the school day, and other uses of the facilities.

Folding partitions and combinations of vinyl and mesh curtains can be effectively used for flexibility and to increase the number of teaching stations.

Planners should be aware that indoor facilities for physical education, athletics, and recreation are difficult and costly to expand at some future date. School planners should know the peak enrollment potential for each space. The anticipated enrollment five to 10 years after completion of construction should serve as a basis for determining the required number of original teaching stations. Long-range planning is imperative to provide for the logical and most economical expansion. The initial design should make provisions for the anticipated construction.

Common Planning Considerations

There are a number of common planning considerations for physical education facilities in public and private schools (see Chapters 1 and 2). These common planning considerations include surface materials (i.e., ceilings, floors, and walls), sound control and acoustics, electrical systems and service, climate control, security, climbing walls, ropes and cargo nets, storage, shower and dressing rooms, folding partitions or curtains, and office space for physical education teachers. Each of these common planning considerations is discussed in detail in the following pages.

Surface Materials

The selection of indoor surface materials for ceilings, floors, and walls becomes complicated because indoor facilities will be subject to hard usage, excessive moisture, and multiple uses. These surfaces must meet minimum standards in terms of acoustical and light-reflecting properties. Geographic location and the availability of certain surface materials are factors to be considered as well. (See Chapter 8 for greater details on indoor surfaces).

Floor Surfaces

The best floor surface to use may depend upon the number of different teaching areas. The main gymnasium area should have either a hardwood or synthetic surface. Wood, preferably maple, is an excellent all-around surface, although it lacks the durability and flexibility that might be demanded by extensive community use of the facility. Synthetic surfaces have proven excellent for all normal game-type activities and also can better accommodate events that put additional stress on the floor such as setting up chairs, tables, booths, and the like. In an auxiliary teaching station, carpeting is often used but not recommend due to the low coefficient of slippage, which increases the chances of joint injury when quick movements are attempted (e.g., knee and ankle). Tile is also not recommended as a play surface due to the high co-efficient of slippage and the lack of adequate resiliency, which increases the chances of joint injury (e.g., knees and hips).

There are at least three distinct types of floor surfacing (e.g., hardwood, resilient synthetic, or common surfaces such as tile, ceramic tile, or rug) required in facilities described in this chapter. Floors in service areas such as locker rooms, shower rooms, toweling rooms, and toilet rooms require a surface impervious to moisture (e.g., concrete or ceramic tile). Classroom, corridor, and office areas may be grouped together for common surfacing (e.g., tile or rug).

Special activity areas require different treatments. For example, a dance gymnasium that is used for instruction in modern dance should have a finished treatment, which will allow dancers to slide or glide across the floor (see Appendix T for greater details on dance areas). In other areas, such as basketball courts, the finish should be of a nonslip nature. Careful consideration should also be given to the location of lines for various activities and floor plates for standards or gymnastic equipment.

Flexibility, durability, and cost are three criteria that have been instrumental in seeing synthetic surfaces challenge hardwood floors for installation in activity areas. The most popular synthetic surfacing materials can be classed into two types: plasticized polyvinyl chlorides (PVCs) and polyurethanes. The PVCs are primarily prefabricated, while the polyurethanes are either poured in place or produced in factory-prefabricated sheets that are adhered down on the site. In general, the polyurethanes possess most of the desirable characteristics sought in a floor surface.

Walls

In addition to segregating specific areas, walls should serve as barriers to sound, light, heat, and moisture. In selecting wall surfacing, considerations should be given to the acoustical properties of the material. In general, moisture-resistant walls with good acoustical properties are recommended. Most modern gymnasiums have smooth surfaces on the lower portion of the walls so they may be used as rebound surfaces. Rough-surfaced walls collect dirt easily and are difficult to clean. Recently, there has been a trend to use color, murals, and graphics to add aesthetic appeal. However, in the elementary gymnasium, the need for walls to hold paper, posters, and/or decals should be considered as well.

In locker rooms, shower rooms, and toilet rooms where high humidity is often present, it is important to select wall surfacing that is moisture-resistant and has good acoustical properties. Walls serving as barriers between toilet rooms, handball courts, squash courts, and other areas where noise is a problem should have a minimum of sound transmission.

Ceilings

Roof design, type of activity, and local building codes should determine the ceiling construction. Ceilings should be insulated to prevent condensation and should be painted to provide pleasing aesthetics and to enhance light reflection. Acoustical ceiling materials are desirable in instructional and activity areas. Dropped ceiling panels susceptible to damage by objects or individuals will require considerable maintenance. False ceilings with catwalks above them have been effectively designed to permit maintenance and repair of lighting and ventilating systems.

Sound Control and Acoustics

The sonic, or audible, environment is the most difficult phase of the total environment to balance and requires the services of an acoustical engineer. In each room, attention must be given to reverberation time. This is influenced by the absorption and reflection qualities of all surfaces within the room. Hard surfaces reflect sound and produce excessive unwanted reflection and reverberations. Thus, the space may be "noisy." Soft or absorbable surfaces turn the sound into another form of energy and can produce areas that are too "dead." Therefore, most areas must have some materials with sound-absorbing qualities in order to balance the sonic environment for good hearing conditions.

Sound Insulation

Unwanted sound or noise may be transmitted into the room by means of ventilating ducts, pipes, and spaces around pipe sleeves. The transmission of sound through ducts can be reduced by the use of baffles or by lining the ducts with sound-absorbent, fire-resistant materials. The ducts may also be connected with canvas to interrupt the transmission through the metal in the ducts. Pipes can be covered with pipe covering and spaces in the pipe sleeves can be filled.

Sound can also be transmitted through the walls, floors, and ceilings. This can be reduced to a desirable minimum by the proper structural design and materials. In conventional wall construction, alternate studs can support the sides of the wall in such a manner that there is no through connection from one wall surface to another. This is sometimes known as double-wall construction. The space inside the walls can be filled with sound-absorbing material to further decrease the sound transmission.

Sometimes, three or four inches of sand inside the walls at the baseboard will cut down the transmission appreciably. Likewise, sound-absorption blankets laid over the partitions in suspended ceiling construction can frequently reduce the sound from one room to another.

Machinery vibration or impact sounds can be reduced by use of the proper floor covering and/or by installing the machinery on floating or resilient mountings. "Sound locks," such as double walls or doors, are needed between noisy areas and adjoining quiet areas. Improper location of doors and windows can create noise problems. It is imperative to pay attention to the acoustical treatment of all areas. Gymnasiums, swimming pools, and dressing locker rooms are frequently neglected.

Materials for Acoustical Treatment

Care must be taken in the maintenance of acoustical materials. Oil paint reduces the sound-absorbing qualities of most materials. Surface treatment for different acoustical areas will vary. The most common treatment of acoustical fiber tile is a light brush coat of water-based paint. Most acoustical materials lose their efficiency after several applications of paint.

Electrical Systems and Service

All electrical service, wiring, and connections should be installed in accordance with the requirements of the National Electric Code of the National Board of Fire Underwriters and the state and local building codes and fire regulations. (See Chapter 5 for additional information.)

The capacity of each individual electrical system should be determined accurately for the obvious reasons of safety and economy. Full consideration should be given to present and future program plans when designing the electrical systems. The increasing use of electrically operated equipment, higher standards of illumination, and special audiovisual equipment should be anticipated.

Illumination

In addition to the amount of light in any given area, the quality of light is of equal importance. Providing efficient illumination is complicated and challenging and the services of an illuminating engineer are recommended in order to obtain maximum lighting efficiency. Gymnasiums, classrooms, corridors, and other specific areas have distinct and different lighting requirements. Planning for electric illumination requires that each area be considered relative to the specific use.

Important Lighting Considerations

In addition to the quantity and quality of light from the various kinds of lighting systems available, additional factors to consider in the selection of an electrical illumination system are maintenance, repair, replacement, and cleaning. The ideal lighting fixture has both an indirect and a direct component, throwing surface light on the ceiling to give it about the same brightness as the lighting unit itself.

There is less need, however, to provide high-ceiling areas with direct-indirect fixtures. In gymnasiums, swimming pools, and similar activity areas, an even distribution of light is required to permit the individual to see quickly and distinctly in any part of the room. It is advisable to provide supplementary lighting on such specialized equipment and areas that may be provided in a main or auxiliary gymnasium. Even with careful planning, it is difficult to make adequate provisions without some compromise.

In some activities, such as aquatics, the very nature of the activity necessitates a separate facility. Night lights, sometimes known as safety lights, that burn continually are recommended for gymnasiums, swimming pools, handball courts, squash courts, and other indoor activity areas. Lobbies, corridors, and some classrooms should also be equipped with night lights. These lights are extremely important for safety and security purposes and should have separate controls.

Provisions for outside lighting should be considered. Exit lights must follow the prescribed codes of the local community and the state. Electrically illuminated exit lights clearly indicating the direction to the exterior should be provided over all exit doors from gymnasiums, combined auditorium-gymnasiums, multipurpose rooms, and other areas such as those containing goals or targets. Dimmers should be installed on the lighting in spectator areas. Supplementary light sources should be shielded from the eyes of participants and spectators in order to provide the proper brightness balance.

Transparent, non-breakable plastic protective covers will protect lighting units in activity areas where balls may be thrown. Vapor-proof lighting units are recommended for damp areas such as toilets, showers, the dressing locker suite, and the swimming pool. Locker-room lights should be spaced to the light areas between lockers.

Incandescent, fluorescent, mercury-vapor, sodium-vapor, and metal halide lighting systems are most commonly used in gymnasium buildings. The incandescent light is instantaneous, burns without sound, and is not affected by the number of times the light is turned on or off. Incandescent lights and fixtures are considerably cheaper in initial cost; are easier to change; and the lamp, within limits, may be varied in size within a given fixture.

Incandescent fixtures, however, have excessively high spot brightness and give off considerable heat, which becomes a problem when high levels of illumination are necessary. Fluorescent lamps have the advantage of long life and can be placed over all exit doors from the building and at the head and foot of exit stairways. Emergency (white) lighting systems should be provided for exits (including exterior open spaces to which the exits lead) in gymnasiums, multipurpose rooms, and other places of assembly or large group activity. This lighting should be on a special emergency circuit. All controls should be located so as to be under the supervision of authorized persons and all other aspects of the installation should meet the specifications prescribed by the Underwriters Exits Code and state and local fire laws and regulations.

Artificial Lighting System

A variety of trends in lighting systems have developed in conventional structures. One system utilizes primarily skylights and is supplemented with conventional artificial light. In such a system, a light sensor assesses the light level coming through the skylight in the working area just above the floor.

At this point, the sensor signals that information to the artificial light system to shine from 0 to 100 percent of the wattage capacity depending upon how much light is coming through the skylights. The sensor in this system can raise or lower the intensity of the artificial light to an acceptable and predetermined candle power dependent on the activity. Installation of skylights plus a light sensor system will add an additional construction cost; however, this installation will reward the institution with energy conservation and cost savings. In addition, without the utilization of a light sensor system, a facility's lights would be required to be on full time whenever the building was occupied. Also, a high percentage of the total kilowatt hours used in a facility are conventionally designed for artificial lighting. A skylight and light sensor system will accrue a significant savings in energy cost. Artificial lights also generate considerable heat and, by reducing the amount of artificial light (heat), a skylight and light sensor system would have a significant impact on savings in air-conditioning cost. Such a system has an approximate theoretical saving projected to reduce air-conditioning costs by one-half and lighting costs by one-third.

Fire-Alarm System

Electrical fire-alarm systems should be separate and distinct from all program-signal or other signal systems and should be designed to permit operation from convenient locations in corridors and from areas of unusual fire hazard. All fire-alarm systems should meet the specifications prescribed by the Underwriters Laboratories and by state and local fire laws and regulations.

Program-Signal System

Gymnasium buildings can be wired for a signal system operated by a master clock or push buttons from the main administrative offices. Secondary controls may be placed in other administrative units of the facility. Program signals should be independent of the fire-alarm system and should not be used as a fire-alarm system. Program signals usually include: buzzers or chimes in the classrooms; bells in corridors, pool, gymnasiums, fields, and dressing-locker suites; and large gongs on the outside of the building. In many instances, signals placed strategically in corridors rather than in individual classrooms are adequate. Electric clocks should be included in all indoor areas in the program-signal system.

Services for Appliances and Other Electrical Equipment

There are many needs for electrical wiring and connections, which require careful analysis and planning. The following are illustrative:

- Basic construction: motors to operate folding partitions, blowers for heaters and ventilating ducts, exhaust fans in gymnasium ceilings or walls.
- Custodial and maintenance services: receptacles for floor-cleaning equipment and power tools.
- Dressing locker rooms: wiring for hair and hand dryers and electric shavers.
- Lounges, kitchenettes, snack bars, and concessions: outlets for refrigerators, water or soft drink coolers, electric stoves, blenders, mixers, coffee urns, and hot plates.
- Office suites: wiring for individual air-conditioners, business machines, floor fans, and other mechanical and electrical equipment.
- Laundry rooms: wiring for washers, dryers, and irons.
- Pools: provision for underwater vacuum cleaners, pumps, and special lighting.
- Gymnasiums: provisions for special lighting effects, spotlights, and rheostats or controls to lower the illumination for certain activities.
- Health suites: receptacles and provision for audiometers, vision-testing equipment, floor fans, and air-conditioning units.

Climate Control

The engineering design of heating, systems should be based on the technical data and procedures of the American Society of Heating, Refrigerating and Air-Conditioning Engineers, Inc. The selection of the type of HVAC systems should be made with special consideration for economy of operation, flexibility of control, quietness of operation, and capacity to provide desirable thermal conditions. The design and location of all climate-control equipment should provide for possible future additions.

Since the number of occupants in any given area of the building will vary, special consideration should be given to providing variable controls to supply the proper amount of fresh air and total circulation for maximum occupancy in any one area. Specially designed equipment and controls are necessary to ensure that climate control in some major areas can be regulated and operated independently of the rest of the facility.

All three mechanical systems—heating, ventilating, and air-conditioning—are interrelated and should be planned together. The services of a competent mechanical engineer should be obtained not only for design, but also for making inspections during construction and for giving operating instructions to the service department. Some problems involved in the installation of HVAC systems include:

- maintaining a minimum noise level,
- maintaining separate temperature control for laboratory areas,
- insulating all steam, hot-water, and cold-water pipes and marking them with a color code,
- exhausting dry air through the locker rooms and damp air from the shower room to the outside,
- providing a minimum of four changes of air per hour without drafts,
- installing locking-type thermostats in all areas, with guards wherever they may be subject to damage,
- placing the thermostats for highest efficiency,
- zoning the areas for night and recreational use, and
- eliminating drafts on spectators and participants.

The geographical location of the proposed facility will dictate to some extent the type of climate control equipment selected for installation. Mechanical ventilation is preferred over open windows. Air-conditioning has been strongly recommended for southern climates; however, year-round uses of facilities make air-conditioning a desirable building feature in other areas. Special rooms such as locker rooms, shower rooms, swimming pools, and steam rooms need special consideration for moisture and humidity control.

Security

The athletic and physical education complex presents a unique security problem. The facilities and the programs attract large numbers of individuals who move at all times during the day and week and through many areas in different directions. It is reasonable to believe that all students and visitors who come to the building have a distinct purpose in coming and should be welcome. This is the type of building that people enter through many outside doors and disperse to offices, classrooms, dressing rooms, activity areas, and spectator galleries. There should be some plan for pedestrian control and for the handling of visitors. Security is accomplished in two ways:

- Constructing the facilities according to a plan that allows for maximum security.
- Adopting an administrative plan for the direction and control of all persons using the building.

The physical layout will facilitate security but will not guarantee it. A good administrative plan will help. However, a good administrative plan cannot completely accomplish effective security if the physical layout does not lend itself to the attainment of such security.

Security Features of Construction

Entrance doors constitute the first barriers against illegal intrusion. Open and descending stairways, walled entries, and deep-set entrances should be avoided. The points of entrance to buildings should be well lighted from dusk until dawn. The corners of the buildings should have floodlights that light the face of the structure. So-called vandal lights should be installed and protected to make them vandal-proof.

Corridors, which are continuous and straight, providing unbroken vision, add qualities of safety and security to the building, its contents, and its users. Corridors are best lined up with entrance doors to provide a commanding view of the doorway from the corridor and of the corridor from the entrance door. There should be an attempt to avoid angular corridors and to eliminate niches or cubbyholes. The use of the night lighting within the building and at its entrances will assist in protection against vandalism and other forms of undesirable conduct. Night lighting will require separate wiring and switches in order to maintain a desirable amount of illumination. Switches for such lighting should be key-controlled to prevent their use by unauthorized individuals. A building chart for day and night "on" and "off" lights should be developed. There should be additional directions for "on" and "off" at every switch and such directions should be changed according to need. A key-station system for night watch checking is desirable.

Security of the Building

Securing the building and its component rooms against illegal entry is the first and most logical consideration in terms of building protection. Good door framing, substantial doors, and heavy-duty hardware and locks hold up against wear and abuse. In their long life and securing qualities, they constitute a reasonable investment. In reducing replacement costs for materials and labor, the installation of good hardware is economical in the long run. To reduce loss through breakage and theft, the additional security factor of quality hardware should never be overlooked at any cost.

A Lock-and-Key System

Enlisting the help of experts in the field of building administration will usually result in a plan that considers some of the following features:

- A building master plan including a lock-and-key system.
- The use of electronic locks with cards.

- Lock-tumbler adjustments so that an area may have its own control and authorization.
- Area division (vertical division) by responsibility or usage for key assignment; or "level" division (horizontal division) for key assignment; or a combination of both vertical and horizontal divisions.
- A policy of not lending keys is recommended. The person to whom the key is assigned signs a pledge to not lend it out. The keys for the facilities should be identified by a distinguishing mark, and a policy should be established with key duplicators in the areas that the duplicators will refuse to duplicate keys carrying such identifying marks.
- An annunciator system for outside or other doors of importance such as swimming pool doors.

Climbing Walls, Ropes, and Cargo Nets

The trend for the last decade has been to involve the elementary students in activities that allow them to develop upper-body strength (e.g., climbing walls [fixed and portable], climbing ropes, and cargo nets). The most recent addition to the elementary school gymnasium has been climbing walls and bouldering walls. These walls are either fixed to the gymnasium wall or portable. The fixed versions should have a resilient landing base and a safety rope system to protect the students from falls. See Chapter 27 for a listing of companies and detailed suggestions for construction of a climbing wall.

The traditional rope-climbing activities have not changed in great detail over the years. The important facility and safety issues include how 1) the rope is fixed to the ceiling, 2) the rope is stored when not in use, and 3) the landing base is established under the rope. Climbing ropes should be attached to a height of 24 feet and drop to about three feet above the floor. If the ceiling is placed below the structural members, the locations of suspended equipment should be planned and eye bolts provided during construction. Ropes should be placed five feet apart, allowing one for each five students in class.

Cargo nets are great fun. The greatest concerns focus on how they are secured to the ceiling or wall and the landing base provided. The landing base should include either a landing pad, similar to those used in the jumping events in track and field, or a specially designed pit under the net filled with foam squares.

Storage

Two types of storage rooms are necessary for every physical education facility. The first is the storage of large pieces of equipment needed in the gym, items such as volleyball standards and official stands, gymnastic equipment, chairs, mats and score tables, which, if left around the gym floor, are a safety hazard. This room should have easy access to the gym floor through a roll-up door. The room should be planned to provide for current equipment and future expansion and should be equipped with safety lights in case of power failure.

Storage rooms are needed for each of the different instructional areas. The room adjoining the gymnasium should be at least 1,000 to 1,200 square feet, 10 feet high, equipped with a roll-up door, and should be directly accessible from the gymnasium floor. Consideration must be given to community use of the facility and separately secured storage of related equipment. Ideally, there would be a separate storage room for each of the programs. The storage areas should have adjustable bins, shelves, racks, and hangers for the best utilization of space and the proper care of equipment and supplies. Space to store out-of-season equipment is essential to prevent loss or misplacement between seasons. An outside entrance assists in the handling of equipment that is used outdoors and/or in connection with a summer playground program.

The second type of room needed is for the storage and repair of small equipment and supplies. Special bins, racks, hooks, and nets, with a work bench for making minor repairs, add greatly to the efficiency of the room. Ideally this room should be located near faculty offices.

Shower and Dressing Rooms

Although it has been standard practice not to include shower, locker, and dressing room facilities in the elementary school, such facilities are essential if the gymnasium is to be used for intramural or interscholastic competition and community usage. The size, number of lockers, showers, and toilet facilities will be dependent on the extent of usage. (See Chapter 6 for greater detail on these areas) If swimming pools are added as part of the school-community complex, such facilities are a must. Provision for outdoor restrooms is desirable if the general public is involved.

Folding Partitions or Curtains

Folding partitions make possible two or more teaching stations in the gymnasium. They should be power-operated, insulated against sound transmission and reverberation, and installed to permit compensation for building settlement. The control should be key-operated. The design and operation must ensure student safety. Partitions should extend from floor to ceiling and may be recessed when folded. Floor tracks should not be used. A pass door should be provided at the end of a partition. When partitions are installed in gymnasiums with open truss construction, the space between the top of the folding doors and the ceiling should be insulated against sound transmission.

Vinyl/mesh combination curtains have become very popular. The curtain is rolled to the ceiling when not in use. The curtains generally are vinyl for the first six feet to eight feet with mesh for the remaining distance to the ceiling. The vinyl comes in a variety of colors.

Office Space for Physical Education Teachers

The office space for physical education teachers should be in close proximity to the gymnasium and locker room areas. It should range from 150 to 250 square feet and include an attached bathroom and shower facility. The office should have an observation window for the gymnasium and outdoor field spaces. Further, the office should be close to or attached to the storage space for the gymnasium. Finally, the office should be designed to include accessibility to a computer and a telephone.

Other General Considerations

It is important for planners to consider other uses of physical education teaching facilities for extracurricular activities for the students and the community in general at the end of the school day. These considerations include:

- Additional space will be necessary if all students are to be given an opportunity to participate in an intramural and/or interscholastic program.
- It is desirable to have such additional special facilities as dance studios (see Appendix T), gymnastics areas, swimming pools (see Chapter 13), and archery ranges in order to expand the offerings of the physical education program. Note: It may be possible for the school to obtain some of these facilities through the cooperative use of existing or proposed facilities owned and administered by some other agency.
- As planning for recreation is considered, the entire school plant becomes a potential space resource and all units should be scrutinized and planned with recreational adaptability in mind.

Specific Planning Considerations for Specific School Buildings

Elementary School

The elementary school is defined as follows for this book—kindergarten through fifth grade. These suggestions are based on input from experienced elementary practitioners and the Council on Physical Education for Children.

Indoor Activity Areas

The elementary school physical education program centers around the teaching of funda-mental movement patterns, rhythmic or dance, fitness activities, games and sports, gymnastic activities, combative, self-testing activities, and aquatics. The design and scope of physical education facilities should reflect the activities included in the elementary physical education curriculum. Additionally, the planners should refer to the National Association for Sport and Physical Education's Council on Physical Education for Children (COPEC) guidelines for facilities, equipment, and instructional materials in elementary physical education (2001). Finally, another good resource for planners is Chapter 33, Facilities, Equipment, and Supplies in Pangrazi and Dauer's *Dynamic Physical Education*.

Physical Education for Elementary School Children

A major consideration fundamental to the planning of an elementary school indoor activity area is the anticipated use by the community. Future years are expected to see more and more community use of these facilities.

Several of the standard planning principles apply particularly to the elementary facility. Such planning principles would include establishing priority use for the facility by giving basic consideration to the primary age group using the facility, allowing for use by children with disabilities, designing for the participants ahead of the spectators, and remembering considerations for maintenance of the facilities.

Location

Elementary schools are often more compact than other schools, and it is desirable to have the activity area apart from the classrooms to reduce noise disturbance. With the increasing use of such facilities by the community, consideration must be given to accessibility from the parking areas. In addition, it should be adjacent to the outdoor play fields. This allows for easier storage of equipment and increases the efficiency of the area to be used as a neighborhood playground in the summer months.

Teaching Stations for Physical Education

Elementary school physical education classes may be organized by a number of methods. The average class size is usually based on the number of pupils in the classroom unit. Because of differences in pupil maturation, physical education periods generally vary from 20 minutes for kindergarten and first grade to 45 minutes for fifth and sixth grades with the school average (for computation purposes) being 30 minutes per class. The formula for computing the number of teaching stations needed for physical education in an elementary school is as follows:

Minimum number of teaching stations equals the number of classroom students times the number of PE periods per week per class (Total number of PE class periods in a school week).

Example:
- Number of classrooms of students: school contains grades K to 6, three classrooms for each grade level, or a total of 21 classroom units.
- Number of physical education periods per week per class: one period per class for physical education each school day during the week equals five periods per week.
- Total number of physical education class periods in a school week: There are five instructional hours in the school day and the length of physical education period is 30 minutes. Thus, a total of ten 30-minute periods each school day may be scheduled for physical education, or a total of 50 periods for the five-day school week.

The teaching station needs would be calculated as follows:

Minimum number of teaching stations equals 21 classroom units times five periods per day, 50 periods per week, equals 105 divided by 50 equals 2.1.

In the above situation, if one classroom section has been dropped each week (bringing the total to 20), then the need would be two teaching stations. Therefore, requiring physical education five periods per week in the school used in the example would necessitate employing two physical education teachers each hour of the day.

In many school systems, the above situation would be too idealistic. More likely, only one physical education instructor would be available (either a specialist, or the classroom teacher, or a paraprofessional in collaboration with one of the other two). This would then drop the number of sessions per week for each classroom unit from 5 to an average of 2.5. One teaching station would handle this setup. If only one teaching station can be provided in the elementary school, then preferably it would be a gymnasium, despite the fact that some other type of auxiliary station might prove superior for instruction in the lower grades. The elementary gymnasium remains the preferred facility because of its heavy use by both the upper grades and the community. If the school system and the community were in need of an indoor swimming pool, this would be the choice for a second teaching station.

The next choice is an auxiliary teaching station, sometimes called a playroom. Particularly when heavy community use is anticipated, another alternative is to build a larger gymnasium and allow for dividing it by a folding partition or vinyl/mesh curtains. Such a setup would provide four possible teaching stations, two on each side of the divider. This area would also allow for two basketball intramural courts, one basketball interscholastic court, three volleyball courts, six badminton courts, and four multi-purpose game circles.

Multipurpose, Cafeteria-Gymnasium Combinations, and Self-Contained Classrooms

Multipurpose rooms and cafeteria-gymnasium combinations have been found to be most impractical for physical education, especially from the standpoint of scheduling. Self-contained classrooms are restrictive in the types of activities that can be offered and have an additional disadvantage. Furniture must be moved whenever activity takes place; but if there is no way to have a separate facility, make sure there is adequate storage space for the tables, chairs, and benches. This storage space should be separate for physical education equipment and for cafeteria equipment. Both spaces should have roll-up doors for ease of transfer of equipment between uses.

If used, such classrooms must provide an unobstructed area of 450 square feet, be of a nonskid surface, have no dangerous projections, and ideally have direct access to an adjoining terrace, part of which should be roofed for protection against rain. These self-contained classrooms would only be used in the lower grades.

The Gymnasium

In planning the elementary school gymnasium, a minimum of 110 to 150 square feet per pupil and a total of at least 4,860 square feet is recommended. Spectator seating (if provided) and storage rooms (ranging in size from 400 to 600 square feet with roll-up doors and a minimum ceiling height of 10 feet) require additional space. Many of the general considerations recommended for secondary school gymnasiums also apply to elementary school facilities.

The specific dimensions of the gymnasium should provide for a basketball court of 42 feet by 74 feet with a minimum safety space of six feet around the perimeter. An area of 54 feet by 90 feet (4,860 square feet) would be adequate. The ceiling should be at least 22 feet high. This space is adequate for activities normally included in the elementary school program and will serve the community recreation program. The gymnasium will be of a larger size if the decision is made to use it as a multiple teaching facility and include a folding partition or vinyl/mesh curtains as part of the design.

Special Floor Markings

The elementary gymnasium floor may have additional markings beyond the traditional game markings (e.g., basketball). These other markings may include, but are not limited to, circles of various sizes and shapes. Floor markings facilitate a variety of activities; however, the number of different markings should be limited to reduce confusion. The dominant lines should intersect the non-dominant lines (e.g., game lines should intersect nongame lines). A non-dominant line should be broken (two inches) prior to intersecting the dominant line and lines should be in different colors.

Buffer/Safety Zones

All playing areas must have buffer/safety zones separating them from walls, bleachers, and adjacent playing areas. The distance should be at least 10 feet (although the NFHS rules stipulation a minimum of three feet but preferably 10 feet, so the range would be three to 10 feet) from the sideline to the nearest obstruction (e.g., wall, bleacher, stage, or adjacent playing area). Facilities without buffer/safety zones around playing areas will expose participants and/or spectators to serious injury.

Auxiliary Teaching Stations

If a second indoor physical education teaching area is built, it should be either a swimming pool or an auxiliary instruction room, sometimes called a playroom. Swimming pools are discussed elsewhere in this text (see Chapter 13). The auxiliary teaching station is most practical when the main gymnasium cannot fulfill all of the school's needs for teaching stations.

At least 80 square feet per primary pupil, with a total minimum of 2,000 square feet of space, is suggested for this unit. A ceiling height of 18 to 22 feet in the clear is preferred, although lower ceilings may be used. One wall should be free of obstruction to be used for target and ball games or throwing practice. A smooth masonry wall will provide an adequate rebounding surface. If included, windows should be of break-proof glass or be protected by a shield or grill and located high enough so as not to restrict activities.

The auxiliary unit should be planned to accommodate limited apparatus and tumbling activities, games of low organization, rhythmic activities, movement exploration, and other activities for the primary grades. Often a 30-foot circle for circle games is located at one end of this room allowing for permanent or semi-permanent equipment at the other end. The equipment could include such items as climbing ropes and poles, ladders, mats, stall bars, rings, large wooden boxes, horizontal bars, and peg boards. These should be located so as not to interfere with other activities or so that they may be easily moved out of the way. A storage room for equipment and supplies should be included. A section of wall can be equipped with hangers for mat storage.

Electrical outlets are required for the use of sound equipment. This room will, for the most part, be used by the lower grades and should be accessible to those classrooms. If the area is to serve the after school recreational program for pupils or community groups, toilet facilities should be accessible.

Use of Playroom

The area should be suitable for preschool and for grades K to 2 or K to 3 for fundamental movement activities including creative games and rhythms, relays, stunts, and climbing and hanging activities.

Size

The area should be a rectangle measuring approximately 50 feet by 40 feet providing 2,000 square feet of space.

Ceiling

The ceiling should be acoustically treated, 18 to 22 feet high (all beams and supports above the minimum height), with suitable fixtures attached to the beams to support hanging equipment.

Walls

Walls below 10 feet should be free from obstruction. A smooth concrete block sealed with epoxy paint works well. Above 10 feet, walls should also be free of obstruction but made of acoustic or slotted concrete block. A wall free from obstruction will provide practice areas for such activities as kicking, striking, and throwing, and a space for the placement of targets and use of visual aids.

Floors

Hardwood maple or synthetic surfaces provide the best floor for general activity use. Both have advantages and disadvantages. The decision should be based on how the floor is to be used. Careful consideration should also be given to the location of lines and the installation of equipment.

Lighting

Fluorescent lighting should supply 35 to 50 foot-candles on the floor and a switch should be installed at each door. Light fixtures should be guarded to prevent breakage.

Windows

If used at all, windows should be placed on only one side of the room to provide natural light. They should be covered with a protective screen. Windowsills should be eight feet above the floor.

Electrical Outlets

Double-service outlets should be installed on each wall.

Equipment Storage Area

At least 400 to 600 square feet should be provided for storage. Cabinets and shelves should be installed. The equipment room should have a double door in order for wide equipment to be moved in or out easily. A telephone for emergency use should be placed in the equipment room.

Mirrors

Three full-length mirrors should be placed at one end of a wall, side by side, for visual analysis of movement.

Bulletin Board

Corkboard should be hung on the wall near the entrance for posting materials and schedules.

Chalkboard

A chalkboard can be wall-mounted to facilitate teaching if this will not interfere with wall-rebounding activities. Otherwise, portable chalkboards can be used.

Drinking Fountain

A drinking fountain should be placed on a wall in the corridor just outside the door to the playroom.

Speakers

Two matched speakers should be placed high on the wall or in the ceiling. A cordless headset with a mike and sound system should be built into a wall.

Paint

Walls should be painted off-white or a very pale color with epoxy paint. However, murals, accent colors, and designs can be used for aesthetics.

Other Items

If the building is equipped with closed-circuit TV, two outlets should be provided for the receiver. There should be a separate entrance for recreational use. The teaching station should be isolated from other parts of the building for evening functions.

Adapted Teaching Station

Local philosophy and state and federal laws vary as to the inclusion of students with disabilities in regular physical education classes. A separate adaptive teaching station would be an ideal setup; however, any special program for such students often has to be accommodated in the regular facilities. (See Chapter 4 for further details.)

Secondary Schools

A secondary school is defined as any of the following for this book—middle school (grades six to eight), junior high school (grades seven and eight), high school (grades 9-12).

Teaching Stations

The type and number of indoor teaching stations for a secondary school depends on the number of students and the specific program of physical education and related activities. In all situations, a gymnasium is required. By determining the number of teaching stations essential for the formal program of instruction, planners will have a basis for calculating other needs. Computation of the minimum numerical requirement is achieved by the following formula:

Minimum number of teaching stations:

700 student times 5 periods per week equals 3,500 Teaching Stations, 30 per class times 30 periods per week equals 900 and 3,500 divided by 900 equals 3.9 teaching stations.

The fraction is rounded to the next highest number, making four teaching stations the minimum requirement. This number would also afford some flexibility of class scheduling.

In computing teaching station requirements for the secondary school, the desired class size must not be set so low as to require an impossible number of teachers and facilities, nor should it be so high that effectiveness is impaired. An average class size of 30 with daily instruction is recommended. However, if the physical education classes meet only two periods per week, the total number of class periods Notes per week in the formula must be adjusted accordingly.

The next step for planners is to determine the degree to which the number of teaching stations for the program of instruction will meet the needs for voluntary recreation, extramural and intramural activities, and interscholastic athletics for girls and boys, as well as the possible use of facilities by the community. The needs must be based upon the season of the year representing the greatest demand for facilities.

The following guide can be used to determine the number of teaching stations needed for activities other than the formal program of instruction in physical education:

Minimum number of teaching stations, or fractions thereof, needed for interscholastic-team practice at peak load, plus minimum number of teaching stations, or fractions thereof, needed for intramural and extramural activities, plus minimum number of teaching stations, or fractions thereof, needed for student recreation, plus minimum number of teaching stations, or fractions thereof, needed for community recreation, equals the total number of teaching stations needed for any specific after-school period.

To illustrate, assume a school has two interscholastic squads, an intramural program, a voluntary recreation group, and no community recreational use of facilities immediately after school during a specific season. The total needs are as follows:

Required teaching stations equals:
two interscholastic,
plus one intramural,
plus one voluntary recreation,
equals four stations

The need for four teaching stations for the after-school program must then be compared to the number necessary for the formal program of instruction in physical education. If the after-school needs are in excess of those for the regular periods of instruction, additional teaching stations should be provided. Careful administrative scheduling can result in maximum utilization of facilities.

Variety of Teaching Stations

A wide variety of teaching stations is possible depending on the number of different activities that would appropriately be included in the physical education program. Among the possible types of indoor teaching stations that might be included are gymnasiums, rhythm rooms, rooms for gymnastics, adapted physical education rooms, wrestling rooms, classrooms, swimming pools, archery ranges, rifle ranges, and racquetball courts.

The problem for some schools is not the lack of an adequate number of teaching stations but rather the lack of facilities to accommodate the desired variety of activities. For a secondary school with 360 students, a divisible gymnasium will create an adequate number of teaching stations for the program of instruction in physical education but may not meet the peak load requirement for after-school activities.

The facility must be planned and designed to serve all program needs as adequately as possible. Whenever a school's teaching requirements are such that a basic gymnasium is inadequate, planners should consider special purpose stations such as auxiliary physical education teaching stations, a natatorium, or a dance studio.

Secondary School Gymnasium

The building or portion of the school that houses the gymnasium should be easily accessible from classrooms, parking areas, and the outdoor activity area. This also makes possible the use of the facility after school hours or during weekends or holidays without having to open other sections of the school.

Size and Layout

For general purposes, allow a minimum of 125 square feet of usable activity space for each individual in a physical education class at peak load. The space requirements and dimensions of a gymnasium floor are significantly influenced by the official rules governing court games, particularly interscholastic basketball and the extent of spectator seating. The minimum dimensions required of a gymnasium for basketball, however, should be expanded, if necessary, to accommodate other activities. In some instances, an entire gymnasium is not required for an activity. Folding, soundproof partitions can be used to divide the area and provide two teaching stations.

Walls and Ceilings

The walls of the gymnasium should be of a material that is resistant to hard use, at least to door height. The finish should be non-marking and have a smooth, nonabrasive surface. All corners below door height should be rounded and there should be no projections into playing areas. Lower portions (10 feet) of the walls should be finished with materials that can be easily cleaned without destroying the finish. Epoxy paint on cement block makes a durable finish.

The ceiling should be 24 feet to the low side of beams or supports with fixtures attached to the beams to support hanging equipment. High ceilings are expensive, and a natural method for cutting construction costs is to minimize ceiling height. If this is in the area for basketball, volleyball, gymnastics, badminton, or tennis, it can be a critical error. However, in an auxiliary gym used for wrestling, dance, combative, weight lifting, or table games, a 15- to 18-foot ceiling is acceptable.

All ceilings should be light in color and, if support beams are below the ceiling, they normally are painted the same color as the ceiling or background. Contrasting colors have been used effectively; however, such color contrast may make it difficult to follow the flight of an object.

Acoustical treatment of ceilings and walls is important where teaching is to take place. To obtain the best results, at least two adjacent surfaces should be treated. Many types of acoustical treatment are available. However, avoid those that will chip or break when hit with a ball.

Lighting

There are many types of lighting systems that will produce the 35 to 50 foot-candles needed for a good teaching and spectator area. For television, the foot-candles should be closer to 200 foot-candles and that requires more sophisticated lighting systems. When selecting a lighting system, compare initial costs, annual replacement costs, and operational or electrical expenses. Some are less expensive to install but very expensive to maintain or operate.

Windows

Windows should generally be avoided. When located to take advantage of the sun for solar heat, the glare may cause serious problems. When windows are on the north side, there are fewer glares, but the loss of heat may be significant. Vandalism is another disadvantage.

Wall Padding

Generally, at the end of the basketball competition courts, there is padding attached to the wall to protect the students from injury when running into the wall. This is true even when a recommended 10-foot safety zone (i.e., the standard for a safety zone for a basketball court is three feet on the sidelines and end lines according to the NFHS rule book) is provided at the end of the court. These pads can be permanently installed or made to be portable. They are generally six feet tall and 16 to 24 feet wide and attached approximately six inches off the floor. The pads can be designed with almost any kind of graphic desired by the school in a wide variety of colors.

Fixed Equipment

If suspended equipment is planned, provision for its attachment should be made before the ceiling is installed. Basketball backstops will need special care in their installation to ensure rigidity and safety. All basketball backstops should be attached to ceilings or walls and swing-up or fold-up models should be used where the backstops might interfere with other activities. In addition to the main court basketball backstops, provision should be made for other backstops on clear sidewalls. Hinged rims that collapse when grabbed are recommended for baskets used for recreational basketball play.

In the interest of safety, such suspension apparatus as bars, rings, and climbing poles and ropes should be so placed as to allow sufficient clearance from basketball backstops and walls. If wall apparatus is desired in the gymnasium, a strip of metal or hardwood firmly attached to the wall at the proper height is recommended. Wherever necessary, floor plates should be installed for fastening movable equipment such as horizontal bars and volleyball standards. If mats are to be hung in the gymnasium, appropriate hangers placed above head level to avoid any injury must be provided. Rubber-tired mat trucks, which may be wheeled into a storage room, are recommended. For safety reasons, padding should be installed on all walls in back of baskets.

Spectator Seating

The extent of the demand for spectator seating depends upon each school and the community it serves. Modern design uses power-driven folding or rollaway bleachers (see Chapter 12 for greater detail), which require little permanent space. If possible, the outer surface of folding bleachers should create a flat, wall-like surface so it may be used for ball rebounding.

The width of each seating space should not be less than 18 inches. Rollaway bleachers most commonly allow 22-inch depths for seats. The number of rows available in rollaway bleachers varies, with 23 rows being the maximum for standard equipment. In some instances, bleachers with 30 rows can be obtained by special order. Planners should investigate local and state codes.

Balconies can be used to increase the total seating capacity beyond the maximum permitted at floor level. The space at both levels should be considered as activity areas when the bleachers are closed. It may be desirable, in some instances, to provide less than maximum seating at floor level so a balcony will be wide enough to serve as a teaching station for specific activities. Balcony bleachers can be installed to telescope from the back to the front so that in the closed position they stand erect, creating a divider wall at the edge of the balcony. This arrangement affords partial isolation of the teaching station and enhances the safety of participants.

Traffic Controls

Good traffic control should permit the efficient movement of students to and from the gymnasium, locker rooms, and other related service areas. All traffic arrangements for spectators should provide direct movement to and from bleachers with a minimum of foot traffic on gymnasium floors. Spectators should have access to drinking fountains, refreshment counters, and toilets without crossing the gymnasium floor. Steep, high stairways should be avoided. Ramps with nonslip surfaces might be substituted in appropriate places. Local and state building codes and standards of the National Fire Protection Association should be consulted.

Foyers

Where finances and space will allow, foyers should be placed so they will serve as entries to gymnasiums and will guide spectators as directly as possible to seating areas. Toilet facilities for men and women, ticket-sales windows, ticket-collection arrangements, checkrooms, public telephones, a refreshment-dispensing room with counter, and lockable display case should be provided, opening directly to the foyer.

Spectator Restrooms

All athletic events that attract spectators require restroom facilities. Restrooms should be designed for proper light, ventilation, and sanitary care. State health codes will influence the number and location of restrooms.

Concessions

Concessions have come to be considered a necessary service for public gatherings. Appropriate space and distribution as well as adequate fixtures for concession stands within the field house should be planned. Since plumbing and electrical services are already available in the field house, the concession stand might be located as a part of or adjacent to the field house. The concessions area will include, but not be limited to, a double sink, garbage disposal, electric range, microwave, refrigerator, ice maker, popcorn maker, freezer, plenty of counter space, and signage.

Other Factors

Provisions should be made for the installation of electric scoreboards, a central sound and public address system, picture projectors, radio and television equipment, high-fidelity equipment, and cleaning machines. Special consideration should be given to locating floor outlets for scoreboards and public address systems adjacent to the scoring table. Wall outlets should be installed near cupped eyes to permit special lighting as needed. Controls for gymnasium lighting should be conveniently located, recessed, and keyed.

Drinking fountains and cuspidors should be accessible without causing a traffic or safety problem. It may be desirable to provide a drained catch-basin, grilled flush with the floor, to care for splash and overflow.

Cupped eyes can be installed in all walls at approximately 15-foot height and 10-foot intervals for decorating convenience. They may also be used for attaching nets and other equipment to walls at appropriate heights. Bulletin boards and chalkboards should be provided where needed. If wall space is available, such boards may be provided for each teaching station. Three full-length mirrors should be placed at one end of a wall, side by side, for visual analysis of movement.

The Auxiliary Gymnasium

Depending on the demands placed on a facility for classes, after-school athletics, intramurals, and student and faculty recreation, more than one gymnasium may be necessary. Careful program scheduling will determine what is best in each situation. However, most schools need at least one auxiliary gym. Room dimensions should be based on the anticipated uses with special attention to the need to accommodate standard-size wrestling mats.

The other type of auxiliary gymnasium closely resembles the main gym, except there is little or no need for spectator seating, and the floor dimensions may be smaller. A 75-foot by 90-foot gym will house two volleyball courts, three badminton courts, three one-wall handball courts, and space for some gymnastic equipment.

The auxiliary gyms can serve a variety of other activities in the instructional, intramural, recreational, or interscholastic program, which cannot all be accommodated after school in the main gymnasium. Some auxiliary gyms are large enough to be divided into two teaching stations. The characteristics of these facilities are similar to those in the gymnasium. A less-expensive type may have a ceiling as low as 18 feet. Activities as wrestling, tumbling, calisthenics, self-defense, and fencing may be conducted in such a room.

Adapted Physical Education Area

Federal legislation requires that special considerations be made for persons with disabilities. Schools must provide programs, which meet their special needs. The adaptive area, therefore, becomes essential (See Chapter 4 for additional information).

Gymnastics Area for the Gymnasium

By planning in detail, the equipment layout for gymnastics, attachment hardware for the floors, walls, and ceilings can be included in the original design and construction. The manufacturers of gymnastics equipment will supply details for the attachment of their equipment as well as suggestions for floor plans or layout for the apparatus with proper safety areas. Preplanning ensures not only in proper installation, but also in savings on the cost of doing the work at a later date.

Storage of gymnastics equipment requires special attention, for example a room adjacent to the gym with a roll-up door. Equipment left out or stored around the edge of the gym is a safety hazard and will shorten the life of the equipment. Mat storage requires either a mat truck or a hydraulic lift to ceiling.

The use of light folding mats will, however, alleviate some of the storage problems. Climbing ropes should be attached to a height of 24 feet and drop to about three feet above the floor. Apparatus may be attached to the exposed beams. If the ceiling is placed below the structural members, the locations of suspended equipment should be planned and eyebolts provided during construction.

Ropes should be placed five feet apart, allowing one for each five students in class. The rings should be at least five feet from the walls. End walls at least 35 feet from the point of attachment will afford safety for the participants. Traveling rings are supported from a height of 18 to 26 feet and are located seven feet apart along a continuous line. Lines should be provided for drawing ropes and rings not in use to the overhead so as not to interfere with other activities.

High bars require both floor and wall or ceiling attachments. Adjustable bars for class instruction can be arranged in a linear series. Bars vary from six to seven feet in length and require 12 feet of unobstructed space extending perpendicular to their long axis. Bars for interscholastic competition are commonly located as individual units.

Free-Standing Gymnastics Area

Rarely will a free-standing gymnastics area be found in a secondary school. These facilities are either privately owned or part of a nonprofit agency (e.g., YMCA, YWCA, or Boys and Girls Club).

The free-standing facility (Figure 22.1) will include:

- Entrance area.
- Lobby space.
- Small proshop.
- Concessions.
- Public restrooms.
- Day care area.
- Balcony for spectator seating for 300.
- Competition/practice area—boys: runway for vaulting with a landing pit, high bar (2) area

Figure 22.1
Sample Layout of a Free-Standing Gymnastics Area

with a landing pit, pummel horse area, parallel bars (2) area, rings area, and floor exercise area shared with girls; girls: runway for vaulting with a landing pit, uneven bar (2) area with landing pit, balance beams (3) area with a landing pit, and a shared floor exercise area.

- Trampoline area with trampoline flush with floor.
- Office space.
- A large storage area at least 600 square feet with a ceiling height of 10 feet and a roll-up door.

Strength and Cardio-Respiratory Area

The current trend in physical education facilities is the addition of a strength and cardio-respiratory area. Student-athletes would use this area for physical education classes before and after school, and community programming after school hours and on the weekends. The details regarding this space can be found in Chapter 17.

Health Instruction

The purpose of health instruction is to provide health information and experiences that will lead to the establishment of attitudes and practices conducive to the conservation, protection, and promotion of individual, community, and world health. This section of the chapter is concerned with the facilities essential to the conduct of health classes, including first-aid and safety instruction.

Elementary School

For the elementary school, the general principle of the self-contained classroom is accepted. However, in order that there be maximum opportunity for health and safety instruction, it is important to have drinking fountains and hand-washing and grooming facilities and that there be ready accessibility to toilets for the exclusive use of each room in the primary grades. In classrooms for intermediate grades, hand lavatories should be provided. In addition to the central storage space for equipment common to all rooms, each room should have storage space for health teaching aids especially suited to that class. A mobile laboratory table or a resource room equipped with facilities for demonstrations in health and science should be available.

Secondary School

The basic space allotment for the health instruction facilities in the secondary school should be in harmony with generally accepted standards for schoolroom size. However, due to the nature of activities involved in health and safety instructional programs, it is recommended that the space allowed for such instruction be increased approximately 35% above requirements for the regular classroom. This will result in a space allotment of 35 square feet per student, including storage space.

The space allotment should be sufficient to allow for such activities as vision and hearing screening, first-aid and safety instruction and practical demonstrations, and for flexible teacher location. In addition to the conventional teacher's desk, provision should be made for laboratory demonstrations.

This indicates the need for a laboratory-demonstration table, which will provide space and facilities for demonstrations. Thus, provisions should be made for water, gas, and electricity as well as storage space for heating devices, test tubes, flasks, beakers, and other equipment essential to such demonstrations. The diversity of teaching procedures requires that regular classroom arrangements (Appendix S for additional information) be used at some times, but at other times floor space be made available for practical instruction such as practice in artificial respiration, splinting, and emergency transportation.

The suggested laboratory method of teaching will require adequate storage space as well as display areas for charts, mannequins, models, and equipment. First-aid equipment such as blankets, bandages, splints, and stretchers will also be needed. For instruction in home nursing, such equipment as incubators, rollaway beds, pans, containers, and bedding will be required.

There should be a large amount of display space for the great variety of educational exhibits, literature, and pupil projects inherent in the health education program. This can be provided by allowing liberal space for tables and shelves and by using all available wall space for bulletin boards and tack boards.

The health instruction laboratory should provide for the optimum use of such additional audiovisual devices as still pictures, slides, motion pictures, radio, and television. This will necessitate a liberal allowance of appropriately located electrical outlets, shades, or curtains that will reduce the outside light and a screen that may be mounted above the chalkboard behind the laboratory desk.

It may be desirable that there be convenient access between the health instruction laboratory and the health service suite in order that each may augment the total health program. For example, when home-nursing classes are meeting in the health instruction laboratory, there will be times when it is desirable to have free but supervised access to both facilities. Similarly, when there is an occasion to have a large number of people using the health service suite, it may be desirable to have access to the health instruction laboratory for seating or other purposes. In some instances, it may be desirable to consider locating the health instruction laboratory near the science laboratories in order to facilitate joint use of equipment and supplies. In other instances, location in the area of the physical education facilities may be desirable.

The secondary school health instruction laboratory should be an example of the ideal classroom environment with special concern for color of walls, lighting, ventilation, temperature and humidity control, order, and cleanliness (see Appendix S for additional information).

Recognition should be given to the desirability of joint planning of school health facilities with public health officials and other community groups who might need access to such facilities, thus strengthening the total community health program. Such arrangements can serve to strengthen the program of all who are concerned with health by providing for dual use of such facilities without duplication and with a minimum of expense.

The following is a checklist for health instruction facilities:

- space for 35 square feet per pupil, maximum of 30 pupils
- flexible teacher location
- provision for various teaching methods, including laboratory demonstration
- flexibility of seating
- hot and cold running water and gas outlet
- educational exhibit space
- storage space
- provision for using audiovisual devices (electrical outlets, window shades, screens)
- access to health service unit exemplary environmental features
- adequate hand-washing facilities, drinking fountains, and toilets
- air-conditioning
- accessible to and usable by persons with disabilities
- planned jointly for community use

Health Services

Health services contribute to the school program by 1) facilitating learning, 2) encouraging pupils to obtain needed medical or dental treatment, 3) adapting school programs to individual pupil needs, 4) maintaining a healthful school environment, and 5) increasing pupils' understanding of health and health problems. Following the principle that program determines facilities, plans would include accommodations for:

- appraising the health status of pupils and school personnel;
- counseling pupils, parents, and others concerning appraisal findings;
- encouraging the correction of remediable defects and the proper adjustment of those identified as not remediable;
- assisting in the identification and education of pupils with disabilities;
- helping to prevent and control disease;

- providing emergency service for injury or sudden illness;
- maintaining a cumulative combined health and accident file for each student.

Health service personnel are not only charged with the responsibility for developing policies and procedures, but should also be consulted in planning programs and facilities. Policies and procedures are essential for the attainment of program objectives through the proper utilization of facilities and the protection of school populations under adverse or disaster conditions.

Health Suite

Whether in a small rural or a large urban school building, the health service suite will be used for a variety of activities. It may be the center for emergency care of injuries or sickness and health appraisals by nurses, physicians, dentists or dental hygienists, and psychiatrists or psychologists. Various types of systematized screening tests, such as tests of vision and hearing, may be conducted in this area.

The health suite is the logical place for conferences concerning a pupil's health problems involving the parent, teacher, doctor, nurse, and physical educator. A part of the suite should be used as a dressing room and another section should serve as a waiting room. Some space should be set aside for the isolation of a pupil when the situation warrants, and accommodations should be provided for pupils on a prescribed rest schedule. The suite will also need to provide space for the health service personnel, plus the necessary space for records and equipment.

The common concerns of school health service personnel and guidance personnel suggest the need for a close, cooperative working relationship. This would indicate the desirability of locating the units in close proximity to each other and the possibility of using a common waiting room.

The school health suite may, in some instances, also serve the community. Thus, the health suite and the adjacent health instruction area may be for well-child conferences and other preschool health activities. They may accommodate classes for expectant mothers and other adult education activities. In those situations where the building and grounds are used for recreation purposes, the unit may serve as an emergency-care and first-aid station for those participating in the recreation program.

The fact that a health service suite is located within the school does not mean that programs for non-school groups will be administered or manned by school personnel. Usually, these community health activities will be under the direct supervision of the official health agency. If community usage of the health service suite is expected, then those who will provide the service should be involved in the planning.

Location

In locating a health service suite, consideration should be given to the variety of activities that will be carried on therein and to conditions that will permit those functions to be carried on conveniently and efficiently. Some factors to be considered in the location of a health service suite are:

- It should be located along a corridor near a main entrance to the building so that it may be completely isolated from the remainder of the building, yet remain conveniently accessible from all parts of the building.
- It should be located on the first or ground floor.
- The location should be in close proximity to the administrative suite. In situations where full-time health service personnel are not contemplated, direct access should be provided between the area and the administrative office, the teacher's lounge, or an adjacent classroom. In the secondary school, advantages will accrue from locating the health classroom and the service suite so that there is convenient access between the two areas. This is especially true when school health facilities are utilized for community health services.
- The location and acoustical treatment should be such that corridor and outside noises are kept to a minimum.
- A maximum amount of natural light should be available.

Rooms

All purposes for which the health service suite is designed may be carried out in one large unit, which may be subdivided into 1) waiting room, 2) examining room, 3) resting rooms, 4) toilet rooms, 5) counseling room, 6) dental health room, 7) isolation room, 8) special screening areas (e.g., vision and hearing), and 9) office area for health service personnel and records. Depending upon the size of the school and its health policies, various combinations of the above spaces may be planned without affecting the efficiency of the services. For example, in smaller elementary schools, all services may be cared for in one room provided proper screening is used and the administrative and health service suite are served by a common waiting room.

In larger schools, and especially in high schools, division of the unit into separate rooms is desirable. Thought should be given to the type of wall construction that provides for rearrangement of space allocation, since change in policies and school population will affect the nature and extent of health services. When remodeling old buildings, the same standards that apply to new structures should be maintained.

Guidelines based on accepted standards are recommended below:

Waiting Room

Schools with 10 or more classrooms or enrollments of 300 or more pupils should provide a waiting room, possibly in combination with guidance and/or administrative offices. It should be directly accessible to the corridor and the examining room. The waiting room should be separated from adjacent rooms by a full-height partition.

The decorations and furnishings should be designed to create a bright and cheerful atmosphere. The size is dependent upon enrollment and established health policies of the school (see Table 22.1).

Examining Room

Schools consisting of six or more classrooms or an enrollment of 180 or more pupils should include an examining room in the health suite. It should be directly connected with bathrooms and the waiting room, and should have access to toilets, the dental space, and any offices that are provided.

The location should provide for natural light and ventilation. The size and arrangement should be such that an uninterrupted distance of 20 feet is available for vision testing. The room should be acoustically treated. If the examining room is to serve as a resting room (in small schools) screened cot areas should be provided. The space should be ample for proper arrangement or storage of the following equipment:

- desk, chair, computer, and possibly a typewriter
- filing cabinets
- platform scale with stadiometer
- vision testing equipment
- movable spotlight
- blankets and linens
- folding screen
- sterilizer and instrument table
- cot or couch
- cabinet for first-aid supplies
- cup and towel dispensers
- wastebasket and foot-operated disposal can
- full-length mirror
- audiometric testing devices

The size of the examining room will be determined by enrollment, the types of activities to be conducted, and the extent of use by medical and other health personnel (see Table 22.1).

Resting Rooms

Resting rooms are essential in all schools. They should be directly connected with the examining room and toilets or be accessible to them from a restricted hallway. Separate resting rooms should be provided for each sex. A screened cot space may be a necessary arrangement in smaller schools. The location should be such that natural light and ven-

Table 22.1
Recommended Sizes in Square Feet of Health-Service Facilities for Schools of Various Sizes

ENROLLMENT	200-300	301-500	501-700	701-900	901-1100	1101-1300
Waiting Room	80	80	100	100	100	120
*Examining Room	200	200	200	240	240	240
**Rest room (total area for boys and girls) 200	200	200	240	240	240

Toilets.......... 48 square feet total area (provide one for girls and one for boys)

OPTIONAL AREAS

Dental Clinic	100 square feet for all schools
Office Space	80 square feet for each office provided
Eye examination	120 square feet minimum for all schools

* Examining room areas include 6 square feet for clothes closet and 24 square feet for storage closets.

** For determining the number of cots, allow one cot per 100 pupils up to 400 pupils, and one cot per 200 pupils above 400. Round out fractions to nearest whole number. Allow 50 square feet of floor space for each of the first two cots and 40 square feet for each additional cot.

*** In schools enrolling 901 to 1,100, a three-cot rest room is suggested for boys and a four-cot rest room for girls, and in 1,101 to1,300-pupil schools, a three-cot rest room is suggested for boys and a five-cot rest room for girls.
Note: For larger schools, add multiples of the above areas to obtain total needs.
State Department of Education, *School Planning Manual*, school Health Service Section, Vol. 37. November, 1954, Richmond Va.

tilation and quiet atmosphere are secured. If there are no full-time health service personnel available, the location should be such that supervision of the area may be conveniently provided from the administrative office or an adjacent classroom. Adequate space should be provided for cots (see Figure 22.3), bedside stands, wastebaskets, and blanket and linen storage.

Rest Rooms

A toilet room with stool and lavatory should be directly connected, or be accessible by a restricted hallway, to the resting rooms in all schools with 10 or more classrooms or with an enrollment of 300 or more pupils. In smaller schools where the resting rooms are a part of the examining room or other space provision should be made for convenient toilet facilities. A rest room with a minimum of 48 square feet should be provided for each sex (see Figure 22.2).

Storage Closets

Storage space, opening off each resting room, should be provided for linens, blankets, pillows, and so forth. In the smaller schools without separate resting rooms, such storage should be provided for in the examining room. A ventilated cloak closet should be provided for school health personnel. If built-in storage facilities are not feasible, space should be allowed for movable storage cabinets.

Isolation Room

An isolation room as an integral part of the health service suite is desirable to insure privacy when required. It should be directly connected with the examining room, but apart from the resting rooms. A space for one cot and the necessary circulation area is sufficient in most instances.

Vision and Hearing Screening Areas

Such areas should be included as a part of the examining room. An uninterrupted distance of 20 feet should be provided for vision testing. Audiometric testing will require an acoustically treated room.

Offices

The provision of office space for health service personnel will depend upon the time they spend in the school. If office space is provided it should be connected with the waiting room, the examining room and, if possible, the corridor. The minimum recommended space for two people is 80 square feet. Provision should be made for maintaining health and accident reports.

Counseling Room

Although such space will not be in constant use, a room where the doctor, nurse, teacher, and parent can discuss a pupil's health is an important unit of the total health facility. Space large enough to accommodate a small table and four or five

Figure 22.2
Health Suite for Elementary School with Seven Classrooms

Figure 22.3
Secondary School Health Suite

chairs is adequate. It may be used as office space for part-time health service personnel.

General Suggestions

The entire suite should present an informal and pleasant atmosphere. Flooring should be of a material that is nonabsorbent, easily cleaned, and light in color. Lavatories used by personnel functioning within the examining room should be operable by the wrist, knee, or foot. Figures 20.2 and 20.3 are examples of some possible health suite arrangements.

Driver Education Areas and Facilities

The program of driver education is generally accepted as a responsibility of the school and, more specifically, as a function of health and safety and physical education departments. The guidelines outlined below are in keeping with approved standards and national recommendations.

Indoor Facilities

For the indoor program, there should be a classroom, a psychophysical laboratory with testing devices, a simulator laboratory, and an office.

Location

All indoor facilities should be on the first floor of the building, near the garage or parking space for the dual-control cars, and near the driving range if one is used.

Classroom

Size

The recommended procedure is to combine the classroom with the laboratory for a combination room of 30 feet by 40 feet. Where separate rooms are used, the classroom should be of standard size.

Furniture and Equipment

In addition to the standard classroom facilities and equipment, such as chalkboard, bulletin board, desk, and chairs, the driver education classroom should provide facilities for the following special equipment:
- VCR and monitor
- bookcases and storage cabinets for videotapes, flip charts, testing equipment, models, and so on.
- demonstration table
- demonstration equipment, including magnetic traffic board, working models, flannel boards, model signs, and signals

Driver Education Laboratory

The laboratory contains equipment needed to test the student's physical, mental, and emo-

tional qualifications required for safe and skillful driving.

Size

When the combined room is not used, the laboratory should be at least 24 feet by 30 feet.

Furniture and Equipment

The needed furniture and equipment will include a demonstration table, chairs, worktables, and spaces to accommodate equipment for testing visual acuity, depth perception, color vision, field of vision, reaction time, steadiness, night vision, and so forth.

Simulator Laboratory

Driver education simulators are accepted as a means of providing the preliminary steps to behind-the-wheel instruction. Because of the nature of the simulator units, facilities for them should be considered as permanent installations, preferably in a separate classroom.

Size

The size of the simulator laboratory will depend on the number of simulator cars to be installed. A typical eight-car installation will accommodate 450 to 500 students per year and a 16-car installation will accommodate 960 to 1,000. The room size for eight cars should be 24 feet by 33 feet and for 16 cars it should be 30 feet by 40 feet.

Furniture and Equipment

The room should be clear of obstructions that might interfere with the projector beam and should be provided with the regular complement of chalkboard, bulletin board, tack board, magnetic board, and so on.

Layout

The cars are arranged in a semicircular fashion with the first row a minimum of 8 feet, preferably 10 feet to 12 feet, from the screen and with the outside cars not exceeding an angle of 30 degrees from the screen. The first row should have the lesser number of cars. A minimum of 24 inches should be allowed between the rows with a 30-inch aisle down each side of the room. Aisle spaces must comply with state safety codes. The projector should be located in the center at the extreme rear of the room, and a 6-foot by 8-foot screen should be placed in the front of the room. Manufacturers' specifications for electrical requirements should be followed. Ordinarily, the standard 120-volt, 60-cycle alternating current is required. It should be supplied through a double outlet located in the vicinity of the recording unit.

Lighting

Soft white fluorescent-light tubes recessed in the ceiling with semi-translucent shields to provide

100-foot-candles of light at desk height should be installed.

Color

Pastel colors should be used. The woodwork and finishing should be compatible with color used on the walls. A reflection factor of 80% is needed for the ceiling and 60% for the walls. The furniture should have a non-glare finish.

Heating and Ventilation

Heating and ventilation should conform to standards required throughout the entire school system.

Outdoor Areas and Facilities
Driving Area

Purpose

Behind-the-wheel instruction provides the skills necessary for safe and efficient driving.

Types

An on-street driving area is recommended for schools where traffic congestion is not a problem. First, driving maneuvers should be conducted in locations such as school driveways where there is no traffic. As ability develops, students get experience driving in situations that approximate normal driving conditions and then, finally, in actual normal traffic situations. Blocked-off streets are sometimes used when street traffic is too heavy and school driveways are not available to teach the first driving maneuvers. Arrangements should be made with the residents of the area and with police officials. Since advanced driving skills are taught where other traffic is involved, streets should not be blocked off for an undue length of time. An off-street driving range is recommended where land is available. Ranges should be laid out to simulate most physical situations associated with driving, such as: traffic signs, signals, and other control devices, parallel and angle parking, upgrade and downgrade situations, and simulated emergency situations. Space should allow for needed skill-test maneuvers. Different types of road surfaces should be provided. If night classes are conducted, the area should be lighted. The size of the driving range should be no smaller than 350 feet by 450 feet.

The multiple-car driving range (see Figure 22.4) has the advantage of accommodating several cars simultaneously under the supervision of one teacher, thus reducing the per-pupil cost. With this type of range, communication between the instructor and students is accomplished by means of a radio or public-address system.

Recommended Equipment and Facilities

- curbs for parking practice
- intersections for various turn maneuvers
- gravel area for driving and turn maneuvers
- streets marked properly
- streets that are both wide and narrow
- all signs—traffic, control signals, stop, warning, yield the right-of-way, regulatory, guide, and information
- upgrade and downgrade roadways
- simulated road surfaces—concrete, asphalt, and gravel
- muddy surface for emergency situations
- signboards found on normal roads
- stanchions, guide-on, and the like for maneuvers

Points to Remember:
- Determine the needs of the student and the objectives of the program.
- Provide as many realistic situations as possible.
- Design the driver-training area equal to the best facilities available.

Figure 22.4
Multiple Car Off Street Driving Range

Jason Winkle, Indiana State University
Thomas H. Sawyer, Indiana State University

Boxing

This section provides readers with information that will allow them to utilize existing space in the physical education area to design a multipurpose boxing facility that meets existing standards for safety and utilization of proper equipment for boxing.

United States Amateur Boxing Inc. (USA Boxing)

United States Amateur Boxing Inc. is the controlling organization for all amateur boxing in the United States. Rules, legislation, and safety regulations are promulgated by USA Boxing and its membership to provide a healthy, safe, and sportsmanlike environment in which young men and women can participate in the sport of boxing throughout the United States.

National Collegiate Boxing Association (NCBA)

The National Collegiate Boxing Association is an umbrella organization under the jurisdiction of USA Boxing that was organized to provide an opportunity for college students to participate in the sport of amateur boxing against other students enrolled in fully accredited institutions of higher learning. Only properly registered students (full-time) from institutions registered with the NCBA may participate in this program, and they may only compete against other full-time college students who meet all the necessary registration requirements. The NCBA is not a member of the NCAA, but is rather an organization of club teams authorized by their respective institutions and registered with both the NCBA and USA Boxing. Numbers of registrations vary from year to year, but there are approximately 30 member clubs (institutions) and over 300 registered participants covering four geographic regions (Northeast, Southeast, Midwest, and Far West). The NCBA conducts educational clinics and annual regional and national championship competitions.

Why a Boxing Facility?

Some may question the use of physical education space for the development of a boxing facility because of boxing reputation as a violent and potentially dangerous sport. Some of those same people would not think of questioning the use of either outdoor or indoor space for an activity such as football, which is statistically far more dangerous than boxing. While one might argue that boxing (amateur as opposed to professional) is one of the safest of the contact sports that is not the purpose of this discussion. Rather, it is to describe how a facility can be organized for learning and practicing boxing fundamentals and techniques that are ideal for the development of physical fitness and self-confidence.

Boxing is now widely accepted and utilized as a fitness activity. It is universally known that boxers are among the best-conditioned athletes, and that boxing fitness activities (punching drills, bag punching, plyometrics, associated calisthenics, rope skipping, shadow boxing, distance running, and interval training) are excellent conditioners that reduce stress and are fun at the same time. Add to this the potential for learning the fundamentals of self-defense, and you have an activity that is hard to beat.

Considerable media attention has been recently given to "white-collar" boxing by young professionals, both male and female. Many of these young men and women have traded their jogging and racquet sport shoes for boxing shoes! It is a relatively inexpensive alternative to many other activities and develops not only aerobic capacity but can also increase strength and muscular endurance. It is also a great opportunity for coed fitness training. Conditioning drills and non-contact offensive and defensive fundamentals can be practiced without regard to gender in an environment that can be designed to push participants to reach beyond their previously self-imposed physical limits. Finally, a properly designed boxing area can be utilized as a multipurpose facility. If it is set up correctly, a boxing space can easily be turned into an aerobics area, a wrestling or gymnastics room, a practice area for cheerleaders, or a conditioning space for just about any team or activity you can name.

How Much Space Is Necessary?

If the space is to be used for boxing only, any space that is 10' x 10' or larger will suffice. All that is necessary is the proper floor covering, heavy and light striking bags, calisthenic stations, and a small equipment storage area. This area could be categorized as an "all-purpose boxing room" and makes use of almost any available space. The size of a boxing exercise/training area can vary from a large field house, armory, or gymnasium, to a small classroom or similar space suitable for small-group instruction. All that is required for boxing drills/practice is some unobstructed space, adequate ventilation, and sufficient lighting.

If a boxing ring is available, or you desire a multipurpose room, then some additional space will be necessary. A space 20' x 20' is required for the ring setup. A good way to organize such a room would be to divide it into the ring area, a striking bag area (heavy and light), and an exercise section. A 30' x 50' space would be sufficient for this type of room. If you are converting an old swimming pool space (e.g., 20 yards x 10 yards) you should have all the space you need for an excellent boxing/multipurpose exercise room.

Converting such existing space as a swimming pool into a boxing room is worth considering. Many older instructional pools that no longer meet specifications as competitive venues occupy more than enough space for an excellent boxing facility.

Older pools of this type are usually at least 75' x 25' (1,875 square feet) with considerable additional space allotted for the pool deck areas. All that is needed is a way to construct a wooden floor over the surface that will support the weight of 25 to 40 participants (100 lbs. per square inch). The buildings and grounds staff of a school along with a local architect can plan and construct this project for less than $10,000. (see Diagram 23.1).

Materials necessary (other than labor) are:

- 2" x 4" studs,
- 2" x 8" floor joists,
- Wooden bridging pieces,
- 1/2-inch plywood and 5/8 inch particle board (installed on top of the floor joists), and
- Ensolite(r) matting to cover the exercise area.

What Equipment Is Necessary?

If a ring is used, or if contact drills are used, the ring or floor area must be covered with a one-inch layer of Ensolite(r) AAC or AL closed-cell foam rubber (or a chemical equivalent). The ring padding must be covered with canvas or some similar material, and be tightly stretched and laced securely in place (USA Boxing, 2005). If no contact drills are anticipated, the floor area could be any type surface, but wood is preferable.

Boxing gloves used for sparring or live contact drills must meet the specifications required by USA Boxing Inc. USA Boxing Official Rules (2007, p. 115) require that the padding inside the gloves be "1/2-inch Latex, 3/4-inch PVC (Husitonic), 3/8-inch PVC (Rubitex- 313 V) and V inch Polyfoam or other products that meet the severity (force of blow) index." For instructional purposes, 16-ounce thumbless or attached thumb gloves are recommended. Remember that the purpose of the gloves (in contact work) is to diminish the impact of a blow and to protect the hands.

The purpose of boxing headgear is to reduce the impact of a blow, reduce/prevent facial cuts, protect the ears, and substantially reduce impact to the head if a fall occurs. Only headgear approved by USA Boxing Inc. should be used (USA Boxing, 2007). Several manufacturers produce headgear to the proper standard.

During any type of contact drills, use of a mouthpiece is mandatory. The mouthpiece reduces the possibility of jaw injuries, cuts to the inside of the mouth, and injuries to the tongue and teeth. A custom-made or individually fitted mouthpiece must be worn by each participant. Examples of the custom-made and individually fitted mouthpieces are the "dentist-molded" and the clear plastic types, respectively (USA Boxing, 2007).

When contact drills are involved, men and women should wear approved groin or chest protection. For men, this means either a foul-proof protection cup or a jock-strap cup. Women should wear a well-fitting breast protector (USA Boxing, 2007).

Handwraps are recommended for all types of striking drills but need not be required (they are mandatory in competition, however). The purpose of the handwrap is primarily to protect the metacarpal bones of the hand. They are not designed or utilized to add force to a blow. Handwraps can be made of cotton gauze, soft surgical gauze or velpeau material. For ease of wrapping, the velpeau type is recommended. Instruction and practice in proper wrapping technique should be given prior to their use.

Heavy bags are vital to the organization of any boxing training facility. They are the single best modality to use for non contact striking/punching drills and are a must in your training area. They are used to simulate an opponent's body and head, and any number of very useful drills can be done with these bags. Several types and sizes are available (canvas, leather, nylon, vinyl) and they can be filled with foam, water, or rags (depending on the type). An inexpensive way to make up a heavy bag is to use a duffle or "sea" bag filled with sawdust, rags, or a combination of the two.

Light striking bags are used for advanced drills and are a "nice to have" item in your facility, but the heavy bags are much more practical. Light bags are used for developing speed, timing, and coordination. They are much smaller than a heavy

Diagram 23.1
Boxing Instruction & Competition

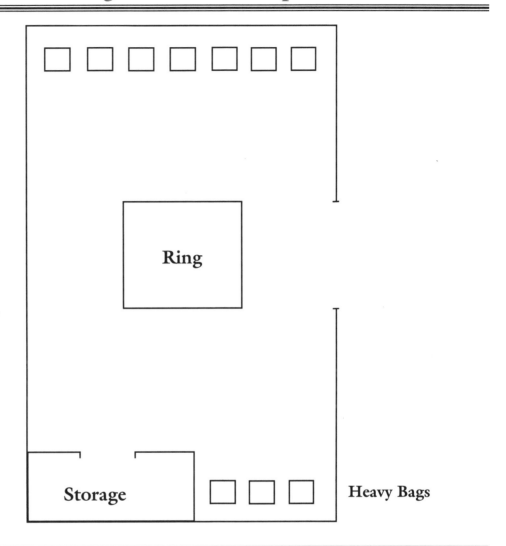

bag, but require that a bag "platform" be anchored to a wall in order to be utilized.

A boxing ring is not necessary for boxing instruction, drills, or conditioning exercises. It is, however, an important piece of equipment if any of your participants are interested in competitive boxing. It is also a good way to control the various boxing contact drills or any sparring that is done. Only rings that meet USA Boxing specifications should be utilized. The ring can be either a platform type, elevated about three feet above the floor (not more than four feet), or a floor type, built directly upon the floor or on a slightly raised platform that is laid directly on the floor. The platform type is recommended for competition, but for training purposes, many prefer the floor type. According to USA Boxing Official Rules (2007, p. 17), "the ring must be not less than 16 nor more than 20 feet square within the ropes, and the apron of the ring floor shall extend beyond the ropes not less than two feet." The ring should be equipped with

four ropes that are wrapped in a soft material, and all turnbuckles must be covered with protective padding.

Miscellaneous Exercise Stations

Depending on the specific purpose of your room and the needs of the participants, the number and types of exercise stations you develop is unlimited. At a minimum, however, are recommended exercise stations requiring individuals to use their own body weight as resistance. Among these are pull-up bars (six to eight), and sit-up and push-up stations. If the floor is not already padded, some type of matting will be necessary at the sit-up station. An area set up for rope skipping and shadow-boxing (two full length mirrors) can also be provided.

Cost of Various Equipment Items

The cost of equipment items for your facility will vary slightly depending on the vendor you use, but the following rough estimates will enable you to establish a budget to get your facility started. The amount of equipment, of course, will depend on the number of participants, but the total costs for this example are based on an expected 25 participants: (based on 2008 dollars)

-Training gloves (16 ounce):
25 pair @ $175/pair $ 4375.00
-Bag gloves: 25 pair @ $10.00/pair = $ 250.00
-Training head gear: 25 @ $70 each $ 1750.00
-Plastic mouthpiece (upper): 50 @ $1.50 each $ 75.00
-Groin protection (boxing cups): 25 @ $15.00 each, $ 375.00
-Female chest guards (with support bra): 25 @ 45.00 each $ 1125.00
-Handwrap: 25@ $5.00 each $ 125.00
-Heavy bags (canvas; unfilled): 8 @ $55.00 each $ 440.00
-Boxing ring (platform type) $ 6,000.00
-Boxing ring (floor type) $ 2,500.00
Total cost (with platform ring) = $14,515.00
Total cost (with floor ring) = $11,015.00

It must be emphasized that these prices may vary from vendor to vendor, and you should shop around for the best price. Your facility does not have to be completely equipped for 25 persons. Depending upon how you organize your exercise / practice sessions, equipment, and exercise stations can be shared and rotated so that you may only have to be equipped for 10 participants or fewer. You may also be able to purchase used equipment, or construct some of your own.

Organization of the Facility

If you intend to set up a boxing room with a ring, remember that a regulation-size ring can be from 16 to 20 feet, inside dimensions of all four sides. Obviously, this means that you will need more space than if you set up the room without a ring. To utilize your available space most efficiently, center the ring on one end of the room, and place heavy bags and light striking bags on the opposite end, thus leaving the space between for drills, calisthenics, plyometrics, or for multipurpose use when the area is not being utilized for boxing. On either end of the room or along the side walls, you can set up permanent pull-up and sit-up stations, using pipe suspended horizontally from the ceiling for the pull-up station and bolted to the floor as an anchor point for feet at the sit-up station. Along one side wall, place full-length mirrors (six by four feet) for shadow boxing and technique drills. This type of arrangement gives you four areas in which to work: a ring area, a bag work area, a calisthenics/conditioning area, and a space in between that can be used as a multipurpose area.

If you decide to set up your facility without a ring, you will save at least 400 square feet of use-able space (not to mention the expense of a ring). This will still enable you to set up three areas for specific fitness training, including aerobics and circuit training. It also allows you to design your facility in a much smaller space than is possible with a ring. The number of exercise stations in your circuit is then left up to your imagination and the available space. The perimeter of this fitness training facility should be set up for specific circuit exercises, with the center area left open for multipurpose use.

Any boxing facility that does not have a ring (or the space for one), but is going to be used for self-defense contact drills or sparring, should be set up to ensure that participants are protected from the perimeter walls and any objects that may protrude from those walls, and that the floor surface being used is properly matted. Floor surface matting has already been discussed (one-inch Ensolite™), and its main purpose is to protect against traumatic injuries to the head resulting from falls or knock-downs. Perimeter walls should also be padded with one-inch Ensolite™ to protect against injuries caused by wall contact. When a ring is not available and the perimeter walls are not matted, you can still conduct contact drills and sparring if you organize the session properly. Participants should form a large circle (16-20 foot diameter) and be instructed to act as a "human ring." This ring should be centered in the exercise area and at least six feet from the perimeter walls. Only two participants should spar at a time, and they should begin in the center. Participants on the perimeter of the ring should be instructed to adjust their positions so as to keep the two sparring individuals inside the ring. Any time either of the two boxers makes contact with the ring's perimeter, the instructor should immediately stop the activity and have the participants begin again, in the center. This not only prevents traumatic contact with the perimeter walls, it stops any punching activity when one individual becomes momentarily disadvantaged.

Equipment Storage Concerns

Equipment should be of high quality and meet all published safety standards required by USA Boxing. Properly cared for, boxing equipment will have a long life and replacement costs will be minimal.

Security of the equipment and, in fact, the entire area, is of paramount importance. The entire facility should be locked when not in use and access limited to instructors, coaches, and maintenance personnel.

There should be adequate and assigned storage areas for all equipment that is moveable and used on a regular basis. Boxing gloves and headgear, for example, should be stored in an area that is open to circulating air so that the equipment can dry properly. Gloves and headgear should be stowed in open wire racks, on open shelving, or in lockers with steel mesh fronts that allow the circulation of air. Both should be washed with saddle soap and dried thoroughly each week. Both should also be treated weekly with a commercial disinfectant or with a solution of 10% carbolic acid and 90% sweet oil (Deeter, Rubino, & Simmons, 1950). Handwraps should be allowed to dry after each use and should be washed weekly. Obviously, athletic supporters, groin protectors, athletic bras, and chest protectors should be washed thoroughly on a regular basis and stored in a dry, clean area. Usually, this will be the responsibility of individual participants.

Safety Concerns

If contact drills or sparring are part of your exercise program, then it is mandatory that the boxing gloves and headgear utilized meet the safety specifications of USA Boxing. It is also essential that any safety equipment worn be properly fitted to the individual. Protective headgear, especially, should be worn so that it provides the maximum protection possible. All headgear should fit snugly and should not change position on the head if pulled, pushed, or struck. The bottom edge of the padded forehead portion of the headgear should sit just above the top of the eyebrow, approximately 1/2 inch above the hairline of the brow. The participant's ears should fit snugly inside the ear openings on the headgear, and the ears should lie flat against the inside surface. There should be an additional heavily padded area on the rear of the headgear. This should be centered on the back of the head and reach down to the top of the neck. If the headgear has cheek guards, they should fit snugly against the cheeks, tight enough so that they cannot slide up into the eye. Finally, the chinstrap should fit under the chin and be as tight as possible, without causing discomfort.

If plastic mouthpieces (uppers only or doubles) are used, they should be softened and molded to the individual's mouth. This can be done by placing the mouthpiece in a cup of water and then heating it in a microwave oven. When the mouthpiece appears to be softened (flaccid), remove it from the hot water and rinse it with cool water. While it is still soft, have the individual bite down on it until it is "molded" to his or her mouth. This may take a few tries, but it is the most inexpensive way to obtain a fitted mouthpiece.

Handwraps should always be worn when striking drills of any kind are being performed. Cloth (velpeau) handwraps are recommended. Further, it is recommended that commercial handwraps can be applied as follows:

- Place the looped end of the wrap over the thumb,
- Bring the wrap over the back of the hand to the big knuckle of the wrist,
- Go underneath the wrist to the base of the thumb in diagonally across the back of the hand to the big knuckle of the little finger,

- Encircle completely the big knuckles of the hand, wrapping well up toward the middle joints of the fingers,
- Go diagonally across the back of the hand to the outside wrist bone,
- Completely encircle the wrist once, angling the wrap slightly upward, stopping at the base of the thumb,
- Completely encircle the thumb once,
- Following the normal contour of the hand, bring the wrap over across the back of the hand to the joint of the little finger,
- Completely encircle the large knuckles of the hand a second time, Carry the wrapping down diagonally across the back of the hand and around to the base of the thumb,
- Pull it up, completely encircling the thumb for a second time, and
- Finally, bring the wrap diagonally over the back of the hand to the wrist, and encircle the wrist once using a small piece of tape (one inch by six inches) to secure the wrap.

Ensure that participants keep their fingers spread and extended throughout the wrapping process. This will prevent the wrap from being too tight, thus cutting off circulation.

When pairing participants for contact drills, there should be as little weight difference between the participants as possible. A reasonable guideline to follow is to allow no more than an eight-pound differential during any sparring or contact drills. It is perhaps even more important to also pair individuals according to their respective skill/experience levels. If a new skill is being learned, it is a good idea to pair an experienced individual with a beginner. The experienced person can control the action and can also act as an assistant instructor for the beginner. If the activity involves sparring or any competitive situations, then it is usually best to pair the individuals according to size (weight) and relative ability.

During any vigorous activity, there is the possibility of injury. There should be a phone located inside the boxing room with clearly posted numbers of the local emergency squad, the school athletic training staff, and the infirmary. In addition, all instructors should be CPR certified and a first-aid kit should always be on hand. Identifying injuries should be the responsibility of the professional staff, but guidelines for handling suspected head injuries should also be clearly posted inside the room. USA Boxing Inc. has published the following guidelines for recognizing a possible head injury:

Observe the athlete for:

- dizziness or headache lasting more than one hour,
- increasing drowsiness,

- loss of consciousness,
- mental disorientation or confusion,
- unusual or strange behavior,
- restlessness or irritability,
- seizure (convulsion),
- blurred vision or loss of vision,
- repeated vomiting,
- blood or watery fluid from ears or nose,
- inability to control urination or bowel movement, and
- inability to move an arm or leg.

If any of these symptoms occur (or persist), medical personnel should be contacted immediately.

Martial Arts

The term "martial art" comprises a wide range of fighting systems that are practiced for physical fitness, sport competition, and self-defense (Borkowski & Manzo, 1999). Lawler (1996) stated that traditionally, martial arts are various Asian fighting systems that teach combat-specific techniques. Most of the modern martial arts have roots that go back to the ancient martial arts of Asia. It is commonly believed that some martial arts started before 2000 B.C. (Winkle & Ozmun, 2001). Differing philosophies, interpretations, and interests of instructors and students have produced the wide range of martial arts practiced today.

Building or renovating a martial arts facility requires extensive planning. This chapter will provide information to assist martial arts facility developers with design and construction decisions. Planners and developers of martial arts facilities must understand at least the general nature of martial arts if they are to make informed decisions. The major classifications of martial arts are summarized in this chapter to provide this knowledge base.

Facility Planning Concepts
(see chapters 1-2 for details)

The goal when constructing or renovating a martial arts facility is to produce a facility that is highly functional, cost effective, aesthetically pleasing, safe, and accessible to all. Failure to adequately plan often results in a facility that costs too much and delivers too little. Sawyer (2005) and others suggest participatory planning (seeking information from all interested individuals, especially the representative user group) is the recommended planning strategy. The first step is to conduct a needs assessment. The needs assessment solicits information from the owners and operators, the target facility users, and staff members. The owner and operator may be a person, a group of people, or an established organization. The owners and operators often provide all or some of the finances for the project, so they expect and deserve the opportunity to influence construction or renovation decisions. They are often the ones to provide a vision for the facility and leadership in organizing and executing both the planning and construction. Staff members provide an excellent source of information on which features should be included in a new martial arts facility. They have practical expertise and experience and can provide many useful recommendations. Gathering information from the target population provides valuable information to determine the demand for martial arts activities and identify which style is most popular. The users or customers are often the best source of information on the desired support facilities, such as parking areas, locker rooms, concessions, and administrative areas.

Armed with data gathered from the needs assessment, the next step is to solicit support from those providing the funding for the construction or renovation project. It is important to present the data collected in a professional and persuasive manner. Oftentimes, important features of a building project are not supported due to a lack of time spent in developing and crafting the justification statements in the proposal. Failing to adequately prepare for this phase of planning could result in a poor presentation and the project being abandoned.

Once a project gets support from a higher authority, establish a planning group or a steering committee. This group will stay actively involved during the entire planning and construction process. It is critical to spend time when making the decision on whom to include on the committee as they will provide guidance, and in some cases make decisions on such issues as:

- renovating an existing facility or building a new facility
- cost limitations and funding sources
- promoting the project
- gathering additional needs assessment data
- site location
- selecting an architectural firm
- approving, rejecting, or modifying architectural firm plans and proposals
- selecting construction contractors
- developing construction schedules and phasing
- specifying material and space requirements
- ensuring code compliance
- identifying and solving design and construction problems
- establishing and implementing maintenance and operation procedures
- determining requirements for support and competition areas

The scope of the project and the complexity of the administrative requirements will determine the magnitude of the planning effort. Whether planning a modest renovation of an existing martial arts room or constructing a new martial arts complex complete with all the support facilities, careful planning will avoid costly mistakes.

Overview of the Martial Arts

Martial arts can be defined as numerous systems of self-defense and offensive techniques that may emphasize sports competition, physical development, mental development, or a combination of these aspects. Initially, most martial arts taught in America were taught in wrestling rooms, gymnasiums, multipurpose rooms, or in the outdoors. This is still the case in most colleges, recreation centers, YMCAs, and other multipurpose facilities. Martial arts facilities, designed specifically for martial arts, are now being included in the design and construction of many of these multipurpose facilities. Many commercial martial arts programs are taught in specialized martial arts facilities.

Whether designing a separate commercial facility or a martial arts area in a larger project, planners must decide if the new martial arts facility will be a general combative facility or a facility designed to accommodate a specific classification of martial arts. In either case, a general knowledge of the major martial arts will help planners make important design decisions. There are almost as many types of martial arts as there are types of ball games. There are too many types and styles of martial arts to discuss the facility requirements for each one. A brief summary of the two major martial arts divisions is provided to assist facility planners in making informed design and construction decisions (see Table 23.1)

Grappling Arts

The grappling arts have achieved a surge in popularity in the past several years due to the television coverage of various mixed martial arts competitions. While the arts that comprise this classification of martial arts have as rich of a history as their striking counterparts, the grappling arts have resurfaced as a mainstream addition to fitness and recreational facility programming. Their popularity has sparked facility designers to consider devoting specialized areas to this activity. While multipurpose rooms can accommodate these arts with some limited modifications and additional equipment, grappling specific areas are recommended for safety reasons. Facility planners must take into consideration the characteristics of these grappling arts when making facility decisions. These arts tend to emphasize throwing skills, joint-locking, falling, and wrestling-type movements. Participants compete against opponents in close proximity with the goal of physically controlling the other.

Striking Arts

The striking arts are systems designed to train participants to make contact with an opponent from a distance (Winkle & Ozmun, 2001). There are numerous systems that meet this criterion. The most commonly practiced striking arts include karate, tae kwon do, kung fu, and kickboxing. Each of these arts is characterized by their need for mobility and various hand and foot striking techniques. An understanding of the nature of striking arts and grappling arts is required to properly design or accommodate a safe training environment.

Facility Concerns

Martial arts facilities tend to be simple structures with large open spaces. However, the two classifications of martial arts systems have distinctly different needs from the perspective of facility design. Flooring is the primary difference in each facility. The grappling arts require floor matting while the striking arts are best suited with a wooden or synthetic floor.

Grappling Martial Arts Facilities

The requirement of floor matting is the distinguishing characteristic of grappling martial arts facilities. Grappling arts often use traditional wrestling rooms with mats and padded walls. These wrestling rooms meet the minimum requirements for grappling martial arts, but a two-layer mat system is recommended for any of the grappling martial arts that require throwing. The standard wrestling mat alone does not provide sufficient protection for high-impact activities like throws. A

Table 23.1
Martial Arts Classification Summary

GRAPPLING ARTS	STRIKING ARTS
Involve throwing skills, joint locks, falling, and wrestling-type activities	Emphasize punching, kicking, and weapon use.
COMMON GRAPPLING ARTS:	**COMMON STRIKING ARTS:**
Judo Jiu-Jitsu Aikido Wrestling/Brazilian Jiu-Jitsu	Tae Kwon Do Karate Kung Fu Kickboxing/Boxing

two-layer mat system with a lower layer of foam-type matting and an upper-layer standard wrestling-type mat is a versatile option. Tatami mats (made of compressed foam) over a spring-loaded base is ideal for the throwing arts.

When designing a dedicated martial arts facility, include specialized matting specifically selected for the intended activity. Non-competitive grappling arts only require a firm mat with shock-absorbing properties. The mat should not be slippery or too rough.

For competitive grappling arts, such as judo, the mat must be a minimum of 14 meters by 14

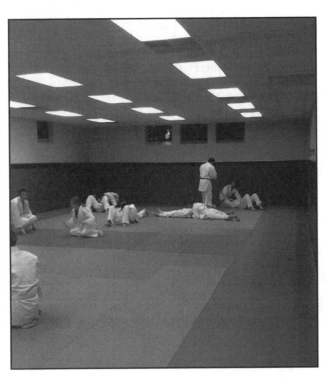

meters and a maximum of 16 meters by 16 meters. The top layer of matting is usually a green-colored tatami. Competition mats must have a smooth surface without gaps between sections. Competition mats must also have a competition zone surrounded by a one-meter danger zone

marked in red. A three-meter zone on the outside of the danger zone is the safety zone. A resilient wooden platform is the preferred base for judo competitions. Competitive judo venues should also include two scoreboards and three timing clocks. Other competitive grappling arts, such as Brazilian Jiu-Jitsu, do not require the wooden platform, only competition quality mats.

Striking Martial Arts Facilities

Karate, kung fu, tae kwon do, and kendo are martial arts that employ mostly striking techniques (Roth, 1974). Karate, kung fu, and tae kwon do all utilize a wide variety of kicks with the feet, punches with the hands, and striking skills with other body parts. The majority of these blows are

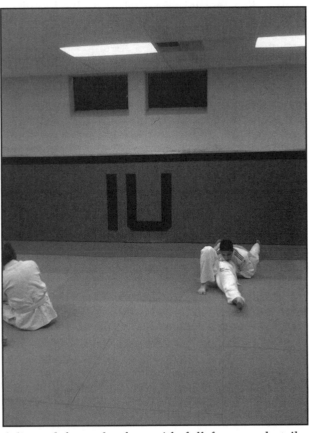

delivered from the feet with full force and strike into a padded surface or stop just short of a human target. Kata, a prearranged series of skills, is also an important aspect for the majority of these styles. Normally, only the advanced students participate in contact competitions where they deliver full-contact blows against an opponent. Additional protective equipment is recommended when practicing striking techniques with an opponent and required for full-contact competition. The emphasis in each of these martial arts is body control, striking power, and precise technique. The punching, kicking, and striking techniques are delivered from either a linear or a spinning and turning motion. Wrestling-type mats are not recommended when throwing circular techniques since the anchor foot must rotate freely. Flexible hardwood or smooth synthetic floors are preferred for striking martial arts.

The American College of Sports Medicine's (ACSM) health/fitness facility standards and guidelines are commonly used by multipurpose facility designers when determining what type of flooring is best suited for certain activities. Guideline #8 states, "Floor surfaces in physical activity areas should provide the proper level of absorption and slip resistance to minimize the risk of users' incurring impact or fall-related injuries" (ACSM, 2007, p. 37). According to ACSM, the critical point regarding flooring is that it meets the criteria of the Deutsches Institute fur Normung (DIN). DIN standards require floors to meet five criteria: shock absorption, vertical deflection, deflective indentation sliding characteristics, rolling load, and ball reflection.

The goal of these standards is to reduce the number of acute and chronic-impact injuries. These floors should have excellent shock absorption, small vertical deformation, and limited sliding characteristics (ACSM, 2007). According to DIN standards (see Appendix H), a floor suitable for activities such as the striking arts should serve both a protective and a material-technical function (ACSM, 2007).

General Features for Martial Arts Facilities

While the primary distinguishing feature of martial arts facilities is the type of flooring and matting required, facility planners must also consider other important features.

Wall Coverings

The selection of appropriate wall coverings is critical. All striking martial arts facilities should have at least a portion of the wall covered with mirrors. Mirrors provide a valuable source of feedback for individuals participating in martial arts. Selecting the best location for the mirrors may be challenging because of conflicting priorities. Placing the mirrors too close to the activity area may result in the mirror being broken. Non-glass mirrors are safer and less likely to get broken, but scratch more easily and tend to give a distorted image. If glass mirrors are to be used, shatter-resistant glass mirrors are recommended. Placing mirrors too far from the activity area may make it difficult for participants to see themselves. Walls that do not have mirrors are often covered with protective wall mats, to a height of six feet.

Water Fountains

Martial arts activities are very demanding physically, and martial arts participants will need to keep hydrated. A recessed water cooler is recommended for all types of martial arts facilities. A recessed water spigot is often desired to make facility sanitation easier. The spigot may be located near or as part of the water cooler.

Ceiling

Martial arts facilities tend to be simple functional facilities with few distractions. The simplest and least expensive ceiling is an open ceiling, the roof or floor above and associated piping, conduit, and ductwork is left exposed. An open ceiling area is normally painted white to give the training room an open-area feeling. The open ceiling has advantages for activities that involve weapons and throws. The longer weapons, bows and swords, may damage an acoustic tile ceiling. Acoustic tiles used in drop ceilings can be equipped with spring-loaded clips that will allow the tiles to be contacted without being knocked out of place. The open ceiling is not as aesthetic as an acoustical tile ceiling, nor does it have as good of acoustic properties. If the facility is to be used primarily as a teaching station, an acoustic tile ceiling may be the ceiling of choice and worth the extra expense. The minimum ceiling height is 12 feet for martial arts facilities, and a higher ceiling is recommended for a martial arts facility used primarily for weapons-oriented activities.

Lighting

The recommended lighting level for martial arts facilities is 50 foot-candles. Recessed lights that have some type of protective covering are recommended. If the facility will be used for martial arts demonstrations or shows, equip the lights with a dimmer switch.

Storage

Providing adequate storage space for the martial arts facility is an important planning decision. Like storage space in many other facilities, storage space in martial arts facilities is often overlooked or reduced as soon as finances become an issue. Specific storage needs vary with each martial arts program, but should include at least some storage for personal items and mesh-type lockers to allow stored gear to dry. The size and type of storage facility required depends upon:

- total space available for construction
- budget constraints
- type of facility (grappling or striking)
- class sizes
- whether the mats will need to be taken up and stored or not
- whether the uniforms will be stored or not
- the style of martial arts to be practiced
- desire to include a trophy case to store and display trophies

If specific storage needs are not available during the planning phase, allow 8 to 10% of the total martial arts facility square footage for storage.

Scoreboard

A scoreboard with a clock is a practical feature for many of the martial arts, especially those that involve competition. The specific features of the scoreboard will depend on which style of martial art will use the scoreboard. If a scoreboard is desired, but funds are not available at the time of design, include the required power source in the plans. Including the power source in the original construction will cost very little and will save both time and money if funds become available to purchase a scoreboard in the future.

Custodial Closet

Martial arts facilities have a lot of skin contact areas that require regular cleaning and disinfecting. Locating a custodial closet in or close to the martial arts facility will facilitate cleaning and sanitation efforts. Rubberized mats require regular cleaning and disinfecting with a liquid disinfectant. A custodial sink is recommended, and a recessed spigot is the minimum source of water for cleaning the martial arts facility. The closet needs to have storage space for mops, buckets, cleaning and disinfecting supplies, and a vacuum cleaner (especially for carpeted facilities).

EQUESTRIAN SPACES

24

Michael G. Hypes, Morehead State University
Julia Ann Hypes, Morehead State University

There are many variables involved in the planning of equestrian facilities. These variables include purpose, budget, image, climate, available material and labor, personal preferences, and future plans, to name a few. These variables make good planning critical to the overall success of the project.

Equestrian facilities incorporate several different components. These components include:
- barns,
- work areas,
- turnout areas, and
- arenas.

Each component serves a specific function in the overall operation of the equestrian program.

Barns

"The atmosphere and safety of all activities within a barn are determined by three main barn features: the brightness and placement of lights, the amount of fresh air, and the material and condition of the aisle floor" (Hill, 2000). Although some people prefer their facility to be plain, no frills and practical, others prefer their facility to make a statement. The image you want to portray with your facility can be a preliminary goal in the planning process. This image goal will guide many of the choices made including architectural style, building materials, interior fittings, equipment, and costs.

Site Considerations

A horse barn's site selection should receive careful consideration. The barn's orientation to wind, sun, and shade should be considered. The ideal orientation would utilize summer breezes for cooling effect while avoiding the harsh winter wind. Trees can be used to:
- provide shade,
- serve as wind breaks, and
- to screen private areas.

Good water drainage is necessary to avoid standing water. Standing water or marshy areas could be breeding grounds for insects and disease, thus making it difficult to maintain a healthy stable environment.

General Construction Issues

A variety of construction materials can be used for barn structures. These materials can range from wood to pre-cast concrete. Safety features should be the main consideration when choosing materials. Whatever choice in materials is made, it is essential that the structure be as fire-resistant as possible.

Many different types or combinations of lighting can be used in a barn. Natural lighting can be used to enhance the overall lighting of the facility through the use of skylights, windows, translucent wall panels, and open doors. Whether incandescent, halogen, fluorescent, or high-intensity discharge lighting is used, it is important to remember that the fixture should be protected from dust and impact. The needed illumination in a given area will dictate the type and amount of fixtures needed.

Another important aspect of any barn is adequate ventilation. Ventilation in barns can be provided by windows, doors, roof vents, and exhaust fans. Adequate ventilation not only keeps barn odor at a minimum, it also helps keep the barn area dry, cool in the summer, and contributes to a healthy stable environment.

The main aisle in a barn receives a large amount of traffic. The surface in the main aisle should be durable and easy to clean. It is important for the safety of the horse and handler that the floor should be relatively smooth and level. The decision as to what type of flooring to use should be based on a balance of your personal preference, cost, availability, maintenance, and durability. Table 24.1 provides a list of the more common flooring surfaces used in barn structures. Each type of flooring has distinct advantages and selection should be based upon your specific needs.

The size and number of components making up the barn will vary not only in relationship to the size of the facility, but also to the requirements placed upon the facility. The following are basic components for a typical barn facility:

- stalls
- feed room
- hay storage
- straw storage/alternative
- bedding
- feed storage
- wash and cleaning room (drying facilities)
- tack room
- utility stall
- manure disposal
- office
- lavatory accommodations
- equipment storage

The relationship of the components should first be concentrated on the horse. The components should also be considered with respect to other facilities, to the site, surrounding buildings, and to each other. Careful planning and placement of these barn components can minimize movement of heavy materials, feed, and tack, thus maximizing efficiency and safety of the facility.

Stalls

The stall is the indoor living space for the horse. It should be large enough to allow the horse to move about freely, lie down, and get up without hindrance from banging into the walls. Each stall should be large enough to accommodate separate areas for a horse's three main activities: eating, lying down, and defecating/urinating. In addition, stalls can be used for:

- tending to sick horses,
- birthing (foaling),
- sheltering horses from extreme weather, and
- keeping horses clean.

The more time a horse spends in a stall, the larger and more spacious the area should be. Table 24.2 identifies some common stall dimensions based on the characteristics of the horse.

Stall doors come in a variety of styles. The door size should be sufficient to allow the horse to be led through the door without rubbing the sides and large enough for a cart to be pushed into the stall for cleaning. Stall doors should be a minimum of four feet wide and eight feet high. The edges of the door opening should be rounded to prevent injury. Horse-proof latches should be utilized on all stall doors. Horse-proof latches are out of reach of the horse or are made in such a way the horse cannot open it. Some of the more common latches include spring bolt, turning, and sliding bolt latches. A lower latch can be used to prevent the horse from pushing the bottom of the door out and possibly injuring itself.

Photo by Michael Hypes
Example of a well-organized utility area

A good stall floor will help reduce the amount of bedding needed. The stall floor should be comfortable for the horse, safe, and easy to clean. The flooring should be fairly easy to install, affordable, and able to withstand the abuse from hooves and acid from urine. Natural soil is the cheapest and easiest floor to install. However, over time, it can become uneven from the horse's movements, pawing, and urination. The size of your horse, function of the stall, and amount of stall use will also contribute to the stall flooring decision. Table 24.3 provides a comparison of different stall floorings.

Flooring can be categorized as a draining or a non-draining surface. A draining floor allows

Table 24.1
Types of Barn Flooring

• dirt	• brick
• wood shavings, chips, shredded bark	• rubber brick
• sand	• rubber tile
• road base	• concrete
• gravel	• asphalt
• wood	• rubber mats

Table 24.2
Common Stall Sizes

Stall Size		
Feet	**Meters**	**Suitable for:**
10 x 10	3 x 3	Pony: under 14.2 hands Usually under 800 pounds
12 x 12	3.7 x 3.7	Standard Horse: up to 16 hands, 800-1,100 pounds
12 x 14	3.7 x 4.3	Large Horse: 16+ hands, 1,100-1,400 pounds
12 x 16	3.7 x 4.9	Draft Horse: more than 16 hands, over 1,400 pounds
12 x 18	3.7 x 5.5	Foaling Stall: up to 1,400 pound mare with foal

Modified from Hill, C. (2000). *Stablekeeping: A visual guide to safe and healthy horsekeeping.*

urine to pass through holes in the material. A non-draining or solid floor is made of material that keeps moisture on top of the flooring, allowing the moisture to be absorbed by the bedding. Bedding provides a comfortable surface for a horse to lie down. It is also used for absorption of urine and as an insulator from the cold. Bedding material should be absorbent, soft, dust-free, easy to handle, and nontoxic. A list of possible types of bedding includes:

- straw,
- pine sawdust,
- pine shavings,
- shredded newspaper,
- hardwood chips, shavings, and
- sand.

Feed Room

This room houses the feed (corn, grains, oats, etc.) for daily use. It should be located close to the stalls for easy human access while still from animal access. Each type of food should have a separate storage bin. Feed and grain storage bins should be lined with galvanized steel for vermin control. It is essential that the feed room be a dry storage area to avoid fungal and mold growth in the feed. Feed spoilage can be costly in dollars and animal health. Hazardous chemicals, cleaners, and disinfectants should be stored away from feed.

Hay Storage

The hay storage area should be directly accessible from the feed room. The size for this area will depend on the size of the facility and the frequency of feeding. The hay should be stored close to the stalls, usually in the loft, where it can be dropped into cribs in each stall. There should be exterior access to this area for ease of storing hay, either brought in from the field or purchased. It is essential that hay storage areas be dry with good ventilation. The storage area should be free of mold and molding or wet hay. Molding hay can cause serious equine illness and wet hay can ignite, leading to deadly fires.

Bedding Storage

A variety of materials may be used for bedding purposes. The type selected may be based on geographical location, personal preference, animal preference, or availability. The area for bedding storage needs to be well ventilated and dry. Bedding such as straw can be stored in a separate facility to minimize the risk of fire.

Tack Rooms

The tack room should be accessible to all stalls. The exact size and arrangement will be dependent upon the number of horses and the purposes for which the horses are being used.

Windows are typically omitted from the tack room, because they take up valuable wall space as well as posing a security risk. Sunlight exposure can also dry and damage leather and other fine tack materials. The tack room should be designed to fit your needs. Some common elements in the tack room include bridle racks, saddle racks, tack hooks, blanket rods, and shelving for various grooming and veterinary items. If a separate barn office is not available, the tack room may include a refrigerator for storing medications and fireproof file cabinets for storing records. Space should also be allotted for the repair and cleaning of tack.

Many items are common to all horses and should be at hand in all tack rooms. Grooming tools are among the common items. These tools include:

- brushes
- curry combs (rubber and metal)
- electric clippers
- extension cords

Table 24.3
Stall Flooring

Material	Advantages	Disadvantages
Soil (clay, dirt)	Relatively inexpensive Provides good traction and cushion	High maintenance, difficult to clean
Gravel, sand	Inexpensive Good traction and cushion	High maintenance, difficult to clean, danger of colic*
Asphalt	Easy to clean Low maintenance	Cold, hard, and abrasive Can be slippery Hard on legs and feet
Concrete	Easy to clean Good traction** Maintenance-free	Cold, hard, and abrasive Hard on legs and feet Slippery if not textured
Wood	Nice sound Warm	Slippery when wet Difficult to clean and disinfect
Draining flooring	Minimal bedding needed Moisture drains through	Urine accumulates under flooring
Conveyor belting	Easy to clean	Very slippery when wet Difficult to handle and install
Rubber mats	Quiet Good cushion and traction Easy to clean	Can be difficult to handle and properly install Can gap and buckle

*Sand is not recommended because the horse can ingest the sand and develop colic.
**good traction if textured

Modified from Hill, C. (2000). *Stablekeeping: A visual guide to safe and healthy horsekeeping*

- scissors
- shedding blades
- soft cloths
- sponges
- sweat scrappers

In addition, all tack rooms should have first-aid kits for both horses and people. Depending upon the type of horse stabled, other assorted items are generally stored in the tack room. These include:

- bell boots
- lead ropes
- leg wraps
- longe lines
- ropes
- saddles
- tail wraps
- blankets
- bridles
- cavassons
- chain lead shanks
- crops

Photo by Michael Hypes

Interior view of stall, feed, and water containers.

Photo by Michael Hypes

Space Utilization
Saint Mary-of-the-Woods College, IN

Photo by Michael Hypes

Example of double-door entry.

- feed bags
- halters
- hobbles

Materials and tools for maintaining and repair of tack should also be kept in the tack room. Materials often needed are:

- awls
- hole punch
- knife
- latigo leather
- neats foot oil
- nylon string
- rivets
- saddle leather
- saddle soap
- sheepskin
- waxed linen string

Cleaning

From tack to facilities to horses, cleaning is an important aspect of barn operations. The function will dictate the space and location required. The cleaning area for equipment can be incorporated

Photo by Michael Hypes

Example of interior stall door

into a tack room or be a separate area. Large, deep sinks, hot- and cold-water sources, and washers and dryers aid in the proper cleaning and disinfecting of blankets and other accessories. By placing plumbing for workrooms and horse washrooms adjacent to or near each other, you can help minimize plumbing headaches and costs.

Manure Disposal

The manure disposal area should be positioned well away from the stalls but be easily accessible. It should be located adjacent to a road

Photo by Michael Hypes
Example of bedding storage

to facilitate collection and dispersal. Care should be taken to assure that run off from manure and bedding disposal areas do not contaminate wells, creeks, or other water resources.

Office

The office space should accommodate a desk, chairs, filing cabinets, and storage space for supplies. A fireproof file cabinet or safe should be considered for record storage. An area for a computer with a dedicated phone line should be considered. The telephone should be fitted with an external bell or extensions, so it may be heard throughout the facility. The office area should be located to provide supervision over the stable yard, deliveries, and arrival of people. The office can be utilized as an additional layer of safety for the facility. It is an appropriate screening area for visitors to the facility. The office should be adjacent to toilet and washroom areas. Some facilities have the office adjacent to or located near sleeping areas.

Turnout Areas

All turnout areas should be safe for the horse. These areas are designed to provide limited exercise space for the horse. Turnout areas include pens, runs, corrals, and paddocks.

The pen is usually the size of a large stall. A pen is typically 16 by 20 feet. The run is longer, 16 by 60 feet, and allows the horse to get more exercise by trotting. A corral can be a square or round pen. The corral is at least 1,600 square feet. These three areas are usually devoid of grass due to concentrated horse traffic. The paddock area is usually a grassy area from 1/2 acre to several acres and is used for short periods of exercise and grazing.

The turnout areas should have fencing designed for horses. Sturdy five- to six-foot perimeter fences, complete with latched gates, should encircle the area. Types of fencing range from vinyl to recycled rubber. The type best suited depends on your specific circumstances and livestock type. One of the most practical and inexpensive fences for a horse farm is a five-foot-high, 12 1/2 gauge,

galvanized 2" x 4" V-mesh. Pipe fences are attractive, easily maintained, and safe when properly constructed.

Competitive Areas

Arenas

Arena sizes vary widely between the disciplines. Working cows and reining typically require the most room. An arena for this purpose should be 100 feet wide by 200 + feet long. Jumping events usually require at least 80 feet wide and 120 feet long and more space is preferable if possible. A large dressage arena is 20 meters by 60 meters (66' x 198') and a small dressage arena is 20 meters by 40 meters (66' x 132').

Roof truss manufacturers use standard dimensions, usually in increments of 10 feet. A standard small covered arena truss is 60 feet wide and spaced 12 feet apart. A good rule of thumb for commercial riding arenas is to construct bigger than what you think you need. This will allow multiple disciplines to utilize the facility or accommodate multiple riding lessons simultaneously.

The proper lighting of arena is an important part of the planning phase. The sheer size of the arena makes it important to plan regarding fixtures, circuit size, and placement.

Jumps

The types of jumps used in Hunter classes are representative of natural obstacles found in the hunt field. These include:

Photo by Michael Hypes
Tack room,
Saint Mary-of-the-Woods College, IN

- post-and-rails,
- stone walls,
- Aiken,
- chicken coop,
- brush,
- plank, and
- white gate.

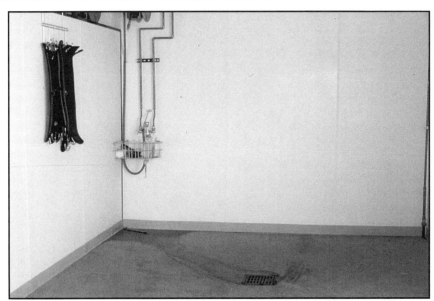

Photo by Michael Hypes
**Wash room,
Saint Mary-of-the-Woods College, IN**

safety of horse and rider in mind. It should collapse easily to prevent injury. This break-away characteristic is based upon the types of cups that hold the rails. The inside dimensions of a cup for a four-inch pole must be a minimum of 1 1/2 inches deep and five inches across. The maximum depth must not exceed one-half the diameter of the pole. (Price, 1998)

The poles (rails) used in many shows are 12-foot or 14-foot lengths. The longer the pole, the greater the weight and the lesser the tendency to pop out of the cups when hit. "Fences designed to test for horizontal distances are called spread fences. They may include the oxer, double oxer, hogback, and triple bar. While these obstacles are of different configurations, they can all be raised and lengthened, as for jump-offs" (Price, 1998, p. 245).

The post-and-rails is a natural rail fence, usually of three cross rails. The chicken coop is a triangular wooden obstacle ranging from perhaps two feet six inches to four feet. The Aiken is a split rail over bushes (Price, 1998).

All jumps should be constructed with the

The Puissance walls are typically constructed of light plywood with the upper elements able to slide off. Paint is used to create illusions for the horse. Table 24.4 provides a summary of the types of fences used in jumping. New variations are appearing all the time; however, these three categories represent most of the jumps currently used.

Figure 24.4
Types of Fences

Uprights are fences built vertical to the ground with all parts placed one above the other. These include gates, planks, walls, straight posts, and rails.

Spread fences require a horse to jump width as well as height. These include parallels, hogbacks, triple bars, double oxers, wall with rails behind, water ditches, and open water jumps.

Combinations consist of two or more elements placed in front of one another. The combination is usually designed with a single or double non-jumping stride between each part.

The double consists of two fences, which may be of any design. A straightforward distance for non-jumping stride in a double is 7.3-8 meters (24-26 feet). For two non-jumping strides 10-11 meters (33-36 feet).

Trebles consist of three elements of any type of fence or combination of striding.

Modified from Holderness-Roddam, J. (1988). *Competitive riding.* New York, NY: Prentice-Hall.

ATHLETIC TRAINING FACILITIES

25

Joe Brown, Emeriti Faculty, Austin Peay State University
Michael G. Hypes, Morehead State University

Athletic training rooms are common features in indoor and outdoor athletic complexes, and their specific purposes depend on the type of activities and facilities they support. For example, in multipurpose recreational facilities, the athletic training room often serves as a first-aid station for recreational athletes. Conversely, in athletic facilities, it serves as a comprehensive athletic medicine facility for interscholastic, intercollegiate, Olympic, or professional athletes. When housed in a community, the athletic training room may serve the "weekend warrior." Therefore, proper planning, plus an understanding of the essential components of an athletic training room, will make it more effective when completed. Accordingly, athletic training room planners should regularly consult with staff athletic trainers during the planning phase to ensure the construction of a sound facility for treating and rehabilitating athletes (Ingersoll & Sawyer, 1999).

While the specific activities performed in an athletic training room are subject to institutional preference along with the availability of financial and facility resources, certain activities are performed in all such facilities. These include team preparation, injury evaluation, injury treatment, injury rehabilitation, and administrative functions. It is important, then, to understand these activities before building, retrofitting, or remodeling an athletic training room. To improve the planning process, general considerations for the athletic training room and/or the requirements of organizations concerned with athletic training facilities should be considered (Ingersoll & Sawyer, 1999).

General Considerations for the Athletic Training Facility

Authors in the 1950s (Bevan, 1956; Morehouse & Rasch, 1958), 1960s (Morehouse & Rasch, 1964; Rawlinson, 1961), 1970s (Brown, 1972; Klafs & Arnheim, 1973), 1980s (Forseth, 1986; Penman & Penman, 1982; Sauers, 1985; Secor, 1984), 1990s (Arnheim & Prentice, 1997; Ingersoll & Sawyer, 1999; Lavoie, 1993; Rankin & Ingersoll, 1995; Ray, 1994), and 2000s (Sabo, 2001; Newell, 2003) have offered a number of options to be considered when contemplating an athletic training facility. While each author offers specific suggestions, a common thread is associated with each one. Generally, these authors agree that the athletic training room is a place specifically set aside for injury care. It has good lighting and ventilation; a constant temperature range; light-colored walls, ceilings, and floors; easily cleaned surfaces; adequate equipment; and ground-fault interrupter (GFCI) electrical outlets located on all walls. It is easily accessible by being near the dressing room, but is not a part of it, nor is it to be used as a passageway to the dressing room or showers. Moreover, these authors support the importance of a facility set aside specifically for the prevention, treatment, and rehabilitation of individuals who may incur injuries.

The Case for Athletic Training Facilities

It is important, then, for organizations without athletic training facilities to promote the need for an athletic training room. First, these management promotion factors include a well-organized plan of action, which outlines why the athletic training room is essential to injury care. These three factors follow:

- Minor injuries often are not reported immediately, because there is no one place or person to whom the injured athlete should report. Moreover, the injured person is often reluctant to be treated for minor injuries in the presence of others. It also is difficult to give minor injuries proper attention during the confusion of dressing and undressing.
- A sanitary and comparatively private environment is generally helpful for treatment of injuries. Organizations are giving more attention to injury prevention, treatment, and rehabilitation

because of the individual's privacy need from a practical and psychological point of view, because of the increased public attention given to sports injury problems, and because injuries adversely affect efficiency. Thus, the presence of an athletic training facility shows an interest in the welfare of athletes.

- A properly fitted athletic training room's cost is minimal when compared with costs incurred for lost time, uniforms, and other equipment (Brown, 1972).

Second, space needed for an athletic training facility must be determined. Forseth (1986) lists five general factors of facility development he obtained from Coates for determining the space needed for the athletic training room. These factors include:

- Program needs such as the number of sports and the type of sports offered at the institution.
- Projected institutional enrollment and the stability of the number of participants from one year to the next.
- Space needed for athletic training instruction.
- Cost per square foot estimates to determine what is feasible under the existing economic status.
- Communication with the architect early in the process to assure a functional athletic training room.

Third, the development of an athletic training facility requires the services of a certified athletic trainer. Such a person has requisite skills in the prevention, treatment, and rehabilitation of athletic injuries. Additionally, the certified athletic trainer has a working knowledge of the national standards for athletic training facilities (Newell, 2003).

Fourth, in retrofitting or remodeling facilities, the athletic training room size will be dictated by a number of unforeseen factors.

Fifth, make sure the athletic trainers are included during the planning phases.

Sixth, emphasize that the primary purpose of an athletic training room is to provide efficient service to large numbers of athletes at one time. Therefore, when building a new facility with a generous budget, the Arnheim and Prentice recommendation, the Penman and Penman formula, and/or Sabo's guidelines for minimal size should be followed.

Seventh, when possible, use the standards of the NATA and/or the American Academy of Orthopaedic Surgeons.

National Athletic Trainers' Association

The most important organization to consult is the NATA, especially if the athletic training room is in an institution that has a certification curriculum. According to Ingersoll and Sawyer (1999), the Commission on Accreditation of Allied Health Education Programs (CAAHEP) suggests specific guidelines for the development of an athletic training room. In this setting, the athletic training room components include team preparation area, injury evaluation/treatment area, rehabilitation area, wet space, maintenance area, storage space, office area, examination space, computer/study/conference area, and a classroom. The specifications for each of these areas are detailed to assist the planner in developing an appropriate floor plan for the athletic training room.

The *team preparation area* will have a tile floor with an appropriate number of floor drains, treatment cabinets with Formica tops, a recessed waste receptacle, drawers, and shelves. The ceiling height should be 11 to 12 feet, but not less than 10 feet. Further, fireproof tiles are a requirement for the ceiling. The walls should be constructed of masonry blocks for durability and sound control and painted with an epoxy paint to seal the blocks so they will be easier to clean. A deep, double-basin sink is suggested. The direct lighting should be with fluorescent tubes. Electrical outlets should be located every six feet on all the walls and those electrical outlets around the sink should be GFCI rated. Finally, this area should have a biohazard waste container and have double doors for entrance and/or exit.

The *injury evaluation/treatment area* requires different space and equipment needs for performing injury evaluations and treatments. This space has therapeutic modality applications, manual therapy, and treatment activities going on at the same time. Typically, this space includes numerous treatment tables that are used to examine body parts, do special tests on joints, and to treat various types of injuries. There should be a suspended curtain system that can, when necessary, be utilized for privacy.

Moveable carts between each table are used for transporting therapeutic equipment (e.g., ultrasound machine, muscle stimulator, etc.) and storing supplies. The specific space needs of the injury evaluation/treatment area include:

- a ceiling with a minimum height of 10 feet (11 to 12 feet is desirable) that is covered with fireproof tiles
- cabinets for storage
- a deep double-basin, stainless-steel sink
- rubberized roll-out sports surface such as Mondo7®,
- masonry block walls covered with epoxy paint
- GFCI-rated electrical outlets at each treatment site and above the counter on either side of the sink,
- direct fluorescent lighting
- biohazard waste containers
- double doors for entering and exiting the area

The *rehabilitation area* includes space for therapeutic exercise equipment. This area should be separate from other areas in the complex because of the noise level and the movement of the exercising athletes. The needs of this area include:

- a rubberized roll-out sports floor surface such as Mondo7®
- free weights
- mechanized strength training equipment for exercising shoulders, arms, backs, hips, thighs, knees, and ankles
- electrical outlets on all walls spaced every 6 feet
- indirect fluorescent lighting
- a 10-foot ceiling equipped with fireproof tiles
- soundproofing in the epoxy-painted masonry block walls
- double-door entrance and/or exit
- audio and video system
- space for running, jumping, and throwing activities

The *wet space (hydrotherapy)* area generally includes whirlpools, ice machines, therapeutic pools, refrigerator, and storage for large drink containers. The area should have:

- non-slip tiled floor
- a minimum ceiling height of 10 feet
- an appropriate number of floor drains
- recessed plumbing for whirlpools
- GFCI electrical supply for whirlpools and ice machines
- storage area for drinking containers
- a deep double-basin stainless-steel sink equipped with storage
- extra ventilation and humidity control
- indirect fluorescent lighting
- close to the athletic trainer's office, so constant visual contact can be maintained

The *maintenance area* is where broken equipment is stored and repaired. The area needs are:

- shelves
- worktable
- concrete floor with a drain
- epoxy-painted masonry block walls
- two, eight-feet roll-up internal and external door entrances
- fireproof tiled eight-foot-high ceiling
- enhanced ventilation
- deep double-basin, stainless steel sink with storage
- GFCI electrical outlets on all walls and an electrical strip above the workbench
- direct fluorescent lighting in the room and over the workbench

- storage space for an electric golf cart and its electrical charger

The *storage space* can never be too large. The storage space requirements include:

- humidity control to protect the stored tape
- locking cabinets
- shelves of various heights and lengths
- concrete floor
- direct fluorescent lighting
- epoxy-painted masonry block walls

Eastern Kentucky University Movable Cart

- double-door entrance, or at least a 36-inch door, or a roll-up door for easy access
- located close to the athletic trainer's administrative office area
- close to loading docks and/or delivery areas

The *office area* contains all medical records and serves as the administrative hub for the athletic training room. The space needs are:

- no smaller than 220 square feet
- located adjacent to the wet and storage areas
- a sight line to all other areas in the facility
- electrical, phone, and computer outlets on all walls
- locking file and storage cabinets
- carpeted floor
- masonry block walls fitted with windows which address each area of the facility
- a fireproof tiled eight-foot ceiling

The *examination space* is oftentimes the second office area that is used as a physician's examination room. The space includes those items in the athletic trainer's office area, an examination table, and single-sink basin provided with storage above and below it. It should have a locking door, and it could best be used for record storage, as there is less traffic.

The athletic training students will use the *computer/study/conference area*. This space should be no smaller than 220 square feet. The space needs include:

- tables for computers and printers
- a conference table
- shelving for a small library
- appropriate furniture for relaxing and studying
- storage lockers for the students' books, coats, and so forth located on the outside wall

The *classroom design* should include considerations outlined in Appendix S, Academic Classrooms and Laboratories. More importantly, the classroom must be dedicated for the use of the athletic training curriculum functions. Additionally, this room should have ample storage for instructional equipment and supplies used in athletic training instruction.

The American Academy of Orthopaedic Surgeons

While the NATA is the parent organization for athletic training standards, another good source is the American Academy of Orthopaedic Surgeons. Their publication, *Athletic Training and Sports Medicine (1991)*, contains suggestions useful for developing a training room when a curriculum is not a factor. The American Academy of Orthopaedic Surgeons suggests that each organization be obligated to provide athletic training room facilities sufficient for enhancing the athlete's health. Furthermore, this athletic training room facility is to be adequately sized; provided with utilities, supplies, and equipment; and staffed by qualified individuals. The services to be provided include preventive measures, assessment of injuries, first-aid administration, emergency care, routine evaluation and treatment, and rehabilitation of injuries. The academy's specific suggestions follow:

- The size and shape of the athletic training room should accommodate the number of individuals served by the facility.
- The athletic training room should be central to all of the activities provided by the organization. Also, the facility must be equally accessible to both men and women.
- The athletic training room should be equipped with the basic utilities of electricity, lighting, temperature control, ventilation, and plumbing.
- The walls in the athletic training room should have a minimum of two electrical outlets.
- The whirlpool area should have GFCI electrical outlets.
- Light fixtures should produce a minimum of 30 foot-candles at four feet above the surface. When illumination varies in intensity, the brightest ar-

eas are to be used for evaluation and treatment of injuries or other conditions.
- Because of the use of warm water in the whirlpools and the hydrocollators, super ventilation must be present.
- The ideal athletic training room temperature is between 68°F and 70°F.
- The basic minimum plumbing requirements include a deep sink with cold and hot water, a whirlpool, and a minimum of one to two floor drains.
- The athletic training room should have a number of locking storage cabinets and closets. Additionally, a telephone, desk, computer, and file cabinet are necessary.
- The athletic training room traffic flow will be determined by the size and shape of the facility, placement of lighting fixtures, location of electrical outlets, site of phone/computer lines, and position of plumbing fixtures.

The athletic training room traffic-flow problems can be improved by:

- placing a bench outside a small athletic training room to reduce congestion in the treatment area,
- locating those services used less often away from the entrance,
- positioning taping tables nearest to the entrance, and
- stationing the trainer's desk so all ongoing activity can be observed.

Basic Elements for Renovating or Retrofitting an Athletic Training Room

Unfortunately, many organizations do not have the money or facilities for the development of an ideal athletic training room or to implement all the recommendations of national organizations. Therefore, it will be necessary to renovate or retrofit present facilities. While these two options do not make it easy to develop the ideal training room, it is still possible to provide a practical and efficient athletic training room. The elements to be considered when planning this facility include size, location, traffic flow, and structural components.

Size

LaVoie (1999) indicates the athletic training room designer, the administrative requirements of the athletic training staff, number of athletes, type of equipment, storage needs, and expansion possibilities should be considered in determining the initial size of the athletic training room. Furthermore, he states that a rule of thumb for the size and shape of the athletic training room is unnecessary. Instead, he relies on excellent communication between the designer and the athletic training staff to develop an athletic training facility that will be both productive and efficient. In a way, he agrees with the American Academy of Orthopaedic Surgeons (1991) who maintain that the size and shape of the athletic training room help determine an ability to accommodate large numbers of athletes at one time. Arnheim and Prentice (1997), however, contend that any athletic training room less than 1,000 square feet is impractical.

Instead, they recommend that the facility be between 1,000 and 1,200 square feet, with 1,200 square feet being the preferred size. According to them, an athletic training room of this size accommodates large numbers of individuals along with the bulky equipment found in athletic training rooms.

Although minimum space requirements have been suggested, Penman and Penman (1982) provide a specific formula for determining a rough estimate of the minimum space needs for an athletic training room. This formula is based on the assertion that each taping or treatment table is sufficient for 20 athletes and occupies approximately 100 square feet, including the table, work area around the table, and counter and storage space. Thus, the minimum space for the athletic training room can be determined by dividing the number of athletes expected at peak times by 20. This will give the number of treatment and/or taping tables needed. Then, by multiplying by 100, the total square footage can be obtained. The formula follows:

Number of athletes at peak ÷ 20 x 100 = Total square footage for treatment/taping table. Sabo (2001) agrees that the athletic training room space needs can be determined by using the Penman formula. However, he suggests a more accurate means for sizing the athletic training room is by dividing the facility into eight functional areas: taping and first aid, hydrotherapy, treatment, rehabilitation, offices, physician's examination room, and storage. His specific recommendations for each of these areas follow:

- The taping and first aid areas are determined by using Penman's formula. However, Sabo does suggest that the minimum space requirements should be large enough for six taping tables to be used at the same time.
- The hydrotherapy area space is calculated by assessing the space needs of equipment in the area. Whirlpool space is based on the assumption that one whirlpool can accommodate three athletes per peak hour. Thus, the number of athletes to be treated during the peak hour is divided by 20 to determine the number of whirlpools needed. This number is multiplied by the square footage of the appropriate whirlpool to determine area needed. To calculate the square footage for the whirlpools, he uses the following guidelines: small whirlpool = 35 square feet,

medium whirlpool = 56 square feet, and large whirlpool = 64 square feet.
- The treatment area should be large enough to house six treatment tables with two of these having privacy curtains. According to Sabo, one treatment table will accommodate three athletes per hour. Consequently, to obtain the number of tables needed, divide by three the number of athletes to be treated during the peak hour. Then, multiply the required tables by 100 to assess the square footage needed in the treatment area.
- The size of the rehabilitation area depends on the amount and kind of equipment housed in this area. The space required for each piece of equipment, working area around the equipment, further expansion, and storage are added together to give approximate space requirements for the rehabilitation room.
- The head athletic trainer's office should be a minimum of 120 square feet.
- The physician's office should be a minimum of 120 square feet.
- The storage area should have at least 100 square feet; however, a more accurate measure is that the room should be large enough to hold one year's worth of supplies.

Location

In locating the athletic training room, working space and traffic flow is of primary importance. When followed, the guidelines listed below will meet these criteria. Ideally, the athletic training room should be:

- Close to bathrooms.
- Close to dressing rooms, but away from the showers.
- Close to water and drainage.
- Easily accessible for both men and women.
- Easily accessible to emergency vehicle loading zones.
- Near participation areas.
- Located on an outside wall.
- Equipped with a street-level double door that can be operated automatically (similar to a handicapped entranceway).
- Provided with a janitorial closet that has a large sink, floor drain, and storage area. This janitorial closet should be adjacent to or within the athletic training room.

Traffic Flow

The layout of the athletic training room is designed to maximize the traffic flow of individuals who are using the various services of the athletic training room. Ideally, according to Arnheim and Prentice (1997), individuals should be able to enter and exit the athletic training facilities from an outside doorway and from the men's and women's locker rooms. The design shown in their textbook illustrates an ideal layout. Some of the characteristics of this design are:

- Saves unnecessary footsteps.
- Provides completely unhampered and uncomplicated traffic lanes.
- Places sensitive equipment away from the traffic lanes.
- Positions the athletic trainer's office in the center of the room so he or she can observe all ongoing activities.
- Locates the physician's office in a far corner so there will be privacy during the physician's examination.
- Furnishes the physician's office with a desk and chair, treatment table, sink, refrigerator, and storage space.

Structural Components

To a large extent, structural features will dictate the configuration of the athletic training room. Accordingly, the following structural component guidelines will be beneficial in making the athletic training room as functional as possible:

- Ceilings should be a minimum of 10 feet in the treatment area so tall athletes can stand on treatment tables as they are being treated. Additionally, the ceilings should be constructed of material that reflects light and deadens sound. Acoustical tiles are excellent for the athletic training room. For best results, the tiles should be white, ivory, cream, or buff color. These colors tend to reduce glare and provide good light reflection.
- Doors must be large enough to accommodate a wheelchair or a stretcher. Generally, a door 36 inches wide is sufficient for most athletic training rooms. However, if the budget is generous, double doors should be installed in at least one entrance. The photo on this page shows the outside double doors leading into the building where the Eastern Kentucky athletic training room is located. These doors have a full glass view and are wide enough for those in wheelchairs or on stretchers to enter or exit through them. Additionally, the surface under the doors is flat, so there will be no problem in moving injured athletes in wheelchairs or stretchers.
- Electrical outlets should be located three to four feet from the floor and spaced at six- to eight-feet intervals. Outlets equipped with ground fault circuit interrupters (GFCI) are required in areas where there is moisture. However, it is best if all electrical outlets in the athletic training room are GFCI equipped because moisture could be present in all areas of the athletic training room.
- Equipment in the athletic training room should

Main Entrance to the Eastern Kentucky University Building, where the Athletic Training Room is Housed, Automatic Double-Wide Doors

be a minimum of a desk and chair, bookcase, locking file cabinet, one or two visitor chairs, a computer and printer, and a desk calculator. When possible, the computer should be connected to the Internet.
- Floors should be sloped toward a drainage area, covered with a nonslip surface, moisture resistant, and easily cleaned and disinfected. Good materials for the floor include concrete, vinyl tile, ceramic tile, and poured liquid floors.
- Illumination in the athletic training room should provide even and efficient light on the work surface. Fluorescent fixtures with diffusers for elimination of flickering and that produce a minimum of 30 foot-candles four feet above the work surface are good choices. For evaluation and treatment areas, 50 to 60 foot-candles four feet above the work surface are recommended.
- Plumbing should follow all applicable building codes and the plumbing area must include at least one floor drain equipped with a trap to prevent odors from entering the athletic training room. The plumbing area has a concrete floor covered with a paint that has been modified to prevent slippage, rubber strips, pitted surfaces, or a rubberized liquid coating. The plumbing area should have a back flow device, a deep sink (preferably a double sink) equipped with hot and cold running water, and at least one whirlpool located in an area with a floor drain. Additionally, all electrical outlets must be GFCI rated, and it is recommended that all equipment used in the plumbing area be approved by the Underwriter's Laboratory as safe for use in wet areas.
- Storage facilities are of prime importance and the storage area should include lock cabinets, lockers, and closets. For best results, the storage facilities should be near the working space, but

out of the traffic flow. Another storage consideration is that the storage area be designed so that it does not require excessive space. An example of efficient utilization of space is the taping and storage table at Austin Peay State University. This taping table shown to the right is 42 inches high, 144 inches long, and 48 inches deep. It will accommodate four to five athletes for taping and it is located near the entrance to the athletic training room and adjacent to the head athletic trainer's office. Beneath the tabletop are lockable cabinets that are used to store tape and other supplies. Directly across from the taping and storage table is a treatment storage cabinet pictured to the right, which is 42 inches high, 84 inches long, and 26 inches deep. This cabinet is approximately six feet from the taping table, making it easy for the trainers to obtain the supplies they need for minor treatment and for preventive taping and wrapping activities. Another good feature of this taping and storage area is its close proximity to the athletic trainer's office and the fact that it facilitates preventing waste of materials and supplies while requiring very little square footage.

Austin Peay State University Taping Table

- Temperature control is provided with heating, ventilating, and air-conditioning (HVAC) units capable of maintaining a constant temperature range of 72° to 78°F and a humidity range of 40 to 50%. Additionally, the temperature control system must be sufficient to change the room air eight to 10 times each hour so vapors from the warm water present in the whirlpools and hydrocollators can be exhausted continuously. Moreover, it is recommended, when possible, that the athletic training room temperature control units be separate from the rest of the building's temperature control units.
- Windows should be installed in such a manner that all activities in the athletic training room can be observed but, at the same time, maintain the privacy of individuals who may be conversing in the office area. One-way mirrors are good choices when privacy and adequate supervision are of primary importance.

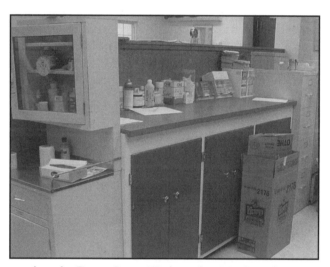

Austin Peay State University Taping Area Storage Cabinet

Equipment Considerations for the Athletic Training Facility

Athletic training rooms contain a variety of equipment with the extent of the equipment being determined by the availability of financial resources and physical facilities. There are three categories of athletic training room equipment: basic, moderate, and ultimate (well-equipped).

Basic Equipment Needs

Basic equipment for the athletic training room consists of a dry and wet heat source, cold source, rehabilitation source, locking supply cabinet, treatment cabinet, training table, and whirlpool.

- Heat lamps provide dry heat for treatment of injuries. If a heat lamp is not available, a heating pad is a good substitute. Both of these dry heat devices are inexpensive and safe for use in the athletic training room equipped with GFCI-equipped electrical outlets.
- A refrigerator is necessary for maintenance of an adequate supply of ice for use in treating injuries. A used refrigerator may be purchased in any locality at a reasonable price; however, just keep in mind that the main feature of this refrigerator is its capacity for making and keeping ice. It is also useful for storing ice bags and cold water.
- A double sink equipped with hot and cold running water, hooked to a trapped drain, and with under the sink storage and counter space of two

to four feet is strongly recommended. Sinks are relatively inexpensive and can be purchased at home centers. Sinks may also be obtained from salvage yards or obtained when someone remodels a home or business.

- A supply cabinet is an essential piece of equipment for the athletic training room. The supply cabinet may be either metal or wood and it may be constructed or purchased secondhand. A suitable closet may be used, but it is important that any supply storage area be kept locked to prevent waste and misuse of athletic training materials. The photo to the right shows a suitable supply cabinet used in the Austin Peay State University athletic training room. The cabinet is 66 inches high (36 inches on the bottom and 30 inches on the top), 18 inches on the bottom section, eight inches deep on the top section, and 30 inches wide.

- The treatment cabinet must have an adequate working surface and space for holding first-aid and other treatment supplies. It should lock to prevent misuse of supplies and to keep the supplies sanitary. A set of regular quart mason jars placed on the cabinet surface is recommended to keep dressing materials clean and available. The size of the treatment cabinet will vary among athletic training rooms; however, a treatment cabinet 78 inches high, 18 to 20 inches deep, and 36 inches wide is adequate for most basically equipped athletic training rooms.

- The training table is the most essential piece of athletic training room equipment, as it is used for examining injuries, applying treatment modalities, and applying protective taping and/or wrapping. The training table is usually constructed of heavy wood and measures 78 inches long, 24 inches wide, and 30 inches high. The top is covered with foam rubber or some other form of padding over which an easily cleaned cloth or other covering is applied. Figure 25.1 shows the pattern for a basic athletic training table.

- The whirlpool is another essential piece of equipment for the athletic training room for its use in applying wet, moving heat to athletic injuries. It is important that the whirlpool is on a concrete surface and that the area has adequate drains plus GFCI-equipped electrical outlets. The photo on the next page shows a whirlpool setup in the Eastern Kentucky University athletic training room. One way of improvising a whirlpool bath is to take an old bathtub and equip it with a portable agitator. Be certain the improvised whirlpool is properly grounded and connected to GFCI electrical outlets.

Austin Peay State University Supply Cabinet

Figure 25.1. Athletic Training Table Pattern

Eastern Kentucky University Whirlpool Setup

Examples of Moderately and Well-Equipped Training Rooms

Examples of a moderately and a well-equipped athletic training room are those at Austin Peay State University (APSU) and Eastern Kentucky University (EKU). One, APSU, is a retrofitted facility and the other, EKU, is a newly built structure.

Austin Peay State University

Austin Peay State University in Clarksville, Tennessee is typical of a moderately equipped athletic training room facility. It was retrofitted from a small athletic training room for football, two locker rooms, three shower rooms, a steam room, a large hallway, a sunken whirlpool and its deck, and an equipment issuing room.

The athletic training room contains 2,138 square feet and it is divided into seven components: head athletic trainer's office; assistant athletic trainer's office; team physician's office; treatment room; taping, wrapping, and weighing room; hydrotherapy room; and storage areas.

Head Athletic Trainer's Office

The head athletic trainer's office has 132 square feet (11 feet by 12 feet). It was retrofitted from an equipment issuing room and it has an entrance door from the hallway and a door leading to the taping table. The door leading to the taping table area has glass so it offers a direct sight line to the taping table area and a partial sight line to the treatment room. Yet the office design allows for privacy when it is needed. It contains:

- a desk and chair,
- a chair for consultations,
- a computer connected to the Internet,
- a printer for the computer,
- a telephone,
- a recording machine for voice mail,
- a calculator,
- two two-drawer and one four-drawer file cabinets,

- a large double-door cabinet that has locking drawers and file cabinets,
- a bookcase with adjustable shelves and a locking cabinet and drawer, and
- a small bookcase with three shelves.

Assistant Athletic Trainer's Office

Two assistant athletic trainers share an office containing 110 square feet (10 feet by 11 feet). The office was constructed from an area in the rehabilitation area. It has two windows and a glass door with a clear sight line to the rehabilitation activities. This office is equipped with

- two desks and chairs,
- one computer with Internet connection,
- one printer,
- a small worktable,
- two file cabinets, and
- bookshelves along one of the walls.

Team Physician's Office

The physician's office has 96 square feet (12 feet by 8 feet) and is located at one end of the treatment area. It has

- a solid door for privacy,
- a telephone,
- a desk and chair,
- an examination table,
- locking storage cabinets along one wall, and
- a sink with hot and cold running water.

Treatment Room

The treatment room is located in a separate room that can be partially observed by the head athletic trainer from his office. It was once a locker room, and it has 345 square feet (23 feet by 15 feet) of space. It has the following treatment modalities:

- Orthotron KT1 exercise table
- Synatron 500 Electrotherapy CTL CTR
- Nemectron 2 ultrasound therapy unit
- Pentium Z station ZSK-8559
- Electrotherapy ultrasound modality
- Two Mettler electronic stimulators
- Z station
- treatment tables
- examination tables
- a hydrocollator and hydrocollator tree
- a computer with printer

Rehabilitation Room

The rehabilitation room was retrofitted from a dressing room. It has 448 square feet (28 feet by 16 feet) of space in which the following pieces of rehabilitation equipment are located:

- a Nemectrodyn Model V
- a Nemectrodyn MDL-2 nerve stimulator device

- an Orthotron II Fitron cycle-ergometer
- a Cybex 2450 upper body exerciser
- a Lifestep 1000
- a cable column rehabilitation device

Taping, Wrapping, and Weighing Room

The taping, wrapping, and weighing room has 228 square feet (19 feet by 12 feet) of useable space. It, like the rehabilitation room and assistant athletic trainer's office, was retrofitted from a room used for dressing and locker space. It has a taping table that is 144 inches long, 42 inches high, and 48 inches deep; a large weight scale; and a storage cabinet that is 84 inches long, 26 inches deep, and 42 inches high. The taping, wrapping, and weighing area is directly to the right of the entrance into the training room and is situated directly adjacent to the head athletic trainer's office. It is separated from the rehabilitation area by a five-inch-thick wooden partition wall that is 60 inches high and 145 inches long. This area is shown in Figures 25.3 and 25.4.

Hydrotherapy Room

The hydrotherapy room was once a shower room. It contains 60 square feet (10 feet by six feet), and it has a full body whirlpool and two extremity whirlpools. It is located adjacent to the treatment area, but it must be entered through a door from the treatment room, making it impossible to supervise its activities from any of the offices or other areas of the athletic training room. It has GFCI electrical outlets and excellent drainage. Additionally, the area has a curb that prevents overflowing water from entering the treatment or storage areas.

Storage Areas

The Austin Peay State University athletic training room has four retrofitted storage areas other than those already mentioned. One of these is a converted shower room containing 84 square feet of useable space (14 feet by 6 feet). It houses the ice machine, and it is where all the drinking and ice containers and the crutches are kept.

Another major storage area is located directly across from the hydrotherapy room in what was once a hall leading from the treatment room area to a steam room and a sunken whirlpool. This area contains 240 square feet (16 feet by 15 feet). It has lockable metal and wooden lockers that are used to store various treatment and rehabilitation supplies and equipment.

The area that was originally a large sunken whirlpool has 255 square feet (17 feet by 15 feet) including the large whirlpool, the whirlpool deck, and the hallway leading to the steam room. The area is utilized mostly for large boxes as well as a variety of protective and preventive equipment.

The former steam room is the most secure storage area, for it has a metal door and is away from any traffic flow. It has 180 square feet (15 feet by 12 feet). It is used to store old records and sensitive supplies and equipment. The room also has temperature and humidity controls not present in the other storage areas.

Eastern Kentucky University

Eastern Kentucky University's new athletic training room is an example of a well-equipped facility, and it demonstrates what can be done when building a new athletic training room. It is located on the first floor of the 40,000-square-foot Harry Moberly Classroom, Wellness, and Conditioning Building. The first floor of the building houses the physical education activity/laboratory, the weight room, and the athletic training room. On the second floor, there is a wellness center, three large classrooms, human performance and computer laboratories, offices, locker rooms, showers, and dressing rooms. Primarily, the building houses the College of Health, Physical Education, Recreation, and Athletics plus the 16 intercollegiate athletic teams.

The athletic training room is located between the weight room and the physical activity/laboratory. It is entered from the main foyer through glass-enclosed double doors that do not have thresholds. The athletic training facility functional areas follow (see photos on the following pages):

- a taping/treatment area
- a rehabilitation area
- a treatment/therapy area
- glass-enclosed office
- therapy storage area
- hydrotherapy cooler storage area
- an in-ground hydrotherapy pool equipped with a treadmill
- rehabilitation storage area
- treatment storage area
- hydrotherapy room

In addition to the areas depicted here, the athletic training facility has three above-ground therapeutic pools in the hydrotherapy area, X-ray room with accompanying equipment and exposure control measures, and private examination rooms. All office doors have either full glass or partial full-length glass so activities can be observed from the office. There are artificial and natural light sources in all areas.

**Eastern Kentucky University
Taping/Treatment Area**

**Eastern Kentucky University
Rehabilitation Area**

**Eastern Kentucky University
Treatment/Therapy Area**

Eastern Kentucky University
Office Area

Eastern Kentucky University
Treatment/Therapy Storage Area

Eastern Kentucky University
Hydrotherapy Cooler Storage Area

Eastern Kentucky University
In-Ground Therapy Pool with Treadmill

Eastern Kentucky University
Rehabilitation Storage Area

Eastern Kentucky University
Treatment Storage Area

Eastern Kentucky University
Hydrotherapy Room

SHOOTING FACILITIES: ARCHERY, RIFLE, AND PISTOL 26

Jason Winkle, Indiana State University

The evolution of modern shooting sports can be traced back to early man's development of bows, arrows, and spears for protection and a way to gather food. Around 3,500 BC, the Egyptians used archery as a weapon of war (*USA Archery, 2008*). Much of the early development of archery was based on designing archery equipment for a military application. In addition to using bows and arrows for weapons, they were also used for leisure activities and contests. Homer, in the *Iliad*, referenced archery contests in which archers shot at tethered doves. During the 14th century in England, archery practice was mandatory for all able-bodied men (Van Dalen & Bennett, 1971). The advent of gunpowder led to the decline of archery as a tool of war and to the increased development of firearm activities. Organized firearms shooting began in Europe when the first shooting clubs were formed. Public shooting matches were first seen in Europe around the 16th century and in America in the early 1700s.

The rules for shooting sports began to standardize when the National Rifle Association (NRA) was founded in the United States in 1871 and the National Archery Association (NAA) was formed in 1879. Numerous disciplines have developed for rifle, pistol, and archery sports; therefore, the facilities, equipment, and procedures used for shooting activities and competitions vary greatly. This chapter will focus on facilities, equipment, and operational procedures required when developing and operating competitive indoor rifle and pistol facilities and both indoor and outdoor archery facilities. The equipment, facility design, and risk management issues associated with these competitive shooting facilities can be applied or adapted to other shooting activities and facilities.

Planning and Designing a Shooting Facility

Whether planning and designing a shooting facility from scratch, remodeling an existing facility to accommodate shooting activities, or renovating an existing shooting facility, detailed planning will avoid costly design mistakes. The major factors that usually determine any facility design are the funding; availability of appropriate space; nature and scope of the program; and quality of the planners, architects, and engineers involved in the project.

Since each planning and design situation is different, the relative importance of each design criteria will vary with each project. Based on guidelines for facility planning and shooting facility specific design criteria, the following are sound general guidelines for planning a shooting facility:

- Participatory planning—Involve the stakeholders in the planning process. This may include establishing a formal planning team.
- Needs assessment—Determine past, present, and future needs and desires as early and as accurately as possible in the design process.
- Site selection—A large, relatively flat area is ideal, since archery ranges are large facilities that usually require a flat shooting area. Consider the type and use of adjacent areas when selecting the shooting facility site. Use of natural land features such as hillsides may provide natural backdrops if available.
- Build to code—Be certain all construction meets governmental (local, state, and national) building codes to include Americans With Disabilities Act (ADA) requirements. If the shooting facility is to be used for competitions, be sure the facility specifications meet or exceed those required by sanctioning agencies. For target archery, the Federation Internationale de Tir a l'Arc (FITA) and the NAA are the recognized sanctioning organizations. These organizations publish detailed rules and specifications for sanctioned archery competitions.
- Support selection—A careful and judicious process should be used when selecting the architect, engineers, contractors, and any other consultants. Select individuals or organizations

that have experience in building shooting or similar facilities and have good references. Do not hesitate to contact previous customers.

- Risk management—When planning a shooting facility, be certain to address security, access control, and buffer zones around shooting areas.

The specific design features for a shooting facility will depend on the availability of an appropriate site, the availability of funds, the type of shooting, and many other factors. Proper prior planning will help ensure a highly functional and efficient shooting facility.

Archery

According to *The American Heritage Dictionary*, "Archery is the art, sport, or skill of shooting with a bow and arrow." Although this may sound simple, many archery disciplines and activities have developed over the years. Competitive archery as we know it today originated in England in the 17th century.

Most early competitions fell into one of three general categories of shooting: butt shooting, clout shooting, or roving. Butt shooting consisted of bowmen shooting from set distances at targets mounted vertically on earthen mounds or butts. Most modern competitive archery programs and competitions are based on butt shooting. Clout shooting involved shooting arrows into the air and having them land on a target mounted flat on the ground. The third type of archery was roving, where archers simulated hunting over rough ground and shooting targets representing animals. Roving is the forerunner of today's field archery programs that focus on hunting-oriented shooting. Field archery shots are often made uphill or downhill and may involve shooting around obstacles.

The most popular and numerous archery ranges are basic outdoor designs often referred to as "place-to-shoot ranges." These unmanned place-to-shoot ranges usually have target distances from 25 to 100 yards and cater to bow hunters. Some ranges include a field archery course that has targets placed in a natural setting and may even have tree stand stations to simulate bow hunting. Archers bring their own equipment and shoot unsupervised. Few specific design features other than a parking lot, outhouse, and possibly a covered pavilion are normally included. Most archery programs in schools, colleges, recreation settings, and the Olympics are based on early forms of butt shooting. The equipment, facilities, and risk-management procedures used for this type of target shooting are well established and clearly defined by the FITA and the NAA. This section will focus on facilities and equipment to support competitive target archery programs. Most of the facility and equipment issues for competitive target archery are applicable to other less structured types of archery shooting.

Outdoor Target Archery Competitions

Most major outdoor target archery competitions in the United States include a FITA Round followed by an Olympic Round. A FITA Round consists of 36 arrows shot at each of four distances (90, 70, 50, and 30 meters for men; 70, 60, 50, 30 meters for women) for a total of 144 arrows. Arrows are generally shot in groups of six (called ends) within a specified time period. Scores are then totaled to determine seeding for the Olympic Round. An Olympic Round is a direct elimination, head-to-head competition shot at 70 meters. The winner of each match advances until a champion is determined. All matches are 18 arrows, except the quarterfinals, semifinals, and finals, which are 12-arrow matches.

Indoor Target Archery Competitions

Indoor tournaments are held for the Recurve (Olympic) and Compound Divisions. Recurve Division events are generally held at either 25 meters or 18 meters. In a 25-Meter Indoor Round, archers shoot 60 arrows at a 60 cm diameter target face. In the 18-Meter Indoor Round, archers shoot 60 arrows at a 40 cm diameter target face. Championship events employ a Grand Indoor Round that starts off with a Combined Indoor Round (both 25-meter and 18-meter rounds) followed by a direct elimination competition for the top 16 archers. These direct elimination matches are 15-arrow matches shot at a special 20 cm diameter target face. Competitions in the Compound Division usually consist of a Combined Indoor Round of 60 arrows shot from 25 meters at 40 cm diameter target face. A Grand Indoor Round, used in championships, consists of a Double Combined Indoor Round. The top 16 archers advance to direct elimination matches made up of 15 arrows at 25 meters.

Target Archery Ranges

Competition target archery ranges must be designed and built to meet or exceed FITA and NAA specifications, the recognized sanctioning organizations for most archery competitions. FITA and NAA have also established standards for Field Archery and Ski-Archery; but these standards are outside the scope of this chapter.

Target archery ranges are often set up on multipurpose outdoor fields or in large multipurpose indoor areas. Some schools, clubs, camps, and other agencies have custom designed permanent archery facilities. The Beijing Shooting Range Hall, used in the 2008 Olympics, is an example of a world-class shooting hall. Whether the shooting facility is a permanent facility or a temporary setup in a multipurpose facility, a classroom or meeting room is recommended if the shooting facility is to be used by a club or for educational purposes.

Outdoor archery ranges are most effectively laid out on level turf oriented north to south with shooting aimed to the north. The actual shooting length of the archery range will vary depending on the shooting event being contested but the range layout is basically the same for all events. The archers shoot from the Shooting Line at targets placed at the prescribed distance. The minimum spacing of the targets for competitions depends upon the number of shooters per lane. If shooters are shooting singly or in pairs, the minimum spacing between targets is 2.5 meters (8 feet, 2 inches) and 3.66 meters (12 feet) if the archers are shooting in threes. All targets should be clearly numbered. Shooting marks, consisting of discs or other flat markers, should be positioned opposite the targets at the shooting line. The shooting marks have the number that corresponds with the target for that lane. A line extending from the shooting line to the target line establishes shooting lanes. A waiting line should be placed at least five yards behind the shooting line. An equipment area may be marked off behind the waiting area. Behind the equipment area a space for athletes is recommended. A 50-yard buffer zone must be roped off behind the targets to keep spectators, competitors, and officials safe (see Figure 26.1).

Traditional targets consisted of a boss of tightly coiled roped straw about four inches thick and four feet in diameter on which is stretched a target face. Targets for both indoor and outdoor target archery competitions are now often made of high-density foam. Targets must be secured to target stands, called butts (buttresses), which are secured to the ground. For indoor archery, targets must be inclined, tilted back, between vertical and 10 degrees. For outdoor archery, targets must be inclined 10 to 15 degrees.

The center of the target for both indoor and outdoor targets must be 130 cm (four feet, three inches) (within 5 cm) above the ground for single target faces. All targets must be inclined at the same angle. The target face consists of 10 rings made out of five different colors. The scoring is 10,9 (gold), 8,7 (red), 6,5 (blue), 4,3 (black), 2,1 (white) from inner circle to outer ring. The rings all have the same thickness (except for the compound competitions where the 10 is made smaller). Target sizes vary at different distances and may be displayed as a single face (see Figure 26.2), triple faces triangular, or triple faces vertical.

Figure 26.1
Sample Archery Range Layout

Figure 26.2
Single-Faced Target

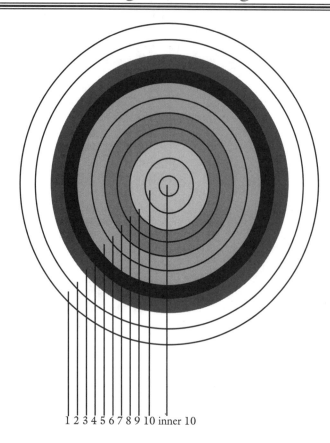

1 2 3 4 5 6 7 8 9 10 inner 10

Venue Support Equipment

If an archery range will be used for competitions, especially FITA- or NAA-sanctioned competitions, additional venue support equipment will be required. The following is a brief description of some of the additional equipment that may be required to host a sanctioned archery tournament:

- Barriers—Some type of physical restraint placed on the range to mark safety buffer zones to keep spectators out of the archers' competition areas and facilitate desired circulation patterns. The barriers may be as simple as a rope suspended between two poles or a fenced-in area with directional signage attached. The barriers must clearly designate safety zones and provide a physical obstruction.
- Scoreboards—A minimum of one large scoreboard is needed for posting scores. For large, sanctioned competitions, smaller scoreboards should be placed near the target butt to display a progressive score for each shooter. For less formal competitions and during match competitions, flip scoreboards may be used.
- Flags—Judges and officials are often separated from the archers and other meet officials. Flags

or a similar device should be available for judges and officials for signaling or requesting assistance.
- Speaker system—Important announcements will need to be made during competitions to archers, coaches, officials, meet organizers, and spectators. A quality speaker system is needed to meet this requirement.
- Timing control equipment—Most archery competitions have time limits for the archers to shoot their ends. Enforcing the established time limits is essential in having a fair competition, so both visual and acoustic time signals are required for most sanctioned competitions. Visual time signals can be given with digital clocks, lights, flags, or other simple visual devices. The acoustical signals may be given with a whistle, air horn, or a similar device.
- Archer identification—Tournament officials, organizers, and spectators need to be able to identify archers competing in the competition. In championship tournaments, archers must wear nametags and have a nameplate displayed at the target area. Even at less formal tournaments, archers must wear some type of identification tag, number, or vest.

- Field glasses—Some type of visual aid is often necessary for competition administrators and officials to spot arrows. Providing field glasses or a telescope at the shooting facility is recommended.

Shooters Equipment

Bows used for target archery are held in one hand and drawn with the other. They may have an adjustable arrow rest on the riser. The bowstring is permitted to have a center serving to fit the arrow nocks, with one or two nock locators, and one attachment to serve as a lip or nose mark. An audible or visual draw checker (clicker) may be used as long as it is not electrical. Stabilizers and torque compensators are allowed, as long as they do not touch anything but the bow itself, and do not interfere with other competitors on the shooting line.

Recurve Bow

A recurve bow is a relatively short bow that was preferred over the longbow by archers who were forced into environments where long weapons could be cumbersome. A recurve bow used for target archery consists of a handle riser and two flexible limbs terminating in nocks supporting a single string.

The distinguishing feature of the recurve bow is that the ends of the limbs curve away from the archer when in the shooting position (See Figure 26.3). This recurve shape reduces loading at full draw (let-off) and will impart more energy to the arrow than a standard longbow of similar top draw weight.

Compound Bow

Compound bows have cams and cables, making the holding weight less than half of the draw weight. Bow hunters favor them because of their greater accuracy, flatter arrow trajectory, and their ease of use. A compound bow with a peak draw weight of 60 pounds or less may be used for target archery competitions. Cables and cable guards are allowed (see Figure 26.4). The bowstring may contain a peep sight or hole for sighting. The bow sight may not have electrical components but may contain lenses and/or multiple aim points. A mechanical string release may be used, as long as it does not attach to the bow and has no electrical components.

Strings

Strings are usually made by twining several strings of Kevlar, Dacron, or polyethylene to make a single cord. Dacron is relatively inexpensive, but prone to creep, meaning that it may stretch and make for inconsistent shots. Dacron is recommended for bows with wooden risers and older bows since the other string materials might put too much stress on the bow. Aramid fibers (Kevlar) have very little stretch, thus giving the arrow

Figure 26.3
The Basic Recurve Bow

Figure 26.4
The Compound Bow

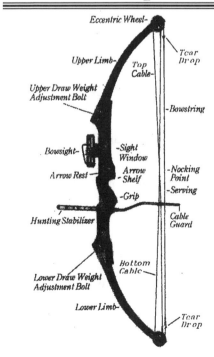

a flatter trajectory. The disadvantage of Kevlar is that these fibers cannot take much shear, so they tend to break more often, usually just below the nocking point. Kevlar fibers are also very susceptible to moisture; therefore, these strings have to be waxed carefully. Polyethylene fibers are the latest addition to string materials. Polyethylene strings last at least as long as those made of Dacron and are less susceptible to moisture than other string materials.

Sights

The sight can come in many forms; but, the most popular sight has a circular sight with a cross-hairs or pin at its center. Some compound bows incorporate a "spirit level" that tells the archer if the bow is tilted.

Arrows

Wooden shafted arrows are still used with longbows and for recreational purposes but are rarely used for competitive target archery. For competitive target archery, arrows of any type may be used as long as the maximum diameter is 9.3 mm (.366 inch) or less. Arrows should be marked with the competitor's initials and all arrows used in an end must be of uniform color, shaft, fletching, and cresting. The most commonly used arrows for target archery are made of aluminum tubes, carbon fibers, or an aluminum/carbon combination (a very thin aluminum tube inside and carbon fibers on the outside).

Aluminum tube arrows are more durable than either of the carbon fiber type arrows. Carbon fiber arrows and aluminum/carbon arrows are nearly impossible to repair if damaged. Aluminum/carbon arrows are the most commonly used arrows for outdoor shooting. All three arrow types are used for indoor shooting.

Vanes, also called the fletching, are the three featherlike attachments near the rear of the arrow that keep the arrow tracking. There are two options for vanes, either plastic vanes or real feathers. Plastic vanes are less affected by moisture and are recommended for outdoor shooting.

General Archery Equipment

A bow, arrows, and a target are required for target archery shooting, but experienced archers rarely shoot with only the bare essentials. Archers or those conducting an archery program, whether highly competitive or recreational, should consider purchasing the following general archery equipment:

- Arm guard—A piece of leather or other durable material that fits over the bow arm that keeps the string from contacting the arm when the string is released.
- Chest guard—Protects the chest and prevents clothing from becoming caught by the string.

- Finger protectors—One of a variety of protective finger stalls, gloves, tabs, or tape methods to protect the fingers on the draw hand.
- Quiver—An arrow-holding device that can be worn on the body or attached to the bow.
- Arrow straightener—A device that measures arrow bend and straightens arrows.
- Grip/arrow pull—A rubber grip that helps in removing arrows from the target.
- Fletching jig—Allows you to fletch a shaft, put vanes on it.
- Nocking jig—Allows you to accurately replace a nock on the arrow shaft.
- Stringer—Recurve archers use this device to string their bows. Compound bows are permanently strung and many longbows have built in stringers.
- Stringing rig—A device you can make your own strings with.
- String server—A device that allows you to create nocking points on the string.

Equipment Care and Maintenance

The Bow

The bow is the most important piece of equipment in archery, so keeping it in good working condition is essential. A sound practice is to never lay the bow on the ground. This can cause dust and other materials to damage or ruin sensitive parts of the bow. If a bow becomes wet for any reason, dry it off as soon as possible even if the finishes are waterproof. Metal bows may rust, reducing bow function. Apply bow wax to preserve the bow's finish.

Bow Strings

This vital part of the bow is perhaps one of the easier areas to damage. To avoid damage, archers should use bow string wax to keep the string waterproof. This will help keep the string in maximum performance condition and prevent it from becoming tangled.

Arrows

Although numerous and somewhat inexpensive, an arrow which has even the slightest malfunction can cause unexpected and unwanted results. Protect the fletching from getting wet or becoming damaged. Repair or discard any damaged arrows. Serious archers should only use arrows deemed to be in perfect condition.

Target Butts

To help prevent fungus growth, mold, and premature deterioration, do not place target butts on damp floors or leave them uncovered in the rain.

Target Faces

Target faces must be in good condition. Remove faces while moistening butts. If the face is torn, use masking tape to bind the tears.

Replacing a Plastic Nock

Nocks may become worn down and will need to be replaced, so inspect the nock regularly.

Replacing a Feather or Vane

Replacing a feather or vane is easy, but restoring an arrow to competition quality is difficult, and requires skill, experience, and the use of a feather jig. Feather replacement is only recommended for arrows that will be used for recreation or practice shooting.

Replacing Arrow Points

The condition of the arrow shaft directly behind the point should be checked when replacing points. If the shaft is damaged, the arrow cannot be repaired unless the shaft is shortened. These salvaged arrows may still be used for school, recreation, and practice purposes, but are no longer suitable for competition shooting.

Storage

The amount of storage required for an archery facility will vary based on many factors. If the archery facility is used for instructional and recreation programs where the program sponsors provide the equipment, well-secured storage will be necessary. If the archery facility is simply an outdoor facility that stocks limited personal archery gear, the storage requirements will be considerably less than a facility that provides equipment. If any bows and arrows are to be stored, they must be stored in a secure area since they could be used as weapons. Archery equipment, especially bows, arrows and targets, must be stored in a dry environment to avoid damage.

Rifle and Pistol

The first consideration when designing an indoor shooting facility is determining what type of shooting will be conducted. Firearm caliber, muzzle velocity, and the nature of the shooting all play an important role in the construction needs of the facility. Firearms commonly used in indoor ranges include air pistols, air rifles, handguns of various calibers, and rifles with muzzle velocities below 3,500 feet per second. Indoor ranges can also be used for a variety of shooting approaches from basic marksmanship to tactical shooting where participants practice defensive shooting skills. While each of the above-mentioned shooting variables have unique facility needs, they all share some common design characteristics.

This section will examine these common design characteristics and design and construction standards for indoor shooting ranges.

Space Needs

Once the types of shooting that will be conducted in a facility have been determined, the focus can shift to designing a facility to adequately and safely house these shooting activities. The largest expense in range development is usually the real estate that comprises the shooting area. Thorough planning to determine space needs is critical to keep development prices from escalating dramatically. Most competition shooting can be accommodated with a range that provides 50 to 100 feet between the target and the firing line. The industry standard length, however, is 84 feet, 4 inches (Navy Environmental Health Center [NEHC], 2002). Be sure to identify all space needs to include support functions such as parking areas, restrooms, storage, office space, lobby area, and circulation space.

Ceiling Height and Construction

An important space consideration is ceiling height in the range. A ceiling that is too low or too high can cause ricochet issues that must be addressed with baffling and other types of ballistic protection. A ceiling height between 10 and 12 feet is recommended (NEHC, 2002). This height provides adequate overhead clearance for downrange shooting as well as keeping lighting, ventilation, and target retrieval systems costs to a minimum.

A slab ceiling is the industry standard. Slab ceilings require few baffles and guards, thus reducing costs. Guards are required, however, for any exposed light fixtures, ducts, conduits, and plumbing. For ceilings other than slab, baffles and guards must be placed at angles that are determined by the length and height of the facility. A 30-degree angle to the ceiling is suggested for baffle placement (United States Corps of Engineers Huntsville Division [CEHND], 1990).

Shooting Stalls

Shooting stalls function as protective dividers between shooters in the range by preventing interference from expelled casings, misdirected shots, and other distractions. In addition to their protective characteristics, stalls also provide a stable mounting position for range equipment. Stalls are typically equipped with a self-controlled target retrieval system to prevent shooters from stepping downrange from the firing line (CEHND, 1990). A stall width between 42 inches and 48 inches is suggested.

Shooting stalls are typically constructed of double-wall steel liners covered in a molded shell. While steel has been the industry standard, a new clear acrylic stall is becoming more popular. The acrylic stall is very popular in academic shooting ranges due to the unobstructed view the clear dividers provide range personnel.

Shooting stalls for shooters

Wall Construction

Range walls provide a protective shell between the interior of the range and the building exterior or adjacent spaces. In addition to their safety function, walls play an important role in noise attenuation. Most range walls are constructed of poured concrete. Concrete block is also acceptable; however, the block should be filled with grout or cement. Unfilled block is sufficient in ballistic security but has poor sound-dampening qualities. Sound-dampening tiles are recommended for the walls from an area 10 feet forward of the firing line to 20 feet in front of the bullet trap.

Flooring

The flooring in shooting ranges needs to be durable enough to withstand the high volume of stray shots that will strike it and smooth enough to prevent erratic ricochets. Most ranges utilize a hardened concrete floor. Absorbent material behind padding for construction is to include floor drains. Excluding floor drains and sloped floors in the shooting area is recommended. Environmental regulations stipulate that all floor drains located between the firing line and the bullet trap must contain filtration systems. These systems tend to be very expensive and require substantial maintenance.

Back wall padding for shooting range

The flooring from the firing line backwards should be covered with a non-slip surface. Moderate traction in these areas is suggested to prevent shooters from losing their footing. Many ranges have a vinyl floor cover in this area to prevent slippage. Carpeting is not recommended as it tends to collect lead dust and is cumbersome to clean (NEHC, 2002).

Bullet Traps

Bullet traps have evolved substantially over the past 50 years. Environmental standards, particularly during the 1980s, have changed to accommodate environmental and safety concerns, but the object of the bullet trap has remained constant. The goal of any bullet trap is to provide a means of decelerating the bullet into a collection chamber. A brief description of the plate and pit trap, Venetian blind trap, steel escalator trap, and the granular rubber trap is provided below:

Absorbent material behind padding for back wall of shooting range

- Plate and pit trap—The first widely accepted bullet traps utilized a steel plate that was secured, at a 45-degree angle, into a deceleration chamber (NECH, 2002). The bullet would strike the angled plate and break apart inside the chamber. While this method accomplished its purpose, it raised environmental concerns due to the generation of lead fragments and lead dust that accompanied a destroyed bullet. Other concerns with this type of trap include high noise levels from bullets striking steel, as well as erratic ricochets.
- Venetian blind trap—The first widely accepted improvement to the plate and pit trap was the Venetian blind trap. The trap utilized a series of impact plates angled at approximately 35 degrees to direct bullets into a deceleration chamber (NECH, 2002). The bullet's velocity and energy is dissipated via friction. Typically this trap was a small freestanding trap, making it a popular model for shooting ranges.

- Steel escalator trap—The next evolution of bullet traps improved on the problem of bullets hitting the front edges of the Venetian trap. This improvement was accomplished by designing a sloping plate that directed bullets into a deceleration chamber. This trap utilizes sloping surfaces to create multiple striking areas where the bullet loses energy and then drops into a collection tray (CEHND, 1990).
- Granular rubber trap—The latest development in high-tech, environmentally sound bullet traps is the granular rubber trap. This trap is constructed with an inclined skeleton of steel that supports a sloped mound of granulated rubber covered with a rubber blanket for containment. This design provides excellent sound attenuation as the bullets strike only rubber. Lead recovery is also simple and safer because the bullets are not destroyed upon impact. Bullets are decelerated and contained in the top 10 inches of the granulated rubber. Erratic ricochets resulting from hitting the trap itself are no longer a problem.

Range Lighting

Shooting range illumination entails general facility brightness and target specific lighting. Fluorescent fixtures typically generate general illumination. A soft light is preferable for general areas of the range. Target-specific lights need to be much brighter and have the ability to be moved to achieve a direct focus on a target. Recommended down range lighting should be approximately 100 foot-candles measured four feet above the floor at target face (NECH, 2002). These lights should be baffled to protect them from misdirected shots. Many shooting experts, however, prefer recessed floor spotlights. Shadowing is typically less of a problem with bottom-illuminated targets. It is important to have protective covers for floor lighting, since stray shots often strike the floor of a range.

Target Retrieval Systems

The purpose of a target retrieval system is to place the target downrange and retrieve it in a safe

Target pulley with cables

and convenient manner. Target retrieval systems allow the shooter to remain behind the firing line. The type of shooting that will be conducted in the range determines the type of retrieval system needed. Most target shooting consists of firing at a stationary bull's-eye target at predetermined distances and then retrieving the target to determine shooting accuracy. Two types of target retrieval systems are commonly used for this purpose, a guide wire system and a steel track system.

These retrieval systems have the following features:

- Guide wire system—This system utilizes a guide wire that is suspended between the bullet trap and the firing line. A target attachment travels along the tight guide wire to place the target downrange or for retrieval. The shooter typically controls the target's movement along the guide wire via a control switch located in the shooting stall. Many models of guide wire systems allow for intermediate target stops for various shooting distances. One limitation of guide wire systems is that they typically don't allow for target oscillation.
- Steel track system—A steel track system is the most common target retrieval choice in commercial and law enforcement facilities. In addition to providing shooters with multiple stops, these systems offer 180-degree turning targets to present tactical situations. A steel track runs along the length of the shooting lane, providing the support structure for an oscillating target system.

Range Control

There are a variety of range control systems on the market, each with unique features. All of these systems, however, serve as the command center for target placement and retrieval. Some systems are controlled from the shooting stall while others utilize a central control booth. The level of sophistication and the capabilities of a control system are dependent upon the type of target system being used and the type of shooting desired.

High school and collegiate ranges typically only require a basic system that is controlled at the shooting stall. These systems contain a forward and reverse toggle switch for target placement as well as a range master call intercom.

A computer-based control center is often utilized in military and law enforcement facilities. These systems offer sophisticated options for tactical training. Training scenarios can be created and downloaded into individual shooting stall systems to provide a personalized shooting session (CEHND, 1990).

Range Ventilation

Exposure to lead in a shooting facility is a major concern for all range planners. Lead, when

**Communication equipment and
target control**

absorbed into the body in certain doses, can be toxic. When a gun is fired, lead dust and fumes are released. The amount of lead dust in the air is greatly increased in a range that uses steel bullet traps.

When a bullet strikes a steel plate, it is destroyed, sending lead fragments and dust into the air. Federal and state health standards regarding permissible exposure to lead (PEL) must be adhered to when developing an indoor range. Ventilation systems should provide airflow from the firing line toward the bullet trap. Exhaust points should be located downrange from the shooter. Heating, ventilating, and air-conditioning (HVAC) systems are especially important in shooting facilities; therefore, shooting facility planners should enlist the services of an experienced HVAC engineer to ensure the ventilation system meets all safety and government standards.

As industry, state, and federal standards continue to tighten, the need to include a state-of-the-art ventilation system increases. Typically, a ventilation system is a large portion of shooting facility development costs. Professional developers recommend spending the money for a highly efficient and effective system rather than one that only meets minimum requirements. This may prevent the need to do a costly upgrade to meet governmental standards in the future.

The Occupational Safety and Health Administration (OSHA) established a PEL limit of 0.05 milligrams per cubic meter of air that is based on an eight-hour time weighted average. More information regarding permissible exposure to lead can be found in the National Institute of Occupational Safety and Health (NIOSH) publication 76-130.

Ballistic Security

Range designers must be cognizant of potential ricochet threats and stray shots that may occur in a range. Misdirected shots can be extremely dangerous if protrusions in the range are not covered with protective baffling and guards. The three primary types of ballistic security used in indoor ranges include re-directive guards, air-space baffles, and steel guards. Each of these security devices has a particular function in the range. Steel guards are most often used in facilities that have slab ceilings. These guards are positioned in a manner that directs any impact toward the bullet trap. Steel guards should be used to protect all protruding light fixtures and duct work.

Re-directive guards serve the purpose of deflecting stray shots in the direction of the bullet trap. These guards are typically located just in front of the bullet trap, as they are the guards that receive the greatest percentage of stray shots. Their composition should match the composition of the bullet trap. Steel bullet traps should utilize steel re-directive guards and rubber air-space guards should be earmarked for rubber traps.

Air-space baffles are a critical safety buffer for indoor ranges. These horizontally suspended panels reduce the risk of injury resulting from a vertically discharged shot by trapping the round in the panel.

These baffles are constructed with a thin layer of rubber that is separated from a steel plate. A misfired shot passes through the rubber surface and strikes the steel plate. After striking the steel plate the bullet bounces back across the air space and re-strikes the rubber face. The baffle decelerates the bullet to where it no longer has the velocity to exit the baffle. The bullet is therefore trapped inside the air space.

The danger zone for vertical shots extends from the firing line to 15 feet downrange. Air-space baffles should be hung at regular intervals for the first 15 feet and then where needed to protect protruding objects. Baffles should be installed with a 30-degree angle in relation to the floor.

Risk Management

Establishing and maintaining sound risk-management policies and procedures is especially important for shooting facilities since weapons are involved. Shooting facility design must consider risk-management issues, including the following:

- Staffing—training (type, duration, & certification), ratios (staff to participants).
- Insurance—waivers (professionally developed), liability (specific to activity and venue).
- Emergency Procedures—first aid, emergency action plan.
- Equipment and supplies—safety checks, handling, storage.
- Facility—inspections, procedures.
- Post rules and signage.
- Ensure that shooters use appropriate protective equipment—eye protection and ear protection.
- Properly locate the activity so that it does not pose a hazard to participants or spectators.
- Provide adequate spacing so that the activity may be performed safely.

SECTION V

TRENDS AND HISTORY

DESIGN TRENDS IN STADIUMS AND ARENAS

27

Todd L. Seidler, University of New Mexico
John J. Miller, Texas Tech University

This chapter will present an overview and analysis of certain recent trends and innovations in stadium and arena design. It is by no means a complete look at these unique sports facilities; many additional trends and innovations are covered in other parts of this book. This chapter will merely try to highlight certain significant trends and concepts that should not be overlooked.

Funding Arenas and Stadiums

By the end of 2012, nearly every American sports team will be playing in a facility that is 20 years old or less (Lemke, 2008). However, building stadiums and arenas today can be tremendously expensive, often running into the hundreds of millions of dollars. The Orlando Magic are expected to open the 2011-2012 season in a new $480 million facility, and the Pittsburgh Penguins are expected to play in a new $290 million multipurpose facility by the 2011-12 season. In 2009, New York's, new Yankee Stadium, Mets Stadium, and the Dallas Cowboys Stadium opened, each costing over $1 billion. Of major concern to the owners of these facilities is the concept of maximizing the revenue generating potential. One of the most significant trends in revenue generation and financing of stadiums and arenas is the selling or leasing of luxury suites, personal seating licenses, and the naming rights to the facility.

Luxury Suites

One of the most dynamic trends that have developed in the design of spectator sport facilities is the inclusion of luxury suites in professional as well as intercollegiate arenas and stadiums. Additionally, suites are now found at rodeo arenas. PGA, LPGA and Senior PGA events, the Kentucky Derby, the U.S. Olympic track and field trials and ATP Tour tournaments, among others. This popularity may be traced to luxury suites becoming a significant tactic to take full advantage of cash flow per seat in most stadium construction projects (Howard &

Crompton, 1995). In 1997, Funk estimated that the 114 teams belonging to the four major leagues (Major League Baseball, the National Football League, the National Basketball Association, and the National Hockey League) realized nearly $1 billion from luxury suite revenues.

This incredible increase in revenue can make a big difference in the profitability of an organization and can provide a huge competitive advantage over other organizations that do not have it. It also has become an essential part of the equation for financing a new facility. Thus, not only are luxury suites a design issue but they are becoming of primary importance for any sport organization aspiring to maximize revenue.

Luxury suites are small, private rooms opening toward the court or field that are usually leased to individuals or companies who desire a semi-private lounge area, typically large enough to accommodate 12 to 20 guests. Suites are normally leased on multiyear contracts and are often furnished and decorated by the tenant. The prevalence of these luxury suites is growing rapidly primarily because they are such good revenue producers. Originally referred to as skyboxes, luxury suites have become a foremost feature of the majority of new stadiums and arenas constructed since the early 1990s (Heistand, 1999). The Houston Astrodome is generally recognized as being the pioneer facility to include luxury suites in sport venues in the late 1960s (Fischer & Ozanian, 1999). However, while the inclusion of luxury suites is an acceptable, almost mandatory, feature of a spectator sport facility today its revenue potential did not become fully recognized for 20 years (Heistand, 1999).

The impetus for the luxury suite trend was the tremendous success of The Palace of Auburn Hills in Detroit and Joe Robbie Stadium, now referred to as Dolphin Stadium, in Miami (Howard & Crompton, 2004). The Palace of Auburn Hills is a good example of how important suites have become to the economics of this type of facility. The original plans called for 100 luxury suites to be built as part of the arena. About one-third of the way through construction, all 100 suites had already been leased. Some quick design changes by the architect produced an additional upper ring of 80 suites, which were also leased by the time The Palace opened. Total construction cost for The Palace was about $70 million. The income from the lease of the suites alone was almost $12 million per year, which allowed for an unheard of six-year payoff (Howard & Crompton, 2004).

As for the Miami Dolphins, they took in gross revenues of nearly $20 million annually from the 216 luxury suites in their stadium. This amount equaled more than 50% of the entire team's 1990 gross revenues (Howard & Crompton, 2004). The financial impact of luxury suites may be exemplified by the Dallas Cowboys, who constructed 360 luxury suites that produced more than $23 million annually in potential revenue in the early 1990s (Gorman & Calhoun, 1994). Then, later in the 1990s, they increased the number of luxury suites to 398, which grossed about $29 million per year (Fischer & Ozanian, 1999). The Cleveland Browns' move to Baltimore was based on the assurance of a publicly funded stadium containing 108 luxury boxes that would be leased for between $55,000 and $200,000. As a result, the Baltimore Ravens (formerly the Cleveland Browns) anticipated earning about $11 million annually from suite leases at the brand new Raven Stadium.

Professional sports teams are not alone in reaping the benefits of luxury suite sales. Despite uncertain economic times and criticism from university circles, major colleges around the country are constructing sport facilities at a tremendously fast pace primarily due to luxury suite income potential. It has been estimated that universities invested between $800 million and $1 billion for new athletic facilities in the five-year period between 1999 and 2005 (Garbarino & Johnson, 1999). For example, Auburn University incorporated 71 executive suites into the football stadium renovation. This allowed Auburn University to entirely balance the $1-million-plus yearly debit created by the expansion. Once the facility construction debt is totally repaid, Auburn will realize an annual profit of close to $1.8 million (Simers & Wharton, 1999). Other prominent university facilities that have used proceeds from luxury suites for construction cost repayment include the University of Oregon's Autzen Stadium, the University of Texas' Darrel K. Royal Memorial Stadium, the University of Michigan's "Big House," Virginia Tech's Lane Stadium, and Texas Tech's Jones/SBC Stadium.

Some of the items that are now being included in the design of luxury suites are full service kitchens, toilets, wet bars, coffee makers, and refrigerators. The Toronto Blue Jays baseball team has been recognized as a leader in designing luxury boxes as an upscale hotel room. Moreover, previous complaints, from those who purchased luxury boxes, included being exposed to too much direct sunlight as well as being so far away from the action on the field that they would have to use binoculars. To counteract these complaints, luxury box windows are now offered with the ability to transition from light to dark depending on the amount of sunlight. A second window feature provides binocular-like properties that allow the spectator the ability to see the action on the field from a distance without eye strain. As such, while luxury suites have become a significant design feature, the ability to update them is essential. In summary, luxury suites not only make the construction of future arenas and stadiums more economically feasible, but are becoming a necessity for many sports organizations to remain financially competitive.

Naming Rights

As with luxury suites, selling the naming rights of sports facilities has gained recent importance in sport facility construction. Naming rights deals are agreements made between stadium owners and large corporations that permit the sponsor to connect a brand name or logo to a stadium for a given period of time. The first naming rights agreement occurred in 1971 when the New England Patriots agreed to have the Schaefer Brewing Company pay $150,000 to rename Patriots Stadium, Schaefer Field. In 1973, the Buffalo Bills signed a 20-year agreement with a frozen food supplier, Rich Products, to rename War Memorial Stadium, Rich Stadium. Between 1995 and 2000, the number and financial magnitude of sport facility naming rights grew dramatically. A primary reason for this escalation was due to the increased number of new sporting venues that were built in the late 1990s. For example, the period from 1991 to 1995 had eight stadium or arena openings compared to a total of eight in the previous 15-year period between 1976-1990 (Waterman, 2002). In 1997, one-third (41 of 113) of the sport stadiums or arenas used by teams in the NFL, NBA, NHL, or Major League Baseball had been named for corporations; however, by 2002, 80 of 121 teams were competing in sports venues that were named for large corporations (Waterman, 2002). According to a businessman who specializes in naming rights agreements, there were three naming rights deals in professional sports totaling $25 million in 1988 (Maher, 2003). Presently, there are 69 pro teams, with anticipated significant increase of intercollegiate teams, who have naming rights deals that total in excess of $3.5 billion (Maher, 2003). Thus, this new strategy was implemented as a way of helping to ease the financial burden of stadium or arena construction.

Below are the names, naming rights sponsor, the name of the team, the average per year that the sponsor pays for the naming rights and the year the agreement will end for 69 professional teams associated with the four major leagues. The cost of naming rights for the professional teams listed below ranges from $620,000 per year (Alltel Stadium) to $10 million per year (Reliant Stadium).

Table 27.1
Cost of Naming Rights

Stadium	Name Sponsor	Home Teams	Avg. $/Year	Expires
Air Canada Centre	Air Canada	Toronto Maple Leafs, Raptors	$1.5 million	2019
Alltel Stadium	Alltel Corp.	Jacksonville Jaguars	$620,000	2007
American Airlines Arena	American Airlines	Miami Heat	$2.1 million	2019
American Airlines Center	American Airlines	Dallas Mavericks, Stars	$6.5 million	2031
America West Arena	America West	Phoenix Suns, Coyotes, Mercury	$866,667	2019
Arco Arena	Atlantic Richfield	Sacramento Kings, Monarchs	$750,000	2007
Bank of America Stadium	Bank of America	Carolina Panthers	$7 million	2024
Bank One Ballpark	Bank One	Arizona Diamondbacks	$2.2 million	2028
Bell Centre	Bell Canada	Montreal Canadiens	N/A	N/A
Cinergy Field	Cinergy	Cincinnati Reds	$1 million	2002
Citizens Bank Park	Citizens Bank	Philadelphia Phillies	$2.3 million	2028
Comerica Park	Comerica	Detroit Tigers	$2.2 million	2030
Compaq Center	Compaq Computer	Houston Rockets, Comets,	$900,000	2003
Compaq Center at San Jose	Compaq Computer	San Jose Sharks	$3.1 million	2016
Conseco Fieldhouse	Conseco	Indiana Pacers, Fever	$2 million	2019
Continental Airlines Arena	Continental Airlines	New Jersey Nets, Devils	$1.4 million	2011
Coors Field	Coors Brewing	Colorado Rockies	N/A	INDEFINITE
Corel Center	Corel	Ottawa Senators	$878,142	2016
Delta Center	Delta Airlines	Utah Jazz, Starzz	$1.3 million	2011
Edison International Field	Edison Intl.	Los Angeles Angels	$2.5 million	2018
Edward Jones Dome	Edward Jones	St. Louis Rams	$2.65 million	2013
FedEx Field	Federal Express	Washington Redskins	$7.6 million	2025
FedEx Forum	Federal Express	Memphis Grizzlies	$4.5 million	2023
Wachovia Center	Wachovia Bank	Philadelphia 76ers, Flyers	$1.4 million	2023
Fleetcenter	Fleet Bank	Boston Celtics, Bruins	$2 million	2010
Ford Field	Ford Motor Co.	Detroit Lions	$1 million	2042
Gaylord Entertainment Center	Gaylord Entertainment	Nashville Predators	$4 million	2018
General Motors Place	General Motors	Vancouver Canucks	$844,366	2015
Gillette Stadium	Gillette	New England Patriots	N/A	2017
Great American Ball Park	Great American Insurance	Cincinnati Reds	$2.5 million	2033
Gund Arena	Owners	Cleveland Cavs, Rockers	$700,000	2014
Heinz Field	H.J. Heinz	Pittsburgh Steelers	$2.9 million	2021
HSBC Arena	HSBC Bank	Buffalo Sabres	$800,000	2026
Invesco Field at Mile High	Invesco Funds	Denver Broncos	$6 million	2021
Jacobs Field	Richard Jacobs	Cleveland Indians	$695,000	2014
KeyArena	Key Corp.	Seattle Supersonics, Storm	$1 million	2010
Lincoln Financial Field	Lincoln Financial Group	Philadelphia Eagles	$6.7 million	2022
M & T Bank Stadium	M & T Bank	Baltimore Ravens	$5 million	2018
MCI Center	MCI	Wash. Wizards, Caps, Mystics	$2.2 million	2017
Mellon Arena	Mellon Financial	Pittsburgh Penguins	$1.8 million	2009
Miller Park	Miller Brewing	Milwaukee Brewers	$2.1 million	2020
Minute Maid Park	Coca Cola	Houston Astros	$6 million	2030
Nationwide Arena	Nationwide Insurance	Columbus BlueJackets	N/A	INDEFINITE
Network Associates Coliseum	Network Associates	Oakland A's	$1.2 million	2003
Office Depot Center	Office Depot	Florida Panthers	$1.4 million	2013
Pacific Bell Park	Pacific Telesis	San Francisco Giants	$2.1 million	2024
Pengrowth Saddledome	Pengrowth Mgmt.	Calgary Flames	$1 million	2016
Pepsi Center	PepsiCo	Denver Nuggets, Colorado Avalanche	$3.4 million	2019
Phillips Arena	Royal Phillips Electronics	Atlanta Hawks, Thrashers	$9.3 million	2019
PNC Park	PNC Bank	Pittsburgh Pirates	$2 million	2020
Pro Player Stadium	Fruit of the Loom	Miami Dolphins, Florida Marlins	COMPANY BANKRUPT	N/A

Table 27.1 Cont.

Stadium	Name Sponsor	Home Teams	Avg. $/Year	Expires
Qualcomm Stadium	Qualcomm	San Diego Padres, Chargers	$900,000	2017
Raymond James Stadium	Raymond James Financial	Tampa Bay Buccaneers	$3.1 million	2026
RBC Center	RBC Centura Banks	Carolina Hurricanes	$4 million	2022
Lucas Oil Stadium	Lucas Oil	Indianapolis Colts	$5 million	2028
Reliant Stadium	Reliant Energy	Houston Texans	$10 million	2032
Rexall Place	Katz Group	Edmonton Oilers	N/A	2013
Safeco Field	Safeco Corp.	Seattle Mariners	$2 million	2019
Savvis Center	Savvis Communications	St. Louis Blues	N/A	INDEFINITE
SBC Center	SBC Communications	San Antonio Spurs	$2.1 million	2022
Staples Center	Staples	Los Angeles Lakers, Kings, Clippers, Sparks	$5.8 million	2019
St. Pete Times Forum	St. Petersburg Times	Tampa Bay Lightning	$2.1 million	2014
Target Center	Target	Minnesota Timberwolves, Lynx	$1.3 million	2005
TD Waterhouse Centre	TD Waterhouse Group	Orlando Magic, Miracle	$1.6 million	2003
Toyota Center	Toyota	Houston Rockets	N/A	N/A
Tropicana Field	Tropicana	Tampa Bay Devil Rays	$1.5 million	2026
United Center	United Airlines	Chicago Blackhawks, Bulls	$1.8 million	2014
U.S. Cellular Field	U.S. Cellular	Chicago White Sox	$3.4 million	2025
Xcel Energy Center	Xcel Energy	Minnesota Wild	$3 million	2024

Source: ESPN.com (Sports Business, 2004).

Three reasons have been identified as to why the Houston Texans were able to command $10 million per year. First, for the next three decades, not only will Reliant Stadium be the home of the Texans, each of three other facilities at the complex will bear the Reliant name. Reliant Park, as the Astrodome complex was renamed, consists of Reliant Stadium, Reliant Astrodome, Reliant Arena (formerly the AstroArena), and Reliant Center, a 1.4 million-square-foot exhibition center. Secondly, the 69,500-seat, retractable-roof stadium also annually holds the Houston Livestock Show and Rodeo, which attracts two million visitors during its two weeks of operation. Third, the stadium hosted the 2004 Super Bowl and is expected to become a part of the Super Bowl rotation. These value-added aspects significantly played an important part in Reliant's motivation to invest a large amount of money for the naming rights. The $10 million per year that Reliant Energy will pay breaks down in the following fashion: the Houston Texans NFL team will receive $7.5 million (75%), the Houston Livestock Show & Rodeo approximately 1.5 million (15%), and Harris County about 1 million (10%) annually until the agreement expires in 2032. Thus, the naming rights for Reliant Stadium will benefit not only the Texans, but also the Rodeo and the county as well in paying off the arena.

While naming-rights deals have become commonplace in professional sports, the trend has recently been seen in intercollegiate athletics. For many years, universities named buildings after munificent donors and prominent alumni. As of the time of this writing, more than a dozen have sold naming rights to major corporations.

For example, Comcast Corporation has a $25 million, 25-year deal to have its name on the Terrapins' new arena in College Park at the University of Maryland (Weinberg, 2003). At Texas Tech University, SBC Communications is paying $20 million over 20 years to have its name on Jones SBC Stadium, and United Supermarkets has a $10 million, 20-year naming rights deal for the United Spirit Arena, where the Texas Tech basketball teams play (Maher, 2003). The Ohio State University plays its basketball games at the Value City Arena, the result of a $12.5 million naming-rights deal with a discount department store chain. While these institutions possess impressive naming rights agreements, the largest intercollegiate deal to date has been a $40 million, 20-year deal for the Save Mart Center at Fresno State University. Recently, the University of Memphis announced that the naming rights for the office of the athletic director as well as the office of Memphis head basketball coach John Calipari had been sold for $100,000 (Tiger Athletics, 2004). As a result, collegiate sports are going to "be the next frontier." The only concerns are which schools are going to be first and how much will they receive (Maher, 2003). It has been estimated that 80% of new stadiums or arenas will be named after a corporation in the near future (Brenner, 1999). As the prices of sports venues increase, new sources of income must be recognized and used to the maximum that the market will bear. Therefore, the importance of naming rights to raise revenue to pay for sport stadiums and arenas will undoubtedly continue, if not increase in the future.

Personal Seating Licenses (PSLs)

A third revenue trend that developed significantly in the 1990s was the concept of personal or permanent seating licenses (PSLs). Personal seating licenses are to individuals what luxury suites are to corporations (Yeomans, 2001). Personal or permanent seating licenses have been primarily associated with new facility construction and are used to assist in financing plans (Irwin, Sutton, & McCarthy, 2002). Personal seating licenses have given athletic organizations a tremendous benefit since they provide the opportunity to pre-sell seats in advance of the actual construction or renovation of the sport facility. This ensures that the organization responsible for the financing of the facility will not have to borrow as much (Irwin, Sutton, & McCarthy, 2002).

Typically, PSLs allow the purchaser the right to buy season tickets in special seating areas such as club seats. Club seats are typically larger, more comfortable, and have more leg room than regular seating. Also, they usually include special considerations such as a wait staff who take orders and deliver food right to the seat and possibly access to certain restaurants or lounges.

First identified by the Dallas Cowboys in 1968, the concept of PSLs did not gain widespread recognition until the Carolina Panthers implemented a highly successful campaign in 1993. Using personal seating licenses, the Panthers were able to raise $125 million prior to playing their first game in the National Football League. By 2002, nearly 30 professional, intercollegiate, and race-car speedways had adopted the personal seating license concept (Howard & Crompton, 2004). For example, the Chicago Bears were able to raise approximately $60 million for 27,500 personal seating licenses to help pay for the renovation of Soldier Field. As stated earlier, other examples of the personal seating license trend are not only limited to professional sports. The Ohio State University recently raised about $20 million from the sale of licensed seating in its new basketball arena while Texas Motor Speedway sold 30,000 personal seating licenses generating $27.5 million of the $110 million construction costs. It is important to note that the trend of personal seating licenses is not without controversy. Because some critics have accused sport organizations of holding ticket holders "hostage" by forcing them to pay large upfront fees, some sport organizations such as the Pittsburgh Steelers have changed the PSL acronym to SBL (stadium builder licenses). This strongly expresses to the ticket holder that the money raised through personal license sales is going directly to construction of the stadium rather than to owner's pockets. Thus, whereas the corporate support and willingness to pay relatively high prices for luxury suites and naming rights, the trend of personal seating licenses, while an important component for paying for a sport facility, seems to be in an evolutionary, more consumer friendly stage.

The Need for Multi-Use Design

The fundamental purpose and design of stadiums and arenas has changed radically in the last decade. These changes are so dramatic that many facilities have become obsolete, and even young ones 10 to 20 years old are facing the wrecking ball. The basic idea behind this change is that modern arenas and stadiums are no longer just places to watch an event, but are now designed to provide a total entertainment experience and optimally host as many different events as possible. For example, in 1999, the Miami Arena hosted all of the home games for the Miami Heat, the Florida Panthers, as well as the University of Miami basketball program. However, since that time, the arena has hosted only an indoor football team, the Miami Moorays, which disbanded in 2005. In fact, the Miami Arena is presently in such a state that their phone number and website have been disconnected (Andriesen, 2007). Thus, it appears that the Miami Arena may be shut down before it is 20 years old.

While many older stadiums were designed for multipurpose use, the users were primarily professional baseball and football teams. Prior to the modern football stadiums in the United States, stadiums such as Fenway Park, Wrigley Field, and Milwaukee County Stadium were sites of competition for the Red Sox/Patriots, Cubs/Bears, and Braves/Packers, respectively. Moreover, teams such as the New York football Giants shared Yankee Stadium with the New York Yankees and the San Francisco 49ers shared Candlestick Park for years. Yet, these two major stadium sports cannot coexist unless a major reconfiguration of the playing field is made for each sport. Such changes often include the leveling of the pitcher's mound, covering the warning track and the infield skin of a baseball field to play football and then reversing the process from football to baseball.

Additionally, the spectator seats need to be reconfigured in an attempt to provide the best viewing for both baseball and football in the same facility. However, many individuals did not believe that such a configuration could be satisfactorily accomplished. As a compromise, Kansas City, Missouri, voted to have a dual stadium complex that would house 78,000 spectators for the Kansas City Chiefs and 42,000 for the Kansas City Royals.

While some dual-sport facilities exist, such as Pro Player stadium in Miami, the majority of newer arenas and stadiums are being planned and built to avoid becoming a white elephant. This is accomplished by designing so that the facility optimally supports many sporting and non-sporting events. For instance, thriving facilities have been used to host a number of diverse events, including a wine-tasting contest at Alamodome, a Beatles tribute show at U.S. Cellular Arena in Milwaukee, and Reliant Stadium was designed for concerts and rodeos as well as professional football. However, some newer facilities, such the KeyArena in Seattle, are still being identified as potential white elephants. Key Arena, which is the home for the Seattle SuperSonics of the National Basketball Association as well as the Women's National Basketball Association Seattle Storm, received its name from naming rights which cost the Key Corporation $1 million annually until 2010 as previously identified in this chapter. Yet, the new owner of the Sonics recently stated that:

> The case may or may not be able to be made that KeyArena is a viable building today. While KeyArena may survive for a few years, certainly five, seven, 10 years from now, KeyArena will not be a state-of-the-art, viable, competitive, tier-one-market building (Andriesen, 2007, p. 1).

Multiuse design is playing a role in intercollegiate sports facilities as well. Due to the escalating pressure to be self-sustaining, universities in the United States have begun to investigate traditional and non-traditional options for revenue streams. For example, college stadiums that have been customarily used only for football now are being renovated to accommodate soccer, lacrosse, field hockey, as well as track and field competitions. With the stress to produce revenue, many of these stadiums may also host motocross events and concerts during non-playing season (Hutchison, 2003).

In order to maximize return on such a large investment as a stadium or arena, every effort must be made to ensure that the facility be able to accommodate as many events and different kinds of activities and generate as much revenue as possible. A list of multiuse sport venues in the United States since 2002 is located in Table 2. The information within this table identifies an important facility trend that combines naming rights of the venue with multiuse designs. Such recent trends include design features that allow a facility to change over from one event to another as quickly as possible. Whereas some older facilities would rely on six to 10 football games or 30 basketball games per year as their main source of revenue, some facilities now schedule from 250 to 600 events per year, including such varied activities such as basketball, soccer, hockey, arena football, concerts, conventions, trade shows, rodeos, monster truck shows, and professional wrestling. It is not uncommon for a poorly designed facility to require up to a full day for a crew to change the set-up from one event to another, whereas a well-designed facility can be transformed in a matter of hours. Not only can this provide a significant cost saving in manpower, but also often means that more than one event can take place in the same day. Several aspects of design that allow a facility to accommodate a wide variety of events and also to quickly alter the set-up for different events include:

- Versatile lighting and sound systems that are designed to adequately handle the wide variety of events.
- Heavy-duty lighting grids that can be lowered to the floor in order to enhance the placement of sound and lighting equipment for concerts.
- Loading ramps that allow semi-trucks to back all the way onto the floor. Even better, some facilities provide floor access for two or more trucks at a time so that one can be loading after a show while another is unloading for the next.
- Versatile, moveable sections of seats that can quickly change the configuration of a facility.
- Fixed, pre-wired camera positions that allow for quick and easy set-up for television broadcasts. Many new arenas are constructed with a full television production studio, which permits a television network to broadcast a game without bringing in their semi-trucks full of production equipment.
- Computerized curtain systems that can quickly change the layout and size of the facility.

Many sport organizations have made a shift in their fundamental mission and have gone from primarily trying to put a winning team on the court/field to providing a great family entertainment experience. This change in thinking has led to many design changes in the arenas and stadiums being constructed today. In general, this has caused a move toward more upscale facilities with greater service, entertainment and convenience for spectators. Some aspects of this trend include the following:

- Providing more rest rooms, especially for women. In the past, many spectator facilities provided only enough rest rooms to satisfy the local code requirements. This often resulted in long lines and frustration on the part of spectators. Many facilities are now being designed with more than twice as many rest rooms as the minimum required. Since some events may draw a disproportionate number of men or women, consideration should be given to designing some rest rooms that can serve either gender simply by changing the sign on the door. Family rest rooms are also becoming common in new stadiums and arenas.
- Taking into consideration the requirements of customers with disabilities. With the advent of the Americans with Disabilities Act, full accommodation of the needs of people with disabilities is now federal law. Recent lawsuits have established new standards for the placement of handicapped seating. All wheelchair-accessible seats should now be located so that users can

see over the heads of the spectators in front of them even when the spectators stand.

- Building larger concourse areas and adding separate concourses to serve different levels. Improved access and less crowding make these areas more attractive. Some concourse areas are being designed to resemble a mini-mall by offering many different choices of food, novelty items and entertainment opportunities. Some concession areas are designed so that customers standing in line still have a direct view of the field while others place closed-circuit televisions so that patrons will not miss the action while spending their money. Opportunities for amusement are becoming more common. These include things such as batting cages, merry-go-rounds, bouncers, museums, and many types of electronic games as well as gift shops. Many facilities strive to provide the atmosphere of an amusement park.

- Improving pedestrian traffic flow into, out of and within the facility. People do not enjoy standing in long lines. This can be accomplished by providing more entrances/exits, as well as wider and more stairways, ramps and escalators.

Table 27.2
Multiuse Professional and Intercollegiate Sport Arenas and Stadiums with Naming Rights

Name	Location
Alerus Center	Grand Forks, North Dakota
Alliant Energy Center	Madison, Wisconsin
Allstate Arena	Rosemont, Illinois
Alltel Center	Mankato, Minnesota
Alltel Arena	North Little Rock, Arkansas
AmericanAirlines Arena	Miami, Florida
AmericanAirlines Center	Dallas, Texas
American Bank Center	Corpus Christi, Texas
Amyway Arena	Orlando, Florida
Androscoggin Bank Colisee	Lewiston, Maine
Arco Arena	Sacramento, California
AT&T Center	San Antonio, Texas
BancorpSouth Arena	Tupelo, Mississippi
Bank of America Arena at Hec Edmundson Pavilion	Seattle, Washington
BankAtlantic Center	Sunrise, Florida
BankUnited Center	Coral Gables, Florida
Big Sandy Superstore Arena	Huntington, West Virginia
Bi Lo Center	Greenville, South Carolina
Blue Cross Arena	Rochester, New York
Budweiser Events Center	Loveland, Colorado
Carrier Dome	Syracuse, New York
CenturyTel Center	Bossier City, Louisiana
Chevrolet Centre	Youngstown, Ohio
Cintas Center	Cincinnati, Ohio
City Bank Coliseum	Lubbock, Texas
Colonial Center	Columbia, South Carolina
Comcast Center	College Park, Maryland
Conseco Fieldhouse	Indianapolis, Indiana
Coors Events Center	Boulder, Colorado
Cox Arena	San Diego, California
Cox Pavilion	Las Vegas, Nevada
Cricket Arena	Charlotte, North Carolina
Deja Blue Arena	Frisco, Texas
Dunkin' Donuts Center	Providence, Rhode Island
EnergySolutions Arena	Salt Lake City, Utah
FedExForum	Memphis, Tennessee
Fifth Third Arena	Cincinnati, Ohio
Ford Arena	Beaumont, Texas
Ford Center	Oklahoma City, Oklahoma
GIANT Center	Hershey, Pennsylvania
Honda Center	Anaheim, California
HP Pavilion at San Jose	San Jose, California
HSBC Arena	Buffalo, New York
I wireless Center	Moline, Illinois
IpayOne Center	San Diego, California
Izod Center	East Rutherford, New Jersey
Jobing.com Arena	Glendale, Arizona

Table 27.2 Cont.

Name	Location
MassMutual Center	Springfield, Massachusetts
McAfee Coliseum	Oakland, California
Mellon Arena	Pittsburgh, Pennsylvania
Nationwide Arena	Columbus, Ohio
Oracle Arena	Oakland, California
Pepsi Center	Denver, Colorado
Pepsi Coliseum	Indianapolis, Indiana
Perani Arena and Event Center	Flint, Michigan
PGE Park	Portland, Oregon
Pharmed Arena	Miami, Florida
Philips Arena	Atlanta, Georgia
Prudential Center	Newark, New Jersey
Quicken Loans Arena	Cleveland, Ohio
Qwest Arena	Boise, Idaho
Qwest Center Omaha	Omaha, Nebraska
RBC Center	Raleigh, North Carolina
Reliant Stadium	Houston, Texas
Reser Stadium	Corvallis, Oregon
S&T Bank Arena	Indiana, Pennsylvania
Safeco Field	Seattle, Washington
St. Pete Times Forum	Tampa, Florida
Santa Ana Star Center	Rio Rancho, New Mexico
Save Mart Center	Fresno, California
Scottrade Center	St. Louis, Missouri
Sears Center	Hoffman Estates, Illinois
SEFCU Arena	Albany, New York
Sommet Center	Nashville, Tennessee
Sovereign Bank Arena	Trenton, New Jersey
Sovereign Center	Reading, Pennsylvania
Sprint Center	Kansas City, Missouri
Staples Center	Los Angeles, California
Taco Bell Arena	Boise, Idaho
Taco John's Events Center	Cheyenne, Wyoming
Target Center	Minneapolis, Minnesota
TD Banknorth Garden	Boston, Massachusetts
Times Union Center	Albany, New York
Toyota Arena	York, Pennsylvania
Toyota Center	Houston, Texas
Toyota Center	Kennewick, Washington
United Center	Chicago, Illinois
United Spirit Arena	Lubbock, Texas
University of Phoenix Stadium	Glendale, Arizona
US Airways Center	Phoenix, Arizona
U.S. Bank Arena	Cincinnati, Ohio
U.S. Cellular Arena	Milwaukee, Wisconsin
U.S. Cellular Center	Cedar Rapids, Iowa
Value City Arena	Columbus, Ohio
Verizon Center	Washington, DC
Verizon Wireless Arena	Manchester, New Hampshire
Wachovia Center	Philadelphia, Pennsylvania
Wachovia Spectrum	Philadelphia, Pennsylvania
Wells Fargo Arena	Des Moines, Iowa
Wells Fargo Arena	Tempe, Arizona
WesBanco Arena	Wheeling, West Virginia
Xcel Energy Center	Saint Paul, Minnesota

Innovations in Materials and Methods of Construction

Recent innovations in the methods of enclosing large areas without support pillars and posts that interfere with spectator sight lines are providing many more options for the construction of stadiums and arenas. Stadiums with retractable roofs, tension fabric structures, air-supported fabric structures, wooden domes, and cable domes are examples of building designs that have been successfully used to enclose large sports facilities.

Retractable Roof Stadiums

One of the biggest innovations in stadium design is the concept of having a stadium that is open to the elements when the weather is nice but can be quickly covered when needed. The first attempt at a retractable roof stadium was Olympic

Photo courtesy Ellerbe Becket

Rogers Centre

Photo courtesy Ellerbe Becket

Chase Field

Stadium in Montreal, built for the 1976 Olympic Games. The original plan was to build a huge concrete mast next to the stadium that would support a fabric roof supported by steel cables. The roof was supposed to have the ability to be lifted off the stadium and suspended from the mast, thereby becoming an open-air stadium (Holleman, 1996). The roof could then be lowered back on top of the stadium to enclose it again when desired. The design never has worked correctly, but this ambitious idea eventually led to the successful designs we are seeing today. It is estimated that adding a retractable roof to the design of a new stadium will increase the cost of a stadium between $40 and $100 million.

Examples

- Rogers Centre—Formerly known as SkyDome, the Rogers Centre was the first stadium to have a fully retractable roof. Located in Toronto, Ontario, it was opened in 1989. The Rogers Centre can completely open or close the entire steel-trussed roof in 20 minutes. This is accomplished by three movable roof sections, two of which slide and another that rotates. The stadium seats 50,600 for baseball, 53,000 for football, and has different seating arrangements for concerts ranging from 10,000 to 70,000. It also contains 161 luxury suites, a 348-room hotel and health club, full broadcast facilities, underground parking, and a 110-by-33-foot video screen. Original estimates of the cost for the Rogers Centre were $184 million (Canadian) but it ended up costing about $585 million. Typically, the roof only has to be closed for about four or five games a season due to inclement weather (Gordon, 1990).

- Chase Field—Opened as Bank One Ballpark for the 1998 season, Chase Field is the home of the Arizona Diamondbacks. Located in downtown Phoenix, it was the first retractable-roof stadium to be built since the Rogers Centre. This air-conditioned, retractable-roof stadium is designed primarily for baseball and seats 48,500. It

has a natural grass field and was built for a cost of $354 million with 68% coming from public financing. With a total of 69 private suites, six party suites and 5,592 club seats, there is something for everybody, including 350 bleacher seats that originally sold for $1 per game. As with many of the new stadiums, it is more than just a place to watch a ballgame. Chase Field contains two micro-breweries and two 10,000-square-foot beer gardens, a mini hall of fame fashioned after Cooperstown, a 4,000-square-foot team store, 110 picnic tables, 212 concession stands, and a swimming pool and spa just beyond the outfield fence.

- Safeco Field—Opened in 1999 Safeco Field's retractable roof allows Seattle Mariner fans to stay dry during the rainy days of the season. While the retractable roof covers the entire ballpark, it does not enclose it, thus giving the stadium an open-air feel. When opened, the roof sits above and behind the right field seats. The roof consists of three panels that glide on 128 steel wheels powered by almost 100 ten-horsepower electric motors. When fully extended, it encompasses almost nine acres and weighs 22 million pounds, yet, at the push of a button can close or open in 10-20 minutes depending on wind and other weather conditions. For protection against lightning the roof is self-grounded and is planned to hold up under six to seven feet of snow as well as winds of up to 70 miles per hour.

- Minute Maid Park—Originally named Enron Field, it was completed in time for the 2000 baseball season. In 2001, Enron declared bankruptcy and the naming rights were sold to the Minute Maid Company for an estimated $170 million for 28 years. Built for a relatively inexpensive $248 million, it seats approximately 42,000 and has a fully retractable steel roof. The roof covers 6.25 acres when closed and is made up of three moveable sections that can be opened in less than 20 minutes. The moving roof panels contain over 5,000 tons of steel as well as an acre of glass to allow for spectacular views even when the roof is closed. Also, the roof has been designed to withstand hurricane force winds. Special amenities within the stadium include a kid's play area, batting cages, more than 60 private suites and 4,850 club seats, a café, retail space and even has a 65,000 lb. full-size locomotive that moves along an 800 ft. section of track after game highlights.

- Miller Park—Home of the Milwaukee Brewers, Miller Park opened in 2001. It possesses many unique features, the most obvious one being the retractable roof. The 12,000-ton, seven-panel roof has a unique fan shape design. The moveable roof panels pivot from a point behind home plate and go along a semicircular track beam powered by 60-horsepower motors. The roof can open or close in ten minutes and sits 175 feet above second base. Miller Park has no air conditioning, but an air-circulation system keeps the ballpark comfortable when the roof is closed. The roof is designed to withstand snow drifts of up to 12 feet.

- Reliant Stadium—This 1.9 million sq. ft. facility opened in August 2002 as the NFL's first retractable roof venue. It is also home to the largest rodeo in the world, the Houston Livestock Show & Rodeo and was built at a cost of $417 million. The roof is comprised of two translucent Teflon-coated fiberglass fabric panels, which separate at the 50-yard line, slide on tracks and rest over each end zone. It can open or close in just seven to ten minutes, depending on wind conditions. The super-trusses used to support the retractable roof transport system are 84 feet tall and 12 feet wide and weigh 3,750 tons. The retractable panels move in opposite directions, similar to the Arizona Diamondbacks' Chase Field's roof, but unlike the two moving panels at Houston's Minute Maid and Safeco Field in Seattle, which travel in the same direction. Miller Park in Milwaukee also has two moving panels, but they retract in a fan-shaped pattern. Even though it weighs an estimated 2,000 tons, high winds can create havoc. To counteract this, operable clamps hold the roof in place to stabilize it.

- University of Phoenix Stadium—Home of the Arizona Cardinals, construction began in July 2003. Opened in August 2006 at a cost of $455 million, it was named by *Business Week* as one of the 10 most impressive sports facilities in the world. The facility seats 63,400 and is expandable to 73,719 with 7,000 club seats and 88 luxury suites called luxury lofts. There is space for an additional 16 suites if needed in the future. The roof consists of two large panels that retract to uncover the entire playing field and has been designed to provide a balance of sun on the field and shade in the seats. An additional innovation is their portable grass field, which can be moved outside until needed.

- Dallas Cowboys New Stadium—Still under construction at the time of this writing, the Arlington, TX stadium will replace Texas Stadium, the Cowboy's home since 1971. Scheduled to open for the 2009 NFL season, it will accommodate 80,000 seats with the possibility for expansion to 100,000. One of the most expensive sports venues ever, it is estimated that the construction cost will exceed $1 billion dollars. The domed stadium will be supported by two steel arches nearly 300 ft. high and 1,290 feet long, the longest single-span arches in the world. A retractable roof and two huge fully retractable glass walls, 120 feet high and 180 feet wide on each end of the stadium will allow for great flexibility.

As of the time of this writing, several other teams are planning or considering construction of retractable-roof stadiums. It appears that the retractable-roof stadium is now coming into its own, and we will probably see many new examples in the coming years.

Trends in Indoor Playing Surfaces

Due to the increase of retractable roofs or domed stadiums, there needed to be playing surfaces that required either no or minimal amounts of sunlight. At first, artificial turf fields were categorized as nothing more than carpets, often laid on hard concrete or asphalt bases. These surfaces were very hard and presented sports participants with extensive opportunities for injury. Often, players would suffer injuries, sometimes career-ending such as Michael Irvin, as a result of being slammed to the ground. In other situations, the footing was too good, thereby creating the potential for ankle, knee, and groin injuries when an athlete's shoe became planted in the carpet. The danger of friction burns when players slid on the carpet with bare limbs posed an additional risk of infection if these abrasions were not treated properly.

In response to these potentially unsafe situations, innovative indoor playing surfaces have evolved to the point that players actually prefer to play on some types of artificial surfaces. Approximately 40 Division I-A schools currently use synthetic turf on their playing fields, according to the NCAA. The majority of colleges still play on natural grass, but the percentage of artificial fields is the highest since 1997. In fact, a 2003 NCAA report showed baseball players experienced nearly identical injury rates on synthetic and natural surfaces. The following information will highlight the improvements of playing surfaces for retractable and/or domed stadiums.

New Breed of Synthetic Turf

The last decade has seen a tremendous improvement in the design and manufacture of synthetic turfs. Many of the old concerns about higher injury rates have been alleviated. The new designs are much softer to fall on and do not produce the friction burns of the previous designs. Most participants report that conditions are more similar to those found on good natural grass fields. The new turfs are typically filled with ground rubber particles and sometimes with sand. Recently, the National Football League Player's Association conducted a survey of playing fields. The FieldTurf surface at Seattle Stadium finished as the third most popular playing surface in the NFL (Waterman, 2003). Additionally, the new FieldTurf playing surface at the Detroit Lions Ford Field ranked as the 11th most popular playing surface (Waterman, 2003). This despite that only nine of the 32 NFL teams had the opportunity to play on it. It is important to note that both of these fields were rated ahead of many natural grass fields and that no other artificial turf field rated higher than 20th. An added feature of FieldTurf is its ability to be installed for football, markings and all, in eight hours or less as well as all the markings can be removed in the equivalent time frame. Therefore, it is also entirely possible that a field conversion from football to another sport may be accomplished in less than eight hours. This would allow a stadium to stage a soccer game or tennis matches on it one day and a football game the next without tearing up the playing field as might occur on natural grass (Waterman, 2003).

Examples of professional football teams that have recently installed FieldTurf at their game or practice facilities are the Atlanta Falcons, St. Louis Rams, Kansas City Chiefs, Houston Texans, New England Patriots, Cleveland Browns, Green Bay Packers, Seattle Seahawks, Detroit Lions, Pittsburgh Steelers, New York Giants, and New York Jets. Additionally, the Florida Marlins and Montreal Expos have, of late, elected to install FieldTurf for their fields. It has become evident that the FieldTurf and similar systems are becoming the preferred design choice for the National Football League and major league baseball.

Removable Natural Grass

Another turf related option that has become a facility design issue in sport stadiums is removable natural grass. This innovative concept was first used in the Silver Dome for the 1994 World Cup Soccer Tournament. A hybrid grass was developed at Michigan State University that was designed to thrive in the low levels of sunlight that could enter through the fabric roof of the Silver Dome. A system of nearly 2,000 interlocking pallets was computer designed and built to provide the regulation soccer field. The pallets were set up in the parking lot where the grass was planted and received plenty of sunlight. Just prior to the first game, they were hauled by trucks and forklifts into the stadium and assembled. The process took two days to complete. The field was a success and got very good reviews.

Photo by Todd Seidler
Pontiac Silverdome

Unfortunately, it was too large an undertaking to make it feasible to move in and out of the stadium on a regular basis so the Detroit Lions continued to play on their AstroTurf field.

The idea of using a removable natural grass field was also hotly debated during the construction of Reliant Stadium, since the field would accommodate both professional football and rodeo. A palletized natural turf field was seen as the solution. It integrates portable turf units of 8 ft. x 8 ft., including a metal drainage base. The units incorporate a growing medium that is reinforced with Reflex mesh elements (small pieces of nylon mesh) that increases field stability, aids in water and air management, and provides a forgiving (non-hard) surface for the athletes (Thompson, 2001). The turf was designed so that any unit can be replaced without affecting the unit next to it (Valentine, 2003). They can be easily replaced so as to resist extreme wear as well as the effects of extended time in shade. The field is completely removed to an outside nursery once a year while the stadium hosts the Houston Livestock Show and Rodeo.

The new University of Phoenix Stadium addressed the problem in a very innovative way. A full-size natural grass field is contained on a moveable, 12-million pound tray 234 feet wide by 400 feet long. The tray rests on tracks and rolls on steel wheel sets powered by small electric motors. The entire field can reside outside of the facility where the grass can absorb sunlight and receive nourishment, maintenance, and grooming. Then, when it is needed, the entire field is moved into the stadium, a process that takes about 45 minutes. This allows for tremendous flexibility and ideal conditions for maintaining strong, healthy grass.

Fabric Structures

A fairly recent development in the area of physical education, recreation, and athletic facilities is the concept of fabric structures. The fabric commonly used is either a Teflon® coated fiberglass or polyester material. The fiberglass fabric is, pound for pound, stronger than steel and is also less expensive. It can be designed to allow either a large amount or very little natural light to penetrate. The fabric can withstand temperatures of 1300 to 1500 degrees Fahrenheit and is not adversely affected by cold or the ultraviolet rays of the sun. Fabric structures offer a number of potential advantages and disadvantages when compared with standard construction.

Advantages
- Lower initial cost—Initial costs are usually lower than with conventional construction. Several factors contribute to this, the primary one being weight. A fabric roof is 1/30 the weight of a conventional steel-truss roof. This reduced weight means that the walls, footings, and foundations are not required to be nearly as strong as in a conventional building.
- Less construction time—The amount of construction time is directly related to the initial cost of the structure. The total time necessary to build a fabric structure is usually less than for a conventional roof.
- Natural lighting—Since the fiberglass fabric material that is used is translucent, it results in a large amount of interior natural lighting. Without using artificial lights during the day, the light intensity inside can vary anywhere from 100 to 1000 foot-candles, depending on weather conditions, design, and choice of fabric. The interior light is considered to be of high quality because it is non-glare and shadow-free.
- Possibly lower energy costs—In some climates or regions, energy costs may be substantially reduced by the fabric's translucency. The large amount of natural light may reduce or eliminate the need for artificial light during the daytime. This may also reduce the need for air-conditioning required to overcome the heat generated by the artificial lights.
- Less maintenance—The non-stick characteristics of Teflon® allow the fabric to be washed clean each time it rains.
- Full utilization of space—Depending on the fabric structure's configuration and support, the area that can be enclosed is almost limitless.

Disadvantages
- Life span—The fabric envelope in use today has a life expectancy of up to 25 years, with longer-life materials being tested. All other items such as the foundation, flooring, and mechanical equipment have the life span of a conventional building.
- Poor thermal insulation—In cold climates there may be an increase in energy cost when compared with conventional construction due to lower insulating properties of the fabric roof. The insulating value of a typical fabric roof is about R-2 but can be increased substantially (see Lindsay Park Sports Centre). The cost of heating is a significant factor and should be evaluated against that for a conventional building over time. During winter months when the heat is required to melt the snow or to cause it to slide off, a safe level of temperature will have to be maintained

at all times, which has an impact on heating costs. If the bubble is not to be heated during inactive hours, it will have to be supervised constantly for the dangers of unexpected snowfall. In the summertime the heat gain of the air-supported structure may pose a cooling problem.
- Acoustic problems—The curved shape of the air-supported structure produces a peculiar acoustic environment. This large reflective surface magnifies crowd noise and can create undesirable noise conditions.
- Restriction due to wind—In winds of hurricane velocity, many codes require that the fabric structure be evacuated.

There are three basic types of fabric structures in use: 1) tension structures, 2) air-supported structures, and 3) cable domes. Tension structures are made by stretching the fabric between rigid supports and/or steel cables. Air structures are sealed buildings that, through the use of fans, maintain a positive internal air pressure that supports the roof. These structures are actually inflated like a balloon and must maintain the positive air pressure to remain inflated. Cable domes are the newest type of fabric structure. The cable dome is actually a modified tension structure that uses a complex network of cables and supports to suspend and hold up the fabric roof.

Tension Structures
Some projects lend themselves more naturally to tension structures than to air-supported structures or cable domes. Some of the conditions in which tension structures may be more favorable are as follows:

- When free and open access from the sides is desirable or required.
- A unique design or aesthetics are of importance.
- The facility will be largely unattended or not monitored.
- Possible deflation of an air structure would constitute a severe operational or safety problem.
- A retrofit to an existing building or structure such as a swimming pool or an outdoor stadium is desired.

Examples
- Knott Athletic, Recreation & Convocation Center—Located at Mount Saint Mary's College in Emmitsburg, MD, the Knott Center is a unique combination of standard construction and a fabric tension structure. Completed in 1987, most of the facility is built with standard brick construction, with the tension-structure field house connected onto one side of the building. The fabric roof covers 30,000 square feet of activity space including a multiple court set-up and a 10-lap-per-mile running track. Rising to a height of 40 feet, the double-layered roof allows for almost exclusive use of natural light during the day. Also included within the facility are four racquetball courts, locker rooms, and a 25-yard pool.

Photo courtesy Bohlin Cywinski & Jackson
Photo by Matt Wargo
Knott Center—exterior

Photo courtesy Bohlin Cywinski & Jackson
Photo by Matt Wargo
Knott Center—interior

- Lindsay Park—The Lindsay Park Sports Centre in Calgary, Alberta, Canada, houses a 50-meter pool, a diving pool, a fully equipped 30,000-square-foot gymnasium, and a 200-meter running track. The roof is unique in that it was designed with insulation that is rated at R-16. This compares with a typical fabric roof that has about an R-2 rating. Despite the great improvement in insulating qualities, the fabric roof is still translucent enough to allow for an interior illumination of about 200 foot-candles. This facility was completed in 1983.
- McClain Athletic Training Facility—Completed in 1988, this field house is located at the University of Wisconsin at Madison, WI. Due to site restrictions, this $9.5 million facility contains a 90-yard football field instead of a full-size field. Most of the field is covered by a 42,000-square-foot fabric-tension roof that admits up to 750 foot-candles of natural light into the structure. When comparing the fabric roof to standard construction, it is estimated that the increased cost for heating and the reduced cost for artificial lighting result in an overall saving of about $21,000 per year. Below the synthetic turf field lies

a full 64,320-square-foot basement that contains locker rooms for football, track, and coaches; weight room; training facilities and therapy pool. The therapy pool is 15 by 40 feet and goes from four to seven feet in depth. Also included in the facility are an auditorium, six meeting rooms, and a film room.

Air-Supported Structures

There are two basic types of air-supported structures; 1) large permanent structures and 2) smaller, more portable structures. These facilities are actually inflated with positive air pressure that is produced by a group of large fans. In conventional buildings, the foundation, walls, and internal columns must support a roof weight of between 10 and 40 pounds per square foot. In air-supported structures, a roof weight of about one pound per square foot is transmitted directly to the ground by the increased air pressure. This increased pressure of about four or five pounds per square foot greater than ambient pressure is usually unnoticed by the building's occupants. While a significant advantage of this type of roofing is the relatively low capital cost some of the disadvantages include relatively short design life and vulnerability to damaging the full enclosure (John, Shear, & Vickery, 2007). Some of the instances when an air structure may be preferable to a tension structure or standard construction are:

- When column-free spans of greater than 150 feet are desired,
- When large, column-free spans are desired at a cost that is greatly reduced compared to conventional structures. In fact, cost per unit area usually decreases as the size of the span increases, and
- When a low silhouette is desired.

Examples
- Dedmon Center—Located at Radford University in Radford, VA, the Dedmon Center was constructed for a cost of $6,750,000 and opened in 1982. Encompassing 110,000 square feet, it has 5,000 temporary seats for basketball. Used for physical education, athletics, and recreation, the center provides five full basketball courts, weight room, pool, locker rooms, and offices.
- DakotaDome—Located at the University of South Dakota in Vermillion, SD, the DakotaDome contains five basketball/volleyball courts, two tennis courts, an eight-lane 200-meter track, four racquetball courts, a six-lane 25-meter pool, locker rooms, classrooms, and the offices for the athletic department. The main floor is a synthetic surface that is used for most court activities and has an artificial turf football field that can be rolled out for football, soccer, and other field events. When the facility is set up for football, there is seating for 12,000 spectators. The entire facility was built for the bargain price of about $51 per square foot in 1978.
- Carrier Dome—The Carrier Dome, located in Syracuse, NY, is the home of Syracuse University

Photo courtesy Sanaki Associates
Dedmon Center

athletics. The stadium seats 50,000 for football and over 30,000 for basketball. Also a great bargain, total construction cost was $27,715,000, which figures out to $554 per seat. This is very inexpensive when compared to conventional covered stadiums. This facility was completed in 1980.

- RCA Dome—Originally called the Hoosier Dome, it first opened in 1984. The home of the Indianapolis Colts, the RCA Dome seats 57,890 for football and was built for a cost of $77.5 million. The versatile facility has been host to many national and international events including the Pan American Games, the World Track & Field Championships, the World Gymnastic Championships and several NCAA Final Fours. This dome was torn down in 2008 to expand the convention center connecting to the new Lucas Oil Stadium.

Other examples:

- Steve Lacy Field house—Milligan College, Milligan, TN–1974,
- Uni-Dome—University of Northern Iowa, Cedar Falls, IA–1975,
- Metrodome—Minneapolis, MN–1982,
- B.C. Place Amphitheater—Vancouver, B.C., Canada–1983, and
- Tokyo Dome—Tokyo, Japan–1988.

Photo courtesy Geiger Engineers
Metrodome

The primary disadvantage of air-supported structures is the need for the constant positive air pressure. Since this positive pressure is what supports the roof, if there is even a temporary loss of pressure, the fabric will hang down on the supporting cables. Although this alone should cause no damage to the facility, this is when the structural system is the most vulnerable. Even light winds, snow, or rain may cause extensive damage to a fabric roof in the deflated position. These facilities must be constantly monitored and all precautions must be taken to ensure that all systems are functioning properly. Since cable domes appear to have the same advantages as the large air-pressure structures but without many of the disadvantages, it is entirely possible that we have seen the last large air-supported structure that will ever be built (see Cable Domes).

Combining Air-Supported and Tension

Another development in the construction of fabric structures is the idea of combining both an air-supported roof and a tension roof in the same building. An example of this concept is the Stephen C. O'Connell Center. This physical education, recreation, and athletic complex is located at the University of Florida at Gainesville. This was the first structure to combine both air-supported and tension roofs in one building. The center or main arena is covered by a large air-inflated roof, while the outer areas of the building are the tension-covered spaces. The main arena has an indoor track and can seat 10,400 spectators for basketball. Located under the tension-supported areas are a gymnastics area, dance studio, weight room, locker rooms, offices, and a 3,000-seat, 50-meter natatorium. Like most fabric structures, this facility was a bargain. The total construction cost was $11,954,418, which comes out to about $49 per square foot. This facility was completed in 1980.

Temporary Air Structures

This section will outline the merits of the smaller and more portable air structures. Air structures work well as environmental covers placed over existing recreational areas and, for many organizations, the bubble is the answer to an increasing need for large, covered activity areas at a nominal cost. Cost savings are in proportion to the size of the space to be covered. Spaces over 300 square feet usually bring a cost savings when compared to conventional roofing. Heat gain seems to present a more severe problem than heat loss and must be considered in warmer climates. There are numerous playing fields within communities and around schools and colleges that lend themselves easily to enclosure by a fabric air structure. Some of the additional advantages and disadvantages of using small air-supported structures are as follows:

Advantages:

- Speed of erection—Once in place, the actual erection of the structure usually takes only one or two days.

However, additional time is required for the ground work, site services, foundation, anchorage, flooring, and installation of mechanical and electrical equipment needed in the initial installation. Only minimal field labor is needed.

- Ease of deflation, inflation, and repair—Deflation and inflation of the fabric bubble usually does not require skilled labor.
- Portability—When deflated and packed, the fabric envelope can be stored in a small space or easily transported elsewhere for storage or use. Depending on the size of the dome, deflation and packing usually require one or two days.
- Adaptability for temporary functions—For temporary use, the air-supported structure has definite physical and financial advantages over a conventional building.
- Long-span and high-ceiling features—Clear and unobstructed spaces are an inherent feature of the air supported domes. Conventional long-span and high-ceiling structures are much more expensive.
- Integrated heating, ventilation, and air-pressure system—The integrated heating, ventilation, and air-pressure system is simple and less expensive than conventional systems. Lengthy ductwork is not required.

Examples

•Memorial Stadium—A portable inflatable fabric bubble is used to cover the entire football field at the University of Illinois in the winter. First erected in 1985, it was purchased for $1.5 million. With an average inside winter temperature of 55 degrees, the field is used heavily by several departments across the campus. The concept of a portable dome over the game field adds extra use to a facility that would otherwise sit empty much of the year.

•University of Santa Clara—The swimming pool at the Thomas E. Leavey Center is covered by a portable air structure. It is removed for use as an outdoor pool in the summer months and then re-inflated for the winter to transform the pool for indoor use.

•Numerous tennis centers, golf driving ranges, pools, and fitness centers.

Cable Domes

Cable domes are the most recent innovation in fabric structure technology. Through a complex system of cables and girders, very large spans can be inexpensively covered by a fabric roof without the need for columns or fans to maintain integrity. Engineers predict that the cable dome concept is feasible for spans of at least 1,000 feet. Cable domes incorporate most of the advantages of fabric structures when compared to standard construction, and fewer of the disadvantages. Many experts in fabric roof technology believe that cable domes will replace the air-supported structure as the fabric roof design of choice for the future. There will probably not be any more large air structures built because of the inherent advantages of the cable dome. Some of these advantages are as follows:

- Huge column-free spans can be covered.
- There is no need for expensive energy-consuming fans.
- A passive system means there is no need for someone to constantly monitor the facility.
- The structure has an extremely low silhouette.

Examples

- Redbird Arena—Opened in 1991, Redbird Arena is on the campus of Illinois State University in Bloomington-Normal, IL. This multipurpose arena can seat 10,500 spectators for basketball, with the ability to provide an additional 1,500 seats on the floor for concerts or commencement. The lower sections of seats are portable bleachers that can be removed to provide 36,000 square feet of space on the main floor. Built for a cost of $20 million, Redbird Arena was the first cable dome to be constructed on a college campus, but probably won't be the last.
- Tropicana Field—Tropicana Field is located in St. Petersburg, FL, and was opened in 1990. This multipurpose stadium was designed primarily for baseball, yet with the flexibility to accommodate football, basketball, soccer, and tennis, as well as concerts and trade shows. In addition to 50 private suites, a variety of seating arrangements allow the facility to function as an 18,000-seat arena or a 43,000-seat stadium for baseball. The unique movable grandstands contain built-in concession stands and public toilets. The fabric roof is 688 feet in diameter and was constructed on a tilt of 60 degrees. This tilt is designed to allow more clearance for the trajectory of fly balls and allows the roof to reach a height of 225 feet in front of home plate. The cable truss roof system is capable of supporting 60 tons of lighting and sound equipment for concerts, yet weighs a mere six pounds per square foot. Tropicana

Photo by Todd Seidler

Redbird Arena

Photo courtesy HOK, Inc.
Photo by George Cott

Tropicana Field

Field was built for a cost of $132 million and is the home of the Tampa Bay Devil Rays.

- Georgia Dome—Located in downtown Atlanta, GA, the Georgia Dome was completed in August 1992. This $210 million structure was the site of both the Super Bowl and the Olympics in 1996. The Teflon-coated fabric roof covers 8.6 acres, weighs 68 tons, and incorporates 11.1 miles of steel support cables. This multipurpose facility seats 70,500 for football and is the home of the Atlanta Falcons. A total of 202 luxury suites are located on different levels around the stadium that range in price from $20,000 to $120,000 per year for a 10-year lease. During the planning process it was estimated that changing the design from an open-air stadium to a fabric-covered dome increased the cost of the project by only 20% or less. In March of 2008, during the SEC Tournament, the dome was actually hit by a tornado that struck downtown Atlanta. It ripped two holes in the roof and delayed a quarterfinal game for about an hour. The remaining games of the tournament were moved to another location while the dome was inspected for safety.

Wooden Domes

Another recent development in encapsulated spaces is the wooden dome. These spherical wooden structures have several advantages over conventional structures. Column-free spans of up to 800 feet are possible, and they are generally easier to build. There are several wooden dome structures around the country ranging from high school gymnasiums to very large stadiums. Some of the advantages of wooden domes when compared with standard construction may include:

- Efficient construction of huge column-free spans,
- Lower initial cost when compared with conventional construction,
- Less construction time,
- Full utilization of space, and
- Good insulation and acoustical properties.

Examples

- Round Valley Ensphere—Located in Eager, AZ, this wooden dome is the only high school domed football stadium in the world. Opened in 1991, it was built for a total project cost of only $11.5 million and is unique in many respects. The 113,000 square feet of unobstructed floor space provides a full-size synthetic turf football field with seating for 5,000; a six-lane, 200-meter, synthetic-surface running track with 100-meter straight away; seven combination basketball, volleyball, or tennis courts; and a softball field; as well as offices, training room, and four full locker rooms. The wooden roof is insulated to a value of R-28 and is very energy and acoustically efficient. One of the most interesting features of the dome is that it contains a large skylight in the center of the roof. This skylight is made of clear Lexan and provides good illumination of the activity areas even on overcast days. At an elevation of over 7,000 feet, the Round Valley area experiences extremes in weather, including snow-packed winters. During these colder months, the skylight also acts as a solar collector, helping to make the Ensphere very energy efficient.
- Walkup Skydome—This laminated wood dome is located in Northern Arizona University in Flagstaff, AZ. Opened in 1977, the Skydome is 502 feet across

Photo courtesy Heery Architects & Engineers
Georgia Dome—exterior

Photo by Todd Seidler
Georgia Dome—exterior

Photo courtesy Rossman, Schneider, Gadberry, & Shay
Round Valley Ensphere—exterior

Photo courtesy TMP Associates, Inc.
Photo by Balthazer Korab, Ltd.
Superior Dome—exterior

Photo courtesy Rossman, Schneider, Gadberry, & Shay
Round Valley Ensphere—interior

Photo courtesy TMP Associates, Inc.
Photo by Balthazer Korab, Ltd.t
Superior Dome—interior

and covers 6.2 acres. It contains a full-size, roll-up, synthetic football/soccer field, a professional-sized ice hockey rink, a 1/5-mile running track, a portable wood basketball court, and has seating for more than 15,000 people. The total construction cost was $8.3 million, or about $620 per seat.

- Superior Dome—Constructed on the campus of Northern Michigan University in Marquette, MI, this state-owned wooden dome was opened in the fall of 1991. With a diameter of 533 feet, the 14-story,

$21.8-million structure was envisioned in 1985 as an Olympic training center. It has a 200-meter track, a full-size football field and is home to the NMU football team, with seating for 8,000 spectators. Designed to be constructed in phases as funding becomes available, the facility will eventually include an additional 5,000 seats; an ice rink for hockey, speed skating, and figure skating; locker rooms; sports medicine facilities; and public use areas.

TRENDS IN EQUIPMENT AND SUPPLIES 28

Jeffrey C. Petersen, Baylor University

In the process of building a new facility or completing major renovations of an existing facility for physical activity or sport, the planning process typically focuses on the building itself. At times the focus may shift to major building systems such as the electrical; heating, ventilating, and air conditioning (HVAC); plumbing; or structural systems. While these aspects of the building or renovation process are important, the needs of facility users must remain the greatest consideration. Although the facility itself needs to be a high priority in the building process, it is also crucial that the equipment and supplies required within the facility are carefully considered and selected. The equipment and supplies are just as vital as the building itself if the facility is to fully serve its intended purposes for the users.

Consider for example a very basic health and fitness center. While a physical space for this center must be created, the space alone will never meet the expectations of the facility users without the procurement of the necessary equipment and supplies.

As the demand for sport and recreation facilities increases, so does the demand for necessary supplies and equipment. When considering the competitive nature of sport organizations (interscholastic, intercollegiate, and professional), as well as the pressure on fitness centers and health clubs to attract and maintain a customer base, it is not surprising that new equipment and supply innovations are regularly entering the sport marketplace. Each athletic program wants to provide the latest equipment innovation that may help their athletes or programs become more successful. Similarly, leaders in the fitness industry search to find the next must-have exercise machine. Identifying trends becomes crucial for success because of both the large capital investments in equipment and the competitive nature of the fitness and sport market. Of course, predicting future trends is just as difficult as predicting a moneymaking stock or predicting what team will win the next Super Bowl. It is more typical to identify equipment or supplies that are experiencing rapid growth in use and popularity. The purpose of this chapter is to examine selected trends impacting the selection and use of equipment and supplies within several venue types. The discussion of various products should in no way be considered a blanket endorsement, because each facility operator or manager must develop her own selection criteria based on the wants and needs of their own consumers.

Supplies and Equipment Defined

A case of athletic tape, a soccer uniform, hockey mouthpieces, football helmets, a case of tennis balls, portable bleachers, a baseball pitching machine, basketballs, a treadmill, wrestling mats, towels, and a pole vault landing pit are all items that might be necessary in a facility used for physical activity and sport. Which of these would be considered a supply and which would be equipment?

According to the Miriam Webster's *Collegiate Dictionary*, equipment is defined as "all the fixed assets other than land and buildings of a business enterprise." A fixed asset is often considered an item with a worth or value above a pre-established dollar value. Equipment could also be defined as durable goods or items used repeatedly over a period of years. Items that have a short duration of use, typically one year or less, are classified as supplies. Many supplies have a one-time-only use, while other supplies may be repeatedly used over a relatively short functional life. Equipment, on the other hand, will have one year of useful service at a minimum.

The cost per item or unit is another method of differentiating between equipment and supplies. Items with higher costs are usually considered equipment; therefore, something as large as a scoreboard and something as small as an external heart monitor may both considered to be equipment. Depending on the established policies of the organization, be it governmental, school, or private enterprise, a price standard may be set to distinguish between supplies and equipment. This may be set at the low end of perhaps $100 per item or at higher levels such as $250, $500 or even $1,000 per item. Items designated as equipment are more closely monitored through item tagging and annual inventory processes. Therefore, the two major considerations in differentiating between supplies and equipment are the cost of the item and the duration of its use.

Another term commonly used that encompasses both equipment and supplies in the planning and building process is FF&E. This is a common acronym for furniture, fixtures, and equipment. The FF&E is a very detail-oriented part of the design process that will often make or break a facility in terms of its overall functionality and appearance.

Cost Considerations

The cost of supplies and equipment is a major consideration in both the initial creation and annual operation of facilities for physical activity and sport. When considering the costs for equipment and supplies, a balance must be maintained between the ultimate wants of the users and the total cost. There is usually a very significant portion of the project cost that should be allocated to properly equip and furnish a facility. Without taking this into consideration, a beautiful facility structure could be constructed, but it would be useless without the necessary equipment and supplies.

Consider, for example, a fitness center. Typically, the greatest equipment cost factor for a new fitness facility would be the cost of the cardio and strength-training equipment. According to a compilation of data from six recently completed facilities compiled by Kevin Stubbs of RDG Sports, a leading architectural firm, the fitness center equipment costs vary greatly (see Table 28.1). There was a rather large range of cost ($20.00 to $51.44 per square foot for equipment), depending on the specific requirements of the clients, but the average of the selected projects was found to be just over $30 per square foot. Note that these estimations only include the exercise equipment, and a facility

of this type would require other furnishings and operational supplies as well.

Equipment Trends for Stadiums, Arenas & Gymnasiums

With the 1990s being a decade of unprecedented growth in professional sport venues in the U.S., it is not surprising that many colleges have also seen this prosperous economic climate as a time to build or expand facilities. With such a high rate of growth in spectator sport venues, several equipment trends have emerged. Most of the trends described in this section focus on enhancing the spectator comfort, the spectator sensory experience, or the use of creative management to reduce direct equipment expenses for the owner or operator.

The development of a myriad of seating options has been one major trend in large spectator facilities, both indoor and outdoor. Gone are the days of standard bleachers with the minimal 18 inches per person seating width allowance. The current trends are expanding not only the seat width, but also the legroom (tread depth) available. Stadium seating now commonly includes various seatback options, different levels of cushioning, custom color schemes, logo or graphic branding incorporations, arm rests, and even cup holders.

As an example, consider Invesco Field at Mile High, the home of the NFL's Denver Broncos. This new facility has an official seating capacity of 76,125 with a total facility size of 1,717,000 square feet. The previous home stadium of the team, Mile High Stadium, had an official capacity of only two less spectators at 76,123, but the total size was less than half the total of the new stadium at only 850,000 square feet. Although this increase of total square footage cannot be completely contributed to seating upgrades, the changes in seating allocation were substantial. The old stadium had an average seat width of 18 inches and legroom of only 31 inches, while the new facility has a 19-inch minimum seat width and 32-33 inches of standard legroom. The club seating area in the stadium boasts 20-inch-wide padded seating with

Table 28.1
Fitness Equipment Costs from Six Recent Building Projects

Facility Area (sq. ft.)	Equipment Cost	Equipment Cost per sq. ft.
1,200	$24,000	$20.00
2,000	$48,000	$24.00
2,500	$100,000	$40.00
6,000	$125,000	$20.83
7,270	$374,000	$51.44
15,000	$360,000	$24.00

K. Stubbs (personal communication, January 18, 2001)

33 inches of tread depth. The new stadium seating also provides the added amenity of cup holders for every seat regardless of the seating section.

In addition to general seating upgrades, the continued trends of both luxury boxes and club seating areas cater to the expanded desire to provide creature comforts such as: food and beverage catering services, television monitors, and full climate control. There has also been increased emphasis in high-quality sound and video systems to enhance the live sport experience.

While watching a sporting event live at the venue was once considered the best place to view sports, television's use of instant replay (begun in the 1960s) has greatly added to the viewing experience. Replays allow the spectator at home to see plays again that may be either spectacular or controversial. Spectators attending an event at the stadium or arena may miss key parts of the game due to lapses in concentration or their sheer distance from an actual play. However, the installation of big-screen LED (light-emitting diode) panels that serve as large video or television monitors can solve these viewing problems for the live event spectator. The use of this video equipment now allows the spectators at the venue to view both the live action and have access as an entire stadium or arena audience to the replays, game statistics, close-up images, and other video information broadcast on the LED big screens.

The number of LED screen installations in sport venues increased enormously throughout the 1990s and the first decade of the 2000s, and this growth is likely to continue. LED displays are not the only video technology available, but other systems such as projection, liquid crystal display (LCD), and cathode ray tube (CRT) are at a significant disadvantage compared to LEDs. First, the power consumption for LED is lower than the previously mentioned systems. The second major advantage to LED displays is that they will typically operate for 100,000 hours before dropping to 50% of their original brightness (Dahlgren, 2000). The LED systems are also much lighter than the CRT display options, making them easier to suspend or mount. The major drop in production cost of the blue and green LEDs has also allowed the price for full-color displays to drop and become more affordable for collegiate programs, and minor league professional venue use. The LED displays have even entered into the interscholastic market with installations now in place at fields and gymnasiums across the United States. High schools of all sizes are investing in the latest scoreboard, matrix and video display technologies as they have become more affordable (Steinbach 2008b). In fact, large-screen LED displays globally are projected to grow from $639 million in 2004 to $755 million in 2010, and the unit sales should rise from 518,067 square feet in 2004 to a projected 1.2 million square feet by the year 2010 (Ankeney, 2005).

Another reason that LED video boards are expanding in use is that three different types of display manufacturing have been developed, each with its own specific applications. The lamp LED method uses a combination of reflector cups and epoxy lenses to intensify and focus the light. These are typically the brightest systems and can be used outdoors where more light intensity is needed. The surface-mounted lamp method utilizes a metal reflector frame that is mounted directly to the board. This method provides a higher resolution and allows for viewing from a wider range of angles. The drawback to the surface-mounted lamp LED display is that it lacks the brightness necessary to provide an optimal image outdoors. The chip-on-the-board method places the LED directly on the board without any type of reflection or lens system. This method is the least expensive, but it is the least light efficient of the three and it is often harder to maintain. The full-color displays in all three manufacturing options are obtained by the blending of light from the combination of red, blue, and green LEDs, creating up to 4.4 trillion colors. The red LEDs continue to be the least costly to produce; therefore, many scoreboard or marquee sign applications of LED technology continue to use red as the primary color (Dahlgren, 2000).

A major factor in the growing popularity of the LED video display would be the competition between colleges and professional sports organizations. Each venue attempts to keep up with or become the leader with the biggest or best video displays available for their patrons. The inclusion of large video display screens is considered standard in new large-scale venue constructions. Another advantage of the LED screens is that older venues

Photo courtesy Daktonics

Indoor LED video display at Thompson-Boling Assembly Center & Arena, home of the University of Tennessee Basketball, in Knoxville, TN with the following LED video features starting from the top, a ringed screen 3'0" x 100'6", four 9'6" x 18'0" main video screens, four scoreboard screens 5'6" x 13'6" and a final ringed screen 3'0" x 58'6".

Photo courtesy Daktonics

Outdoor application of LED video technology at Kauffman Stadium, home of the Kansas City Royals. This was the world's largest high definition (HD) LED video display in 2008 with a display size of 105'0" x 85'0".

can easily add these displays to upgrade the facility. This can have a major impact on spectators' impressions of the facility. The wide range of size options (from 6' x 8' at the small end to the 85' x 105' mammoth screen installed at Kauffman Stadium, see photo above) allows each stadium to create a more customized fit for its particular needs. Other recent LED video innovations include the use of long, narrow screens, called fascia displays, such as the two 300' x 5' video displays located along the face of the upper deck of the US Cellular Field, home of the Chicago White Sox. These US Cellular fascia displays, installed in 2003, are used primarily for promotional and advertising purposes but can also display scoring or other data. Another example of LED fascia board display is shown at Dolphins Stadium in the photo below.

In addition to the use of LED technology for the traditional scoreboard and the new fascia board displays, the use of LED and other video displays has spread to the scorer's table of basketball arenas. In 2005, the NBA's Portland Trailblazers

Photo courtesy Daktonics

An example of a fascia or ribbon board LED display at Dolphins Stadium in Miami, FL. This display runs between the two suite levels and circles the entire stadium with dimensions of 3'6" x 2,117'6".

installed a 58-foot-long rear-projection system at the Rose Garden's center court consisting of 16 digital displays encased in padded modules that provide advertising, statistics and other information (Popke, 2006). This technology trend signals the next step in sports venue signage, one that creates more sponsorship and advertising revenue opportunities for the sport organization while also enhancing the spectator experience. This scorer's table technology has also gone to full LED displays and has spread to the collegiate level such as the LED display at UCLA's Pauley Pavilion detailed in the photo below.

Another trend impacting equipment in spectator venues is contracting and outsourcing portions of the typical functions associated with the venue. According to Peter Bendor-Samuel, considered a leading outsourcing authority, outsourcing occurs

Photo courtesy Daktonics

An LED scorer's table application on the John Wooden Court, home of UCLA basketball, provides full-color video display on a 2'0" x 57'0" format.

when an organization transfers the ownership of a business process to a supplier. Heywood (2001) more precisely defines the outsourcing process as the "transferring of an internal business function or functions, plus any associated assets, to an external supplier or service provider who offers a defined service for a specified period of time, and at an agreed but probably qualified price" (p. 27). The key aspect is the transfer of control. Outsourcing differs from contracting where the buyer retains control of the process and tells the supplier how to do the work. It is the transfer of ownership that defines outsourcing, and at times, makes it a challenging process. In outsourcing, the buyer does not instruct the supplier how to perform its task. The buyer clearly communicates the desired results and leaves the process decisions for accomplishing those results with the supplier.

Within stadiums and arenas, typical operational aspects that may be outsourced include services such as: concessions, laundry and facility maintenance. One of the advantages of outsourcing can be significant savings in major equipment expenditures. When organizations or teams owning or operating these facilities outsource, the equipment and supplies required can be significantly reduced. For example, at a venue where concessions are outsourced, only a space allocation with water and electrical supply would be provided. The outsourced supplier for concessions would provide all the necessary equipment for the preparation, storage, and sales of all products. Outsourcing of concessions operations has expanded to over 50% of collegiate arenas and stadiums with companies like Sodexho-Marriott and Aramark dominating this sector (Steinbach, 2000). According to the Outsourcing Research Council, operations and facilities outsourcing had an 18% growth rate in 1999 in the corporate sector (Raiford, 1999). This trend will continue to impact the equipment needs for major venues in the future. The needs for equipment will not decrease, but outsourcing will shift the responsibility of equipment search research/selection, purchase and maintenance on the outsourcing supplier. Additionally, outsourcing of management and leadership functions in the sport realm have been increasing in the area of municipal parks and recreation for sports instruction, league and tournament play (Bynum, 2007). This trend has also impacted management outsourcing of fitness facilities at Jewish Community Centers by Club One Fitness in order to revitalize the viability of many of these locations nationwide (Popke, 2008).

Gymnasiums are facilities in secondary schools throughout the country that serve as both a primary activity space for physical education as well as a primary spectator venue for interscholastic sports. As spectator venues, gymnasiums require safe and ample seating, while as a teaching and practice area, the need is for maximum useable floor space. The most common solution to these two needs has been the telescoping bleachers unit. Most gyms have these seating structures, however current requirements in the Uniform Building Code (UBC) and the Americans with Disabilities Act (ADA) are most likely not met if your bleachers were installed before 1990. The replacement of older models of bleachers has become a growing trend in the renovation and improvement of gyms.

The older model bleachers have some serious deficiencies in regard to safety and risk management. Many old bleacher models have open-space area between the seat and the foot rest or tread area. This is a space that small children can often fit through to fall under the structure, or where an adult could slip a foot or a leg into and be injured. Additionally, many old units lack designated aisles, and require that the seating area itself double as an access route up and down the bleachers. The rails on many older units consist of a single or double bar that has a large open area where children could fall through. Older bleacher units often require manual operation to open and close. This process exposes workers to a greater risk of injury. In fact, the rate of injuries associated with bleacher

seating, estimated by the U.S. Consumer Product Safety Commission, averages 18,815 injuries each year since 1999, while 1999 saw a record high of 22,063 injuries (Steinbach, 2008a).

Because of the significant issues with many older bleacher units, it is not surprising that bleacher replacement is becoming a popular trend. Steel remains the primary structural component of the units, but seats can be made of wood, vinyl-coated metal, or of molded plastic for standard seating. Tip-up seating with chair backs, either padded or unpadded, is another option for telescoping bleacher units. The price for new bleachers ranges from the entry level $90 to $100 per gross seat to as much as $350 per seat for fold-up padded seating with chair backs (Kocher, 1996).

The specific UBC regulations impacting bleacher seating begin with row limitations. A maximum of 16 rows is allowed if the bleachers load only from the top or only from the bottom. No row limitations exist if the bleacher section can load from both the top and bottom. Whenever there are more than 11 rows of seating, aisles are required, and no more than 20 seats can separate each aisle. Aisle steps cannot exceed nine inches without providing an intermediate step, and since the typical bleacher rise between rows is more than nine inches these intermediate steps are almost always required. A minimum aisle width of 42 inches is necessary if servicing seating areas on both sides, or 36 inches wide if seating is only to one side. When considering railings, the aisles require discontinuous rails that allow spectators to move laterally as well as up and down the aisle. These rails must also have an intermediate rail 12 inches below the top of the rail for shorter spectators (Scandrett, 1998). These P-shaped railings usually attach to the riser face in the center of the aisle and must be attached and removed each time the units are moved. The end railings prevent falls and must have no gaps greater than six inches.

The ADA requirements also specify that the seating areas provided for those with wheelchairs be spread throughout the facility rather than all congregated together for nay facility with a spectator capacity greater than 300. Wheelchair seating is to be an integral part of the seating plan, and a companion seat must be provided adjacent to each wheelchair seating location (U.S. Department of Justice, n.d.). The number of wheelchair spaces for spectator seating should be reviewed carefully to maintain ADA compliance. The required amount of wheelchair seating locations, according to the Uniform Federal Accessibility Standards section 4.12, are detailed in Table 28.2. For example, a gymnasium with a seating capacity of 1300 spectators must provide 20 wheelchair locations plus one additional location for every 100 seats over the initial 1,000. Therefore, this example gymnasium would require a total of 23 wheelchair locations plus 23 companion seating spaces (Access Board, n.d.).

Table 28.2
Accessibility Spaces for Stadium, Arena, or Gymnasium Spectator Seating

Capacity of Seating Area	Number of Required Wheelchair Locations
50 to 75	3
76 to 100	4
101 to 150	5
151 to 200	6
201 to 300	7
301 to 400	8
401 to 500	9
501 to 1000	2% of total
Over 1000	20 plus 1 for each 100 over 1000

Bleacher replacement (see Chapter 12) can improve a gymnasium facility not just by improving the facilities compliance with ADA and UBC, but also by creating an improved facility appearance. Many models have color options to enhance the aesthetic image of the facility. The use of mechanical opening and closing greatly reduces the injury risk for personnel in facility set-up and teardown. The risk-management benefits and ADA compliance associated with bleacher replacement help make this improvement not only a desired trend but, in many cases, a necessity.

Several suppliers of bleachers and other gymnasium components have taken safety a step further, going beyond the code language to help mitigate injury risk with specialized bleacher accessories and innovations. The bleacher enclosure, as one of these innovations, has gained increasing popularity among athletic directors within the past five years. Bleacher enclosures are available either as heavy-gauge nylon curtains or collapsible wood walls with lockable access doors on the exposed bleacher ends. In either form, they attach to the bleacher system and move in and out with its telescoping motion to deter unwanted access underneath the opened bleachers (Steinbach, 2008a).

Equipment Trends for Fitness Venues

A 2008 report from the National Sporting Goods Association described a rise of 27.5% from 1998 to 2007 in the number of individuals working out in a health or fitness club. Additionally, total revenues in 2006 for the U.S. health club industry were $17.6 billion, and total fitness equipment sales were approximately $4.7 billion (Archer, 2007). With this great desire of individuals to use exercise equipment, public and private institutions must continue to focus efforts on meeting these fitness needs with their selection of exercise equipment for both strength and cardio training.

One major consideration in the selection of fitness equipment is the cost. Table 28.3 identifies the average cost of 12 selected weight machines over three time periods. The 1995 pricing from Hasler and Bartlett, is compared to the average prices obtained from price quotes for two lines of selectorized machines in 2004 and from three lines of both selectorized and plate loaded machines in 2008. Over this 13-year period, the total price for these 12 selectorized machines has increased by 49.2%. While the plate loaded weight machines have a lower total price, it should be noted that these prices do not include the weight plates required for use, and three of the included machines are not available in a plate loaded configuration. This data demonstrates the overall trend of rising costs for weight-training equipment. The recent trend in rising global steel prices has greatly impacted the overall cost of the weight machines and plates. For example, hot-rolled sheet steel rose from an average of $400 per metric ton in 2007 to $1,154 per metric ton in June of 2008 representing a 189% increase in market price (Cohen, 2008). In response to rising prices, the purchase of used strength equipment is growing. Key issues to consider in purchasing used strength equipment are aesthetics, function, and liability considerations; although risk factors are generally fewer for strength equipment than for cardio equipment (Broadhag, 2006).

Cardio equipment has also continued to see rises in product prices. The National Sporting Goods Association (2008b) reported pricing trends from 2003 to 2007 remaining stable for treadmills, while average prices for exercise bikes rose 16.1% and elliptical machine prices rose 35.3%. While cost is one major factor in equipment selection, the needs and wants of the users cannot be overlooked.

According to the Fitness Products Council, four of eight major fitness trends identified related directly to equipment. One of the most significant trends is the explosive growth of the aerobic exercise equipment. A 63% increase in use for Americans was noted from 1987 to 1997 with 67.3 million people reporting regular workouts with cardio equipment. Within this increased use of

Table 28.3
Total-Body Weight Workout Sample Equipment Costs

Weight Equipment	1995 Selectorized Average Cost Per Unit	2004 Selectorized Average Cost Per Unit	2008 Selectorized Average Cost Per Unit	2008 Plate-Loaded Average Cost Per Unit
Lower Body				
Leg Press	$4,783	$4,510	$4,841	$3,148
Seated Leg Curl	$2,459	$2,975	$3,611	$1,985
Leg Extension	$2,388	$2,663	$3,645	$1,878
Multi-Hip	$2,406	$2,550	$4,285	N/A
Mid Section				
Abdominal	$2,394	$2,713	$3,461	N/A
Lower Back	$2,729	$2,763	$3,668	N/A
Upper Body				
Arm Curl	$2,081	$2,563	$3,378	$1,921
Triceps Extension	$2,256	$2,563	$3,425	$2,038
Chest Press	$2,546	$2,813	$3,885	$2,081
Shoulder Press	$2,414	$2,813	$3,885	$2,038
Rowing	$2,281	$2,813	$3,918	$2,061
Lat Pulldown	$2,044	$2,663	$3,918	$2,065
Total Cost	$30,781	$34,398	$45,919	$19,215

cardio machines, the treadmill was still the most-used piece of equipment with 36.1 million regular users in 1997. Weight training increased 127% from 1987 to 1997 among American women for a total of 16.8 million (*Trend Setting*, 1999).

There can also be significant variance in the equipment preferences based on the demographic traits such as age and gender. This is evident in the results of a survey of nearly 1,200 collegiate recreation providers (see Table 28.4). The top preference of males at these colleges was free weights, while the female top preference was treadmills.

Weight training has a variety of equipment options from free weights, to plate-loaded machines, to selectorized (weight stack and pin) machines. While novice lifters typically prefer the selectorized machines, there continues to be a significant amount of growth in the use of free weights as well as the plate-loaded systems.

One trend within the strength training modes is a continued focus on safety and risk management. Some selectorized systems have incorporated shrouds that cover much of the weight stack and many moving parts to reduce to risk of injury. On the free weight side, changes in the plate designs, such as the addition of grip slots, has made for easier handling of the weights. The creation of multisided plates and dumbbells that will not roll have also increased the safety in handling free weights, as displayed in the photo on the following page (Brown, 2007).

Another major trend in weight-training equipment is the continued integration of computer-chip technology on many selectorized systems. For ex-

Table 28.4
Workout Equipment Preferences by Gender

Choice of Equipment	Males	Females
First Choice	Free Weights	Treadmills
Second Choice	Bikes	Steppers
Third Choice	Treadmills	Elliptical
Fourth Choice	Steppers	Bikes

(Patton 1999, August)

Butterfly chest press as a typical selectorized weight machine.

Plate-loaded Smith Machine

ample, some systems are able to read users' swipe cards or other input devices and can set resistance levels and record results based on a prescribed workout routine from a personal trainer.

The increasing use of aerobic or cardio machines is another current trend. The "big three" pieces of cardio equipment expected in any fitness center are treadmills, ellipticals, and cycles (Peavey, 2008). Since walking may be the most popular of all forms of aerobic exercise, it is not surprising that the treadmill is still a very popular piece of exercise equipment. Cycling machines have also been a mainstay of cardio exercise machines, but they have continued to diversify. Cycling equip-

ment now includes many options such as the traditional exercise cycle, air resistance cycle, spin cycle, and recumbent cycle (see photo on the next page). Other equipment innovations, such as elliptical machines, are also popular cardio options that offer nonimpact aerobic training. While some cardio equipment users may exclusively train on one type of machine, other users tend to enjoy using a variety of machines to avoid stagnation or boredom in their exercise programs. Because of the varied use of aerobic exercise equipment, it is difficult to predict what machine might become the next top-choice machine, but it is almost certain that there will be other creative innovations.

Key trends in cardio equipment revolve around the use of technology for entertainment, tracking workout progress, and personalization (McDonnell & Tucker-Rhodes, 2007). The continued integration of computer technology within cardio machines is related to decrease in price and size for these innovations. The use of direct pulse monitoring while using the cardio machines began in the 1980s, but the development of computer programming that can alter the speed or resistance level of the machine to keep the person exercising within a specified target heart rate is definitely a great step forward in customizing workouts. The computerized workout routines that focus on optimal fat-burning pulse zones (typically 65% of maximal heart rate (MHR)) or optimal cardiovascular benefit zones (typically 80% MHR) are becoming common options on many cardio machines. Additionally, many cardio machines contain other preprogrammed workouts, such as interval or hill sessions. Some manufacturers have installed fitness protocols used in military, law enforcement, or firefighting fitness assessments. Other cardio machine

Selectorized weight machine with shroud to provide protection from many moving parts during use.

**Free weight plates designed with
risk-management features**

technologies emerging include "smart chips" that can be individually preprogrammed by a personal trainer for the creation and saving of customized workouts. These chips are plugged into ports on the control console of the equipment.

At the same time, there are many users of these machines who simply wish to get on and work out at a steady rate or pace without using these programming options. For those types of users, the manual operation or quick-start options are also available to allow a very basic workout. According to King (2003), approximately 80% of exercisers use these manual or quick-start settings; however, several factors contribute to the continued development of high-tech programming on cardio machines. These include the ability to cater to specific customer wants and needs, the ability to respond to more highly educated exercisers, and the creation of unique sales tool for a manufacturer.

The entertainment of individuals using exercise equipment is a current trend that will likely continue to expand in the future. Cardiovascular exercise areas in the past may have provided reading material, a room-wide stereo system, and perhaps a television. More recent trends involve the use of multiple video display screens and FM band audio programming for individual headset listening of either the video programming or music. The addition of wireless broadband technology has also been adapted to fitness applications, allowing institutions to customize audio and video entertainment and to include internal promotions as well. Numerous video monitors, coupled with individual audio broadcasting systems, are now trademarked as comprehensive systems such as Cardio Theater and Broadcast Vision. With the drop in LED screen technology prices, these systems have been moving from large group monitors to small individual screens directly mounted to each cardio machine. These systems meet users' needs by allowing them to select their own programming in news, business, or entertainment. The video portion of these systems can play network or cable programming or they can play specific workout, motivational, or educational programming.

Entertainment while using cardio equipment has also moved into the interactive realm. New options are available such as stationary cycles combined with video gaming devices. The level of cycle performance directly impacts the performance in the video game in this technology termed "exergaming." Some systems have been developed for both individual applications and group competition, where up to 16 riders can compete on the same system. Other technology moved toward virtual reality, where scenery simulation products that create beach scenery, trails, or palm-lined streets that are projected onto video displays. The landscape moves on the monitor according to the rate of performance on the cardio equipment, and the virtual hills are synchronized with the incline on a treadmill or the resistance level on a cycle.

In addition to the expansion of audio and video entertainment options while exercising,

**The three most common exercise bikes (from left to right)
a standard excercise cycle, a recumbent cycle, and spin cycle**

The treadmill is still one of the most popular cardio machines.

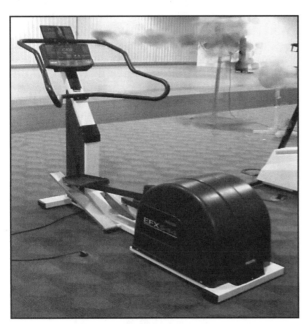

The elliptical machine provides a non-impact cardio workout.

personal computers have been modified for ease of use while exercising. Computers and display monitors have been modified to allow for operation while exercising on a treadmill, stepper, or elliptical trainer. This technology allows the exerciser to access the Internet via a touch screen or modified mouse. Increased use of computer technology has also led to an increase in the use of wireless computer network technology or Wi-Fi. Fitness equipment manufacturers such as Nautilus and FitLinxx have moved to the lead of the wireless-network revolution in fitness. Their systems are typically composed of two parts: a wireless device

attached to individual pieces of cardio or resistance equipment, and a wireless fitness tracking kiosk where patrons can obtain personalized data about their workouts (Picozzi-Moran & Brown, 2006). These technology trends allow for an increase in individual choice in the entertainment and feedback options while exercising. It is likely that market forces will continue to drive an expansion of these trends.

Automated External Defibrillators (AEDs)

Automated External Defibrillators (AEDs) are portable emergency medical devices that deliver an electric shock to the heart in order to halt sudden cardiac arrest (SCA). SCA is the onset of a chaotic and unproductive heart rhythm, and the AED works to restore a normal heart rhythm. Published studies have proven that defibrillation within the first few minutes of cardiac arrest can save up to 50 percent of victims. Sudden cardiac arrest causes the death of more than 250,000 Americans annually; however, an estimated 20,000 could be saved each year with prompt use of AEDs (National Conference of State Legislatures, 2008). The AED uses a two-electrode system. Once the electrodes are in place, the AED itself will analyze the heart rhythm and determine if an electric shock is necessary (see photo below). If the AED determines the victim is shockable, then the AED instructs the responder to push the shock button. The AED will also instruct the responder to repeat the procedure if necessary.

Much of the growing movement to place AEDs in facilities used for sport, recreation, physical education, and fitness has been in response to the passage of federal legislation, the Cardiac Arrest Survival Act (House Resolution 2498), in 2000. This federal law requires all federal buildings,

A Typical AED device with electrodes displayed.

nationwide, to provide an AED. The law also provides nationwide Good Samaritan protection that exempts from liability anyone who renders emergency treatment with a defibrillator to save someone's life. This legislation has raised the standard for what would be considered customary treatment for a victim of sudden cardiac arrest. Many public facilities, such as airports, professional stadiums ,and arenas, now have AEDs on the premises. They also have personnel trained in the use of AEDs on staff due to the large number of spectators present at sporting events.

In the school setting, AEDs are becoming more prevalent on campuses. The state of New York in 2002 became the first state in the nation to require automated external defibrillators in schools. This state statute requires school districts, boards of cooperative educational services, county vocational education, and extension boards and charter schools to keep at least one functional AED on their premises. It also requires that an AED must be available at school-sponsored athletic events, whether on campus or off site. It is likely that other states may soon follow in requiring schools to provide AEDs in the future. At the college level, there are similar AED needs for both large spectator events in sport as well as for campus fitness and recreation centers.

In the fitness club setting, the state of Illinois became the first state to pass legislation in 2004 that requires all clubs to provide at least one AED and at least one staff member trained in its use. Additional states mandated similar legislation requiring AEDs in health clubs including: New York in 2004, California in 2005, and Massachusetts, Michigan, and New Jersey in 2006 (National Conference of State Legislatures, 2008).

AEDs were approximately $3,000 per unit in 2000 when the original federal AED legislation was passed. According to Richard Lazar of the Early Defibrillator Law and Policy Center in Portland, Oregon, the cost for each AED in 2004 was about $2,200 and training might run $100 per person (Kufahl, 2004). Prices in 2008 ranged from $1,275 to $2,780 for an AED. It would be expected that the increased placement of these devices might create market conditions that would allow for a further reduction in the price of the AEDs in the future, therefore, more facilities can provide them for their users.

Extreme Sports

Adventure-oriented sports continue to grow in popularity and bring unique requirements for facilities and equipment. The media exposure of extreme sports through competitions such as ESPN's X Games and numerous other network spin-offs continues to help fuel interest in and give credibility to these activities. Although some of the events such as street luge may have limited appeal to mass participation, activities such as rock climbing and skating (skateboarding and in-line skating) have large levels of participation. In fact, these activities are attracting so many participants that instead of being viewed as "extreme sports," it might be better to consider them extremely common.

The number of participants in skateboarding, according to the SkatePark Association of the United States of America (SPAUSA), tops more than nine million regular users. There are approximately 650,000 serious climbers and perhaps millions of people starting the sport annually. Added to this impressive total is inline skating that has over 75,000 members within the USA Hockey Inline with at least 2.5 million playing inline hockey informally (Ahrweiler, 2001). When including the number of inline skaters for informal cardiovascular exercise and the additional recreational street and skatepark skaters, there is a significant population with sporting and recreational needs in this area.

Skateboarding and inline skating opportunities can be enhanced through the creation of skateparks as designated areas developed for safe, supervised, and exciting riding. More than 300 public skateparks were constructed in the U.S. in 1999 with double that number expected in 2000 (Ahrweiler, 2001). Skateboarding continues to see incredible growth in participants with a 74.1% increase in total participants from 1998 to 2007 (National Sporting Goods Association, 2008a).

While some skateparks are elaborate concrete build-in-place systems, there are also modular park components available. These components could be considered the equipment necessary to create a skatepark from an available asphalt or concrete space. The modular components can be made out of concrete, wood, or a combination of steel framing, polyethylene, and zinc plating. These components combine elements such as angled and curved ramps, rails, curbs, and bumps to create fairly comprehensive parks suitable for both skateboard and inline skate use. The modular components have even been assembled into portable units such as the "Flip Side" in Caledon, Ontario. This portable system of seven ramp structures and grind rails is transported to various locations throughout the summer in this Toronto suburb.

Inline hockey has allowed the expansion of the traditionally "northland" sport of hockey to be adapted to sun-belt states without the requirement of ice. Inline hockey can be played indoors or outdoors, and the facility space can often be converted for modified soccer use. Equipment needed to create a usable facility includes the dasherboards, goals, and a smooth base surface. The dasherboards are commonly constructed from wood, fiberglass, or plastic. One change is that the Plexiglas upper portion of the boards seen in ice hockey is often replaced with coated fencing or netting for inline hockey. The preferred surface is smoothly finished concrete, but portable vinyl tiling systems, such as Sport Court or other similar products, can also provide a good playing surface.

The over 300 dedicated climbing gyms and the multitude of fitness clubs and recreation centers with climbing wall components have their own unique equipment requirements. The equipment required for the use of a climbing structure might consist of a variety of mountable holds (fiberglass or resin fixtures for hands or feet), belay systems (safety harness), ropes and rope hardware, helmets, and climbing shoes. Most climbing structures are custom-built walls or free-standing structures, but in some instances, existing wall space of adequate height and structural soundness can be adapted into a functional climbing surface. One current trend is the conversion of underutilized racquetball courts into climbing facilities (Steinbach, 2008c). Of course, the custom climbing areas are much more impressive in appearance and in realistic climbing features. Regardless of the climbing-wall type, the ability to alter the holds creates immense flexibility for the climbing wall to be configured for both novice and experienced climbers. This changeability also helps to keep climbers motivated and interested in the climbing experience. The clientele of climbing walls continues to expand, especially for young people. A total of 60% of all artificial wall-climbing participants are 17 years old or younger, with six- to 11-year-olds the most frequent participants (Popke, 2005).

Supply Trends

It is far more difficult to trace supply trends within sport facilities and sport and fitness organizations. Changes in the market for particular supplies, be it towels, athletic tape, or basketballs, would be more likely to be researched by the manufacturers and those practitioners in the field than those in the facility planning process. The specific supply needs also vary greatly based on the nature of the organization. A tennis club has far different supply needs than an arena league football team. Similarly, the maintenance department for a major stadium has far different supply needs than the baseball team that plays at the stadium.

One innovation that can now greatly influence the selection and purchase of supplies regardless of the program or department is the explosive growth of the use of the Internet. The Internet can be used to research products, obtain price quotes, and even place orders for almost any supply needed in the realm of sport and recreation. The use of standard search engines can be used to locate supplies, but the development of sport specific supply websites can also be effective. Athleticsearch.com can be used to research product information from a multitude of suppliers as well as give access to articles from trade magazines and other sources. The bidding and purchasing process can be facilitated through sites like Athleticbid.com that contact multiple vendors and allow them to place bids on your specified needs.

Vendor Websites

The following list of equipment vendor websites may be useful for the case study exercises and for general product research. This listing of vendors is only a small segment of the total market, and any listing or omission from this listing is in no way to be construed as an endorsement or lack thereof of any products or services.

www.athleticainc.com—in-line hockey
www.body-masters.com—weight equipment
www.boldr.com—climbing walls
www.broadcastvision.com—exercise entertainment systems
www.daktronics.com—scoreboards and LED displays
www.diamond-vision.com—LED video display boards
www.ecybex.com—cardio and weight machines
www.edgewalls.com—climbing walls
www.hammerstrength.com—weight machines
www.humanemfg.com—rubber mats and flooring
www.irongrip.com—weight plates
www.keiser.com—performance equipment
www.lifefitness.com—fitness equipment
www.nautilus.com—weight machines
www.netpulse.com—exercise entertainment systems
www.nicros.com—climbing walls
www.nustep.com—performance equipment
www.paramount.com—weight machines
www.power-lift.com—weight machines
www.power-systems.com—performance equipment
www.precor.com—elliptical machines
www.quantumfitness.com—fitness equipment
www.quinton.com—treadmills
www.spohnranch.com—skate park components
www.stairmaster.com—cardio machines
www.startrac.com—cardio machines
www.truefitness.com—cardio machines
www.yorkbarbell.com—free weights
www.werksanusa.com—barbells
www.wwsport.com—sport supply

Thomas H. Sawyer, Indiana State University
Michael G. Hypes, Morehead State University

The Council on Facilities and Equipment (CFE) focuses on concerns regarding facilities and equipment in relationship to physical activity and sport. The CFE works to develop policies, standards, guidelines, and innovations to ensure the safest and most effective means for quality health, physical education, recreation, dance, sport, and fitness facilities and equipment for the young through the aging populations. This chapter describes the development of the CFE and facility and equipment standards.

Initial Interest in Facilities

Aside from Dr. Edward M. Hartwell's comprehensive report on gymnasium construction in 1885 and occasional articles in *The American Physical Education Review* (the official publication of the American Association for the Advancement of Physical Education [AAAPR]), no concerted effort was made by the profession to consider facilities (Rice, Hutchinson, & Lee, 1958). In the early 1920s the Society of Directors of Physical Education in College (College Physical Education Association) appointed a committee, of which Dr. George L. Meylan was chairman, to consider physical education facilities. Its work was published in booklet form in 1923, entitled *Physical Education Buildings for Education Institutions, Part I, Gymnasiums and Lockers* (Hackensmith, 1966). The committee remained active, and following Meylan in the chairmanship was Harry A. Scott until 1927; A.R. Winters from 1927-28; and Albert H. Prettyman, from 1928-1945 (VanDalen, Mitchell, & Bennett, 1953).

The halt in the construction of facilities during the depression was only temporary, and as soon as the federal government entered the picture, building programs were resumed on a grander scale than before. In its early stages, many obvious and absurd mistakes were made in architectural planning (VanDalen, et al., 1953; Rice, et al., 1958; & Hackensmith, 1966). This led to government provision of expert guidance in planning facilities. In addition, the National Recreation Association and the Recreation Division, Work Project Administration, issued many pamphlets as guides in planning recreation facilities. The College Physical Education Association also initiated the practice of collecting and filing architectural plans of college facilities that were made available to the profession on request (Hackensmith, 1966).

By the end of the 1930s, the degree of interest in the planning and construction of facilities was demonstrated by many publications on the subject, including Herbert Blair's *Physical Education for the Modern Junior and Senior High School* (1938), Emil Lamar's *The Athletic Plant* (1938), George Butler's *The New Play Areas-Their Design and Equipment* (1938), Fredrick W. Leuhring's *Swimming Pool Standards* (1939), and Ruth Eliott Houston's *Modern Trends in Physical Education Facilities for College Women* (1939).

Early Physical Education Facilities

Many gymnasiums were erected after the Civil War, starting with the Dartmouth building of 1867, which cost $24,000. Following that, Princeton replaced its earlier red shack with a $38,000 "gym," the finest of its day. Bowdoin's gymnasium had no heat, and the men dressed for class even in zero weather, changing to cotton shirts and tights and cloth slippers. In 1870, the University of Wisconsin built a $4,000 gymnasium (the first state university to build one). The Yale gymnasium of 1875 had eight long "bathtubes" lined with zinc, which the students used only on payment of a special fee. Then 1879 brought the wonder gymnasium of the age—Harvard's $110,000 Hemenway Gymnasium—followed in 1878 by the University of California's modest $12,000 Harmon Gymnasium. During the 1960s and 1970s, many colleges that could not afford gymnasia fitted up vacant rooms as drill halls (Rice et al., 1958).

In the women's colleges, physical education classwork got underway in this period by using the outdoors, corridors, assembly halls, and storerooms. One school used a privately owned gymnasium in the local community—Radcliffe at Sargent's Gymnasium. Vassar was the only college that started its physical education work with a special building constructed for that purpose. In 1860 it built a "Hall of Calisthenics" with footprints painted on the floor to indicate where the students should stand during their exercise periods. Mt. Holyoke built a gymnasium by 1865 that cost $1,900. Other gymnasiums that were constructed included one at Smith in 1875, Bryn Mawr, by 1885; Goucher, by 1888; and Mills College, by the end of the century. Goucher College constructed the first swimming pool for women in 1888, although it did not list swimming as an activity for students until 1904. Vasser built the second pool in 1889, and Smith installed a "swimming bath" in 1892 that could be used by two to five students at a time and was used for over 30 years; Bryn Mawr built its pool in 1894, and by the end of the century, Radcliffe College had built one. There were no pools for women or men in any coeducational college or coeducational university of this era (Rice, 1929; Rice et al., 1958).

The coeducational colleges/universities lagged far behind the women's colleges in procuring facilities for women students. As a rule, the women were permitted to use the men's facilities on occasion, and in many schools a large room in the women's dormitory was set aside for a women's gymnasium (Hackensmith, 1966).

American Alliance for Health, Physical Education, Recreation, and Dance

The American Alliance for Health, Physical Education, Recreation and Dance (AAHPERD) was founded on November 27, 1885, when William Gilbert Anderson, a physical training instructor in Brooklyn, New York, invited a group of people who were working in the gymnastic field to come together to discuss their profession. These 60 people talked informally of methods of teaching, the best system of measurements, normal-training classes, and the manufacture of apparatus. After a demonstration of new exercise methods, they embarked on the formation of a permanent organization that was named the Association for the Advancement of Physical Education (AAPE). Forty-nine people, all teaching physical education, enrolled as members of the organization with a pledge to meet the next year at the same place. The first convention ran full-circle with discussions, speeches, a demonstration, enrolling members, adoption of a plan of organization, and election of officers.

At the second meeting in 1886, a formal constitution was adopted, and the name was changed to the American Association for the Advancement of Physical Education (AAAPE). The name was later changed to the American Physical Educa-

tion Association (APEA). In 1937, the APEA and the Department of School Health and Physical Education of the National Education Association were formally amalgamated to form the American Association for Health and Physical Education (AAHPE). The following year, recreation was added to the title, and the American Association For Health, Physical Education and Recreation (AAHPER) continued until 1974 when the American Alliance for Health, Physical Education, and Recreation was reorganized. Dance was added to the title in 1979.

The early years of the alliance focused on defining and exploring the field of physical education and encouraging its inclusion in the schools. By the close of the century, the organization had grown in number of members from 49 to 1,076 and was spreading throughout the nation. As the years went by, the alliance grew in structure, size, and scope as it worked toward the acceptance of the study of physical education.

In late 1896, the AAPE approved a plan to begin publishing a quarterly magazine, the *American Physical Education Review,* which became the *Journal of Health and Physical Education* in 1930 and becoming the *Journal of Physical Education, Recreation, and Dance* in the '70s. The journal is published nine times a year. In 1930, the Association began publishing the *Research Quarterly,* now called the *Research Quarterly for Exercise and Sport.*

The years following World War 11 saw an emphasis on two key issues. One was the need for adequate and well-planned facilities, and the other was the pressing need for improved professional preparation of teachers. The alliance also continued its interest, which had developed during the War, in federal legislation relating to physical education and health services.

The decade of the 1950s was notable for a prodigious expansion of AAHPER activities, evident in three areas: conferences, consultant services, and publications. During this time, AAHPER also provided significant support and service to the cause of fitness. In 1958, the Alliance developed the Youth Fitness Test, which was the first program of testing with national norms that applied to the fitness levels of America's school-age children.

In 1965, a second national study was conducted, and the norms for the test were revised. It was during this year that the President's Council on Fitness joined with AAHPER, using the Youth Fitness Test, to initiate and promote the Presidential Physical Fitness Award.

In 1980, AAHPERD developed the Health-Related Fitness Test, where the items on the test battery related to major health risk factors. From 1980 through spring 1988, the alliance sponsored its Youth Fitness Test and the Health-Related Fitness Test. The Physical Best Program was developed in 1988 and contains both the health-related test and the teaching of fitness concepts.

The alliance went through growing pains in the late '80s and launched two major initiatives to explore its future. One, the Blue Ribbon Task Force, devoted three years of study to the structure and function of the alliance in an attempt to analyze its effectiveness for meeting member needs. Somewhat overlapping this effort was an experimental project focusing on autonomy. This project, called the AAHE Experiment, used a different method of accounting for cost of doing business and revenue sources. It allowed AAHE to experiment with more autonomous decision-making as well as taking responsibility for those decisions. This experiment, along with the outcome of the Blue Ribbon Task Force, resulted in Model III, a move toward autonomy for all national associations. The American Alliance for Health, Physical Education, Recreation, and Dance (AAHPERD) is an educational organization designed to support, encourage, and provide assistance to member groups and their personnel nationwide as they initiate, develop, and conduct programs in health, leisure, and movement-related activities.

AAHPERD seeks to:
- encourage, guide, and support professional growth and development in health, leisure, and movement-related programs based on individual needs, interests, and capabilities;
- communicate the importance of health, leisure, and movement-related activities as they contribute to human well-being;
- encourage and facilitate research that will enrich health, leisure, and movement-related activities, and disseminate the findings to professionals and the public;
- develop and evaluate standards and guidelines for personnel and programs in health, leisure, and movement-related activities;
- coordinate and administer a planned program of professional, public, and government relations that improves education in areas of health, leisure, and movement-related activities; and
- conduct other activities for the public benefit.

AAHPERD is composed of five national associations and the Research Consortium, including:
- American Association for Physical Activity and Recreation (AAPAR)
- American Association for Health Education (AAHE)
- National Association for Girls and Women in Sport (NAGWS)
- National Association for Sport and Physical Education (NASPE)
- National Dance Association (NDA)

American Association for Physical Activity and Recreation History 1949-2009

The American Association for Physical Activity and Recreation evolved out of the General Division of the American Association for Health, Physical Education, and Recreation. In 1949, the General Division was created as the fourth division of AAHPER, joining the Health Education Division, Physical Education Division, and the Recreation Division. This reorganization plan consolidated the general sections to eliminate duplication of functions and service. At the time of its formation, the General Division included 12 sections, three of which originated in the AAHPER well before 1930.

These 12 sections were:
- Aquatics
- Administration and Supervision
- Athletics Boys and Men
- Athletics Girls and Women
- Camping and Outdoor Education
- Dance
- Measurement and Evaluation
- Professional Education
- Professional and Public Relations
- Research
- Students
- Therapeutics

The General Division's substructures fluctuated in number through the years, beginning with the addition of the Research Council in 1952. General Division councils and sections were differentiated by functions. The sections operated primarily to plan and conduct programs at the annual AAHPER conventions in their specialized interest area.

The General Division 1970 Operating Code stated that "The purpose of the General Division shall be to provide leadership and coordination to those groups developing programs and fostering education activities under its auspices" and to:
- Provide an organizational structure to serve groups whose professional interest and activities relate to two or more existing AAHPER divisions or whose professional interests do not readily lend themselves to inclusion in other divisions.
- Promote flexibility in serving the many and varied professional interests and levels of the AAHPER membership by providing opportunity for growth of new and continuing professional interest groups.
- Recognize inter-divisional professional interests and activities and to encourage communications and cooperation among the divisions of AAHPER.
- Coordinate and lend intra-divisional support to professional interests and programs.

On April 16, 1973, the AAHPER Representative Assembly approved the Reorganization Committee's Model II to change AAHPER from an association to an alliance. This gave the eight AAHPER divisions and their structure self-determination of association status and placement. The premise was that the alliance would "provide unity with diversity," allowing the associations full control over their professional programs, while being a united structure of related disciplines. It is within these concepts and at that time that the Association for Research, Administration, and Professional Councils (ARAPC) had its origin. In October 1974, the Alliance Board of Governors defined the term "society" as an alliance structure, and further stated that all societies would be housed in ARAPCS, formerly the General Division of the American Association for Health, Physical Education, and Recreation. The name change took place during the early 1960s. ARAPCS was composed of those councils and a professional society that did not clearly fit into the other national associations—National Association for Sport and Physical Education, National Association for Girls and Women in Sports, American Association for Leisure and Recreation, and American Association for Health Education.

In spring 1994, ARAPCS changed its name to the American Association for Active Lifestyles and Fitness (AAALF). This name change was designed to more clearly define the focus and mission of the association. With its 12 councils and one society, AAALF has a broad range of interests and programs. All professional activities are carried on through the special interest areas of its councils. With this format, most of the income received by AAALF is allocated directly to the councils/society for their professional activities, which maximizes allocations for program content.

American Association for Physical Activity and Recreation

The American Association for Physical Activity and Recreation (AAPAR), formerly AAALF, is one of five national associations within the American Alliance for Health, Physical Education, Recreation, and Dance (AAHPERD). The goal of AAPAR and its 11 councils (Adapted Physical Education Council, Aquatics Council, College and University Administrators Council, Council on Aging and Adult Development, Council on Facilities and Equipment, Council on Outdoor Education, Measurement and Evaluation Council, Physical Fitness Council, Safety and Risk Management, and Professional Recreation Council) is to promote active lifestyles and fitness for all populations through support of research, development of leaders, and dissemination of current information. The membership is provided the latest information in the field, professional development opportunities, career networking and contacts, an annual national convention, regional workshops/ conferences, publication opportunities, advocacy of mission, leadership opportunities, professional recognition, and headquarters support staff.

The Birth of the Guide for Planning Facilities for Athletics, Recreation, Physical and Health Education

At the meeting of the Board of Directors of the American Alliance for Health, Physical Education, and Recreation in Washington, D.C. in April 1945, favorable action was taken on a proposal by Caswell M. Miles, AAHPERD vice-president for recreation, that a grant be obtained to finance a national conference on facilities. Subsequently, a request for $10,000 to finance the first facilities conference was placed before Theodore R. Bank, president of The Athletic Institute. The project was approved and the money appropriated to finance the first conference. The conference was held at Jacob's Mill, West Virginia. As a result of this conference, the *Guide for Planning Facilities for Athletics, Recreation, Physical and Health Education* was published that same year.

The second conference was held from May 5-12, 1956, at the Kellogg Center for Continuing Education at Michigan State University in East Lansing. The second conference, like the first, was financed by The Athletic Institute. The second edition (1956) of the *Guide* was the result of this second conference.

The third edition (1965) was prepared at the third conference, which was financed jointly by AAHPER and The Athletic Institute and held at the Biddle Continuing Education Center, Indiana University, in Bloomington from January 15-24, 1965. The fourth conference was held two years later, from April 29-May 8, 1967, at Indiana University. Among those invited were a number of outstanding college and technical personnel engaged in planning and conducting programs of athletics, recreation, outdoor education, and physical and health education. In addition, invitations were extended to a number of specialists responsible for planning and constructing facilities for these programs. These specialists included city planners, architects, landscape architects, engineers, and schoolhouse construction consultants.

At the 1974 facilities committee meeting, five members were assigned the task of restructuring the *Guide* (fourth edition) in such a way that it would serve as a more practical tool for school administrators, physical education heads, architects, planning consultants, and all others interested in planning new areas and facilities or checking the adequacy of those already in use.

During recent years, there have been many new developments in facility planning and construction. These have been due to a number of factors. The need for improving education, recreation, and fitness opportunities for the youth of the nation has been highlighted by many groups. The extensive work of the President's Council on Physical Fitness is one illustration of the growing national interest in health, physical education, and recreation activities. Much of the research and attention devoted to facility planning and construction during the past three decades has been due to the increased leisure time in society and a growing realization that recreation, and especially physical activity, is a fundamental human need essential to the well-being of all people.

The Athletic Institute and AAHPERD Council on Facilities, Equipment, and Supplies initiated the fifth edition (1979) of the *Guide* following a careful review of the fourth edition (1974). A blue-ribbon steering committee was appointed by the Council. Edward Coates of Ohio University and Richard B. Flynn of the University of Nebraska at Omaha were appointed as co-editors and contributing authors. Professionals well-known for their expertise in facility planning and construction were invited to assist in a complete rewrite.

The sixth edition (1984) of *Planning Facilities for Athletics, Physical Education, and Recreation* represents a continuing effort on the part of The Athletic Institute and AAHPERD to keep the text current and relevant. Richard B. Flynn of the University of Nebraska at Omaha was selected as editor and contributing author. Chapter input was solicited from carefully chosen leaders in the field as well as from outstanding architects. Efforts were made to incorporate the most recent advances in facility planning and construction. Certain program areas, such as planning for the handicapped, were expanded, while outdated or irrelevant materials were deleted.

Richard B. Flynn, who edited the seventh edition, was selected to serve as editor and contributing author for the eighth edition (1993). This edition carried the same title as the seventh edition (1988). Many of the same contributors volunteered to revise their sections. The text was revised but not expanded.

For the ninth edition (1999), a new editorial team was put together by the Council on Facilities and Equipment to do a complete overhaul of the book. The editorial team consisted of Thomas H. Sawyer, Ed.D. (Indiana State University), Editor-in-Chief; Bernie Goldfine, Ph.D. (Kennesaw State University); Michael G. Hypes, D.A. (Indiana State University); Richard L. LaRue, D.P.E. (University of New England); and Todd Seidler, Ph.D. (University of New Mexico); There were 21 authors involved in writing the 29 chapters. The name of the text was changed to *Facility Development for Physical Activity and Sport: Concepts and Applications*, in order to reflect an expanded content aimed at a broader audience.

The 10th edition (2002) used the same editorial team led by Thomas H. Sawyer. This edition was revised and expanded to 37 chapters, including a chapter describing the newest Japanese Olympic Training Center. The book was published by Sagamore Publishing/AAALF publications. The 11th edition was published in 2005 with the same editorial team that was used for the 10th edition.

Evolution of the Council on Facilities and Equipment 1955-2009

In 1955, AAHPER established the Council on Equipment and Supplies, with Thomas E. McDonough (Emory University, Georgia) as chairman and Charles Heilman (Drake University, Iowa) as secretary. The purpose of the council was to assist physical educators, athletic coaches, and recreation leaders in the selection, purchase, and care of equipment and supplies. Since its organization, the council has secured the cooperation of manufacturing companies and stimulated professional interest through exhibits of equipment and supplies at conferences and conventions. In 1959, AAHPER and the Athletic Institute cosponsored a third National Workshop on Equipment and Supplies for Athletics, Physical Education, and Recreation at Michigan State University, whose report was made available in 1960. The name of the council was changed (1976) to reflect its work in the area of facilities: Council on Facilities, Equipment, and Supplies.

In 1993, the Council on Facilities, Equipment, and Supplies changed its name to the Council on Facilities and Equipment (CFE). The new name better identified the Council's focus on concerns relating to facilities and equipment in relationship to physical activity. CFE works to develop policies, standards, guidelines, and innovations to ensure the safest and most effective means for quality health, physical education, recreation, dance, sport, and fitness facilities for the young through the aging populations.

The purposes of the CFE are:
- To initiate a national cooperative effort to improve the quality of the facilities and equipment for health, physical education, recreation, and dance;
- To improve the quality of undergraduate and graduate instruction in facilities and equipment design and planning;
- To present research findings and to review needed research projects for possible endorsement and development by the council;
- To prepare and disseminate information to aid members to keep abreast of current innovations, promising practices, comparative data and practical ideas;
- To cooperate with related professions (architecture, engineering, construction, manufacturing), representing the alliance in all matters within its purview and proposing and implementing joint projects with other councils within AAALF;
- To initiate and conduct state, district, and national conferences on facilities and equipment issues;

- To plan and develop needed publications through the alliance; and
- To provide consultant services for referral to potential users and developers of facilities.

    Who Should Be a Member:

- Those teaching courses or a unit within a course in facilities planning;
- Any HPERD professional who has an interest in facility planning; and
- Any professional who plans, designs, and manages facilities, and manufacturers of equipment involving fitness, physical activity, and sport.

    CFE Membership Services:

- Consultant service for potential users, planners, and designers of physical activity facilities and equipment;
- Research on current trends in physical activity facilities and equipment;
- Programs and site visits of facilities at the annual AAHPERD national conference;
- Newsletter, *Focus on Facilities*, published semi-annually. It contains news about ongoing projects within the council and important happenings in facility and equipment development;
- Awards given to members who contribute significantly to the CFE;
- World Wide Web connection is http://www.aahperd.org/aaalf.html; and
- Publication of state-of-the-art textbook used in educating undergraduates and graduates in the field of facilities and equipment; available from AAHPERD Publications.

Future of the Council on Facilities and Equipment

The CFE sees great potential for its newest version of the facility development book. The expanded book provides greater detail for students, professionals in the field, consultants, and architects than previous editions. Further, CFE will develop a second book entitled *Facility Management for Activity, Health and Sports*. The Council will also develop two certifications with examinations based on both textbooks along with online courses. Finally, CFE will develop a new online journal.

CFE LEADERSHIP AND AWARDS

Leadership in Facilities and Equipment since 1920

The following professionals have been on the council since 1920:

Leaders in Facilities, Equipment, and Supplies

1920-23	George L. Meylan
1924-27	Harry A. Scott
1927-28	A.R. Winters
1928-45	Prettyman
1928-45	Caswell M. Miles

Chairpersons of the Council on Equipment and Supplies [CES]

1954-56	Thomas E. McDonough
1956-59	Charles Heilman
1959-60	D.K. Stanley
1960-61	Robert Weber
1961-62	James C. Loveless
1962-63	John A. Friedrich
1963-64	William Theunissen
1964-65	John Fox
1965-66	Maurice A. Clay
1966-67	Wayne Brumbach
1967-68	Richard B. Westkaemper
1968-69	Joseph M. Pease

1969-70	John Nettleton
1970-71	James Delamater
1971-72	Alexander Petersen
1972-73	O.N. Hunter
1973-74	Ghary M. Akers
1974-75	Richard B. Flynn

Chairpersons of the Council on Facilities, Equipment, and Supplies (CFES)

1975-76	James E. Sharman
1976-77	Edward Coates
1977-78	James Mason
1978-79	Marty McIntyre
1979-80	Margaret Waters
1980-81	Mike Collins
1981-82	Robert L. Case
1982-83	Edward T Turner
1983-84	Ernest A. White
1984-85	Dan Gruetter
1985-86	Jack Lynn Shannon
1986-87	Larry Horine
1987-88	Armond Seidler
1988-89	Harvey White
1989-90	David Stotlar
1990-91	Maureen Henry
1991-92	Todd Seidler

Chairpersons of the Council on Facilities and Equipment [CFE]

1992-93	Brad Strand
1993-94	Marcia Walker
1994-95	Richard J. LaRue
1995-97	Thomas H. Sawyer
1997-99	Robert Femat
1999-2001	Bernie Goldfine
2001-2003	Michael G. Hypes
2003-2005	Thomas Horne
2005-2007	Jeff Peterson
2007-2008	Julia Ann Hypes
2008-2009	Michael G. Hypes
2009-2011	Michael G. Hypes
2011-2013	Lawrence Judge

The CFES or CFE Award Winners

Honor Award

1979	Richard B. Flynn
1980	Edward Coates
1981	Edward Shea
1982	Martin McIntyre
1983	Margaret H. Aitken
1994	Armond Seidler
1995	James Mason
1996	Harvey White

1997	Todd Seidler & Marcia Walker
1998	Edward Turner
1999	Thomas H. Sawyer
2000	Hervy LaVoie
2001	Donna Thompson
2002	Thomas H. Sawyer
2003	Richard LaRue
2004	No Award
2005	Michael Hypes
2006	No Award
2007	Todd Seidler
2008	Michael Hypes
2009	Bernie Goldfine

Professional Recognition Award

1994	Edward Turner
1995	Larry Horine
1996	Alexander Gabrielsen
1997	Arthur Mittelstaedt
1998	Alison Osinski
1999	Dave Stotlar
2000	Richard LaRue
2001	Thomas Sawyer
2002	Todd Seidler
2003	Susan Hudson
2004	Bernie Goldfine
2005	Hal Walker
2006	No Award
2007	Michael G. Hypes
2008	Bernie Goldfine
2009	Gary Rushing

Chairperson Citations

2009	Chris Neumann & Sam Iverson
2008	Jeff Peterson
2007	Thomas Sawyer

Lifetime Achievement Award

| 2008 | Edward Turner |

EQUIPMENT AND FACILITY DESIGN STANDARDS 30

Thomas H. Sawyer, Indiana State University

Standards

Standards are the basis by which fitness, physical activity, recreation, sport products, and facilities can be harmonized between companies, between sports associations, trade associations, and between countries. Standards that have been developed over the past 50 years have provided a uniform approach to producing devices and parts used in fitness, physical activity, recreation, and sport equipment and in the construction elements of a facility. Standards have also provided sports organizations with consistency among levels of a sport and variations of the game itself. This has perhaps been the weakest aspect of standardization, as various sport organizations have similarities and differences that become the competitive edge for control of that market.

A standard is something established for use as a rule or basis of comparison in measuring or judging capacity. A standard applies to some measure, principle, model, etc., with which things of the same class are compared in order to determine their quantity, value, or quality. A standard has a set of criteria used to test or measure the excellence, fitness, or correctness of something.

Standards for facilities and equipment are established by associations, societies, trades, or federal and state governments. The American Society for Testing and Materials (ASTM) is an example of a society that establishes standards. From the work of 132 technical standards- writing committees, ASTM (http://www. astm.org) publishes standard specifications, tests, practices, guides, and definitions for materials, products, systems, and services. ASTM also publishes books containing reports on state-of-the-art testing techniques and their possible applications. These standards and related information are used throughout the world.

Mandatory and Voluntary Standards

Standards may be either mandatory or voluntary. The status of a standard depends on the sponsor's organizational standing (i.e., governmental or voluntary non-governmental). A mandatory standard is developed by a federal agency such as the Environmental Protection Agency (EPA) and Occupational Safety and Health Administration (OSHA). The voluntary standard is developed by a professional non-profit agency. A violation of a mandatory standard carries a penalty. In addition to standards, other written documents control the unity and uniformity of equipment and facility development; including legal codes or regulations, technical specifications, guides, and literature and learned treatises.

Legal codes are developed by elected public officials, such as the National Bureau of Standards, EPA, and OSHA. Further, each state or local government has its own building codes. Technical specifications and guidelines are developed by voluntary organizations such as the American Society of Testing and Materials (ASTM) or American National Standard Institute (ANSI), which create standards through committee or trade group processes. Many other professional, trade, and organizational associations also promulgate standards, specifications, or guides that are used to measure a standard of care. Literature and learned treatises document common knowledge in a variety of ways, including professional journals, magazines, reference books, textbooks, and reports.

Standard of Practice

A standard of practice is a usual practice accepted by the national or local government regarding some aspect of equipment or facility design or usage. It is a usage or practice of the people, which, by common adoption and acquiescence and by long and unvarying habit, has become compulsory and has acquired the force of law with respect to the place or subject matter to which it relates. It is considered a customary practice that prevails within a geographical area.

Standard of Care

In laws of negligence, the standard of care is that degree of care that a reasonably prudent person should exercise in the same or similar circumstances. If a person's conduct falls below such standard, legal or customary, he or she may be liable in damages for injuries or damages resulting from his or her conduct.

Evolution of Standards

The development of standards began in earnest at the conclusion of World War II. The movement was enhanced by the efforts of the National Bureau of Standards to establish partnerships with ASTM, ANSI, and other groups to standardize materials and methods used by private industry and government. During the 1950s and '60s, automation of the workplace increased the need for greater standardization of materials and methods. The computer age has again increased the need for yet greater collaboration between government and the private sector in the development of additional standards as well as the modification of previous ones.

The development of standards in the fitness, physical activity, recreation, and sport area began in the early 1970s. The F-8 Committee on Sports Equipment and Facilities was organized by ASTM. The initial standards promulgated by the F-8 Committee dealt with footwear and football helmets. Ten years after the F-8 Committee was developed, the Committee on Skiing and Amusements was established. Over the years, a wide range of standards has been developed that influence fitness, physical activity, recreation, and sport. These standards have also made equipment and facilities safer for participants.

Though such standards have been through the gauntlet of objections and reservations, they are here to stay. Some fear standards may inhibit creativity, negatively affect the growth of the sport, and increase its cost. When participants are engaged in a sport they seem to want to use something to protect themselves. When they do, that something should meet reasonable and meaningful requirements, demonstrating that it provides the protection. The cost of debilitating injuries is reduced by this common denominator.

Organizations Advancing Standards

American National Standards Institute (ANSI)

ANSI is another significant organization that develops standards. It is a nonprofit, privately funded membership organization that coordinates the development of U.S. voluntary national standards and is the U.S. member body to non-treaty international standards bodies, such as the International Organization for Standardization (ISO) and the International Electrotechnical Commission (IEC) through the Institute's U.S. National Committee (USNC). ANSI serves both the private and public sectors' need for voluntary standardization. The voluntary standards system contributes to the overall health of the economy and the competitiveness of U.S. industry in the changing global marketplace.

ANSI was founded in 1918, prompted by the need for an "umbrella" organization to coordinate the activities of the U.S. voluntary standards system and eliminate conflict and duplication in the development process. The institute serves a diverse membership of over 1,200 companies; 250 professional, technical, trade, labor, and consumer organizations; and some 30 government agencies. The ANSI federation is guided by the national culture and the free enterprise system. For over 70 years, the U.S. voluntary standards system has been administered successfully by the private sector, through ANSI, with the cooperation of federal, state, and local governments. Standards exist in all industries, including telecommunications, safety and health, information processing, petroleum, banking, and household appliances. ANSI's key functions as stated are to:

- Coordinate the self-regulating, due-process consensus-based, U.S. voluntary standards system;
- Administer the development of standards and approve them as American National Standards;
- Provide the means for the U.S. to influence development of international and regional standards;
- Disseminate timely and important information on national, international, and regional standards activities to U.S. industry; and
- Promote awareness of the growing strategic significance of standards technology and U.S. global competitiveness.

A standards board is a standing organization within ANSI, having planning and coordination responsibilities on a continuing basis for a defined scope of activity under the purview of, and advisory to, ANSI's Executive Standards Council (ExSC). Standards boards serve in a purely advisory capacity. They do not develop standards, nor do they have authority over the activities of accredited standards developers. Membership within ANSI is a prerequisite to service on a standards board. The standards board has responsibility for establishing overall planning and coordination for national and international standards activities in the safety and health area. Further, it reviews the standards activity of applicants for accreditation and the initiation of new standards activities by accredited standards developers. It reviews applications for accreditation of International Standards Organization's U.S. Technical Advisory Group (TAG) Administrators and makes recommendations to the ExSO regarding approval of TAG Administrators, TAG membership lists, and accreditation. The board also reviews lists of candidates for American National Standards and recommends the addition of directly and materially affected interests, and it makes recommendations to the ExSO concerning suggested changes to ANSI procedures.

The scope of the standards board includes protection of the health and safety of employees and the public using buildings, machinery, and other equipment; hazardous materials; workplaces (including construction sites); vehicular traffic; public and recreation areas; homes and schools; and occupational and non-occupational hazards. Hazards include such things as explosion; fire; radiation (other than ionizing); mechanical, physical, chemical, and environmental hazards; disease; and inadequate or polluted air. Specifically included are personal protective equipment, including personal protection devices for attenuating noise, practices or devices to prevent or minimize fire, explosion or mechanical hazards, safe work practices, and provision for accident reporting and recording. Specifically excluded are building codes and acoustical (other than personal protective devices), electrical, process industry, and nuclear energy standards.

American Society of Testing and Materials (ASTM)

One of the first materials specifications was found in the Book of Genesis: "Make thee an ark of gopher wood; rooms shalt thou make in the ark, and shalt pitch it within and without with pitch." Prior to the 19th century's industrial revolution, craftsmen told their suppliers in similarly basic language what kinds of materials they desired. Craft experience was indeed key, because artisans had no instruments to measure the tensile strength, chemical composition, and other characteristics of a given material.

The industrial revolution opened a new chapter in the history of material specifications. Locomotive builders, steel rail producers, and steam engine builders who used revolutionary new materials, such as Bessemer steel, could no longer rely on craft experiences of centuries past. Manufacturers encountered numerous quality problems in such end products as steel rails, because suppliers furnished inferior materials. American rails were so poorly made, in fact, that many railroad companies preferred British imports, which were more expensive but reliable.

To avoid such problems, some manufacturers issued detailed descriptions of material to ensure that their supplies met certain quality standards. However, suppliers in many industries, such as construction and metallurgy, objected to standard material specifications and testing procedures, because they feared that strict quality controls would make customers more inclined to reject items and default on contracts.

The Pennsylvania Railroad, the largest corporation of the 19th century, played a key role in the quest for standard specifications. Its efforts in this field were initiated by Charles Dudley, who received his Ph.D. from Yale University in 1874, and who later became the driving force behind ASTM. Dudley organized the railroad's new chemistry department, where he investigated the technical properties of oil, paint, steel, and other materials the Pennsylvania Railroad bought in large quantities. Based on his research, Dudley issued standard material specifications for the company's suppliers.

What is ASTM?

Organized in 1898, ASTM has grown into one of the largest voluntary standards development systems in the world. ASTM is a not-for-profit organization that provides a forum for producers, users, ultimate consumers, and those having a general interest (representatives of government and academia) to meet on common ground and write standards for materials, products, systems, and services. From the work of 132 standards-writing committees, ASTM publishes standard test methods, specifications, practices, guides, classifications, and terminology. ASTM's standards development activities encompass metals, paints, plastics, textiles, petroleum, construction, energy, the environment, consumer products, medical services and devices, computerized systems, electronics, and many other areas. ASTM Headquarters has no technical research or testing facilities; such work is done voluntarily by 35,000 technically qualified ASTM members located throughout the world. More than 10,000 ASTM standards are published each year in the 72 volumes of the *Annual Book of ASTM Standards*. These standards and related information are sold throughout the world.

What Is an ASTM Standard?

As used in ASTM, a standard is a document that has been developed and established within the consensus principles of the society and that meets the approval requirements of ASTM procedures and regulations. Some of the specific standards developed that relate to fitness, physical activity, recreation, and sport facilities and equipment are E-5 Fire Standards, F-6 Resilient Floor Coverings, F-8 Sports Equipment and Facilities, F-14 Fences, F-21 Filtration, F-24 Amusement Rides and Devices, F-26 Food Service Equipment. F-27 Snow Skiing, and F-30 Emergency Medical Services.

What Types of Standards Does ASTM Produce?

ASTM develops six principal types of full-consensus standards. They are:

- Standard test method—A definitive procedure for the identification, measurement, and evaluation of one or more qualities, characteristics, or properties of a material, product, system, or service that produces a test result.

- Standard specification—A precise statement of a set of requirements to be satisfied by a material, product, system, or service that also indicates the procedures for determining whether each of the requirements is satisfied.
- Standard practice—A definitive procedure for performing one or more specific operations or functions that does not produce a test result.
- Standard terminology—A document comprising terms, definitions, description of terms, explanation of symbols, abbreviations, or acronyms.
- Standard guide—A series of options or instructions that do not recommend a specific course of action.
- Standard classification—A systematic arrangement or division of materials, products, systems, or services into groups based on similar characteristics such as origin, composition, properties, or use.

Why Are ASTM Standards Credible?

Many factors contribute to the quality and credibility of ASTM standards. Those factors include:

- A voluntary, full-consensus approach that brings together people with diverse backgrounds, expertise, and knowledge;
- A balanced representation of interests at the standards-writing table;
- Intense round-robin testing to ensure precision;
- Strict balloting and due-process procedures to guarantee accurate, up-to-date information; and
- An atmosphere that promotes open discussion.

What is Meant by Full-Consensus Standards?

Full-consensus standards are developed through the cooperation of all parties who have an interest in participating in the development and/or use of the standards. Standards can be developed through varying degrees of consensus. Examples include:

- Company Standard—consensus among the employees of a given organization (principally within such departments as design, development, production, and purchasing).
- Industry Standard—consensus among the employees of a given industry (typically developed by a trade association).
- Professional Standard—consensus among the individual members of a given profession (typically developed by a professional society).

- Government Standard—consensus often among the employees of a government agency or department.

ASTM develops full-consensus standards with the belief that input from all concerned parties in the development of a standard will ensure technically competent standards having the highest credibility when critically examined and used as the basis for commercial, legal, or regulatory actions.

Is the Use of ASTM Standards Mandatory?

ASTM standards are developed voluntarily and used voluntarily. They become legally binding only when a government body makes them so, or when they are cited in a contract.

Who Uses ASTM Standards?

ASTM standards are used by thousands of individuals, companies, and agencies. Purchasers and sellers incorporate standards into contracts; scientists and engineers use them in their laboratories; architects and designers use them in their plans; government agencies reference them in codes, regulations, and laws; and many others refer to them for guidance.

Who Writes ASTM Standards?

ASTM standards are written by volunteer members who serve on technical committees. Through a formal balloting process, all members may have input into the standards before they are published by ASTM.

Anyone who is qualified or knowledgeable in the area of a committee's scope is eligible to become a committee member. ASTM currently has 35,000 members representing virtually every segment of industry, government, and academia.

What Are ASTM Technical Committees?

They are the specific arenas in which ASTM standards are developed. There are 132 ASTM main technical committees, and each is divided into subcommittees. The subcommittee is the primary unit in ASTM's standards development system, as it represents the highest degree of expertise in a given area. Subcommittees are further subdivided into task groups. Task group members do not have to be ASTM members. Many task groups seek non-ASTM members to provide special expertise in a given area.

How Are ASTM Standards Developed?

Standards development work begins when a need is recognized. Task group members prepare a draft standard, which is reviewed by its parent subcommittee through a letter ballot. After the subcommittee approves the document, it is submitted to a main committee letter box. Once approved at the main committee level, the document is submitted for balloting to the society. All negative votes cast during the balloting process, which must include a written explanation of the voter's objections, must be fully considered before the document can be submitted to the next level in the process. Final approval of a standard depends on concurrence by the ASTM Committee on Standards that proper procedures were followed and due process achieved. Only then is the ASTM standard published.

How Long Does It Take to Develop a Standard?

It usually takes about two years to develop a standard, although some committees have produced their standards in a year or less. Progress depends entirely on the urgency of the need, the complexity of the job, and the amount of time committees devote to the work.

How Does Someone Initiate a New Standards Activity in ASTM?

A written request, which describes the proposed activity and lists individuals, companies, and organizations that might have an interest in it, should be submitted to ASTM headquarters. The ASTM staff then researches the project to assess whether there is adequate interest, to discover if parallel activities exist in other organizations, and to determine where the activity would appropriately fit within the ASTM structure.

The process of organizing a new activity includes holding a planning and/or organizational meeting, depending on the activity's complexity. These meetings ensure that all affected interests have an opportunity to determine the need for the activity, participate in the development of a title, scope, and structure, and identify areas that need standardization.

Does ASTM Offer Continuing Technical Education?

ASTM provides continuing education and training in the use and application of ASTM standards through technical and professional training courses. ASTM members propose ideas for the courses, work with staff to establish course outlines, and serve as instructors. Attendees learn the practical application of standards and benefit from the instructors' technical expertise and knowledge of standards development.

Occupational Safety and Health Administration (OSHA)

OSHA (a federal agency) has become extensively involved in standards development. The impetus to develop a new standard can come from a variety of sources: OSHA's own initiative, the U.S. Congress, information from the National Institute for Occupational Safety and Health (NIOSH), a referral from EPA's Toxic Substances Control Act (TSCA), public petitions, or requests from OSHA advisory committees.

The standard-setting process can begin in a number of ways—with publication in the *Federal Register* of a request for information (RFI), an advance notice of proposed rule-making (ANPRM), or a notice of proposed rule-making (NPRM). Through an RFI or an ANPRM, OSHA seeks information to determine the extent of a particular hazard, current and potential protective measures, and the costs and benefits of various solutions.

Recently, OSHA has begun to develop some new standards through a negotiated rule-making process. Under this process, the agency forms an advisory committee composed of representatives from the various interest groups that will be affected by the new standard. These labor and industry representatives meet with OSHA to hammer out an agreement (consensus standard) that will serve as the basis for a proposed rule. This process is used to resolve long-standing differences that, until negotiated rule making, could not be resolved. OSHA is using this process to draft proposed rules for steel erection in construction and fire protection in shipyards.

Information from these sources, as well as injury and fatality data, is then used to develop a proposal. Formal proposals are published in the *Federal Register* with notice of a public comment period over the next 60 to 90 days. Occasionally, requests are made to extend the comment period or to hold a public hearing.

Finally, OSHA uses all this information to prepare and publish a final standard in the *Federal Register*, or, in some cases, to determine that no standard is needed. Standards usually take effect in 90 days or less, although some provisions (such as requirements for detailed programs) may be phased in over a longer period.

International Environment, Health and Safety (IEH&S) and International Audit Protocol Consortium (IAPC)

New International Environment, Health, and Safety (IEH&S) requirements are also being developed. These requirements include Great Britain's BS7750, the European Union's (EU) Environmental Management Audit Scheme (EMAS), the International Standards Organizations's (ISO) 9000 quality assurance and quality management standards, and the ISO 14000, a global environmental management standard.

Companies are compelled to comply with these environmental management standards for reasons that reach beyond fear of legal reprisal;

strong economic and political forces are at work. Consumers are increasingly demanding that companies' products and manufacturing processes be environmentally responsible. One of the goals of the ISO 14000 standards will be to provide a precise "green" measuring tool for a concerned public. Governments, particularly those in the EU, are also favoring the "green" company. Companies without an ISO 14000 certification could be shut out of some international markets.

Fitness, Health, Racquet and Sport Clubs

American College of Sports Medicine (ACSM)

The ACSM has published a second edition of the book entitled *Health Fitness Facility Standards and Guidelines,* which suggests that the "book now sets a clear standard of comparison for use in legal proceedings." These standards are as follows:

"Standard #1: A facility must be able to respond in a timely manner to any reasonably foreseeable emergency event that threatens the health and safety of facility users. Toward this end, a facility must have an appropriate emergency plan that can be executed by qualified personnel in a timely manner.

Standard #2: A facility must offer each adult member a preactivity screening that is appropriate to the physical activities to be performed by the member.

Standard #3: Each person who has supervisory responsibility for a physical activity program or area at the facility must have demonstrable professional competence in that activity program or area.

Standard #4: A facility must post appropriate signage alerting users to the risks involved in their use of those areas of a facility that present potential increased risk(s).

Standard #5: A facility that offers youth services or programs must provide appropriate supervision.

Standard #6: A facility must conform to all relevant laws, regulations, and published standards." (ACSM, 5-10)

However, IHRSA, the International Health, Racquet, and Sportclubs Association (see below) has rejected the guidelines. The Association for Worksite Health Promotion (formerly the Association for Fitness in Business) is developing its own standards and certification process in a reaction to ACSM's failure to recognize the AFB's previous contributions to health and fitness certification standards.

There is a veritable alphabet soup of professional certifications from associations wishing to increase their memberships, improve their images, or turn a profit. The ACSM book defers to the state or local codes when it comes to more technical standards.

The ACSM is a medically based organization with a research focus. In the 14 years since the ACSM issued its initial exercise recommendations, the percentage of people complying has not changed substantially. The medical model works in a hospital or testing lab, but not necessarily in clubs or corporate health promotion or municipal fitness programs.

International Health, Racquet, & Sportsclub Association (IHRSA)

IHRSA, is a not-for-profit trade association representing 2,500 health and sports clubs worldwide. It is the largest club association in the world. More than 1,800 IHRSA member clubs offer some form of reciprocal access through the association's "Passport" program, which provides members the opportunity to use another club when they travel.

A club must agree to abide by the IHRSA Code of Conduct and comply with the association's membership standards. A member of IHRSA has the mission to enhance the quality of life through physical fitness and sports. It endeavors to provide quality facilities, programs, instruction, and strives to instill in all those served an understanding of the value of physical fitness and sports to their lives.

IHRSA recognizes the following international certifying agencies:

- Aerobics and Fitness Association of America
- Aerobic Pipeline International
- American Aerobics Association /International Sports Medicine Association
- American College of Sports Medicine
- American Council on Exercise
- Cooper Fitness Institute
- IDEA: The Association for Fitness Professionals
- National Academy of Sports Medicine
- National Association for Fitness Certification
- National Dance Exercise Instructors Training Association
- National Federation of Professional Trainers
- National Strength and Conditioning Association
- Ontario Fitness Council
- Sinai Corporate Health

National Fire Protection Association (NFPA)

The NFPA publishes the Life Safety Codes and will be jointly developing and publishing the first edition of the International Fire Code. This agreement comes after negotiations between the

International Code Council (ICC) and NFPA. The ICC's three model code organizations, include the Building Officials and Code Administrators International, the International Conference of Building Officials, and the Southern Building Code Congress International. Representatives have been appointed by the ICC and NFPA to participate in the development of codes. It will be processed through NFPA's International Conference of Building Officials (ICBO).

ICBO is a leading code organization that established a *Uniform Building Code* (UBC) in 1927. That code contained a little over 200 pages of text, whereas the 1994 version involves three volumes and more than 2,600 pages. Modern codes are steadily moving to performance-type codes rather than the specification type because of the proliferation of types of materials, methods, and machinery used today. Such codes also reflect public policy, which has changed in the past 70 or more years. Contemporary society has looked to codes not only to ensure safety of life and limb, but increasingly to safeguard public welfare or well-being and security. Goals for many public issues, such as air and water quality, energy conservation, recycling, and disabilities, have led to a number of codes that affect recreation, physical activity, and sport facilities.

Codes and standards are sometimes viewed as interchangeable terms. Indeed, a code meets the above definitions of a standard. Codes, or parts thereof, are frequently characterized as being either prescriptive or performance-based. Prescriptive code requirements are definitive and easily measurable, such as the minimum width of an exit corridor, maximum slope for a specific type of roof covering, minimum air gap for back flow prevention, minimum size of grounding conductor, etc. Performance code requirements, on the other hand, use terms that describe the desired result, such as watertight enclosure, smoke removal, safe-for-the-intended-use, etc. Some of these terms have companion standards as part of the code, such as those for smoke dampers, stairway identification signs, and waterproof paper, while others do not. Adopted standards in this context can be thought of as specification codes.

A review of the 1927 *Uniform Building Codes* reveals that 28 standards were incorporated by reference. These documents were promulgated by various organizations including ASTM, the American Concrete Institute, the National Board of Fire Underwriters, the National Fire Protection Association, and others.

Standards are incorporated into the UBC under a code change procedure involving a proposal, a review by a code change committee in a public hearing, and a vote at a final hearing by the assembled membership at the annual meeting. Anyone can propose a code change and argue for or against any code change.

The Building Officials and Code Administrators International (BOCA) and the Southern Building Code Congress International (SBCCI), the respective publishers of the *National Building Code* (NBC) and the *Standard Building Code* (SBC), have similar histories of employing adopted standards in their codes. Together with ICBO, the International Code Council (ICC) has been formed as a consortium of these organizations. The ICC published the *International Building Code* (IBC) in 2003 with subsequent editions in 2006 and 2009, with no further publications of the UBC, NBC, and SBC after 1997.

European Committee for Standardization (CEN)

CEN is the European standards organization that coordinates all European country standards organizations. It has secretariats in various subject areas that in turn relate to ISO Technical Committees. CEN has been the initiator of EC 1992. This is the array of regulatory and standards initiatives that leads to the common European internal market. EC 1992 also requires testing and certifications requirements. It sets forth alternative approaches to testing, certification, and proving conformity with the regulatory directives that are set out. It identifies organizations that will perform conformity assessment functions and U.S. testing and certifying organizations. This has implications on many sports products and ultimately facilities used for international events.

International Standards Organization (ISO) or International Organization for Standardization (IOS)

The ISO is the worldwide body, and ANSI is the member body of this group representing the United States. Approaching the 21st century, ISO sees a world in which global trade between nations continues to grow at a rate three to four times faster than national economies; a world in which the design, manufacture, marketing, and customer service operations of a growing majority of individual enterprises are distributed across many countries; and a world in which electronic communications have dramatically increased technical collaboration between experts in academia, governments, and industries from all countries.

The increasingly rapid development of technology in many sectors will continue to present major opportunities as well as underlying dangers for the general welfare of society It will therefore be incumbent on all social and economic partners to collaborate closely in guiding the applications of appropriate technologies toward sustainable economic development and global prosperity.

In this rapidly evolving scenario, globally applicable standards will play a key role. Such standards, whether developed by ISO or others, will become primary technical instruments supporting international commerce. In this context, ISO intends to be recognized globally as an influential and innovative leader in the developments of globally applicable international standards that meet or exceed the expectations of the community of nations. It will strive at all times to perfect the application of consensus and transparency principles in standardization, and in this way promote the values of rationality, utility, safety, and environmental protection for the benefit of all peoples.

Standardization is essentially an economic undertaking made possible by the achievement of widespread agreements on the coherent and mutually beneficial use of science, technology, and business knowhow. The prime object of ISO and its governance is laid down in the ISO statutes (i.e., to promote the development of standardization and related activities in the world with a view to facilitating international exchange of goods and services and to developing cooperation in the sphere of intellectual, scientific, and economic activity).

National Spa and Pool Institute (NSPI)

The National Spa and Pool Institute has for 30 years been the source of standards for the design, construction, and operation of public as well as residential pools and spas. The organization has a membership of designer-engineers along with manufacturers, builders, contractors, equipment, and chemical manufacturers and suppliers and retailers in every aspect of the pool and spa industry. Many representatives of Health Departments also belong.

In 1996, efforts began to rewrite the ANSI/SPI-11991 standard for public pools as well as other pool and spa standards. This rewrite has undergone a conflict because of the various concerns for safety. At present, the technical committee of NSPI has assumed the rewrite function and the broad base of interests originally invited to serve are now reviewers.

World Waterpark Association (WWA)

The federal government has had standards for waterparks since they became popular over a decade ago. In 1991, the WWA published *Splash Magazine* as a developer's reference. Concurrently, it established a risk management and safety committee. Representatives of this committee were invited by the National Spa and Pool Institute to sit on the public pool standards rewrite committee. After a year of deliberations, it was decided that water slides and flumes should have a standard apart from any public pool standard. As a result, a WWA committee was established in 1997 to write a draft of a standard under the cooperative auspices of NSPI, which is an accredited member of ANSI. This standard is now being circulated.

Sport Indoor and Outdoor Facility Standards

The following organizations establish standards for facilities and equipment for amateur and professional sports in the United States.

Amateur Sports (include, but not limited to):

- National Federation of High School Activities Associations,
- National Collegiate Athletic Association,
- National Junior College Athletic Association,
- Amateur Athletic Union,
- Little League Baseball,
- American Softball Association, and
- United States Olympic Committee and its various National Governing Bodies.

Professional Sports (include, but not limited to):

- National Football League,
- National Basketball Association,
- National Hockey League,
- Major League Baseball,
- Professional Golf Association,
- Ladies Professional Golf Association,
- United States Tennis Association, and
- American Bowling Congress.

Professional Involvement in Standards

Professionals in the fitness, physical activity, recreation, sport, and related fields are not as involved in standards as they could and should be. Standards organizations involve only a small percentage of the professionals directly involved in the teaching, researching, planning, administering, operating, and maintaining of fitness, physical activity, recreation, and sport facilities and activities, regardless of jurisdiction or the type of entity. Many standards applicable to fitness, physical activity, recreation, and sport are developed by manufacturers, medical specialists, businessmen, lawyers, and others.

Professionals have not been aware of these standards organizations nor familiar with how to become involved. Organizations such as the American Alliance for Health, Physical Education, Recreation, and Dance and the National Recreation and Park Association have not specifically designated professionals to serve as their representatives to these organizations. It is imperative that in the future more professionals be appointed or volunteer to lend their expertise to the standards process.

Governmental Involvement in Standards

Governmental agencies have a long history of involvement in standards. Apparently, many of their efforts now tend to be catalytic in evolving standards. This is a significant change over the past 50 years. In most cases they have encouraged producers to regulate their own industries. Where such efforts have failed the government, both state and federal agencies have moved to provide regulations and supportive standards to protect the health, safety, and well-being of the public.

The government usually provides standards in the form of legislation that goes beyond the base line or minimum level of requirement. As a result, industries and professions are becoming more conscious in recognizing that if they themselves do not develop standards, somebody else will.

Guidelines

A guideline is a standard or principle by which to make a judgement or determine a policy or course of action. A guideline is developed after a standard has been established. The guideline is a series of procedures to ensure the maintenance of the standards.

APPENDIX A

(Note: All appendices reprinted from the 10th edition of *Facilities Planning for Health, Fitness, Physical Activity, Recreation, and Sports: Concepts and Applications*)

Facility Specification Guide

Compliments of Athletic Business, National Collegiate Athletic Association, and the National Federation of State High School Associations

Baseball	438
Basketball	439
Hockey	440
Racquetball/Handball	441
Squash	441
Women's Lacrosse	442
Men's Lacrosse	442
Track and Field	443-445
Swimming and Diving	446-447
Team Handball	448
Field Hockey	448
Tennis	449
Badminton	449
Soccer	450
Softball	451
Football	452-453
Volleyball	453

FACILITY SPECIFICATION GUIDE
BASEBALL

LEGEND
- BASE LINES, BATTER'S BOX, CATCHER'S BOX, FOUL LINE, PITCHER'S PLATE, COACH'S BOX
- ○ ON-DECK CIRCLE
- - - - BASE LINES
- – – – GRASS LINES

(Reprinted with permission of the NCAA.)

YOUTH LEAGUE

SANDY KOUFAX (AABC) AND PONY LEAGUE

BABE RUTH AND SENIOR LEAGUE

ALSO:
MICKEY MANTLE
CONNIE MACK
JUNIOR LEGION
HIGH SCHOOL
310' RADIUS
360' OPTION

HOME PLATE

PITCHER'S PLATE

(Diagrams courtesy of USA Baseball.)

For more information contact:

USA Baseball
Hi Corbett Field
3400 E. Camino Campestre
Tucson, AZ 85716
(520) 327-9700
Fax: (520) 327-9221
www.usabaseball.com

American Amateur Baseball Congress
118 Redfield Plaza
P.O. Box 467
Marshall, MI 49068
(616) 781-2002
Fax: (616) 781-2060
www.voyager.net/aabc

National Collegiate Athletic Association
6201 College Blvd.
Overland Park, KS 66211-2422
(913) 339-1906
www.ncaa.org

FACILITY SPECIFICATION GUIDE

BASKETBALL

PROFESSIONAL COURT

HIGH SCHOOL & COLLEGE COURT

Note: The optimum length of the high school court is 84 feet. If court is less than 74 feet long, it should be divided by two lines, each parallel to and 40 feet from the farther end line.

(Reprinted with permission of the NCAA.)

National Basketball Association
Olympic Tower
645 Fifth Ave.
New York, NY 10022
(212) 826-7000
www.nba.com

National Federation of State High School Associations
P.O. Box 20626
Kansas City, MO 64195-0626
(816) 464-5400
Fax: (816) 464-5571
www.nfhs.org

National Collegiate Athletic Association
6201 College Blvd.
Overland Park, KS 66211-2422
(913) 339-1906
www.ncaa.org

FACILITY SPECIFICATION GUIDE
HOCKEY

PROFESSIONAL

COLLEGE AND HIGH SCHOOL

(Diagram courtesy of the NCAA.)

For more information contact:

National Hockey League
75 International Blvd., Room 300
Rexdale, Ontario M9W 6L9
(416) 798-0809
Fax: (416) 798-0819
www.nhl.com

National Federation of State High School Associations
P.O. Box 20626
Kansas City, MO 64195-0626
(816) 464-5400
Fax: (816) 464-5571
www.nfhs.org

National Collegiate Athletic Association
6201 College Blvd.
Overland Park, KS 66211-2422
(913) 339-1906
www.ncaa.org

FACILITY SPECIFICATION GUIDE

RACQUETBALL/ HANDBALL

FRONT AND
SIDE WALL
HEIGHT: 20'0''

REAR WALL
HEIGHT:
AT LEAST 14'0''

For more information contact:

**United States Racquetball
Association**
1685 W. Uintah
Colorado Springs, CO 80904-2921
(719) 635-5396
Fax: (719) 635-0685
www.racquetball.org

SQUASH

NORTH AMERICAN COURT   **INTERNATIONAL COURT**   **DOUBLES COURT**

For more information contact:

**United States Squash Racquets
Association**
23 Cynwyd Road, P.O. Box 1216
Bala-Cynwyd, PA 19004
(610) 667-4006
Fax: (610) 667-6539
www.us-squash.org/squash

FACILITY SPECIFICATION GUIDE

WOMEN'S LACROSSE

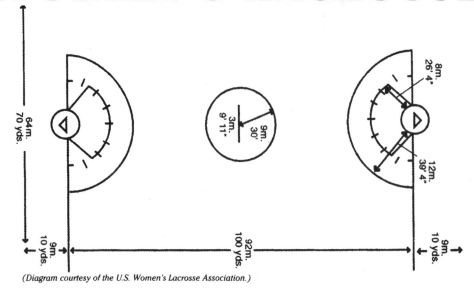

(Diagram courtesy of the U.S. Women's Lacrosse Association.)

For more information contact:

U.S. Women's Lacrosse Association
35 Wisconsin Circle, Suite 525
Chevy Chase, MD 20815
(301) 951-8795
Fax: (301) 951-7082
www.USWLA.org

US Lacrosse Inc.
113 W. University Pkwy.
Baltimore, MD 21210
(410) 235-6882
Fax: (410) 366-6735
www.lacrosse.org

MEN'S LACROSSE

1997
The Lacrosse Field of Play

(Diagram courtesy of the NCAA.)

For more information contact:

US Lacrosse Inc.
113 W. University Pkwy.
Baltimore, MD 21210
(410) 235-6882
Fax: (410) 366-6735
www.lacrosse.org

National Collegiate Athletic Association
6201 College Blvd.
Overland Park, KS 66211-2422
(913) 339-1906
www.ncaa.org

FACILITY SPECIFICATION GUIDE
TRACK & FIELD

POLE VAULT LANDING AREA DETAIL

LONG JUMP/TRIPLE JUMP PIT PLAN

HIGH JUMP DETAIL

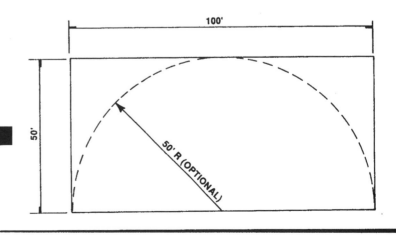

All diagrams reprinted with permission of the USTC&TBA.

For more information contact:

**U.S. Tennis Court and
Track Builders Association**
3525 Ellicott Mills Drive, Suite N
Ellicott City, MD 21043-4547
(410) 418-4875
www.ustctba.com

FACILITY SPECIFICATION GUIDE
TRACK & FIELD

Dimensions for track and field events appearing in the following diagrams are based on requirements set forth by the National Federation of State High School Associations (NFHS). There are variations of requirements for facilities governed by the National Collegiate Athletic Association (NCAA), USA Track and Field (USAT&F) or the International Amateur Athletic Federation (IAAF). Please consult the appropriate governing body or the U.S. Tennis Court and Track Builders Association (USTC&TBA) for specific information.

TRACK USE ONLY

400 METER EVENTS

HURDLE SETTING

	EVENT	NO. OF HURDLES	HURDLE HEIGHT (INCHES)	START TO FIRST HURDLE	BETWEEN HURDLES	LAST HURDLE TO FINISH
B O Y S	55 M	5	39	13.72 M (45 FT)	9.14 M (30 FT)	4.72 M (15.46 FT)
	110 M	10	39	13.72 M (45 FT)	9.14 M (30 FT)	14.02 M (45.98 FT)
	300 M	8	36	45 M (147.62 FT)	35 M (114.83 FT)	10 M (32.81 FT)
G I R L S	75 M	7	30/33	13 M (42.67 FT)	8.5 M (27.90 FT)	11 M (36.08 FT)
	100 M	10	30	13 M (42.67 FT)	8.5 M (27.90 FT)	10.5 M (34.46 FT)
	200 M	10	30	16 M (52.50 FT)	19 M (62.33 FT)	13 M (42.67 FT)
	300 M	8	30	45 M (147.62 FT)	35 M (114.83 FT)	10 M (32.81 FT)

STAGGERED STARTS
STAGGER		
#	FEET	METERS
1	10.996	3.352
2	21.99	6.703
3	32.99	10.054
4	43.98	13.406

FACILITY SPECIFICATION GUIDE
TRACK & FIELD

STEEPLECHASE HURDLES

START

WATER JUMP — 65'
M.L RADIUS 155.5'
FOR STEEPLECHASE

FINISH

100'

Distance for Junior
Events—2,000m

SHOT PUT PAD (HIGH SCHOOL)

THROWING   SECTOR
90° RADIUS

1/4" STONE CHIPS
12" DEPTH

TOE BOARD

2" WIDE PAINTED STRIPE OR
3/4" RECESSED CIRCLE

1/8" SAWCUTS

4" REINFORCED CONCRETE
SLAB WITH
LIGHT BROOM FINISH

1/8" SAWCUTS

10'

10'

NOTE: INSTALL 1/8" SAWCUTS ON
RECESSED CIRCLE ONLY

DISCUS CAGE
(HIGH SCHOOL)

60°

20' - 24'   4' - 5'

(a)   (a)

10'-10'6"   10'-11'

10'-11'

10'-11'

(b)   (b)

(b)

HEIGHT: 10' - 12'
FRONT OPENING: 20' - 24'
4' - 5' : DISTANCE CORNER
          POST TO SECTOR LINE
10' - 11' : DISTANCE CENTER
            OF CIRCLE TO FENCING

JAVELIN THROW

70' - 0"   50' - 0"

26' - 3" R

13' - 1 1/2"

4'

STOP BOARD

FACILITY SPECIFICATION GUIDE
SWIMMING & DIVING

INTERNATIONAL AND NATIONAL COMPETITION

There are a number of sanctioning organizations for national and international amateur competition. Included here are the facility standards of FINA (the Federation Internationale de Natation Amateur) and one of its U.S. affiliates, United States Swimming Inc.

FINA STANDARDS
• Length—50m. When touch panels or electronic timing devices are used, the pool must be of such length that ensures the required distance between the panels.
• Width—25m preferred.
• Depth—1m minimum.
• Number of lanes—8. For Olympic Games and World Championships, 10 lanes are required.
• Width of lanes—2m minimum with spaces of 0.2m outside first and last lanes. A lane rope must separate these spaces from the first and last lanes.

U.S. SWIMMING STANDARDS
• Length—Long course, 164'½" (50m); short course, 82'¼" (25m) or 25 yds.
• Width—Eight lanes, 8'2½" (2.5m) minimum (centerline to centerline), with approximately 1'6" (0.45m) outside first and last lanes.

• Water depth—For national championships and international competition, 6'7" (2m) throughout the course. Minimum water depth for racing starts during competition and practice shall be measured for a distance 3'3½" (1m) to 16'5" (5m) from the end wall. Starting requirements and height of starting blocks shall be as follows: (1) In pools with water depth less than 3'6" (1.07m) at the starting end, the swimmer must start from the deck or from within the water; (2) In pools with water depth 3'6" (1.07m) to less than 4' (1.22m) at the starting end, starting platforms shall be no more than 18" (0.46m) above the water surface; (3) In pools with water depth 4' (1.22m) or more at the starting end, starting platforms shall meet the following height requirements: A. Long course: The front edge of the starting platforms shall be no less than 1'8" (0.50m) nor more than

2'5½" (0.75m) above the surface of the water. B. Short Course: The front edge of the starting platforms shall be not higher than 2'6" (0.762m) above the surface of the water.

NOTE: Local, state and municipal statutes, ordinances, rules and regulations may have depth limitations in conflict with the above. The LSC and all member clubs should check for this at all times.

For more information contact:

United States Swimming Inc.
One Olympic Plaza
Colorado Springs, CO 80909
(719) 578-4578
Fax: (719) 575-4050

STANDARD DIMENSIONS FOR PUBLIC SWIMMING POOLS

The following are the currently recommended standard dimensions for Class B and Class C public swimming pools, not designed for sanctioned competition.

MINIMUM DIMENSIONS FOR DIVING PORTION OF CLASS B AND C POOLS
(This drawing does not show the shallow portion of the pool)

NOTE: L₄ is a minimum dimension to allow sufficient length opposite the board. This may of course be lengthened to form the shallow portion of the pool

POOL TYPE	RELATED DIVING EQUIPMENT		MINIMUM DIMENSIONS							MINIMUM WIDTH OF POOL AT:		
	MAX. DIVING BOARD LENGTH	MAX. BOARD HGT. OVER WATER	D₁	D₂	R	L₁	L₂	L₃	L₄	L₅	PT. A	PT. B	PT. C
VI	10'	26" (⅔ meter)	7'-6"	8'-6"	5'-6"	7'-6"	8'-0"	10'-6"	7'-0"	29'-0"	16'-0"	16'-0"	16'-0"
VII	12'	30"(¾ meter)	7'-6"	9'-0"	6'-0"	3'-0"	9'-0"	12'-0"	4'-0"	28'-0"	16'-0"	20'-0"	20'-0"
VIII	16'	1 Meter	8'-6"	10'-0"	7'-0"	4'-0"	10'-0"	15'-0"	2'-0"	31'-0"	20'-0"	22'-0"	22'-0"
IX	16'	3 Meter	11'-0"	12'-0"	8'-6"	6'-0"	10'-6"	21'-0"	0	37'-6"	22'-0"	24'-0"	24'-0"

L2, L3 and L4 combined represent the minimum distance from the tip of the board to pool wall opposite diving equipment.

For board heights exceeding 3 meters, see Article 3.5.4.

* NOTE: Placement of boards shall observe the following minimum dimensions. With multiple board installations minimum pool widths must be increased accordingly.

Deck level board to pool side ....8'
1 meter board to pool side ....10'
3 meter board to pool side ....11'
1 meter or deck level board to 3 meter board ....10'
1 meter or deck level to another 1 meter or deck level board ....8'
3 meter to another 3 meter board ....10'

DEPTH
• Swimming—In Class B and C pools, water depths at the shallow end of the swimming area shall be 3' minimum with 3'6" minimum for racing pools. Exceptions may be made in a recessed area of the main swimming pool, outside of the competitive and/or swimming course, when the pool is of an irregular shape with the permission of the state or local authority.
• Diving—Class B and C pools intended for diving shall conform to the minimum water depths, areas, slopes and other dimensions shown in Article 4.7 and shall be located in the diving area of the pool so as to provide the minimum dimensions as shown in Article 3.6.1. Competitive diving equipment shall not be installed in Class B and C pools.

There shall be a completely unobstructed clear vertical distance of 13' above any diving board, measured from the center of the front end of the board. This area shall extend horizontally at least 8' behind, 8' to each side and 16' ahead of point A. (See diagram.)

According to a spokesperson for the National Spa and Pool Institute (NSPI), this standard has been approved by the American National Standards Institute. American National Standards, once approved, may be revised at any time. Make sure that you have the latest edition of this standard by ordering the NSPI-1 Standard for Public Swimming Pools from the NSPI.

For more information contact:

National Spa and Pool Institute
2111 Eisenhower Ave.
Alexandria, VA 22314-4678
(703) 838-0083
Fax: (703) 549-0493
www.poolspaworld.com

FACILITY SPECIFICATION GUIDE
SWIMMING & DIVING

The following are NCAA standard pool dimensions. These are recommended dimensions for collegiate competition only, and specifications are subject to annual review and change.

POOL CROSS-SECTION

LONGITUDINAL SECTION
DIAGRAMMATIC ONLY

CROSS SECTION
DIAGRAMMATIC ONLY

DIVING CHART

LONG COURSE SWIMMING POOL

• Preferred—The racing course should be 164'1½" (50m, 2.54cm) in length by 75'1" (22.89m) in width, providing for eight 9' (2.74m) lanes with additional width outside lanes 1 and 8. A minimum water depth of 7' (2.13m) is desirable for competition. Optional markings: nine 8' (2.44m) lanes or ten 7' (2.13m) lanes.
• Acceptable—The racing course may be 164'1½" (50m, 2.54cm) in length by 60' (18.29m) in width, providing for eight 7' (2.13m) lanes with additional width outside lanes 1 and 8. The water depth may be no less than 4' (1.22m) at the starting end of the racing course and no less than 3'6" (1.07m) at the opposite end. However, a water depth of no less than 4' (1.22m) is recommended throughout the entire length of the racing course.

SHORT COURSE SWIMMING POOL

• Preferred—The racing course should be 75'1" (22.89m) in length by at least 60' (18.29m) in width, providing for not less than eight 7' (2.13m) lanes with additional width outside lanes 1 and 8. A minimum water depth of 7' (2.13m) is desirable for competition.
• Acceptable—The racing course may be 82'1¼" (25m, 2.54cm) in length by at least 45' (13.72m) in width, providing for six 7' (2.13m) lanes with additional width outside lanes 1 and 6. The water depth may be no less than 4' (1.22m) at the starting end of the racing course and no less than 3'6" (1.07m) at the opposite end. However, a water depth of no less than 4' (1.22m) is recommended throughout the entire length of the racing course.

DIVING POOL

• Preferred—The diving facility should be 60' (18.29m) in length by 75'1" (22.89m) in width. It should be equipped with two 1-meter and two 3-meter springboards and a diving tower, providing takeoff platforms at 5, 7.5 and 10 meters. Recommended dimensions for diving facilities are specified in the table on the left.
• Acceptable—The diving facility may be separated from or incorporated with the swimming pool. Recommended dimensions for diving facilities are specified in the table on the left.
Note: The above dimensions may be incorporated in "L," "T," "Z," and "U" shaped pools.

NCAA Recommended Dimensions for Diving Facilities		Dimensions are in Feet	SPRINGBOARD				PLATFORM			
			1 Meter		3 meters		5 meters	7.5 Meters	10 Meters	
Revised to March 3, 1991		LENGTH	16'		16'		20'	20'	20'	
		WIDTH	1'8"		1'8"		5'	5'	6'7"	
		HEIGHT	3'4"		10'		16'5"	24'8"	32'10"	
			Horiz.	Vert.	Horiz.	Vert.	Horiz.	Vert.	Horiz.	Vert.
A	From plummet BACK TO POOL WALL	Designation	A-1		A-3		A-5	A-7.5	A-10	
		Minimum	5'		5'		4'2"	5'	5'	
		Preferred	6'1"		6'1"		4'2"	5'	5'	
A/A	From plummet BACK TO PLATFORM plummet directly below	Designation					A/A5	A/A7.5	A/A10	
		Minimum					2'6"	2'6"	2'6"	
		Preferred					4'2"	4'2"	4'2"	
B	From plummet to POOL WALL AT SIDE	Designation	B-1		B-3		B-5	B-75	B-10	
		Minimum	8'3"		11'6"		10'8"	14'	17'3"	
		Preferred	8'3"		11'6"		12'4"	14'10"	17'3"	
C	From plummet to ADJACENT PLUMMET	Designation	C-11		C-331		C-531	C-7.5531	C-107.55531	
		Minimum	6'7"		7'3"		7'5"	8'3"	9'1"	
		Preferred	7'1"		8'3"		8'3"	8'3"	9'1"	
D	From plummet to POOL WALL AHEAD	Designation	D-1		D-3		D-5	D-7.5	D-10	
		Minimum	29'7"		33'8"		33'8"	36'2"	44'4	
		Preferred	29'7"		33'8"		33'8"	36'2"	44'4"	
E	On plummet from BOARD TO CEILING	Designation		E-1		E-3		E-5		E-10
		Minimum		16'5"		16'5"		10'8"	10'8"	13'2"
		Preferred		16'5"		16'5"		11'6"	11'6"	16'5"
F	CLEAR OVERHEAD behind and each side of plummet	Designation	F-1	E-1	F-3	E-3	F-5	E-5	F-7.5	E-7.5	F-10	E-10
		Minimum	8'3"	16'5"	8'3"	16'5"	9'1"	10'8"	9'1"	10'9"	9'1"	13'2"
		Preferred	8'3"	16'5"	8'3"	16'5"	9'1"	11'6"	9'1"	11'6"	9'1"	16'5"
G	CLEAR OVERHEAD ahead of plummet	Designation	G-1	E-1	G-3	E-3	G-5	E-5	G-7.5	E-7.5	G-10	E-10
		Minimum	16'5"	16'5"	16'5"	16'5"	16'5"	10'8"	16'5"	10'8"	19'9"	13'2"
		Preferred	16'5"	16'5"	16'5"	16'5"	16'5"	11'6"	16'5"	11'6"	19'9"	16'5"
H	DEPTH OF WATER at plummet (minimum required)	Designation		H-1		H-3		H-5	H-7.5	H-10	
		Minimum		11'		12'		12'2"	13'6"	14'10"	
		Preferred		11'6"		12'6"		12'6"	14'10"	16'5"	
J-K	DISTANCE AND DEPTH ahead of plummet	Designation	J-1	K-1	J-3	K-3	J-5	K-5	J-7.5	K-7.5	J-10	K-10
		Minimum	16'5"	10'10"	16'5"	11'10"	19'9"	11'10"	26'3"	13'2"	36'2"	14'
		Preferred	16'5"	11'2"	19'9"	12'2"	19'9"	12'2"	26'3"	14'6"	36'2"	15'7"
L-M	DISTANCE AND DEPTH each side of plummet	Designation	L-1	M-1	L-3	M-3	L-5	M-5	L-7.5	M-7.5	L-10	M-10
		Minimum	5'	10'10"	6'7"	11'10"	19'11"	11'10"	12'4"	13'2"	14'10"	14'
		Preferred	9'11'	11'2"	8'3"	12'2"	11'6"	12'2"	14'10"	14'6"	17'3"	15'7"
N	MAXIMUM SLOPE OF REDUCE DIMENSIONS beyond full requirements	Pool depth Ceiling Ht.	30 degrees 30 degrees		Note 1: Dimensions C (plummet to adjacent plummet) apply for Platforms with widths as detailed. For wider Platforms increase C by half the additional width(s). Note 2: All dimensions rounded up, even if only fractionally greater than the enxt lowest inch.					

For more information contact:

National Collegiate Athletic Association
6201 College Blvd.
Overland Park, KS 66211-2422
(913) 339-1906
www.ncaa.org

Reprinted with permission of the NCAA.

FACILITY SPECIFICATION GUIDE

TEAM HANDBALL

(Measurements in centimeters)

For more information contact:

United States Team Handball Federation
1903 Powers Ferry, Suite 230
Atlanta, GA 30339

FIELD HOCKEY

For more information contact:

National Federation of State High School Associations
P.O. Box 20626
Kansas City, MO 64195-0626
(816) 464-5400
Fax: (816) 464-5571
www.nfhs.org

FACILITY SPECIFICATION GUIDE

TENNIS

TRUE PLANE SLOPE REQUIREMENTS:
SIDE TO SIDE → *(preferred)*
END TO END
DIAGONAL

The recommended court slope should be:

Fast Dry:
Minimum 1" in 30' (0.28%) (preferred)
Maximum 1" in 24' (0.35%)

Hard Courts:
Minimum 1" in 10' (0.833%) (preferred)
Maximum 1" in 8.33' (1%)

⊙ MARKER FOR SINGLES STICKS OR SINGLES NET POSTS

LINE WIDTH: 2" 5CM
4" 10 CM
NOTE BASE LINES CAN BE 4" WIDE

(Reprinted with permission of the USTC&TBA.)

Lines should not vary more the 1/4" (.64cm) from exact measurement.

For more information contact:

U.S. Tennis Court and Track Builders Association
3525 Ellicott Mills Drive, Suite N
Ellicott City, MD 21043-4547
(410) 418-4875
www.ustctba.com

United States Tennis Association
70 W. Red Oak Lane
White Plains, NY 10604
914/696-7000
www.usta.com

BADMINTON

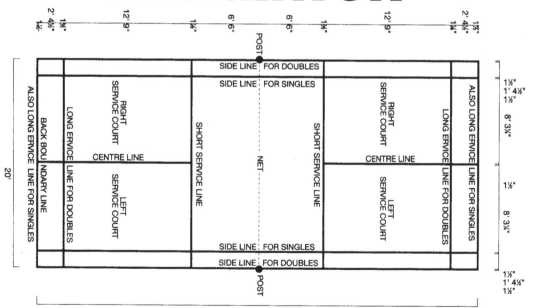

For more information contact:

USA Badminton
One Olympic Plaza
Colorado Springs, CO 80909
(719) 578-4808
Fax: (719) 578-4507
www.usabadminton.org

Note: Court can be used for both singles and doubles play.
Dimensions determined by the International Badminton Federation.

FACILITY SPECIFICATION GUIDE

SOCCER

LAW I. — THE FIELD OF PLAY
The Field of Play and appurtenances shall be as shown in the following plan:

Note: For players under 16 years of age, the size of the field of play, as well as the width between the goal posts and the height of the cross-bar may be modified.

OUTDOOR FIELD

Note: The length of the touch line must be greater than the length of the goal line.

INDOOR FIELD

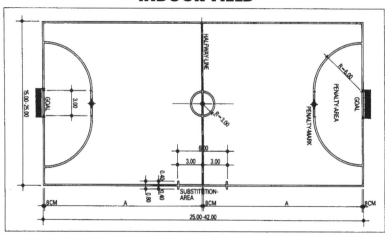

For more information contact:

United States Soccer Federation
1801-1811 S. Prairie Ave.
Chicago, IL 60616
(312) 808-1300
www.us-soccer.com

American Youth Soccer Organization
5403 W. 138th St.
Hawthorne, CA 90250
(800) USA-AYSO
Fax: (310) 643-5310
www.ayso.org

US Youth Soccer
899 Presidential Drive, Suite 117
Richardson, TX 75081
(800) 4-SOCCER

FACILITY SPECIFICATION GUIDE
SOFTBALL

OFFICIAL DIMENSIONS FOR SOFTBALL DIAMONDS

Skinned infields:
A 55' (16.76m) and 60' (18.29m) radius may be used with the front center of the 46'' (14.02m) pitcher's plate as the center point of the arc. The 60' (18.29m) is recommended for 60' bases.
For 65' bases, a 65' (19.81m) radius is recommended.

Backstop should be a minimum of 25' (7.62m) or a maximum of 30' (9.14m) from home plate.

(Diagrams courtesy of the Amateur Softball Association of America.)

DISTANCE TABLE

ADULT

GAME	DIVISION	BASES	PITCHING	FENCES Minimum	FENCES Maximum
Fast Pitch	Women	60' (18.29 m)	40' (12.19 m)	200' (60.96 m)	250' (76.20 m)
	Men	60' (18.29 m)	46' (14.02 m)	225' (68.58 m)	250' (76.20 m)
	Jr. Men	60' (18.29 m)	46' (14.02 m)	225' (68.58 m)	250' (76.20 m)
Modified	Women	60' (18.29 m)	40' (12.19 m)	200' (60.96 m)	
	Men	60' (18.29 m)	46' (14.02 m)	265' (80.80 m)	
Slow Pitch	Women	65' (19.81 m)	50' (15.24 m)	265' (80.80 m)	275' (83.82 m)
	Men	65' (19.81 m)	50' (15.24 m)	275' (83.82 m)	315' (96.01 m)*
	Co-Ed	65' (19.81 m)	50' (15.24 m)	275' (83.82 m)	300' (91.44 m)
	Super	65' (19.81 m)	50' (15.24 m)	325' (99.06 m)	No Max
16 Inch Slow Pitch	Women	55' (16.76 m)	38' (11.58 m)	200' (60.96 m)	
	Men	55' (16.76 m)	38' (11.58 m)	250' (76.20 m)	
14 Inch Slow Pitch	Women	60' (18.29 m)	46' (14.02 m)		
	Men	60' (18.29 m)	46' (14.02 m)		

YOUTH

GAME	DIVISION	BASES	PITCHING	FENCES Minimum	FENCES Maximum
Slow Pitch	Girls 10-under	55' (16.76 m)	35' (10.67 m)	150' (45.72 m)	175' (53.34 m)
	Boys 10-under	55' (16.76 m)	35' (10.67 m)	150' (45.72 m)	175' (53.34 m)
	Girls 12-under	60' (18.29 m)	40' (12.19 m)	175' (53.34 m)	200' (60.96 m)
	Boys 12-under	60' (18.29 m)	40' (12.19 m)	175' (53.34 m)	200' (60.96 m)
	Girls 14-under	65' (19.81 m)	46' (14.02 m)	225' (68.58 m)	250' (76.20 m)
	Boys 14-under	65' (19.81 m)	46' (14.02 m)	250' (76.20 m)	275' (83.82 m)
	Girls 16-under	65' (19.81 m)	50' (15.24 m)	225' (68.58 m)	250' (76.02 m)
	Boys 16-under	65' (19.81 m)	50' (15.24 m)	275' (83.82 m)	300' (91.44 m)
	Girls 18-under	65' (19.81 m)	50' (15.24 m)	225' (68.58 m)	250' (76.02 m)
	Boys 18-under	65' (19.81 m)	50' (15.24 m)	275' (83.82 m)	300' (91.44 m)
Fast Pitch	Girls 10-under	55' (16.76 m)	35' (10.67 m)	150' (45.72 m)	175' (53.34 m)
	Boys 10-under	55' (16.76 m)	35' (10.67 m)	150' (45.72 m)	175' (53.34 m)
	Girls 12-under	60' (18.29 m)	35' (10.67 m)	175' (53.34 m)	200' (60.96 m)
	Boys 12-under	60' (18.29 m)	40' (12.19 m)	175' (53.34 m)	200' (60.96 m)
	Girls 14-under	60' (18.29 m)	40' (12.19 m)	175' (53.34 m)	200' (60.96 m)
	Boys 14-under	60' (18.29 m)	46' (14.02 m)	175' (53.34 m)	200' (60.96 m)
	Girls 16-under	60' (18.29 m)	40' (12.19 m)	200' (60.96 m)	225' (68.58 m)
	Boys 16-under	60' (18.29 m)	46' (14.02 m)	200' (60.96 m)	225' (68.58 m)
	Girls 18-under	60' (18.29 m)	40' (12.19 m)	200' (60.96 m)	225' (68.58 m)
	Boys 18-under	60' (18.29 m)	46' (14.02 m)	200' (60.96 m)	225' (68.58 m)

Note: The only difference between college and high school is the pitching distance.

high school   fast pitch male .... .46'
                  slow pitch male .... .46'
                  slow pitch female .... .46'
                  fast pitch female .... .40'
college   .... .43'

For more information contact:

Amateur Softball Association of America
2801 N.E. 50th St.
Oklahoma City, OK 73111
(405) 424-5266
www.softball.org

FACILITY SPECIFICATION GUIDE
FOOTBALL

PROFESSIONAL

(Diagram courtesy of the NFL.)

DIAGRAM OF FIELD

COLLEGE

GOAL POST DETAIL

PYLON DETAIL

RECOMMENDED YARD-LINE NUMBERING

END ZONE DETAIL

(Diagrams courtesy of the NFHS.)

For more information contact:

National Football League
410 Park Ave.
New York, NY 10022
(212) 758-1500
www.nfl.com

National Collegiate Athletic Association
6201 College Blvd.
Overland Park, KS 66211-2422
(913) 339-1906
www.ncaa.org

FACILITY SPECIFICATION GUIDE

FOOTBALL

HIGH SCHOOL

(Diagram courtesy of the NFHS.)

Note: Both team boxes may be on one side between the two 45- and 20-yard lines. End lines and sidelines should be at least 4 inches wide. Other field dimensions should be 4 inches wide.

Note: Recommend the area between team boxes and sidelines be solid white or marked with diagonal lines.

Note: Inbounds lines should be 24'' long and 4'' wide.

Note: Recommend the field slope from center to each sideline at 1/4-inch per foot.

Note: A 4-inch wide broken restraining line may be put around the entire field, 2 or more yards from boundaries.

For more information contact:

National Federation of State High School Associations
P.O. Box 20626
Kansas City, MO 64195-0626
(816) 464-5400
Fax: (816) 464-5571
www.nfhs.org

VOLLEYBALL

Note: NFHS rules require standards to be 3' (1m) outside the court.

(Reprinted with permission of USA Volleyball.)

In the interest of safety for age group and scholastic competition, the height of the net shall be that specified for male competition. This height requirement shall not be modified.

For more information contact:

USA Volleyball
3595 E. Fountain Blvd.
Colorado Springs, CO 80910-1740
(719) 637-8300
www.volleyball.org

The following net heights are currently in practice for the below indicated age groups and scholastic levels of competition:

AGE GROUPS	GIRLS	BOYS/COED
18 years and under	2.24m (7'4⅛")	2.43m (7'11⅝")
16 years and under	2.24m (7'4⅛")	2.43m (7'11⅝")
14 years and under	2.24m (7'4⅛") or 7'0"	2.24m (7'4⅛")
12 years and under	2.10m (7'0") or 6'6"	2.10m (7'0") or 6'6"

SCHOLASTIC LEVELS	GIRLS	BOYS/COED
Grades 1 thru 6 (Elementary School):	1.85m (6'1")	1.85m (6'1")
Grades 7 and 8 (Middle School):	2.24m (7'4⅛")	2.24m(7'4⅛")
Grades 9 thru 12 (Sr. High School):	2.24m (7'4⅛")	2.43m (7'11⅝")

APPENDIX B

Listing of Skatepark Builders, Consultants, and Designers

American Ramp Company
fax. 417. 206.6888
www.arc-ramp.com

Ramps R Us
fax. 417. 206.6888

Anywhere Sports Productions
ph:310.823.1826 - 949.360.6970
fax. 949.360.7303

Benshoof, Withers,& Sandgren Ltd.
818.952.7606
fax. 818.952.7607
www.bwsla.com

BG Consultants Inc.
785.749.4474
fax. 785.749.7340
www.bgcons.com

Big Daddy Inc.
714.893.5621
fax 714.893.5631
www.bigdaddyinc.com

Cissell Design Group
ph: 203.245.4250
fax. 203. 245.7684
www.cissell-design.com

Dave Duncan Designs
714.960.8636
fax. 714.848.6343

FSU Inc., Functional Sculptures Unlimited
1.888.753.2124 - 719.229.7970
kpatterson@fsuinc.org

Grind Co.
310.330.0554
fax. 310.330.0409
www.grindco.net

Hirsch & Associates
Chuck Foley
714.776.4340
fax 714.776.4395
www.hha.landarch.com

Land Image Landscape Architects
530.899.1913
fax 530.899.1920

Lawrence R. Moss & Associates
818.248.5200
fax.818.248.6574
www.lrmassoc.com

Mark Podgurski Enterprise
814.349.5633
fax. 814.349.5643
office@woodwardcamp.com

Monkey Manufacturing
530.223.7400
fax. 530.223.7418
johnpfarr@msn.com

Pierce Enterprises
571.633.7583
fax. 517.631.6365

Purkiss Rose Landscape Architects
714.871.3638
fax.714.871.1188
www.skateparkdesigner.com

Ramptech Inc.
703-492-2378
fax 703.492.1023
www.ramptech.com

Robo Ramps
ph & fax 909.247.5289

Skateparks Inc.
781.544.2020
fax 781.545.6021

Spectrum Skatepark Creations Ltd.
604.905.3467
www.mountain-inter.net/
spectrum

Spohn Ranch
626.330.5803
fax 626.330.5503
www.spohnranch.com
Suburban Rails
740.593.8145
fax 740.592.5235
www.suburbanrails.com

Team Pain
ph & fax 407. 695.8215
www.teampain.com

Trueride
218.525.2625
fax 218.525 2850
www.trueride.com

Twister Skate Designs
619.226.6241
fax. 619.226.6010

Vertical Consultants
330.782.1456
fax. 330.533.1413

VPI Industries
John Tyson (JT)
ph & fax : 707.537.6803
www.access1.net/vpi

Vertical Skateramps
www.verticalskate.ch

Wally Hollyday Designs
562.438.7122
fax 562.856.5445
www.skatedesign.com

Wormhoudt Landscape
  Architecture Inc.
831.426.8424
fax 831.426.8411
www.skateparks.com

APPENDIX C

Planning Checklist for Outdoor Spaces

The following is an abbreviated list of items to be considered during the planning process:

Circulation

- Types: Vehicle (cars, trucks, buses, maintenance, etc.); pedestrians (handicapped, different teams); participants (different teams, players, coaches, officials, etc.); main entry; secondary entries; control and security points, etc.
- Roadway: Type of vehicles (trucks, cars, buses, etc.); quantity of traffic (conduct survey); type of roadway system (single or two directional); roadway width (vehicle size and number of lanes); surface systems (materials); protection devices (bollards, guard rails, etc.); etc.
- Parking: Type of vehicles (trucks, cars, buses, etc.); quantity of vehicles; sizes (length and width) of vehicles; drainage (surface or subsurface, water collection/detention areas); snow removal (storage areas); protection devices (bollards, guard rails, tire bumpers, etc.)
- Walkways: Type of use (pedestrian and/or vehicle); walkway widths; surface system (materials); elevation changes (walks, ramps, stairs and lifts); railings.

Activity Areas

- Landscaping: Type of surfaces (grass, etc.); type of plantings (ground cover, shrubs, plantings, etc.); etc.
- Game Standards: Applicable Association regulations for each sport; etc.
- Activity Configuration: Areas (separate or combined activity); orientation; flexibility; etc.
- Surfaces: Type (natural, synthetic, or combination); grading and drainage (surface and subsurface); etc.

Sports Areas

- Diamonds: Type of sport(s); type (game and/or practice); size; quantity; etc.
- Courts: Type of sport(s); type (game and/or practice); size; quantity; etc.
- Fields: Type of sport(s); type (game and/or practice); size; quantity; etc.
- Ranges: Type of sport(s); type (game and/or practice); size; quantity; etc.

Structures

- Tickets: Type (fixed or portable); surfaces for portable types (pads); utilities; quantity of units (location on site); etc.
- Security: Type (fixed or portable); surfaces for portable types (pads); utilities; quantity of units (location on site).
- Medical Treatment: Type (fixed portable); surfaces for portable types (pads); utilities; quantity of units (location on the site); etc.
- Storage: Type (fixed or portable); Surfaces for portable types (pads); utilities, quantity of units (location on site); type of storage (equipment and tools); etc.
- Communications: Type (fixed or portable); utilities (supplemental); quantity of units (location on site); type of systems; etc.
- Concessions: Type (fixed or portable-owner or vendor-supplied); surfaces for portable types (tent pads, trailer pads, etc.); utilities; quantity of units (location on the site); etc.
- Seating: Type (standing and/or seats); persons (spectators, teams, officials, etc.); natural (beams, sloped areas, etc.); artificial (prefabricated bleachers, type of seat, guard rails, etc.); etc.

Signage

- Vehicle: Type (direction, information, safety, etc.); etc.
- Pedestrian: Type (direction, information, safety, etc.); etc.
- Activity: (by sport, area, etc.); etc.
- Scoreboard: activity (single or combined use); type (manual or electronic); size; etc.

Barriers

- Vehicle: Type (sound, visual, safety, etc.); natural (plantings, berms, depressed areas, etc.); artificial (walls, fending, railings, etc.);
- Person: Type (sound, visual, safety, etc.); natural (plantings, berms, depressed areas, etc.) artificial (walls, fencing, railings, etc.) etc.
- Security: Type (gates, juxtaposition, or open); etc.

Utilities

- Power: Site lighting (pedestrian and vehicle); activity lighting; structures (tickets, security, storage, communications, concessions, etc.); etc.
- Water: Irrigation; sanitary; drinking fountains (hot and cold), etc.
- Sanitary: Type of units (fixed or portable); etc.
- Storm Drainage: Type (surface and subsurface); etc.
- Communications: Scoreboards; team sidelines to observation booth; public address for game; telephones for public and private use; broadcasting for television and radio; portable communications for security personnel; emergency; etc.

Equipment Evaluation Considerations

The following system analyzes the most common exercise equipment used in the fitness industry.

- ❖ Purchase Price ranges will be designated by $ / $$ / $$$; variables that increase the cost of the equipment will also be identified.
- ❖ The maintenance requirements, ease of use and learning curve of operating equipment, popularity of equipment will be designated by: L-Low/M-Medium/H-High
- ❖ The clientele typically using the equipment will be reflected by:
  G- General Population
  SN- Special Needs – Wheel Chair bound (WCB), Rehabilitation (R), or Senior Citizens (SC)

Equipment	Cost	Maintenance (and Variables)	Learning Curve	Popularity	Clientele	Variables that increase cost
Treadmills	$$$	H •Deck replacement •Belt replacement •Motor replacement •Self-lubricating deck	M	H	G	•Number of diagnostic features •Number of programs •Elevation options •Heart rate functions •Entertainment features
Ellipticals	$$	L •Ramp replacement •Elevation assembly replacement	L	H	G	•Heart rate functions •Entertainment features
Stair Steppers	$	L	L	L/M	G	Heart rate function
Recumbent/ Stationary Bikes	$	L	L	L	G/SN- Rehabili- tation	Heart rate function
Upper and Lower Body Ergometers	$$$	M •Calibration	L	M	G/SN- WCB	
Rowing Machines	$	L	L	L	G	

Planning Checklist for Indoor and Outdoor Spaces

Lobby/Entrance
- peak traffic rate entering and exiting
- energy conservation
- door size
- lobby size
- seating arrangements
- public restrooms
- floor surfaces
- lighting
- ADA requirements
- ticket booth
- concessions

Control area
- number of patrons at peak periods
- number of staff at peak loads
- computers, cash registers, automated check-in
- towel service
- locker registration
- TV surveillance
- light controls
- door monitor system/panel
- fire annunciator panel
- public address system
- emergency alarm system/panel
- equipment issue/return/storage;
  equipment to be stored;
  storage cabinets;
  separate issue and return functions;
  peak load considerations; staffing
- building directory
- phone system

Strength training area
- number of mechanized weight machines
- electrical needs
- flooring considerations
- mirrors
- audio/visual accommodations
- control center
- desk and computer
- storage space and cabinets
- clocks
- peak load considerations
- HVAC considerations
- platforms

Free Weight area
- benches
- weight racks
- dumbbells and racks
- weight platforms
- chalk holders and chalk
- floor considerations
- control area

- desk and computer
- mirrors
- HVAC considerations
- audio and visual considerations
- peak load considerations

Fitness Testing
- treadmill
- exercise bike
- monitoring equipment
- desk and bed
- storage cabinets
- sink and counter space
- computer
- telephone
- tack board
- special electrical or HVAC requirements

Cardiorespiratory area
- treadmills
- bicycles
- rowing machines
- stair climbers
- arm ergometers
- wall weight racks
- dumbbells
- floor surface
- audio and visual accommodations
- desk and computer
- storage
- HVAC considerations
- peak load considerations

Aquatics center
- competition pool
- teaching pool
- handicapped pool
- diving well
- diving boards
- diving platform
- underwater windows
- underwater sound
- filtration and sanitation
- vacuum
- lane lines
- bulkheads
- moveable floors
- lifeguard stands
- HVAC considerations
- lighting
- handicapped pool lift
- whirlpool for divers
- spectator seating
- rescue equipment
- grab rails and ladders

- acoustic treatment
- wall graphics
- staring platforms
- timing devices, scoreboard, diving scoring, PA system
- deck space and drainage
- corrosion resistant fittings
- emergency telephone or call button
- storage
- control center, desks, computers
- office, desks, computers
- telephones
- automated pool chemical control
- tile or no tile
- pumps and auxiliary pumps
- heater and auxiliary heater
- main drains
- access to pipes

Dependent Care
- number of children
- number of aging adults
- state requirements
- number of staff
- adjacent play areas in and out
- adjacent toilet facilities
- audio and visual accommodations
- office, desk, computer
- storage and storage cabinets
- indoor and outdoor play spaces

Pro shop
- display windows
- adjustable wall display system
- adjustable display shelving
- adjustable display lighting
- office
- control area, computer, cash register, visual surveillance
- door alarm system for shoplifting

Food Service
- juice bar
- vending
- seating area
- small kitchen with microwave, range, dishwasher, hot water booster, garbage disposal, range hood, refrigeration, sink and counter space
- health requirements
- tiled floor with drains

Gymnasium/Multipurpose Space
- activities to be accommodated
- peak number of people
- floor and wall inserts required
- lighting requirements

- folding partitions or dividing curtains, motorized or manual
- baskets and back stops—portable or permanent, motorized or manual
- batting cages
- golf cages
- scoreboards
- seating, portable or permanent
- wall pads
- flooring considerations
- wall graphics
- drinking fountains
- PA system
- large storage area, roll-up doors
- public rest rooms
- concessions
- portable stage
- press box
- press (media) room
- built-in audio-visual hook-ups
- computer hook-ups
- ceiling and wall-mounted projection screens
- video monitoring
- loading dock with roll-up door
- adjacent meeting areas
- adjacent locker rooms
- large janitorial space
- adjacent training room
- climbing wall area
- indoor jumping and throwing areas

Running track (indoor)
- laps per turn
- elevated or floor level
- number of lanes
- type of surface
- adjacent strength training, cardiovascular areas
- radius at turns
- banked curves
- automated banking
- lane markers
- pacer lights

Dance areas
- number of participants at peak loads
- audio accommodations
- acoustics
- ballet bars
- mirrors
- dance floor
- storage
- HVAC considerations
- emergency telephone or call button

Handball/Racquetball/Squash Courts
- number of courts
- competition courts

- spectator seating
- instructor observation area
- type of wall and ceiling system
- type of floor system
- glass or solid walls
- remote lighting
- stripping
- other activities—wall soccer, walleyball, dancercise, etc.
- lighting
- securing valuables
- accessing lighting
- HVAC considerations
- acoustics

Combative/Wrestling Room
- number of participants
- padded walls
- padded floor
- no glass areas
- no protruding fixtures
- remote HVAC sensing
- hanging bag
- hanging rope for climbing

Locker rooms
- number of lockers
- type of lockers and locker system
- tile floor with drains
- grooming area—number of sinks, mirrors, hair dryers, soap dispensers, towel dispensers, waste receptacles, non-slip floor, water resistant electrical receptacles
- handicapped area
- family changing areas
- benches or stools—fixed or moveable
- HVAC considerations
- swimming suit drying system
- permanent lockers
- dressing booths

Rest Rooms
- health code requirements
- handicapped area
- family changing areas
- non-slip floor
- floor drains
- mechanical exhaust
- diaper changing areas
- toilet partitions
- disposable seat covers
- sanitary napkin dispensers and disposals
- vandal-proof partitions
- corrosion resistant fittings
- automatic flush

Showers
- number of people to accommodate at peak loads
- individual showers
- hose bibb
- soap dispensers
- soap dishes
- handicapped accommodations
- non-slip floor
- floor drains
- corrosion resistant fittings
- water-proof membrane as required
- HVAC considerations

Shower drying areas
- number of people
- floor drains
- towel racks or hooks
- non-slip floor surface

Steam Room
- number of people
- steam convector units with cover plates, electric or gas
- waterproof membranes
- observation window
- emergency call button
- remote temperature control
- floor drains
- tiled room
- mechanical exhaust
- shower in steam room
- corrosion resistant fittings
- lighting
- hose bibb
- unisex or separate facilities

Sauna
- number of people
- exterior shower adjacent the sauna
- waterproof membranes
- observation window
- emergency call button
- remote temperature control
- floor drains
- redwood interior, all boards screwed into frame
- mechanical exhaust
- protective covering over rocks
- corrosion resistant fittings
- lighting
- hose bibb
- unisex or separate facilities

Tanning room
- number of units
- type of units

- adjacent a changing area
- wash-up or grooming area

Massage room
- number of massage tables
- heat lamps
- towel, cleaning, and disinfectant storage cabinets

Laundry
- projected volume/required staffing
- number and size of washers
- number and size of extractor units
- number and size of dryer units—gas or electric
- sorting and folding area
- floor drains
- soiled linen area
- carts
- linear feet of linen storage shelving & cabinets required
- HVAC considerations
- office, desk, computer

Administrative areas
- number of offices
- size of offices
- contents

Other miscellaneous areas
- janitorial spaces and break areas
- general storage
- classrooms
- maintenance area
- mechanical areas
- elevators and elevator equipment spaces
- hallways
- stairwells

Outdoor Activity Areas
- sport fields, practice and games
- basketball courts
- sand volleyball courts
- golf course
- tennis courts
- archery and shooting ranges
- ice hockey/skating
- outdoor aquatic center
- playground
- spectator seating
- concessions
- security lighting
- game lighting
- security fencing
- observation areas
- press boxes
- storage buildings and areas
- scoreboards
- ticket booths
- pump houses
- rope courses
- challenge courses
- fitness courses
- picnic areas
- horseshoes
- croquet area
- bocci area
- shuffle board area
- parking—zoning requirements, adjacent existing facilities, surface or garage parking, handicapped spaces, security lighting, landscaping buffers, asphalt or concrete, entering and exiting, pedestrian areas

APPENDIX D

Existing Facility Assessment and Future Planning Checklist

Check appropriate facility being assessed:
- ❏ Cardiovascular Center
- ❏ Strength Weight Area
- ❏ Group Exercise Room
- ❏ Selectorized Weight Equipment area
- ❏ Indoor Cycling Studio
- ❏ Other _____

Rating System:

	Rating MR/YES D/NO	Comments regarding Deficiencies
MR/YES – Meets Requirements (Fitness Facility Industry Standards)		
D/NO – Deficiency (Does not meet Industry Standards)		

❏ Facility Appearance
    Well maintained (No visual signs of structural deterioration) _____ _____
    Well cleaned _____ _____
    Ambiance—Inviting and creates a sense of energy _____ _____
❏ Facility Space Assessment
    Adequate Space to support activity _____ _____
    Appropriate Traffic Flow throughout space _____ _____
❏ Compliant with local, state, federal, and ADA requirements:
    Width of Entrances _____ _____
    Water Fountain levels _____ _____
    Aisle widths _____ _____
    Appropriate Signage _____ _____
❏ Ample Storage for:
    Program related accessories _____ _____
    Cleaning and Maintenance supplies _____ _____
❏ Monitor Station appropriately located to activity _____ _____
❏ Electrical:
    Lighting:
        No dark spots in facility _____ _____
        Candle illumination appropriate for activity _____ _____
    Electrical Supply:
        Adequate number of breakers for present needs as well as
    future expansion requirements _____ _____
        Dedicated breakers for equipment, as required by
    Manufacturer (110 or 220) _____ _____
        Sufficient # of wall outlets for present and future
    expansion requirements _____ _____
❏ HVAC System Analysis:
    Air Exchange Ratio is 8-10 per hour _____ _____
    Humidity is 60% or less _____ _____
    Appropriate Temperature—68-72 degrees _____ _____
    Separate HVAC control for designated activity space _____ _____
❏ Flooring:
    No signs of visible wear of the flooring surface or hazards _____ _____
    Appropriate flooring for activity (DIN standards) _____ _____
        Surface is antibacterial, slip resistant, etc. _____ _____
❏ Ceiling:
    Adequate ceiling height for designated activity _____ _____
    Condition of ceiling tiles, if applicable. _____ _____
❏ Walls:
    All apparatus, fixtures, mirrors, shelving, securely
    attached to walls? _____ _____
❏ Sound (Controllable ambient noise levels)
❏ Entertainment
    Variety of entertainment options offered, when appropriate for
    appropriate venues—TV, stereo? _____ _____
❏ Equipment _____ _____
    Storage of items and placement of equipment do not
    block walkways, entrances, emergency exits, etc.? _____ _____
    State of the art of equipment in place. _____ _____
    No equipment replacement required. _____ _____
❏ Appropriate cleaning and maintenance systems in place. _____ _____

Assessment completed by:_____ Date completed: _____

APPENDIX E

Indoor Activity Area Planning Checklist

Checklist for Planning and Designing Indoor Activity Areas

A checklist has been prepared to aid those responsible for planning facilities for athletics, physical education, health and recreation. The application of this checklist may prevent unfortunate and costly errors.

General

_____ 1. A clear-cut statement has been prepared on the nature and scope of the program, and the special requirements for space, equipment, fixtures, and facilities have been dictated by the activities to be conducted.

_____ 2. The facility has been planned to meet the total requirements of the program, as well as the special needs of those who are to be served.

_____ 3. The plans and specifications have been checked by all governmental agencies (city, county, and state) whose approval is required by law.

_____ 4. Plans for areas and facilities conform to state and local regulations and to accepted standards and practices.

_____ 5. The areas and facilities planned make possible the programs that serve the interests and needs of all the people.

_____ 6. Every available source of property or funds has been explored, evaluated, and utilized whenever appropriate.

_____ 7. All interested persons and organizations concerned with the facility have had an opportunity to share in its planning (professional educators, users, consultants, administrators, engineers, architects, program specialists, building managers, and builder)—a team approach.

_____ 8. The facility will fulfill the maximum demands of the program. The program has not been curtailed to fit the facility.

_____ 9. The facility has been functionally planned to meet the present and anticipated needs of specific programs, situations, and publics.

_____ 10. Future additions are included in present plans to permit economy of construction.

_____ 11. All classrooms and offices are isolated from background noise.

_____ 12. Ample numbers and sized storage areas are built-in flush with walls at all teach stations.

_____ 13. No center mullions or thresholds are on storage room doorways.

_____ 14. All passageways are free of obstructions; fixtures are recessed.

_____ 15. Storage areas are well ventilated, dry, and cool.

_____ 16. Buildings, specific areas, and facilities are clearly identified.

_____ 17. Locker rooms are arranged for ease of supervision.

_____ 18. Offices, teaching stations, and service facilities are properly interrelated.

_____ 19. Special needs of the physically handicapped are met, including a ramp into the building at a major entrance.

_____ 20. All "dead space" is used.

_____ 21. The building is compatible in design and comparable in quality and accommodation to other campus structures.

_____ 22. Storage rooms are accessible to the play area.

_____ 23. Workrooms, conference rooms, and staff and administrative offices are inter-related.

_____ 24. Shower and dressing facilities are provided for professional staff members and are conveniently located.

_____ 25. Thought and attention has been given to making facilities and equipment as durable and vandal-proof as possible.

_____ 26. Low-cost maintenance features have been considered.

_____ 27. This facility is a part of a well-integrated Master Plan.

_____ 28. All areas, courts, facilities, equipment, climate control, security, etc., conform rigidly to detailed standards and specifications.

_____ 29. Shelves are recessed and mirrors and supplies are in appropriate places in restrooms and dressing rooms.

_____ 30. Dressing space between locker rows is adjusted to the size and age of students.

_____ 31. Drinking fountains are placed conveniently in locker room areas or immediately adjacent areas.

_____ 32. Special attention is given to provision for locking service windows and counter, supply bins, carts, shelves, and racks.

_____ 33. Provision is made for repair, maintenance, replacement, and off-season storage of equipment and uniforms.

_____ 34. A well-defined program for laundering and cleaning towels, uniforms, and equipment is included in the plan.

_____ 35. Noncorrosive metal is used in dressing, drying, and shower areas, except for enameled lockers.

_____ 36. Antipanic hardware is used where required by fire regulations.

_____ 37. Properly placed house bibbs and drains are sufficient in size and quantity to permit flushing the entire area with a water hose.

_____ 38. A water-resistant, covered base is used under the locker base and floor mat and where floor and wall join.

_____ 39. Chalkboards and/or tackboards with map tracks are located in appropriate places in dressing rooms, hallways, and classrooms.

_____ 40. Book shelves are provided in toilet area.

_____ 41. Space and equipment are planned in accordance with the types and number of enrollees.

_____ 42. Basement rooms undesirable for dressing, drying, and showering, are not planned for those purposes.

_____ 43. Spectator seating (permanent) in areas that are basically instructional is kept at a minimum. Rollaway bleachers are used primarily. Balcony seating is considered as a possibility.

_____ 44. Well-lighted and effectively displayed trophy cases enhance the interest and beauty of the lobby.

_____ 45. The space under the stairs is used for storage.

_____ 46. Department heads' offices are located near the central administrative office which includes a well-planned conference room.

_____ 47. Workrooms are located near the central office and serve as a repository for departmental materials and records.

_____ 48. Conference area includes a cloak room, lavatory, and toilet.

_____ 49. In addition to regular secretarial offices established in the central and department chairmen's offices, a special room to house a secretarial pool for staff members if provided.

_____ 50. Staff dressing facilities are provided. These facilities also may serve game officials.

_____ 51. The community and/or neighborhood has a "round table" for planning.

_____ 52. All those (persons and agencies) who should be a party to planning and development are invited and actively engaged in the planning process.

_____ 53. Space and area relationships are important. They have been considered carefully.

_____ 54. Both long-range and immediate plans have been made.

_____ 55. The body comfort of the child, a major factor in securing maximum learning, has been considered in the plans.

_____ 56. Plans for quiet areas have been made.

_____ 57. In the planning, consideration has been given to the need for adequate recreational areas and facilities, both near and distant from the homes of people.

_____ 58. Consoles for security, information, and checkout have been ideally located.

_____ 59. Every effort has been exercised to eliminate hazards.

_____ 60. The installation of low-handing door closers, light fixtures, signs, and other objects in traffic areas has been avoided.

_____ 61. Warning signals—both visible and audible—are included in the plans.

_____ 62. Ramps have a slope equal to or greater than a one-foot rise in 12 feet.

_____ 63. Minimum landings for ramps are five-by-five feet, extend at least one foot beyond the swinging arc of a door, have at least a six-foot clearance at the bottom, and have level platforms at 30-foot intervals on every turn.

_____ 64. Adequate locker and dressing spaces are provided.

_____ 65. The design of dressing, drying, and shower areas reduces foot traffic to a minimum and establishes clean, dry aisles for bare feet.

_____ 66. Teaching stations are related properly to service facilities.

_____ 67. Toilet facilities are adequate in number. They are located to serve all groups for which provisions are made.

_____ 68. Mail services, outgoing and incoming, are included in the plans.
_____ 69. Hallways, ramps, doorways, and elevators are designed to permit equipment to be moved easily and quickly.
_____ 70. A keying design suited to administrative and instructional needs is planned.
_____ 71. Toilets used by large groups have circulating (in and out) entrances and exits.
_____ 72. All surfaces in racquetball, handball, and squash courts are flush.
_____ 73. At least one racquetball, handball, or squash court has a tempered glass back and side wall.
_____ 74. All vents in racquetball, handball, and squash courts are located in the back one-third of the ceiling.
_____ 75. Standard size doors are utilized on racquetball, handball, and squash courts.
_____ 76. All aspects of safety are planned carefully for the weight areas.
_____ 77. Racks are provided for all lose plates, dumbbells, and barbells in weight areas.
_____ 78. Special attention is paid to acoustical treatment in weight areas.
_____ 79. Ample walk areas for traffic flow are planned around lifting areas in weight rooms.
_____ 80. Concession areas are planned for and built flush with existing walls.
_____ 81. Adequate numbers of concession areas are planned.
_____ 82. Concession stand cash-handling methods have been planned carefully.
_____ 83. Storage and maintenance has been planned for concession areas.
_____ 84. Classrooms are planned by instructors, students, and maintenance staff.
_____ 85. Classrooms are planned for the numbers of users and the styles of teaching to be utilized in the room.
_____ 86. Careful attention has been paid to storage areas in classrooms.
_____ 87. Faculty offices should be private and secured.
_____ 88. Storage areas and windows are planned in faculty offices.
_____ 89. Laboratories need to be planned for both teaching and research utilization.
_____ 90. Ample space and subdivisions within laboratories are planned carefully.

Climate Control

_____ 1. Provisions made throughout the building for climate control—heating, ventilating, and refrigerated cooling.
_____ 2. Special ventilation is provided for locker, dressing, shower, drying, and toilet rooms.
_____ 3. Heating plans permit both area and individual room control.
_____ 4. Research areas where small animals are kept and where chemicals are used have been provided with special ventilating equipment.
_____ 5. The heating and ventilating of the wrestling gymnasium has been given special attention.
_____ 6. All air diffusers adequately diffuse the air.
_____ 7. Storage area ventilation is planned carefully.
_____ 8. Humidity and ventilation are balanced properly in racquetball, handball, and squash courts.
_____ 9. Thermostats are located out of the general users' reach and/or are secured.
_____ 10. The total energy concept has been investigated.

Electrical

_____ 1. Shielded, vapor-prooflights are used in moisture-prevalent areas.
_____ 2. Lights in strategic areas are key-controlled.
_____ 3. Lighting intensity conforms to approved standards.
_____ 4. Adequate numbers of electrical outlets are placed strategically.
_____ 5. Gymnasium and auditorium lights are controlled by dimmer units.
_____ 6. Locker room lights are mounted above the space between lockers.
_____ 7. Natural light is controlled properly for purposes of visual aids and to avoid glare.
_____ 8. Electrical outlet plates are installed three feet above the floor unless special use dictates other locations.
_____ 9. Controls for light switches and projection equipment are located suitably and are interrelated.
_____ 10. All lights are shielded. Special protection is provided in gymnasium, court areas, and shower rooms.
_____ 11. All lights must be easily accessible for maintenance.
_____ 12. The use of metal halide and high pressure sodium lighting has been investigated.
_____ 13. All areas have been wired for television cable and computer hookups.
_____ 14. Indirect lighting has been utilized wherever possible.
_____ 15. All teaching areas are equipped with a mounted camera, 25-foot color monitor, and tape deck securely built-in flush with the existing walls.

Walls

_____ 1. Movable and folding partitions are power-operated and controlled by keyed switches.

_____ 2. Wall plates are located where needed and are attached firmly.

_____ 3. Hooks and rings for nets are placed (and recessed in walls) according to court locations and net heights.

_____ 4. Materials that clean easily and are impervious to moisture are used where moisture is prevalent.

_____ 5. Shower heads are placed at different heights; four feet (elementary) to seven feet (university) for each school level.

_____ 6. Protective matting is placed permanently on the walls in the wrestling room, at the ends of basketball courts, and in other areas where such protection is needed.

_____ 7. Adequate numbers of drinking fountains are provided. They are properly placed (recessed in wall).

_____ 8. The lower eight feet of wall surface in activity areas is glazed and planned for ease of maintenance.

_____ 9. All corners in locker rooms are rounded.

_____ 10. At least two adjacent walls in dance and weight areas should have full-length mirrors.

_____ 11. Walls should be treated acoustically 15 feet and above.

_____ 12. Walls are reinforced structurally where equipment is to be mounted.

_____ 13. Flat wall space is planned for rebounding areas.

_____ 14. Walls should be flat with no juts or extruding columns.

_____ 15. Pastel colors are utilized on the walls.

_____ 16. Windows should be kept to a minimum in activity areas.

Ceilings

_____ 1. Overhead support apparatus is secured to beams that are engineered to withstand stress.

_____ 2. The ceiling height is adequate for the activities to be housed.

_____ 3. Acoustical materials impervious to moisture are used in moisture-prevalent areas.

_____ 4. Skylights are gymnasiums, being impractical, are seldom used because of problems in waterproofing roofs and of controlling sun rays.

_____ 5. All ceilings except those in storage areas are acoustically treated with sound-absorbent materials.

_____ 6. Ceilings should be painted an off-white.

Floors

_____ 1. Floor plates are placed where needed and are flush-mounted.

_____ 2. Floor design and materials conform to recommended standards and specifications.

_____ 3. Lines and markings are painted in floors before sealing is completed (when synthetic tape is not used).

_____ 4. A cove base (around lockers and where all and floor meet) of the same water-resistant material that is used on floor is found in all dressing and shower rooms.

_____ 5. Abrasive, nonskid, slip-resistant flooring that is impervious to moisture is provided on all areas where water is used (laundry, swimming pools, shower, dressing, and drying rooms).

_____ 6. Floor drains are located properly, and the slope of the floor is adequate for rapid drainage.

_____ 7. Hardwood floors are utilized in racquetball, handball, and squash courts.

_____ 8. Maintenance storage is located in areas with synthetic floors.

_____ 9. Floors should be treated accoustically when possible.

_____ 10. Hardwood floors should be utilized in dance areas.

APPENDIX F

Cleaning and Maintenance Equipment Record Sheet

Brand/Kind of equipment _____ Purchase date of equipment_____

Delivery date of equipment _____ Length of Warranty_____ Warranty Ex. Date:_____

Serial # of equipment _____ Internal Organizational Inventory #_____

Code

All Cleaning, Maintenance, and Repairs must be completed in accordance with Equipment Manufacturer's Recommendations
C -Cleaning – Daily, Weekly, Biweekly, or Monthly service
L-Lubrication – Rails, etc.
MI-Maintenance Inspection -Cardiovascular and Weight Equipment (Cables, Weight Stack attachments, bolts on benches, condition of running belts, etc.)
R -Repair
O- Other

Date Task was completed	Type of task completed (Refer to code system)	Name of Staff Member or Vendor completing task	Comments: (ex: Description of repair or status update)
Ex: 05/11/04	0- Arrival of new treadmill	Mr. Exercise	Scratch on Console –Waiting for replacement. Under warranty!

APPENDIX G

Surface Selection Process

A systematic approach must be followed to conduct a search to determine the appropriate surface. The following guidelines will assist in the decision-making process:

- **Definition:** Define the characteristics required to meet specified needs. These characteristics should be material, system, and activity-specific, such as, the effects of sunlight on synthetic materials, the internal filtration of water through the system, or the bounce of a ball on the surface, respectively. This task may seem research-intensive, but it usually isn't since many of these questions already have been addressed by the manufacturers in their literature.
- **Solicitation:** Don't allow a cost limitation to prevent review of all available systems. Request information from as many manufacturers as possible to obtain literature. The information contained in the literature will provide you with a broad knowledge of different systems, a basis to compare systems, and instill a curiosity to question system design. Project costs as well as material estimates should be obtained. References, list of installers, and locations of systems should be furnished with the literature.
- **Comparison:** Review and compare each system after receiving the manufacturers' literature. Categorize the information by type and desirable qualities, such as natural versus synthetic or resiliency, etc. A table of desirable attributes is most helpful in comparing the systems.
- **Visitation:** After the type of products has been narrowed to a few systems, the sports professional should plan to visit various sites to inspect the products, as well as discuss the performance and maintenance factors with the users.
- **Selection:** Select a system based on research to this point. Although this may be the system eventually purchased, other factors still have to be considered and may influence the final selection.
- **Quality:** Defining the quality of a system may become difficult since several systems may be very close in design. Quality refers to the materials as well as the installation of the system.
- **Manufacturers:** What type of reputation does the manufacturer have? Ask for references, but don't be surprised if they give the manufacturer and the installer high marks. Some manufacturers have provided products to clients at reduced rates in exchange for their marketing assistance. How many years has the manufacturer been

in business? What type of technical support is available through the manufacturer and the local representative? Ask for information regarding the manufacturer's method of monitoring quality control in the plant as well as in the field.
- **Installer:** The installer should be recommended by the manufacturer to be assured that the installer is familiar with the products and installation. The installer should be asked questions similar to those asked of the manufacturer.
- **Maintenance:** Since maintenance can be a considerable portion of the operating budget, it is important to define the extent of the system. Questions, such as these will help with planning: What type of maintenance is required? What is the frequency of each type of maintenance?
- **Initial Cost:** What is the "total" initial cost of the system? Ask if two systems are considered the same, then why is one system more costly than the other? It may be that the quality of the materials or the system or both are the reason for the cost reduction. In some instances, the product name will increase the cost of the system, or hidden costs will be identified by the low bidder after the work has been awarded.
- **Life Cycle Cost (LCC):** This is a comparative analysis of each type of surface which considers the initial cost, the operation and maintenance cost, the operation and maintenance cost, and the replacement cost, if necessary, during an established time period. The figures generated from the analysis provide the anticipated total costs. Generally, the more expensive systems (initial cost) will be comparable to the less expensive systems when all factors are considered.
- **Bidding:** When the owner is required to conduct competitive bidding for products or services, attention should be directed to the written specifications, to insure that the products and methods of installations are clearly and accurately described. Too often the specifications make assumptions which permit systems of lesser quality to be considered as equals and therefore acceptable.
- **Installation/Installer:** Up until this point, the owner has had control over the selection process. However, this phase is where additional expertise will be required. It is in the owner's interest to require the manufacturer to perform periodic on-site supervision of the installer to insure compliance with the manufacturers' specifications.

APPENDIX H

DIN Standards

DIN refers to a set of standards developed by the Otto-Graf Institute, an affiliate of Stuttgart University, in Stuttgart, Germany. DIN standards are used to govern quality control and performance for a wide range of products, including sports floors. For sports floors, there are six quality control and performance tests. A floor system MUST PASS ALL SIX TESTS to receive DIN Certification. Installing a floor system that is fully DIN Certified ensures the highest possible athletic performance, injury prevention, and durability.

DIN Requirements for Sports Floors:

1. *Force Reduction or Shock Absorption*—This measures a floor's ability to absorb the shock of an impact. A solid concrete slab is used as a reference point. The minimum allowable score for a sports floor on this test is 53% force reduction. For Aerobic floors, a high force reduction value is desirable.

2. *Standard Deformation or Resilience*—This measures a floor's ability to deflect or "give" when impacted by the Artificial Athlete-Stuttgart. The minimum allowable score for a sports floor on this test is 2.3 millimeters.

3. *Deformation Control*—This measures a floor's ability to control the area spread of the deformation as outlined in the previous test. The maximum allowable score for a sports floor on this test is 15%. This means that a maximum of 15% of an impact's deformation can be spread to a point 500 millimeters (20 inches) from the point of impact.

4. *Ball Rebound*—This measures a floor's ability to provide a suitable surface for ball bounce. The minimum allowable score for a sports floor on this test is 90%. This means that a sports floor must produce a ball rebound height of at least 90% as compared to a concrete floor.

5. *Behavior Under Rolling Load*—This measures a floor's ability to withstand the weight of a rolling load, such as that of bleachers or other portable equipment. To pass this test, a sports floor must be able to withstand the trauma caused by a rolling cart carrying 1500 n (337 lbs.), without damage. This weighted cart is rolled over the sports floor 300 times. After the test, the sports floor is disassembled to examine the condition of the components. A floor passes the test only if none of the components have been damaged.

6. *Sliding Behavior*—This measures a floor's ability to control the sliding of the athletes who are playing on the floor. In short, a DIN certified floor must provide a surface that does not slide excessively as to cause an athlete to loose control and fall, while also providing a surface that will allow sliding when a severe force is exerted

DON'T BE MISLED!

There are several terms currently used to identify athletic floor systems as "DIN floors." Of these terms, "DIN Certified" is the only label used to identify a floor system that has PASSED ALL REQUIRED TESTS. The terms "DIN Approved", "DIN Compliant", and "DIN Tested", have been used to label floors that have passed as few as one of the required tests. If a floor is not "DIN Certified" it is not a DIN floor. All of Superior's DIN floors are fully DIN Certified.

APPENDIX I

Indoor Activity Dimensions

Ceiling Activity	Play Area in Feet	Safety Space in Feet*	Total Area in Feet	Minimum Height
Archery	5 3 60	15e	5 3 75	12
Badminton	20 3 44	6s, 8e	32 3 60	24
Basketball				
Jr. High instructional	42 3 74	6s, 8e		24
Jr. High interscholastic	50 3 84	6s, 8e		
Sr. High interscholastic	50 3 84	6s, 8e	62 3 100	
Sr. High instructional	45 3 74	6s, 8e	57 3 90	
Neighborhood E. Sch.	42 3 74	6s, 8e	54 3 90	
Community Junior H.S.	50 3 84	6s, 8e	62 3 100	
Community Senior H.S.	50 3 84	6s, 8e	62 3 100	
Competitive— College & University	50 3 94	6s, 8e	62 3 110	
Boccie	18 3 62	3s, 9e	24 3 80	
Fencing, competitive	6 3 46	9s, 6e	18 3 52	
instructional	4 3 30	4s, 6e	12 3 42	12
Handball	20 3 40			
Racquetball	20 3 40			20
Rifle (one pt.)	5 3 50	6 to 20 e	5 3 70 min.	20
Shuffleboard	6 3 52	6s, 2e	18 3 56	12
Squash	18.5 3 32			12
Tennis				
Deck (doubles)	18 3 40	4s, 5e	26 3 50	
Hand	16 3 40	41/2s, 10e	25 3 60	
Lawn (singles)	27 3 78	12s, 21e	51 3 120	
(doubles)	36 3 78	12s, 21e	60 3 120	
Paddle (singles)	16 3 44	6s, 8e	28 3 60	
(doubles)	20 3 44	6s, 8e	32 3 60	
Table (playing area)			9 3 31	
Volleyball				24
Competitive and adult	30 3 60	6s, 6e	42 3 72	
Junior High	30 3 50	6s, 6e	42 3 62	
Wrestling (competitive)	24 3 24	5s, 5e	36 3 36	

Safety space at the side of an area is indicated by a number followed by "e" for end and "s" for side.

APPENDIX J

Park and Recreation Open Space Standards

PART 1—GENERAL

1.01 Introduction:

This document is intended as a tool for designers and citizens to use while planning the renovation or development of play areas within the Seattle Parks and Recreation (SPR) System. The standards may appear excessive if the project they are being applied to is small, or they may appear to lack specific details required of large complex projects. SPR may require some, all or additional requirements are met.

1.02 Definitions:

Play Area—For the purposes of this document, the term "play area" shall refer to any place or space specifically and primarily intended for recreational use by children, generally between the ages of 2 and 12.

Designer—The design professional responsible for the assembly of the documents required to implement the intent of the Play Area Design including construction drawings and specifications. The Designer must be licensed in the State of Washington to practice design appropriate to the task, including but not necessarily limited to: Architects, Landscape Architects, and Civil Engineers. The Designer may be a volunteer, a paid consultant, or be provided by SPR.

Design Team—For the purposes of these guidelines, a group of interested volunteers and/or paid individuals, who have committed to participating in the design process by attending working meetings, public meetings, and performing various research and consensus building tasks, to achieve a common goal of developing or renovating a Play Area. The group requires some organization, and can consist of any interested parties plus the Designer.

1.03 References:

SPR adheres to the standards of several nationally recognized organizations, as well as internal documents, where the design, construction, and maintenance of Play Areas are involved. The following documents are hereby incorporated as part of these guidelines:

A. Published Documents:

1. American Society for Testing and Materials (ASTM) "Standard Consumer Safety Performance Specification for Playground Equipment for Public Use," F1487 (most recent edition).
2. .U.S. Consumer Product Safety Commission (CPSC) "Handbook for Public Playground Safety," Publication No. 235 or (most recent edition).
3. U.S. Architectural and Transportation Barriers Compliance Board, Americans with Disabilities Act (ADA),Accessibility Guidelines for Buildings and Facilities; Play Areas; October 2000, amended November 2000, (or most recent edition).
4. City of Seattle "Standard Specifications for Road, Bridge, and Municipal Construction," (most recent edition).
5. City of Seattle "Standard Plans for Municipal Public Works Construction," (most recent edition).

B. Other specifications may be provided by City Staff, during the course of design and design review, including storm drainage, concrete, irrigation, and others that may be deemed necessary for the acceptable completion of the design of the project.

1.04 Quality Control:

SPR system has Play Areas in all types of settings, some nestled among trees, and others surrounded by downtown traffic. All of the Play Areas in the system, however, must be considered within the greater urban context. The extent of use is generally higher than you might find within other municipal settings, and the large number of facilities within the system dictates that with sometimes limited resources and high use, maintenance attention can at times be less than ideal. The quality ideal that the SPR aims for in acceptable Play Area Design balances Function and Aesthetics with Safety, Accessibility, Durability, and Maintainability. With these considerations in mind, the following quality control measures must be upheld during the process of designing Play Areas;

A. Designer Selection:

SPR requires that the design of Play Areas be performed with the guidance of a professional licensed by the Stateof Washington to practice design within an area of specialty appropriate to the task. Generally this has meant either an Architect, Landscape Architect, or Civil Engineer must be retained to assume the responsibility for performing the essential tasks of producing and assembling the documentation necessary to design and construct the Play Area (refer to PART 2—PRODUCTS).

Selection of a Designer is typically as follows:

1. *Paid Consultant*—Where a group of interested citizens or SPR cannot produce an individual who meets the required qualifications, a Request for Qualifications or Proposals (RFQ or RFP) may issued, soliciting the services of a paid consultant.
2. *Parks Staff*—Qualified Park staff support may be provided on certain projects.
3. *Volunteer*—An interested party meeting the above qualifications may voluntarily provide the necessary services to see the process through.

B. Public Involvement

The City of Seattle has a blanket policy of Public Involvement for all Public Works performed on public property. Generally this requires that notification be made within the geographic neighborhood or potentially impacted area, followed by a comment period and most often a Public Meeting where comment and discussion can take place. Public notifications and meetings may be required on multiple occasions depending on the scale and complexity of the project, on new development, or on projects proposing considerable changes to the use or character of public property.

C. Internal SPR Review

SPR has a system in place for reviewing capitol improvements of all types. For Play Areas, it is expected that the PROVIEW Project Review Committees (composed of Administrative, Program, and Professionals), and Technical Review Committee (composed of Technical Staff and Shops Representatives), each have an opportunity to review and comment on the direction and progress of the design process. The scale and complexity of the project will usually have a direct bearing on the number and frequency of review sessions required by each review body.

D. Review by Other City Departments

Depending upon whether various criteria are met (or in some cases not met); other City Departments may require an opportunity to review the direction and progress of the design process, or require permit-ting. These Departments may include Public Utilities, Transportation, Design Commission, Arts Commission, Landmarks Board, Public Works, or others.

E. Review by Other Agencies

Although infrequently required for Play Area design, it may become necessary to submit for review or permit with State or Federal Agencies, particularly where shoreline, riparian, or other ecologically sensitive, regulated natural systems are involved.

F. Adherence to accepted standards for Safety, Accessibility, Durability, and Maintainability.

PART 2—PRODUCTS

2.01 General

This Section will focus on the physical products required by the SPR during the design process.

2.02 Pre-Design

Prior to beginning the production of visual representations of the project, it is important to produce the following preliminary documentation to aid in the actual design.

A. Design Program

Generally a planning tool, this document outlines the basic intent of the project and defines certain specific boundaries, physical, regulatory, fiscal, and conceptual, as well as time constraints. This document may include the results of citizen surveys if available. Citizen groups or the SPR may produce this document directly, depending upon the primary funding source.

B. Site Analysis

Assuming a project location has been selected and approved by the SPR; the Consultant or Design Professional will produce, with the aid of Park Staff and Citizen Neighbors of the Park, a comprehensive analysis of the site. At a minimum, this document will identify existing conditions including solar orientation and wind conditions, vegetation, pedestrian and vehicular traffic patterns, use patterns both formal and informal, known improvements such as surface materials, site furniture, and underground utilities. Use a common scale of measurement appropriate to the task.

2.03 Schematic Design

A. Preliminary Schematics

Rough sketches showing various options based on requirements and parameters set forth in the Design Program and Site Analysis, as well as input at public meetings. Rough estimates of cost to construct should be calculated for each scheme. Review of Preliminary

Sketches by the Design Team should result in revisions that develop a preferred alternative.

B. Preferred Alternative

This is typically a color rendering illustrating the alternative that has drawn the consensus of the Design Team for use in presentation to the Public and various reviewers. This drawing should be proportional and to scale (except reproductions), showing all key elements to be included in the finished project.

C. Cost Estimate

As the Preferred Alternative is developed from the Preliminary Schematics, an accurate estimate of the cost to construct the project must be maintained.

D. Approved Schematic Design

A graphic representation and cost estimate of the approved project design intent, as reviewed, revised, and accepted. Often the Preferred Alternative is an elaborate illustration produced for presentation and cannot easily be revised, however a photocopy with redlined revisions reflecting the consensus drawn through the review process and an adjusted cost estimate may be accepted as the Approved Schematic Design. If wholesale revisions have not been required, the Preferred Alternative may still be used for public presentation of the proposed project.

2.04 Design Development

Design development is the intermediate stage between schematic design and the construction documents where further research and development of the design begins to identify specific details of the project that may result in necessary changes to the physical appearance, functionality, and cost to construct of a project. Design Development is performed by the Designer (usually a registered Landscape Architecture firm) and (an Artist, if there is a known art component integrated into the design), and produces documentation consisting of measured drawings and details of construction, outline specifications for materials and workmanship, and cost estimates. This documentation is reviewed by the Design Team and the SPR to insure that the approved intent of the project as defined by the Design Program is adhered to and that all required standards for safety, accessibility, durability, and maintainability are upheld. For smaller, less complex projects, this phase may be waived.

2.05 Construction Documents

Project scale and complexity will define the level of detail required in the preparation of Construction Documents; however the following provides a complete example;

A. Construction Documents

Measured scale drawings produced on an appropriate title block which provides all of the detail necessary to construct the project as proposed, revised, and approved through Design Development. The drawings must be clear and concise, with plan views separated by trade as appropriate (i.e., existing conditions and demolition, layout, grading and drainage, irrigation, planting, play equipment and site furniture). Separate drawing sheets should be used to identify specific details to be used in construction. The details should be organized in a logical manner by trades as indicated above.

B. Specifications

SPR uses a CSI-based, five-digit specification system consisting of 16 Divisions. Division 0 & 1 are the primary and general requirements, Divisions 2 through 16 are technical specifications.

The level of written specification required will depend on the size, complexity, and implementation mechanism being utilized to construct the work. Below are some examples.

1. City of Seattle Department of Finance Public Bid For projects bid through the Planning and Development Division, the primary City Contract language (Division Zero or "boilerplate" will be provided by the SPR, as will the basic framework of the General Requirements (Division 1). It is the Designer's responsibility to provide all technical specifications.

2. Department of Neighborhoods Contract
   Used by Citizen Groups operating under contract with the Department of Neighborhoods through the Neighborhood Matching Grant Fund, the SPR requires that approved technical specifications be attached as an addendum to the D.O.N. contract.

3. Volunteer Construction
   Typically used in the installation of landscaping and play equipment. In the case of landscaping, the SPR will provide technical specifications to be utilized. In the case of play equipment, the manufacturer's installation instructions and specifications, as well as the reference documents named above in Paragraph 1.03 shall guide the work.

C. Inspection Plan

Identify primary construction systems requiring inspection. Examples are concrete formwork prior to pour, pressure testing irrigation lines prior to backfill, safety inspection of play equipment.

D. Cost Estimate

An accurate cost estimate broken down by trades and identifying each separate construction system within each trade, showing quantity, unit price, and total system cost. Trade categories should show a subtotal. Contractor markups can be shown per line item or as a multiplier to the subtotal. Unit price can be expressed as a line unit or broken down by Labor, Equipment, and Materials.

E. Schedule

A reasonable critical path schedule based on the trade and construction system breakdown used in the estimate should be prepared to complete the Construction Document phase. Identify all major milestones and incorporate inspection plan. Identify clearly the division of labor anticipated for projects which include multiple implementation mechanisms, for example physical participation by citizen volunteers, donated contractor work, manufacturers certified installers, and bid work.

PART 3—EXECUTION

3.01 General

This Section describes the sequence of events expected by the Department of Parks and Recreation during the design process for Play Areas, as well as specific physical and programmatic considerations, which are generally required.

3.02 Pre-Design

A. Citizen Initiated Projects

Neighborhood groups, once they have organized and formulated the intent to proceed with the renovation or development of a play area, should contact the SPRs Planning Unit to arrange with Parks Staff initiation of the design process.

B. Design Program

Projects initiated through the Cumulative Reserve Fund or Pro Parks Levy will have the Design Program generated internally though the Departments Planning Unit. Citizen initiated projects may develop their own Design Program with the assistance of the Planning Unit.

1. Content
The Program should, at minimum, be broken down into three sections as follows:

a. Background—Describes the basic history of the facility, explanation of the need for improvement or new development, and the source of funding for the work.
b. Description—Provides a description of the existing condition of the facility, placing emphasis on those aspects that most require attention. Provide a statement of intent to correct the inadequacies.
c. Design Considerations—Physical

C. Parks Review

D. Revisions

3.03 Schematic Design and Estimate

A. Public Involvement Process (PIP)

B. Parks Review

C. Revisions

3.04 Design Development / Construction Documents and Estimate

A. Parks Review

B. Other City Departments Review / Permitting

C. Revisions

Implementation Strategies

1. Bidding and Contracting

2. Volunteer Construction

a. Skilled Labor
b. Unskilled Labor
c. Power Equipment

3. Donated Contractor Services

4. Parks Forces

Design Standards for: Baseball and Softball Field Layouts

	BASEBALL		SOFTBALL	
	Regulation, Colt & Babe Ruth Leagues	Pony League	Regulation	Little League
Outfield Radius	375'	300'	300'	180'
Hood or Hoop Style Backstop distance from Home Plate	14'-6"	14'-6"	14'-6"	14'-6"
Distance from Pitcher's Rubber to Home Plate	60'-6"	54'	46' 40'(Women)	46'
Radius of Pitcher's Rubber to Skinned Infield	95'	80'	65' or 70'**	65'
Wing Fences: 1. Length 2. Height	96' 10'	96' 10'	60' 10'	60' 10'
Dugouts	All Dugouts shall be at least 30' long, gated for baseball with entrance at least 40' from backstop, and usually open at one end for all types of backstops.			
Distance between bases	90'	80'	60'or 65'**	60'
Outfield Fences: 1. Distance from Home Plate 2. Height	375' 8'	300'* 8'	300'* 8'	180' 8'
Bleachers (minimum)	2@8'x9' sections each side	2@8'x9' sections each side	2@8'x9' sections each side	2@8'x9' sections each side

*Outfield fences are optional
**Some leagues play 60', some 65' bases; infield grass should be cut back accordingly.

Design Standards for: Sport Fields

Regulation Football 120 yards (360') in length x 53.3 yards (160') in width includes two 10-yard (30') end zones. Requires 15' of clearance from end lines and sidelines to vertical fixed objects. Goal posts are behind end zones, 120 yards (360') apart.

Regulation Soccer 110-120 yards (330'-360') in length, by 65-75 yards (195'-225') in width. Requires 15' of clearance from end lines and sidelines to vertical fixed objects. Goal posts are on end lines. For other than regulation size fields, length is more critical than width.

Combined Football/Soccer Same as regulation football.

Flag Football 100 yards (300') in length x 40 yards (120') in width includes two 10-yard (30') end zones. Goal posts not required for kicks.

Rugby 160 yards (480') in length x 75 yards (225') in width includes two 25-yard (75') goal zones. Goal posts are 25 yards (75') in from end lines.

Field Hockey 100 yards (300') in length x 60 yards (180') in width. Goal posts are 100 yards (300') apart.

La Crosse 110 yards (330') in length x 60-70 yards (180-210') in width. Goals are 15 yards (45') in from end lines and 80 yards (240') apart.

Design Standards for: Athletic Field Lighting

SECTION I: Introduction:

Seattle is one of the mostly densely populated areas on the West Coast, therefore, Seattle Parks and Recreation (SPR) is committed to supporting growth management and comprehensive planning goals by providing an inventory of athletic facilities within Seattle that are safe, high-quality fields. Due to the City of Seattle's geographic location and environmental conditions, the use of synthetic surfaces and field lighting greatly increases the Park system's scheduling capacity. The decision to light athletic fields comes with impacts to the immediate residents and area neighbors, even when utilizing the latest technologies. The Joint Athletic Facilities Development Program (JAFDP) and these lighting design standards reflect the commitment to both providing safe, high-quality facilities and the recognition that these facilities impact the communities in which they are located.

Within this context, this document outlines the issues requiring consideration during the design phase of an athletic field lighting project. It also outlines design standards on technical issues such as levels of field lighting, addresses obtrusive light and establishes design parameters for materials, all while allowing flexibility with regard to emerging technologies.

SECTION II: Definitions

Common Lighting Systems: The key technical issues to consider when selecting a preferred lighting system include: Illumination Levels, Uniformity, Obtrusive Light Levels, Daylight Appearance (pole number, fixture density), Lamp Type (affects color rendition), Initial Capital Investment and Operating and Maintenance Costs.

- **Full Cut-off**— "Full Cut-off" Lighting Systems incorporate a downward aiming array of fixtures set close to the supporting pole, arrayed around the field-side of the pole at various heights. Individual fixtures are composed of a reflector enclosed within an essentially open-bottomed, box-like structure. "Full cut-off" refers to the fact that the lamp placement inside the box and above the plane of the bottom opening eliminates, or cuts off, all direct light above the plane of the fixture opening. "Full Cut-off" system designs may incorporate both metal halide and high-pressure sodium lamps of 1000 watts each.
- **Pros** (compared to "Shielded Aimable"): No glare above the plane of the fixture. Minimal sky glow (some glow is produced by reflected light, which varies by field surface). Visually unobtrusive at the mounting point (fewer fixtures, mounted close in), in daylight.

- **Cons** (compared to "Shielded Aimable"): Uniformity on larger surfaces is more difficult to achieve. More spill light behind the pole. Difficult to adjust. Does not allow for a reduction in pole quantities. Typically higher initial capital outlay. Poles must be close to the playing surface.
- **Shielded Aimable**—"Shielded Aimable" Lighting Systems incorporate a parabolic (somewhat dome-shaped) metal reflector around the lamp that results in a controlled beam spreads. Fixtures are arrayed on supporting cross-arms extending outward from the pole. The term "shielded" refers to two typical components—the parabolic reflector, which to some degree shields the lamp as viewed from off-site and separate visors and shutters that, can be bent or hinged to tighten the beam spread and further shield the lamp. The term "aimable" refers to the fact that the individual fixtures are mounted on an armature such that they can be specifically targeted at a pre-determined point on the surface to be lighted. Although high-lift equipment is required to do so, each fixture can be re-aimed or have its individual visors and/or shutters adjusted, added to, or removed, if necessary. "Shielded Aimable" systems are produced almost exclusively with metal halide lamps with either a 1000 or 1500 watt power output.
- **Pros** (compared to "Full Cut-off"): High degree of uniformity regardless of field size or shape. High degree of control of spill light behind the pole. Adjustability of "problem" fixtures (on-field or off). Typically lower number of poles required. Typically lower initial capital outlay.
- **Cons** (compared to "Full Cut-off"): Higher glare below the plane of the fixture. Moderate glare above the plane of the fixture. High resultant sky glow from direct and reflected sources. Visually dense at mounting point (numerous fixtures arrayed on cross-arms), in daylight.

Illuminance: The density of the flow of light falling on a surface. This document refers to illuminance as measured in foot-candles (fc), which is defined as one lumen uniformly distributed over an area of one square foot.

- **Horizontal** illuminance is the normal design criteria used for design calculations and measuring field lighting levels for athletic field lighting projects. It is calculated by measuring the amount of light falling on the horizontal plane 36 inches above the surface.
- **Vertical** illuminance is critical for sports where the ball spends most of the time in the air (such as baseball, football and softball). Vertical levels are typically calculated in four directions and at various heights above the playing field. It is also used to calculate spill light levels.

Environmental Zones (defined by the Illuminating Engineering Society of North America, IESNA):

Zone	Description	Light trespass (maximum levels at the residential property line)* Initial/Maintained
E1	Areas with intrinsically dark landscapes, such as national parks and areas of outstanding beauty.	0.14 fc / 0.1 fc
E2	Areas of low ambient lighting, such as suburban or rural residential areas.	0.42 fc / 0.3 fc
E3	Areas of medium ambient brightness, such as urban residential areas.	1.1 fc / 0.8 fc
E4	Areas of high ambient brightness, such as dense urban areas with mixed residential and commercial uses.	2.1 fc / 1.5 fc

*As a comparison, a 30-foot street lamp located 10 feet from a residential property line would have a vertical illumination level, at six feet above grade, of 1.3 fc at the residential property line (Reference page 2-17).

- **Initial** illuminance is the measurable output of the fixture with a new arc tube (light source) installed.
- **Maintained** illuminance is the average output of the fixture following an initial burn-in period. The initial burn-in period is approximately 100 hours.

Illumination—Off Site:
- **Ambient Light** describes the existing light levels in a neighborhood given off from streetlights, building lights, etc.
- **Spill light** is the light that falls beyond the athletic field being illuminated. Spill light is expressed in foot-candles (fc) and is normally measured in the vertical plane.
- **Glare** is light that hinders or bothers the human eye due to the eye's difficulty in adjusting to different levels of light. Direct glare from a light source is typically an important issue in the design and operation of athletic field lighting installations, both in terms of players and nearby populations. Topography and vegetation can change the impacts of glare. There is no industry standard for measuring glare once a project is completed. However, there may be design steps that may mitigate the effects of glare, such as increased pole height.
- **Sky glow** is the haze or glow of light emitted above the lighting installation and reduces the ability to view the darkened nighttime sky. This is a combination of light emitted directly from the light source and reflected light that casts upward from the surface being illuminated. The level of sky glow is also impacted by atmospheric conditions; clouds and moisture increase the effects of sky glow.

Levels of Play Classifications—IESNA set forth four illumination classifications based on the level of play being accommodated on a lighted athletic field. Recommended levels for social or recreational sports range from 20 to 50 foot-candles; levels for professional play with large spectator attendance and television coverage can reach 300 foot-candles. Field illumination for SPR athletic fields will conform to either Level III or Level IV standards, depending on the anticipated use of the field.
- **Level I** illumination is for competition play before a large group of spectators' attendance (approximately between 5,000 and 10,000 spectators).
- **Level II** illumination is for competition play with up to 5,000 spectators.
- **Level III** illumination is for competition play with some provision for spectators, such as permanent bleachers for 5—100 spectators.
- **Level IV** illumination is for competition or recreational play only with no provision for spectators.

Uniformity: Uniformity measures the relationship between the brightest area on the field and the darkest area on the field. Allowable variations are set to ensure player safety and are established based on the level of play classification determined for the field.

SECTION III: Design Considerations

Site Considerations:

1. **Light Levels**—Meeting illumination levels for safe play on the field while minimizing lighting impacts off site is the priority design consideration for athletic field lighting projects.
- On field light levels: Projects will be designed to meet field surface illumination levels necessary for the safe play of the sports that will be played at the project site.
- Off site light levels: Project design will include analyses of spill light, glare and sky glow.

2. **Park Amenities**—Replacement and new lighting projects may present an opportunity to consider additional park amenities which might be appropriate for the site, such as comfort stations, drinking fountains, security lighting, seating and ADA access.

3. **Topography**—The surrounding topography will be considered when selecting a project's lighting system in an effort to minimize impacts of obtrusive light as well as for aesthetic considerations such as impact to views.

4. **Traffic and Parking**—Increased scheduling of a athletic field may cause periodic traffic congestion and constrain available parking. These issues will be considered during a project design through the public involvement process and/or State Environmental Policy Act (SEPA) analysis. Additionally, the Department will work with sports organizations, field users, and community organizations to provide site-specific information as to preferred traffic routes and parking areas.

5. **Vegetative Screens**—Tall shrubs and trees may be considered as screens to reduce glare and spill light.

6. **Wildlife**—Potential impacts of lights on wildlife varies for each proposed site. Analysis of these potential impacts is performed as part of any required SEPA process.

Programming Considerations

1. **Capacity**—All SPR athletic fields where lights exist or will be installed should be evaluated and monitored with respect to the type of sports, age group, field dimensions, type of surface, etc. by the scheduling staff to maximize the opportunities and improve the management of the entire system.

2. **Noise**—In order to practice a "Good Neighbor" policy in and around parks where lights exist or will be installed every precaution should be taken to minimize the type and amount of noise a surrounding neighbor may be exposed to. Therefore, the Department will work closely with user groups and encourage them to practice being the best neighbor possible while using park facilities.

3. **Programming**—While recognizing that user needs vary, the Department will attempt to balance the needs of users with the impacts to and needs of the neighboring community. Hours of operation for lighted athletic fields are addressed in the Department's Scheduling and Use Policy.

Maintenance and Operational Considerations

1. **Energy Costs**—The cost of energy will be an ongoing challenge and therefore the type of lighting systems installed at each athletic field site should be analyzed for short and long-term energy consumption needs. Current data regarding use patterns, alternative uses, types of lamps used and the level of lighting to accommodate the users at a given location are all considerations.

2. **Safety of Users and Neighbors**—On and off field safety will be considered in the design and development of athletic fields. Close coordination with user groups and good communication with neighbors to address issues and concerns should be on-going. Attention should also be given to ensure user safety after field lights are turned out.

3. **Maintenance**—A maintenance plan outlining on-going services and upkeep will be a critical part of the lighting program and therefore project design should consider issues related to future maintenance. In addition, a well-organized inspection program to monitor and evaluate the efficiency and effectiveness of each lighting system should be developed for each site.

SECTION IV: References

• These Lighting Design Standards are based on the 2001 Ballfield Lighting Study, and the various technical references therein, (The Study) prepared by McGowan Bros. Engineers for SPR.

SECTION V: Standards for Illumination Levels

Illumination levels are determined based on the level of play being accommodated at the project site. The lighting consulting engineer shall verify the level of play with SPR prior to initiating design. The athletic field lighting project must conform to the following standards for illuminance levels, uniformities and light loss factors.

In general, SPR facilities will be built to Level IV illumination standards. Certain baseball/softball athletic fields that can accommodate tournament play with spectator attendance will be built to Level III illumination standards, such as Lower Woodland.

Criteria	Level III Baseball/Softball	Level IV Baseball/Softball	Level III Soccer/Football	Level IV Soccer/Football
Minimum Maintained Average Horizontal Illuminance	50 fc (infield) 30 fc (outfield)	30 fc (infield) 20 fc (outfield)	30 fc	20 fc
Horizontal Uniformity (max: min)	2.5:1 or <	3:1 or <	2:1 or <	4:1 or <
Horizontal Uniformity (CV)	0.21 or <	0.25 or <	0.25 or <	0.3 or <

SECTION VI: Standards for Addressing Obtrusive Light

Spill Light: The Environmental Zone for City projects shall be E3. Only the pre-curfew limitations will be considered, in accordance with the lighting study. Therefore, projects at newly lighted sites shall conform to a maximum maintained vertical illuminance level for spill light that does not exceed 0.8fc (initial 1.1fc) at the residential property line. The lighting designer shall undertake initial vertical illuminance calculations on a line along the edge of the properties and roadways as defined by the City to establish compliance with the 0.8fc level. The levels shall be calculated vertically at five feet above grade. At sites with existing lighting systems, every effort will be made during the design of replacement system to meet this standard. However, in order to encourage an expeditious replacement of these out-of-date systems, projects may deviate from this spill light level.

Glare Analysis: Although glare is very subjective and difficult to measure in the field, it can be analyzed during the design phase. Therefore, as part of the luminaire and mounting height selection process, the lighting designer will review candlepower curves and determine the appropriate luminaire mounting height and optical system so that no greater than 12,000 candlepower from any given luminaire is visible from the residential property line. [This analysis is outlined in The Study, page 2-40].

Sky Glow Assessment: As it is nearly impossible to measure sky glow in the field, it shall be assessed during the design stage to ensure that the calculated maintained average lighting level on a horizontal plane above the lights shall not exceed five percent of the maintained calculated average lighting level on the field surface. We recognize, however, that this method does not ac-count for the reflected light from the field surface or the atmospheric conditions.

SECTION VII: Standards for Materials

Improvements in technology will be considered when choosing appropriate materials.

- **Lighting System:** Full Cutoff, Shielded Aimable, or a hybrid of these two systems will be used for all SPR athletic field lighting projects.
- **Lamp Wattage:** SPR athletic field lighting projects will consider both 1000 watt and 1500 watt lamp systems, and choose the optimal system based on the design considerations list in SECTION III.
- **Pole Material:** SPR athletic field lighting projects will consider galvanized steel and concrete poles, and choose the optimal material based on the design considerations list in SECTION III. Wooden poles are not acceptable due to the susceptibility to twisting and rotting.
- **Safety Lighting:** All lighted facilities shall provide pedestrian-scale lighting of sufficient intensity and duration to allow all participants to exit the site safely at the conclusion of any scheduled evening use. Consideration will be made regarding ADA compliant routes of travel and common points of pedestrian and emergency access and egress from the site. The pedestrian lighting should be designed to incorporate "full cut-off" type fixtures at heights that discourage vandalism but are within the height restriction of land use development standards for the site. Cost effectiveness shall be maximized by utilizing the athletic field lighting poles where possible, and by designing fixture heights that minimize the number of additional poles necessary to achieve the intent.
- **Control System:** All SPR athletic field lighting projects will include an on-site control switch that can allow lights to be operated at the site. Projects

will also be designed to allow individual fields to be lighted separately so that all facility lights are not required to be on when a limited number of fields are in use.

SECTION VIII: Project Design

Lighting Design: Lighting design shall be based on the performance criteria defined by the City. It is the responsibility of the lighting designer to meet the required lighting criteria. The City takes no responsibility for any misinterpretation of these standards. The performance of the installed athletic field lighting system will be field measured as described in SECTION IX.

Project Design Team: A City approved Electrical Engineering firm with thorough knowledge of sports lighting systems, power distribution and controls systems shall undertake all athletic field lighting projects. The electrical engineer shall be registered in the State of Washington. The electrical engineer shall be responsible for the preparation of the construction design drawings(s), technical specifications and the review of the supplier's pole and lighting submittals.

The design team shall design foundations to suit the local soil conditions present. An independent geotechnical engineer registered in the State of Washington shall approve the foundation designs. The City may supply a soil report. Where geotechnical information is not provided, the design team shall confirm the soil conditions.

Codes and Standards: All electrical design shall be performed in accordance with the latest edition of the National Electrical Code (NEC) and any applicable Washington State or local codes and amendments. All engineering shall follow the latest edition of standards and codes, and shall be performed under the direction of engineers competent to practice in those fields. Although the Non-Residential Energy Code (NREC) does not directly apply to athletic fields, energy consumption and energy efficiency shall be given the utmost importance in design.

Design Process: A standard design process has been established to minimize confusion and streamline the design.

1. The City selects a qualified electrical engineering firm for the specific sports lighting project.
2. The engineering firm's project team meets with the City to discuss the project specifics and criteria to be followed.
3. A project schedule is developed after the engineer records all discussions and key issues. The engineer submits notes (i.e., memorandum of understanding) to all key persons involved in the project.
4. The engineer determines the specific lighting electrical loads.
5. The engineer meets with the local utility company to establish either a new or upgraded service including supply voltage and service location.
6. The engineer develops the electrical design drawings, specifications and cost estimates.
7. The drawings, specifications and cost estimate are reviewed with the City, Revisions are made as required and a reproducible set of drawings and digital set of specifications are issued to the City for their bid process. The drawings shall be signed and sealed by the engineer.
8. The engineer provides bidding assistance and shall be available to respond to any questions from bidders. The engineer shall issue addendum as required.
9. After award, the engineer shall review and comment on vendor lighting and technical information submitted.
10. The engineer shall provide construction administration services.
11. Following construction, the engineer shall measure and record all illumination levels in accordance with IESNA LM-5 (Refer to the SECTION on Performance Verification later in this memorandum). This document shall become a part of the project's permanent record.

Drawings and Specifications: Drawings detailing the entire sports lighting installation shall be produced for each installation. At a minimum, the consultant shall supply the following items. [Supplemental specifications may be produced for each contract to compliment these Lighting Design Standards.]

- **Site Plan**—Showing the fields, pole locations, conduit, wiring, pull boxes, service locations, lighting control cabinet and other features necessary to properly construct the facility.
- **Details**—One-line diagram, lighting control schematic, panel schedules, pull box details, conduit trench detail, control cabinet details, equipment elevations and other detail needed to properly construct the facility.
- **Drawings**—Drawings shall be prepared in AutoCAD format and shall include the following information:
- Initial and Maintained Illuminance Designs: The sports field being illuminated shall be presented at a 1:30 scale, or larger showing all illuminance levels at a grid spacing of 10 feet. Grid points shall be calculated at three feet above grade. Grid points shall extend to the edge of the primary play area (PPA) as defined by the City.
- **Summary Table:** A summary table shall be included on the drawing showing the number of grid points, the design average illuminance levels and uniformities achieved (as noted in Table 1), luminaire model

number(s) and types, lamp types(s), wattage and lumen output, light loss factors, tilt factors and other information as deemed necessary.

- **Pole Location:** Pole locations and luminaire mounting heights and total number of luminaries on each pole shall be presented on the drawings. Pole locations shall be dimensioned to key control points.
- **Spill Light Levels:** Off-site vertical illumination (light trespass) levels at 20-foot intervals on the boundary lines defined by the City shall be shown on the drawing. Levels shall be shown in vertical foot-candles calculated at five feet above grade with the meter oriented in the vertical position facing the lights.
- **Glare Levels:** The field being illuminated shall be shown to match the appropriate Maintained and Initial Designs and 12,000 candle power points (as shown in The Study, page 2-40). All luminaire aiming points, pole locations, and number of fixtures on each pole, fixture types and NEMA beam patterns shall also be shown.
- **Candlepower cut sheets:** The lighting supplier shall provide luminaire candlepower cut sheets showing the vertical and horizontal axial candlepower at five-degree increments. These candlepower curves shall be supplied for each luminaire used. An independent testing company shall verify and supply the vendor's candlepower cut sheets.
- **Consultant Information:** Lighting supplier's name, lighting designer's name, phone number, date of design, project title and location, and bar scale shall be included on each drawing.

SECTION IX: Performance Verification

Lighting:

- The engineer shall field measure illuminance levels and document findings in accordance with LM-5. Spill light levels shall also be measured and documented and nighttime digital pictures taken at key points along the residential boundary.
- Where the lighting installation does not meet the required performance levels the engineer shall coordinate re-aiming by the supplier. Re-testing will be required where fixtures are re-aimed. Illumination level measurements shall take place after the lights have been in operation for a period of 50 to 100 hours of operations.
- The engineer shall inspect the installation of the sports lighting equipment for general conformance to the performance requirements. Upon completion, the engineer shall submit a drawing showing the final measured illumination levels, uniformities and spill light levels along with properly labeled nighttime digital pictures from the residential boundary looking at the lights. A letter of compliance shall accompany the measured levels.

Electrical Systems:

- The entire electrical installation shall be inspected by the engineer of record or his designated representative for general conformance to the design. Deficiencies shall be listed in writing and submitted to the contractor for correction. Upon correction of deficiencies. The engineer shall submit notification of substantial completion to the City.
- After completion of the installation, the engineer shall prepare a final set of record drawings commonly referred to as "as-builts: that shall take into account all changes through construction. The record drawings shall be incorporated into an Operation and Maintenance (O&M) manual, which shall include all pertinent information, shop drawing product information, and other salient data deemed necessary to document the installation.

Geotechnical:
- All foundation installations shall be inspected and approved by a geotechnical engineer. The geotechnical engineer shall provide a copy of the foundation design and backfill attached to a letter approving the installation.

Design Standards for: Wood Flooring for Gyms and Multi-Purpose

PART 1—GENERAL

1.01   *Intent*

To provide a floating maple floor system with a consistent ball bounce, good shock absorbing qualities and have no dead spots.

1.02   *Performance Standards*

To be a "DIN" Certified floor system for the attributes listed in 1.02, B below. To meet the "DIN" standards for:

1. Shock absorption—53% minimum to no more than 63% of concrete. Concrete equals 0%.
2. Ball bounce—98% minimum.
3. Deflection—vertical deformations @ point of impact - minimum 0.091".
4. Deflective Indentation—@ 20" from point of impact 15% maximum.
5. Friction—0.5 - 0.7 range.
6. Rolling load—337.6 lbs.

PART 2—PRODUCTS

2.01   *Manufacturers:*

The following manufacturers are acceptable using flooring systems that meet or exceed the above standards:

A.   Robbins Sports Surfaces, Greater Seattle Floors, 5517 6th Ave South, Seattle Washington 98108, 206-763-7004, twells@gsfloors.com.

B.   Connor Sports Flooring Corporation, Doug Grove, 4721 E. Carmen St, Phoenix, AZ, 85044, 800-383-0156, dgrove@connerfloor.com.

C.   Superior Floor Company, Inc, 901 E Thomas St, Wausau, Wisconsin, 54403, 715-842-5358.

D.   Action Floor Systems, LLC, 800-746-3512, info@actionfloors.com

E.   Horner-Western Hardwoods, Inc, Dick Ferry, 206-367-3717, 512 NE 165th St, Seattle Wa. 98155

2.02   *Material*

A.   Flooring to be second and better Northern Hard Maple, MFMA grade marked, edge grain, of 25/32" thick by 11/2" or 21/4 " wide , 33/32" thick preferred

B.   Playing surface to have painted game lines per STD DTL #09900.51 for layout and color. Provide two coats sealer and minimum two coats finish high solids modified polyurethane gymnasium floor finish system, such as, Hilyard Golden Seal system. Three coats of finish preferred. Sand and clean between each coat. Install game lines after the first coat of sealer, sanded.

C.   Subfloor system: shall meet the performance standards listed in 1.02 above for the total system.

D.   Vapor barrier (not retarder) system—sealed at all penetrations and laps.

E.   Wall base—galvanized steel or clear anodized aluminum, 3" x 4" x 1/4" or 3" x 6" x 1/4" angle, spaced 3/8" away from wall. Shop form all outside and inside corners. Wall base to be easily removable for floor repair and refinishing using metal wall inserts and screws.

PART 3—EXECUTION   Not Used

Park and Recreation Open Space Standards

Table 1
Estimated Facility Costs

Facility	Construction Costs	Est. Weekly Maintenance
Baseball	$ 90,000-200,000	16-20 hours
Soccer	$ 60,000-95,000	12-16 hours
Tennis	$ 25,000-55,000	1-2 hours per court
Basketball	$ 30,000-45,000	.5-1 hour per court
Volleyball	$ 6,000-10,000	.5-1 hour per court
Swimming Pool	$100,000-150,000	30-40 hours
General Park	$ 50,000-70,000	17-21 hours
BMX	$ 10,000-25,000	10-12 hours
Skatepark	$100,000-150,000	2-3 hours
Play Ground	$ 20,000-30,000	2-3 hours
Paved Trail	$ 32,000 per linear 1000 feet @ 8' width	

Table 2
Acres Required Per 1,000 Residents

Facility Category	Total Acres
Sports Fields (i.e., soccer, multi/use, baseball, softball)	4.4
Courts (i.e., tennis, basketball, volleyball)	.3
Outdoor Recreation (i.e., skatepark, BMX, trails, fishing access, etc.)	8.5
Leisure (i.e., playgrounds, picnic, general park land)	.8
Other Recreational Facilities (i.e., swimming pool, hockey, outdoor events venue)	1.5

Table 3
Design Standards for: Baseball and Softball Field Layouts

	BASEBALL		SOFTBALL	
	Regulation, Colt & Babe Ruth Leagues	Pony League	Regulation	Little League
Outfield Radius	375'	300'	300'	180'
Hood or Hoop Style Backstop distance from Home Plate	14'-6"	14'-6"	14'-6"	14'-6"
Distance from Pitcher's Rubber to Home Plate	60'-6"	54'	46'	46'
			40'(Women)	46'
Radius of Pitcher's Rubber to Skinned Infield	95'	80'	65' or 70'**	65'
Wing Fences: 1. Length	96'	96'	60'	60'
2. Height	10'	10'	10'	10'
Dugouts	All Dugouts shall be at least 30' long, gated for baseball with entrance at least 40' from backstop and usually open at one end for all types of backstops.			

Table 3 Cont.

Distance between bases	90'	80'	60'or 65'**	60'
Outfield Fences:				
1. Distance from Home Plate	375'	300'*	300'*	180'
2. Height	8'	8'	8'	8'
Bleachers (minimum)	2@8'x9' sections each side	2@8'x9' sections each side	2@8'x9' sections each side	2@8'x9' sections each side

*Outfield fences are optional
**Some leagues play 60', some 65' bases; infield grass should be cut back accordingly.

Recreation, Park, and Open Space Standards and Guidelines

The National Recreation and Park Association (NRPA) recognizes the importance of establishing and using park and recreation standards as:

- A national expression of minimum acceptable facilities for the citizens of urban and rural communities.
- A guideline to determine land requirements for various kinds of park and recreation areas and facilities.
- A basis for relating recreational needs to spatial analysis within a community-wide system of parks and open space areas.
- One of the major structuring elements that can be used to guide and assist regional development.
- A means to justify the need for parks and open space within the overall land-use pattern of a region or community.

The purpose of these guidelines is to present park and recreation space standards that are applicable nationwide for planning, acquisition, and development of park, recreation, and open space lands, primarily at the community level. These standards should be viewed as a guide. They address minimum, not maximum, goals to be achieved. The standards are interpreted according to the particular situation to which they are applied and specific local needs. A variety of standards have been developed by professional and trade associations which are used throughout the country. The standard derived from early studies of park acreages located within metropolitan areas was the expression of acres of park land per unit of population. Over time, the figure of 10 acres per 1,000 population came to be the commonly accepted standard used by a majority of communities. Other standards adopted include the "percent of area" approach, needs determined by user characteristics and participation projections, and area use based on the carrying capacity of the land. The fact that some of the standards have changed substantially is not an indication of their obsolescence. Changes are a measure of the growing awareness and understanding of both participant and resource (land, water, etc.) limitations. Parks are for people. Park, recreation, and planning professionals must integrate the art and science of park management in order to balance such park and open space resource values as water supply, air quality.

Activity/ Facility	Recommended Space Requirements	Recommended Size and Dimensions	Recommended Orientation	No.of Units Per Population	Service Radius	Location Notes
Badminton	1620 sq.ft.	Singles-17' x 44' Doubles- 20' x 44'	Long axis north-south	1 per 5000	1/4-1/2 mile	Usually in school, recreation center or church facility. Safe walking or bike access.
Basketball 1.Youth 2. High School 3. Collegiate	2400-3036 sq.ft. 5040-7280 sq.ft. 5600-7980 sq.ft.	46-50' x 84' 50' x 84' 50' x 94' with 5' unobstructed space on all sides	Long axis north-south	1 per 5000	1/4-1/2 mile	Same as badminton. Outdoor courts in neighborhood and community parks plus active recreation areas in other park settings.
Handball (3-4 wall)	800 sq.ft. for 4-wall 1000 for 3-wall	20' x 40' Minimum of 10' to rear of 3-wall court. Minimum 20' overhead clearance	Long axis north-south Front wall at north end.	1 per 20,000	15-30 minute travel time	4-wall usually indoor as part of multipurpose facility. 3-wall usually outdoor in park or school setting.
Ice hockey	22,000 sq. ft. including support area	Rink 85' x 200' (minimum 85' x 185') Additional 5000 sq.ft. support area	Long axis north-south if outdoor	Indoor-1 per 100,000 Outdoor-depends on climate	1/2-1 hour travel time	Climate important consideration affecting no. of units. Best as part of multipurpose facility.
Tennis	Minimum of 7,200 sq.ft. single court (2 acres for complex)	36' x 78'. 12' clearance on both sides; 21' clearance on both ends.	Long axis north-south	1 court per 2000	1/4-1/2 mile	Best in batteries of 2-4 located in neighborhood/ community park or adjacent to school.
Volleyball	Minimum of 4,000 sq.ft.	30' x 60' Minimum 6' clearance on all sides.	Long axis north-south	1 per 5000	1/4-1/2 mile	Same as other court activities (e.g., badminton)
Baseball 1. Official 2. Little League	3.0-3.85 A minimum 1.2 A minimum	Baselines-90' Pitching distance 60 1/2' foul lines-min. 320' Centerfield-400' Baselines-60' Pitching distance -46' Foul lines- 200' Centerfield- 200'-250'	Locate home plate to pitcher throwing across sun and batter not facing it. Line from home plate through pitchers mound run east-north-east.	1 per 5000 Lighted 1 per 30,000	1/4-1/2 mile	Part of neighborhood complex. Lighted fields part of community complex.
Field Hockey	Minimum 1.5A	180' x 300' with a minimum of 6' clearance on all sides.	Fall season-long axis northwest to southwest. For longer periods north-south.	1 per 20,000	15-30 minutes travel time	Usually part of baseball, football soccer complex in community park or adjacent to high school.

Activity/ Facility	Recommended Space Requirements	Recommended Size and Dimensions	Recommended Orientation	No. of Units Per Population	Service Radius	Location Notes
Football	Minimum 1.5 A	160' x 360' with a minimum of 6' clearance on all sides.	Same as field hockey.	1 per 20,000	15-30 minutes travel time.	Same as field hockey.
Soccer	1.7-2.1 A	195' to 225' x 330' to 360' with a minimum 10' clearance all sides.	Same as field hockey.	1 per 10,000	1-2 miles	Number of units depends on popularity. Youth soccer on smaller fields adjacent to schools or neighborhood parks.
Golf driving range	13.5 A for a minimum of 25 tees.	900' x 690' wide. Add 12' width for each additional tee.	Long axis south-west-northeast with golfer driving toward northeast.	1 per 50,000	30 minutes travel time.	Part of a golf course complex. As separate unit may be privately owned.
1/4-Mile Running Track	4.3 A	Overall width-276' Length-600.02' Track width for 8 to 4 lanes is 32'.	Long axis in sector from north to south to north-west--south-east with finish line at northerly end.	1 per 20,000	15-30 minutes travel time.	Usually part of high school, or in community park complex in combination with football, soccer, etc.
Softball	1.5 to 2.0 A	Baselines-60' Pitching distance-46' min.40' women. Fast-pitch field Radius from home plate-225' Between foul lines. Slow-pitch-275' (men) 250' (women).	Same as baseball.	1 per 5,000 (if also used for youth baseball.)	1/4-1/2	Slight differences in dimensions for 16" slow-pitch. May also be used for youth baseball.
Multiple Recreation Court (basketball, volleyball, tennis)	9,840 ft.	120' x 80'	Long axis of courts with primary use is north-south.	1 per 10,000	1-2 miles	
Trails	N/A	Well-defined head maximum average grade is 5% not to exceed 15%. Capacity rural trails-40 hikers/day/mile. Urban trails-90 hikers/day/mile.	N/A.	1 system per region	N/A	

Activity/ Facility	Recommended Space Requirements	Recommended Size and Dimensions	Recommended Orientation	No.of Units Per Population	Service Radius	Location Notes
Archery Range	Minimum 0.65 A	300' Length x Minimum 10' wide between targets. Roped clear space on sides of range minimum 30', clear space behind targets minimum of 90' x 45' with bunker.	Archer facing north = or -45 degrees.	1 per 50,000	30 minutes travel time.	Part of regional or metro park complex.
Combination Skeet and Trap Field (8 stations)	Minimum 30 A	All walks and structures occur within an area approximately 130' wide by 115' deep. Minimum cleared area is contained within 2 superimposed segments with 100-yard radii (4 acres). Shot-fall danger zone is contained within 2 superimposed segments with 300-yard radii (36 acres).	Center line of length runs northeast-southwest with shooter facing northeast.	1 per 50,000	30 minutes travel time.	Part of regional/ metro park complex.
Golf	50-60 A	Average length vary 600-2700 yds.	Majority of holes on north-south axis.	--	1.2 to 1 hour travel time.	9-hole course can accommodate 350 people/day. 18-hole course can accommodate 500-550 people/day. Course may be located in community or district park, but should not be over 20 miles from population center.
1. Par 3 (18 hole)	Minimum 50 A	Average length 2250 yards		1/25,000		
2. 9-hole standard	Minimum 110 A	Average length 6500 yards		1/50,000		
3. 18-hole standard						
Swimming Pools	Varies on size of pool and amenities. Usually 1/2 to 2 A site.	Teaching-minimum of 25 yards x 45' even depth of 3 to 4 feet. Competitive-minimum of 25m x 16m. Minimum of 27 square feet of water surface per swimmer.	None-although care must be taken in sitting of lifeguard stations in relation to afternoon sun.	1 per 20,000 (Pools should accommodate 3 to 5% of total population at a time.)	15 to 30 minutes travel time.	Pools for general community use should be planned for teaching, competitive and rec-recreational purposes with enough depth (3.4m) to accommodate 1m and 3m diving boards. Located in community park or school site.
Beach Areas	N/A	Beach area should have 50 sq.ft. of land and 50 sq.ft. of water per user. Turnover rate is 3.	N/A	N/A	N/A	Should have sand bottom with slope maximum of 5% Boating areas completely segregated from swimming.

(Reprinted with permission)

Builders, Consultants, and Designers

Anywhere Sports Productions
ph: 310.823.1826 - 949.360.6970
fax. 949.360.7303

Benshoof, Withers,& Sandgren Ltd
818.952.7606
fax. 818.952.7607
www.bwsla.com

BG Consultants Inc
785.749.4474
fax. 785.749.7340
www.bgcons.com

Big Daddy Inc
714.893.5621
fax 714.893.5631
www.bigdaddyinc.com

Cissell Design Group
ph: 203.245.4250
fax. 203. 245.7684
www.cissell-design.com

Dave Duncan Designs
714.960.8636
fax. 714.848.6343

FSU Inc, Functional Sculptures
  Unlimited
1.888.753.2124 - 719.229.7970
kpatterson@fsuinc.org

Grind Co
310.330.0554
fax. 310.330.0409
www.grindco.net

Hirsch & Associates
Chuck Foley
714.776.4340
fax 714.776.4395
www.hha.landarch.com

Land Image Landscape Architects
530.899.1913
fax 530.899.1920

Lawrence R. Moss & Associates
818.248.5200
fx.818.248.6574
www.lrmassoc.com

Mark Podgurski Enterprise
814.349.5633
fax. 814.349.5643
office@woodwardcamp.com

Monkey Manufacturing
530.223.7400
fax. 530.223.7418
johnpfarr@msn.com

Pierce Enterprises
571.633.7583
fax. 517.631.6365

Purkiss Rose Landscape Architects
714.871.3638
fax.714.871.1188
www.skateparkdesigner.com

Ramptech Inc
703-492-2378
fax 703.492.1023
www.ramptech.com

Robo Ramps
ph & fax 909.247.5289

Skateparks Inc
781.544.2020
fax 781.545.6021

Spectrum Skatepark Creations Ltd
604.905.3467
www.mountain-inter.net/spectrum

Spohn Ranc
626.330.5803
fax 626.330.5503
www.spohnranch.com

Suburban Rails
740.593.8145
fax 740.592.5235
www.suburbanrails.com

Team Pain
ph & fax 407. 695.8215
www.teampain.com

Trueride
218.525.2625
fax 218.525 2850
www.trueride.com

Twister Skate Designs
619.226.6241
fax. 619.226.6010

Vertical Consultants
330.782.1456
fax. 330.533.1413

VPI Industries
John Tyson (JT)
ph & fax : 707.537.6803
www.access1.net/vpi

Vertical Skateramps
www.verticalskate.ch

Wally Hollyday Designs
562.438.7122
fax 562.856.5445
www.skatedesign.com

Wormhoudt Landscape
  Architecture Inc
831.426.8424
fax 831.426.8411
www.skateparks.com

APPENDIX K

Metric Conversion Formulas

Converting from Metric to English:

To Obtain	Multiply	By
Inches	Centimeters	0.3937007874
Feet	Meters	3.280839895
Yards	Meters	1.093613298
Miles	Kilometers	0.6213711922

Converting from English to Metric:

To Obtain	Multiply	By
Centimeters	Inches	2.54
Meters	Feet	0.3048
Meters	Yards	0.9144
Kilometers	Miles	1.609344

APPENDIX L

General Resources for Planning Facilities

Books and Guides

DeChiara, J., & Callendar, J. H. (2001). *Time-Saver standards for building types* (5th ed.). New York: McGraw-Hill.

Earthman, G.I. (2009). *Planning educational facilities: What educators need to know.* Lanham, MD: Rowman & Littlefield Publishing Group.

Gillis, John (Ed.). (2004). *National Federation court and field diagram guide.* Indianapolis, IN: National Federation of High School Associations.

Gonsoulin, Sid (Ed.). (2001). *Outstanding sports facilities* (4th ed.). Corvallis, OR: National Intramural Recreational Sports Association.

Kowalski, T.J. (2001). *Planning and managing school facilities* (2nd ed.). *Westport, CT: Bergin & Garvey.*

National Collegiate Athletic Association Rules and Interpretations Guides, Indianapolis, IN:
- —Baseball
- —Basketball
- —Illustrated Basketball
- —Football
- —Field Hockey
- —Golf
- —Gymnastics
- —Ice Hockey
- —Lacrosse
- —Rifle
- —Skiing
- —Soccer
- —Softball
- —Swimming & Diving
- —Track & Field/Cross Country
- —Tennis
- —Volleyball
- —Water Polo
- —Wrestling

National Federation of High School Rules and Interpretations Guides, Indianapolis, IN: http://www.nfhs.org:
- —Baseball
- —Basketball
- —Football
- —Field Hockey
- —Golf
- —Gymnastics
- —Ice Hockey
- —Lacrosse
- —Skiing
- —Soccer
- —Softball
- —Swimming and Diving
- —Tennis
- —Volleyball
- —Track and Field/Cross Country
- —Wrestling

NIRSA. (2009). *Campus recreational sports facilities: Planning, design and construction guidelines.* Champaign, IL: Human Kinetics.

Piersol, J., & Smith, H.V. (2008). *Turf maintenance facility design and management.* Hoboken, NJ: John Wiley & Sons, Inc.

Tharrett, S.J., McInnis, K.J., & Peterson, J.A. (2006). *ACSM's health/fitness facility standards and guidelines.* Champaign, IL: Human Kinetics.

Periodicals

Athletic Business. Published monthly by Athletic Business Publications, 1842 Hoffman Street, Suite 201, Madison, WI 53704, (608) 249-0186. http://www.athleticbusinessmagazine.com

Athletic Management. Published bimonthly by College Athletic Administrator, Inc., 438 West State Street, Ithaca, NY 14850, (607) 272-0265. http://www.athleticmanagement.com

Club Industry. Published monthly by Sportscape Inc., Framingham Corporate Center, 492 Old Connecticut Path, Third Floor, Framingham, MA 01701, (508) 872-2021. http://www.clubindustry.com

Fitness Management. Published monthly by Leisure Publications, Inc., 3923 West 6th Street, Los Angeles, CA 90020, (213) 385-3926. http://www.fitnessworld.com

Journal of Physical Education, Recreation and Dance. Published monthly except in July by American Alliance for Health, Physical Education, Recreation and Dance, 1900 Association Drive, Reston, VA 22091, (703) 476-3400. http://www.aahperd.org

Parks and Recreation. Published monthly by National Recreation and Parks Association, 3101 Park Center Drive, Alexandria, VA 22302, (703) 820-4940. http://www.nrpa.com

The Physician and Sports Medicine. Published monthly by McGraw-Hill Co., 4530 W. 77th Street, Minneapolis, MN 55435, (612) 835-3222. http://www.physsportsmed.com

Tennis Industry. Published monthly by Sterling Southeast Inc., 3230 West Commercial Blvd., Fort Lauderdale, FL 33309, (305) 731-0000. http://www.tennisindustry.com

APPENDIX M

Associations Pertinent to Planning

Aerobics & Fitness Association of America
http://www.afaa.com

American Alliance for Health, Physical Education, Recreation and Dance (AAHPERD)
http://www.aahperd.org

American College of Sports Medicine
http://www.acsm.org

American Council on Exercise
http://www.ace.org

American Heart Association
http://www.aha.org

International Council for Health, Physical Education, Recreation, Sport, and Dance (ICHPER-SD)
http://www.ichpersd.org

IDEA Health & Fitness Association
http://www.ideafit.com

International Health, Racquet, and Sportsclub Association
http://www.cms.ihrsa.org

Maple Flooring Manufacturers Association
http://www.maplefloor.org

National Archery Association
http://www.usarchery.org

National Association of Concessionaires
http://www.naconline.org

National Collegiate Athletic Association
http://www.ncaa.org

Employee Services Management Association
http://www.esmassn.org

National Athletic Trainers Association
http://www.nata.org

National Federation of State High School Associations
http://www.nfhs.org

National Golf Foundation
http://www.ngf.org

National Institute for Occupational Safety and Health
http://www.cdc.gov/niosh

National Intramural-Recreation Sports Association
http://www.nirsa.org

National Recreation and Park Association
http://www.nrpa.org

National Rifle Association
http://www.nra.org

National Strength and Conditioning Association
http://www.nsca.org

National Swimming Pool Foundation
http://www.nspf.org

National Wellness Association
http://www.nationalwellnessassociation.org

National Wellness Institute
http://www.nationalwellness.org

President's Council on Physical Fitness and Sports
http://www.fitness.gov

Professional Golfers Association
http://www.pga.org

Sporting Goods Manufacturers Association
http://www.sgma.com

United States Badminton
http://www.usabadminton.org

United States Fencing
http://www.usfencing.org

United States Golf Association
http://www.usga.org

United States Gymnastics
http://www.usa-gymnastics.org

United States Handball
http://www.ushandball.org

United States Racquetball
http://www.usra.org

United States Squash
http://www.ussquash.org

United States Tennis Association
http://www.usta.org

**United States Tennis Court and
Track Builders Association**
http://www.ustctba.com

United States Track and Field
http://www.usatf.org

United States Volleyball
http://www.usvolleyball.org

Wellness Council of America
http://www.welcoa.org

YMCA of the USA
http://www.ymca.org

YWCA of the USA
http://www.ywca.org

APPENDIX N

Associations Pertinent to Planning for Accessibility

American Council of the Blind
(chapters in states)
http://www.acb,org

Arthritis Foundation
http://arthritis.org

Disabled American Veterans
(state and local units)
http://www.dav.org

**Muscular Dystrophy
Association of America**
http://www.mda.org

National Association of the Deaf
(local chapters)
http://www.nad.org

**National Association of the
Physically Handicapped**
(local chapters)
http://www.naph.net

**National Easter Seal Society for
Crippled Children and Adults**
http://www.easterseals.com

National Multiple Sclerosis Society
http://www.nationalmssociety.org

National Paraplegia Foundation
(state and local chapters)
http://www.ninds.mh.gov

Paralyzed Veterans of America
(state and local chapters)
http://www.pra.org

United Cerebral Palsy Association, Inc.
http://www.ucp.org

APPENDIX O

Track and Field Layouts
OVERALL DIAGRAM OF FIELD EVENTS

STANDARD 400M TRACK

Compliments of the National Collegiate Athletic Association

APPENDIX P

Retrofitting or Replacing Facilities

The practice of buying-using-discarding has become an unacceptable practice today. This not only applies to paper, aluminum cans, and glass, but to facilities as well (CEFP, 1985). Due to the high cost of new construction, upper level administration, whether it be in the private sector, at a university, municipal agency, or in a public school system, has the responsibility of making the wisest use of existing buildings. In meeting this obligation, it is necessary for administrators, with input from knowledgeable resource persons, to consider the feasibility of either renovating or retrofitting an existing building, or of constructing a new facility.

By definition, the renovation of an existing facility is the rehabilitation of the physical features of that building, including the rearrangement of spaces within the structure. Retrofitting, on the other hand, is the addition of new systems, items, features, materials, and/or equipment to a facility which were not installed at the time the building was constructed. These changes may be minor, or they could be significant to the point of changing the primary function of the facility.

To accurately ascertain whether renovation, retrofitting, or new construction is the most prudent alternative, administrators have a myriad of factors to consider. One of the more important is the effect that the construction process has relative to ongoing programs. Consideration must be given to program modifications and adaptions that may occur during the construction process. A close scrutiny of the advantages and disadvantages of both the present and the possibility of a new building should be undertaken. The following is an adequate representation of the factors to consider:

Cost Considerations
- What is the cost of new construction to provide comparable space?
- What is the cost of construction needed to bring the existing facility up to compliance with safety codes/accessibility?
- Does the cost of renovation or retrofitting exceed 50 percent of the cost of new construction?
- Will the increased cost of maintaining an older building justify renovation instead of constructing a new facility?
- Could the existing facility be sold or leased to a private entity to help defray the cost of new construction?

- If the amount of construction time becomes critical, which method, renovation or new construction, could be completed in the least amount of time?

Site Considerations
- Is a site available, and how effectively does the site meet the agency's immediate and long-range goals?
- Is the location of the present structure easily accessible?
- Is the parking adequate at the present site?
- How efficient is the sewer and storm water control?
- How is the soil-bearing performance of the present site?
- What is the general condition of the grounds?
- Is there sufficient area for all program activities?
- Are vehicular drives well located for safe ingress and egress?
- Are the existing utilities on or near the site adequate to provide the needed services?

Architectural and Structural Considerations
A certified architect and engineer should be sought to determine the following structural factors:
- Is the present facility aesthetically appealing and structurally sound?
- Does the existing facility meet current and long-range program goals and, if not, would renovation or retrofitting realistically elevate the facility to acceptable standards?
- What is the availability of utilities?
- How energy efficient is the present facility? Does it meet all updated energy codes?
- Are there signs of deterioration of footings, foundations, or piers?
- Are structural members adequate and in serviceable conditions?
- Is the exterior masonry sound? Are there structural cracks, water damage, or defective mortar?
- What is the condition of the roof and roofing surfaces, roof drains, and skylights?
- What is the condition of flashing, gutters, and downspouts?
- What are the conditions of doors and windows?

- What are the conditions of door hardware and panic devices?
- What are the locations, numbers, types, and condition of plumbing fixtures?
- What is the condition and capacity of the present water supply, sewage lines, and drainage systems?
- Is the present HVAC System adequate and energy efficient? Does it meet updated codes?
- What is the condition and adequacy of lighting and power distribution systems?
- Do the existing light fixtures provide adequate illumination in all areas?
- Are stairways, circulation patterns, and exits safe and adequate in number?
- What is the present condition of fire alarms and inter-communication systems?

Educational Considerations

- Is the building now meeting the agency's program?
- What is the current inventory of rooms and their sizes?
- Are laboratories adequately served by all required utilities?
- Is the library adequate to house the required book collection and to provide media and related services?
- Are food service facilities adequate to meet present and projected needs?
- Are physical education, recreation, and athletic areas usable or capable of being retrofitted if required?

Community Considerations

- Will the renovation of the building be consistent with present zoning requirements and policies?
- What are the plans for the area served by the program as projected by city or area planning agencies?
- Is the building on or eligible for placement on the National Register of Historic Places?
- Will a new facility constitute a political problem with businesses in the private sector?

Before deciding on the wisdom of renovation, retrofitting, remodeling, or replacing, factors concerning the existing and proposed facilities should be evaluated in detail, both individually and collectively. It also would be beneficial for administrators to project a reasonable life expectancy of the facility, taking into account factors such as:

—increased or decreased populations served by the programs within the facility,

—growth and development of areas surrounding the facility, and

—the potential reorganization, community rezoning, or consolidation of schools in the district.

A decision on whether renovation or retrofitting is advantageous over new construction then should be rendered, based on a composite of all the factors. (Figure 1)

Figure 1
Facility Evaluation

FACILITY EVALUATION

APPENDIX Q

Sample ASHRAE Standards

ANSI/ASHRAE/IESNA 90.1-1989—Published standard
Addenda 90.1b-1992, 90.1c-1993, 90.1d-1992, 90.1e-1992, 90.1f-1995, 90.1g-1993, 90.1I-1993, 90.1m-1995 to ASHRAE/IESNA 90.1-1989 (Addendum 90.1n-1997 approved for publication by ASHRAE BOD 97/07/03 [Publication pending])

Energy Efficient Design of New Buildings Except Low-Rise Residential Buildings
1 PURPOSE
  1.1 The purposes of this standard are to: new buildings so that they may be constructed, operated, and maintained in a manner that minimizes the use of energy without constraining the building function nor the comfort or productivity of the occupants;
    (a) provide criteria for energy efficient design and methods for determining compliance with these criteria; and
    (b) provide sound guidance for energy-efficient design.
  1.2 This standard shall not be used to circumvent any safety, health, or environmental requirements.
2 SCOPE
  2.1 This standard sets forth design requirements for the efficient use of energy in new buildings intended for human occupancy. The requirements apply to the building envelope, distribution of energy, systems and equipment for auxiliaries, heating, ventilating, air conditioning, service water heating, lighting, and energy managing.
ASHRAE Standard
  2.2 This standard applies to all new buildings or portions of buildings that provide facilities or shelter for human occupancy and use energy primarily to provide human comfort, except single- and multi-family residential buildings of three or fewer stories above grade.
  2.3 This standard does not apply to:
    (a) areas of buildings intended primarily for manufacturing or commercial or industrial processing:
    (b) buildings or separately enclosed identifiable areas having an combination of dedicated space heating, service water heating, ventilating, air-conditioning, or lighting systems whose combined peak design rate of energy usage for these purposes is less than 3.5 Btu/(h ? ft2) of gross floor area; or
    (c) buildings of fewer than 100 ft2 of gross floor area.
  2.4 Where specifically noted in this standard, certain other buildings or elements of buildings may be exempt.
Standing Standard Project Committee 90.1 (Project Committee originally authorized 83/01/23 and changed to standing committee 83/09/16) (TPS revised 97/07/02)
  Maintenance and revision of ASHRAE/IESNA 90.1 with revised TPS.
  Energy Standard for Buildings Except Low-Rise Residential Buildings
  1 PURPOSE. The purpose of this standard is to provide minimum requirements for the energy-efficient design of buildings except low-rise residential buildings.
  2 SCOPE.
  2.1 This standard provides:
  ASHRAE Standard
    (a) minimum energy-efficient requirements for the design and construction of:
      1. new buildings and their systems,
      2. new portions of buildings and their systems, and
      3. new systems and equipment in existing buildings.
    (b) criteria for determining compliance with these requirements.

2.2   The provisions of this standard apply to:

(a) the envelope of buildings provided that the enclosed spaces are:
1. heated by a heating system whose output capacity is greater than or equal to 3.4 Btu/h · ft2 (10 W/m2), or
2. cooled by a cooling system whose sensible output capacity is greater than or equal to 5 Btu/h · ft2 (15 W/m2);

(b) the following systems and equipment used in conjunction with buildings
1. heating, ventilating, and air-conditioning,
2. service water heating,
3. electric power distribution and metering provisions,
4. electric motors and belt drives, and
5. lighting.

2.3   The provisions of this standard do not apply to:

(a) single-family houses, multi-family structures of three stories or fewer above grade, manufactured houses (mobile and modular homes),
(b) buildings that do not use either electricity or fossil fuel, or ASHRAE Standard
(c) equipment and portions of building systems that use energy primarily to provide for industrial manufacturing or commercial processes.

2.4   Where specifically noted in this standard, certain other buildings or elements of buildings shall be exempt.

2.5   This standard shall not be used to circumvent any safety, health or environmental requirements.

APPENDIX R

Facility Maintenance
Thomas J. Rosandich, Jr.

Most maintenance managers will agree that maintenance requirements are almost never given adequate consideration when facilities are designed. Even when some consideration is given to maintenance during the design phase, changes in design during construction often nullify the original plans. The construction contractor is most usually concerned with completing the building in the manner that will generate the most profit, and as such, is not usually concerned with maintenance and repair requirements once the warranties expire. Further, there is a natural tendency on the part of architects to focus on the visual aesthetics of the design, often at the expense of more utilitarian concerns such as cost efficiency in operations (Beisel, 1998).

Given that the largest cost of a sports facility is borne through the many years of operation following construction and commissioning, maintenance professionals (typically the designated facility maintenance manager) need to participate in the design process. These maintenance professionals should remain involved until the project is completed. So while there should be no question at this point that the maintenance manager can have a lot to offer in terms of the planning of the facility, further discussions are in order as to the practical considerations for operations and maintenance (O&M) in the project planning. This chapter looks at some of the design requirements for the sports facility from the perspective of the maintenance manager. The first part relates specifically to maintenance and support areas and the second to general "generic" maintenance concerns for the facility as a whole.

Design Considerations for Maintenance and Operations

Physical education, athletic, and recreational facilities should be maintained in a sanitary and hygienic condition. The very nature of many of the activities conducted within these facilities and the many uses of water within them magnifies the need for consistent, superior custodial care. Unless custodians are provided with adequate and convenient facilities and equipment, the prospects of achieving the desired level of sanitation are significantly diminished.

Among the facilities required by the maintenance and custodian staff for the care and operation of sports facilities include workshops; storage for tools, spare parts, and supplies; janitorial closets; laundry facilities; office and administrative space; and staff break rooms with locker facilities. The following discussion looks briefly at design considerations for these specific O&M areas within the multipurpose sports facility.

Central Custodial Complex

The size and configuration of the custodial complex in any sports facility is contingent upon a number of factors, the first of which is the size of the building and the nature of the programs being conducted. The needs of a small, privately held health club, for example, will vary markedly in both size and scope from those of a multipurpose municipal facility or a university sports complex.

But even between facilities of comparable size, the nature of the organization that owns them will have a significant impact on the size and composition of the custodial complex and the way that it is managed. For example, the physical education, intercollegiate sports, and recreational facilities of a major university can be very similar in size to that of a national sports complex or a municipal stadium. However, in the university situation, there will typically be less space given over to operations and maintenance within the sports facility itself, because it is likely that elsewhere on campus will be a centralized buildings and grounds operation that will be responsible for the heavy maintenance activities of the entire university. Thus, within the sports facility there may, at most, be a small work space with a storage area for tools and spare parts, which would be totally insufficient for a free-standing, independent operation of comparable size.

Free-standing sport facilities, such as a municipal civic center or a national sports complex, will typically have a self-contained operation for O&M activities. Instead of a small work area for on-site repairs, a free-standing sports facility will need expansive work spaces with a much larger variety of tools and storage for spare parts. Nevertheless, O&M facilities of all types do have a number of elements in common.

Examples of a central custodial complex.

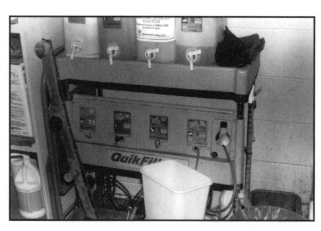

One approach for the allocation of administrative and support space for O&M operatives is described by Bronzan (1974). In large facilities, a central custodian headquarters should be planned to include a toilet, shower, lavatory, and dressing area with individual lockers. This unit should also have a separate break and meal area equipped with a sink, hot-and-cold water supply, microwave oven, and a small refrigerator. Additionally, a small, apartment-size breakfast table and chairs should be provided.

While there is no question that a properly furnished break area and locker room facilities for the O&M staff are appropriate, there is a definite need for a separate O&M office. The area for the administrative office in a typical collegiate facility should be about seven square meters. It is important to note, however, that this space allocation for the administrative office is a minimum, and that the size of the space allocated will grow as the complexity and size of the O&M operation grows. The administrative area should have enough office space to accommodate a desk, filing cabinets, and communications equipment. With today's communication technology capabilities, the administrative office must have a networked computer (either a networked personal computer or a terminal in the case of a mainframe operation) with a printer. Traditionally, the office of the O&M supervisor has been physically located in the workshop or storeroom area. However, because of advances in

the application of communications equipment and powerful management tools, such as networked micro-computers, the physical presence of the supervisor in the workshop area is no longer a necessity (de Booij, 1993).

A further case can be made that, because of the coordination required between the different administrators who manage the sports facility, the office of the maintenance supervisor should be located in the same area as other administrators. Regardless, however, of where the office of the maintenance manager is physically located, the office (and those of the other facility administrators) should be hard-wired for communications and micro-computer networking.

There is little point in having the maintenance manager's office hard-wired for data and communications if the work areas of the operatives are not. Thus, each of the main components of the O&M complex, such as the workshop area, storage for spare parts and supplies, and the administrative office, should similarly be hard-wired for data and communications and should have a desk area that can accommodate a micro-computer and communications equipment.

With the exception of the manager's office as outlined above, ideally the rest of the maintenance offices and workshops will be grouped together in one of the service areas of the building. General characteristics of the O&M area include direct or easy access to the exterior of the building, preferably with a loading dock to facilitate the handling of deliveries, which will often arrive by truck. The landing area at the loading dock should be spacious enough to allow the easy movement of cargo pallets and bulky containers and to allow sorting and organization of materials being received before they are moved into storage.

The storerooms and workshop areas should be located close to each other. This will reduce work hours wasted in retrieving parts and supplies before they are used. In addition to easy access to the exterior of the building, the custodial complex should be easily accessed via wide and level (i.e., without impediments) corridors. Wherever feasible, the doors between service and storage areas should "line-up," so custodial operatives do not have to turn corners with cumbersome loads.

Access to the central custodial complex and its various work and storage areas should be through double doors. If some material other than steel is used for these doors (for aesthestic reasons, for example), they should be equipped with kick plates and bumper guards. The service or freight elevator, in the case of a multi-story building, should also be situated in close proximity to facilitate logistic operations. Such elevators should have a ceiling, if possible, of 10 feet and should be as wide as possible. Quite simply, such elevators are going to have to handle the largest pieces of equipment being moved between floors of a multi-story sports facility and should be planned accordingly. Such appropriate logistical considerations will typically yield dividends in the cost-efficient use of personnel and are discussed further below.

However, while easy access to the custodial complex is desirable, the area must still be secured against unauthorized entry. Bear in mind that the typical sports facility will have large numbers of participants and spectators passing through the building and to have them enter service areas, either intentionally or otherwise, is undesirable.

These are the general guidelines for O&M facilities within the building. Each individual area is discussed below.

Maintenance Workshops

Among the most obvious concerns of the maintenance manager during the design phase of the sports facility are the work and support areas that will be utilized by the maintenance crews. The size and location of their work areas will have a significant impact on how well O&M workers can do their jobs. The argument could be made that perhaps the most important of all of the facilities in the custodial complex is the workshop area.

The workshop itself should be situated against an outside wall of the building in the service area, which will allow an exhaust fan to vent outdoors the hazardous fumes and odors generated by activities conducted within. Preferably it should also be situated immediately adjacent to the loading dock entrance and service reception area and have access to the core of the building.

The floor should be of hardened concrete and have a non-corrosive drain. There should also be sufficient open floor space between such permanent fixtures as the storage bins and shelving, work bench, and slop sink to allow free movement around large pieces of equipment that may be brought to the workshop for servicing. The door into the workshop area itself should be a lockable sheet-metal type without a floor sill or threshold.

Because of the level of noise generated in the workshop area with power tools, the walls should be of sufficient thickness to inhibit the transmission of sound to surrounding spaces. The walls should also be finished with a stain-resistant and easy-to-clean surface.

As stated earlier, the actual size of the workshop area will depend on whether it is a self-contained operation and how much activity it will be required to handle. Regardless of the size, however, some common characteristics should be considered. The first is a spacious workbench equipped with vises, small mounted power tools such as grinders, and a non-skid surface. The workbench area should be well lit by fluorescent lighting in the 100-lumen range that are mounted directly overhead. There should be sufficient electrical outlets around the room, particularly in the workbench wall near the vises and bench-mounted power tools. Also depending on the type of operation, sufficient floor space may be needed to mount free-standing equipment such as pipe-threaders and certain types of woodworking tools.

The maintenance workshop area should be both air conditioned and well ventilated. Because maintenance personnel use highly toxic and volatile substances such as paint, solvents, and cleaners, the workshop areas and central storage areas have exhaust fans that operate automatically and are vented to the outside.

Another area that needs to be considered is the tool room (also known as a tool crib). While maintenance workers frequently have a set of commonly used tools assigned to them, such as those contained in a lockable tool box, many specialized or very expensive tools and equipment are not assigned to individual craftsmen on a permanent basis. Examples of the specialized tools required for building maintenance may include welding equipment, a variety of metering devices (such as volt meters), and certain power tools. Because these types of tools and equipment are typically high-value items, access needs to be controlled and sign-out procedures employed as with any other inventory item. It is therefore cost effective from a labor standpoint to have the tool room physically located near the workshop area and/or combined with other stockroom activities such as the spare parts store room.

Storage

Storage falls into a gray area between strictly O&M concerns and sports activity and program concerns. On the one hand, storage space is needed for tools, spare parts, and consumables, such as cleaning supplies and dispenser items (toilet paper, paper towels, and hand soap) to support O&M activities. On the other hand, sufficient storage space is needed to support program activities in the building, such as that required for sports equipment, uniforms, and ancillary activities.

Experienced administrators of the various activity programs and experienced supervisors of storage and distribution rooms agree that the most prevalent fault in the planning of these facilities is the failure to allocate sufficient space. As a result, programs suffer in one way or another, and students do not enjoy all of the benefits they should receive. Operations costs increase disproportionately. Thus, it is useful to consider all the storage requirements for a sports facility for both O&M and sports and activity programs concurrently.

Storage for O&M Operations

A wide variety of spare parts and consumable supplies is required to keep any building functioning properly. Examples of spare parts required for a typical sports complex can range from light bulbs, ballasts, filters, and fan belts for air-handling units to replacement modules for scoreboards. Consumables similarly include a wide variety of materials, ranging from equipment lubricants, chemicals such as chlorine for the pool, cleaning supplies required for custodial work, and dispenser items required for the restrooms and locker rooms. Secure tool storage and space for storing bulky maintenance equipment, such as scaffolding and/or hydraulic lifts, are also needed.

There are a number of considerations in determining the size and location of storage and supply rooms to support O&M operation. Obviously, whether the O&M operation is self-contained is one of them. Another is whether the supply room is run on an open-stock or closed-inventory basis and how much inventory is dispersed to other storage locations around the facility, such as in janitorial closets.

If the nature of the organization is such that the sports facilities are a self-contained operation, then the space required for the storage of O&M-related equipment and supplies will obviously be greater. More space must be set aside for larger quantities of tools and supplies and for bulky equipment such as scaffolding. If the sport facilities are, for example, part of a centralized O&M operation on a university campus, it is likely that the high-value tools and equipment, such as lifts and scaffolding, will be kept elsewhere at a central location.

Whether the supplies are run on an open-stock or closed-inventory basis is another consideration. Low-value, high-usage standard stock items such as nails, nuts and blocks, paints, and lubricants are frequently designated open-stock items. Maintenance personnel can obtain them directly from bins without a requisition form, and there is no control over who takes them or what job they are used on. Such items can be stored right in the workshop area, for example, which will further enhance efficiency of the O&M operation. While such an arrangement reduces the need for separate storage space and an inventory clerk, it also invites increased pilferage by employees.

Perhaps the best use of an open-stock situation is in operations where maintenance is centralized, such as on a large university campus. As explained earlier, it is likely that a central O&M complex will serve the whole campus with sufficient volume and value of materials to require a closed-inventory system within the central maintenance complex. Thus, the sports facility, which is at best a peripheral operation, will likely have a smaller workshop area and tool crib with an open stock of standard-issue items.

A self-contained sports facility, such as a municipal stadium or national sports complex, on the other hand, will likely have a closed-inventory system or a combined open-stock, closed-inventory system. Because high-value tools and spare parts required for O&M operation must be retained on the premises, there is a need for access control and accountability and thus for an established inventory system and issue clerk. However, in terms of operational efficiency, it still makes sense in this type of an operation to place some items such as standard issue nuts and bolts in workshop areas and to disperse restroom cleaning supplies and equipment to the janitorial closets. The point is, however, that the space given over to this storage will be markedly greater.

In terms of the physical characteristics of storage areas and supply rooms, these should be situated in close proximity to the areas that they service. For example, tool and spare parts issue should be close to the workshop area, with the space required determined by the criteria discussed above.

The storerooms require temperature and humidity control, as inventory items frequently have specific requirements for storage. The floors should be of hardened concrete with a non-slip surface that is easy to clean. The room should be brightly lit with luminaries located between rows of shelving to ease identification of inventory, which is frequently described on small punch cards or tags affixed to the shelving.

For limited-access storage, there should be a distribution window that can be easily secured when the inventory clerk steps away from the service area to retrieve an item. Near the distribution window should be space enough for a desk and filing cabinet, which should be hard-wired for communications and networked computer equipment (de Booji, 1993). The distribution window should have a counter upon which any transactions can be completed.

Doorway access to the stockroom should be planned to accommodate the largest pieces of equipment or machinery that will enter the area. Unless otherwise indicated, a doorway that is at least 60 inches wide and 84 inches high is recommended, with thresholds that are flush with the floor. The doors will also require good-quality, tamper-proof locks and should be of fire-resistant sheet metal.

Shelving is an obvious requirement for the storage of supplies and inventory. These requirements include adjustable steel shelving with a depth of between 18 to 24 inches and a width of 36 to 48 inches. The first shelf should be at least six inches off the floor and the top shelf no less than 12 inches from the ceiling. So far as possible, shelves should be adjustable and standard sizes used.

Sports Equipment Storage and Repair

In most sports facilities, storage and work areas for sports activity and team equipment is separate from that used for general facility O&M. Regardless, many of the physical descriptions of the space required and fixtures contained in the storage rooms used for spare parts and supplies in the O&M operations are also applicable to storage areas for the sports and activity program. It should be noted that virtually all professional teams and most collegiate programs have professional equipment managers whose responsibility includes inventory control and servicing of team clothing and equipment. Just as a maintenance professional should be included in the design process to review the facilities program from an O&M perspective, so too should the equipment manager be consulted with respect to sport equipment storage and repair areas.

It is recommended that the space given over to the storage of sports equipment include a small area to facilitate the repair of program-related equipment. A well-equipped work area can result in considerable savings over an extended period of time, and sports operations tend to work at a higher level of efficiency with this capability.

Examples of equipment that should be housed in a workshop of this type include a small workbench similarly equipped to that in the main facility workshop area described above. Some of the equipment will vary, because the nature of the work to be done is quite different. Examples of equipment that should be included in this work area are racquet-stringing machines and sewing machines for uniforms. Additionally, the laundry facility will typically be located in or near the equipment manager's facility.

As custodial workers are frequently asked to set up and remove equipment used in various sports activities, of particular interest to the maintenance manager are the location and characteristics of equipment storage rooms situated about the building. Generally, an equipment storage facility should be located adjacent to each major activity area in the building. Each of these auxiliary storage units should be designed to accommodate equipment anticipated to be used in that particular area, such as hydraulic basketball and other game standards in the main gymnasium, racing lanes and recall lines in the swimming pool area, and gymnastics equipment and mats in their specific area. In all cases, design considerations include doors of sufficient size to accommodate bulky equipment (preferably "lined up" to reduce the number of corners to be negotiated when moving equipment), no door sills or thresholds, and appropriate shelving needs.

Janitorial Closets

The janitorial closet is the staging area for all custodial or housekeeping work. If the custodian works out of a room that is disorganized and dirty, it is likely that the cleaning effort will suffer accordingly. Also, much of the damage to custodial equipment occurs in the janitorial closet. An example of this is how mop buckets are frequently wheeled into the closet and not emptied, or floor scrubbing equipment is not cleaned after use. Thus, every effort should be made to design janitorial closets that will facilitate the custodial work (Walker, 1990). In determining the number of janitorial closets, a number of variables need to be considered, such as:

- the number of floors within the facility,
- the type of floor finishes to be maintained,
- the proposed use of the areas, and
- the number of restrooms in the facility.

There should be at least one six-square-meter custodial room for each 930 square meters of floor space, and at least one such room on each floor of the facility. The room should be designed with a large enough open area where equipment can be assembled and checked and janitorial carts properly stocked prior to starting a job (Walker, 1990). Each janitorial closet should have a service sink with a pop-up drain and a temperature-mixing type of faucet; floor sinks are preferable to large wall sinks for this purpose. Shelves and hanging boards should be constructed in each janitorial closet to facilitate the storage of supplies and tools (Flynn, 1985, 1993). Hanging boards, however, should be designed so that wet mops do not rest flush against the wall. Lastly, the janitorial closet should have a good level of illumination (at least 50 lumens) so that equipment can be properly cleaned after the job and before being stowed, and the fine print on chemical containers can be read (Walker, 1990).

While the foregoing is a general guide to the dimensions required for janitorial closets, the general rule of thumb is that the closet should have sufficient space both relative and particular to the area that is being served. High-volume activity areas with greater traffic flow have greater requirements and will need a larger space to accommodate the supplies and equipment needed to properly service them (Bronzan, 1974). Additionally, areas serviced on a seven-day cleaning schedule will require 35 to 40% more supplies than those cleaned on a five-day schedule, which would suggest a larger space allocation.

As an example of how the size of a janitorial closet should be determined in part by the area being serviced, consider the open floor space required to store floor maintenance equipment. A closet located in a corridor that features tile flooring would require an area large enough for power scrubbing equipment, whereas one in the vicinity of a carpeted office complex could get by with the smaller area required for a commercial-grade vacuum cleaner. Janitorial closets should also be located in or next to restroom and locker room complexes for a number of reasons. First, this location provides a water and sewage source for the mop sink and thus is cost effective from a design and construction standpoint. The second reason is that locker rooms and restrooms typically must be cleaned more often, and work hours are saved if the supplies and equipment are positioned near these areas. And finally, such a location facilitates storage of restroom cleaners, maintenance supplies, and dispenser stock.

As another example of the need to service high-volume traffic areas, a small room should be located near each entrance of the building to store maintenance supplies and tools (Flynn, 1985, 1993). Quite simply, everyone who enters or leaves the building will do so through one or more designated entries, which leads to excessive wear in these areas. The first 12 feet on the inside of an entry doorway is called "the walk-off area" and functions exactly as the name implies: it is within this radius that dust, dirt, oil from the parking lot, and water from rain and melting snow are deposited. Thus, a well-conceived maintenance plan will call for the regular policing of this area to prevent soiling materials from spreading beyond the walk-off area. To facilitate this frequent cleaning, a small custodial storage area should be situated nearby.

The failure to provide janitorial closets in the proper location and of the proper size can be illustrated by the following example. A building was constructed in which the janitorial closets were only 1.5 square meters in size, most of which was taken up by the mop sink. As a result, most of the supplies and power cleaning equipment had to be stored in the basement of the building, and carting supplies and equipment to the place where they were needed each night amounted to 30 hours of labor per five-night workweek. This amounted to an additional three-fourths of a worker-year labor expense, which would have been unnecessary if the facility were properly planned. Additionally, because of operating conditions that arose from this situation, pilferage of supplies and theft of equipment increased, leading to the additional requirements of building a lock-up room in the basement of the building and the administrative controls (and expense) to run it.

Laundry Room

In most physical education, sport, and recreational facilities, it is now more cost effective to establish in-house laundry facilities than to contract out for cleaning uniforms and towel services.

As the operation of the laundry most frequently devolves to the custodial staff, and the laundry facility itself is most likely to be situated within the maintenance support areas of the building, it is appropriate to consider planning guidelines for the laundry operation along with the rest of the O&M facilities.

So far as possible, the laundry facility should be physically located on the ground level of the building against an outside wall to facilitate venting of the dryer. Non-skid concrete floors are recommended, since the floors in the laundry should be hardened and impervious to water. Floors should be sloped to a drain trough that leads to non-corrosive drains. The slope should be 1/8 inch per linear foot. The planarity of the floor is important, since puddles can be dangerous. Floor materials should extend up the walls at least 12 inches, with corners rounded or covered. The thickness of the floor should comply with the equipment manufacturer's recommendations, but in any case, the floor should be able to withstand heavy, vibrating equipment.

As with other maintenance and service areas, the laundry facility should have double-hinged, double-doors without a threshold or a sill to facilitate the installation of laundry equipment during construction and the subsequent movement of laundry carts and supplies in and out of the premises. As a laundry is a noisy place, the walls and ceilings should have good sound absorption or non-transmission properties and yet be impervious to water. The wall finish should also be easy to clean and stain resistant.

While the floor space required for the laundry is contingent upon the size of the machines and the projected work load, sufficient space should be included in the plan for the storage of supplies and sorting/folding tables. Lizarraga (1991) provides guidelines by noting that the size of the laundry facility is determined by the size of the workload. The capacity of laundry equipment is determined by weight (pound). To calculate the number and the size of the machines that will be required, compare the anticipated daily quantities of articles to be cleaned multiplied by their respective weights with the poundage capacity of the machines under consideration, which will give the number of loads they can handle per day. Most process formulas will handle two loads per hour. Facilities with multiple goods classifications (i.e., nylon game uniforms and cotton-blend towels) should opt for two or more machines. Drying equipment needs to be matched up with the washers/extractors and typically has a larger capacity. For example, a 50-pound dryer is a good match with a 35-pound washer.

Once the number and types of machines have been determined, it is a relatively simple matter to size them, as the dimensions of the units can be easily obtained from prospective vendors. The machines should be mounted a minimum of two feet away from the walls and with a minimum of

18 inches between machines. Generally, however, sufficient space should be left around them for circulation and work and for equipment servicing as may be required. Combine this with the space required for processing the work and storage to determine the net useable footage required for the laundry.

As with all equipment, access to utilities needs to be considered in the plan. While hot and cold water, sewage, and electricity are obvious, gas driers are the most cost efficient to use, so an appropriate hook-up is in order. The room should also have good ventilation and air circulation in addition to outdoor vents for exhaust generated by the equipment.

In terms of the equipment itself, programmable microprocessor controls on the laundry equipment are highly recommended. Also recommended are liquid detergent supply systems that can provide pre-set, automatic injections of chemicals, as such devices may serve to remove judgement calls by operators, especially if the operators are part-time helpers (such as students) (Lizarraga, 1991).

Generic Concerns for Building Maintenance

While the foregoing discussion focused on the design parameters of the facilities specifically required for the O&M effort, aspects of sports facility design as a whole should be considered from the maintenance standpoint. These are really non-specific issues that can nonetheless produce significant operating costs. Many of these considerations are quite simple, yet because of their very simplicity, they are easily overlooked as more obvious design considerations hold the attention of the architect and design committee.

We have touched on such matters as building logistics in discussing the custodial complex, yet so much staff time is spent moving equipment around the typical sports facility that further, more specific attention is warranted. Simple accessibility to equipment and fixtures requiring maintenance tends to get short shift in the design process, with potentially disastrous consequences.

Standardizing Building Fixtures and Equipment

By now it should be clear that the variety of building finishes, fixtures, and equipment in a multipurpose sports facility can be staggering. Similarly, the need to inventory and control spare parts and consumable supplies for the maintenance effort can be a very large undertaking. However, by making a conscious effort to standardize building fixtures and equipment during the design phase, the costs of acquiring and carrying building spares can be significantly reduced.

Such reductions are accomplished in two ways. The first is the direct savings realized through a reduction in stocking spare parts. Standardization of finishes and fixtures allows the maintenance manager to reduce the number of items carried in the spare part inventory, which means a smaller financial burden in carrying costs. As a simple example, consider the effect of standardizing light fixtures. If all the fluorescent light fixtures in the building are the same, the number and variety of ballasts and lighting tubes that must be kept on hand can be considerably smaller than if there were a variety of different fixtures scattered throughout the building. Standardization also prevents the cost of wasted labor that results from bringing the wrong replacement tube to the fixture; the chances of this increase with a wide disparity in fixtures.

The second reduction is more indirect, but significant nonetheless. A smaller inventory requires less room for storage. Additionally, a smaller inventory is easier to administer and control, reducing administrative costs and loss through mishandling and pilferage. Concerted efforts can be made in many areas in standardizing building fixtures, including light fixtures and switches, breaker switches and boxes, bathroom fixtures and dispensers, locker room equipment, door hardware, locks and keys, and moveable equipment.

Logistical Concerns

Operating costs can also be realized by taking into account the needs of the maintenance staff in logistical operations. Logistical operations pertains to the handling of furnishings, equipment, and materials within the facility.

One area that tends to distinguish sports facilities from other types of buildings is the nature of the equipment contained within. A multi-station weight machine is, by its very nature, a very heavy and bulky piece of equipment to move around, particularly without disassembly. Gymnastics apparatus and mats, wrestling mats, and portable basketball goals are other examples of heavy, unusually configured equipment that is frequently moved around the building. An awareness of these characteristics is important during the design phase of the facility. For example (and as stated on several occasions already), the doors between spaces should line up to reduce cornering, and the doors from the loading dock (or main access from the exterior of the building), and equipment storage rooms should be double doors with flush sills and sufficient height to facilitate equipment movement.

Other design considerations from a purely operational point of view include using ramps between levels in the sports hall, provided the change in level is not too significant. Another approach is to ensure that freight or building service elevators are of sufficient size (including height) to facilitate the movement of equipment between floors. Similarly, making stairwells and landings large enough to handle bulky items, such as boxes of supplies or furniture, will help with logistical concerns.

Lastly, the design phase must recognize all the activities that will take place within the facility. For example, food service or concessions within the building will require the movement of groceries into and garbage out of the building, preferably through service passages.

The author is aware of one sports facility in southwest Asia that was built at a cost in excess of $80 million, in which virtually all of these concerns were ignored in the preliminary plan. Fortunately, once construction was underway, a design review was able to rectify the worst of the errors, but only at considerable additional expense. Had not the design errors been caught, the only access to a second-floor food-service facility would have been via the VIP elevator. A worker seeking to get on board with a bag of garbage when the elevator was already occupied by a member of the Royal Family would have been problematic at best. Similarly, the design included three steps between each wing of the building and no way to move equipment between them. It was a situation rectified by the addition of a ramp after the fact.

Access of Building Operating Equipment

As unfortunate as the logistical situation was in this facility, service access to building operating systems was even worse. There was no way to access light and sound fixtures over the pool or the gymnasium floor because of a novel roof design.

The roof in the facility was a translucent, Teflon-coated fiberglass structure designed as an Arabian tent. But the design did not include access by service passages or catwalks to the fixtures suspended from the ceiling. Lights were changed, for example, by erecting scaffolding or using a personal hydraulic lift, both of which were expensive and time consuming. Unfortunately, the hydraulic lift could not be utilized in the pool area, which necessitated the erection of scaffolding in the swimming pool. Thus, the only way to change the lights was to drain the pool. This is a classic case of the architect's placing aesthetics before the more pragmatic

and mundane concerns of operating the building, with quite costly consequences.

The point of this discussion is that maintenance requirements of building operating systems must be considered during the design of a facility. By taking into account such operational requirements as easy access to equipment, particularly control panels and lubrication ports, which require frequent attention, accompanying labor costs can be substantially reduced.

Utilities

In addition to access to control panels and operating systems for routine maintenance, the astute placement of electrical outlets for cleaning equipment and water spigots for hoses can effectively reduce labor hours in the maintenance effort.

Most floor-care equipment requires electrical outlets, whether they are power scrubbers or vacuum cleaners. Therefore, the placement of electrical outlets needs consideration, particularly in corridors, lobbies, and activity areas. Inappropriately situated outlets can cause considerable additional operating expense, both for labor (the need to continually move power cords) and for supplies (the need to purchase excessive numbers of extension cords). Additionally, the need for exterior outlets on the building should not be overlooked. For example, certain types of window-washing equipment require access to power, as do many other types of maintenance and custodial equipment, such as blowers for grass clippings.

Water spigots on the exterior of the building should be treated similarly to electrical outlets on the interior of the building. Water hoses are commonly used for washing down sidewalks and exterior windows, particularly those located near the ground. Thus, careful consideration to the number and placement of spigots similarly warrants close attention in the design phase.

Windows

The whole topic of windows deserves special mention. The arrangement and proportioning of windows is called fenestration. Consideration of the relationships of lighting, color, use of materials, acoustics, and climate control cannot ignore the importance of fenestration. The size and placement of windows cannot be left to chance, personal whims, or merely traditional use.

The generous use of windows has been in vogue in the past few decades, at least in part because of the pleasing visual effects obtained by the architect. But the excessive use of glass in a sports facility may give rise to a host of problems, including high operating costs from heat gain and loss and inordinate cleaning costs.

Glass is a poor insulator. It causes significant heat gain during summer months through the greenhouse effect and a corresponding increase in air-conditioning costs. During the winter, the process is reversed, and large glass areas cause

Emergency lighting.

significant heat loss with a similar increase in operating costs. Similarly, large amounts of glass tend to increase maintenance costs as dirt is more visible. Any person who has glass patio doors, for example, can attest to how much attention they require when weather conditions make handprints and streaks more visible. In commercial buildings such as sports facilities, the amount of cleaning required depends on many variables, such as the local environment (rainfall, dust, and pollution) and the extent of the maintenance effort (or, how dirty you are willing to let the glass get?).

Two basic methods are usually used for window cleaning; "over the roof" or "up from the ground." In both cases, special equipment is required for any structure in excess of one story. The cost for these systems can vary from as little as $15 for a garden hose and squeegee with a six-foot handle to as much as $50,000 for a scaffold for "over the roof" work. Regardless of the system used, plans for water and electrical power sources for window-washing equipment should be included in the design phase.

It should be noted that in sports facilities, if windows are to be incorporated in the design, they should be at least 1/16th of the floor area. Additionally, it is recommended that windows be placed nearer the ceiling than the floor. For a multipurpose gymnasium designed to accommodate both international-level volleyball and team handball, the minimum total area of glass windows would be approximately 66 square meters (over 700 square feet) located some 7 to 12 meters (22 to 40 feet) off the ground. Under these circumstances, accessibility and labor costs related to maintaining an appropriate appearance must be considered during the design phase.

Returning to the sports facility in southwest Asia cited earlier, the architect achieved a stunning visual effect with a bank of blue-tinted windows two meters wide and 50 meters long extending the length of the sports hall wall some 15 meters from the ground and cantilevered at an angle of approximately of 140 degrees to the roof line. However, the design made accessing the windows extremely difficult, and in the six years that the author observed the building, the windows were never washed. The result was an originally unique visual effect that was severely degraded because the design did not take maintenance into consideration.

APPENDIX S

Academic Classrooms and Laboratories

Thomas H. Sawyer

The nature of institutions of higher education and their objectives and functions will determine in large measure the type, number, size, and relative importance of classrooms and teaching/research laboratories. In institutions offering only services courses in physical education, the need for classrooms and teaching/research laboratories will seldom, if ever, be required. However, classrooms, teaching/research laboratories, and testing equipment become integral components for both physical education-teacher education and adult fitness programs.

A lack of appropriate laboratory space and equipment for teaching/research has hampered many institutions of higher education gaining accreditation from the National Council on Accreditation of Teacher Education (NCATE) and the National Association for Sport and Physical Education (NASPE) in the teacher preparation programs and from expanding their program opportunities in non-teaching areas (i.e., adult fitness, fitness, exercise science). Institutions with graduate programs have a greater need for the development of teaching/research laboratories. Such facilities are required not only to provide learning experiences for students but also to attract and retain capable research scholars. Therefore, it is not possible to determine the appropriate square footage for a laboratory space. Each institution and its faculty working together should determine what the need shall be for this space. Yet there are some generic considerations for such laboratories that will be outlined in this chapter.

Learning Objectives

After reading this chapter, the student will be able to
- design a multimedia classroom with distance education capability,
- lay out an exercise physiology laboratory,
- design a biomechanics laboratory, and
- plan a motor development/learning laboratory.

Classrooms

Classrooms need to be designed for multiple uses—from the traditional lecture method aided by multimedia technology to distance education delivery. This requires greater planning and the involvement of multimedia (i.e., sound, video, and graphics) and computer technicians. Classrooms are no longer simple square rooms with adequate lighting, environmental controls, and a blackboard and screen. They have become high-tech instructional spaces.

The ideal classroom is tiered similarly to a theater. The total number of seats will be determined by reviewing typical class sizes over the past five years. Each row should have a counter with the following at each student site—a microphone (for use in televised programming), computer hook-up to mainframe, a 110 V receptacle with appropriate surge protection, comfortable chairs that can be easily accessed, and space for books and paper. The planner needs to consider providing an appropriate number of handicapped seats.

In the rear or on the side of the room there will be a control room. In the front of the room should be a large counter with a built-in TV monitor, overhead projector, and computer, and controls for the audio-visual equipment. Behind the counter will be a combination screen and grease board that is recessed into the wall and can be pulled out when needed. When not in use, the wall will become a backdrop with an appropriate background for telecasting.

Distance Education Classroom System Features

The following features are needed for a distance education classroom system:
- Three color cameras expandable to four with 123 zoom lens 460 lines of resolution;
- Overhead color Elmo camera graphics stand @ 450 lines of resolution;
- Multiple wall-mount monitors for easy student viewing of slides, computer graphics, satellite feeds, and videotape playback;
- One microphone, with expansion capability exceeding 70 microphones, for every two students. This allows student participation in the classroom (16 microphones with 14 for 28 students in classroom, one for instructor, and one for guest);
- Automatic microphone mixing;

- 35 mm slide-to-video conversion for displaying slides locally and at distant locations;
- PC/MAC multimedia computer (minimum 128 mb RAM and 30 gb hard drive with a DVD-RAM, CD-RW, 31/2" disk, and Zip drive) to video converter for PowerPoint and multimedia presentations;
- Computer interface for multimedia such as CD-RW and DVD disks;
- Videocassette for playback with freeze frame capability;
- Multiple VCRs for recording class (one S-VHS VCR playback for presentation, one S-VHS VCR for master record, and five VHS VCR record for library tapes);
- Character generator and video writer for highlighting 35 mm slides, computer graphics, or video stills;
- Sound system for playback of videocassette, CD-ROM or future DVD, computer audio files, audiocassette, and CD player;
- Switching and mixing control of video and audio for all sources;
- Telephone interface for telephone call in or teleconferencing;
- Wireless microphone for instructor;
- Wired microphone for guest;
- Integrated control system for use by instructor and/or for control of videocassette recorders, camera pan and tilt heads, camera lenses, audio, telephone interface, slide to video converter, video source selection, codec;
- AMX integrated control system for simplified operation and full system control;
- Supplemental lighting;
- A system with the ability to use satellite, fiber, codec, or web video and audio as either a source feed or signal distribution for maximum flexibility and adaptability for future technology; and
- A system with room for expansion to accommodate future requirements and technologies.

The Distance Education system consists of six distance education classrooms connected to a central control center. The system designed for each classroom provides multiple local and remote student participation with complete computer, 35 mm slide, videotape, and other multimedia sources. Each classroom has the capability of using satellite, codec, video via fiber, video via the web, or a combination of any of these. Further, the system is designed for video conferencing with two to four people in a room. It has limited capability to expand to either three cameras or two cameras and a single videocassette machine. Finally, each classroom has an option for an overhead graphics camera stand.

Technology is changing rapidly. No matter how well you plan today, it will become outdated in a very short period of time. Therefore, when planning this technical space, consider the importance of upgrading the systems in the future and plan for the capability of upgrading the technical components. This planning should include not only the technical equipment itself, but the spaces in which the equipment is installed.

Computer Classrooms/Laboratories

This is a space that will be outdated weeks and even months before construction is completed, no matter how much futuristic planning is completed. Computer technology changes dramatically about every three months. The space requirements also change fairly rapidly.

Science Laboratories

A number of science laboratories should be considered when planning for HPERD teaching facilities. These include exercise physiology, biomechanics, and motor learning and development. Each of these laboratories has special needs.

Exercise Physiology
(Human Performance) Laboratory

This space will be used for laboratory classes, research, and human performance testing for a variety of service programs. The size of the actual laboratory ranges from 400 sf to 2,000 sf. This laboratory can never be too large.

The following components maybe necessary for this space:
- Small office space (200 sf) is needed for the instructor.
- An environmental chamber is needed, with separate environmental controls that are easily accessible for maintenance.
- A hydrostatic pool recessed to floor level should have a service crawl space, a winch on an I-beam to suspend and move the chair, and appropriate outlets for cables from the computer to the sensor attached to the chair.
- The outlets to the computer station should be surge protected.
- The filter area for the hydrostatic pool must be easily accessible to service personnel.
- The floor in the hydrostatic area and locker areas should be tile, and the floor in the exercise areas should be multipurpose synthetic flooring.
- The hydrostatic area and locker rooms should have an appropriate number of drains in the floor to rapidly remove water.
- Two small locker rooms are necessary, with toilet facilities for a maximum of ten people.
- At least one treadmill recessed to floor level is needed (preferably two), with a service crawl space and a ramp to install and remove treadmill.
- The treadmill(s) should have appropriate 110 or 220 wiring in the recessed area.

- Electrical outlets should be located at the floor level for data-gathering machines.
- Both the hydrostatic area and the main laboratory area should have sinks, counter tops, and storage cabinets.
- Additional electrical outlets should be placed around the perimeter of the laboratory to accommodate other exercise equipment that needs surge protected, electricity.
- All electrical outlets near the water supplies must be GFI types.
- All computer stations must be hardwired to the mainframe computer.
- All separate spaces within the laboratory area must be capable of closed-circuit TV.
- Privacy drapes should be suspended from the ceiling for private sections.
- The height of the room with a recessed treadmill will be 10 feet and 14 feet with a treadmill that is not recessed and has a platform constructed around its perimeter.
- If the research conducted deals with taking and analyzing biopsies and blood samples, a small chemical laboratory will have to be constructed separate from the main space.
- Appropriate storage space is necessary.
- The environment in the laboratory must be conducive to exercise—temperature 68-72 degrees Fahrenheit, 60% or less, and 8 to 12 exchanges per hour.

    > (Note: Air exchanges should have an appropriate mix of outside and inside air. This mix is usually 10 percent outside air and 90 percent inside air, though a ratio of 40 to 60, outside to inside, is preferred. The specific ratio of outside to inside air (recirculated air) is most often governed by local engineering codes. These codes should be followed when any air-handling system is installed.)

- Lighting should be indirect to avoid glare on the computer monitors.
- Appropriate security should be provided to protect all computers and equipment.
- A sprinkler system should not be installed in this space. Use an appropriate substitute that will not harm the computers.

Biomechanics (Kinesiology) Laboratory

There are many areas in the field of biomechanics in which research may be conducted. The type of research may range from cinematography to human engineering. The size of the space ranges from 600 sf to 2,000 sf. This space can never be too large.

The following components may be necessary for this space:

- An office space (200 sf);
- A force platform set into the floor in an area where various activities from jumping to running can take place without hindering other activities in the laboratory;
- Ceiling height of at least 16 feet;

Indiana State University's hydrostatic pool.

- Suspended theater lighting;
- An environment conducive to exercise and cinematography—temperature 68-72 degrees Fahrenheit, 60% or less, and 8 to 12 exchanges per hour;
- Computer stations for laboratory use and digitizing movement;
- All computer stations hardwired into the main frame and all electrical outlets surge protected;
- Possibly a dark room to develop film and appropriate storage space;
- Multipurpose synthetic flooring;
- Nets and background drapes suspended from the ceiling that can be lowered and raised electronically;
- Appropriate storage space;
- Indirect lighting (except for theater lights) to avoid glare on the computer monitors;
- Appropriate security to protect all computers and equipment;
- No sprinkler system, but an appropriate substitute that will not harm the computers.

Motor Learning or Development Laboratory

Much of the research equipment found in exercise physiology and biomechanics laboratories can be used in research in motor learning or development and psychology of sport. However, a separate room or facility is necessary, at least 600 sf

Electronics for hydrostatic weighing, Indiana State University laboratory.

to 1,000 square feet with at least a 12-foot ceiling. The arrangement of the equipment in the room will depend on the research underway at the moment.

The following components maybe necessary for this space:

• An office space (200 sf);
• An environment conducive to movement activities—temperature 68-72 degrees Fahrenheit, 60% or less, and 8 to 12 exchanges per hour;
• Multipurpose synthetic flooring;
• Curtains and nets suspended from the ceiling that can be lowered and raised electronically;
• Four to six telephone-size cubicles with a counter top, chair, light, and electrical outlets;
• Sound proofing and separate environmental controls;
• Counter top spaces around the perimeter of the laboratory with storage below and above;
• A number of computer stations that are directly wired into the main frame and the outlets surge protected;
• No sprinkler system, but an appropriate substitute that will not harm the computers;
• Appropriate storage space;
• Indirect lighting to avoid glare on the computer monitors; and
• Appropriate security to protect all computers and equipment.

Technician's Office and Workshop Area

The science laboratories in HPERD are very technical, and many researchers and teachers are unable to repair equipment when it malfunctions. This means contacting a repair service. The cost of the repair and other customary charges are expensive and the work not always timely. Therefore, serious consideration should be given to hiring a technician to maintain the expensive equipment in all the laboratories. If this option is taken, a technician's office and workshop must be designed.

The following components may be necessary for this space:

• An office space (200 sf) with computer, phone, cable TV, and electrical outlets;
• A workshop space (200 sf) with a work bench with multiple outlets, storage cabinets, drawer space, pegboard on wall to hang tools and parts;
• A concrete floor with a painted coarse finish and a floor drain;
• A double-deep sink and cabinets below and above;
• Temperature of 68-72 degrees Fahrenheit, 60% or less, and 8 to 12 exchanges per hour;
• No sprinkler system, but an appropriate substitute that will not harm the computers;
• Appropriate storage space;
• Indirect lighting to avoid glare on the computer monitors; and
• Appropriate security to protect all computers and equipment.

Suggestions for Purchasing Equipment

The manufacture and sale of research equipment has become a very competitive business. As a result, a wide range of the same kind of equipment is frequently available under different brand names. Before purchasing large expensive units, it is worth the time and effort to investigate carefully the various makes. The annual meetings of professional societies generally include exhibits by manufacturers of research equipment appropriate to the particular area of investigation. Consultation with a colleague in the same field who has used the equipment is a good idea before making a purchase.

In considering particular pieces of equipment, determine the following: (a) whether students or trained researchers are to use the equipment; (b) initial and annual servicing cost; (c) whether the equipment is electronically compatible with other equipment now in use or contemplated (often it is more economical to purchase units that match others from the same company so that the responsibility for servicing them rests with one company); (d) what power supply is needed; (e) ease with which the instrument may be calibrated, and whether other equipment is needed for the calibration; (g) what service the company is willing to provide and where the service centers are located; and (h) levels of noise, vibration, and heat generated by the equipment. Unbiased answers to these and other questions can sometimes best be found by having discussions with other researchers who have used such installations.

Exercise Physiology Laboratory Equipment Needs

The equipment for the Exercise Physiology Laboratory includes

**Electronics use in
Indiana State University's
motor learning laboratory.**

- crash cart,
- ECG defibrillator,
- spine board,
- treadmill(s),
- stair climber(s),
- bicycle ergometer(s),
- pneumotachmeter,
- gas meter,
- telemetering apparatus,
- electronic gas analyzer(s), either paramagnetic or electrochemical,
- infrared analyzer,
- multichannel recorder,
- Douglas bags,
- barometer,
- thermocouples,
- face mask with two-way non-rebreathing valve,
- disposable pneumotach,
- one-way, T-shaped non-rebreathing valve with mouthpiece and saliva trap,
- metabolic cart,
- cardiopulmonary diagnostic system,
- cardiotachmeter,
- pedometers,
- telepedometer,
- biomotometer,
- accelerometers,
- actometer,

- caltrac,
- electromyography, and
- computers, monitors, and printers (laser).

Biomechanics Laboratory Equipment Needs
The equipment for the biomechanics laboratory includes:
- force platform,
- other types of force measuring devices,
- high-speed motion picture camera, motor-driven, 50-500 frames per second,
- stroboscopic equipment,
- videotape recorder with two channels and play-back capacity,
- oscilloscope,
- electronic counters,
- amplifiers compatible with measuring and recording devices,
- digitizing equipment,
- computers, monitors, printers (laser),
- mirrors, and
- metal storage cabinets.

Motor Learning and Development Laboratory Equipment Needs
Equipment for the motor learning and development laboratory includes:
- multichannel recorders,
- standard electric clocks,
- interval timer,
- steadiness units,
- electronic counters,
- variable power supply,
- electronic kits,
- audio amplifiers,
- microphone,
- audio oscillator,
- oscilloscope,
- telemetry transmitter,
- telemetry receiver,
- voltage stabilizer,
- battery charger,
- seashore test,
- magnetic tape recorder, and
- storage cabinets.

APPENDIX T

Dance Spaces

Dance in education is not a new idea. At all education levels it has existed by virtue of dedicated individuals. In the elementary schools, dance activities under a number of aliases—eurhythmics, rhythms, play party games, singing games, and folk dance—have been offered. Coming into the elementary school curriculum as an offshoot of the playground movement, the dance materials presented were usually happenstance (with a few exceptions in experimental schools). A classroom teacher may have been interested in folk dance or been faced with the necessity to prepare a May Day, a pageant, or a festival.

Within the past few years, many privately administered elementary schools and some public schools have made provisions for dance in the curriculum. By and large, existing physical education facilities are used.

Since the turn of the century, folk dance (usually European in origin) has been offered in physical education classes for girls in secondary schools. When folk dance lessons were first introduced, they were often limited in content and skill, and were, as in the elementary school, an outcome of the playground movement. Toward the end of the 19th century, a few secondary schools in large cities had gymnasiums that were primarily equipped for gymnastics and other sports using limited-size courts. The use of these areas for dance was spasmodic and usually occurred in preparation for special events.

In the 1920s dance in education was materially advanced when Margaret H'Doubler initiated the first dance major at the University of Wisconsin. During this period, clog and tap dance assumed a leading role in dance education, and Henry Ford promoted a return to the formal square dances of an earlier day, such as the Lancers (NDA, 1985).

By the 1930s, the country was sufficiently removed from its pioneer beginnings to acknowledge the joy and value of square dancing. The teaching of social dance was heavily emphasized as a means of implementing the social values of physical education. Modern dance—stemming from natural dance and from the influences of Martha Graham, Doris Humphrey, Charles Weidman, and others—began a slow but steady growth in curricular offerings. In 1931, great impetus was given to dance in education with the establishment of the National Section on Dance within the American Association for Health, Physical Education, and Recreation (NDA, 1985).

The advancement of physical education programs was not without trauma for teachers and administrators. Until World War I, with its emphasis upon fitness and recognition of the recreational needs of service personnel, it was difficult to finance facilities and staff for physical education. Immediately after the war, mobility and better communications enhanced the athletic program and, as the result of athletic needs, more gymnasiums and stadiums were built. The need for a gymnasium in secondary schools was thereby placed on a firm basis. The depression of the late 1920s and early 1930s, however, curbed these programs and the extensive expansion of facilities. World War II not only emphasized fitness and the recreational needs of service personnel but added a new dimension-recreational needs of war workers in factories, shipyards, and munition plants. The Cold War and the possibility of increased leisure time have reiterated the needs for enriched curricula and additional facilities.

Until recently, studios for dance at the secondary school level had dropped in priority behind athletic and aquatic facilities. At the beginning of the 20th century, dance was often better off than were sports in the low-ceilinged basement rooms and narrow hallways. As gymnasiums were built primarily for basketball programs, dance was relegated to a low priority in the use of these facilities both for class and after-school clubs. Moreover, the finish or seal on gymnasium floors made certain dance activities uncomfortable and precluded others. Within the past 10 to 15 years, there has been a growing consciousness of the needs of girls in secondary schools. As dance has proved its worth as a physiologically demanding and aesthetically rewarding activity, consideration is being given to the employment of specialized teachers and the provision of specialized areas for teaching dance at the secondary level.

Gradually, clog and tap dance, natural dance, and later ballroom and square dance as well as modern dance have appeared in the secondary school curriculum. Of significance is the increasing interest of boys in the various forms of dance, especially modern jazz. Frequently, dance programs at the secondary school level are the result of grants from the National Endowment for the Arts (NDA, 1985).

As was true in elementary and secondary schools, facilities for dance education at the college level have developed slowly. The gymnasium dominated the scene, with dance scheduled "catch-as-catch-can" during available hours. As emphasis upon dance in teacher preparation increased and as colleges and universities became more involved in all phases of the arts, auxiliary rooms were planned for dance and related activities.

Basic Dance Facility Assumptions

The essential facilities should be supplied in sufficient quantity and quality to provide for all dance activities in the required and elective curriculums and in extracurricular programs. Particular attention should be given to adequate provision for dance performance, observation, and audience spaces.

Related portions of the activity complex should be provided and meet acceptable standards. These will include (NDA, 1985):
- Box office,
- Construction rooms for costumes, props and sets, and music (composing and recording),
- Costume storage areas,
- Custodial space,
- Laundry, cleaning and drying facilities,
- Listening areas,
- Locker-dressing rooms with make-up areas,
- Office space,
- Parking area,
- Public lavatories,
- Rest rooms (remote from toilets and showers),
- Shower area,
- Storage spaces (props and sets),
- Toilets, and
- Training room.

The following should be provided and meet established standards (NDA, 1985):
- Electrical installation,
- Lighting equipment,
- Acoustics,
- Ventilation,
- Heating,
- Floors,
- Walls,
- Sanitation,
- Safety,
- Drinking fountains,
- Sound systems,
- Filming and taping facilities,
- Installation of fixed equipment,
- Movable equipment, and
- Lines of traffic.

Dance facilities should be designed to serve both genders. Further, the dance facility should be readily accessible to outside entrances and be a unit unto itself even if it is attached to, or a part of, another building. Finally, the dance complex should be constructed, decorated, and furnished in an aesthetically pleasing manner and suitable for the pursuit of dance as an art form.

Criteria for Determining Facility Needs

The following criteria can be used to determine the dance facility needs when planning either a stand-alone dance facility or one for inclusion in a larger complex (NDA, 1985):

Total facilities should be determined according to the amount of emphasis placed on various aspects of the dance curriculum, such as classes needed and areas for individual work and for extracurricular and concert practice.

Based on the design of the dance curriculum, facilities should be considered in terms of:
- Auxiliary space and equipment,
- Classroom space,
- Dance teaching space,
- Office space,
- Performance space,
- Practice space and choreography,
- Rehearsal space, and
- Research space.

Preferably three distinct areas should be provided: one area for folk and social dance, one area for modern dance, and one area for ballet.

Construction of Modern Dance and Ballet Areas

The following information is provided to assist in the development of state-of-the-art modern dance and ballet areas (NDA, 1985):

Dimensions
- A minimum of 100 square feet per person is recommended. An area of 3,000 square feet will accommodate 30 students.
- If an area is to serve as an informal theater and instructional area, it should be between 4,800 and 5,000 square feet to accommodate both the class and the needs of the theater section.
- Ceiling height of 16 to 24 feet is recommended for all dance areas. Full height is essential for large dance areas (over 2,400 square feet) and 16 feet is minimum height for small dance areas. There is a feeling of height when the ceiling is high. Some dancers prefer a height of 16 to 18 feet, but consideration must be given to the total construction in the dance areas. In some

Example of a dance exerciser instructor's elevated platform.

instances, any change in the roof line may add prohibitive expense.

Floors
- Dance activities require air space between floor and foundation, and "floating" and/or spring floors for resiliency.
- Floors should be of hardwood (such as maple) of random lengths, and tongue-and-grooved; they should be laid with the grain going in one direction.
- Portable floors (Marly or stage-step) provide flexibility for use when both ballet and modern dance need to be accommodated.
- Floors should be non-slip and constructed for easy cleaning.
- The finish should provide a smooth surface upon which dancers can glide with bare feet or soft sandals. Tung or linseed oil is considered by most to be a satisfactory finish; an alternative might be several coats of wood sealer. No chemical dust mops should be used to clean such floors, only a slightly damp mop.

Doors
There should be wide double doors to permit traffic flow into and out of the room. The sills of such doors should be level with the floor to allow for moving large equipment such as a piano.

Walls
- Walls should be smooth and easily maintained.
- Consideration should be given to having one unobstructed wall of neutral background for filming purposes.
- Stress factors of the walls should be considered to support ballet barres and mirrors.
- Thin walls are inadequate.
- It is desirable to sound-proof walls especially in listening areas.

Lighting
- Incandescent light is preferable to fluorescent light.
- Rheostat lights that also serve as houselights during performances should be controlled from wall switches as well as from the light control board.
- Consideration should be given to natural lighting. Large windows contribute to an aesthetically and psychologically desirable atmosphere. The best location for windows is the north wall to avoid direct sunlight.
- Windows should be curtained so the studio can be darkened for film showing and studio performances.
- When total construction necessitates no windows, the aesthetics may be improved by the use of a pastel color on the walls or draperies serving both aesthetic and acoustical purposes.

Acoustics and Sound Equipment
- When one studio is directly over another or over offices, acoustical treatment is necessary.
- Placement of sound equipment, such as a record player, turntable, microphones, and speakers should be considered in the initial planning in terms of both performance and security.
- An adequate number of speakers, installed in or near ceiling height, should be located so participants can hear both music and instruction.
- Heavy equipment should be placed on stands of table height equipped with rollers.
- Electrical outlets should be spaced on every wall and located close to where equipment will be used. Four-plex outlets are needed close to the area where most equipment is used (e.g., video-tape recorders, tape deck and amplifiers for performance, and stage manager's desk for cueing lights).

Storage Space
- Locked storage space for sound equipment should be adjacent to the dance area and locked. Storage rooms should have double doors and a flush threshold for easy movement of large equipment, such as a piano.
- Built-in storage space for records, sound equipment, tapes, and musical instruments should be provided.
- A sound-proof area for use of students and instructors in listening to recordings and tapes and viewing videotapes is highly desirable. This area should have adequate acoustics, ventilation, and electrical outlets.

Photos by Tom Sawyer

Ballet bar and mirrors.

Wiring
- Heavy-duty wiring is essential for all dance facilities. Wiring should be capable of carrying a portable light board as well as phonographs, additional speakers, tape recorders, and projectors. Wall outlets should be plentiful.
- Television conduits should be installed at the time a building is constructed.

Temperature and Ventilation
- Temperature should be maintained at 65° to 72° F (22°-26° C). The thermostat should be located in the studio areas.
- The air should be well circulated, and consideration should be given to the use of natural air. Humidity should be no greater than 95%.
- Mechanisms for heating and circulating of air should be as nearly silent as possible to avoid interfering with the quality of sound and its reception.

Accessories
- Leaf-fold mirrors, which can be folded for protection or curtained during performances, may be installed along two adjoining walls so that movement can be analyzed from two directions. Wall mirrors at least six feet high should be installed flush with the wall and raised 1 or 1 1/2 feet from the floor.
- Ballet barres should be made of wood, preferably oak or aluminum, and be smooth in texture. The minimum length to accommodate one dancer is five feet. Barres from 40 to 42 inches in height may be installed permanently; they should extend six to eight inches from the wall. If feasible, consider double barres—one at 36 inches, and one at 42 inches. If necessary, barres may be placed in front of mirrors. The barre supports may be screwed into recessed floor sockets just in front of the mirror, thus facilitating the removal of the barre and supports when not needed.

- Custom-made percussion cabinets mounted on rollers are a fine accessory. They may have a carpeted top surface, slide-out drawers lined with felt for small instruments, and larger partitions to accommodate cymbals and drums.
- Heavy sound equipment should be built-in or placed on stands of table height equipped with rollers for ease of transportation.
- Since moving affects the tuning of a piano, this instrument should be placed where it will not have to be moved. A piano should be placed on an inside wall where it will not be subject to extreme heat or cold, and be protected by a suitable cover and lock. It should be placed on a heavy-duty dolly if it is to be moved frequently.
- Chalkboards and tackboards are useful accessories.
- Telephone.
- A glass-enclosed exhibit case for photographs, costumes, costume plates, manuscripts, and other items may be installed near the dance area. A building foyer may be utilized.
- The atmosphere for dance should be conducive to artistic endeavors. Soft colors, clear lighting, and spaciousness are pleasing to both dancers and spectators.

Construction of Folk and Social Dance Areas
The following information is provided to assist in the development of state-of-the-art folk and social dance areas (NDA, 1985):

Dimensions
- An area of 5,400 square feet (54 ft. x 100 ft. is suggested) will accommodate a class of approximately 60 students.
- Dance areas are generally rectangular with a length-width ratio of approximately 3 to 2 (for example, 90 feet x 60 feet).
- Ceiling height should be in proportion to the size of the room but never lower than 12 feet.
- An outside entrance into a main corridor of the building will provide for traffic flow of the relatively large groups using the area.

Floors
Floors as described in the section on ballet and modern dance are necessary. However, an epoxy finish, rather than tung oil, will enable the use of street shoes without damage to the floor.

Lighting and Ventilation
- Acoustics and sound equipment (see above),
- Storage space (see above),
- Wiring (see first point under wiring, above), and
- Temperature and ventilation (see above).

Accessories

- Racks for coats and books should be installed either within the dance area or along the outside corridor wall.
- Tackboards, chalkboards, and display cases are highly desirable.

Dance Production Areas

While a well-equipped theater is the ideal dance performance area, it is not always possible to have such a facility. The alternative is to provide a large area for both instructional and performance activities. The area may be equipped with a balcony for observation of classes and for audience seating during performances. Other seating arrangements such as portable bleachers may also be desirable. A large area may be equipped to provide for arena or proscenium staging, or both.

Photos by Tom Sawyer

The proscenium arch surrounds the stage like a picture frame.

Arena Stage Area

The planning for an arena stage area should include performance space, seating, lighting, sound equipment, control booths, and wiring. The following describes the specifics needed in each area:

Performance Space

The performance area should contain between 875 and 1,200 square feet (NDA, 1985).

Seating Space

The most desirable seating capacity for performances should accommodate 300 to 500 people. The entire performing area should be visible from all seats. The seating arrangement should be flexible. Seats may be on movable risers so space may be used in a variety of ways. Raked seating is essential. Adequate entrances, exits, and exit lights should be provided for performers and audience in accordance with local fire codes.

Lighting

Lighting should be available from all directions. It should be possible to use gels on all lighting instruments except house lights. All lights should be on separate dimmers. A sufficient number of electrical outlets should be available. When possible, all lights should be operated from a single console within the control booth.

Sound Equipment

Equipment should be operated from a control booth. Speakers for amplification should be placed so both performers and audience can hear. Backstage monitors should be used.

Control Booths

Provision should be made for control booths or . . . areas with full view of the stage area to operate lights and sound.

Wiring

Wiring should be adequate to carry a portable light board, a phonograph, tape recorder, speaker system, projector, and follow spots (see local electric codes).

Proscenium Stage Area

The planning for a proscenium stage area should include performance space, seating, curtains, teasers, battens, lighting, sound equipment, control booths, and live musicians. The following describes the specifics needed in each area:

Performance Space

The minimum performance area should be 1,200 square feet (30 feet by 40 feet). The two wing areas combined should be equal to the amount of visible stage space. Space should be provided for musicians, chairs, and lighted music stands. Placement of musicians should not interfere with the visibility of the stage or the sound of the music (NDA, 1985).

Seating Space

A balcony with permanently installed raked seating is desirable, with the possibility of portable risers below. The entire performing area should be visible from all seats. The number of seats should be planned for estimated size of audience.

Curtains, Teasers, Battens

Hand control is preferable to a mechanically controlled front curtain. Side curtains (legs) or flats should be provided on both sides of the stage for entrances and exits. Flexible tracks to move the curtain horizontally should be considered. Asbestos teasers and tormentors are needed for safety and masking. Battens to be used for hanging scenery, sky drop, or film screen should be suspended above the visible stage area. Provision should be made for lowering and raising battens for the attachment of scenery. Lines should be attached to a pin rail located at one side of the stage. Metal grids are also usable. The back wall should be free of visible obstructions and painted white for projections. Curtains and flats should be light, absorbent, and of neutral or dark color.

Lighting Equipment

Provision should be made for side lighting, front lighting, and overhead border lighting. Three separate circuits should be provided to be used singly or in combination. There should be front ceiling beam lighting, balcony lighting, or both. Crawl space should be provided in the ceiling above the beams to permit focusing and repair work. It should be possible to use gels on all lights except house lights. All instruments should be on separate dimmers. A sufficient number of electrical outlets should be located in floor pockets or wall spaces in the wings. A low wattage light should be installed for cueing performers and crew members at the side of the front stage. When possible, all lights should be operated from a single console within the control booth.

Sound Equipment

Equipment should be operated from the control booth. Speakers for amplification should be placed so both performers and audience can hear. An intercom should be used to link the backstage, dressing rooms, and control booth. Telephones to handle outside calls should be located in the box office and backstage. The backstage phone should be equipped with a signal light.

Live Musicians

If feasible, space should be allocated for performance appearances.

Control Booths

Control booths for lights, sound, and projections should be centered at the audience end of the facility and should include soundproofing, a large window for viewing the stage, built-in counters and shelves for storing equipment, and an intercom for communication with the backstage area.

Auxiliary Areas

The following auxiliary areas need to be included in the planning process for a dance facility:

Costume Room

A costume room for constructing, fitting, cleaning, and storing should be a minimum of 400 square feet and be equipped with or accessible to:

- Built-in cabinets with shelves and drawers, and racks for hanging and storing costumes.
- Cleaning machine,
- Control room with toilet facilities,
- Cutting table,
- Double door with a flush threshold to facilitate moving costume racks,
- Dress forms,
- Ironing boards and steam irons,
- Laundry tubs and drying facilities,
- Sewing machines,
- Tackboard and chalkboard affixed to one wall,
- Three-way mirror, and
- Washing machine and dryer.

Dressing Rooms

Dressing rooms should be provided for men and women. They should be equipped with costume racks, chairs, wash basins, lighted mirrors, toilets and showers, and a first-aid kit.

Make-up Room

The make-up room should be located between the men's and women's dressing rooms and be furnished with lighted mirrors, built-in shelves, make-up tables, chairs, wash basins, and storage space.

Scene and Prop Room

The scene and prop room should be located as close to the stage area as feasible. It should be a minimum of 400 to 500 sf and have a ceiling height of at least 16 feet, although 24 feet is preferable. The floor should have a paint-resistant surface. Proper ventilation is necessary to avoid fumes from paint and glue. The room should be furnished with built-in bins and shelves for storage of nails, brushes, screws, paints, and glues; a pegboard mounted flush with the wall for hanging tools; a built-in workbench; a wash sink; outlets for electrical tools; and a chalkboard and tackboard. Storage space for props should be a minimum of 500 sf with a 16- to 24-foot ceiling; it should be easily accessible to the backstage area (NDA, 1985).

Box Office (Ticket Booth)

The box office should have locked racks for tickets, a locked drawer for currency, a telephone with an outside line, and an intercom to the backstage area.

Foyer

It is desirable to provide a social area where the audience and performers may meet following a production. It should be situated adjacent to the performing area and include attractive decorations, a comfortable seating arrangement, display cases, and an adjoining small kitchen for preparing refreshments.

Additional Instructional and Laboratory Facility Needs Based on the Size of the Dance Program and Curriculum

Three areas need to be planned for in the dance facility, including teaching space, office space, and auxiliary space.

Teaching Space

The following are planning considerations for dance teaching areas:

- There should be a minimum of one large teaching and performance area. This area should have a 24-foot ceiling and resilient floors, and be equipped with special lighting for performance, sound equipment, a communications media, an observation balcony, and good ventilation and lighting.
- Two additional areas should be provided: an area for ballet and modern dance, and an area for jazz, social, and folk dance.
- Provision should be made for well-designed and well-equipped classrooms and seminar and lecture rooms for instructional use.
- In addition to the performance area, there should be rehearsal space that is somewhat larger than the area designed for performance.
- There should be an area for practice and choreography that is equipped with phonographs, tape machines, and video-tape equipment.
- A library and reference room with an adjoining study area for books, music, records, tapes, and copying machine should be available.
- Provision should be made for a soundproof recording studio large enough to accommodate a piano and small orchestra, turntables and tape recorder. It should have built-in shelves for storage and be not less than 300 square feet.
- Storage space for musical instruments should be provided.

Office Space

The dance facility office space should include the following:

- There should be a centralized office for unified administration.
- A private office and conference space for the director of the dance program should be available.
- There should be office space for faculty members and for technical personnel.
- Supporting space for office equipment and storage should be provided.
- Laboratory space for faculty should be available.

Auxiliary Space

Additional auxiliary space might include the following:

- It is desirable to have a reception-social room (with adjoining kitchen) for use by students, faculty, and community groups on special occasions.
- Locker-shower areas should be available for students and faculty of both genders.
- A faculty conference room should be provided.
- A rehabilitation or therapy room is desirable.

Adaptation of Dance Facilities and Equipment

Since local conditions may demand modification of ideal dance facilities while a dance program is being developed, this section describes some of the adaptations that may be feasible.

Elementary School

Current Practices

Small gymnasiums are used most frequently, with cafeteria-gymnasiums, multipurpose rooms, and auditorium-gymnasiums following in close order. The size of classes ranges from 25 to 70 pupils, with 30 being the average size.

With regard to floor surfaces used for the instruction of dance, hardwood predominates, with linoleum tile running second. The floors in winter should be heated.

As far as equipment was concerned, all elementary schools but one have a record player with convenient electrical outlets, but just over half the schools report having sufficient recordings. The same is true of movable tables with rollers for record players, and of controlled speeds and amplification of recordings. Tape recorders are available in approximately half the elementary schools. There is some evidence of percussion equipment, principally rhythm band instruments, with a few elementary schools having either a Chinese tom-tom or a Gretsch dance drum. Three-fourths of the elementary schools report chalkboards and nearly half of them report bulletin boards in use as teaching aids. Approximately half of the elementary schools cite that storage space is available for recordings and percussion instruments.

Use of Limited Facilities and Equipment

Practically speaking, it is impossible to secure ideal dance facilities in all situations at the elementary school level. Community socio-economic conditions virtually negate such a dream. Lack of ideal facilities and equipment is no reason to omit dance experiences for children. An outstanding authority on children's movement experiences has stated that a multipurpose room is quite adequate for the dance program. Another expert found that children can be taught to move lightweight classroom furniture efficiently so that dance space is available. By constant attention to opportunities for renovations in a school (or a school system), one may ask for use of renovated space, for installation of bulletin boards and electrical outlets, and even for changes in floor surfaces. Teacher initiative is a priority if space for dance is to be acquired.

Recommendations

Dance areas for elementary school children should be large enough to accommodate approximately 30 students. Rooms below ground level are inadvisable, because of possible dampness and lack of adequate ventilation. As increasing numbers of elementary schools are built on a one-floor plan with outdoor exits for individual classrooms, basement facilities will gradually vanish.

Hardwood is advised for dance floors. Tile floors, which frequently are laid directly on cement or concrete, are cold to the touch, often slippery, and conducive to injury. Because tile flooring allows no resiliency for foot action, it can lead to painful shin splints.

There is no answer to the exact type of dance facility that should be provided. Except under unusual circumstances, economics rule out the provision for a dance studio. The combination gymnasium-lunch room is not recommended because of loss of time for classes before, after, and during lunch hours, and the health hazards of dust on food and lunch debris in the activity area. The stage-auditorium, stage-gymnasium, small gymnasium, multipurpose room, or large playroom may be used if adequate electrical outlets and wiring for record players, tape recorders, and minimal stage lighting can be provided.

The rather informal dance programs presented at the elementary school level can often be accommodated by seating the children on the floor and visitors on chairs around three sides of one end of the dance area. Usually storage space for recordings and simple percussion equipment is available in, or adjacent to, such areas. Many physical education items can be used in the dance program. Jumping ropes, balls, boxes, benches, mats, and other play apparatus lend themselves to creative uses.

Dance for children has become an established activity in elementary school programs. It can only take place, however, when space and equipment are provided, time is allocated, and leadership is available.

Secondary School

Current Practices

It is extremely difficult to secure detailed information on dance programs at the secondary school level. The size of areas used for dance varies from extremely small to extremely large, with a rectangular shape being most common. In height, the areas vary from eight feet to 40 feet. Record players and tape recorders are usually available. Percussion instruments, drums predominating, are also in use. Some secondary schools have closet space set aside for costumes and even a full costume room. Ballet barres and mirrors are in use. Wooden floors predominate. One secondary school

reports that excellent additional practice space is available, and several schools note that smaller additional space is available, and several secondary schools note that smaller additional space is available only when not in use by other groups.

Use of Limited Facilities and Equipment

Few secondary schools have specialized facilities for dance. One reason is that there has not been adequate emphasis on dance in the secondary school curriculum. There is some indication, however, that specialized concentrations (dance, sports, aquatics, gymnastics) in teacher preparation, and a cultural emphasis upon the arts are beginning to alter this pattern, particularly in suburban areas and in certain consolidated school districts. As these programs begin to establish their value, obtaining facilities will become easier.

Meanwhile, the standard gymnasium can be used. Teachers who are interested in providing dance experiences for their students can plan curricular units, secure a few portable barres, borrow a record player and/or tape recorder from the audiovisual supply room, find storage area for a few percussion instruments, and secure space for a costume closet. The floor with the usual gymnasium seal on it is not ideal but can be used. The battle for time allotments and space assignment is perennial. Interest and effort can perform wonders.

Recommendations

A minimum dance facility should provide 100 square feet per student, one dimension to exceed 60 feet; full-length mirrors at a corner for analysis of skill from two directions; a speaker system designed to distribute sound evenly throughout the room; a control system for record players and microphones; and practice barres on one wall at heights of 34 inches and 42 inches. For modern dance, the floor should be of hard northern maple that has been sealed and then buffed with a fine abrasive. Additional suggestions follow (NDA, 1985):

Equipment. As in the case of the elementary school, physical education equipment such as balls, ropes, and gymnastic apparatus may be used. Stall bars, if available, are an excellent substitute for ballet barres and a fine medium for creative activity.

By wise planning, basic equipment (recordings, percussion instruments, and portable lighting boards) can be floated from school to school for production use.

Portable percussion racks made in an industrial arts department solve the problems of easy storage and efficient class and program use. Portable mirrors, six feet tall and eight feet wide, can be constructed 1 1/2 feet from the floor on rollers and moved into the dance area if wall-mounted mirrors are not feasible. Portable ballet barres of lightweight aluminum are desirable when unobstructed wall space is at a premium.

Floors. Poor floors should be covered by Marly dance flooring rather than a ground cloth.

Areas. Investigation of the following areas may reveal available spaces for dance: adaptive rooms, gymnastic rooms, weight control rooms, recreational game rooms. Careful pre-planning of new facilities suggests the possibility of combining two or more of these. Two community resources are feasible-churches and local theater groups. Churches are now interested in dance. Either temporary or permanent use of a large classroom or a church auditorium may be possible. Community theatre groups are adding dance experiences for all age levels to their gamut of activities. It may be possible to arrange for use of their areas during the school day.

The possibility of pooled resources in the performing arts—dance, drama, music—opens wide potential in the development of excellent facilities, economy in their use by several departments, and rich experiences in multimedia.

Performing Arts for Modern Dance or Ballet

The following specific recommendations are made for modern dance and ballet areas (NDA, 1985):

- The stage should be situated at the end of the room that can best provide entrances for the dancers. The dancers' entrances should be out of the audience's view.
- The stage can be formed by curtains or flats.
- A back curtain should have a center opening and be hung at least three feet forward of the back wall to provide crossover space for the performers.
- In the case of a raised stage, the front curtain should be set back about four feet from the raised edge to provide an apron (forestage).
- Side curtains or flats should be provided.
- If curtains cannot be used, an open stage is advisable. The folding mats used in physical education can be set on edge to form entrances and exits. Flats and portable screens are alternative possibilities.

Performing Area for Folk and Social Dance

The following specific recommendations are made for folk and social dance areas (NDA, 1985):

- Roll-away bleachers can be installed at one end of the room.
- Provision should be made for storage of folding chairs, which can be placed along the side walls.
- An auxiliary performing space can be a patio or other outdoor area, such as a dance green or a broad, level surface at the entrance to a school building, which can be adapted for occasional use for dance performances. Marly dance floorings may be placed on the cement surface to protect the dancer's feet and legs.

As in the case of elementary schools, specific dance facilities are not feasible in all secondary schools. Dance is possible, however, depending on the teacher's interest, effort, and ability to adapt to the situation.

College/University

As new facilities have been constructed and older facilities remodeled in the larger colleges and universities, there seems to be little excuse for omission of areas specifically planned for dance. The increasing emphasis upon dance as a major field and the increasing interrelationships among the performing arts have placed dance in a position of importance in college planning.

REFERENCES

Access Board. (n.d.). Retrieved February 4, 2001, from http://www.access-board.gov/508.htm

Access Board. (n.d.). Retrieved February 6, 2001, from http://www.access-board.gov/ufas/ufas-html/ufas.htm#intro

Access Board. (n.d.). Uniform federal accessibility standards. Retrieved Nov 1, 2008, from http://www.access-board.gov/ufas/ufas-html/ufas.htm#4.32

Achampong, F. (1999). *Workplace sexual harassment law.* Westport, CT: Quorum Books.

AEDs now required in New York schools. Retrieved from Available: http://www.padl.org/articles.php3?id = aedsnyschools.htm

Agoglia, J. (2004, January). State of the industry: Taking the industries pulse for 2003-2004. *Club Industry,* 17-20.

Agron, J. (2001, April). Dwindling support. *American School & University: Facilities, Purchasing and Business Administration,* p. 24, 26-28, 30, 32.

Agron, J. (2001, April). Rising to the challenge. *American School & University: Facilities, Purchasing and Business Administration,* 50b, 50d, 50f, 50h.

Ahrweiler, M. (2001, January/February). Extremely mainstream. *Recreation Management,* 12-17.

Ahrweiler, M. (2004). Special supplement: Recreation management's complete guide to sports surfaces and flooring. *Recreation Management.* http://recmanagement.com/features.php?fid = 200407fe00&ch = 2

American Academy of Orthopaedic Surgeons. (2007). *First responder* (4th ed.). Sudbury, MA: Jones and Bartlett.

American Red Cross. (2001). *Emergency response.* Yardley, PA: Staywell.

American Red Cross. (2007b). *Lifeguarding.* Yardley, PA: Staywell.

American Safety and Health Institute. (2007). *Complete emergency care.* Champaign, IL: Human Kinetics.

American Society for Testing and Materials. (1995). *Standard consumer safety performance specification for playground equipment for public use.* (F1487). West Conshohocken, PA: Author.

American Society for Testing and Materials. (2007). *Standard consumer safety performance specification for playground equipment for public use* (1487). West Conshohocken, PA: Author.

American Society for Testing and Materials. (2004). *Standard test method for shock-absorbing properties of playing surface safety systems and materials.* (1292). West Conshohocken, PA: Author.

American Society for Testing and Materials (2005). *Standard consumer safety performance specification for public use play equipment for children six months to 23 months.* West Conshohocken, PA: Author.

Americans With Disabilities Act of 1990, Pub. L. No. 101-336, 2, 104 Stat. 328 (1991).

Ammon, R., Jr., Southall, R. M., & Blair, D. A. (2004). *Sport facility management: Organizing events and mitigating risks.* Morgantown, WV: Fitness Information Technology, Inc.

Andriesen, D. (2007, March 20). Arenas and elephants: How much is too much? Retrieved on March 3, 2008 from http://seattlepi.nwsources.com/basketball/308250_arena20.html.

Andrus, S. (1990). Manual labor. *CAM Magazine, 2*(5), 61-64.

Ankeney, J. (2005, April). Large-format LED Displays. *Sound & Video Contractor, 23*(4), 54-56.

Anonymous (1998). Making indoor air quality work for you. *Public Management, 80*(8), A10.

Appenzeller, H. (2000). Risk assessment and reduction. In H. Appenzeller, & G. Lewis (Eds.), *Successful sport management* (2nd ed.) (pp. 313-321). Durham, NC: Carolina Academic Press.

Armitage-Johnson, S. L. (1994). Equipment maintenance. In T. R. Baechle (Ed.), *Essentials of strength training and conditioning.* Champaign, IL: Human Kinetics.

Arnheim, D. D., & Prentice, W. E. (1997). *Principles of athletic training* (9th ed.). Boston: WCB/McGraw Hill.

ASLA (1998). Landscape Architecture. Retrieved from http://www.asla.org/asla

Atchison, J. (2003). Top 10 annuals for landscaping. *Sportsturf, 19*(7), 30.

Australia's Green Olympics. Retrieved May 17, 2004, from http://www.about-australia.com/spgreen.htm

Author. (1992, November). Blowing hot air. *Energy Ideas, 1*(5), 1-7.

Author. (1993, February). It's a small world after all. *Energy Ideas, 1*(8), 6-8.

Author. (1993, March). Sports vs. efficiency (OT). *Energy Ideas, 1*(9), 8-9.

Author. (2003). ASHRAE studies impact of IAC on classroom performance. HVAC/R Industry News. Retrieved from http://www.hvacmall.com/news/article_01180.htm

Author. (2003). CREON2000 disinfection unit studied under NIH grant. HVAC/R Industry News. Retrieved from http://www.hvacmall.com/news/article_01200.htm

Author. (2003). Sanuvox ultraviolet air purifier reduces school district air contaminants by 66%. HVAC/R Industry News. Retrieved from http://www.hvacmall.com/news/article_00973.htm

Australia's Green Olympics. Retrieved on May 17, 2004 from http://www.aboutaustralia.com/spgreen.htm

Aquatics International. (2003). July/August, *The history of aquatics.* Los Angeles, CA: Hanely-Wood, LLC.

Azar, B. (1999). The top ten most common mistakes that retailers make. *Employee Services Management, 42*(3), 37-38.

Baechle, T. R. (Ed.). (1994). *Essentials of strength training and conditioning.* Champaign, IL: Human Kinetics.

Bannon, J. J. (1978). *Leisure resources: Its comprehensive planning.* Englewood Cliffs, NJ: Prentice-Hall.

Barkely, J. T. (1997). Surfacing. A Fitness, Recreational Facility and Parks and Recreation Web Magazine Retrieved from http:www.sandfordgroup.com/.

Beijing Olympics (2008). Retrieved from: http://en.beijing2008.cn

Bennis, W., & Nanus, B. (1997). *Leaders: Strategies for taking charge.* New York: HarperBusiness.

Berry, D. W. (1990). Maryland study shows simple signage works. *Aquatics, 2*(6), 16-20.

Bevan, R. (1956). *The athletic trainer's handbook.* Englewood Cliffs, NJ: Prentice-Hall, Inc.

Bishop, W. (1997). Athletic flooring. Cornerstones: A Fitness Recreational Facility and Parks and Recreation Web Magazine. Retrieved from http://www.sandfordgroup.com/

Boeh, Thomas. (1989). A program for selling. *CAM Magazine, 3*:10, 53-55.

Bower, M. (1980). *Foil fencing* (4th ed.). Dubuque, IA: William C. Brown.

Bowers, L. (1988). Playground design: A scientific approach. In L. D. Bruya (Ed.), *Play spaces for children: A new beginning* (pp. 22-48). Reston, VA: AAHPERD.

Branvold, S. E. (1992). The utilization of fence signage in college baseball. *Sport Marketing Quarterly, 1*:2, 29-32.

Breems, M. (2001). Quality above depends on quality below. *Sportsturf, 17*(12), 10.

Brenner, S. (1999, July). Editorial column. *Team Marketing Report,* 2.

Bridges, F. J., & Roquemore, L. L. (1999). *Management for athletic/sport administration* (2nd ed). Decatur, GA: ESM Books.

Brinnell, Johann. (n.d.). Retrieved from http://www.fwkc.com/.

Broadhag, K. (2006, June). Purchasing used strength equipment. Fitness Management. Retrieved August 18, 2008, from http://fitnessmanagement.com/articles/article.aspx?articielid=1804&zoneid=13

Bronzan, R. T., & Stotlar, D. K. (1992). *Public relations and promotion in sport.* Daphne, AL: United States Sports Academy.

Brown, B. J. (1972). *Complete guide to the prevention and treatment of athletic injuries.* West Nyack, NY: Parker Publishing Company.

Brown, G. (2003, August). Increased retention with entertainment systems. *Fitness Management,* 32-33.

Brown, G. (2007, October). Investing in free weights. *Fitness Management, 23*(10), 48-51.

Brown, M. T. (2003). Risk identification and reduction. In D. J. Cotten, & J. Wolohan, (Eds.), *Law for recreation and sport managers* (3rd ed.) (pp. 308-319). Dubuque, IA: Kendall/Hunt.

Brownell, E. O. (1999). How to keep your service edge. *Employee Services Management, 41*(5), 39-40.

Bruntland, G. (1987). *Our common future: The world commission on environment and development.* Oxford: Oxford University Press.

Bruya, L., & Wood, G. (1997). Why provide supervision on the playgrounds. In S. Hudson, & D. Thompson (Eds.), *Playground safety handbook* (pp. 38-48). Cedar Falls, IA: National Program for Playground Safety.

Bucher, C. A., & Krotee, M. L. (1993). *Management of physical education and sport* (10th ed.). Boston: Mosby Year Book.

Buisman, K., Thompson, A. F., & Cox, A. T. (1993). Risk management. *Athletic Management.* July, 1992. 3,10-16.

Byl, John. (1990). *Organizing successful tournaments.* Champaign, IL: Leisure Press.

Bynum, Marvin. (November 2004). Analyze These. *Athletic Business,* p. 131-134, 136.

Bynum, Marvin. (July 2004). Continental Divide. *Athletic Business,* p. 84-86, 88, 90, 92.

Bynum, M. (2007, September). Outside help. Athletic Business. Retrieved November 2, 2008, from http://athleticbusiness.com/articles/article.aspx?articleid = 1627&zoneid = 39

Civil Rights Act of 1964; 42 U.S.C. §2000e-5–2000e-9.

Clayton, R. D., & Thomas, D.G. (1989). *Professional aquatic management* (2nd ed.). Champaign, IL: Human Kinetics.

Clement, A. (1988). *Law in sport and physical activity.* Indianapolis, IN: Benchmark Press.

Codring v. Board of Education of Manhasset Union Free School Dist., 435 N.Y.S.2nd 52 (App. Div. 1981).

Cohen, A. (1991). Back to the future. *Athletic Business, 15*(7), 31-37.

Cohen, A. (1993). Security check. *Athletic Business, 17*(3), 41-44.

Cohen, A. (1998, September). Beneath the Surface. *Athletic Business,* p.56-58, 60-62, 64, 66.

Cohen, A. (2000, July). Feet First. *Athletic Business,* 47-48, 50, 52, 54-55.

Cohen, A. (2002, May). Reflections. *Athletic Business,* 48-50, 52-55.

Cohen, A. (2002, November). Keeping up appearances. *Athletic Business,* 105-108.

Cohen, A. (2003, April). Out of the box. *Athletic Business,* 71-76, 78.

Cohen, A. (2008, October). Nerves of steel. Athletic Business. Retrieved November 3, 2008, from http://athleticbusiness.com/articles/article.aspx?articleid = 1880&zoneid = 50

Conklin, A. R. (1999). Facility Follies. *Athletic Business, 23*(9), 28-30.

Cooper, Jay. (2004, July). The Changing Face of Sports Surface Selection. Retrieved from http://www.sandfordgroup.com/

Council on Physical Education for Children (COPEC). (2001). *Guidelines for facilities, equipment, and instructional materials in elementary physical education.* Reston, VA: National Association for Sport and Physical Education.

Dahlgren, S. (2000, November). Making the grade. *Athletic Business,* 77-78, 80-82.

Dahlgren, S. (2000, September). LEDing the way. *Athletic Business,* 73-81.

Davidson, P. (2007). It's lights out for traditional bulbs. USA Today (available online): http://www.usatoday.com/money/industries/energy/environment/2007-12-16-light-bulbs_N.htm

Dea, F. (2008, August). An outsourcing checklist. *Associations Now, 4*(9), 35-35. Retrieved November 30, 2008, from SPORTDiscus with Full Text database.

Dethlefs, D. (1991). Multiple cheers. *College Athletic Management, 3*(3), 28-33.

Di Pilla, Steven. (2001, April). Minimizing 'slip & fall.' *Facilities Design and Management,* 48.

Dougherty, N. J., & Bonanno, D. (1985). *Management principles in sport and leisure services.* Minneapolis: Burgess Publishing Company.

Driscoll, Terri. (2000, October). In Goodman, J., (Ed.), *Cushion extends life: Facilities design and management,* p. 54, 56.

Drucker, P. (1993). *Management* (3rd ed.). NY: HarperCollins.

Eickoff-Shemek, J. (2002). Minimizing legal liability: Risk management for health fitness facilities (Part 2) [Videotape] Risk Management for Health/Fitness Programs and Facilities. Standards and Guidelines. Champaign, IL: Human Kinetics.

Ellis and Associates. (2007). *International lifeguard training program* (3rd ed.). Sudbury, MA: Jones & Bartlett.

Ensman, R. G., Jr. (1999). Fun and games: Solving problems with playful brainstorming techniques. *Employee Services Management, 42*(2), 9-10.

ESPN Sports Business. (2004). Retrieved May 5, 2004, from http://espn.go.com/sportsbusiness/s/stadiumnames.html

Evenden, E. S., Strayer, G. D., & Englehardt, N. I. (1938). *Standards for college buildings*. New York City: Teachers College, Columbia University.

Ewing, S. (1999). Music influences consumers to buy. *Employee Services Management, 42*(3), 5-6.

Farmer, P. J., Mulrooney, A. L., & Ammon, Jr., R., (1996). *Sport facility planning and management*. Morgantown, WV: Fitness Information Technology, Inc.

Farmer, P. J., Mulrooney, A. L., & Ammon, R., Jr. (1999). *Sport facility planning and management*. Morgantown, WV: Fitness Information Technology. Inc.

Farrell, P., & Lundegren, H., M. (1978). *The process of recreation programming: Theory and technique*. New York: John Wiley & Sons, Inc.

Fischer, D., & Ozanian, M. (1999, October 20). Cowboy capitalism. *Forbes, 164*, 171-177.

Florida Department Of Health. (2004). Chapter 64E-9.018, *Public Pool Service Technician Certification*. Public Swimming Pools and Bathing Places. State of Florida.

Flynn, R. B. (Ed.). (1985). *Planning facilities for athletics, physical education and recreation* (7th ed.). Reston, VA: American Alliance for Health, Physical Education, Recreation and Dance.

Flynn, Richard B. (1993). *Facility planning for physical education, recreation, and athletics*. Reston, VA: The Facilities Council of the Association for Research, Administration, Professional Councils and Societies.

Ford, R. (2006). *Certified pool operator handbook*. Colorado Springs, CO: National Swimming Pool Foundation.

Forseth, E. A. (1986, Spring). Consideration in planning small college athletic training facilities. *Athletic Training*, 23-25.

Frost, R. B., Lockhart, B. D., & Marshall, S. J. (1988). *Administration of physical education and athletics: Concepts and practices* (2nd ed.). Dubuque, IA: Wm. C. Brown.

Frost, R. B., Lockhart, B. D., & Marshall, S. J. (1988). Administration of Physical Education an dAtletcs: Concepts and Practices (3rd ed.). Dubuque, IA: Wm. C. Brown Company.

Frost, R. B., & Marshall, S. J. (1977). *Administration of physical education and athletics: Concepts and practices* (2nd ed.). Dubuque, IA: Wm. C. Brown Company.

Funk, D. (1997). Economics of professional sports franchises: The role of luxury suites and club seats in the construction of sports stadiums and arenas in North America. Paper presented at the annual conference of the North American Society for Sport Management, San Antonio, TX.

Future trends in fitness equipment. (1997, November). *Joe Weider's Muscle & Fitness*, 26.

Garbarino, E., & Johnson, M. S. (1999). The different roles of satisfaction, trust, and commitment in customer relationships, *Journal of Marketing, 63*(2), 70-87.

Gabrielsen, M. A. (1987). *Swimming pools* (4th ed.). Champaign, IL: Human Kinetics.

Girdano, D. A. (1986) *Occupational health promotion: A practical guide to program development*. New York: Macmillian.

Goodbody, J. (1969). *The Japanese fighting arts*. South Brunswick, NY: A. S. Barnes and Company.

Goodman, Julie. (2000, October). Cushion extends life. *Facilities Design & Management*, 54,56.

Goodstein, L. D., Nolan, T. M., & Pfeiffer, W. J. (1993). *Applied strategic planning: A comprehensive guide*. New York: McGraw-Hill.

Gordon, J. (1990). The suite smell of success. *Skybox, 1*(2), 6-9.

Gorman, J., Calhoun, K., & Rozin, S. (1994). *The name of the game: The business of sports*. New York: John Wiley & Sons, Inc.

Greenwood. Essential of strength training & conditioning. In Strength and Conditioning Professional Standards and Guidelines (pp. 549-566). Retrieved from http://www.ncsa-lift.org/Publications/standards. Shtml

Gunsten, Paul H. (1978). *Tournament scheduling: The easy way.* Winston-Salem, NC: Hunter Textbooks, Inc.

Hamar, Doug. (November 2000). In Dahlgren, S., Making the Grade. *Athletic Business, 77-78,* 80-82, 84.

Hamel, G., & Prahalad, C. K. (1994). *Competing for the future.* Boston: Harvard Business School Press.

Hammel, D. (2003, September). New green building standards are gaining popularity. Recreation Management. Retrieved May 17, 2004, from http://recmanagement.com/issuecontents.php?si = 200309

Harassment cases soar in the nineties. (1999, April 1). *USA Today,* 1.

Hard Questions, Critical Answers. (March 1998). Building Operating Management. Retrieved from http://www.facilitiesnet.com/

Hasenkamp, T., & Lutz, B. (2001, March). The dash for splash. *Athletic Business,* 55-56, 58, 60.

Hasler, A. E., & Bartlett, M. (1995, September). Equipped for exercise. *Athletic Business,* 47-54.

Heidrich, K. W. (1990). *Working with volunteers.* Champaign, IL: Sagamore.

Heistand, M. (1999, May 26). Skyboxes gain mass appeal. *USA Today,* 3C.

Helitzer, M. (1992). *The dream job sports publicity, promotion, and public relations.* Athens, OH: University Sports Press.

Helson, C. M. (1997). Keeping control when outsourcing your store. *Employee Services Management 40*(8), 30-31.

Helson, C. M. (1998). Employee stores keep growing. *Employee Services Management, 41*(3), 11-14.

Hendy, T. (1997). The nuts and bolts of playground maintenance. In S. Hudson, & D. Thompson (Eds.), *Playground safety handbook* (pp. 60-70). Cedar Falls, IA: National Program for Playground Safety.

Heywood, J. B. (2001). *The outsourcing dilemma: The search for competitiveness.* London: Pearson Education Limited.

Hoffman, A. N., & O'Neill, H. M. (1993). *The strategic management casebook and skill builder.* Minneapolis/St. Paul: West.

Holleman, M. A. (1996). Scoring with stadiums. *Athletic Business, 20*(9), 45-49.

Holzrichter, Doug. (2001, January). Gymnasium makeovers. *Athletic Business,* 59-60, 62-65.

Horine, L., & Stotlar, D. (2003). *Administration of physical education and sport* (5th ed.). Dubuque, IA: Wm. C. Brown.

Howard, D. R., & Crompton, J. L. (1995). *Financing sport.* Morgantown, WV: Fitness Information Technology, Inc.

Howard, D., & Crompton, J. (2004). *Financing sport* (2nd. Ed). Morgantown, WV: Fitness Information Technology.

Howe, D. K. (2000, March/April). Nine trends of the 1990s. *American Fitness,* 12-13.

Huddleston, E. (2001, November). The sweet smell of success. *Athletic Business,* p. 63-64, 66, 68, 70.

Hudson, S., Olsen, & Thompson, D. (2004). *Playground safety.* Cedar Falls, IA: University of Northern Iowa.

Hudson, S., Thompson, D., & Olsen, H. (2008). *Planning playgrounds.* National Program for Playground Safety. Cedar Falls, IA.

Hussey, D. E. (1991). *Introducing corporate planning: Guide to strategic management.* New York: Pergamon.

Hutchison, C. (2003). More than sports. *PanStadia International Quarterly Report, 10*(2), 64-67.

Illinois Park & Recreation Association. (1995). *A guide to playground planning.* Winfield, IL.: Author.

Indiana Administrative Code. (2003). 410 IAC 6-2.1, *Swimming and wading pool rule.* Indiana State Department of Health.

Ingersoll, C., & Sawyer, T. (1999). Sports medicine and rehabilitation. In *Facilities planning for physical activity and sport: Guidelines for development* (9th ed.). Dubuque, IA: Kendall-Hunt.

Inter, F. (2007). Mounting concerns. Fall issue, *Waterpark Resorts Today.* Los Angeles, CA: Hanely-Wood, LLC.

International Association of Skateboard Companies. [On-line]. Available: http://www.iasc.com

Jensen, C. R., & Overman, J. O. (2003). *Administration and management of physical education and athletic programs.* Prospect Heights, IL: Waveland Press, Inc.

Jewell, D. (1992). *Public assembly facilities* (2nd ed.). Malabar, FL: Krieger.

John, G., Shear, R., & Vickery, B. (2007). *Stadia: A design and development guide* (4th ed.). Boston, MA: Architectural Press.

Johnson, D. K., & Patterson, D. S. (1997, December). Window and curtain walls: Out with the old? Building Operating Management. Retrieved from http://www.facilitiesnet.com/.

Johnson, R. (1991). All in one. *College Athletic Management, 3*(3), 28-33.

Jones, T. E (1990, April). Choosing Court Colors. *Athletic Business,* 70-71.

Kaiser, R., & Robinson, K. (1999). Risk management. In B. van der Smissen, M. Moiseichik, V. Hartenburg, & L. Twardzik (Eds.), *Management of park and recreation agencies* (pp. 713-741). Ashburn, VA: NRPA.

Kaplan, D. (1998). ABS: A new way to pay. *Sport Business Journal, 1*(1), 3.

Keller, I. A., & Forsyth, C. E. (1984). *Administration of high school athletics.* Englewood Cliffs, NJ: Prentice Hall, Inc.

Kennedy, M. (2000, October). A well-grounded plan. *American School and University: Facilities, Purchasing and Business Administration,* 30, 32, 34.

King, J. M. (2003, November). Cardio machine programming. *Fitness Management,* 34-37.

Klafs, C. E., & Arnheim, D. D. (1973). *Modern principles of athletic training* (3rd ed.) (pp. 33-42). St. Louis, MO.

Kocher, E. (1996, April). Gymnasium facelifts. *Athletic Business,* 39-42.

Kollie, E. (2004). Sports flooring solutions for your athletic facility. *School Planning & Management, 43*(6), 55-61.

Krenson, F. (1988). Crowd-pleasing arena design. *Athletic Business, 12*(9), 66-69.

Kroll, Karen. (2002, December). Steps to selecting the best floor. *Building Operating Management.* Retrieved from http://www.facilitiesnet.com/

Kroll, K. (December 2003). Ceilings—Blocking the talk: acoustics in the workplace. *Building Operating Management.* Retrieved from http//www.facilitiesnet.com/

Kufahl, P. (2004, January). Political push. *Club Industry,* 21-23.

Lavallee, A. R., & Westervelt, S. (2004). Rehab: Asphalt tennis courts. A brief overview of methods and costs. Retrieved October 23, 2004 from http://www.xsports.com/rehab.html

LaVoie, H. (1993). Ancillary Areas. In R. B. Flynn, (Ed.), *Facility planning for physical education, recreation, and athletics* (pp. 147-148). Reston, VA: The Facilities Council of the Association for Research, Administration, Professional Councils and Societies: An Association of the American Alliance for Health, Physical Education, Recreation, and Dance.

Law-Heitzman, B. (1998, Jan./Feb.) A new tool saves lives. Aquatics International, Los Angeles, CA: Hanely-Wood, LLC.

Lewis, G., & Appenzeller, H. (1985). *Successful sport management.* Charlottesville, VA: The Michie Company.

Lewis, W. (1994). Weeding out unwanted growth: Weed problems on athletic fields can be nipped in the bud by implementing a total weed management program. *Athletic Management, 6*(3), 28.

Logan, W., & Petras, H. (1975). *Handbook of the martial arts and self-defense.* New York: Funk and Wagnalls.

Mack, M. G., Hudson, S., & Thompson, D. (1997, June). A descriptive analysis of children's playground injuries in the United States 1990-1994. *Journal of the International Society for Child and Adolescent Injury Prevention, 3,* 100-103.

Maher, J. (2003, June 28). What's in a name? American Statesman. Retrieved May 5, 2004, from http://www.utwatch.org/oldnews/aas_erwin_6_28_03.html

McArthur, S. (1992). Don't throw in the towel. *Athletic Business, 16*(7), 49-50.

McCarron, C. (2001, April). Reuse, recycle, rebuild. *Athletic Business, 25*(4), 55-62.

McDonnell, A., & Tucker-Rhodes, R. (2007, December) 2007 end-of-year review: Equipment. Fitness Management. Retrieved July 28, 2008, from http://fitnessmanagement.com/articles/article.aspx?articleid=2275&zoneid=13

McPherson, D. (2004). Flooring your members. *Fitness Management, 18*(5), 43.

Meagher, J. (1985). Eliminating the negative in sports facility design. *Athletic Business, 9*(1), 32-35.

Minnesota Building Codes and Standards Division. (2001). Printouts: Bleacher seating. Retrieved from http://www.admin.state.mn.us/buildingcodes/printouts/bleachers.html

Molnar, D., & Rutledge, A. (1986). *Anatomy of a park* (2nd ed.). New York: McGraw-Hill.

Moran, B. (1999, June). Mission essential: NIRSA conference highlights recreation's power to recruit and retain. *Recreational Sports & Fitness*, 14-18.

Morehouse, L. E., & Rasch, P. J. (1958). *Scientific basis of athletic training* (pp. 216-224). Philadelphia: W. B. Saunders Company.

Morehouse, L. E., & Rasch, P. J. (1964). *Sports medicine for trainers* (2nd ed.) (pp. 214-223). Philadelphia: W.B. Saunders Company.

Moussatche, H., Languell-Urquhart, J., & Woodson, C. (2000, September). Life cycle costs in education: Operations & maintenance considered. *Facilities Design & Management*, 20, 22.

Mula, R. M. (1998). Employee vendor fairs. *Employee Services Management, 41*(10),31-32.

Mull, R. F., Bayless, K. G., Ross, C. M., & Jamieson, L. M. (1997). *Recreational sport management* (3rd ed). Champaign, IL: Human Kinetics.

National Facilities Conference. (1962). *Planning facilities for health, physical education, and recreation.* Chicago: The Athletic Institute.

National Facilities Conference. (1966). *College and university facility guide.* Washington, DC: The Athletic Institute and the American Association of Health, Physical Education and Recreation.

National Facilities Conference. (1966). *Planning facilities for health, physical education, and recreation.* Chicago: The Athletic Institute and the American Association of Health, Physical Education and Recreation.

Navy Environmental Health Center. (2002). *Indoor Firing Ranges Industrial Hygiene Technical Guide* (Technical Manual NEHC-TM6290.99-10 Rev. 1). Portsmouth, VA: Author.

NCAA Guides. (2004). Indianapolis, IN: National Collegiate Athletic Association.

National Conference of State Legislatures. (2008, February). State laws on heart attacks, cardiac arrest and defibrillators. Retrieved August 25, 2008, from http://www.ncsl.org/programs/health/aed.htm

National Inline Hockey Assocation (USA). [On-line]. Available: http://www.niha.com

NCAA Rule Books for Baseball, Football, Soccer, and Lacrosse. (2000). Indianapolis, IN: National Collegiate Athletic Association.

National Intramural Recreational Sports Association. (2001). *NIRSA aquatic directors handbook.* Corvallis, OR: NIRSA National Center.

National Safety Council. (2008). *First responder: Skills in action.* New York, NY: McGraw Hill.

National Sporting Goods Association (retrieved from the web June 17, 2007) http://www.nsga.org/i4a/pages/index.cfm?pageid = 3346

National Sporting Goods Association. (2008a). 2007-1998 sports with over 15% change in participation. Retrieved November 11, 2008, from http://www.nsga.org/files/public/2007-1998.pdf

National Sporting Goods Association. (2008b). 2007-2003 sports equipment by average price. Retrieved November 11, 2008, from http://www.nsga.org/files/public/averagepricechangein5yearts.pdf

National Swimming Pool Foundation. (1997). *Official swimming pool design compendium* (5th ed.). San Antonio, TX: National Swimming Pool Foundation.

Neville, W. (1994). *Serve it up: Volleyball for life.* Mountain View, CA: Mayfield.

Neuman, D.J. (2003). *Building type basics for college and university facilities.* Hoboken, NJ: John Wiley & Sons.

Noyes, B., & Skolnicki, J. (2001) A modest proposal. *Athletic Business, 24*(8), 51-58.

Olguin, M. A. (1991). Vital marketing. *Fitness Management, 7*:3, 45-47.

Olson, J., Hirsch, E., Breitenbach, O., & Saunders, K. (1987). *Administration of high school and collegiate athletic programs.* Philadelphia: Saunders College Publishing.

Otto, C. (2006, May). Recreational Water-Illness-Prevention = Healthy Swimming. *Journal of Environmental Health*, Volume 68, Number 9.

Paley, N. (1991). *The strategic marketing planner.* New York: AMACOM.

Parkhouse, B. L. (1991) *The management of sport: Its foundation and application.* St. Louis, MO: C. V. Mosby Year Book.

Parkhouse, B. L. (2001). *The management of sport: Its foundation and application* (3rd ed.). Dubuque, IA: McGraw-Hill.

Patton, J. D. (1999, April). Fitness in flux. *Athletic Business*, 51-54.

Patton, R. W., Corry, J. M., Gettman, L. R., & Schovee, G. J. (1986). *Implementing health/fitness programs.* Champaign, IL: Human Kinetics.

Patton, W., Grantham, William C., Gerson, Richard F., & Gettman, L. R. (1989). *Developing and managing health/fitness facilities.* Champaign, IL: Human Kinetics.

Peavey, H. (2008, February). Beyond the Big Three. *Fitness Magazine, 24*(2), 58-59.

Penman, K. A., & Penman, T. M. (1982, September). Training rooms aren't just for colleges. *Athletic Purchasing and Facilities,* 34-37.

Perfetti, R. & Ch'uan, T. C. [On-line]. Available: http://www.maui.net/ ~ táichi4u/overview.html

Peterson, J. A., & Tharrett, S. J. (1997). *ACSM's health/fitness facility standards and guidelines* (2nd ed). Champaign, IL: Human Kinetics.

Peterson, James A. (1991). Ten steps to effective publicity. *Fitness Management,* 7:12, 41.

Peterson, James A. (1991). The power and nature of publicity. *Fitness Management,* 7:12, 39.

Petersen, J. C. (1997). Indoor activity space and ancillary space analysis for New Mexico high schools. Unpublished doctoral dissertation, The University of New Mexico, Albuquerque.

Picozzi-Moran, A., & Brown C. (2006, October). Wireless dedication. Athletic Business. Retrieved Sept 22, 2008, from http://athleticbusiness.com/articles/article.aspx?articleid = 1275&zoneid = 47

Piper, J. (1998, March). Complete performances. Building Operation Management. Retrieved from http:// www.facilitiesnet.com/

Piper, J. (2000, August). Flooring: The real bottom line. Building Operation Management. Retrieved from http://www.facilitiesnet.com/

Piper, J. (2003, December). Flooring for today, tomorrow. Building Operation Management. Retrieved from http://www.facilities.net.com/

Pollar, O. (1997). Effective delegation. *Employee Services Management, 40*(9), 13-16.

Popke, M. (2000, October). Skate nation. *Athletic Business,* 67-74.

Popke, M. (2001, May). Mixing it up. *Athletic Business,* 46-50, 52.

Popke, Michael. (2006, September). Tread Carefully. *Athletic Business,* p.76-80, 82-83.

Popke, Michael. (2007, November). The Fix Is In. *Athletic Business,* p. 56-57.

Popke, M. (2008, March). Competitive spirit. *Athletic Business, 32*(3), 34-44. Retrieved November 30, 2008, from SPORTDiscus with Full Text database.

Popke, M. (2006, May). Scoring opportunities. Athletic Business. Retrieved September 8, 2008, from http://athleticbusiness.com/articles/article.aspx?articleid = 1198&zoneid = 53

Popke, M. (2005, September). High times. Athletic Business. Retrieved September 22, 2008, from http:// athleticbusiness.com/articles/article.aspx?articleid = 1065&zoneid = 50

President Clinton signs cardiac arrest survival act. Retrieved from http://www.padl.org/articles. php3?id = newlegis005

Project Adventure. [On-line]. Available: http://www.pa.org

Prouty, D. (1999). Project Adventure: A brief history. In J. C. Miles & S. Priest (Eds.), Adventure Programming (pp. 93-101). State College, PA: Venture Publishing.

Puhalla, J., Krans, J., & Goatley, M. (2003). *Baseball and softball fields.* Hoboken, NJ: J.W. Wiley, 4.

Raiford, R. (1999, June). Into uncharted territory: Outsourcing redirects the future of business for facilities professionals. *Buildings,* 40-42.

Railey, J. H., & Railey, P. A. (1988). *Managing physical education, fitness and sports programs.* Mountain View, CA: Mayfield.

Railey, Jim H., & Tschauner, Peggy Railey. (1993). *Managing physical education, fitness, and sports programs* (2nd ed.). Mountainview, CA: Mayfield.

Rankin, J., & Ingersoll, C. (1995). *Athletic training management: Concepts and applications.* St. Louis, MO: Mosby.

Rawlinson, K. (1961). *Modern athletic training.* Englewood Cliffs, NJ: Prentice-Hall, Inc.

Ray, R. (1994). *Management strategies in athletic training.* Champaign, IL: Human Kinetics.

Rehabilitation Act of 1973; 29 U.S.C. §791.

Roberts, C. (2000, September). Ceilings: Form, function and ROI. Building Operating Management. Retrieved from http://www.facilitiesnet.com/.

Robledo, R., & Kozen, K. (2008, February). President signs pool-safety law (p. 16). *Aquatics International,* Hanely Wood LLC. Washington, D.C.

Rogers, D. (2000). To the top: Challenge courses for persons with disabilities. *Parks & Recreation*, Vol. 35, 3.

Rohnke, K., Rogers, D., Wall, J., & Tait, C. (2007). *The complete ropes course manual.* Dubuque, IA: Kendall Hunt.

Roth, J. (1974). *Black belt karate.* Rutland, VT. Charles E. Tuttle Company, Inc.

Russell, R. V. (1982). *Planning programs in recreation.* St. Louis: C. V. Mosby.

Russo, F. (2000). Marketing events and services for spectators. In Appenzeller, H., & Lewis, G. (Eds.), *Successful sport management* (2nd ed.) (151-162). Durham, NC: Carolina Academic Press.

Sabo, J. (2001, May). Design and construction of an athletic training facility. *NATA NEWS*, 10-22.

Sagar, H. R. (2007). Tall orders. Athletic Business, September. Retrieved at http://athlethicbusiness.com/articles/.

Sandorti, C. C. (1995). Court cents, *Volleyball Magazine, 6*(8), 114-115, 140.

Sapora, A., & Kenney, H. (1961). *A study of the present status, future needs and recommended standards regarding space used for health, physical education, physical recreation and athletics.* Champaign, IL: Stipes.

Sauers, R. J. (1985, September). Safety built into a flexible design. *Athletic Business*, 62- 63.

Saunders, K. (2001). Rotational field worth taking a look. *Sportsturf, 17*(11), 24.

Schackter, D. (1983). Using advertising to help boost ticket sales. *Athletic Purchasing and Facilities*, 7:8, 38,40,42.

Schmid, S. (1993). Premium coverage. *Athletic Business, 16*(4), 39-42.

Schroeder, C. L. (1999). Staffing your store. *Employee Services Management, 42*(8), 37-39.

Secor, M. R. (1984). Designing athletic training facilities or where do you want the outlets? *Journal of Athletic Training*, 19:5, 19-21.

Shaffer, A. L. (1999). Taking stock. *Club Industry, 15*(7), 49-51.

Shank, M. D. (2002). *Sports marketing: A strategic perspective.* Upper Saddle River, NJ: Prentice Hall.

Shaw, L. G. (1976). *The playground: The child's center learning space* (MH 20743034A1). Gainsville, FL: The Bureau of Research, College of Architecture, University of Florida.

Simers, T. J., & Wharton, D. (1999, October 10). How the game was played. *Los Angeles Times Magazine*, 28-31, 128-131.

Sol, N., & Foster, C., (1992). *ACSM's health/fitness facility standards and guidelines.* Champaign, IL: Human Kinetics.

Sol, N., & Foster C., (1997). *Health/fitness facility standards and guidelines.* American College of Sports Medicine, Champaign, IL: Human Kinetics Books.

Solomon, J. (2002). *An insider's guide to managing sporting events.* Champaign, IL: Human Kinetics.

Solomon, J. D. (2004, April 1). Public wises up, balks at paying for new stadiums. *USA Today*, p. 13A.

Stadiums & Arenas: Club Seat Breakdown. (2003, July 17-23). *Street & Smith's Sport Business Journal*, 10-11.

Staff. (1998). Stadiums: Today's bargaining chips. *Sports Business Journal, 1*(1), 19-36.

Staff. (1996). Scoring with stadiums. *Athletic Business, 20*(9), 51-54.

Staff. (2000). Key facility elements to meet the growing demands of multipurpose arenas. *Athletic Business, 24* (1), 37 - 41.

Staff. (2000). Stretched stadiums: Division I schools expand home venues. *Athletic Business, 24*(9), 44 - 47.

Starfish Aquatics Institute. (2006). *StarGuard, best practices for lifeguards* (3rd ed.). Champaign, IL: Human Kinetics.

Steinbach, P. (2000, April). Stands that deliver. *Athletic Business*, 93-98.

Steinbach, P. (2004, March). Sudden impact. *Athletic Business*, 51-52, 54, 56, 58.

Steinbach, P. (2002, July). Great plane. *Athletic Business*, 79-80, 82, 84, 86.

Steinbach, P. (2002, January). Beauty & brawn. *Athletic Business*, 58-65.

Steinbach, P. (2008a, April). A step further. Athletic Business. Retrieved November 6, 2008, from http://athleticbusiness.com/articles/article.aspx?articleid = 1743&zoneid = 21

Steinbach, P. (2008b, January). Matrix revolution. Athletic Business. Retrieved October 30, 2008, from http://athleticbusiness.com/articles/article.aspx?articleid = 1707&zoneid = 20

Steinbach, P. (2008c, December). Peak interest. Athletic Business. Retrieved November 3, 2008, from http://athleticbusiness.com/articles/article.aspx?articleid = 1929&zoneid = 10

Sternloff, R. E., & Warren, R. (1984). *Park and recreation maintenance management* (2ⁿᵈ ed.). New York: John Wiley and Sons.

Stiehl, J., & Ramsey, T. (2004). *Climbing walls: A complete guide.* Champaign, IL: Human Kinetics.

Stoll, S., & Beller, J. (1989). The professional's guide to teaching aerobics. Englewood Cliffs, NJ: Prentice Hall.

Strand, B. N. (1988). A space analysis of physical education activity areas and ancillary areas in big ten universities. Unpublished doctoral dissertation, University of New Mexico, Albuquerque, NM..

Straus, D. C., & Kirihara, J. (1996). Indoor microbiological garden: A microscopic line separates good and bad IAQ. Retrieved from: http://www.facilitiesnet.com/

Surface America. (2008). Picking the right gymnasium floor. Retrieved from: www.surfaceamerica.com

Tarlow, P. E. (2002). *Event risk management and safety.* New York: John Wiley & Sons.

Thompson, C. (2001, October 6). First-class Reliant Stadium nears completion. Retrieved on May 3, 2004, from http://www.chron.com/cs/CDA/story.hts/sports/fb/nfl/1077737

Thompson, D., & Hudson, S. (1996). *National action plan for the prevention of playground injuries.* Cedar Falls, IA: National Program for Playground Safety.

Thompson, D., Hudson, S., & Olsen, H. (2007). *S.A.F.E. Play Areas: Creation, Renovation, and Maintenance.* Champaign, IL: Human Kinetics.

Tiger Athletics. Retrieved May 5, 2004, from http://gotigersgo.collegesports.com/genrel/042604aaa.html

Trais, R. A. (1973). *The hand is my sword.* Rutland, VT: Charles E. Tuttle Company, Inc.

Trend setting. (1999, February). *Joe Weider's Muscle & Fitness*, 23.

Turner, E. (1994). Vital signs. *Athletic Business, 18*, 65-67.

Uniform Accessibility Standards. Retrieved from http://www.access-board.gov/ufas/ufas-html/ufas.htm#4.1.1

United States Army Corps of Engineers. (1990). *USACE Design Manual for Indoor Firing Ranges* (CEHND 110-1-18). U.S. Army Corps of Engineers Huntsville Division.

USA Archery. Retrieved from: http://usarchery.org

U.S. Department of Justice. (n.d.). Retrieved from February 19, 2001, from http://www.usdoj.gov/crt/ada/enforce.htm

U.S. Department of Justice. (n.d.). Accessible stadiums. Retrieved Nov.18, 2008, from http://www.ada.gov/stadium.pdf

United States Consumer Product Safety Commission. (2001). *Handbook for public playground safety.* Washington, D.C.: Author.

United States Professional Tennis Association, Rules Committee. (1996). Tennis rules. New York: USPTA.

United States Lifesaving Association. (2005). *Guidelines for open water lifeguard agency certification.* USLA Website (Certification Section), USLA.ORG.

United States Tennis Association. Retrieved from http://www.usta.com

United States Volleyball Association, Rules Committee. (1997). Volleyball rules. New York: USVA.

Urban, Peter. (1981). *The karate dojo* (12ᵗʰ ed.). Rutland, VT. Charles E. Tuttle Company, Inc.

Valentine, P. (2003, May). Out in front. *PanStadia International Quarterly, 9*(4).

Van Dalen, D. B., & Bennett, B. L. (1971). *A world history of physical education.* Englewood Cliffs: Prentice-Hall, Inc.

van der Smissen, B. (1990). *Legal liability and risk management for public and private entities: Sport and physical education, leisure services, recreation and parks, camping and adventure activities.* Cincinnati: Anderson.

Veterans Readjustment Assistance Act of 1974.

Viklund, Roy. (1995, July). High-performance floors. *Athletic Business*, 41-47.

Vocational Rehabilitation Act of 1973; amended 1974.

Walker, M. L. (1989). A space analysis of physical education activity and ancillary areas in selected small colleges and universities. Unpublished doctoral dissertation, University of New Mexico, Albuquerque, NM.

Walker, M. L., & Seidler, T. L. (1993). *Sports equipment management.* Boston, MA: Jones and Bartlett.

Walker, M. L., & Stotlar, D. K. (1997). *Sport facility management.* Sudbury, MA: Jones and Bartlett.

Waterman, S. (2003, February), Magic carpet. *PanStadia International Quarterly Report, 9*(3).

Waterman, S. (2003, November). The naming game. *PanStadia International Quarterly Report, 10*(2), 52-57.

Weinberg, A. (2003, March 23). Biggest college sports arena naming deals. Retrieved May 5, 2004, from http://www.forbes.com/2003/03/24/cx_aw_0320ncaa.html

Whalin, G. (1997a). Fourteen questions to ask before you buy a point-of-sale system. *Employee Services Management, 40*(9), 30-31.

Whalin, G. (1997b). Using cutting-edge retail trends in employee stores. *Employee Services Management, 40*(1), 26-27.

Which Dance Floor? (2001). Retrieved from http://www.stagestep.com/

Whitney, T. (1992). A house divided. *Athletic Business, 16*(3), 44-51.

Wikipedia. (2008). List of sports venues with sole naming rights. Retrieved on February 8, 2008 from: http://en.wikipedia.org/wiki/List_of_sports_venues_with_sole_naming_rights#United_States.

Wilbur, R. A. (1999). Teams. . . friend or foe? *Employee Services Management, 42*(5), 9-11.

Wilkinson, H. T. (2002). Topdressing a baseball field. *Sportsturf, 18*(2), 27.

Williams, J. (2005). *Engineering Tribology.* New York, NY: Cambridge University Press.

Wilson, S. (2000). Crowd pleasers. *Athletic Management12:4,* 31-35.

Winderbaum, L. (1977). *The martial arts encyclopedia.* Washington, D.C.: INSCAPE Publishers.

Wolfe, R. (1987). Designing facilities to meet future needs. *Athletic Business, 11* (9), 48-55.

Wolkoff, M. J. (1985). Chasing a dream: The use of tax abatements to spur urban economic development. *Urban Studies, 22,* 305-315.

Wong, G. M. (2001). *Essentials of amateur sports law* (2nd ed.). Dover, MA: Auburn House Publishing Company.

Yeomans, M. (2001, June 16). Heinz' naming rights deal. *Pittsburgh Tribune Review,* p. 1C.

York, R. O. (1982). *Human service planning.* Chapel Hill, NC: The University of North Carolina Press.

YMCA of the USA. (2001). *On the guard II* (4th ed.). Champaign, IL: Human Kinetics.

YMCA of the USA. (2003). *YMCA aquatic management.* Champaign, IL: Human Kinetics.

YMCA of the USA. (2008). *YMCA pool operations manual* (3rd ed.). Human Kinetics, Champaign, IL.

Zimmerman, B. (2008). Indoor climbing gets serious. *Fitness Management.* March issue. Retrieved at www.fitnessmanagement.com

GLOSSARY OF TERMS

Access. A way or means of approaching, entering, getting, using, and so on.

Acoustical Engineer. Individual responsible for the design of large and small spaces that are appropriate for good sound (e.g., being able to hear in any seat in a large arena or aquatic complex, or not damaging to one's ears while playing racquetball).

Acoustical Treatments. Applications designed to control/absorb sound.

Addendum. A written or graphic instrument issued by the architect prior to the execution of the contract that modifies or interprets the bidding documents by additions, deletions, clarifications, or corrections. An addendum becomes part of the contract documents when the contract is executed.

Advertising Rights. Rights sold to various entities who wish to advertise to the spectators within the sports facility.

Aesthetics. A branch of philosophy dealing with the nature, creation, and appreciation of beauty.

Aggregate. Any hard material (usually sand and rock) for mixing in graduated fragments with a cementing material to form concrete, plaster, and the like.

Alternate Bid. The amount stated in the bid to be added to or deducted from the amount of the base bid if the corresponding change in the work, as described in the bidding documents, is accepted.

Ancillary Areas. Areas that provide support functions for the primary building attractions.

Angle of Reflection. The angle between the reflected ray and the normal or perpendicular to the point of reflection.

Angle of Refraction. The angle between the refracted ray and the normal or perpendicular drawn to the point of refraction.

Annunciator. An electronically controlled signal board that indicates to the building control center which courts/areas are occupied at any time.

Application for Payment. A contractor-certified request for payment of amount due for completed portions of the work and, if the contract so provides, for materials or equipment delivered and suitably stored pending their incorporation into the work.

Appraisal Survey. A method of evaluating the existing community resources, programs, and services in accordance with some established standards or criteria.

Architect. Designation reserved, usually by law, for a person or organization professionally qualified and duly licensed to perform architectural services, including, but necessarily limited to, analysis of project requirements; creation and development of the project design; preparation of drawings, specifications and bidding requirements; and general administration of the construction contract.

Architectural Barriers. Obstacles that prevent parties from entering a facility or any architectural restraint that hampers moving throughout a building.

Area-Elastic Surfaces. Allow for dispersion of impact, where a bouncing object, or an individual jumping, is felt approximately 20 inches around the point of impact.

Area of Deflection. The amount of impact that is felt in the vicinity of the points of contact.

Asphalt. A brown or black solid bituminous substance obtained largely as a residue from certain petroleum and which is insoluble in water. It is used in paving, roofing, and paints and varnishes, and in combination with other materials for floor tiles.

Asset-Backed Securities. Investments secured by expected revenue.

Attractive Nuisance. It is a doctrine that holds if a person creates a condition on his or her premises that may reasonably be construed to be the source of danger to children, he or she must take precautions as a reasonably prudent person would take to prevent injury to children of tender ages whom he or she knows to be accustomed to frequent the area.

Baffles. A mounting or partition used to check the transmission of sound waves.

Base Bid Specifications. The specifications listing or description of those materials, equipment, and methods of construction upon which the bid must be predicated, exclusive of any alternate bids.

Base Bid Sum. The amount of money stated in the bid as the sum for which the bidder offers to perform the work described in the bidding documents, prior to adjustments for alternate bids which are also submitted.

Bearing (Azimuth). A direction stated on compass degrees.

Bequests and Trusts. Agreements made with specific individuals that upon their deaths a certain amount of their estates will be given to the organization.

Berm (or Dike). A narrow shelf, path, or ledge, as along the top of a scarp or along a road.

Bid. A complete and properly signed proposal to do work or designated portion thereof for the amount or amounts stipulated in the proposal and submitted in accordance with the bidding documents

Bid Bond. A form of bid security executed by the bidder and by a surety to guarantee that the bidder will enter into a contract within a specified time and furnish any required performance bond and labor and material payment bond.

Bidder. A person or entity who submits a bid, generally one who submits a bid for a prime contract with the owner, as distinct from a sub-bidder, who submits a bid to a prime bidder. Technically, a bidder is not a contractor on a specified project until a contract exists between the bidder and the owner.

Bidding Documents. The bidding documents include an invitation to bid, instructions to bidders, the bid form, other bidding and contracting forms, and contract documents, including any addenda issued prior to receipt of bids.

Bid Form. A form furnished to a bidder to be completed, signed, and submitted as the bidder's bid.

Bid Opening. The opening and tabulation of bids submitted within the prescribed bid time and in conformity with the prescribed procedures.

Bid Price. The amount stated in the bid for which the bidder offers to perform the work.

Bond. An interest-bearing certificate issued by a government or corporation, promising to pay interest and to repay a sum of money (the principle) at a specified date in the future.

Bond Period. Most government projects and some larger projects require the contractor to post not only a performance bond, but a one-year (or some other specified time) warranty on the quality of the work.

Brightness. The luminous intensity created by direct emission of light from a source by transmission through a translucent medium or by reflection from a surface. The unit of brightness is the foot-lambert.

Brightness Balance. Specified limitations of brightness differences and brightness ratios within the visual fields which, if observed, will contribute toward visual comfort and good visual performance.

Brightness Contrast. The relationship between the brightness of an object and its immediate background.

Brightness Difference. The difference in brightness among the various reflecting surfaces and light sources within the total visual field as measured in foot-lamberts.

Brightness Ratio. The ratio of two brightnesses in the field of view.

British Thermal Unit. The quantity of heat (252 calories) required to raise the temperature of one pound of water one degree Fahrenheit at or near its point of maximum density (62 to 63 percent).

Broken-Back Track. Track configuration that features a more square track with short straightaways and rounded ends made of double curves.

Builder's Risk Insurance. A specialized form of property insurance that provides for loss or damage to the work during the course of construction.

Building Permit. A permit issued by appropriate governmental authority allowing construction of a project in accordance with approved drawings and specifications.

Bulletin. A document issued by the architect after the contract is awarded. It may include drawings and other information used to solicit a proposal for change in the work. A bulletin becomes part of the contract documents only after being incorporated in a change order. A bulletin may also be referred to as a request for a change.

Bulkhead. An upright partition separating two parts in protection against fire or leakage; as a wall or embankment holding back earth, fire, or water.

Candlepower. The luminous intensity or illuminating capacity of a standard candle, as of a lamp measured in candles.

Cash Allowance. An amount established in the contract documents for inclusion in the contract sum to cover cost of prescribed items not specified in detail, with provision that variations between the established amount and the final amount of the prescribed items will be reflected in change orders.

Cash Discount. The amount that can be deducted from a seller invoice for payment within a stipulated period of time.

Cash Donation. Donation of cash to an organization for a general or specific use in return for a personal tax deduction.

Casing. The act or process of encasing a frame, as of a window or a door.

Caulking. To fill in the seams or cracks with a filler.

Certificate of Insurance. A document issued by an authorized representative of an insurance company stating the types, amounts, and effective dates of insurance in force for a designated insured.

Certificate of Substantial Completion. A certificate prepared by the architect on the basis of an inspection stating that the work or a designated portion of the work is substantially complete as of a particular date. This establishes the date of substantial completion with respect to the responsibilities of the owner and the contractor for security maintenance, heat, utilities, damage to the work, and insurance.

Certificates of Participation. Involves a governmental entity buying a facility. The government entity then leases portions of the facility to the general public.

Certification of Occupancy. A document issued by a governmental authority certifying that all or a designated portion of a building complies with the provisions of applicable statutes and regulations, and permitting occupancy for its designated use.

Chair Rail. An encircling band on the walls around the room at chair height to protect walls from damage by chairs contacting them.

Chamfer. The surface formed by cutting away the angle formed by two faces of timber, stone, or metal; to furrow; to channel; to flute; to bevel.

Change Order. A written order to the contractor signed by the owner and the architect, issued after the execution of the contract, authorizing a change in the work or an adjustment in the contract sum or the contract time. The contract sum and contract time may only be changed by a change order. A change order signed by the contractor indicates the contractor agreement therewith, including the adjustment in the contract sum or the contract time.

Changes in the Work. The changes ordered by the owner within the general scope of the contract, consisting of additions, deletions, or other revisions, which result in the contract sum and the contract time being adjusted accordingly. All such changes in the work shall be authorized by a change order, and shall be performed under the applicable conditions of the contract documents.

Checkpoint. An obvious feature shown on the map that helps orienteers determine their progress along the course.

Chlorinate. To combine chlorine with water for purification.

Circuit Breaker. A device that automatically interrupts the flow of an electric current.

Civil Engineer. Individual who is responsible for the following tasks: grading and land movement plans, geometric layout of new improvements, plans for new roads and street pavements, utility plans, and plans for water collection system and sanitary sewers.

Code. It is a legal requirement legislated by federal, state, and/or local government describing legally how a building must be built, including electrical, mechanical, and structural. In many jurisdictions, they are generically titled building codes.

Comprehensive General Liability Insurance. A broad form of liability insurance covering claims for bodily injury and property damage, which combines under one policy coverage for all liability exposures (except those specifically excluded) on a blanket basis and automatically covers new and unknown hazards that may develop. Comprehensive general liability insurance automatically includes contractual liability coverage for certain types of contracts.

Concession. Authority, granted under contract with mutually acceptable provisions by all parties concerned, given by recreation departments to operators permitting them to provide services and/or to sell commodities to patrons of recreation areas and facilities.

Concessionaire Exclusivity. The sale of the exclusive rights for all concessions within a spectator facility for a specified number of dollars over a specified period of time.

Condemnation. To pass an adverse judgment on; disapprove of strongly; censure; to prove guilty of wrong-doing; to declare unfit for service or use; to condemn private property for public use, the processes by which government exercises its rights of eminent domain.

Condenser. That which makes dense, concentrates, or compresses.

Convector. A medium of convection; the transmission of heat or electricity by the mass movement of the heated or electrified particles, such as air, gas, or liquid currents.

Construction Document Phase. This phase is based on the design development phase. The architect prepares final drawings and construction specifications.

Construction Phase. The final phase is the construction phase. The architect shall 1) visit the site at least twice monthly at appropriate intervals at various stages of construction, 2) certify payments for work completed, 3) have the authority to reject work that does not conform to the contract documents, and 4) review.

Contingency Allowance. A sum included in the project budget that is designated to cover unpredictable or unforeseen items of work, or changes in the work subsequently required by the owner.

Contract. A legally enforceable promise or agreement between two or among several persons.

Contract Award. A communication from an owner accepting a bid or negotiated proposal. An award creates legal obligation between the parties.

Contractor's Liability Insurance. Insurance purchased and maintained by the contractor to protect the contractor from specified claims that may arise out of or result from the contractor operations under the contract, whether such operations are by the contractor or by any subcontractor or by anyone directly or indirectly employed by any of them, or by anyone for whose acts any of them may be liable.

Contract Sum. The sum stated in the owner-contractor agreement, which is the total amount payable by the owner to the contractor for the performance of the work under the contract documents. The contract sum may be adjusted only by a change order.

Control. One of several events to be visited by the orienteer.

Control Card. A card carried by orienteers used to verify that the competitor visited the control.

Control Description (Clue Card). A sheet or card with a brief description of the control location, control number, and other clues for locating controls. The International Orienteering Federation control symbols are the internationally recognized symbols for orienteering.

Control Marker. A distinct marker that identifies the control, usually a three-dimensional orange and white nylon marker.

Control Punch. A small clipper used to make a distinctive mark on the control card to verify visiting the control.

Cost Plus Fee Agreement. An agreement under which the contractor (in an owner-contractor agreement) is reimbursed for the direct and indirect costs or performance of the agreement and, in addition, is paid a fee for services. The fee is usually stated as a stipulated sum or as a percentage of cost.

Critical Path Method (CPM). A charting of all events and operations to be encountered in completing a given process, rendered in a form permitting determination of the relative significance of each event, and establishing the optimum sequence and duration of operations.

Crowned Field. A curved field with the summit or highest point (crown) at the middle, running lengthwise. (A football field is crowned for the purpose of drainage.)

Dado. A term applied to the lower portion of walls when decorated separately.

Date of Agreement. The date stated in the agreement. If no date is stated, it could be the date on which the agreement is actually signed, if this is recorded, or it may be the date established by the award.

Date of Substantial Completion. The date certified by the architect when the work or a designated portion thereof is sufficiently complete, in accordance with the contract documents, so the owner can occupy the work or designated portion thereof for the use for which it is intended.

Decibel. The unit for measuring the relative loudness of sounds (as compared with the loudness of a sound that can just be heard by the ear).

Deck. A platform or floor, like a ship's deck or a swimming-pool deck.

Deduction. The amount deducted from the contract sum by a change order.

Deductive Alternate. An alternate bid resulting in a deduction from the base bid of the same bidder.

Desiccant. A substance that absorbs humidity.

Design. The architectural form, pattern, or scheme of construction of health, physical education, or recreation areas, facilities, and their units.

Design-Build Process. A process in which a person or entity assumes responsibility under a single contract for both the design and construction of the project.

Design Development Phase. This phase is based on the results of the schematic design phase. The architect prepares, during this phase, drawings including floor plans, mechanical and electrical systems, and structural design; outline of materials to be used; landscape designs; parking lot designs; and other such documents as may be appropriate.

Dewpoint. The temperature at which moisture will condense out of the air.

Diatomaceous. Containing or consisting of diatoms or their fossils (a number of related microscopic algae, one-celled or in colonies, whose walls consist of two parts or valves and contain silica).

Discomfort Glare. Glare that produces discomfort; it does not necessarily interfere with visual performance or visibility.

District. The district is a large geographical planning unit of a large city, comprising a number of communities.

Drainage. Surface and subsurface removal of water and groundwater. When properly designed, surface and subsurface irrigation eliminates standing water and relieves saturated turf. Further, it will maintain the proper amount of subsurface moisture.

Drawings. Graphic and pictorial documents showing the design, location, and dimensions of the elements of a project. Drawings generally include plans, elevations, sections, details, schedules, and diagrams. When capitalized, the term refers to the graphic and pictorial portions of the contract documents.

Easement. A right or privilege that a person may have on another's land, as the right-of-way.

Eaves. The lower part of a roof projecting beyond the face of the wall.

Economy. Costs are kept at a minimum compatible with program needs, durability of materials, low maintenance, and attractiveness.

Egress. A way out to grade level around a building.

Electrical Contractor. The individual who will provide all electrical wiring, boxes, switches, receptacles, equipment hook-ups, conduit for all telephone wires, computer cable, television cable, security wiring, and public address system.

Elevation. A geometrical projection on a plane perpendicular to the horizon; an elevated place; the distance above or below the zero level or ground level.

Eligible Individuals. Those individuals who have a physical or mental impairment that substantially limits a major life activity.

Eminent Domain. The legal right of federal, state, and local governments to take any property required for public purpose. The right implies that the land must be taken by due process of law, and that the owner from whom the land is taken receives reasonable compensation.

Environment. The aggregate of all the external conditions, surroundings, and influences affecting the place or individual.

Equal Quadrant Track. This type of track configuration features two 100-meter straightaways and two 100-meter curves.

Equipment. Movable furnishings as opposed to stationary property; relatively permanent articles, furnishings, machinery, and devices used in administering, operating, and maintaining recreation programs and services.

Escutcheon. A shield or plate as around a keyhole.

Estimate. A forecast of construction cost, as opposed to a firm bid, prepared by a contractor for a project or a portion thereof. A term sometimes used to denote a contractor application or request for a progress payment.

Estimate of Construction Cost, Detailed. A forecast of construction cost prepared on the basis of a detailed analysis of material and labor for all items of work, as contrasted with an estimate based on current area, volume, or similar unit costs.

Extra. A term sometimes used to denote an item of work involving additional cost.

Facade. The face or elevation of a building.

Facilities. Areas, structures, and fixtures essential to accommodate the program.

Fee. A term used to denote compensation for professional ability, capability, and availability or organization, excluding compensation for direct, indirect, and/or reimbursable expenses, as an agreement based on a professional fee plus expenses. Sometimes denotes compensation of any kind for services rendered.

Field House. A facility providing enclosed and unobstructed space adaptable to various physical education and recreation activities, services, demonstrations, and meetings. It is often located on, or near, a playfield or athletic field. The term also refers to a service building used by people using the athletic field.

Fixed Limit of Construction Cost. The maximum construction cost established in the agreement between the owner and the architect.

Fixed Turning Radius, Wheel to Wheel. The tracking of the caster wheels and large wheels of a wheelchair when pivoting on a spot.

Fixture. Something firmly attached, as a part or an appendage, such as a light fixture; equipment affixed to the surface of a building in such a manner that its removal would deface or mar the surface. (Legally, it is the property of the building.)

Flashing. Sheets of metal or other material used to waterproof joints and cages, especially of a roof.

Fluid Mechanics. The study of the flow properties of liquids and gases.

Flush. Unbroken or even in surface; on a level with the adjacent surfaces; having no indentation.

Fluting. The vertical channeling on the shaft of a column.

Foot-Candle. The illumination at a point on a surface that is one foot from and perpendicular to a uniform point source of one candela (candle); a lighting term used to denote quantity.

Foot-Lambert. A unit of brightness of a surface or of a light source. One foot-lambert equals one lumen per square foot. Candelas (candles) per square inch is an optional term for a unit of brightness of a light source. One candela (candle) per square inch equals 452 foot-lamberts.

Foot-Pound. A unit of energy equal to the amount of energy required to raise a weight of one pound a distance of one foot.

Force Account. A term used when work is ordered, often under urgent circumstances, to be performed without prior agreement as to lump sum or unit price cost thereof and is to be billed at the cost of labor, materials and equipment, insurance, taxes, and so forth, plus an agreed percentage for overhead and profit.

Foreseeability. The reasonable anticipation that harm or injury is a likely result from certain acts or omissions.

Fulcrum. The support or point of support on which a lever rotates.

Fullers Earth. A clay-like, earthy substance used as a filter medium.

Function. Measuring satisfaction of purpose, where function is the particular purpose for which a person or thing is specifically fitted or used or for which a thing exists.

Furring. The leveling of a floor, wall, or ceiling, or the creating of air spaces with thin strips of wood or metal before adding boards or plaster; the act of trimming or lining.

Gable. The triangular portion of a wall, between the enclosing lines of a sloping roof.

Gallery. A communicating passage or wide corridor for pictures and statues; upper story for seats.

General Conditions. That part of the contract documents that sets forth many of the rights, responsibilities, and relationships of the parties involved, particularly those provisions that are common to many construction projects.

General Contractor. Individual responsible for constructing and finishing floors, walls, ceilings, steel structure, built-in cabinets, sidewalks, driveways, doorways, windows, and other things not completed by the electrical and mechanical contractors.

General Obligation Bonds. A full-faith and credit obligation bond. Refers to bonds that are repaid with a portion of the general property tax.

Glare. The sensation produced by brightnesses within the visual field that are sufficiently greater than the brightness to which the eyes are adapted to cause annoyance, discomfort, or loss in visual performance and visibility.

Glaze. Any impervious material produced by fire used to cover the body of a tile to prevent absorption of liquids and gases, to resist abrasion and impact, or to give a more pleasing appearance.

Glazed Tile. A hard, dense tile that has been glazed to prevent absorption, to increase its beauty, or to improve ease of cleaning.

Gradient. The grade or rate of ascent or descent; a rate of increase or decrease of a variable magnitude, or the curve that represents it.

Grid. A framework of parallel bars; a grating.

Groundskeeping. The management and maintenance of the outdoor spaces, including landscaped grounds and play spaces.

Guaranteed Maximum Cost. The sum established in an agreement between owner and contractor as the maximum cost of performing specified work on the basis of cost of labor and materials plus overhead expenses and profit.

Guidelines. An indication or outline of policy or conduct.

Gutter. A trough or channel along or under the eaves of a roof to carry off rainwater; also around the upper edge of a swimming pool.

Gymnasium. A building or part of a building devoted primarily to group activities, such as basketball, gymnastics, volleyball, and dancing. It is equipped with gymnastic apparatus, a court area for playing athletic and game activities, dressing-room facilities, and seating arrangements for spectators.

Gymtorium. A combination facility designed to be used as a gymnasium or auditorium. Other combination facilities are cafetoriums (cafeteria and auditorium) and gymnateria (gymnasium and cafeteria).

Header. A wooden beam placed between two long beams with the ends of the short beams resting against it.

Hose Bibb. A faucet with the nozzle bent downward and threaded for hose connections.

Humidity. Moisture content of the air expressed in percentage of maximum.

Hydrology. Refers to the study of the patterns of water flow above and below the surface.

Inclusion (Designing for). A concept that supports full facility and full program access to all people.

Indirect Expense. Overhead expenses (e.g., general office expense) indirectly incurred and not directly related to a specific project.

Indirect Lighting. The act of reflecting light off the ceiling to create a clean and pleasant form of light arrangement in an indoor space.

Indoor Air Quality. A product of the quality of the fresh air introduced into the ventilation system and the quality of the existing indoor air that is recycled.

In-Kind Contribution. An organization, business, or craftsman donates equipment or time to the project in return for a tax deduction.

Instructions to Bidders. Instructions contained in the bidding documents for preparing and submitting bids for a construction project or designated portion thereof.

Integral. The result of integrating parts into a whole; necessary for completeness; essential; whole or complete.

Integration. Functional interrelationship, the process of making whole.

Interior Designer. This individual will assist in selecting paint colors, wallpaper, rugs (color, texture/thickness), furniture, accessories, artwork, and other items to make spaces comfortable, functional, and aesthetically pleasing.

Invitation to Bid. A portion of the bidding documents soliciting bids for a construction project.

Invited Bidders. The bidders selected by the owner, after consultation with the architect, as the only ones from whom bids will be received.

IP Telephony. The use of an IP network to transmit voice, video, and data.

Irrigation. Surface and subsurface supplemental watering. When properly designed, surface and subsurface irrigation provides an even distribution of water for plants and turfgrass.

Jam. A side post of a doorway, window frame, fireplace, and the like.

Join. A place or part where two things or parts are joined together.

Joint Ventures. A joint venture is a project with multiple parties involved in its planning and operation.

Labor and Material Payment Bond. A bond of the contractor in which a surety guarantees to the owner that the contractor will pay for labor and material used in the performance of the contract.

The claimants under the bond are defined as those having direct contracts with the contractor or any subcontractor.

Landmark. An easily recognized, obvious feature in the landscape.

Landscape Architect. Individual who provides information such as specifications and designs for landscaping a building or green area, types of trees to be planted, types of flowers to be planted, number of walkways, specifications and designs for the irrigation system, and types of grass to be planted or sod to be installed.

Landscape Architecture. The art or science of arranging land, together with spaces and objects upon it, for safe, efficient, healthful, pleasant human use.

Latent Heat. The heat liberated or absorbed by a substance as it changes phase at a constant temperature and pressure.

Lease Agreements. A program to lease facilities to other organizations during the off-season or additional spaces within the facility not used for the sporting activity, such as office space or retail space.

Legend. A section of a map that provides an interpretation of map symbols.

Letter of Agreement. A letter stating the terms of an agreement between addressor and addressee, usually prepared to be signed by the addressee to indicate acceptance of those terms as legally binding.

Letter of Intent. A letter signifying an intention to enter into a formal agreement, usually setting forth the general terms of such agreement.

Liability. The responsibility of one who is bound in law and justice to do something that may be forced by action; a condition that gives rise to an obligation to do a particular thing to be enforced by court action; a responsibility between parties that the courts recognize and enforce; an unintentional breach of legal duty causing reasonably foreseeable damage.

Liability Insurance. Insurance that protects the insured against liability on account of injury to the person or property of another.

Life Insurance Packages. A program to solicit the proceeds from a life insurance policy purchased by a supporter to specifically benefit the organization upon the death of the supporter.

License. A formal permission to do something; a document indicating certain permission; freedom to deviate from strict conduct, rule, or practice; generally may be permitted by common consent.

Light. Visible radiation, generally considered to be the electromagnetic radiations of wave lengths between 380 and 780 millimicrons, which are the violet and red ends of the visible spectrum, respectively.

Lintel. The horizontal timber or stone that spans an opening, as over doors or windows.

Louver. An aperture or frame with louver boards fitted in a slatted panel for ventilation.

Low Bid. A bid stating the lowest bid price for performance of the work, including selected alternates, conforming with bidding documents.

Lowest Responsible Bidder. A bidder who submits the lowest bona fide bid and is considered by the owner and the architect to be fully responsible and qualified to perform the work for which the bid is submitted.

Lumen. A unit of measure for the flow of light.

Luminaries. Floodlight fixtures with a lamp, reflector, and so on.

Luxury Suites. These areas have been designed for VIP use and leased by large corporations to wine and dine their clients as well as to provide them entertainment.

Magnetic Lines. Lines on an orienteering map pointing toward magnetic north.

Master Map. Large orienteering map near the start line that shows the course and controls.

Mechanical Contractor. Individual who is responsible for all plumbing (hot and cold water, sewage), humidity control, heating and cooling systems, ventilation systems, and pumps.

Mechanical/Electrical Engineer. The individual who provides such information as: specifications for heating and air conditioning equipment, drawings and specification for power and lighting, determinations of plumbing requirements, and the design of any communication system (e.g., security, public address, music, closed-circuit television, etc.).

Mechanic Lien. A lien on real property created by statute in all states in favor of persons supplying labor or material for a building or structure for the value of labor or material supplied by them. In some jurisdictions, a mechanic lien also exists for the value of professional services. Clear title to the property cannot be obtained until the claim for the labor, materials, or professional services is settled.

Modification. This is a written amendment to the contract signed by both parties. It is a change order. It is a written interpretation issued by the architect. Finally, it could be a written order for a minor change in the work issued by the architect.

Mullion. A slender, vertical dividing bar between the lights and windows, screens, and so forth.

Municipal Bonds. Bonds issued by a government or a subdivision of a state.

Named Insured. Any person, firm or corporation, or any of its members specifically designated by name as insured(s) in a policy, as distinguished from others who, although unnamed, are protected under some circumstances.

Naming Rights. Corporations vie for the right to place their name on the facility for a specific sum of money for a specific number of years.

Negligence. The omission of that care which a person of common prudence usually takes of his or her own concerns.

Negotiating Phase. Phase in which the architect assists the owner in obtaining bids or negotiating proposals and assists in awarding and preparing contracts for construction.

Nonconforming Work. Work that does not fulfill the requirements of the contract documents.

Non-Equal Quadrant Track. This track configuration resembles a stretched or compressed oval shape with two straightaways of one length and two curves of another length.

Non-Guaranteed Bonds. These bonds are sold on the basis of repayment from other designated revenue sources.

Nonslip. Having the tread so constructed as to reduce skidding or slipping.

Nonslip Tile. Incorporates certain admixtures such as abrasive granules in the body or in the surface of the tile.

NorCompass (Thumb Compass). An orienteering compass that attaches to the left thumb of the orienteer.

Opaque. Does not transmit light; substances that will not allow light through.

Open Space. A relatively underdeveloped area provided within or near urban development to minimize feelings of congested living.

Optimal Thermal Environment. Provides conditions that make it possible to dissipate body heat in the most effortless manner. Combines radiant temperature where surface and air temperature are balanced; air temperature between 64° and 72° F, humidity between 40 and 60%; and, a constant air movement of 20 to 40 linear feet/minute at a sitting height.

Orienteer. A person who participates in the sport of orienteering.

Outrigger. Any temporary support extending out from the main structure.

Owner-Architect Agreement. Contract between owner and architect for professional services.

Owner-Contractor Agreement. Contract between owner and contractor for performance of the work for construction of the project or portion thereof.

Owner's Representative. The person designated as the official representative of the owner in connection with a project.

Park. An area permanently dedicated to recreation use and generally characterized by its natural, historic, and landscape features. It is used for both passive and active forms of recreation and may be designed to serve the residents of a neighborhood, community, state, region, or nation.

Park District. A subdivision of state government exercising within its jurisdiction the authority of a municipality. It may operate and maintain parks, recreation programs, police forces, airports, and other such facilities and programs as may be designated in the act establishing the district.

Parking Fees. Fees generated from parking lots that surround the spectator facility.

Park-School. An area cooperatively planned by school and municipal authorities to provide programs of education and recreation for day-by-day use by the people of a neighborhood or community.

Parkway. Essentially an elongated park with a road running through it, the use of which is restricted to pleasure traffic. The parkway often serves to connect large units in a park system and is rarely found except in large cities.

Performance Bond. A bond of the contractor in which a surety guarantees to the owner that the work will be performed in accordance with the contract documents. Except where prohibited by statute, the performance bond is frequently combined with the labor and material payment bond.

Permeable. That which can be permeated; open to passage or penetration, especially by fluids.

PERT Schedule. An acronym for project evaluation review technique. The PERT schedules the activities and events anticipated in a work process.

Pilaster. A rectangular feature in the shape of a pillar, but projecting only one-sixth of its breadth from a wall.

Plan. A two-dimensional graphic representation of the design, location, and dimensions of the project, or parts thereof, seen in a horizontal plan viewed from above.

Playfield. A recreation area designed to serve the needs of a community or neighborhood having a population of 10,000 to 15,000 persons. Its essential features are a community recreation building, areas for sports and games, a playground for children, picnic areas, public parking, and, occasionally, a swimming area.

Point Elastic Surfaces. Maintain impact effects at the immediate point of contact on the floor, with the ball, object, or individual.

Point-to-Point Orienteering. A type of orienteering where controls must be visited in a specific order and speed in completing the course determines the winner.

Post Sleeves. Metal pipe, installed at ground level or slightly below, which receives posts to facilitate various activities.

Preconstruction Conference. A meeting between the contracting agency and the contractor(s) prior to the commencement of construction to review the contract items and make sure there is an understanding of how the job is to be undertaken.

Preferred/Premium Seating. VIP seating located within the luxury suites or in the club areas of the stadium that are the most expensive seats in the facility.

Prequalification of Bidders. The process of investigating the qualification of prospective bidders on the basis of their experience, availability, and capability for the contemplated project and approving qualified bidders.

Prime Contract. Contract between owner and contractor for construction of the project or portion thereof.

Progress Payment. Partial payment made during progress of the work on account of work completed and/or material suitably stored.

Project. The total construction of which the work performed under the contract documents may be the whole or a part, or it could also include the total furniture, furnishings, and equipment.

Project Cost. Total cost of the project including construction, professional compensation, real estate, furnishings, equipment, and financing.

Property Damage Insurance. Insurance coverage for the insured's legal liability for claims for injury to or destruction of tangible property, including loss of use resulting therefrom, but usually not including coverage for injury to or destruction of property which is in the care, custody, and control of the insured.

Property Insurance. Coverage for loss or damage to the work at the site caused by perils of fire, lightning, extended coverage perils, vandalism, and malicious mischief and additional perils. Property insurance may be written on 1) the completed value form in which the policy is written at the start of a project in a predetermined amount representing the insurable value of the work and adjusted to the final insurable cost on completion of the work, or 2) the reporting form in which the property values fluctuate during the policy term, requiring monthly statements showing the increase in value of work in place over the previous month.

Public Accommodations. A facility operated by a private entity, whose operations affect commerce. The private entity that owns, leases or leases to, or operates a place of public accommodation.

Public Liability Insurance. Insurance covering liability of the insured for negligent acts resulting in bodily injury, disease, or death of persons other than employees of the insured, and/or property damage.

Rabbet. A groove or cut made in the edge of a board in such a way that another piece may be fitted in to form a point.

Ramps, Ramps With Gradients. Because the term "ramp" has a multitude of meanings and uses, its use in this text is clearly defined as ramps with gradients (or ramps with slopes) that deviate from what would otherwise be considered the normal level. An exterior ramp, as distinguished from a "walk," would be considered an appendage to a building leading to a level above or below existing ground level. As such, a ramp shall meet certain requirements similar to those imposed upon stairs.

Ray. A single line of light coming from a luminous point.

Readily Achievable. Easily accomplishable and able to be carried out without much difficulty or expense. It constitutes a lower standard than undue burden.

Reasonable Accommodations. Requires that employers and facilities make an accommodation if doing so will not impose an undue hardship on the operation of the business or facility.

Record Drawings. Construction drawings revised to show significant changes made during the construction process, usually based on marked-up prints, drawings, and other data furnished by the contractor to the architect.

Reflectance (Reflection Factor). The percentage of light falling on a surface that is reflected by that surface.

Reflected Glare. Glare resulting from specular reflections of high brightness in polished or glossy surfaces in the field of view. It usually is associated with reflections from within a visual task or areas in close proximity to the region being viewed.

Reflection Factor. The percentage of light reflected by a given surface.

Refrigerants. Any of the various liquids that vaporize at a low temperature, used in mechanical refrigeration.

Regulations. An order issued by an executive authority of a government and having the force of law.

Reimbursable Expenses. The amounts expended for or on account of the project which, in accordance with the terms of the appropriate agreement, are to be reimbursed by the owner.

Release of Lien. An instrument executed by a person or entity supplying labor, material, or professional services on a project that releases that person or entity for a mechanic lien against the project property.

Resident Engineer. An engineer employed by the owner to represent the owner interests at the project site during the construction phase.

Resilience. The ability to bounce or spring back into shape, position, and so forth.

Restaurant Rights. The sale of the exclusive rights for all the restaurants within a spectator facility.

Retainage. A sum withheld from progress payments to the contractor in accordance with the terms of the owner-contractor agreement.

Revenue Bonds. A bond that can be backed exclusively by the revenue occurring from the project or from a designated revenue source, such as a hotel/motel tax, restaurant tax, auto rental tax, or a combination of these taxes and others.

Reverberation. Reflection of light or sound waves.

Riser. The vertical distance (and pieces) between the steps in a stairway.

Rolling Load. The capacity of a floor to withstand damage from external forces, such as bleacher movement, equipment transport, or similar activities.

Safety Direction (Panic Azimuth; Safety Bearing). A compass bearing or direction to guide the orienteer directly to a road, major trail, or settlement if lost or injured.

Schedule of Values. A statement furnished by the contractor to the architect reflecting the portions of the contract sum allocated to the various portions of the work and used as the basis for reviewing the contractor applications for payment.

Schematic Design Phase. This phase is based on the program developed by the project committee and submitted to the architect. The architect will prepare, for approval by the owner, schematic design documents, including drawings (floor plans and mechanicals), scale model, project development schedule, and estimated costs.

Score Orienteering. A type of orienteering where controls blanket the course, and each is assigned a point value based on the distance to the controls and how difficult they will be to find. The individual or team with the most points in the prescribed time is the winner.

Service Building. A structure affording the facilities necessary to accommodate the people using recreation facilities such as a golf course, swimming pool, or ice-skating rink. It may contain dressing rooms, lockers, toilets, shower rooms, check and storage rooms, a lobby or lounge, and a repair shop. Also, the term is used in reference to buildings that facilitate the operation and maintenance of the recreation system, such as greenhouses, storage buildings, and garages.

Shadow. The space from which light from a given source is excluded by an opaque object; the area of comparative darkness resulting from the interception of light by an opaque object.

Sheathing. The inner covering of boards or waterproof material on the roof or outside wall of a frame house.

Shelter House. A building, usually located on a playground or playfield, equipped with such features as an office for the director, space for storage, toilets, and a craft or play room.

Shop Drawings. Drawings, diagrams, schedules, and other specific data specially prepared for the work by the contractor or any subcontractor, manufacturer, supplier, or distributor to illustrate some portion of the work.

Sill. A heavy horizontal timber or line of masonry supporting a wall; a horizontal piece forming the bottom frame of a door or window.

Site Analysis. The gathering of information and data about a site and adjacent properties. Its purpose is to find a place for a particular use or find a use for a particular place.

Ski Orienteering. Orienteering conducted on cross-country skis.

Sleeper. A piece of timber, stone, or steel, on or near the ground to support some superstructure.

Soft Space. Space in a facility that requires little or no special provisions (such as plumbing or expensive finishes), and therefore is space that is easily vacated and converted.

Special Authority Bonds. These bonds have been used to finance stadiums or arenas by special public authorities, which are entities with public powers that are able to operate outside normal constraints placed on governments.

Specifications. A part of the contract documents contained in the project manual consisting of written requirements for material, equipment, construction systems, standards, and workmanship.

Sponsorship Packages. Corporate support programs pursued whereby large local and international firms are solicited to supply goods and services to a sporting organization at no cost or at a substantial reduction in the wholesale prices in return for visibility for the corporation.

Staggered. Arranged so that alternate intervals are used, as to space or time.

Stanchion. An upright bar, beam, or post used as a support; one of a pair of linked, upright bars.

Standards. Norms established by authority, research, custom, or general consent to be used as criteria and guides in establishing and evaluating programs, leadership, areas, facilities, and plans; as measures of quantity, quality, weight, extent, or value.

Stile. A vertical piece in a panel or frame, as a door or window; a set of steps used in climbing over a fence or wall.

Stipulated Sum Agreement. A contract in which a specific amount is set forth as the total payment for performance of the contract.

Structural Engineer. Individual concerned with determining possible structural systems and materials, providing cost of preferred systems and materials, and designing final structure to meet architectural requirements.

Sub-Bidder. A person or entity who submits a bid to a bidder for material or labor for a portion of the work at the site.

Subcontract. An agreement between a prime contractor and a subcontractor for a portion of the work at the site.

Subcontractor. A person or entity who has a direct contract with the contractor to perform any of the work at the site.

Successful Bidder. The bidder chosen by the owner for the award of a construction contract.

Superintendent. The contractor representative at the site who is responsible for continuous field supervision, coordination, completion of the work and, unless another person is designated in writing by the contractor to the owner and the architect, for prevention of accidents.

Supplementary Conditions. A part of the contract documents that supplements and may also modify, change, add to, or delete from provisions of the general conditions.

Supplementary Lighting. Providing additional lighting on such areas as those containing goals and targets.

Supplier. A person or entity who supplies material or equipment for the work, including that fabricated to a special design, but who does not perform labor at the site.

Survey. A cooperative undertaking that applies scientific methods to the study and treatment of current recreation data, problems, and conditions. The limits of a survey are prescribed before execution, and its facts, findings, conclusions, and recommendations are made common knowledge and provide a base for intelligent, coordinated action.

Synthetic. Artificial; not real or genuine; a substance produced by chemical synthesis.

Tanbark. Any bark containing tannin (used to tan hides) and, after the tannin has been extracted, it is used to cover tracks, circus rings, and dirt floors in field houses.

Template. A short piece placed in a wall under a beam to distribute the pressure; also a beam spanning a doorway, or the like, and supporting joists.

Terra Cotta. Clayware having the surface coated with fine slip or glaze; used in the facing of large buildings for relief ornament or statues.

Terrazzo. A type of flooring made of small chips of marble set irregularly in cement and polished.

Thermodynamics. The branch of physics dealing with the transformation of heat to and from other forms of energy, and with the laws governing such conversions of energy.

Thermostat. An apparatus for regulating temperature, especially one that automatically controls a heating unit.

Threshold. A piece of wood, stone, metal, or the like placed beneath a door; doorsill; the entrance or beginning point of something; the point at which a stimulus is just strong enough to be perceived or produce a response, as the threshold of pain.

Topographical Map. A precise map that designates altitude of the land with contour lines.

Topography. Refers to the surface features of a site including variations in elevation.

Trade (Craft). An occupation requiring manual skill or members of a trade organized into a collective body.

Trade Shows. Expositions that generate sales for a particular industry.

Trail Orienteering (Control Choice). A modified type of orienteering designed for orienteers with disabilities.

Translucent. Transmitting light, but scattering it so that details cannot be distinguished through the translucent medium.

Transparent. Allowing light to pass through so that objects behind can be seen distinctly.

Underpinning. A supporting structure of the foundation, especially one placed beneath a wall.

Undue Hardship. Requiring significant difficulty or expense, considering the employer size, financial resources, and the nature and structure of the operation.

Unglazed Tile. A hard, dense tile of homogenous composition deriving color and texture from the materials of which it is made.

Unit Price. The amount stated in the bid as a price per unit of measurement for materials or services as described in the bidding documents or in the proposed contract documents.

Utility. The degree to which an area, facility, or instrument is designed to serve its purpose, and degree to which it is used; percent of usage during the workday adapted or available for general use or utility.

Vendor/Contractor Equity. Vendor or contractor returns to the owner a specific percentage of the profit generated by the firms during the construction process.

Vestibule. A passage hall or chamber between the outer door and the interior of a building.

Vetting. Checking the orienteering course before competition.

Vinyl Tile. Asphalt tile impregnated with vinyl.

Visual Task. Conventionally, designates those details and objects that must be seen for the performance of a given activity, and includes the immediate background of the details or objects.

Vitreous. Of, pertaining to, or derived from glass; like glass, as in color, brittleness, and luster.

Wainscot. A wood lining or paneling on the lower part of the walls of a room.

Waiver of Lien. An instrument by which a person or organization who has or may have a right of mechanic lien against the property of another relinquishes such right.

Walk-Off Area. The first 12 feet on the inside of an entry doorway that functions exactly as the name implies; it is within this radius that dust, dirt, oil from the parking area, and water from rain and melting snow are deposited.

Walkway. Because the terms "walk" and "walks" have a multitude of meanings and uses, their use in this text is clearly defined as a predetermined, prepared surface; exterior pathway leading to or from a building or facility, or from one exterior area to another, placed on the existing ground level and not deviating from the level of the existing ground immediately adjacent.

Warranty. Legally enforceable assurance of quality or performance of a product or work of the duration of satisfactory performance.

Weephole. To permit or let drops of water or other liquid exude from inner containers, from such sources as condensation or overflow.

Wilderness. A rather large, generally inaccessible area left in its natural state available for recreation experiences. It is void of development, except for those trails, sites, and similar conditions made by previous wilderness users. (No mechanical transportation permitted).

Workers' Compensation Insurance. Insurance covering the liability of an employer for compensation and other benefits required by workers' compensation laws with respect to injury, sickness, diseases, or death arising from their employment.

Zone Heating. To mark off or divide building areas for the purposes of area climate control.

Architectural Drawings

Axonometric Projection. A drawing where the angles can vary depending on the needs of the person drawing it. Axonometric projections tend to offer a view from higher up, and thus are especially helpful in showcasing building interiors with the ceiling pulled away, allowing rooms to be shown within the context of the entire building plan.

CAD Drawings. Computer-aided design has quickly become a staple of building design, as it allows the creation and manipulation of two- and three-dimensional representations of a building. A plan drawn from an eye-level view can be "entered" by the viewer, with perspective automatically maintained by the computer as the client performs the "walk-through." Additionally, the point of view can be changed, allowing architects and clients to immediately see how their designs translate into actual future use.

Cutaway. Similar to an axonometric projection and shows the building from an oblique angle. Where it differs is in its representation of both interior and exterior building elements.

Elevation. A two-dimensional view of a building's external face drawn on a vertical plane; typically, four elevations will be used to show the building from each of four compass points.

Floor Plan. A drawn-to-scale overhead view of each floor looking down from an imaginary plan cut three to four feet above the floor. The plans show circulation paths and recreational and support paths as well as doorways, window openings, furniture, and counters. Elements located above the plane of the cut are usually shown using dashed lines (e.g., suspended running tracks, balconies, overhead cabinets).

Isometric Projection. Drawings drawn with a 30-60-90 triangle, so the subject is always in proportion.

Reflected Ceiling Plan. Ceilings are detailed on a specific drawing type called the reflected ceiling plan, which is a drawing using a similar cut as the floor plan but higher up the wall looking up and down.

Rendering. A perspective or elevation drawing, showing building materials, colors, shadows, textures, and natural features of the site.

Section. Similar to a floor plan, except that its imaginary cut is vertical, not horizontal. It is therefore most frequently used to detail arena bowls and stadium grandstands.

Site plan. An aerial view of the entire project site including the facility, parking lots, pedestrian ways, conceptual landscaping ideas, and other site amenities.

Structural Elements

Building Walls. Often used to bear loads. However, building walls do not always serve to bear the weight of higher elements. For example, in post-and-beam construction vertical elements (columns or posts) support horizontal beams or lintels, which are beams that bridge an opening such as a door or window.

Cantilevers. A beam that is supported only at one end by means of downward force behind a fulcrum to eliminate obstructed-view seats but forces stadium decks to be stacked farther from the field, in order to provide support for the extended portion of the beam. Cantilevered beams are also used extensively in the construction of staircases and balconies.

Ceiling. The underside of a roof.

Ceiling Plenum. The space between a false ceiling and a structured ceiling.

Clerestories. (Clearstories) are traditionally walls containing windows that are vertically above a low roof line and topped with the uppermost rooftop.

Coffered ceiling. This type of ceiling utilizes sunken square or polygonal ornamental panels.

Colonnade. A colonnade is a series of regularly spaced columns.

Columns, Stanchions (Upright Structural Members), Load-Bearing Walls. Typically building floors and roofs are supported by columns, stanchions, and load-bearing walls.

Coping. Similar to an eave with a similar purpose, although the term is used liberally to represent a variety of treatments that cover the top of a wall.

Curtain Wall. Exterior cladding used as a non-load-bearing wall.

Demi-columns. Half-columns that are half sunk into walls.

Eave. An overhanging portion of a roof to keep rain from running down exterior walls. An eave is sometimes called a soffit.

Engaged columns. A wall that encases a column or part of a column.

Fascia. The horizontal band that joins the roof to the eave.

Fenestration. It refers to the arrangement, proportioning, and design of all openings, including windows, doors, and skylights.

Frame Construction. In frame construction, the weight is borne by the framework encased within a facing or cladding of light material.

Inflatable Structures. A class of tensile structure supported by difference in pressure between the air inside and the air outside. Air is pumped in using fans, with air escape prevented by the use of airlocks at entrances. Inflatable structures enjoy applications from big-league stadiums to practice football fields to tennis courts, both temporary and permanent.

Long-Span Spaces. Long-span spaces or large-volume spaces are column-free spaces used for arenas, field houses, and ice rinks because of the open height required to accommodate sport-specific activities, as well as vertical height for spectator seating.

Parapets. A low wall projection located at the edge of a building's roofline.

Pilasters. A pilaster projects only slightly from walls.

Skylights. Glass structures set into the ceilings to let in light.

Soffit. The underside of any architectural element, including balcony overhangs, and staircases. It also refers to the inner curve of an arch, which is a curved means of spanning an opening, used in place of a lintel.

Span. The horizontal distance between the supports of an upper floor or roof.

Spine. A building spine is the backbone of a building's floor plan. Most often the main circulation pathway in an arena or recreation center.

Suspended Ceilings. A false ceiling suspended below a structured ceiling.

Tensile and Membrane Structures. Flexible systems made of thin, coated fabrics supported by a series of masts and stabilized by cables. These structure are often used as roofs over stadium spectator areas and as domes over stadiums and arenas.

Truss. A rigid frame composed of a series of triangular metal or wooden members that is often used to support flat roofs over long-span spaces. Trusses also support horizontal members in pitched-roof construction, such as purlins, which in turn support rafters, the sloping members that support the roof covering. Rafters are joined together at the apex of a pitched roof.

Vault. An arched ceiling.

Material Elements

Bricks. Bricks are made of fired or sun-baked clay, allow architects to make aesthetic statements by selecting a certain color or by specifying more than one color and setting them in various patterns, sometimes interspersed with concrete blocks and stones.

Brick Veneer. Sliced brick pieces affixed with mortar to a concrete load-bearing wall. It is also known as face brick or finish brick.

Concrete. A combination of cement, sand, water, and various sizes of stone. It is used for foundations, structural beams, floors, walls, sidewalks, parking areas, and many other applications. *Note.* Structurally, concrete is notable for its high compression capability and for its poor tension characteristics.

Concrete blocks. Concrete masonry units (CMU) can be worked to different textures similar to rustication. Most common textures are split-faced and ground-faced.

Gunite. A popular swimming-pool shell material consisting of cement, sand, and water that is sprayed onto a mold.

Masonry. This refers to work with brick and stone, offers many aesthetic options, both in the variety of colors and textures of natural materials and in the different ways these materials are cut.
Ashlar masonry—hewn blocks of stone, wrought to even faces and square edges, and laid in horizontal courses (tiers) with vertical joints.
Quarry-faced masonry—stones left in their quarry state and not made even and square.
Polygonal masonry—masonry utilizing blocks having irregular shaped faces.

Mortar. Similar to concrete, except it does not have stones. It is used to bind bricks and concrete blocks together, to fill interior spaces of concrete-block walls and in some forms, as a ceiling coating.

Reinforced Concrete. This type of concrete has rebar (steel reinforcing bars) added to give the concrete slab or beam the ability to withstand tensile stresses. The rebar in reinforced concrete can be put into tension in the factory (e.g., prestressed or pre-tensioned concrete pre-cast) or on-site (post-tensioned concrete or cast-in-place or tilt-up panels).

Rustication. This is a technique used to lend more texture to exterior surfaces, involves the use of large blocks separated by deep mortar joints.
Banded rustication—only the horizontal joints are emphasized.
Smooth or chamfered rustication—smooth faces separated by beveled joints.

Shotcrete. This material is similar to gunite, except it contains stones.

Stucco. This is a plaster made of gypsum (hydrous calcium sulfate), sand, water, and slaked lime.

Terrazzo. This is a floor surface made of cement mortar and marble chips, which after hardening is ground and polished.

Tile. There are three types of tile: ceramic tile (glazed fired clay), quarry tile (unglazed semivitreous tile extruded from shale or natural clay), and composite tile (vinyl).

Who Does What?

Aquatic Design Engineers (Pool Consultants). Persons who design swimming pools and natatorium spaces.

Architectural Designer. This person works with architects and engineers during the initial concept/schematic design phases to integrate building systems (mechanical, electrical, plumbing, and structural) into the building concept.

Building Systems. Building systems include electrical, mechanical, plumbing, and structural aspects of a building.

Construction Manager. S/he supervises all contractors and works with the entire design team to ensure that the project can realistically be built within the allocated budget. Further, this person is charged with keeping costs down and ensuring the project stays on schedule.

Consultants. Specialists in a specific field employed to assist the architectural team in developing a facility, such as: acoustic (sound and sound barriers), audiovisual, ice rink, and lighting.

Interior Architect. This is a licensed architect specializing in interior space design.

Interior Decorator. This is a specialist in accessories and color schemes for upholstery.

Interior Designer. This is a specialist in space planning, interior casework, furniture, interior finishes, and furnishings.

Landscape Architect. This is an architect specializing in vehicular and pedestrian circulation as well as foliage and site grading.

Land Use Planner. This person recommends the best spot for a facility and develops site design documents for master plans, and analyzes a site's location and related physical constraints.

Project Architect. This person converts concept, schematic designs into construction documents and coordinates the site, architectural, specialty, and engineering disciplines.

Project Engineer. Working with the project architect, the project engineer integrates the building systems with the design.

Project Executive (Principal-in-Charge). This person provides professionals to complete work in a timely manner and should be contacted regarding legal or staffing questions. He or she may be a licensed architect, engineer, or planner.

Project Manager. This person directs all of the personnel assigned to the project, including designers, architects, engineers, and consultants. He or she is heavily involved during the feasibility study phase and manages ongoing financial tasks such as budgets and schedules. The project manager hosts regular project meetings, reviews design details from a cost and buildability perspective, seeks participation of the design team, provides ongoing feedback to the design team, works with the design team to resolve design issues, and ensures that the contract documents become an integral part of the comprehensive design and construction process. Finally, the project manager is a facilitator and mediator.

Design and Construction Overview

Change Orders. Change orders are formal documents ordering changes in the construction plans. These changes originate from any of the following requested by owner, site conditions, fire marshal, building inspector, contractor, document omission, or document error.

Construction/Project Management Contracts. Advantages—provides for effective communication, elimination of the general contractor, efficient use of joint expertise in all phases of work, construction may begin early in process, work can be bid sequentially, thus allowing for company expenditures, and high cost of extras potentially reduced; Disadvantages—success of project depends to a great extent on skill of project manager, conflict in control of design and building process, total financial commitment unknown until end of project, procedures result in extra fees to design team, and process necessitates mutual respect of all involved.

Design/Build (Turnkey) Contracts. Advantages—total cost commitment known in advance, very competitive process, builder responsible for all errors, little administration work required by client, the proposal is a single package, and time frames can be dramatically compressed; Disadvantages—builder is in control of all project actions, unless client produces detailed list of requirements, little control over product and process, power of design team reduced as working for builder, liability issues become cloudy as design team, and quality of end product can be compromised.

Engineering Systems. Structural—clear span demands, wall projections/pilasters, and internal environmental effects; Mechanical—verification of environmental conditions, air conditioning requirements, detect impact on structural, electrical systems, noise generation, and review of operating costs; Electrical—lighting levels, direct, indirect, verification of ceiling heights, and determination of specialized electrical systems.

Master Plan. General site master planning—primary objectives, site characteristics (sun, wind, topographic), massing of facilities, functional characteristics, access and transportation characteristics, connection to services and utilities, and zoning; Building specific master planning—primary objective, priorities of development, phasing requirements, and interface with feasibility study.

Needs Analysis. The needs analysis consists of technical audit, physical inspection, history and tradition of organization and community, building systems, quality of building finishes, disability access, user requirements, program requirements, safety issues, security issues, and health issues.

Project Cost. The project cost is equal to construction cost + soft costs. Typical construction costs include enclosed building, landscape/sitework, demolition, utility service, fixed equipment, furniture, fixtures, equipment, and art/graphics. Typical soft costs include architect/engineer fees, building permits, testing and inspection fees, special consultants, sewer connection fees, maintenance endowment, parking replacement fund, construction financing, legal fees, in-house administration, other finance fees, and contingency.

Project Team - Design Phase. A project team consists of the following professionals: owner, fund-raiser, zoning consultant, legal counsel, surveyor, soils engineer, environmental consultant, special consultants (e.g., programmer, master planner, interior designer, aquatic consultant, acoustic consultant, theater consultant, graphic designer), architect, structural engineer, mechanical engineer, plumbing engineer, civil engineer, estimator, landscape engineer, interior designer, interior decorator, construction manager, and contractors.

Punch List. A list of items that needs to be completed before the project is complete, including aesthetics, quality of construction/finish, code requirements, levels and plumbness, structural deflections, engineering systems, building systems, and maintenance requirements.

Schedule/Budget/Contingency. This includes identifying total project schedule-design period, bidding phase, contract award, and construction; identifying total project budget-planning and design costs, administration costs, furniture and equipment costs, building costs, and site and utilities costs; and contingencies.

Site influences. The following are the most common site influences during the planning phase: adjacent properties, boundaries of sites, relationships to adjoining streets and roadways, existing trees and vegetation, orientation, wind, sun, shadow and microclimatic control, adjacent building heights, pedestrian and vehicular flow on-site and off-site, utilities and services (water, gas, electricity, sewer, telephone), soils, subsoils, water table, contours, and topography.

Stipulated Sum Contracts. Advantages—architect in close contact with client, time-tested traditional contract, sequential phasing of design, bidding and construction, best price at time of tender, capital commitment known at time of bid; Disadvantages—sequential process, thus time frame longer, creation of powerful adversary with the general contractor, and changes are expensive and time consuming.

INDEX

A
ABA (Architectural Barriers Act), 40
academic classrooms, laboratories, 508–512
access
    allowing locker room traffic flow, 81–82
    designing for control, 20–21
    to playgrounds, 210
accessibility standards
    See also Americans With Disabilities Act (ADA)
    accessible buildings, 39–47
    aquatic facilities, 190
    associations pertinent to planning for, 493
    bleachers, 180
    challenge courses, 278–279
    playgrounds, 201–202, 204–205
    signage, 98
    spectator seating, 411–412
    strength and cardiovascular training facilities (SCF), 253
    walking trails, 230
accidents
    injuries in common sports (table), 283
    from winter sports, 287–288
acoustic ceiling panels, 25
acoustics
    in auditoriums, 222
    dance spaces, 515
    indoor facilities for physical education, 324–325
    and sound considerations, 57–58
    squash courts, 154–155
ACSM (American College of Sports Medicine), 432
ADA. See Americans With Disabilities Act (ADA)
administration
    area checklist, 460
    offices, 87
adventure programming facilities, 265–280
advertising, bidding for construction contracts, 16–17
AEDs (automated external defibrillators), 192, 416–417
aerobic training equipment, 257–258, 412–416
aerobics rooms, 57, 119
aesthetics
    landscape design, 122
    parking lot design, 133–134
air
    leakage through buildings, 67–68
    purification systems, 62–63
air quality, 27, 37–38, 61, 197-198
air-conditioning equipment, 60
air-handling systems, 60
air-supported structures, 401–402
alarms, 59, 71
American Academy of Orthopaedic Surgeons, 366
American Alliance for Health, Physical Education, Recreation and Dance (AAHPERD), 420–421
American Association for Health and Physical Education (AAHPE), 420

American Association For Health, Physical Education and Recreation (AAHPER), 420–426
American Association for Physical Activity and Recreation (AAPAR), 422
American Association for the Advancement of Physical Education (AAAPE), 420
American College of Sports Medicine (ACSM), 432
American National Standards Institute. See ANSI
American Physical Education Association (APEA), 420
American Society for Testing and Materials. See ASTM
American Society of Heating, Refrigerating and Air-Conditioning Engineers (ASHRAE) air quality standards, 62–63
American work styles of (table), 85
Americans With Disabilities Act (ADA)
    accessibility standards, 39–47, 40–41
    aquatic facilities, 192
    playground standards, 203–204
    signage guidelines, 98
    spectator seating, 411–412
    tennis court requirements, 139
    toilet requirements. See Americans With Disabilities Act (ADA)
    wet facilities and dry areas, 80
Americans With Disabilities Act Accessibility Guidelines (ADAAG), 40, 41
ammonia (refrigerant), 295
amphitheaters, 238
ancillary areas
    See also laundry, locker rooms, storage
    generally, 73–75
    specialization in, 94–96
Anderson, William Gilbert, 420
animal-baiting areas, 237
ANSI (American National Standards Institute)
    accessibility standards, 40–41
    organization, standards described, 427–429
aquatic centers (natatoriums), 226
aquatic facilities
    aquatic design and operation concerns, 199–201
    emergency management design considerations, 194–198
    history and trends, 187–188
    legal considerations, 192–193
    lighting, 55
    planning, 188–189
    planning checklist, 457–458
    pool design supervision issues, 198–199
    pool temperature, 190–191
    types and components, 189–192
    waterfronts (in camps), 296–302
archery ranges, 235, 239, 378–383
architectural firms, selecting, 12
architectural signage, 100
Architectural and Transportation Barriers Compliance Board (ATBCB) Access Board, 40–42
Architectural Barriers Act (ABA), 39

area-elastic sport flooring, 106–108
arenas
See also stadiums
equipment trends for, 410–414
funding, 389–397
horse, 360
LED screens, video boards, 409–410
multi-use design, 393–395
naming rights, 390–393
art centers, 226
artificial waterfronts, 298–300
arts and craft rooms, 224
ASHRAE standards (samples), 497–498
Asset Lifecycle Model for Total Cost of Ownership Management, 34
Association for Experiential Education (AEE), 280
Association for the Advancement of Physical Education (AAPE), 420
associations. See organizations, or specific association
ASTM (American Society for Testing and Materials)
building sustainability standards, 34
organization described, 427
playground standards, 203, 206, 215–216
standards of, 429–431
wall padding specifications, 22
athletic facilities
See also specific facility type
ancillary area design, 95
athletic fields
design standards for, 476–481
lining, 130
athletic training facilities
equipment, 369–371
examples of, 371–376
generally, 363–369
audio communications systems, 58–59
auditorium stages, 224
audits, energy, 66
Austin Peay State University athletic training facility, 371–372
automated external defibrillators (AEDs), 194, 416–417
automation systems, building, 70–71
AZ-50 (refrigerant), 295

B
back offices, 86
backstops in baseball fields, 171, 174
badminton courts, 146, 449
Bank, Theodore, ix, 422
barns, horse, 355
baseball fields
design standards for layouts, 483–484
designing, 167–172
specification guide, 438
topdressing, 128
basketball
area in recreation centers, 223
court design, 21–22, 146–147
court surfaces, 106
specification guide, 439
batting cages, 171–172
Bermuda grass, 126
bicycle
facilities, pathways in parks, 232–233
parking, 133
biological contaminants, 63
biomechanics (kinesiology) laboratories, 510, 512
biometric identification, 20
bird feeding stations, 238
Blair, Herbert, 419
bleachers
See also spectator seating
designing, 175–181

locating safely, 23
trends in, 411–412
boat ramps, 234–235
boating, 295
bocce ball courts, 233–234
bodyweight exercise equipment, 258–261
boilers, 60
box offices, 518
boxing facilities, 345–350
branding in locker rooms, 90
bridle paths, 233
brightness (illumination), 51–53
Building for Environmental Economic Sustainability (BEES), 34
building materials, and safety, 24–25
buildings
See also specific building type
automation systems, 70–71
codes. See codes, standards
envelope, energy management, 67–70
operation and maintenance, 67–70
and playgrounds, 211–212
sustainable operations, 27–38
bullet traps, 384–385
bullpens, 172
Butch, Matthew, 129
Butler, George, 419

C
cable domes, 403–404
Cable Microcell Integrators (CMIs), 59–60
calcium chloride (coolant), 292
campfire rings, 235
camping areas, 239
camps
campgrounds, 295–296
waterfronts, 296–302
campus recreational sports centers, 241–246
canoeing, 295
carbon reduction, 27
card readers for access control, 20–21
cardio equipment, 412–416, 457
cargo nets, 328
carpool/vanpool programs, 133
Carrier Dome (Syracuse, NY), 401–402
casting, 295
CCTV (Closed Circuit Television) systems, 26
ceilings
additional considerations, 117–120
athletic training facilities, 368
designing, 105–106, 114–115
indoor facilities for physical education, 324
martial arts facilities, 353–354
planning checklist, 465
safe materials, 25
secondary school gyms, 333
squash courts, 154
strength and cardiovascular training facilities (SCF), 252, 254
CEN (European Committee for Standardization), 433
certification
building programs, 31
future developments, 424
track facilities, 319
challenge course adventures, 273–280
change orders, 17
Chase Field (Phoenix), 397
checklists
air quality, 64
challenge courses, 278–279
existing facility assessment and future planning, 461
flooring surface selection, 111–114
outdoor, indoor spaces, 455–460

planning sports fields, 173–174
strength and cardiovascular training facility design, 250–253
strength training equipment, 263
Chemical Hazards Act, 129–130
chemicals
for aquatic facilities, 197
contaminants, 27, 63
handling safely, 129–130
circulation control, 21
civil rights, legislation for the disabled, 40–44
classrooms
designing, 342
and equipment, 508–512
climate control, 464
climbing towers, 239, 270
climbing walls, 265, 266–273, 328, 417–418
Closed Circuit Television (CCTV) systems, 26
CMI (Cable Microcell Integrator) systems, 59–60
coasting, tobogganing, 292
Coates, Edward, ix, 423
codes
See also regulations, standards
bleacher construction, 176–181
compliance with fire, safety, health, 26
communication, electronic, 58
community areas in recreation centers, 225
community centers, 221–223
community gardens, 238-239
community involvement in parks planning, 219–220
comprehensibility, readability of signs, 98–99
computer classrooms/laboratories, 511
computer entertainment systems, 415–416
computer rooms, 225
computer-regulated access control, 20
concession areas, 164–165, 334
condenser cooling tower systems, 61
conference rooms, 88–90
construction
approaches, phases, 16–18
documents, 14–16
double-wall, 58
sustainable, 27–38
contaminants, physical, chemical, biological, 27, 63
contracts, awarding construction, 17
controls
building automation systems, 70–71
lighting, 56
costs
equipment generally, 407–408
green building, 32–35
indoor tennis courts, 142
initial, vs. life-cycle, 66
life cycle, 467
naming rights for arenas, stadiums (table), 391–392
Council on Facilities and Equipment (CFE), xv, 423–426
counseling rooms, 340, 342
CPSC. See U.S. Consumer Product Safety Commission (CPSC)
croquet courts, 158–159
cross-country skiing, 289–290
culverts, 124
curling, 235
custodial complexes, 501–503

D
DakotaDome (Vermillion, SD), 401
Dalcher, Steven, 187
Dallas Cowboys New Stadium, 398
dance spaces, 25, 513–521
day camps, 295–296
Dedmon Center (Radford, VA), 401, 402
design

facility master plans, 4–16
standards. See standards
sustainable, 27–38
universal and accessible, 39–47
design teams, 12
development laboratories, 510–511, 512
DIN (wood athletic floors) standards, 106–107, 147, 468
disabled persons
See also accessibility, Americans With Disabilities Act (ADA)
civil rights legislation for, 40–44
eliminating architectural barriers, 219
discus, 312–313, 315, 445
distance education classroom system features, 508–509
diving boards, 187, 447
diving wells, 187
documents
construction, 14–16
playground maintenance, inspections, 215–216
dog parks, 234
domestic hot water, 61, 69
doors and access control, 20–21
double-wall construction, 58
drainage
baseball, softball fields, 167–168
landscape, 123–126
playgrounds, 209
sand volleyball courts, 150
slanting courts, 147
sports fields, 164, 173
drawings, working and as-built, 14–15, 18
dressing rooms, school physical education facilities, 328
drinking fountains
accessibility standards, 47
along trails, 230
martial arts facilities, 353
in playlots/miniparks, 229
in recreation centers, 221
driver education areas, facilities, 342–344
dryers, washers, 92–94
drying areas for showers, 79–80
dugouts, 23

E
Eastern Kentucky University athletic training facility, 372–376
Economic Calculator for Assemblies, 34–35
education
See also specific building or room type
campus recreational sports centers, 239–246
and recreation areas in parks, 234–239
EEOC (U.S. Equal Employment Opportunity Commission), 41–43
electrical management, 49–57, 464–465
electronic card readers for access control, 20–21
electronic timing systems, 59
elementary schools, physical education facilities, 328–332
elevators, 59
emergency
alarms, generators, 59
aquatic facilities, design considerations, 192, 197–198
lighting, 56
personnel, signage for, 101–102
rescue craft for waterfronts, 301
energy
costs, and building design, 32–35
efficient lighting, 49–57
management, 65–67
monitoring, 71
reducing, conserving, 27–28
energy accounting, 67
energy audits, 66
Energy Independence and Security Act of 2007, 53
Energy Star certification program, 31

environment, impact of buildings on, 35–36
environmental climate control, 61–62
EPA (Environmental Protection Agency), 427, 431
equestrian spaces, 355–361
equipment
    cleaning, maintenance equipment record sheet, 466
    climbing, 270–272
    cost considerations, 408
    evaluation considerations, 456
    repair work order (sample), 263
    storage, 24, 90–92, 503
    suggestions for purchasing, 511
    and supplies defined, 407–409
    vendor websites, 418
European Committee for Standardization (CEN), 433
examining rooms, 339
exercise facility surfaces, 119
exercise physiology laboratory equipment, 511–512
exit lighting, 56
extreme sports parks, 282
extreme sports, trends in, 417–418

F
fabric structures, 399–404
facial recognition systems, 20
facilities
    See also specific facility type
    ancillary areas, 73–96
    bicycle, 230–231
    builders, consultants, designers, 488
    building accessible, 39–47
    checklists. See checklists
    maintenance. See maintenance
    master plans, 4–16
    mixed-use, 73–74
    multi-use, 218–219
    planning, 3–4, 19–26
    rebuilding, renovating, or reinvesting, 218
    retrofitting or replacing, 495–496
    specialized rooms, 221–226
    specification guide for, 437–453
    standards. See standards
    sustainable design, construction, operations, 27–38
facility managers, duties related to safety, 19
family camps, 296
family locker rooms, 83–84
farms, 238–239
Federal Energy Management Program (FEMP), 35
fencing
    aquatic facilities, 197
    baseball, softball fields, 164
    courts, 159–160
    equestrian spaces, 360–361
    safety, 4
    sports fields, 163–164
fiber optics for electronic communication, 58
field hockey fields, 172–173, 448, 475
field spaces
    See also specific field type
    fencing, 163–164
    generally, 161
    safety and, 161–163
    service areas, 164–167
fire
    alarms, 59, 326
    emergencies and aquatic facilities, 192
    regulations, outside door requirements, 20
fitness clubs
    ancillary area design, 96
    equipment trends for, 412–416
    standards, 432

fitness tests, 420, 457
fitness-testing equipment, 261
flooring
    additional considerations, 117
    athletic facilities, 95
    climbing walls, 268
    dance spaces, 515
    design standards for, 482
    DIN (wood athletic floors) standards, 106–107, 468
    gyms, 147
    ice hockey rinks, 291–294
    indoor facilities for physical education, 323–324
    locker rooms, 80
    materials, 24
    planning checklist, 465
    recreation gymnasiums, 221
    shooting ranges, 384
    squash courts, 153–154
    strength and cardiovascular training facilities (SCF), 252, 254
    surfaces, 106–120
fluorescent lighting, 53–54, 155
Flynn, Richard B., 423, ix, x
football fields
    designing, 172–173, 475
    irrigation and drainage, 124
    specification guide, 452–453
foot-candles (illumination), 50
forests
    See also parks and recreation
    developing, 239
front offices, 86
full-consensus standards, 430
functional analysis in planning, 14
funding
    arenas, stadiums, 391–398
    parking systems, 134

G
game rooms, 222
gang showers, 77
gardens, 238–239
generators
    electrical, 59
    hot water, 69
Georgia Dome (Atlanta, GA), 404
glare
    lighting and, 51–53
    and windows, 115
glass
    in basketball facilities, 146
    in doors, windows, 24–25
glycol (coolant), 292
Goldfine, Bernie, xiii, 139, 423
golf courses, 231–232
Gonzales, Rick, 27
government regulation, 35, 435
grandstands. See bleachers
graphics. See signage
grappling arts, 351–352
grass, 351
    See also synthetic turfs
    irrigation and drainage of, 123–126
    parks, 235
    removable natural, 401
    tennis courts, 141
green design, 27–28, 30–31, 36–38, 198–199, 219
Green Globes program, 31, 35
greenhouse gases (GHG), 27
greenhouses, 238
grooming stations in locker rooms, 79
grounding lighting systems, 56

groundkeeping, 128–130
group camps, 296
guardrails on bleachers, 176, 178–179, 181
Guide for Planning Facilities for Athletics, Recreation, Physical and Health Education (AAHPER), 422
guidelines
   See also codes, standards
   described, 435
gymnasiums
   auxiliary, 224
   basketball courts in, 146–147
   buffer zones, 22
   equipment trends for, 408–412
   flooring. See flooring
   history of, 419–420
   illumination recommendations (table), 51–52
   locating storage space, 24
   planning checklist, 458
   in recreation centers, 221
   in schools, 330–335
gymnastics areas, 224, 225, 335–337

H
halide lighting, 54, 154
hammer throw, 311, 312–313, 314, 315
handball courts, 150–157, 441, 448, 458–459
Hartwell, Dr. Edward M., 419
H'Doubler, Margaret, 513
health club standards, 432
health instruction facilities, 337–338
health services in schools, 338–342
heat convection, conduction, radiation, 68
heat pumps, 69
Heilman, Charles, 423
HEPA filters, 37–38
herb gardens, 236
high jump, 309–310, 443
Historic Preservation Act (1966), 42
historical markers, 236
hockey specification guide, 440
home plates on baseball fields, 169
horizontal circulation control, 21
horseback
   bridle paths, 231
   equestrian spaces, 355–361
Houston, Ruth Eliott, 419
Hudson, Susan, 201
human performance laboratories, 509–510
humidity control, 26, 64, 291
HVAC (heating, ventilation and air conditioning) systems
   in aquatic facilities, 198
   in indoor facilities for physical education, 326–327
HVAC-R (heating, ventilation, air conditioning, and refrigeration) systems
   air quality, 62–63
   design, building considerations, 60–61
   trends in, 64–65
hydraulic lifts, 59
hydrostatic pressure, aquatic facilities, 194
hydrotherapy areas, 367
Hypes, Julia Ann, 355
Hypes, Michael G., x, xv, 3, 97, 175, 355, 419, 423

I
ice skating, hockey rinks, 290–294
ID cards for accessing facilities, 20
IHRSA (International Health, Racquet, & Sportsclub Association), 432
illumination. See lighting
implementing master plans, 11–18
incandescent lighting, 53–54

indoor
   activity area planning checklist, 462–465
   activity dimensions, 471
   buffer zones, 21–23
   facility standards, 434
   illumination recommendations (table), 51–52
   jumping, throwing facilities, 318
   recreation and community centers, 219–226
   recreational, intramural, informal sports activities, 244–246
   recreational sports centers, 239–246
   running tracks, 317–319
   skateboard parks, 287
   spaces checklist, 457–460
   surfaces, 105–120
   water use, 69
indoor air quality (IAQ), 62–63
information desks, 223
injuries in common sports (table), 283
inline hockey, 417
inline skating, 281, 417
insurance
   See also liability issues
   carriers (table), 282
intelligent buildings and temperature control, 61
International Audit Protocol Consortium (IAPC), 431–432
International Building Code (IBC), 176, 178
International Environment, Health & Safety (IEH&S), 431–432
International Health, Racquet, & Sportsclub Association (IHRSA), 432
International Organization for Standardization (IOS), 433–434
International Standards Organization (ISO) standards, 431–432, 433–434
Internet systems, 416
interpretive centers, 237–238
Invesco Field (Denver), 408–409
IOS (International Organization for Standardization), 433–434
IP telephony, 59
irrigation
   landscape, 123–126
   sports fields, 164, 173
ISO (International Standards Organization) standards, 433–434

J
janitorial closets, 94, 503–504
javelin, 311, 315, 445
Judge, Lawrence W., xv, 247, 305

K
Kentucky bluegrass, 126
kitchens in recreation centers, 222
Knott Athletic, Recreation & Convention Center (Emmitsburg, MD), 400

L
laboratories, classrooms, 508–512
lacrosse fields, 172–173, 442, 475
Lamar, Emil, 419
land use and site analysis, 14
landscape
   design and planning, 7
   design generally, 121–123
   grass. See grass
   irrigation and drainage, 123–126
   parking lot design, 130–135
lap pools, 187
LaRue, David A., 121
LaRue, Richard L., x, 39, 121, 423
laundry areas, 92–94, 460, 504–505
lavatories in locker rooms, 79
laws. See legislation
LED screens, video boards, 409–410

LEED- (Leadership in Energy and Environment Design) certified
    building, 28–29, 31–33, 35, 219
LEED Green Building Rating System, 117
legislation
    See also specific law or act
    aquatic facility-related, 190–191
    civil rights, for the disabled, 40–44
lemmon lines, 301
Leuhring, Fredrick W., 419
liability issues
    for playgrounds, 214–215
    for skateparks, 282
life cycle
    of building products, 34
    flooring cost, 108–110
lifeguard stations, 300
lighting
    design considerations, 49–57
    energy management, 70
    and facility surfaces, 116
    fixtures, 25
    indoor facilities for physical education, 325–326
Lindsay Park (Calgary, Alberta), 401
lobbies, 225
locker rooms
    designing, 25–26, 75–85
    flooring, ceilings, walls, 117–118
    planning checklist, 459
    in recreation centers, 221–222
lockers, 76–77
locks, 21, 58, 77
long jump, 310–312, 443
luxury suites in arenas, stadiums, 389–390

M
maintenance
    air quality checklists, 64
    challenge courses, 280
    closet design, 94
    equipment record sheet, 466
    facility, 499–507
    filter, 61
    flooring cost, 113
    grasses, turfs, 128–130
    lighting systems, 54–55
    and operational needs, designing for, 13
    parking lots, 134
    playgrounds, 206–208, 215–216
    signage, 102
marinas, 232–233
martial arts facilities, 350–354
massage areas, 82–83, 459–460
master plans, 4–18
Material Safety Data Sheets (MSDS), 129–130
McClain Athletic Training Facility (Madison, WI), 401
McDonough, Thomas E., 423
meeting rooms, 88–90, 223–224
mercury-vapor lighting, 54
metric conversion formulas, 489
Meylan, Dr. George L., 419
Miles, Caswell M., 422, ix
Miller Park (Milwaukee), 398
Minimum Guidelines and Requirements for Accessible Design
    (MGRAD), 40
Minnesota Building Codes, Standards Div. bleacher construction
    requirements, 177–178
Minute Maid Park (Houston), 397–398
mirrors
    martial arts facilities, 353
    in strength and cardiovascular training facilities, 256–257
    in weight rooms, dance studios, 25

Mohs, Friedrich, 106
Mohs scale of surface hardness, 106
monitoring
    energy management, 66–67
    pool chemicals, 195–196
    using building automation systems, 70–71
Moravek, Jim, 64
motor learning laboratories, 510–512
motorcycle parking, 132
multipurpose
    classrooms, 223–224
    facilities, ancillary area design, 96
music rooms, 224

N
naming rights for arenas, stadiums, 390–393, 395–396
natatoriums (aquatic centers), 224
National Archery Association (NAA), 377
National Athletics Trainers' Association (NATA), 364–366
National Building Code (NBC)
    bleacher construction, 177, 178
    standards, 433
National Collegiate Boxing Association (NCBA), 345
National Fire Protection Association (NFPA)
    bleacher construction, 177, 179
    codes and standards, 433
National Program for Playground Safety (NPPS), 203
National Rifle Association (NRA), 377
National Spa and Pool Institute (NSPI), 434
natural areas, 239
natural lighting, 54
natural preserves, 236
nature centers, 237
nature trails, 235
negligence, preventing, 19
neighborhood parks, 229
neighborhood recreation centers, 219–220
NFPA. See National Fire Protection Association (NFPA)
night lighting, 56
noise
    See also acoustics
    building considerations, 57–58
NSPI (National Spa and Pool Institute), 434

O
occupancy levels, and activity area sizes, 80
Occupational Safety and Health Organization. See OSHA
open spaces
    and outdoor facilities, 226–239
    park and recreation standards, 470–473
operations
    challenge courses, 277–278
    climbing facility, 270–271
    maintenance, 505–507
    strength and cardiovascular training facilities (SCF), 261–264
    sustainable, 36
organizations
    advancing standards, 428–435
    pertinent to planning, 491–492
orientation of sports fields, 163
OSHA (Occupational Safety and Health Organization), 431
outdoor
    buffer zones, 23
    education and recreation areas, 234–239
    facilities and open spaces, 226–239
    facility standards, 434
    jumping, throwing facilities, 309–315
    laboratories, 236
    lighting, 55–56
    recreational, intramural, informal sports centers, 240–246
    running tracks, 307–309

skills and sports areas, 239
spaces checklist, 457–462
water use, 69–70
outsourcing, 412–413

P
padding obstructions, 23
paddle courts, 144–145
paddle tennis courts, 143
paddleball, 150
paint, 49
park-and-ride parking, 133
parking lot design, 121, 130–135
parklands, 227–228
parks
citywide, district, 229–230
dog, 234
neighborhood, community, 229
open space standards, guidelines, 484–487
special-use areas, facilities, 230–234
parks and recreation
general planning issues, 217–220
indoor recreation and community centers, 219–226
outdoor education and recreation areas, 234–239
outdoor facilities and open spaces, 226–234
pedestrian traffic flow, 23–24
performing arts areas, 233
personal seating licenses (PSLs), 393
Petersen, Jeffrey C., 73, 407
photography rooms, 224
physical contaminants, 63
physical education
ancillary area design, 95–96
campus recreational sports centers, 241–246
picnic sites, 236
pistol ranges, 383–386
pitchers mounds, 170
platform tennis courts, 145–146
playgrounds
equipment selection, 211–213
final design, equipment installation, 213–214
liability issues, 214–215
maintenance, repair, inspections, 215–216
planning, 201–211
surfacing, 203–208
playlots/miniparks, 228–229
playrooms, 331
point-elastic sport flooring, 106–108
pole vault, 310, 311, 443
pools. See swimming pools
portable grass, 127
predevelopment reviews, 13
preschool centers, 224
President's Council on Physical Fitness, 423
press boxes, 166, 180
Prettyman, Albert H., 421
procedures, operational and maintenance, 68–70
program statements, 6, 7, 8
programs
adventure, 265–267
planning, 13
public accommodations, and accessibility, 45–47
Public Assembly Facilities (Jewell), 19
public schools
driver education areas, facilities, 342–344
health instruction facilities, 337–338
health services, 338–342
planning facilities, 323–337
punch lists, 17–18

Q
quarts lights, 54

R
R-134a, R-22 (refrigerants), 293
racks, weight, 256–257
racquet standards, 432
racquetball courts
designing, 150–157, 458–459
specification guide, 441
surfaces, 119–120
ramps
for accessibility, 40, 44, 46
boat, 232–233
pool, 190
skatepark, 283–286
RCA Dome (Indianapolis), 402
readability, comprehensibility of signs, 98–99
recordkeeping for playground maintenance, inspections, 215–216
recreation centers, 219–226, 239–244
recreation facilities. See parks and recreation
recreational aquatic facilities, 187–188
recycling building materials, 36
Redbird Arena (Bloomington-Normal, IL), 403
regional site analysis, 9
regulations
See also codes, standards
of bleacher construction, 176–181
of sustainable building, 35
Rehabilitation Act of 1973, 40
relative humidity, 64
Reliant Stadium (Houston), 398, 399
request for proposals (RFPs), 12
research for facility development, 13
reserved parking, 131, 132
resistance training equipment, 256–257
resting rooms in schools, 339–340
restrooms
See also toilets
arenas, stadiums, 394
planning checklist, 459
in schools, 340
sports fields, 166
retrofitting
athletic training rooms, 366–369
bleacher construction, 180–181
or replacing facilities, 495–496
reviews, predevelopment, 13
RFPs (request for proposals), 12
rifle ranges, 236, 383–386
risk management
flooring, 114
planning facilities for, 19–26
shooting ranges, 397
Rogers, Donald, 39, 265
Rogers Centre (Toronto), 397
rolling load of flooring, 108, 468
rooms
See also specific room type
multipurpose, 221
ropes courses, 273, 328
Rosandich, Thomas J. Jr., 499
Round Valley Ensphere (Eager, AZ), 404, 405
rugby fields, 172–173, 475
running tracks
See also track and field
layouts, 494
planning checklist, 458
specification guide, 444–445

S
Safeco Field (Seattle), 397
safety
  See also security
  buffer zones, 21–23
  flooring, 114
  landscape design, 122–123
  parking lots, 135
  planning facilities for, 19–26
  playgrounds, 201–206
safety glass, 24–25
sailing, 295
sand volleyball courts, 149–150
sanitation, aquatic facilities, 194–195
Sanuvox UV Air Purifier, 63
saunas, 82, 459
Sawyer, Thomas H., x, 3, 121, 161, 239, 281, 295, 305, 323, 345,
  419, 423, 427, 508
science laboratories, 509–511
scoreboards, 59, 166, 354, 409–410
Scott, Harry A., 419
Seattle Parks and Recreation (SPR) System open space standards,
  470–473
security
  See also safety
  and access control, 20–21
  aquatic facilities, 197
  campus recreational sports centers, 246
  facility, 59
  indoor facilities for physical education, 327–328
  monitors in parking lots, 130–131
  playgrounds, 210
Seidler, Todd, x, xiii, 19, 423
senior citizen centers, 224
sensors, occupancy and light-level, 56
shooting facilities, 377–386
shooting ranges, 236, 239
shot put, 311, 312, 313, 318, 445
showers
  indoor facilities for physical education, 328
  in locker rooms, 77–78
  planning checklist, 459
  in recreation centers, 221–222
  in schools, 95–96
  surfaces, 117–118
shuffleboard courts, 157–158
sick building syndrome, 64
signage
  cross-country courses, 319
  outdoor, indoor spaces, 455
  parking lots, 134
  planning, 26, 97
  playgrounds, 202
  squash courts, 155
  strength and cardiovascular training facilities (SCF), 255
site analysis, 9–11, 14
  nature centers, 237
  parks, 234–236
  playgrounds, 210–212
skateboard parks, 417
skateparks, 281–287, 454
skeet ranges, 236
skiing areas, 289–290
sledding areas, 287–289
smoke alarms, 59
snow sport areas, 289–290
snowboard hills, 289–290
soccer fields, 23, 172–173, 450, 475
softball fields
  See also baseball, softball fields
  layouts, 474
  specification guide, 451

sound
  See also acoustics
  absorption by walls, ceilings, 114–115
  and acoustical considerations, 57–58
Sound Transmission Class (STC), 115
specification guide for facilities, 437–453
specifications, construction, 15
spectator seating
  See also bleachers
  secondary school gyms, 334
  sports fields, 173
  stadiums, arenas, 411–412
  track and field, 316
sports
  See also specific sport
  extreme, 417–418
  injuries in common (table), 283
  winter areas, 287–294
sports centers, campus recreational, 239–246
sports club standards, 432
sports fields
  See also arenas, stadiums
  design standards for, 475
  drainage, 124–126
  lighting, 55–56
sports grasses, turfs, 126–128
springboards, 187
sprinkler systems. See irrigation
squash courts, 150–157, 441, 458–459
stables, 231
stadiums
  See also arenas
  equipment trends for, 408–412
  funding of, 389–396
  LED screens, video boards, 409–410
  retractable roof, 396–398
staff locker rooms, offices, 84, 87
stages in auditoriums, 222
stalls
  horse, 356–359
  shooting, 383–386
Standard Building Code (SBC), bleacher construction, 177–178
standard phrases, 99
standards
  See also codes
  accessibility, 40–43
  air quality, 62
  aquatic facilities, 191
  baseball, softball field layouts, 474
  challenge courses, 279–280
  climbing wall, 272
  DIN (wood athletic floors), 106–107, 147, 468
  generally, 427–428
  organizations advancing, 428–435
  outdoor facilities and open spaces, 226–227
  park and recreation open space, 470–473
  playground, 201–202
  of practice, of care, 427–428
steam rooms, 82, 118–119, 459
steeplechase hurdles, 316–317, 445
Stienhaus, Bob, 129
storage
  areas in recreation centers, 223
  design considerations, 90–92
  for facility maintenance, 502–504
  locating, 24
strategic planning, 47
strength and cardiovascular training facilities (SCF)
  area surfaces, 119
  checklist, 457
  designing, 247–256
  equipment selection, 256–261

operations, 261–264
in schools, 337
stretching equipment, 258–261
striking arts, 351, 352–353
supercenters, 219, 221
Superior Dome (Marquette, MI), 405
supervision of facilities, 25–26
supplies
See also equipment
trends in, 418
surfaces
aquatic facility decks, 194
courts. See specific court type
indoor, 107–120
selection process, 467
trends in indoor, 398–399
surfacing, playground, 203–208, 213–214
sustainable design, construction, operations, 27–38
swimming pools
See also aquatic facilities
pool design supervision issues, 198–199
specification guide, 446–447
synthetic flooring, 107–114
synthetic turfs, 127–128, 163, 398–399

T
tanning rooms, 459
teaching stations, 323, 329, 331–333
team rooms, 90
teams, design, 12
teams courses, 277
Telecommunications Act of 1996, 42
temperature control
athletic training facilities, 369
in building envelope, 67–70
dance spaces, 518
ice hockey rinks, 290–294
strength and cardiovascular training facilities (SCF), 255
strength and cardiovascular training facility, 251
temporary air structures, 402–403
tennis courts, 139–143, 449
tension structures, 400–402
thermal factors, and air quality, 63–64
Thompson, Donna, 203
ticket booths, 518
timing systems, 59
togganing, coasting, 290
toilets
See also restrooms
accessibility standards, 47
in locker rooms, 78–79
towers (track and field), 315–316
track and field
See also specific activity
cross-country courses, 319–321
equipment, 316–317
finish line towers, press boxes, 315–316
indoor jumping, throwing facilities, 318–319
layouts, 496
outdoor jumping facilities, 309–311
outdoor throwing facilities, 311–315
site selection, facility layout, 305–309
specification guide, 443–445
trails in parks, 230–231, 235
trampolines, 24
tree nurseries, 236
tribometers, 114
triple jump, 310–312, 443
trophy cases, 25
Tropicana Field (St. Petersburg, FL), 403–404
turfs. See sports grasses, turfs

Turkish baths, 82
Turner, Ed, x

U
Uniform Building Code (UBC)
bleacher construction, 178–179
codes, 435
universal design, 40, 44, 278
University of Connecticut athletic facility, 29
University of Phoenix Stadium, 398, 400
U.S. Consumer Product Safety Commission (CPSC)
bleacher construction guidelines, 180–181
playground guidelines, standards, 201–202, 204
U.S. Equal Employment Opportunity Commission (EEOC), 41–43
U.S. Forest Service accessibility standards, 42
U.S. Green Building Council (USGBC), 28, 31
USA Boxing, 345
utilities
maintenance, 506
offices, 87
outdoor, indoor spaces, 456
planning, 65–67
playgrounds, 209

V
vanities, grooming stations, 79
vendor websites, 418
ventilation
shooting ranges, 385–386
squash courts, 154–155
systems, 60–61
vertical circulation control, 21
video conference rooms, 90
Virginia Graeme Baker Pool and Spa Safety Act, 190
volleyball courts, 147–150, 453

W
waiting rooms, 339
Walker, Hal, 105
walking trails, 230
Walkup Skydome (Flagstaff, AZ), 404–405
walls
climbing, 266–273
dance spaces, 517
designing, 114–115
indoor facilities for physical education, 324
martial arts facilities, 353
planning checklist, 465
safe materials, 23–24
secondary school gyms, 333–334
shooting ranges, 384
strength and cardiovascular training facilities (SCF), 251–252, 254–255
surface types, 105–106, 117–120
warning track, baseball fields, 170–171
washers, dryers, 92–94
waste
minimizing construction, 37
reducing non-biodegradable, 27
water
conserving, 27
domestic hot water, 61, 69
drinking fountains. See drinking fountains
harvesting, 37
irrigation and drainage of landscape, 123–126
jumps, 309
to laundry areas, 93
optimization, 71
parks, 186, 223
and playground design, 210
pools. See aquatic facilities
treatment of HVAC-R systems, 61–62

water sports areas, 239
waterfronts (in camps), 296–302
Weaver, Tony, 105
Web-to-telephone calling, 59
weight rooms, 22–23, 25, 457
weight throw, 318
weight training equipment, 256–257
weight-training equipment trends, 412–416
whirlpools, 82, 367, 370
Whole Building Design Guide, 33
windows
    designing, 115–116
    maintenance, 506–507
    secondary school gyms, 333

Winkle, Jason, 345, 377
winter sports areas, 236, 287–294
Winters, A.R., 419
wood flooring, 107–114, 482
wooden domes, 404–405
working drawings, construction phase, 14–15
workout equipment trends, 412–416
WWA (World Waterpark Association), 434

Y
Yarger, Leland, 185

Z
Z-lockers, 76